CENSORSHIP LIBRARIES AND THE LAW

COMPILED AND WITH
AN INTRODUCTION BY
HAIG BOSMAJIAN
UNIVERSITY OF WASHINGTON

Foreword by Nat Hentoff

Neal-Schuman Publishers, Inc.

Published by Neal-Schuman Publishers, Inc.
23 Cornelia Street
New York, New York   10014

Printed and bound in the United States of America.

Library of Congress Cataloging in Publication Data

Bosmajian, Haig A.
   Censorship, libraries, and the law.

   Includes bibliographical references and index.
   1. Libraries—United States—Censorship—Cases.
I. Title.
KF4774.A7B67   1983   342.73'0853   83-2162
ISBN 0-918212-54-5   347.302853

CONTENTS

FOREWORD

by Nat Hentoff

THERE IS a Federal District Judge in Boston, Joseph Tauro, whose
passion for the First Amendment would have greatly gratified James
Madison. In 1978, Tauro presided over a school library censorship
case that is included in this invaluably comprehensive compilation of such
cases. The trial, involving one poem in the anthology, *Male and Female Under
Eighteen*, was attended by more than a hundred students at Chelsea High
School (where the poem was under attack). Taking every available seat in the
courtroom, the kids watched in fascination as *their* right to read the poem was
contested by the school board's asserting *its* right to protect the students from
the words and the ideas in the poem.

Judge Tauro was delighted that the kids had come. For maybe the first
time in the lives of most of them, the First Amendment was not some abstract
notion but an actual part of their own experience.

During his subsequent decision, Tauro connected the First Amendment
with another dimension of the students' experience. The library. "There," he
said, "a student can literally explore the unknown, and discover areas of
interest and thought not covered by the prescribed curriculum. The student
who discovers the magic of the library is on the way to a life-long experience of
self-education and enrichment. That student learns that a library is a place to
test or expand upon ideas presented to him, in or out of the classroom."

To some people, that may sound flowery, but for me, who practically lived
in the library as I was growing up in the 1930s, Tauro was understating the
case. And more to the present point, traveling around the schools, as I often
do, I know a lot of kids who agree with the judge that the doors to the library
are indeed the doors to the wondrously unknown.

But there are times, increasingly, when forces alien to knowledge and
wonder—certain school boards, certain principals—try to "sanitize" the
library. To remove books that offend *them* and therefore, they say, are not
suitable for students.

This had happened in the case before Judge Tauro (*Right to Read Defense
Committee* v. *School Committee, Etc.*), and he declared that the "offending"
poem, and the book in which it was included, must stay in the school library.
Tauro declared: "What is at stake here is the right to read and be exposed to
controversial thoughts and language—a valuable right subject to First
Amendment protection."

The right to read! The First Amendment, as written, says nothing explicit
about the right to read. However, said Judge Tauro, this right is implicit in the
First Amendment; among other sources of support for his position, he cited a
1969 Supreme Court decision, *Tinker* v. *Des Moines School District*, which is the
American Magna Charta of young people's First Amendment rights.

That case had to do with whether three students, during the Vietnam War,

v

had the right to wear black armbands in school as a symbolic protest against the war. School officials in Des Moines scoffed at the notion that these kids had the First Amendment right to wear those pieces of black cloth. And so, the school officials suspended them.

The Supreme Court of the United States disagreed with the school officials and ringingly affirmed the First Amendment rights of students, adding:

> In our system, state-operated schools may not be enclaves of totalitarianism. . . . In our system, students may not be regarded as closed-circuit recipients of only that which the state wants to communicate. They may not be confined to those sentiments that are officially approved. In the absence of a specific showing of constitutionally valid reasons to regulate their speech, students are entitled to freedom of expression of their views.

That sounds just fine. But nonetheless, in the years after *Tinker*, school boards and other agents of the state kept censoring books in school libraries. And the Supreme Court was silent. After all, *Tinker* said students were entitled to freedom of expression; it didn't say anything about the right to read. And indeed, the Supreme Court did not directly address the question of school library censorship until 1982, when, for the first time, it ruled on the matter in *Board of Education, Island Trees Union Free School Dist.* v. *Pico.*

At last, Judge Tauro's assertion that there is a First Amendment right to read, in a school situation, was affirmed on high. Speaking for a plurality of the Supreme Court, Justice William Brennan declared that there is indeed a right "to receive information and ideas." (This, one would assume, is a First Amendment right extending to all citizens, not just students, and therefore to all public libraries, not just school libraries.)

But where does it say in the First Amendment that there is such a right to receive ideas? The answer, according to Brennan, is that the right "is an inherent corollary of the rights of free speech and press that are explicitly guaranteed by the Constitution, in two senses. First, the right to receive ideas follows ineluctably from the *sender's* First Amendment right to send them. . . . More importantly, the right to receive ideas is a necessary predicate to the *recipient's* meaningful exercise of his own rights of speech, press, and political freedom."

Put another way, the publisher of a book, the writer of a book, and the librarian (as the disseminator of the book) are all exercising their First Amendment rights to communicate ideas. Simultaneously, students, or anybody using a public library, have a constitutional right of access to ideas that will better enable them, so they believe, to speak and write more effectively.

It's an indivisible First Amendment circle.

However, the Supreme Court decision in *Pico* is by no means an unalloyed triumph. Censorship, and attempts at censorship, are going to continue in both school and public libraries. This book by Haig Bosmajian will be of value for many years ahead to help perfect your defenses against would-be censors and your understanding of the political dynamics of the continuing thrust to suppress ideas.

First, exactly what did the Supreme Court decide in *Pico* regarding this crucial right to receive ideas? By a 5—4 decision, the Court declared that while school boards can *remove* books from school libraries for vulgarity or educational unsuitability, "our Constitution does not permit the official suppression of ideas."

So, for the first time in American history, students and parents fighting what they claim to be censorship now have a Supreme Court-backed right to go to court. There, they will have to prove that a particular book was removed from the shelves because school board members disagreed with the *ideas* in that book. (Political ideas, or social ideas and values.) If, however, parents and students cannot prove, at trial, that the school board's *motivation* in expelling the books was indeed to create an orthodoxy of ideas in the school library, the books will remain banned.

Having done this much to clarify the right to read as it applies to school libraries, the High Court stopped. And thereby it has allowed, and one might say it has encouraged, further library censorship on two fronts. Writing for the plurality of the Court, Justice Brennan could not have been more clear as to the limits of the *Pico* ruling:

> Nothing in our decision today affects in any way the discretion of a local school board to choose books to *add* to the libraries of their schools. Because we are concerned in this case with the suppression of ideas, our holding today affects only the discretion to *remove* books.

It is as if Justice Brennan had never heard of preselection censorship.

But one of the Justices in the minority certainly had. William Rehnquist gleefully pointed to Brennan's grave lapse of logic:

> If Justice Brennan truly has found a [First Amendment] "right to receive [a diversity of] ideas". . . this distinction between acquisition and removal makes little sense. *The failure of a library to acquire a book denies access to its contents just as effectively as does the removal of the book from the library's shelf.* [Emphasis added].

For example, two librarians in Minnesota decided, as they told me, that they were not going to order any more Judy Blume books. Their principal was very pleased to hear it. Judy Blume, I was told by the librarians, is "too much trouble" to have in a library.

For another example, the head librarian in an Illinois High School is utterly convinced that abortion is murder and she will not order any books for the school library that, as she puts it, may encourage students to commit murder. That is, no books that might be interpreted as being "pro" abortion.

In Massachusetts, a school official with direct responsibility for library purchases is just as convinced, on the other hand, that "anti-abortion books have no business being in a school library because they promote, she says, a religious point of view. And so she sees to it there are no such books in the library of her school.

According to the *Pico* decision, preselection censorship of this kind is permitted by the Supreme Court, whether perpetrated by school boards or by others with authority over school library books.

Yet, as Justice Rehnquist points out, "If a school board's removal of books might be motivated by a desire to promote favored political or religious views"—or to exclude certain political or religious views—"there is no reason that its acquisition policy might not also be so motivated. And yet the 'pall of orthodoxy' cast by a carefully selected book-acquisition program apparently would not violate the First Amendment under Justice Brennan's view."

There is another huge exception to "the right to read" in the *Pico* decision. Justice Brennan emphasized that "the curricula of the Island Trees schools" were not at issue in the case. "On the contrary," Brennan went on to say, "the only books at issue are *library* books, books that by their nature are optional rather than required reading. Our adjudication of the present case thus does not intrude into the classroom, or into the compulsory courses taught there."

But many books attacked by would-be censors, and sometimes removed by actual censors, *are* on required reading lists. In most of the cases concerning *Huckleberry Finn* in recent years, for example, the demand was not only to remove Mr. Twain's novel from the library but also from the curriculum.

As another member of the minority in *Pico,* Chief Justice Burger, wrote: "It would appear that required reading and textbooks have a greater likelihood of imposing 'a pall of orthodoxy' over the educational process than do optional reading [in the school library]."

Burger, who believes there are no First Amendment barriers to the censoring of school library books, was making the "pall of orthodoxy" point just to indicate—correctly—the illogic of Brennan's plurality opinion. In school libraries, according to Brennan, school boards "may not remove books" from the shelves "simply because they dislike the ideas contained in those books and seek their removal to 'prescribe what shall be orthodox in politics, nationalism, religion, or other matters of opinion.' "

But what about those books that are both in school libraries and are also used in the classroom? According to *Pico,* attempts to banish those books from the *library* can be fought under the First Amendment. But there is no First Amendment defense against censors who remove the very same books from *classrooms* in order to "prescribe what shall be orthodox" in those places of learning.

So, in the years ahead, along with actual court battles over books removed from school libraries, many of us will be engaged in trying to ward off attempts to censor curriculum books and attempts to censor other books by making sure they never get into the library in the first place.

For these battles, it will be useful to know the modern history of censorship of books in American libraries—particularly as illuminated in the leading cases included in this book. Reading the often frustrating and yet often glorious accounts of these confrontations should make librarians more confident of their ability to deal with any future assaults on the freedom to read. And no library is immune to such an assault.

Reading the cases and the commentary, moreover, provides a challenge to those librarians who themselves are sometimes tempted to interfere with the freedom to read. Reading the rationales for suppression of ideas that are given by school boards, and sometimes by judges, may cause some librarians to see parallels in their own reasons for not ordering certain books or for suggesting that others be removed.

At the July 1982 convention of the American Library Association in Philadelphia, soon after the *Pico* decision had been announced, a questionnaire was handed out to ALA members. Prepared by the Young Adult Services Intellectual Freedom Committee, the sheet asked whether the librarian filling it out had ever:

- not purchased teenage sex books from a conservative religious point of view, such as *How To Be Happy Though Young,* because a staff member found them personally repugnant . . .
- not purchased a popular young-adult title such as [Judy Blume's] *Forever* because it might be unpopular with parents . . .
- reviewed potentially controversial materials and recommended that they not be purchased because of poor characterization, poorly developed plot, or due to other violations of the "Law of Literary Merit," even though there are other *noncontroversial* materials already in the collection that also violate the "Law of Literary Merit.'" [Emphasis added.]

As they were reading the questionnaire, some librarians, looking rueful, were nodding affirmatively.

By and large, however, librarians, especially in recent years, have been more heroic in defending the First Amendment than any other group, including journalists. You will see some of their names in these pages; you will see some of their faces in the mirror.

And the value of these librarians, though they are in combat to defend everyone's right to read, is of particular and durable importance to young folks. For years, during the tortuous odyssey of the *Pico* case, Irene Turin, an Island Trees librarian, was practically ostracized by the school board and some school officials because she had, from the beginning, spoken out against the suppression of the books that had led to the case being brought to court.

At one point, I asked Irene Turin why she stayed, why she endured the slights of her "superiors." She is not, after all, a masochist. Irene Turin told me she had spoken out in the first place, and then refused to leave during all those years, because she felt it was important for kids to know that there are adults who do care about free speech and the freedom to read. Adults who care enough to put themselves at risk—so that kids can have the freedom to read.

Long after the children in the Island Trees schools have children of their own, I expect many will remember Irene Turin, and that ought to mean that they will also care, really care, about others' freedom of expression and right to read, as well as their own.

In 1952, Georges Bernanos, who left France because he refused to live under the Nazi occupation, wrote a book called *Tradition of Freedom,* and toward the end, he wrote:

I have thought for a long time now that if, some day, the increasing efficiency of the technique of destruction finally causes our species to disappear from the earth, it will not be cruelty that will be responsible for our extinction . . . but the docility, the lack of responsibility of the common man, his base, subservient acceptance of every common decree.

The horrors which we have seen, the still greater horrors we shall presently see, are not signs that rebels, insubordinate, untameable men, are increasing in number throughout the world, but rather that there is a constant increase, a stupendously rapid increase, in the number of obedient, docile men.

Clearly, the most effective way to insure an even greater increase in the number of obedient, docile men and women is to teach them, beginning with their schooling, that free inquiry is forbidden. That they do not have the freedom to read because the authorities will decide for them what they can read and what they cannot read.

The authorities, it may further be decreed, will police the shelves of all our public libraries, and everyone—from grade school on—will learn only what he is permitted to learn.

And in time, the writings of James Madison and Thomas Jefferson will be removed from the shelves because those writings are dangerous, even revolutionary.

On the front line of the battle against that kind of future are librarians, and there will have to be even more of them on that front line. As a librarian in Minnesota—not one of the two who have decided to precensor Judy Blume—has said: "I wish professionals would become more courageous. I realize there are jobs on the line, but being courageous is the most important role we can play. Because if we don't, who will?"

INTRODUCTION

by Haig Bosmajian

"ONE OF the liberties we Americans prize most highly is our freedom to read what we wish and when we wish," declared Supreme Court Justice William Brennan in a speech delivered in 1963 to a group of librarians. "It is hard to realize," continued Justice Brennan, "that nothing in the body of the Constitution or the Bill of Rights says anything in terms about a freedom to read, or to listen, or even to think. Yet we know that such liberties are there just as surely as if they were expressly written into the First Amendment."[1]

While it may be hard to realize that in the body of the Constitution and the Bill of Rights there is no specific mention of the freedoms to read, to listen, and to think, it is even more difficult to accept that the United States Supreme Court never decided a case dealing directly with library censorship and the right to read until June 1982; and even then, in a 5-4 decision, the dissenting Justices argued, among other things, that the Supreme Court was not the place to decide school library censorship issues.[2] Though hundreds of efforts—some successful—are made yearly to censor and remove "objectionable" books and periodicals from library shelves, the Supreme Court had previously never spoken on the issue of book banning in the libraries.[3] Reporting on 2,178 items that were censored during the decade from 1966 to 1975, one study concluded that two thirds of library censorship attempts were either successful or partially successful; the disputed books and periodicals were either removed from the libraries or retained with limited access.[4] While books such as *The Catcher in the Rye, The Grapes of Wrath, Brave New World,* and *Of Mice and Men* have been successfully banned from school libraries without the courts ever having decided whether the censorship was constitutional, and while the lower courts have been deciding library censorship cases involving such books as *Catch 22, Go Ask Alice, Soul on Ice, Slaughterhouse Five, Male and Female Under 18, The Fixer,* and others, the banning of these books from school libraries was an issue the Supreme Court had avoided.

This situation becomes especially hard to accept after listening to Justice Brennan who had emphasized twenty years earlier the importance of the rights to read and listen: "For the freedom to speak would be meaningless without the corollary freedom to listen. And in the same way freedom of the press which we have cherished throughout history would be a hollow right without a corresponding freedom to read without fear of prosecution, censorship, or suspicion. The author and publisher are only as free to write and to print as their readers are to read."[5]

In 1972, the United States Supreme Court was given the opportunity to hear a library censorship case, but refused to grant certiorari; Justice William O. Douglas, however, argued that the case should be heard "because the issues raised here are crucial to our national life."[6] The case involved the banning of

Down These Mean Streets to junior high school students, though it was made available to their parents. Douglas questioned the constitutionality of the New York School Board's order that the book not be made directly available to students who requested it from the library.

After asserting that the "First Amendment involves not only the right to speak and publish, but also the right to hear, to learn, to know," Douglas observed: "At school the children are allowed to discuss the contents of the book and the social problems it portrays. They can do everything but read it. This in my mind lessens somewhat the contention that the subject matter of the book is not proper." Only Justice Potter Stewart joined Douglas in arguing that the case should be heard. As a result, the lower court's decision stood, and the censorship was held constitutional.

Where Justice Douglas saw the free discussion of the "contents of the book and the social problems it portrays" as reason to support his position against the banning of the book, the lower court saw the same free discussion as reason to justify its conclusion that the book banning was not unconstitutional, the United States Court of Appeals stating: "There is here no problem of freedom of speech or the expression of opinions on the part of parents, students or librarians. As we have pointed out, the discussion of the book or the problems which it encompasses or the ideas it espouses have not been prohibited by the Board's action in removing the book."[7] Ten years later, the four Supreme Court Justices dissenting in *Board of Education* v. *Pico*, Chief Justice Burger and Justices Powell, Rehnquist, and O'Connor, took the same position that the banning of the several books involved in that case did not interfere with the students' freedom of speech; referring to the banned books, the Chief Justice said that the students "are free to discuss them in the classroom or elsewhere."[8]

While the Supreme Court prior to 1982 had not dealt with the library censorship issue, it had provided relevant arguments in numerous cases related to such matters as distribution of literature, post-office censorship, advertising, and the banning of controversial speakers, arguments which have subsequently been used by the lower courts in deciding cases involving the banning of books from libraries. Several lower courts have relied heavily in their library-censorship opinions on what the Supreme Court has had to say in the cases involving the right to receive information, the right to hear, and the free-speech rights of minors. Even those lower courts which upheld library censorship practices gave a nod of recognition to these Supreme Court decisions.

The importance and relevance of the Supreme Court's opinions in the nonlibrary censorship cases to the lower courts' library-censorship decisions is well illustrated in *Minarcini* v. *Strongsville City School Dist.* in which the United States Court of Appeals, Sixth Circuit, declared unconstitutional the Strongsville, Ohio, School Board's action removing from the school library *Catch 22* and *Cat's Cradle*.[9] After stating that "here we are concerned with the right of students to receive information which they and their teachers desire them to have" and that "First Amendment protection of the right to know has frequently been recognized in the past," the Court of Appeals drew on Supreme Court Justice Harry Blackmun's 1976 opinion in *Virginia State Board of Pharmacy* v. *Virginia Citizens Consumers Council, Inc.,* Blackmun asserting:

Freedom of speech presupposes a willing speaker. But where a speaker exists, as in the case here, the protection afforded is to the communication, to its source and to its recipients both. This is clear from the decided cases. In *Lamont...,* the Court upheld the First Amendment rights of citizens to receive political publications sent from abroad. More recently, in *Kleindienst...,* we acknowledged that this Court has referred to a First Amendment right to "receive information and ideas," and that freedom of speech " 'necessarily protects the right to receive.' " And in *Procunier...,* where censorship of prison inmates' mail was under examination, we thought it unnecessary to assess the First Amendment rights of the inmates themselves, for it was reasoned that such censorship equally infringed the rights of noninmates to whom correspondence was addressed. There are numerous other expressions to the same effect in the Court's decisions. . . . If there is a right to advertise, there is a reciprocal right to receive the advertising, and it may be asserted by these appellees.[10]

The Court of Appeals concluded: "We believe that the language just quoted, plus the recent cases of *Kleindienst* v. *Mandel, supra,* and *Procunier* v. *Martinez, supra,* serve to establish firmly both the First Amendment right to know which is involved in our instant case and the standing of the student plaintiffs to raise the issue."

Another federal court, however, in deciding that the School Board of Directors' order to remove *Dog Day Afternoon* and *The Wanderers* from the school library was constitutional, did not find *Virginia State Board of Pharmacy* and the "right to receive information" argument persuasive or applicable in this library censorship case: "The right to receive information in the free speech context is merely the reciprocal of the right of the speaker. . . . Plaintiffs do not contend, nor could they reasonably argue, that the publishers of certain works have a constitutionally protected right to have their works purchased by the Vergennes High School Library or retained on the open shelves after purchase. The students' right to review those works through the school library, expressed as the constitutional right to receive information, is no broader."[11]

While the District Court decided to uphold the Board of Directors' banning of the books, it did at the same time reassert the necessity for freedom of expression in our schools and libraries: "A library is a vital institution in the continuing American struggle to create a society rich in freedom and variety of thought, broad in its understanding of diverse views and cultures and justifiably proud of its democratic institutions. The life and utility of a library are severely impaired whenever works can be removed merely because they are offensive to the personal, political or social taste of individual citizens, whether or not those citizens represent the majority of opinion in the community." The District Court then went on to say that while it did not "entirely agree with the policies and actions" of the School Board, it did not find "that those policies and actions directly or sharply infringe upon the basic constitutional rights of the students of Vergennes Union High School."

With no United States Supreme Court decisions and guidelines on library censorship, the lower courts struggled with a variety of arguments, at times the courts using the same facts and premises but arriving at different conclusions. In upholding the banning of *Down These Mean Streets* from all the junior high school libraries in New York's Community School District No. 25, the United

States Court of Appeals argued that the removal of a book that had already been purchased and shelved in the library was not unconstitutional.[12] On the other hand, a United States District Court, in deciding that *Male and Female Under 18* could not be banned from a high school library, argued that the school committee that ordered the book off the library shelf "was under no obligation to purchase *Male and Female* for the High School library, but it did. It is a familiar constitutional principle that a state, though having acted when not compelled, may consequently create a constitutionally protected interest."[13] The District Court cited from the opinion of the United States Court of Appeals, Sixth Circuit, which had found unconstitutional a school board's banning of *Catch 22, Cat's Cradle,* and *God Bless You, Mr. Rosewater,* the Appeals Court having asserted: "Neither the state of Ohio nor the Strongsville School Board was under any federal constitutional compulsion to provide a library for the Strongsville High School or to choose any particular books. Once having created such a privilege for the benefit of its students, however, neither body could place conditions on the use of the library which were related solely to the social or political tastes of school board members."[14]

In *Salvail* v. *Nashua Board of Education,* another United States District Court used the argument described above in finding that the removal of *Ms.* magazine from the Nashua (New Hampshire) High School library was a contravention of a student's First Amendment rights: "The duties of school boards must be exercised 'consistently with federal constitutional requirements.' *Morgan* v. *McDonough.* . . . It is a familiar constitutional principle that a state, having so acted when not compelled, may consequently create a constitutionally protected interest."[15]

The availability of the banned books from sources outside the school library has been cited by the lower courts (a) in arguments justifying the censorship and (b) in arguments against the censorship. While the *Bicknell* court argued that the Board's action did not abridge the students' constitutional rights of free expression, because "students remain free to purchase the books in question from private bookstores, to read them in other libraries . . . ," the *Minarcini* court saw the removal of the books from a school library as "a much more serious burden upon freedom of classroom discussion than the action found unconstitutional in *Tinker* . . . ," and, continued the court, "we do not think this burden is minimized by the availability of the disputed book in sources outside the school. Restraint on expression may not generally be justified by the fact that there may be other times, places, or circumstances available for such expression." In deciding that *Ms.* magazine could not be removed from the school library, the District Court stated in *Salvail* that "the defendants' contention as to the limited impact of the removal of MS magazine to the high school population, members of which are free to purchase or to read the publication in a public library, is without merit."

In deciding to reverse a lower court's judgment against students who had objected to the removal of *Down These Mean Streets, The Naked Ape, Soul on Ice, Go Ask Alice,* and other books from the school library, Judge Newman of the United States Court of Appeals, Second Circuit, stated that the availability of the banned books elsewhere was not decisive: "The symbolic effect of a school's action in removing a book solely because of its ideas will often be more significant than the resulting limitation upon access to it. The fact that the books barred from the school library may be available elsewhere is not decisive. What is significant is that the school has used its public power to perform an act clearly indicating that the views represented by the forbidden books are unacceptable. The impact of burning a book does not depend on whether every copy is on the fire. Removing a book from a school library is a less offensive act, but it can also pose a substantial threat of suppression."[16]

But to Judge Mansfield, sitting on the same Appeals Court, the availability of the books elsewhere argued against finding for the students; Mansfield said in his dissenting opinion that not only were students free to discuss the ideas of the books on the school premises, they "may also be able to purchase the books outside of school or borrow them from a public library. In short, there are no First Amendment or other constitutional interests at stake...."

The *Minarcini, Salvail,* and *Pico* courts' position that one cannot justify banning materials on the grounds that those materials are obtainable elsewhere was reflected earlier in the United States Supreme Court's opinion in *Kleindienst* v. *Mandel.* Even though the majority of the Court decided against allowing Belgian journalist and Marxist theoretician Ernest Mandel to enter the United States to deliver a series of lectures, primarily because the Court felt that the Attorney General had sufficient reasons to bar Mandel, the same majority emphasized in its opinion that the Court recognized the First Amendment right to "receive information and ideas." Indeed, the Court appeared to reject the Government's argument that those who wanted to be informed of Mandel's ideas could go to some other source, such as his publications; in the words of the majority of the Court, "While alternative means of access to Mandel's ideas might be a relevant factor were we called upon to balance First Amendment rights against governmental regulatory interests—a balance we find unnecessary here.... —we are loath to hold on this record that existence of other alternatives extinguishes altogether any constitutional interest on the part of appellees in this particular form of access."[17]

Yet, in his 1982 *Pico* dissenting opinion, Justice Rehnquist, joined by the Chief Justice and Justice Powell, declared, "After all else is said ... the most obvious reason that petitioners' removal of the books did not violate respondents' right to receive information is the ready availability of the books elsewhere. Students are not denied books by their removal from a school library. The books may be borrowed from a public library, read at a university library, purchased at a bookstore, or loaned by a friend. The government as educator does not seek to reach beyond the confines of the school. Indeed, following the removal from the school library of the books at issue in this case, the local public library put all nine books on display for public inspection. Their contents were fully accessible to any inquisitive student."[18]

The United States District Court which held that the school board's removal of *Male and Female Under 18* from the high school library was an infringement on the First Amendment rights of students and faculty cited *Red Lion Broadcasting Corp.* v. *FCC,* in which the United States Supreme Court had said, "It is the purpose of the First Amendment to preserve an uninhibited marketplace of ideas in which truth will ultimately prevail.... It is the right of the public to receive suitable access to social, political, esthetic, moral and other ideas and experiences which is crucial here."[19] The District Court cited from *Red Lion* to support its position that "what is at stake here is the right to read and be exposed to controversial thought and language—a valuable right subject to First Amendment protection."[20]

Allowing students to freely discuss the subject matter and contents of a book, in and out of the classroom, has led the lower courts to conclude that (a) the book itself could not be banned from the school library and (b) the book could be banned from the school library. In arguing that the United States Supreme Court should hear the case involving the banning of *Down These Mean Streets*, Justice Douglas had said, in 1972, "The Board . . . contends that a book with such vivid accounts of sordid and perverted occurrences is not good for junior high students. At trial both sides produced expert witnesses to prove the value or harm of the novel. At school the children are allowed to discuss the contents of the book and the social problems it portrays. They can do everything but read it. This in my mind lessens somewhat the contention that the subject matter of the book is not proper."

Though the Board's allowing of students to freely discuss the contents of the book led Justice Douglas to the conclusion that the book should also be made available for discussion, this allowance led two United States District Courts to the conclusion that the book could be banned. The District Court which had found against the students in *Pico* argued: "Significantly, the school board's actions here involved no religious question, either free exercise or establishment; nor was there a ban on teaching of any theory or doctrine; nor has there been a restriction imposed on classroom discussion, or a penalty inflicted on any teacher or librarian. Moreover, these restrictions have denied no student the right to silent or open speech as did the restrictions in *Tinker*. . . ; they have not inhibited discussion in the classroom or elsewhere in the schools; and they have focused upon no particular student or group."

In finding for the high school Board of Directors which had ordered the removal of *Dog Day Afternoon* and *The Wanderers* from the school library, the District Court noted in *Bicknell* that "there has been neither evidence nor argument in this case that the Board's actions have in fact abridged the student plaintiff's constitutional rights of free expression. Students remain free to purchase the books in question from private bookstores, to read them in other libraries, to carry them to school and to discuss them freely during the school day. Neither the Board's failure to purchase a work nor its decision to remove or restrict access to a work in the school library violate the first amendment rights of the student plaintiffs before this court."

As the District Courts in *Pico* and *Bicknell* and the Supreme Court Justices dissenting in *Pico* saw it, the fact that students were free to discuss the contents of the books demonstrated that their First Amendment freedoms were not abridged by the banning of the books. To others, such as Justice Douglas, allowing students to discuss the language and content of *Down These Mean Streets* carried with it the corollary of allowing the students to have access to the book through their school library, or at least of not removing the book from the library shelf simply because it offended the sensibilities of some board members or citizens of the community.

Can a book be removed from the school library shelves because members of a school board or of the community find the language and content of the book "disgusting," "filthy," or "vulgar"? In *Right to Read Defense Committee,* involving the banning of *Male and Female Under 18,* the District Court said that the "defendants' case was premised on the assumption that language offensive to the Committee and some parents had no place in the Chelsea education system" and the Court then quoted from *Keefe* v. *Geanakos* (a case dealing with a teacher's use of "vulgar" language in a high school English class studying the uses of language), in which Judge Aldrich had said, "With the greatest respect to such parents, their sensibilities are not the full measure of what is proper education." The District Court argued that if *Male and Female Under 18* "may be removed by a committee hostile to its language and theme, then the precedent is set for removal of any other work. The prospect of successive school committees 'sanitizing' the school library of views divergent from their own is alarming, whether they do it book by book or one page at a time."

The *Pico* District Court, however, in upholding the ban on *Go Ask Alice, Black Boy, Soul on Ice,* and several other books, asserted that the school board's action "has restricted access only to certain books which the board believed to be, in essence, vulgar. While removal of such books from a school library may, indeed in this court's view does, reflect a misguided educational philosophy, it does not constitute a sharp and direct infringement of any first amendment right."

In reversing the District Court's judgment in *Pico,* Judge Sifton of the Court of Appeals expressed concern about the imprecision of the "charges" against the books involved in this case:

> Whatever may be said in favor of the good intentions of the school officials in this case . . . little may be said in support of their sensitivity or precision in dealing with the first amendment issues in this case. On the substantive side, the criteria used for removal suggested by the evidence suffer excessive generality and overbreadth. Whatever definiteness there may be in a complaint that a book is "filth" . . . there is certainly no precision, sufficient to provide the kind of reasonably clear guidance necessary for free and open debate, in the complaints that books are "anti-Christian" or "anti-American." See *Keyishian* v. *Board of Regents.* . . . The very nature of this broad brush approach must inevitably be to suggest that the school officials' concern is less to cleanse the libraries of all books containing material insulting to members of one or another religious group or which evidences an inaccurate view of the nation's history, than it is to express an official policy with regard to God and country of uncertain and indefinite content which is to be ignored by pupils, librarians and teachers at their peril.

Judge Sifton expressed concern not only about the vagueness of the "charges" against the books but also about the "erratic, arbitrary and free-wheeling manner in which the defendant school officials proceeded in this case." He observed that the "books were removed from the school library shelves before any concerned school official had read them, solely on the basis of mimeographed quotations collected by anonymous readers whose editorial comments revealed political concerns reaching far beyond the education and well-being of the children of the Island Trees Union Free School District."[21]

Judge Mansfield of the Appeals Court appeared to give credence to the practice of determining the suitability of books for high school students on the basis of excerpts taken from the books and not on the basis of taking the work as a whole. Mansfield stated in his *Pico* dissent: "...adopting the Supreme Court's practice in similar cases, see e.g. *Federal Communications Commission* v. *Pacifica Foundation...*, I have set forth in the margin those portions of the text of the books which led the Board to investigate their suitability as educational tools and to discontinue eight of the books. Despite Judge Sifton's conclusion that the excerpts leave 'no great sense of confidence in the literary accuracy of the quotations,' I find, upon reading the books, that except for minor errors the quotations are indeed accurate. I also note that some of the books contain additional indecent statements not found in the original excerpts." Judge Mansfield cites, for example, eight excerpts from Bernard Malamud's *The Fixer;* one extended quotation from Eldridge Cleaver's *Soul on Ice;* the following three excerpts from Alice Childress's *A Hero Ain't Nothin' But a Sandwich:* "[p.] 10 Hell no! Fuck the society. [pp.] 64-65 The hell with the junkie, the wino, the capitalist, the welfare checks, the world...yeah, and fuck you too! [pp.] 75-76 They can have back the spread and curtains, I'm too old for them fuckin bunnies anyway."

The four dissenting Supreme Court Justices approached the "vulgarity" issue in *Pico* in much the same manner as Judge Mansfield, with Justice Powell attaching to his dissenting opinion the offending excerpts from the several books and Chief Justice Burger stating in his dissenting opinion: "The plurality also tells us that a book may be removed from a school library if it is 'pervasively vulgar.' But why must the vulgarity be 'pervasive' to be offensive? Vulgarity might be concentrated in a single poem or a single chapter or a single page, yet still be inappropriate. Or a school board might reasonably conclude that even 'random' vulgarity is inappropriate for teenage school students. A school board might also reasonably conclude that the school board's retention of such books gives those volumes an implicit endorsement. Cf. *FCC* v. *Pacifica Foundation,* 438 U. S. 726 (1978)."

But the practice of determining the value of a book on the basis of isolated passages and words was discarded years ago by the United States Supreme Court and most lower courts. When in 1933, Judge Woolsey decided that James Joyce's *Ulysses* was not obscene, he did so by taking into account the work as a whole, not various "obscene" passages in the book. In the landmark *Roth* decision, the United States Supreme Court Court found nothing wrong with the trial judge's instructions to the jury when he said: "The books, pictures and circulars must be judged as a whole, in their entire context, and you are not to consider detached or separate portions in reaching a conclusion."[22] The requirement that a book must be taken as a whole in determining whether it is obscene has been incorporated into subsequent Supreme Court obscenity tests, such as the *Memoirs* test and the *Miller* test.[23] But in their *Pico* dissents, Judge Mansfield and the four dissenting Supreme Court Justices depart from this criterion.

In setting "forth in the margin" the passages from the several books at issue in *Pico,* Mansfield states that he is "adopting the Supreme Court's practice in similar cases, e.g. *Federal Communications Commission* v. *Pacifica Foundation...*" It is noteworthy, however, that in the *Pacifica Foundation* case, the Supreme Court appended to its opinion the *entire* George Carlin "dirty words" selection which had been aired over a New York radio station; the Supreme Court looked at the "work" as a whole, in its entirety, not merely at a passage or two. In fact, in his opinion, Justice John Paul Stevens pointed out that the "dirty words" would probably not be banned if aired in another context: "It is appropriate, in conclusion, to emphasize the narrowness of our holding. This case does not involve a two-way radio conversation between a cab driver and a dispatcher, or a telecast of an Elizabethan comedy. We have not decided that an occasional expletive in either setting would justify any sanction or, indeed, that this broadcast would justify a criminal prosecution."[24] If several vulgar words could be aired on radio or television in the context of an Elizabethan comedy or some other classical piece of literature, even if children are likely to be listening, perhaps as a "captive audience," then justifying the banning from a school library or classroom significant works of literature, such as *Catch 22*, *The Fixer* or *Slaughterhouse Five*, becomes extremely difficult, especially when the students are not a "captive audience" in the library.

In rejecting a lower court's ruling that Kurt Vonnegut's *Slaughterhouse Five* "be forthwith removed from the defendant's school library," the Court of Appeals of Michigan noted in *Todd* v. *Rochester Community Schools* that "obscenity, although not raised in the pleadings, and declared not to be an issue in the trial court's June 9, 1971 judgment, is pervasive in the lower court's opinion."[25] The lower court's condemnation of the book on the basis of isolated passages and words was rejected by the Appeals Court: "In his findings of fact, the trial judge did indeed cite many words which, if standing alone, would offend some person's sensibilities. Yet each and every example advanced by the trial court was taken totally out of context. This is constitutional error." And, said the Appeals Court, "although the trial court did not expressly rule that *Slaughterhouse Five* was obscene, his June 9, 1971 judgment strongly suggests that possibility. We are constrained to hold that *Slaughterhouse Five* is clearly not obscene under present constitutional tests."

It is noteworthy that in none of the library censorship cases dealt with in this book was it ever established, nor even argued in some cases, that the banned books were "obscene," as that term has been defined by the United States Supreme Court. The language in the books removed from the school libraries was condemned more vaguely as "filthy," "vulgar," or "indecent"; the subject matter may have been "offensive," "anti-Christian," or "un-American," but none of the books was ever determined to be obscene.

Concerned that those calling for the removal of the books involved in *Pico* were motivated to ban the books more because of the content than the objectionable language, Judge Newman said in his 1980 *Pico* concurring opinion: "Ideas and the language used to express them always are related. See *Cohen* v. *California*. . . . Because of that relationship First Amendment values would be imperiled if a motivation concerned with the language of a book were permitted to justify an act of suppression also motivated by the book's political content."[26]

In deciding against the school board in *Pico*, Justice Brennan expressed a similar concern, that it was possible that the books in that case had been banned because the school board disliked the ideas in the books: "Our Constitution does not permit the official suppression of *ideas*. Thus whether petitioners' removal of books from their school libraries denied respondents their First Amendment rights depends upon the motivation behind petitioners' actions. If petitioners *intended* by their removal decision to deny respondents access to ideas with which petitioners disagreed, and if this intent was the decisive factor in petitioners' decision, then petitioners have exercised their discretion in violation of the Constitution. To permit such intentions to control official actions would be to encourage the precise sort of officially prescribed orthodoxy unequivocally condemned in *Barnette*. On the other hand, respondents implicitly concede that an unconstitutional motivation would *not* be demonstrated if it were shown that petitioners had decided to remove the books at issue if it were shown that petitioners had decided to remove the books because those books were pervasively vulgar."

Whether upholding the banning of books from the libraries or declaring such censorship unconstitutional, the courts have had to deal with the Supreme Court's landmark 1969 *Tinker* decision, in which the majority gave First Amendment protection to students who wore black armbands to school as a means of communicating their opposition to the Vietnam war. Also, the courts have had to grapple with the question of whether the marketplace of ideas and the right to receive information, which apply to the public in general, apply also to students in the schoolhouse.

In *Tinker* the Court declared that "First Amendment rights, applied in light of the special characteristics of the school environment, are available to teachers and students. It can hardly be argued that either students or teachers shed their constitutional rights to freedom of speech or expression at the schoolhouse gate. This has been the unmistakable holding of this Court for almost 50 years."[27] When in 1943 the Court had decided in *Barnette* that students of the Jehovah's Witness faith could not be required to take part in the flag salute ritual at school, the high court said that "the Fourteenth Amendment, as now applied to the states, protects the citizen against the State itself and all of its creatures—Boards of Education not excepted. These have, of course, important, delicate, and highly discretionary functions, but none that they may not perform within the limits of the Bill of Rights. That they are educating the young for citizenship is reason for scrupulous protection of Constitutional freedoms of the individual, if we are not to strangle the free mind at its source and teach youth to discount important principles of our government as mere platitudes."[28]

When in 1978 a United States District Court decided that the book *Male and Female Under 18* could not be banned from the Chelsea, Massachusetts, high school library, the court was reflecting the thinking of *Tinker* and *Barnette:* "Students have a right to express themselves in non-disruptive political protest..., and the right not to be forced to express ideas with which they disagree.... In short, the First Amendment is not merely a mantle which students and faculty must doff when they take their place in the classroom."[29]

However, the United States Court of Appeals, which decided that it was not unconstitutional for a New York school district to order its junior high school libraries to make *Down These Mean Streets* directly available only to the parents of the students, declared that "the appellant conveniently ignores the factual setting of *Tinker* but would have us apply its test. Since the shelving of *Down These Mean Streets* did not create any disruption or disorder, it is argued, it should remain on the shelf. There is here no problem of freedom of speech or the expression of opinions on the part of parents, teachers, students or librarians. As we have pointed out, the discussion of the book or the problems which it encompasses or the ideas it espouses have not been prohibited by the Board's action in removing the book."

Arguing that the United States Supreme Court should hear the case involving *Down These Mean Streets,* Justice Douglas relied, in part, on *Tinker:* "The First Amendment is a preferred right and is of great importance in the schools. In *Tinker,* the Court held that the First Amendment can only be restricted in the schools when a disciplinary problem is raised. No such allegation is asserted here. What else can the School Board now decide it does not like? How else will its sensibilities be offended? Are we sending children to school to be educated by the norms of the School Board or are we educating our youth to shed the prejudices of the past, to explore all forms of thought, and to find solutions to our world's problems?"

In their 1982 *Pico* opinions, both Justices Brennan and Blackmun rely heavily on *Tinker,* Blackmun stating: "In my view, we strike a proper balance here by holding that school officials may not remove books for the *purpose* of restricting access to the political ideas or social perspectives discussed in them, when that action is motivated simply by the officials' disapproval of the ideas involved. It does not seem radical to suggest that state action calculated to suppress novel ideas or concepts is fundamentally antithetical to the values of the First Amendment. At a minimum, allowing a school board to engage in such conduct hardly teaches children to respect the diversity of ideas that is fundamental to the American system. In this context, then, the school board must be able to show that its action was caused by something more than a mere desire to avoid the discomfort and unpleasantness that always accompany an unpopular viewpoint, *Tinker* v. *Des Moines School Dist...,* and that the board had something in mind in addition to the suppression of partisan or political views it did not share."

The four Justices dissenting in *Pico,* however, did not see *Tinker* as applicable; nor did they appear to object to allowing the school board "unfettered" discretion to "transmit community values" through the Island Trees schools. Of the relevance of *Tinker,* Justice Rehnquist wrote, "But as this language from *Tinker* suggests, our past decisions in this area have concerned freedom of speech and expression, not the right of access to particular ideas. We have held that students may not be prevented from symbolically expressing their political views by wearing of black arm bands ... and that they may not be forced to participate in the symbolic expression of saluting the flag. ... But these decisions scarcely control the case before us. Neither the District Court nor the Court of Appeals found that petitioners' removal of books from the school libraries infringed respondents' right to speak or otherwise express themselves."

Apparently willing to give the school board "unfettered" discretion, the dissenters appear to agree with the position expressed by the school committee which attempted to ban from the school library *Ms.* magazine, "claiming an unconstrained authority to remove books from the shelves of the school library."[30] According to the Justices dissenting in *Pico,* the appropriate response by those who objected to the school board's removal of *Go Ask Alice,*

The Fixer, Soul on Ice, A Hero Ain't Nothin' But a Sandwich, and other books from the high school libraries was to remove the board members who supported the ban on the books by voting against them at the next election. In the words of Chief Justice Burger, "How are 'fundamental values' to be inculcated except by having school boards make content-based decisions about the appropriateness of retaining materials in the school library and curriculum. In order to fulfill its function, an elected school board *must* express its views on the subjects which are taught to its students. In doing so those elected officials express their views of their community; they may err, of course, and the voters may remove them. It is a startling erosion of the very idea of democratic government to have this Court arrogate to itself the power the plurality asserts today." What the Chief Justice and the other *Pico* dissenters failed to take into account, and what the *Barnette* majority recognized forty years earlier, was that "there are village tyrants as well as village Hampdens, but none who acts under color of the law is beyond the Constitution."[31]

While the Justices dissenting in *Pico* denied that any "right to receive information and ideas" was guaranteed to students, Justice Brennan emphasized that "the First Amendment rights of students may be directly and sharply implicated by the removal of books from the shelves of a school library." It was Brennan's position that "just as access to ideas makes it possible for citizens generally to exercise their rights of free speech and press in a meaningful manner, such access prepares students for active and effective participation in the pluralistic, often contentious society in which they will soon be adult members. Of course all First Amendment rights accorded to students must be construed 'in light of the special characteristics of the school environment.' *Tinker.* . . . But the special characteristics of the school *library* make that environment especially appropriate for recognition of the First Amendment rights of students."

The First Amendment rights of minors were discussed in another context by Supreme Court Justice Powell in his 1975 majority opinion declaring unconstitutional a Jacksonville, Florida, ordinance which prohibited the showing at drive-in theaters of films depicting any nudity. Powell rejected the city's argument that the ordinance was an exercise of the city's police power to protect children. Delivering the opinion of the Court, Powell stated that "minors are entitled to a significant measure of First Amendment protection. . . , and only in relatively narrow and well-defined circumstances may government bar public dissemination of protected materials to them. . . ." Powell's argument could easily be applied to the rights of students to have access to controversial books in the school library: *"Speech that is neither obscene as to youths nor subject to some other legitimate proscription cannot be suppressed solely to protect the young from ideas or images that a legislative body thinks unsuitable for them. In most circumstances the values protected by the First Amendment are no less applicable when government seeks to control the flow of information to minors."*[32] [Italics mine] While Justice Powell spoke out in 1975 against suppressing speech "solely to protect the young from ideas or images that a legislative body thinks unsuitable for them," in 1982 Powell argued in his *Pico* dissenting opinion that a school board was not required "to promote ideas and values repugnant to a democratic society or to teach such values to *children.*"

"Protecting" people, whether they be students or nonstudents, from such "objectionable" books as *Catch 22, The Fixer, Soul on Ice,* and *Slaughterhouse Five* by removing such books from our libraries, in or out of the schoolhouse, does not reflect much confidence in those Americans who would be exposed to such literature. If a society is to remain free, however, the citizenry must ultimately be trusted to make their own decisions related to the books, magazines, and newspapers they wish to read. Supreme Court Justice Potter Stewart has observed that "censorship reflects a society's lack of confidence in itself" and that the Constitution "protects coarse expression as well as refined, and vulgarity not less than elegance. A book worthless to me may convey something of value to my neighbor. In the free society to which our Constitution has committed us, it is for each to choose for himself."[33] The book censors, however, deny us the freedom to choose. Unlike Justice Douglas, who has written, "I have the same confidence in the ability of our people to reject noxious literature as I have in their capacity to sort out the true from the false in theology, economics, politics, or any other field,"[34] the censors question the abilities of others to choose.

When in 1967 the United States Supreme Court struck down as unconstitutional New York's teacher loyalty oaths, Justice Brennan declared in the opinion of the Court, "Our nation is deeply committed to safeguarding academic freedom, which is of transcendent value to all of us and not merely to the teachers concerned. That freedom is therefore a special concern of the First Amendment, which does not tolerate laws that cast a pall of orthodoxy over the classroom."[35] Similarly, surely the First Amendment does not tolerate laws, orders, or actions by high or petty officials that "cast a pall of orthodoxy" over our libraries.

NOTES

1. William Brennan, Jr., "Law, Liberty and Libraries," *Book Selection and Censorship in the Sixties,* ed. Eric Moon (New York: Bowker, 1969), p. 268.
2. *Board of Education* v. *Pico,* 42 CCH S.Ct. Bull. B3921, 50 *LW* 4831 (1982).
3. For discussion of the paucity of library litigation see Robert O'Neil, "Libraries, Liberties and the First Amendment," *University of Cincinnati Law Review* 42 (1973): 213–216.
4. L. B. Woods, *A Decade of Censorship in America* (Metuchen, N. J.: Scarecrow Press, 1979), pp. 155–156.
5. Brennan, p. 268.
6. *Presidents Council, Dist. 25* v. *Community School Bd. No. 25,* 409 U.S. 998 (1972).
7. *Presidents Council, Dist. 25* v. *Community School Bd. No. 25,* 457 F.2d 289 (1972).
8. *Board of Education* v. *Pico,* 42 CCH S.Ct. Bull. B3921, 50 *LW* 4831 (1982).
9. *Minarcini* v. *Strongsville City School Dist.,* 541 F.2d 577 (1977).
10. *Virginia State Bd. of Pharmacy* v. *Virginia Citizens Consumers Council, Inc.,* 425 U.S. 748 (1966).
11. *Bicknell* v. *Vergennes Union High School Bd. of Directors,* 475 F.Supp. 615 (1979).
12. *Presidents Council, Dist. 25* v. *Community School Bd. No. 25,* 457 F.2d 289 (1972).
13. *Right to Read Defense Committee* v. *School Committee, Etc.,* 454 F.Supp. 703 (1978).
14. *Minarcini* v. *Strongsville City School Dist.,* 541 F.2d 577 (1977).
15. *Salvail* v. *Nashua Board of Education,* 469 F.Supp. 1269 (1979).
16. *Pico* v. *Board of Ed., Island Trees Union Free School Dist.,* 638 F.2d 404 (1980).
17. *Kleindienst* v. *Mandel,* 408 U.S. 421 (1972).
18. *Board of Education* v. *Pico,* 42 CCH S.Ct. Bull. B3921, 50 *LW* 4831 (1982).
19. *Red Lion Broadcasting Co.* v. *FCC,* 395 U.S. 367 (1969).
20. *Right to Read Defense Committee* v. *School Committee, Etc.,* 454 F.Supp. 703 (1978).
21. *Pico* v. *Board of Ed., Island Trees Union Free School Dist.,* 638 F.2d 404 (1980).
22. *Roth* v. *United States,* 354 U.S. 476 (1957).
23. *Memoirs* v. *Massachusetts,* 383 U.S. 413 (1966); *Miller* v. *California,* 413 U.S. 15 (1973).
24. *FCC* v. *Pacifica Foundation,* 438 U.S. 726 (1978).
25. *Todd* v. *Rochester Community Schools,* 200 N.W.2d 90 (1972).
26. *Pico* v. *Board of Ed., Island Trees Union Free School Dist.,* 638 F.2d 404 (1980).
27. *Tinker* v. *Des Moines School Dist.,* 393 U.S. 503 (1969).
28. *West Virginia State Bd. of Education* v. *Barnette,* 319 U.S. 624 (1943).
29. *Right to Read Defense Committee* v. *School Committee, Etc.,* 454 F.Supp. 703 (1978).
30. *Salvail* v. *Nashua Board of Education,* 469 F.Supp. 1269 (1979).
31. *West Virginia State Bd. of Education* v. *Barnette,* 319 U.S. 624 (1943).
32. *Erznoznik* v. *Jacksonville,* 422 U.S. 205 (1975).
33. *Ginzburg* v. *United States,* 383 U.S. 463 (1966).
34. *Roth* v. *United States,* 354 U.S. 476 (1957).
35. *Keyishian* v. *Board of Regents,* 385 U.S. 589 (1967).

CENSORSHIP
LIBRARIES
AND THE
LAW

PART ONE

School Library
Censorship Cases

*The California State Supreme Court decides
that the Selma Union High School District of
Fresno County may purchase twelve copies of the
Bible in the King James version for the library
of the high school, the court declaring: "The
mere act of purchasing a book to be added to
the school library does not carry with it any
implication of the adoption of the theory or
dogma contained therein, or any approval of the
book itself, except as a work of literature fit
to be included in a reference library."*

Evans v. Selma Union High School
Dist., 222P. 801 (1924)

PER CURIAM. Plaintiff brought this action
to enjoin the trustees of the Selma union high
school district of Fresno county from carrying
into effect a resolution for the purchase of 12
copies of the Bible in the King James version
for the library of the high school. George
Enos was permitted to intervene, and filed a
complaint which alleged substantially the same
matters and sought the same relief as that of
plaintiff. Both complaints rest on the contention that the King James version of the Bible
is a book of a sectarian character, and that
its purchase for the library of a public school
is therefore contrary to constitutional and
statutory provisions in this state.

The trial court held that the Bible in the
King James version was not a publication of
sectarian, partisan, or denominational character, and accordingly gave judgment for the defendants. This appeal is from that judgment.

The Constitution of this state provides (article, 1, § 4) that--

   "The free exercise and enjoyment of religious profession and worship, without discrimination or preference, shall forever be
   guaranteed in this state."

It prohibits (article 4, § 30) appropria-
tions, grants, or payments of public moneys in
aid of any "religious sect, church, creed, or
sectarian purpose," or to support or sustain
any school or other institution "controlled by
any religious creed, church, or sectarian denomination whatever." In section 8 of article
9 it provides that--

   "No public money shall ever be appropri-
   ated for the support of any sectarian or denominational school, or any school not under
   the exclusive control of the officers of the
   public schools; nor shall any sectarian or
   denominational doctrine be taught, or instruction thereon be permitted, directly or
   indirectly, in any of the common schools of
   this state."

Political Code, § 1607 (subdivision 3), as

added by St. 1917, p. 736, § 6, makes it the
duty of boards of education and school
trustees--

   "to exclude from school and school libraries all books, publications, or papers
   of a sectarian, partisan, or denominational
   character."

Section 1672 of the same Code provides that--

   "No publication of a sectarian, partisan,
   or denominational character must be used or
   distributed in any school, or be made a part
   of any school library; nor must any sectarian or denominational doctrine be taught
   therein."

The question before us is different from
those dealt with in the reported cases which
consider the question of Bible instruction in
the public schools. We have examined with care
all decisions cited by counsel and all that our
independent research has discovered, and not
one of them deals with the precise question now
under consideration, namely, the placing of the
Bible in a public school library. These decisions all deal with questions growing out of
the use of the Bible in devotional exercises or
for religious instruction or as a text-book in
the public schools; for that reason we do not
discuss these decisions in detail in arriving
at our conclusion, although some of these decisions consider and decide whether or not the
Bible is sectarian. In our opinion, for the
reasons hereafter stated, it is clear that for
reference and library purposes in the public
schools, it is not a book of the class prohibited by our statute.

It will be seen from the provisions of our
statutes above quoted that they do not in terms
exclude from these schools "religious" books as
such. Indeed, there is nothing in our statutes
aimed at religious works. To be legally objectionable they must be "sectarian, partisan,
or denominational in character." It is under
our Code provisions that this question immediately arises, and their terms must be construed
with their intent and purpose in view and the
mischief at which they were aimed. The terms
used are "sectarian," and "denominational."
"Sect," strictly defined, means "a body of persons distinguished by peculiarities of faith
and practice from other bodies adhering to the
same general system" (Standard Dict.), and "denominational" is given much the same definition. But the term "sect" has frequently a
broader signification, the activities of the
followers of one faith being regarded as sectarian as related to those of the adherents of
another. Since the object of these Code provisions was to exclude controversial matters of
any kind from the school libraries, in so far
as that object could be attained by the exclusion of printed matter of partisan tendency, we
have no doubt that the term "sectarian" was
used in its broad signification. The purpose
was to bar from school libraries books and other publications of factional religion--those
whose character is "sectarian, partisan, or de-

3

nominational." As a book on almost any subject may adopt a partisan tone, so a book on religion, instead of confining itself to broad principles and simple fundamentals, may emphasize particular points -- those upon which differences of opinion have arisen. In a word, a book on any subject may be strongly partisan in tone and treatment. A religious book treating its subject in this manner would be sectarian. But not all books of religion would be thus excluded. The fact that it was not approved by all sects of a particular religion, nor by the followers of all religions, would not class it as sectarian for library purposes. There is no religion that has found universal acceptance, and therefore no book of religion that has.

The correctness of this view of the meaning of these Code sections is indicated by their origin. Since 1851 the statutes of this state have excluded books of a sectarian character from public school libraries. Stats. 1851, pp. 491, 495, art. 3, § 5; Stats. 1852, pp. 117, 125, art. 6, § 3; Stats. 1855, p. 229, 237, § 33; Stats. 1863, pp. 194, 210, § 67; Stats. 1869-70, pp. 824, 835, 839, 842, §§ 42, 58, 71. Political Code, § 1607 (3), was derived from section 42 (subd. 11) of the Act of 1870, the language of which shows the class of publications in the mind of the Legislature. It required the school authorities to exclude from schools and their libraries "books, tracts, papers or catechisms of a sectarian character." As originally adopted into the Code (Pol. Code, § 1617, subd. 12, enacted March 12, 1872) this language was shortened to "books, publications or papers of a sectarian character." The words "partisan or denominational" were inserted after "sectarian" by Code Amendments 1873-74, p. 81, and its present number (1607) was given the section by an amendment in 1917 (Stats. 1917, p. 736).

Political Code, § 1672, which has remained the same since its adoption in 1872, was derived from section 58 of the same Act of 1870, which referred to "books, tracts, papers, catechisms or other publications of a sectarian or denominational character." Thus we think the history of these sections indicates the class of "books" and "other publications" at which the statute was aimed.

Turning to the character of the King James version, it appears that the original manuscripts of the Bible have been lost for centuries. Those available for translation are themselves "versions," and either copies or translations or still older texts. There have been numerous English translations, but those most generally in use to-day are the King James version, and its subsequent English and American revisions, and the Douai version.

The Douai version consists of a translation of the New Testament made in the English College at Rheims, published there in 1582, and of the Old Testament published at Douai in 1609.

The King James version is a translation made at the direction of James I of England, and published at London in 1611. The work was done by a commission of forty-seven scholars drawn largely from the universities of Oxford and Cambridge. The work of its revision by English and American committees was begun in 1870, and the revised New Testament published in 1881, and the revised Old Testament in 1884.

The Douai version is based upon the text of the Latin Vulgate, the King James version on the Hebrew and Greek texts. There are variances in the rendering of certain phrases and passages. The Douai version incorporates the Apocrypha, which are omitted from the texts of the Testaments in the King James version, though in many editions they have been printed between the two Testaments. The Douai version was the work of Catholics, and is the translation used by the Roman Catholic Church in English-speaking countries. The King James version and its revisions are the work of Protestants, and are used in Protestant churches.

The contention that the Bible in the King James translation is a book of a sectarian character rests on the fact that there are differences between it and, among others, the Douai version; that it is of Protestant authorship; that it is used in Protestant Churches; and that it is not approved by the Catholic Church. According to such a test the Bible in any known version or text is sectarian. In fact, until all sects can agree upon the manuscript texts that should be used, no English version of the Bible not "sectarian" in this view can be produced.

The statute, however, deals with publications of a sectarian character. It makes the character of the book the test of whether it is "sectarian," not the authorship or the extent of its approval by different sects or by all. That the authors of religious books belong to a sect or church does not necessarily make their books of a sectarian character. Nor does the fact that the King James version is commonly used by Protestant Churches and not by Catholics make its character sectarian. Its character is what it is, a widely accepted translation of the Bible. What we have said of the King James translation is equally applicable to the Douai version. Both are scholarly translations of the Bible, and neither is a book "of a sectarian character" within the meaning of the statute relating to school libraries. Both are eligible to a place on the shelves of our public school libraries for reference purposes. Each version has claims. Regarded merely as literature, the King James version is a recognized classic. For centuries it has been the version most generally used in Protestant Churches in England and America. The Douai version has merits of its own. It is the text approved by one of the world's greatest churches. Many children base their religious education upon its text. We do not assume to decide the comparative merits of the two versions. We do, however, hold that either or both may be purchased for and placed in a public school library without violation of the law of this state.

If it were a fact that the King James version of the Bible was sought to be placed in the public school library to the exclusion of all other versions of the Bible, or if it appeared to be a fact that this particular version or any other version of the Bible was to be used as a text-book for a prescribed course of study or to be used in reading therefrom to the pupils as a part of school exercises, it might then be well argued that such circumstances amounted to an implied declaration that this version was the only true version of the Scriptures, and that all others were false in so far as not in accord therewith. So used and under such circumstances it might be justly claimed to be used as a basis for sectarian instruction. Such are not the facts in the case at bar. The mere act of purchasing a book to be added to the school library does not carry with it any implication of the adoption of the theory or dogma contained therein, or any approval of the book itself, except as a work of literature fit to be included in a reference library. For aught that appears in the instant case the library in question may already contain copies of the Douai version of the Bible as well as copies of the Talmud, Koran, and teachings of Confucius. If the Douai version and these other books are not already in the library, we have no right to assume that they will not be added thereto in the future. That such action would be legal and appropriate we have no doubt.

We are not required in this case to decide, nor are we to be understood as deciding, the question of whether or not the use of the Bible for class instruction amounts to the teaching of sectarian or denominational doctrine, nor to consider whether or to what extent its reading may be made a part of the exercises in the schools, without offending the provisions of the state Constitution and statutes.

The judgment is affirmed.

All concur.

After considering the charge that Oliver Twist *and* The Merchant of Venice *are "objectionable because they tend to engender hatred of the Jew as a person and as a race," the Supreme Court, Kings County, New York, decides that these two works cannot be banned from the New York City Schools, libraries or classrooms, declaring that the Board Of Education "acted in good faith without malice or prejudice and in the best interests of the school system entrusted to their care and control, and, therefore, that no substantial reason exists which compels the suppression of the two books under consideration."*

Rosenberg v. Board of Education of City of New York, 92 N. Y. S. 2d 344 (1949)

DI GIOVANNA, Justice.

This is an application pursuant to Article 78 of the Civil Practice Act for review of a determination permitting and allowing the use of "Oliver Twist" by Charles Dickens and "The Merchant of Venice" by William Shakespeare, in the secondary schools of the City of New York as approved reading and study material.

In exercising its duty under Section 2516, subd. 3, of the Education Law, the respondents select text books regarded as preferable for instruction of pupils in English and English literature. These two books were selected together with many others.

Petitioner charges that the two books are objectionable because they tend to engender hatred of the Jew as a person and as a race.

It is not contended herein that the respondents, collectively or individually, approved the books because of anti-religious or anti-racial inclinations. As a matter of fact, because of public discussion concerning books of this nature, respondents have expressly required teachers to explain to pupils that the characters described therein are not typical of any nation or race, including persons of the Jewish faith, and are not intended and are not to be regarded as reflecting discredit on any race or national group.

Except where a book has been maliciously written for the apparent purpose of promoting and fomenting a bigoted and intolerant hatred against a particular racial or religious group, public interest in a free and democratic society does not warrant or encourage the suppression of any book at the whim of any unduly sensitive person or group of persons, merely because a character described in such book as belonging to a particular race or religion is portrayed in a derogatory or offensive manner. The necessity for the suppression of such a book must clearly depend upon the intent and motive which has actuated the author in making such a portrayal.

Literary value of a work of fiction does not depend upon the religious or national origin of the characters portrayed therein. If evaluation of any literary work is permitted to be based upon a requirement that each book be free from derogatory reference to any religion, race, country, nation or personality, endless litigation respecting many books would probably ensue, dependent upon sensibilities and views of the person suing.

Public education and instruction in the home will remove religious and racial intolerance more effectively than censorship and suppression of literary works which have been accepted as works of art and which are not per se propaganda against or for any race, religion or group. Removal from schools of these books will contribute nothing toward the diminution of anti-religious feeling; as a matter of fact, removal may lead to misguided reading and unwarranted inferences by the unguided pupil.

Educational institutions are concerned with the development of free inquiry and learning. The administrative officers must be free to guide teachers and pupils toward that goal. Their discretion must not be interfered with in the absence of proof of actual malevolent intent. Interference by the court will result in suppression of the intended purpose of aiding those seeking education.

The Court therefore finds that respondents, in exercising their judgment, did not abuse their discretion; that they acted in good faith without malice or prejudice and in the best interests of the school system entrusted to their care and control, and, therefore, that no substantial reason exists which compels the suppression of the two books under consideration. Motion for review is denied and the petition is dismissed.

In deciding that Slaughterhouse-Five *or the* Children's Crusade *could not be banned from the libraries and classrooms of Michigan schools, the Court of Appeals of Michigan declares:* "Vonnegut's literary dwellings on war, religion, death, Christ, God, government, politics, and any other subject should be as welcome in the public schools of this state as those of Machiavelli, Chaucer, Shakespeare, Melville, Lenin, Joseph McCarthy, or Walt Disney. The students of Michigan are free to make of Slaughterhouse-Five *what they will.*"

Todd v. *Rochester Community Schools,* 200 N. W. 2d 90 (1972)

BRONSON, Presiding Judge.

On March 24, 1971, plaintiff, Bruce Livingston Todd, filed a complaint for a writ of mandamus against the defendant, Rochester Community Schools, in the Oakland County Circuit Court. Mr. Todd's complaint alleged that one of his minor children was enrolled in a course of instruction referred to as "Current Literature" which was being taught in a Rochester public high school. Plaintiff averred that part of the curriculum in said course was the study of *Slaughterhouse-Five or The Children's Crusade,*[1] a novel by the contemporary American author, Kurt Vonnegut, Jr.

The gravamen of plaintiff's complaint was that *Slaughterhouse-Five* "contains and makes reference to religious matters" and, therefore,"the use of such book as a part or in connection with any course of instruction by a public school district or system is illegal and contrary to the laws of the land; namely, the First and Fourteenth Amendments of the United States Constitution."[2] Predicated on these factual allegations, Mr. Todd requested that the Oakland County Circuit Court issue a writ of mandamus compelling the defendant school district to cease utilizing *Slaughterhouse-Five* "as a part of a course of instruction in the Rochester Community Schools." In his complaint, Mr. Todd did not allege that *Slaughterhouse-Five* was obscene nor that it had no literary value.

On March 31, 1971, defendant answered plaintiff's complaint. In its pleading the Rochester Community Schools affirmatively stated that the novel at issue, along with several others, "is used in connection with a general secular course of instruction entitled 'Current Literature' and the fact that the same might incidentally refer to religious matters does not render its use in violation of the First and Fourteenth Amendments of the Constitution of the United States." Defendant further contended that the selection of books to be used in its course of instruction was a matter exclusively within its administrative powers and not subject to judicial supervision nor review.[3]

Subsequent to answering, defendant filed a motion for summary judgment of no cause of action on the basis that there was no genuine issue as to any material fact and that the Rochester Community School District was entitled to judgment as a matter of law. GCR 1963, 117.2(3). A hearing on this motion was held on April 7, 1971, before the Honorable Arthur E. Moore, Circuit Judge for the County of Oakland. At this time the parties stipulated to allow the novel into evidence, formally waived pretrial, and agreed to accept the court's decision predicated upon the pleadings, briefs and motions, with the book itself constituting the sole evidence.

On May 13, 1971, the court filed a nine-page opinion granting plaintiff's requested relief "if necessary". On May 20, 1971, in the trial judge's temporary absence, the Presiding Judge of the Oakland County Circuit Court entered a judgment of mandamus. However, on May 28, 1971, the trial judge, on his own motion, set aside the May 20, 1971 judgment so he could make more appropriate findings of fact and law. GCR 1963, 517.1. A new hearing was held before Judge Moore on June 5, 1971. On June 9, 1971, a final opinion and order granting plaintiff a judgment of mandamus was issued.[4]

On June 18, 1971, defendant filed a claim of appeal as a matter of right. On July 16, 1971, this Court granted the American Civil Liberties Union of Michigan permission to file a brief *amicus curiae*.[5]

After thorough study of the proceedings below, including a careful scrutiny of *Slaughterhouse-Five*, and aware that some of the legal questions suggested by these proceedings have apparently never been squarely passed upon by any other court in this country, we are constrained to reverse the trial court's judgment and permanently dissolve the previously issued judgment of mandamus. The reasons for our actions follow.

Initially we consider what we believe should have been the proper disposition of this matter in the court below. As previously indicated on March 31, 1971, defendant filed a motion for summary judgment pursuant to GCR 1963, 117.2(3). Technically, defendant's requested relief was more properly predicated upon the authority of GCR 1963, 117.2(1). For reasons we are about to delineate, we hold that even if all the factual allegations pleaded in the instant complaint are taken to be true, Bielski v. Wolverine Insurance Co., 379 Mich. 280, 283, 150 N.W.2d 788, 789 (1967), plaintiff still has "failed to state a claim upon which relief can be granted" and defendant should prevail as a matter of law.

Our Court considered the nature of GCR 1963, 117.2(1) in Major v. Schmidt Trucking Co., 15 Mich.App. 75, 166 N.W.2d 517 (1968). In *Major*, Judge Charles Levin, writing for a unanimous panel, observed that:

"A motion under GCR 1963, 117.2(1) asserts that the opposing party's pleading fails to state a claim upon which relief can be granted. The motion may be granted only

where it appears on the face of the challenged pleading that the pleader cannot recover." *Major, supra*, at 78, 166 N.W.2d at 518.

See, also, Bloss v. Williams, 15 Mich.App. 228, 231, 166 N.W.2d 520 (1968); Johnston's Administrator v. United Airlines, 23 Mich.App. 279, 286, 178 N.W.2d 536 (1970). The fact that defendant chose to support its motion by appending an affidavit is perfectly proper inasmuch as the combining of subparts of GCR 1963, 117 has been approved. Durant v. Stahlin, 375 Mich. 628, 644, 135 N.W.2d 392 (1965). But it was not necessary for defendant to affix an affidavit with its motion for summary judgment to prevail inasmuch as plaintiff's complaint pleads an alleged cause of action heretofore unknown to our law.[6] Plaintiff's theory will remain an unwelcome stranger to our jurisprudence unless and until the United States Supreme Court or our State Supreme Court dictate otherwise.

Pursuant to GCR 1963, 820.1(1) and (7) we grant defendant's requested summary judgment of no cause of action and reverse the trial court's judgment of mandamus.

Plaintiff's complaint specifically pleads only that *Slaughterhouse-Five* is used in a public school and "contains and makes reference to religious matters." We have been cited to no authority, nor has our own research uncovered any, which holds that *any* portion of *any* constitution is violated simply because a novel, utilized in a public school "contains and makes reference to religious matters". This concept is legally repugnant to what we believe is the time-tested rationale underlying the First and Fourteenth Amendments. By couching a personal grievance in First Amendment language, one may not stifle freedom of expression. Vigorously opposed to such a suggestion, we stand firm in rendering plaintiff's theory constitutionally impermissible.

If plaintiff's contention was correct, then public school students could no longer marvel at Sir Galahad's saintly quest for the Holy Grail, nor be introduced to the dangers of Hitler's *Mein Kampf* nor read the mellifluous poetry of John Milton and John Donne. Unhappily, Robin Hood would be forced to forage without Friar Tuck and Shakespeare would have to delete Shylock from *The Merchant of Venice*. Is this to be the state of our law? Our Constitution does not command ignorance; on the contrary, it assures the people that the state may not relegate them to such a status and guarantees to all the precious and unfettered freedom of pursuing one's own intellectual pleasures in one's own personal way.

We hasten to point out that plaintiff did not allege that the Rochester public schools were intentionally taking action which was derogatory to Christianity. Nor did plaintiff aver that defendant was attempting to "establish" any specific religious sect in preference over another; nor one over all others; nor none at all. Had plaintiff's complaint suggested such a state of affairs, the question before the Court would be substantially different. But in this case the evidence is undisputed that the novel in question, and the Bible, were being utilized as literature. There is no allegation nor proof that *Slaughterhouse-Five* was being taught subjectively, or that the religious or antireligious view contained therein were espoused by the teachers.

Portions of the trial court's rulings were as follows:

"40. It is hereby ordered that the book, 'Slaughterhouse Five or The Children's Crusade', be forthwith removed from the defendant's school library.

"41. It is further ordered that the book may not be fostered, promoted or recommended for use in the defendant's school system; and defendant is ordered to desist accordingly.

"42. It is further ordered that the book is banned from the school library only so long as is necessary to prevent its use as promoted or recommended reading material in the courses of study in defendant's school system.

"43. The book may be returned to the library shelves of the defendant school if and when the defendant has definitely and conclusively withdrawn and desisted from the promotion, recommendation and use of the book in educational courses of the defendant school system. This mandamus order may then be amended for that specific purpose on appropriate motion of counsel."

In rendering his decision the trial court relied solely upon School District of Abington Tp. v. Schempp, 374 U.S. 203, 83 S.Ct. 1560, 10 L.Ed.2d 844 (1963). *Schempp* held that a statute requiring daily Bible reading without comment in public schools violated the First Amendment, even though participation by each pupil was voluntary. *Schempp* is totally dissimilar to the case at bar. *Schempp* turned upon the fact that reciting a prayer in public schools had no connection whatsoever with secular education. Saying the prayer was an end in itself. Such conduct had as its primary purpose the advancement of religion; the relationship between prayer and education was non-existent.[7] This cannot be said about *Slaughterhouse-Five*. In our opinion, Mr. Vonnegut's novel is an anti-war allegory which dwells on the horror of the Allied fire-bombing of Dresden[8] and which makes ancillary use of religious matter only for literary reasons. But whatever our insight or ability as critics, we are strongly persuaded that, as judges, we are correct in holding that *Slaughterhouse-Five* is not violative of the *Schempp* test:

"The test may be stated as follows: what are the purpose and the primary effect of the enactment? If either is the advancement or inhibition of religion then the enactment exceeds the scope of legislative power as circumscribed by the Constitution. That is to say that to withstand the strictures of the Establishment Clause there must be a secular legislative purpose and a primary effect that neither advances nor inhibits religion. * * *" Abington School District v. Schempp, 374 U.S. 203, 222, 83 S.Ct. 1560, 1571, 10 L.Ed.2d 844, 858 (1963).

See, also, Board of Education of Central School District No. 1 v. Allen, 392 U.S. 236, 243, 88 S.Ct. 1923, 1926, 20 L.Ed.2d 1060, 1065 (1968); Walz v. Tax Commission of City of New York, 397 U.S. 664, 90 S.Ct. 1409, 25 L.Ed.2d 697 (1970). Mr. Justice Brennan's concurring opinion in *Schempp* is highly instructive as to the proper interpretation of that decision:

"The holding of the Court today plainly does not foreclose teaching *about* the Holy Scriptures or about the differences between religious sects in classes in literature or history. Indeed, whether or not the Bible is involved, it would be impossible to teach meaningfully many subjects in the social sciences or the humanities without some mention of religion. *To what extent, and at what points in the curriculum, religious materials should be cited are matters which the courts ought to entrust very largely to the experienced officials who superintend our Nation's public schools. They are experts in such matters, and we are not.* We should heed Mr. Justice Jackson's *caveat* that any attempt by this Court to announce curricular standards would be 'to decree a uniform, rigid and, if we are consistent, an unchanging standard for countless school boards representing and serving highly localized groups which not only differ from each other but which themselves from time to time change attitudes.' * * *" (Emphasis supplied.) Abington School District v. Schempp, *supra*, 374 U.S. at 300-301, 83 S.Ct. at 1612 (Brennan, J., concurring).

Our scrutiny of Zorach v. Clauson, 343 U.S. 306, 72 S.Ct. 679, 96 L.Ed. 954 (1952); Illinois ex rel. McCollum v. Champaign County Board of Education, 333 U.S. 203, 68 S.Ct. 461, 92 L.Ed. 649 (1948); Torcaso v. Watkins, 367 U.S. 488, 81 S.Ct. 1680, 6 L.Ed.2d 982 (1961); Engel v. Vitale, 370 U.S. 421, 82 S.Ct. 1261, 8 L.Ed.2d 601 (1962), and the famous Everson v. Board of Education of Ewing Township, 330 U.S. 1, 67 S.Ct. 504, 91 L.Ed. 711 (1947), all of which authoritatively construe the First Amendment's religion clauses, leads us to conclude that the learned trial judge misapplied the teachings of the First Amendment and the specific holding of *Schempp*.[9]

Obscenity, although not raised in the pleadings, and declared not to be at issue in the trial court's June 9, 1971 judgment, is pervasive in the lower court's opinion.

In his findings of fact, the trial judge did indeed cite many words which, if standing alone, would offend some person's sensibilities. Yet each and every example advanced by the trial court was taken totally out of context. This is constitutional error. Ackerman

v. United States, 293 F.2d 449 (C.A. 9, 1961);
Haldeman v. United States, 340 F.2d 59 (C.A.
10, 1965); People v. Stabile, 58 Misc.2d 905,
296 N.Y.S.2d 815 (1969). To be constitutionally obscene, the matter scrutinized must be
judged in its entirety. Roth v. United States,
354 U.S. 476, 77 S.Ct. 1304, 1 L.Ed.2d 1498
(1957); Excellent Publications, Inc. v. United
States, 309 F.2d 362 (C.A. 1, 1962); State v.
Hudson County News Co., 41 N.J. 247, 196 A.2d
225 (1963). As *amicus curiae* correctly
points out, even the Bible may be considered
profane or vulgar if certain passages are considered piecemeal and without due regard given
to the entire text.[10]

The Supreme Court has clearly held that it
is incumbent upon a court to employ a constitutional test to determine whether a given work
is "obscene" in the legal sense. A Book Named
"John Cleland's Memoirs" v. Massachusetts, 383
U.S. 413, 86 S.Ct. 975, 16 L.Ed.2d 1 (1966).
In Jacobellis v. Ohio, 378 U.S. 184, 84 S.Ct.
1676, 12 L.Ed.2d 793 (1964), the Court eloquently articulated the dangers of a Balkanized
obscenity standard. Neither the trial court
nor this Court has any legal prerogative to refuse to follow the rulings of the United States
Supreme Court when it decides a question which
requires interpretation of the Federal Constitution. Scholle v. Secretary of State, 360
Mich. 1, 104 N.W.2d 63 (1960); Union Central
Life Insurance Co. v. Peters, 361 Mich. 283,
105 N.W.2d 196 (1960). See, also, People v.
Gonzales, 356 Mich. 247, 262-263, 97 N.W.2d 16
(1959); People v. Temple, 23 Mich.App. 651,
661, 179 N.W.2d 200 (1970).

Although the trial court did not expressly
rule that *Slaughterhouse-Five* was obscene,
his June 9, 1971 judgment strongly suggests
that possibility. We are constrained to hold
that *Slaughterhouse-Five* is clearly not obscene under present constitutional tests. Roth
v. United States, *supra*; Jacobellis v. Ohio,
supra; Redrup v. New York, 386 U.S. 767, 87
S.Ct. 1414, 18 L.Ed.2d 515 (1967); People v.
Wasserman, 27 Mich.App. 16, 183 N.W.2d 313
(1970); People v. Billingsley, 20 Mich.App. 10,
173 N.W.2d 785 (1969); Wayne County Prosecutor
v. Doerfler, 14 Mich.App. 428, 165 N.W.2d 648
(1968).

Courts cannot permit themselves the luxury
of refusing to adhere to a constitutional standard of review. When a court momentarily for-
gets this fact, as we did in Grand Rapids City
Attorney v. Bloss, 17 Mich.App. 318, 169 N.W.2d
367 (1969), a higher court usually terminates
this judicial forgetfulness. Bloss v. Dykema,
398 U.S. 278, 90 S.Ct. 1727, 26 L.Ed.2d 230
(1970).

Judges are mortal and therefore are heir to
the delightful differences which make up the
human species. Nevertheless, when passing upon
an alleged obscenity issue, we must strive to
put aside our personal predilections and
strictly adhere to the authoritative United
States Supreme Court decisions.[11]

In *Redrup*, *supra*, the Court found the
paperback books *Lust Pool* and *Shame Agent*
not to be obscene. We believe that it is ludi-

crous to consider *Slaughterhouse-Five* in the
same literary niche as *Lust Pool* and *Shame
Agent*. If the latter are not convicted because of their alleged profanity, then the
former should never even stand trial.
Slaughterhouse-Five is Sunday school reading
compared to these paperbacks. We do not wish
to demean Mr. Vonnegut by making such ridiculous comparisons. That he is a serious writer
has been attested to by those whose literary
credentials are more impressive than our
own.[12]

"Obscenity" is a mercurial matter. As Mr.
Justice Harlan recently said for the Court in
Cohen v. California, 403 U.S. 15, 25, 91 S.Ct.
1780, 1788, 29 L.Ed.2d 284, 294 (1971):

"[I]t is nevertheless often true that one
man's vulgarity is another's lyric. Indeed,
we think it is largely because governmental
officials cannot make principled distinctions in this area that the Constitution
leaves matters of taste and style so largely
to the individual."

We concur.

We hold that, as a matter of law, *Slaughterhouse-Five* is not obscene in the constitutional sense. Under the authority granted us
by GCR1963, 820.6, we find as a matter of fact
that *Slaughterhouse-Five* is not obscene, profane, or vulgar in the constitutional sense.
We believe it to be a serious work of quasi-
fiction by an acknowledged legitimate writer.
The book's dominant theme is anti-war. The
subject, war, slaughter, bombing, may be obscene: the telling of the tale is not.[13]

Defendant and *amicus curiae* urge that the
real issue underlying this case is that a circuit judge, or any government official, has no
lawful right to impose his own particular value
judgments on our citizenry in matters which are
traditionally protected by the penumbra of the
First Amendment. They argue that that, in
fact, is what happened here and meticulously
cite the trial record for factual support. For
the reasons outlined below we entertain no
doubt that defendant and *amicus curiae* are
legally correct and that the trial court abused
its discretion in entering this traditionally
sacred area.

One of the reasons that our constitutions
have wisely precluded sovereign interference
with an individual's right to read, think,
speak, observe, and pray as he desires is the
fact that these concepts are so arbitrary and
diverse that they are foreign to standardiza-
tion and any possible test of right-wrong.
Government has no legitimate interest in controlling or tabulating the human mind nor the
fuel that feeds it.

In his May 11, 1971 opinion, the trial judge
stated:

"The Court did read the book as requested
for determination of factual matters and
issues of law alike, and unfortunately did
thus waste considerable time. At points,
the Court was deeply disgusted. How any

educator entrusted during school hours with the educational, emotional and moral welfare and healthy growth of children could do other than reject such cheap, valueless reading material, is incomprehensible. Its repetitious obscenity and immorality, merely degrade and defile, teaching nothing. Contemporary literature, of real educational value to youth abounds, contains scientific, social and cultural facts, of which youth need more to know, today.

"Certainly, it is unnecessary for any school system to search out and select obscenity, pornography, or deviated immorality in order to teach modern literature.

"Modern desire for complete licentious freedom has evidently led some educators into the fallacy that degradation of subject matter in reading and thought, is a necessary part of freedom in modern education. Does the modern trend of education permit mental prostitution, and encourage mental deviation? If so, this is a sad distortion of educational purpose."

While the May 11, 1971 opinion was subsequently superseded by a later one, the former is instructive insomuch as it allows this Court the opportunity to follow the trial judge's judicial thought process. Clearly, the trial judge found *Slaughterhouse-Five* to be a "bad" book, totally worthless and utterly lacking in any merit, literary or otherwise. But as Shakespeare reminds us in language antedating almost all of our sacred precedent, "There is nothing either good or bad, but thinking makes it so." (Hamlet, Act II, Scene 2, line 259). This Court cannot, in good conscience, nor in adherence to our constitutional oath of office, allow a non-educational public official the right, in absence of gross constitutional transgressions, to regulate the reading material to which our students are exposed. Our Constitution will tolerate no supreme censor nor allow any man to superimpose his judgment on that of others so that the latter are denied the freedom to decide and choose for themselves.

The reasons for such a philosophy are basic to the American system of jurisprudence. Judges pass on the law not upon morals. It is, then, perhaps ironic that the most able articulation of judicial non-intervention in matters of conscience and personal conviction was penned by the distinguished English playwright Robert Bolt. In *A Man for All Seasons*, Sir Thomas More, the sacred ancestor of our judiciary, is infused by Mr. Bolt with the following language:

"More: * * * The law, Roper, the law. I know what's legal not what's right. And I'll stick to what's legal.
"Roper: Then you set man's law above God's!
More: No, far below; but let *me* draw your attention to a fact--I'm *not* God. The currents and eddies of right and wrong, which you find such plain sailing, I can't navigate. I'm no voyager. But in the

thickets of the law, oh, there I'm a forester. I doubt if there's a man alive who could follow me there, thank God * * *." *A Man for All Seasons*, 37 (Vintage Books, N.Y., 1960).

What does the law say when it speaks to this precise issue? No American jurist ever stated the basic premise better than Mr. Justice Jackson in his now classic opinion in West Virginia State Board of Education v. Barnette, 319 U.S. 624, 642, 63 S.Ct. 1178, 1187, 87 L.Ed. 1628, 1639 (1943):

"If there is any fixed star in our constitutional constellation, it is that no official, high or petty, can prescribe what shall be orthodox in politics, nationalism, religion or other matters of opinion * * *."

It is clear from the trial court's May 11, 1971 opinion that he viewed reading *Slaughterhouse-Five* as a "waste (of) considerable time". He found the novel to be "deeply disgust(ing)", "cheap, valueless reading material", repetitious in its obscenity, "incomprehensible", "immoral", "defil(ing)" and totally non-instructive. He further said "Certainly, it is unnecessary for any school system to search out and select obscenity, pornography, or deviated immorality in order to teach modern literature." Capsulized, the trial judge found *Slaughterhouse-Five* to be "rubbish".

Turning again for guidance to Mr. Justice Jackson,[14] we approvingly cite and adopt the following language from his scholarly dissent in United States v. Ballard, 322 U.S. 78, 95, 64 S.Ct. 882, 890, 88 L.Ed. 1148, 1158 (1944):

"But that is precisely the thing the Constitution put beyond the reach of the prosecutor, for the price of freedom of religion or of speech or of the press is that we must put up with, and even pay for, a good deal of rubbish."[15]

We are concerned that in this case the trial court, in attempting to adjudicate this matter, substituted its own judgment of what is "right" and "moral" for that of the student, the teacher, and the duly constituted school authority.[16] Such action is resolutely forbidden by the Constitution. It is for the lawfully elected school board, its supervisory personnel and its teachers to determine the local schools' curriculum. The judicial censor is *persona non grata* in formation of public education. Epperson v. Arkansas, 393 U.S. 97, 104, 89 S.Ct. 266, 270, 21 L.Ed.2d 228, 234 (1968). "The vigilant protection of constitutional freedoms is nowhere more vital than in the community of American schools," Shelton v. Tucker, 364 U.S. 479, 487, 81 S.Ct. 247, 251, 5 L.Ed.2d 231, 236 (1960), but the trial court's actions in this case abridge these priceless, guaranteed academic freedoms and "cast a pall of orthodoxy over the classroom." Keyishian v. Board of Regents, 385 U.S. 589, 603, 87 S.Ct. 675, 683, 17 L.Ed.2d 629, 640 (1967). We cannot approve such action by the judiciary nor any other government official. U.S.Const., art. VI, cl. 2; Sweezy v. New Hampshire, 354 U.S. 234, 250, 77 S.Ct. 1203, 1211-1212, 1 L.Ed.2d 1311, 1324-1325 (1957). Schools are an institution, indeed the only institution, in which our youth is exposed to exciting and competing ideas, varying from antiquity to the present.

It is the trial court's right to select the reading matter which he personally consumes. That is a matter purely for his own conscience, preference and appetite. On the other hand, the judicial garb should never be mistaken for the accoutrements of a censor and the black robes of the trial court may not exclude, from public school students, the light of ideas-- irrespective of their varied hues. See, American Bar Association "Statement on the Freedom to Read," reprinted in *The First Freedom*, Robert B. Downs, ed. (American Library Association, 1960). Sweezy v. New Hampshire, *supra*; Shelton v. Tucker, *supra*.

The Supreme Court has clearly indicated that book censorship is an odious practice. In Hannegan v. Esquire, Inc., 327 U.S. 146, 157-158, 66 S.Ct. 456, 462, 90 L.Ed. 586, 593 (1946), the Court observed:

> "Under our system of government there is an accommodation for the widest varieties of tastes and ideas. What is good literature, what has educational value, what is refined public information, what is good art, varies with individuals as it does from one generation to another. There doubtless would be a contrariety of views concerning Cervantes' Don Quixote, Shakespeare's Venus and Adonis or Zola's Nana. *But a requirement that literature or art conform to some norm prescribed by an official smacks of an ideology foreign to our system.*" (Emphasis supplied.)

The Court has characterized the classroom as "the 'marketplace of ideas.'" The Nation's future depends upon leaders trained through wide exposure to that robust exchange of ideas which discovers truth 'out of a multitude of tongues, [rather] than through any kind of authoritative selection.'" Keyishian v. Board of Regents, *supra*, 385 U.S. at 603, 87 S.Ct. at 683, 17 L.Ed.2d at 640. See, also, Tinker v. Des Moines Community School District, 393 U.S. 503, 512, 89 S.Ct. 733, 739, 21 L.Ed.2d 731, 741, (1969).

Vonnegut's literary dwellings on war, religion, death, Christ, God, government, politics, and any other subject should be as welcome in the public schools of this State as those of Machiavelli, Chaucer, Shakespeare, Melville, Lenin, Hitler, Joseph McCarthy, or Walt Disney. The students of Michigan are free to make of *Slaughterhouse-Five* what they will.

Reversed. Summary judgment of no cause of action is entered in this Court in favor of defendant Rochester Community Schools.

No costs, a public question being involved.

O'HARA, Judge (concurring in result).

Judge Brennan and I concur only in the result reached by Judge Bronson. We are not prepared to endorse his opinion.

We feel the basic point involved here is not whether the book in question is *per se* obscene or pornographic as those terms have been judicially defined by the United States Supreme Court. This is made clear by the following finding of the trial judge.

> "The issues in this case have to do solely with the doctrine of separation of religion and state, and there is nothing before the court on which to rule concerning mere obscenity, pornography * * *."

There is no doubt, as the trial court noted, that certain *characters* in the novel express sentiments that are derogatory of the religious beliefs of a very sizable segment of our society. However, the novel in question is merely listed as one of a number of books reflective of a current literary style. It is not alleged that the teacher of the course advocated, approved or promulgated concepts offensive to established religious beliefs or organized religious sects.

This, of course, is precisely the point. Writings, contemporary as well as of ages past, have attributed to characters beliefs and expressions highly antagonistic to established religious beliefs. Manifestly, many of these writings have attained classical status. As we view the constitutional test, a public educational institution cannot espouse as part of its teaching program such expressions of belief *pro* or *contra* as representative of the beliefs of the institution. In the presentation of reading material, the public institution is well within its teaching function to list the particular books the faculty regards as valuable to the full exposure of the student to conflicting views of religious beliefs. To advocate the views doctrinally as those of the institution is quite another thing. It is not alleged that defendant in this case espoused any antireligious views as opposed merely to making available course material.

We find no violation of the "establishment" clause of the First Amendment.

The judgment granting mandamus against defendant school system is reversed. The case is remanded to the trial court for entry under directions to grant defendant motion for summary judgment.

No costs.

NOTES

* MICHAEL D. O'HARA, former Supreme Court Justice, sitting on the Court of Appeals by assignment pursuant to Const. 1963, art. 6, § 23 as amended in 1968.

1. The novel was published in 1969 by the

Delacorte Press, Inc., of New York.

2. The quoted textual passages in this paragraph of the opinion are taken verbatim from paragraphs 4 and 5 of plaintiff's complaint.

3. The "Current Literature" course offered by the Rochester Community Schools was not part of the prescribed curriculum but was an elective. Some of the other literature which was required reading for the course was: *Arsenic and Old Lace*, *The Detective Story*, Herman Hesse's *Steppenwolf*, *The American Dream*, short stories by J. D. Salinger, and selected poetry by James Dickey, Allen Ginsberg, Lawrence Ferlinghetti, and Howard Nemerov. The supplemental reading list for the course included: *Love Story* by Erich Segal, *Walden II* by B. F. Skinner, *Catch-22* by Joseph Heller, *Waiting for Godot* by Samuel Beckett, *Catcher in the Rye* by J. D. Salinger, *The Andromeda Strain* by Michael Crichton, *Who's Afraid of Virginia Woolf?* by Edward Albee and *The Power and the Glory* by Graham Greene. Since plaintiff apparently did not find these writings to violate the First and Fourteenth Amendments, we express no judicial opinion as to their constitutional validity. Nor is such necessary.

4. The May 13, 1971 and June 9, 1971 opinions by Judge Moore are meticulous and thorough. We commend him for his steadfast adherence to GCR 1963, 517.1. Relevant portions of both opinions will be set out later in this opinion.

5. This Court wishes to express its gratitude to the American Civil Liberties Union of Michigan for its valued assistance as *amicus curiae*.

6. The complaint is herein set out in full: "NOW COMES, BRUCE LIVINGSTON TODD, a resident of the County of Oakland, residing at 753 Charlesina, Oakland Township, Oakland County, Michigan, and complaint [*sic*] of the ROCHESTER COMMUNITY SCHOOLS, A Body Corporate, Defendant herein, named pursuant to RJA 600.4401 and GCR [1963] 710, as follows:
"1) One of Plaintiff's children is lawfully enrolled in the Rochester Community Schools and is attending the prescribed classes of instruction pursuant to the curriculum requirements and specifications.
"2) As a part of said curriculum is a course of study referred to as 'Current Literature'.
"3) As a part of said 'Current Literature' course of instruction is the offered reading of a book titled, 'Slaughterhouse-Five' or 'The Children's Crusade' believed to have been authored by one Kurt Vonnegut, Jr. and published by Dell Publishing Company, Inc. of New York, New York.
"4) Said book contains and makes reference to religious matters.
"5) The use of such book as a part of or in connection with any course of instruction by a Public School District or System is illegal and contrary to the laws of this land; namely, the First and Fourteenth Amendments of the Constitution of the United States, pursuant to the determinations of the Supreme Court of the United States, to-wit: Engel v. Vitale, 370 U.S. 421; 82 S.Ct. 1261; 8 L.Ed.2d 601 (1962), and DeSpain v. DeKalb County Community School District, 7 Cir., 384 F.2d 836 (1967), *et al.*
"6) Plaintiff herein has often requested of Defendant herein that said book, to wit: 'Slaughterhouse-Five' or 'The Children's Crusade', be withdrawn from and as a part of the curriculum offered by Defendant has failed and refused to do so, and Defendant continues to employ said book as a part of its offered course of instruction contrary to the laws of this land.
"WHEREFORE, Plaintiff prays that a Writ of Mandamus be issued adjudging said book, 'Slaughterhouse-Five' or 'The Children's Crusade' to be unlawful and unfit for use as a part of a course of instruction offered by Defendant, The Rochester Community Schools; or
"In the Alternative
"That this Court issue its Order to Show Cause pursuant to the Petition and Affidavit of Bruce Livingston Todd, Plaintiff herein, the originals of which are attached hereto and made a part of this Complaint and that said matter be brought on for an immediate hearing and determination by this Honorable Court."

7. As Mr. Justice Brennan so ably articulated in his concurring opinion in *Schempp*, *supra*:
"* * * What the Framers meant to foreclose, and what our decisions under the Establishment Clause have forbidden, are those involvements of religious with secular institutions which (a) serve the essentially religious activities of religious institutions; (b) employ the organs of government for essentially religious purposes; or (c) use essentially religious means to serve governmental ends, where secular means would suffice. * * *" 374 U.S. at 294-295, 83 S.Ct. at 1609-1610, 10 L.Ed.2d at 899.
"The holding of the Court today plainly does not foreclose teaching *about* the Holy Scriptures or about the differences between religious sects in classes in literature or history. Indeed, whether or not the Bible is involved, it would be impossible to teach meaningfully many subjects in the social sciences or the humanities without some mention of religion. To what extent, and at what points in the curriculum, religious materials should be cited are matters which the courts ought to entrust very largely to the experienced officials who superintend our Nation's public schools. They are experts in such matters, and we are not. We should heed Mr. Justice Jackson's caveat that any attempt by this Court to announce curricular standards

would be 'to decree a uniform, rigid and, if we are consistent, an unchanging standard for countless school boards representing and serving highly localized groups which not only differ from each other but which themselves from time to time change attitudes.'* * *" 374 U.S. at 300-301, 83 S.Ct. at 1612-1613; 10 L.Ed.2d at 902-903.

8. Kurt Vonnegut, Jr. personally witnessed this carnage while in a Nazi prisoner of war camp. See, Slaughterhouse-Five at 1; 93 Time 108-109 (April 11, 1969).

9. The Michigan Supreme Court apparently stands four-square with the *Schempp* test. See, Advisory Opinion re: Constitutionality of P.A. 1970, No. 100, 384 Mich. 82, 180 N.W.2d 265 (1970), which has been overruled on the issue of "parochiaid." See, generally, Downey and Roberts, Freedom From Federal Establishment (1964) and Church, State and Freedom (1967), by Leo Pfeffer.

10. See, *e.g.*, Genesis 19:33.

11. To insure objective, rather than subjective, review the Fifth Circuit Court of Appeals has held that expert testimony is required on community obscenity standards. United States v. Groner (C.A. 5, Jan. 11, 1972) rehearing en banc granted March 28, 1972.

12. See, *e.g.*, Granville Hicks, *Saturday Review* (March 27, 1969).

13. The following sentiment of Kurt Vonnegut, Jr. is perhaps self-explanatory:

"Addressing his editor, Seymour Lawrence, Vonnegut says: 'Sam--here's the book, It is so short and jumbled and jangled, Sam, because there is nothing intelligent to say about a massacre.'" Saturday Review, p. 25 (March 27, 1969).

14. Lest it be thought that somehow Justice Robert Jackson was incapable of taking a firm, "moral" stance on an issue, we have not forgotten that it was this legal giant, perhaps the most eloquent man ever to wear the robes of a Justice of the United States Supreme Court, who successfully headed the prosecution of the chief Nazi war criminals at Nuremberg.

15. Similarly, see the recent decision in United States v. Head, D.C., 317 F.Supp. 1138, 1146 (1970), in which the Court said:
"The whole thrust of the First Amendment is to shelter expression from the value judgments of those in power; when any judge or prosecutor attempts to assess speech, he must do so in his own coin--a coin that is by definition suspect."

16. "The law knows no heresy, and is committed to the support of no dogma * * *." Watson v. Jones, 80 U.S. (13 Wall.) 679, 728, 20 L.Ed. 666, 676 (1872).

A United States District Court decides against New York students who had requested the court to declare unconstitutional the school board's order to remove all copies of Down These Mean Streets *from the school libraries of all schools under the jurisdiction of the school board.*

Presidents Council, Dist. 25 v. *Community School Bd. No. 25*, No. 71-C-601 (E. D. N. Y., August 4, 1971)

This is a civil rights action brought pursuant to 42 U.S.C. §1983, jurisdiction being grounded on 28 U.S.C. §1343. Plaintiffs,[1] in their amended complaint, claim that defendants,[2] acting under color of state law, have deprived them of rights secured to them by the First Amendment, and of due process of law as guaranteed by the Fourteenth Amendment. They seek an injunction and declaratory relief.

A hearing was held on the motion for a preliminary injunction on June 1, 1971. Subsequently, plaintiffs moved for summary judgment or alternatively for both a temporary and permanent injunction, praying further that any additional hearing which the court might find necessary be consolidated with a trial on the merits pursuant to F.R.Civ.P. Rule 65(a)(2). Defendants Community School Board No. 25 and Antoinette McCarthy have moved to dismiss the complaint or alternatively for summary judgment. Several briefs have been submitted *amicus curiae*.[3] A hearing was held on July 16, 1971, at which all of the above mentioned motions were argued.

Plaintiffs' claim arises out of the following circumstances: on March 31, 1971, defendant Community School Board (Board), of Community School District No. 25 (District), meeting in executive session, voted five to three to remove all copies of *Down These Mean Streets*, a novel by Piri Thomas, from the school libraries of all schools under the jurisdiction of the Board. This resolution was duly adopted at a public meeting held on April 19, 1971, where it again passed by a vote of five to three.[4] According to a direction contained in the resolution defendant Community Superintendent Meagher (Superintendent) had the book removed from those school libraries which had copies.[5]

Plaintiffs allege that the resolution adopted by the Board, and the action taken by the Superintendent in compliance with that resolution, deprive all of them of ". . . their rights to academic freedom under the First

Amendment . . ." (Amended Complaint,¶16), and further deprive the teacher, librarian and principal plaintiffs of ". . . their liberty to freely practice their profession in accordance with professional standards in violation of the due process clause of the Fourteenth Amendment." (Amended Complaint ¶17). Accordingly, plaintiffs request that the court declare the resolution adopted by the Board unconstitutional, and order the defendants to replace the book on the shelves of the libraries from which it was removed, and enjoin them from interfering with other school libraries within their jurisdiction which desire to purchase the book.[6]

The following facts are either conceded by all parties or uncontested:

1. The Board is the duly and legally elected Community School Board of Community School District No. 25.
2. Cormac K. Meagher is the duly appointed Community Superintendent of Community School District No. 25, chosen by the Board.
3. The power of the state to determine matters relating to the education of students, including the prescription of a curriculum and the selection of textbooks and other instructional material, has been delegated by the New York State Legislature to the duly elected Community School Boards in New York City.[7]
4. The resolutions adopted by the Board at the public meetings held on April 19, 1971 and June 2, 1971 were duly adopted by the Board.
5. *Down These Mean Streets*, by Piri Thomas, was removed from the school libraries of Junior High Schools 185, 189 and 218 pursuant to the resolution adopted by the Board on April 19, 1971, by defendant Superintendent, and other schools in the District were barred from placing the book on their library shelves.
6. The students at Junior High Schools 185, 189 and 218 range in age from 11 to 15 years.
7. (a) The state has provided administrative procedures for the review of arbitrary actions on the part of Community School Boards.[8]
   (b) Final administrative action is reviewable under Article 78 of the New York Civil Practice Law and Rules.

Discussion

Plaintiffs are divided into three sets: (a) the students; (b) the parents and guardians; and (c) the teachers, librarian and Principal. The rights of each of these sets, and their possible infringement, must be discussed separately, since they differ one from another as alleged and argued by plaintiffs' counsel.

Plaintiff students claim that they have a right to know, or right of access to publications, under the First Amendment. They claim

the right to read *Down These Mean Streets* without restriction, citing *Tinker* v. *Des Moines Independent Community School District*, 393 U.S. 503, 89 S.Ct. 733 (1969). They see *Ginsberg* v. *New York*, 390 U.S. 629, 88 S.Ct. 1274 (1968) as requiring the Board to make the book available absent a finding of obscenity. Further, they find the resolution of June 2, 1971, called by them the "parent option plan," an abridgment of their First Amendment rights under *Lamont* v. *Postmaster General*, 381 U.S. 301, 85 S.Ct. 1493 (1965).

Tinker held that high school students were "...entitled to freedom of expression of their views," 393 U.S. at 511, 89 S.Ct. at 739, in demonstrating their opposition to the Viet Nam war. It is significant that in *Tinker* the Court dealt with and spoke of a right of *expression*. It said nothing of the corollary right of *access* to publications, i.e., the right to know.[9]

A child's First Amendment right of access to reading material is not co-extensive with the right of adults. *Ginsberg* v. *New York, supra*, 390 U.S. at 636-37, 88 S.Ct. at 1279. In *Ginsberg*, the Court rejected appellant's argument "...that the scope of the constitutional freedom of expression secured to a citizen to read or see material concerned with sex cannot be made to depend on whether the citizen is an adult or a minor." 390 U.S. at 636, 88 S.Ct. at 1279. Rather, the Court approved a distinction between children and adults when constitutional liberties and their exercise are involved: "...we have recognized that even where there is an invasion of protected freedoms the power of the state to control the conduct of children reaches beyond the scope of its authority over adults." [Citing *Prince* v. *Massachusetts*, 321 U.S. 158, 170, 64 S.Ct. 438, 444 (1944)] 390 U.S. at 638, 88 S.Ct. at 1280. The Court then went on to uphold the New York statute attacked by the appellant, which statute made criminal the furnishing to children of sexually-oriented reading matter which would concededly have been constitutionally protected reading matter were the rights of an adult involved.[10] *Ginsberg* in no way stands for the proposition advanced by plaintiffs in reliance upon it: that if a state cannot totally ban a book it cannot bar its school libraries from loaning it.

This court must thus conclude that the students had no constitutional right to have *Down These Mean Streets* freely available to them in the school libraries. On the contrary, the Board, acting pursuant to its statutory powers, had discretion to order the book or refuse to do so, to put it on the school library shelves or remove it therefrom. The Board has the general power to determine curriculum, which must of necessity include the selection of reading matter to be available in the schools, subject only to certain powers of the Chancellor of the New York City School System.

Having no right to have the book available to them in school, no right is abridged by the institution of the "parent option system." In *Lamont* v. *Postmaster General*, 381 U.S.

85 S.Ct. 1493 (1965), the Court struck down a statute requiring addressees to whom unsealed Communist propaganda is consigned to perform an "official act" in order to receive the propaganda through the mail. The Court considered this requirement "...an unconstitutional a-bridgment of addressee's First Amendment rights," in that it would tend to chill the exercise of those rights. As the exercise of a child's First Amendment right of access within a public school is subject to the discretionary power of the Board, and the Board may constitutionally ban the book from the schools entirely, the Board, in adopting the "parent option system," is not infringing any right but rather granting one where none before existed.

Plaintiff parents concede that "...the state has a legitimate interest in the education of its minor citizens..." (Plaintiffs' Memorandum of Law, filed May 19, 1971, p. 4). However, they claim that this interest must submit to the superior right of the parents and guardians "...to direct the upbringing and education of the children under their control." (Id.)[11] Plaintiffs cite *Meyer* v. *Nebraska*, 262 U.S. 390, 43 S.Ct. 625 (1923) and *Pierce* v. *Society of Sisters*, 268 U.S. 510, 45 S.Ct. 571 (1925), as support for their position. The rationale underlying Justice McReynolds' decisions for the Court in *Meyer* and *Pierce* has been decisively rejected in later cases.[12] The concept of the Due Process Clause of the Fourteenth Amendment as being a grab-bag of substantive rights has held little currency for over thirty years. However, the question of whether or not the holdings in *Meyer* and *Pierce* retain any validity is not before this court. This is so because the language of both of those opinions makes it clear that the Court, in holding as it did, had no intention of abridging, and indeed specifically recognized, the power of the state to dictate a curriculum for use in public schools.

In *Meyer*, the Court struck down a Nebraska statute which made it illegal to teach a foreign language to students who had not completed their eighth grade. Meyer, originally the defendant in the case, was a teacher in a parochial school maintained by the Zion Evangelical Lutheran Congregation. Finding that the statute in question violated Meyer's rights under the Due Process Clause of the Fourteenth Amendment, the Court stated that "[h]is right thus to teach and the right of parents to engage him so to instruct their children, we think, are within the liberty of the amendment." 262 U.S. at 400, 43 S.Ct. at 627. The rights of parents, however, were not without substantial limitations:

...The power of the state to compel attendance at some school and to make reasonable regulations for all schools, including a requirement that they shall give instructions in English, is not questioned. *Nor has challenge been made of the state's power to prescribe a curriculum for institutions which it supports.* Those matters are not within the present controversy. [Emphasis supplied.] 262 U.S. at 402, 43 S.Ct. at 628.

Pierce involved an Oregon statute requiring every parent or guardian of a child between the ages of 8 and 16 years to send the child to a public school. Two suits, both involving organizations which ran private schools, challenged the constitutionality of the statute. The Court, citing *Meyer*, again found the statute under scrutiny to be void as in violation of the Due Process Clause. The specific right which the Court found to be unconstitutionally infringed was the right of the defendant organizations to run schools. 268 U.S. at 543, 45 S.Ct. at 573.

Despite the holding of the Court, the opinion carefully affirmed the state's general power over the education of children. It said:

No question is raised concerning the power of the state reasonably to regulate all schools, to inspect, supervise and examine them, their teachers and pupils; to require that all children of proper age attend some school, that teachers shall be of good moral character and patriotic disposition, that certain studies plainly essential to good citizenship must be taught, and that nothing be taught which is manifestly inimical to the public welfare. 268 U.S. at 543, 45 S.Ct. at 573.

Meyer and *Pierce*, then, cannot be read to stand for the broad proposition advanced by the plaintiffs: that parents' rights to direct the education of their children are necessarily superior to the rights of the state. In *Prince* v. *Massachusetts*, 321 U.S. 158, 64 S.Ct. 438 (1944), the Court dealt with the parent-state conflict in a more modern manner. In that case the guardian of a minor child had been convicted of violating a penal statute regulating the labor of children, in that she had permitted her ward, a small girl, to sell the publications of the Jehovah's Witnesses on the streets at night. The appellant argued that the statute (a) violated her First Amendment right to free exercise of her religion, and (b) violated her rights as a parent and guardian under the Due Process Clause, citing *Meyer*. Characteristic of the change in judicial philosophy which had intervened, the Court commented on the appellant's Due Process claim: "The due process claim, as made and perhaps necessarily, extends no further than that to freedom of religion, since in the circumstances all that is comprehended in the former is comprehended in the latter." 321 U.S. at 164, fn. 8, 64 S.Ct. at 441, fn. 8. In rejecting the appellant's claim, the Court referred to the protection given by the Court in *Pierce* and *Meyer*, stating that "...neither rights of religion or parenthood are beyond limitation." 321 U.S. at 166, 64 S.Ct. at 442. After detailing the instances in which the state's power over the education, rearing and upbringing of a child had been upheld, the Court concluded that

"...the state has a wide range of power for limiting parental freedom and authority in things affecting the child's welfare." 321 U.S. at 167, 64 S.Ct. at 442.

Having decided that there is no absolute right in the parent to control all aspects of his child's education in the public schools, this court can find no substance or precedent for the argument that the parent has a specific right to control what literature shall be available to the child in school. No cases have been cited to the court, nor has the court been able to find any, which would substantiate that claim. It must thus be concluded that as between the state, represented here by the Board, and the parents, it is the state, under its general power to control curriculum in the public schools, which has discretion over the choice of library books.

Plaintiff teachers, librarian, and Principal claim a loss of "academic freedom" caused by the removal of the books, and further, an interference with their "right" to freely practice their profession in accordance with professional standards. They cite *Keefe* v. *Geanakos*, 418 F.2d 359 (1st Cir. 1969) and *Parducci* v. *Rutland*, 316 F.Supp. 352 (M.D. Ala. 1970) in support of their claim.

In *Keefe*, an English teacher assigned an article in the *Atlantic Monthly* as required reading for his English class. The school authorities found the article offensive and were about to take disciplinary action against the teacher when he brought suit to restrain them from so doing. The lower court refused to enjoin the disciplinary proceedings, but the Court of Appeals reversed. The reversal was based on procedural due process problems which are unrelated to the instant discussion. *Parducci* is similar. There, a teacher was discharged for assigning to her high school class a certain short story repugnant to the school authorities. The district court ordered her reinstatement.

Both *Keefe* and *Parducci* involved procedural due process problems of notice that are not present here. This court will not attempt to divine the attitudes of the courts involved were they to be presented with cases not including such problems. It is true that in both cases the courts ruled on the suitability of the literature in question for the minds of high school students, finding that the respective article and story were indeed suitable. Nevertheless, this court has no need to do so, as no employee, teacher or otherwise, has been disciplined or threatened with discipline in the instant proceeding. Nor have any teachers been instructed not to assign the book. Thus, it is apparent that no right of academic freedom has been infringed.

As for plaintiff teachers' contention that they have a "right" to freely practice their profession according to professional standards, no authority has been cited and none found. If by so stating plaintiffs intimate that they seek to resurrect the discredited theory of "substantive" due process (see *supra*, n. 12),

their argument must fail. The cases which have been cited by plaintiffs as general support are inapposite.[13]

After due consideration, this court must conclude that the claim of plaintiffs herein presents no federal question. The court has not considered the educational value of the book or the harm it might inflict on young children. The court refuses, as requested by the defendant Board, to consider whether there is a factual basis for its resolution of June 2, 1971. These issues are not relevant to the instant claim. They may be discussed and litigated elsewhere. Plaintiffs have available administrative and state remedies, since their claim is not of constitutional magnitude. In the final analysis, they have their right to challenge Board policy at the next election of Board members.

Findings of fact and conclusions of law as required by F.R.Civ.P. Rule 52(a) are included in the body of this opinion.

The Clerk is directed to enter judgment dismissing the complaint and it is

SO ORDERED.

JACOB MISHLER
U.S.D.J

NOTES

1. Plaintiffs are (a) Presidents Council District 25, an organization of presidents and past presidents of various parent and parent-teacher associations in Community School District No. 25; (b) three students, one attending Junior High School 185, and the other two attending Junior High School 189, both schools being within Community School District No. 25 and under the jurisdiction of the defendant Community School Board (Board); (c) seven parents and guardians of minor children attending Junior High Schools 185, 189, and 218, all within the Community School District No. 25 and under the jurisdiction of the Board; (d) two teachers working at Junior High School 189, which school is within Community School District No. 25, and under the jurisdiction of the Board; (e) a librarian at Junior High School 185, which school is within Community School District No. 25, and under the jurisdiction of the Board; and (f) the Principal of Junior High School 189, which school is within Community School District No. 25, and under the jurisdiction of the Board.

2. Defendants are (a) Community School Board No. 25, the duly elected school board of Community School District No. 25, Queens, New York; (b) Cormac K. Meagher, duly appointed Community Superintendent of Community School District No. 25; and (c) Antoinette McCarthy, individually and as a representative for the Committee for Parents' Rights in Public Education. [Mrs. McCarthy was not an original defendant, but

moved to intervene as such subsequent to the filing of the complaint, which motion was granted.]

3. The *amici* are: (a) Hyman Rosner, Betty Louise Felton, James O'Hara, and Edna Turner, minority members of Community School Board No. 25; (b) Local 2 of the American Federation of Teachers (AFL-CIO); and (c) the Author's League of America .

4. The resolution adopted by the Board at its public meeting of April 19, 1971, reads as follows:

> The Superintendent is hereby directed to remove "Down These Mean Streets" by Piri Thomas from all student libraries in the district.
> The Board hereby instructs Dr. Meagher to immediately appoint a professional committee to recommend to the Board guidelines for the selection of books.

5. "Down These Mean Streets" is an autobiographical novel describing the childhood of a boy in Spanish Harlem. It gives a vivid picture of the material and cultural deprivation to which the boy was subject, the sordid existence of which he partook, and the bitter humor with which he and his fellows attempted to leave their lot. It is revealing in its exposition of the racial tensions between Blacks, Whites and Puerto Ricans. Homosexual and heterosexual acts are candidly described with a liberal sprinkling of four letter words in past, present and future tenses.

6. At a special public meeting held subsequent to the initiation of the suit, (the original complaint was filed on May 19, 1971), the Board adopted, by a 5-0 vote, with three abstentions, a resolution modifying the original resolution adopted on April 19, 1971. The text of this resolution, passed at the public meeting on June 2, 1971, is as follows:

> The district copies of *Down These Mean Streets* shall be kept at the schools which previously had the book in their respective libraries, and shall be loaned directly to the parents of the children attending these schools who request the book.
> The Superintendent shall establish and forthwith put into effect a procedure for the implementation of the above.

On June 25, 1971, the plaintiffs filed an amended complaint realleging everything that had been contained in the original complaint, but also alleging the passage of the above resolution, and alleging that it too was unconstitutional on the grounds already discussed. The amended prayer seeks to have both resolutions declared unconstitutional, and to have the operation of both enjoined.

7. N.Y. Education Law, § 2590-e.
...each community board shall have the

power and the duty to:
...
3. determine matters relating to the instruction of students, including the selection of textbooks and other instructional materials; provided, however, that such textbooks and other instructional materials shall first have been approved by the chancellor.

8. New York Education Law §§310 and 2590-1.

9. It is also significant that the Court put distinct limits on the exercise of the students' right of free expression:

> "...[b]ut conduct by the student, in class or out of it, which for any reason--whether it stems from time, place, or type of behavior--materially disrupts classwork or involves substantial disorder or invasion of the rights of others is, of course, not immunized by the constitutional guarantee of freedom of speech." 393 U.S. at 513, 89 S.Ct. at 740.

10. The Court had previously intimated that such a position would be taken, were the case to arise, as it subsequently did. *See Jacobellis* v. *Ohio*, 378 U.S. 189, 195, 84 S.Ct. 1676, 1682 (1964).

11. The argument that parents' rights are superior to those of the state is a double-edged sword. There are admittedly many issues in educational policy upon which parents will differ. Were each child to be educated solely in accordance with its parents' views on education, public education as such would become impossible.

12. *See, e.g., West Coast Hotel* v. *Parrish*, 300 U.S. 379, 57 S.Ct. 578 (1937); *Day-Brite Lighting, Inc.* v. *Missouri*, 342 U.S. 421, 72 S.Ct. 405 (1952); *Williamson* v. *Lee Optical Co.*, 348 U.S. 483, 75 S.Ct. 461 (1955); and see McCloskey, *Economic Due Process and the Supreme Court: An Exhumation and Reburial*, 1962 Supreme Court Review 34.

13. *Keyishian* v. *Board of Regents*, 385 U.S. 589, 87 S.Ct. 675 (1967), held that a statute providing for dismissal of university personnel for seditious statements or acts was void for vagueness. *Slochower* v. *Board of Higher Education*, 350 U.S. 551, 76 S.Ct. 637 (1956), held that dismissal of a publicly employed professor for refusal to testify before a Congressional committee violated his right to procedural due process. *Vought* v. *Van Buren Public Schools*, 306 F.Supp. 1380 (E.D. Mich. 1969), while sustaining the schools' right to promulgate a regulation forbidding possession of obscene material on school grounds, held that a student could not be expelled on the charge of such possession without a hearing.

An elected school board orders all copies of Down These Mean Streets *removed from all junior high school libraries in New York's Community School District No. 25. Parents and students in the district challenge the board's action and seek an injunction against the school board. The United States Court of Appeals, Second Circuit, decides for the school board, declaring: "There is here no problem of freedom of speech or the expression of opinions on the part of parents, students or librarians. As we have pointed out, the discussion of the book or the problems which it encompasses or the ideas it espouses have not been prohibited by the board's action in removing the book....To suggest that the shelving or unshelving of books presents a constitutional issue, particularly where there is no showing of a curtailment of freedom of speech or thought, is a proposition we cannot accept."*

Presidents Council, Dist. 25 v. *Community School Bd. No. 25,* 457 F.2d 289 (1972)

MULLIGAN, Circuit Judge:

This is an appeal from an order of Chief Judge Jacob Mishler, United States District Court, Eastern District of New York, dismissing plaintiffs' civil rights action which was brought pursuant to 42 U.S.C. § 1983 and 28 U.S.C. § 1343, seeking an injunction and declaratory relief against Community School Board No. 25, Queens, New York, Cormac K. Meagher, Community Superintendent of Community School District No. 25, and Antoinette McCarthy, a representative of the Committee for Parents' Rights in Public Education. We affirm.

The plaintiffs-appellants in this case are the Presidents Council, District 25, an organization of presidents and past presidents of various parent and parent-teacher associations in the district, three junior high school students enrolled in schools in the district, seven parents and guardians of minors who attend junior high schools in the district, two teachers, a librarian and the principal of a junior high school, all within the district and under the jurisdiction of the Board. This litigation commenced as a result of the decisions of the duly elected Community School Board (hereinafter Board) of Community School District 25 (hereinafter District), which in executive session on March 31, 1971, voted five to three to remove from all junior high school libraries in the District all copies of *Down These Mean Streets*, a novel by Piri Thomas. At a public meeting on April 19, 1971 the resolution was again duly adopted by a vote of five to three. Pursuant to the resolution the defendant community superintendent had the book removed. At a public meeting of the Board on June 2, 1971 a

resolution was unanimously passed permitting the book to be kept at those schools which previously had the book in their libraries but making it available on a direct loan basis to the parents of children attending these schools.

It is conceded by the parties in this suit that the Board was duly and legally elected and that the resolutions were duly adopted by the Board at the public meetings of April 19 and June 2, 1971. It is further uncontested that the students at the three junior high schools affected (Junior High School Nos. 185, 189 and 218) range in age from 11 to 15 years. The parties do not dispute that in New York City the selection of textbooks and other instructional material has been delegated by the Legislature of the State of New York to the Community School Board.[1] It is also clear that there are administrative procedures available to review the decisions of the Community School Boards in New York.[2] Any final administrative action is reviewable under Article 78 of the New York Civil Practice Law and Rules.[3]

The book, which has created the controversy and provoked the action of the Board, *Down These Mean Streets*, is an autobiographical account by Piri Thomas, of a Puerto Rican youth growing up in the East Side Barrio (Spanish Harlem) in New York City. Predictably the scene is depressing, ugly and violent. The argot of the vicinage is replete with four letter and twelve letter obscenities unreported by Tom Swift or even Tom Jones. Acts of criminal violence, sex, normal and perverse, as well as episodes of drug shooting are graphically described. The book has been made available to the court and in a soft cover reprint is available to the public for an investment of $1.25. Presumably the educational value of this work, aside from whatever literary merit it may have, is to acquaint the predominantly white, middle-class junior high school students of Queens County with the bitter realities facing their contemporaries in Manhattan's Spanish Harlem. Some parents objected to the public school library stocking the book, which they claimed would have an adverse moral and psychological effect on 11 to 15 year old children, principally because of the obscenities and explicit sexual interludes. The plaintiffs on the other hand have supplied affidavits from psychologists, teachers, and even children who claim the book is valuable and had no adverse effect on the development of the children of the District. One thirteen year old boy solemnly swears and assures us that the book has "literary merits" and is not a "corruptive influence."

Since the Legislature of the State of New York has by law determined that the responsibility for the selection of materials in the public school libraries in New York City is to be vested in the Community School Board (n. 1, *supra*), and the Commissioner of Education of that State has defined the purposes of the public school library,[4] and in further view of the procedures for administrative and state court review provided in New York (nn. 2 and 3, *supra*), we do not consider it appropriate for this court to review either the wisdom or the efficacy of the determinations of the Board. Our function is purely one of constitutional adjudication on the facts and the record before us: has the Board transgressed the first amendment rights of the plaintiff teachers, parents, librarian and children. In its most recent pronouncement on the subject the Supreme Court has stated: "By and large, public education in our Nation is committed to the control of state and local authorities. Courts do not and cannot intervene in the resolution of conflicts which arise in the daily operation of school systems and which do not directly and sharply implicate basic constitutional values." Epperson v. Arkansas, 393 U.S. 97, 104, 89 S.Ct. 266, 270, 21 L.Ed.2d 228 (1968) (footnote omitted).

After a careful review of the record before us and the precedents we find no impingement upon any basic constitutional values. Since we are dealing not with the collection of a public book store but with the library of a public junior high school, evidently some authorized person or body has to make a determination as to what the library collection will be. It is predictable that no matter what choice of books may be made by whatever segment of academe, some other person or group may well dissent. The ensuing shouts of book burning, witch hunting and violation of academic freedom hardly elevate this intramural strife to first amendment constitutional proportions. If it did, there would be a constant intrusion of the judiciary into the internal affairs of the school. Academic freedom is scarcely fostered by the intrusion of three or even nine federal jurists making curriculum or library choices for the community of scholars. When the court has intervened, the circumstances have been rare and extreme and the issues presented totally distinct from those we have here. See Developments in the Law--Academic Freedom, 81 Harv.L.Rev. 1045, 1051-1054 (1968).

In Epperson v. Arkansas, *supra*, the court did strike down a state statute which made it unlawful for a teacher in any state supported school to use a text book that teaches that men are descended from a lower order of animals. The court vitiated the statute on the specific ground that the State may not adopt programs or practices in its public schools or colleges which 'aid or oppose' any religion." 393 U.S. at 106, 89 S.Ct. at 271. "The State's undoubted right to prescribe the curriculum for its public schools does not carry with it the right to prohibit, on pain of criminal penalty, the teaching of a scientific theory or doctrine where that prohibition is based upon reasons that violate the First Amendment." *Id.* at 107, 89 S.Ct. at 272. Here, patently we have no religious establishment or free exercise question, and neither do we have the banning of the teaching of any theory or doctrine. The problems of the youth in the ghetto, crime, drugs and violence have not been placed off limits by the Board. A book has been removed but the librarian has not been penalized, and the teacher is still free to discuss the Barrio and its problems in the classroom. The action

of the Board does not even preclude the teacher from discussing *Down These Mean Streets* in class or from assigning it for outside reading. In those libraries which have the book, the parent can borrow it and, if he sees fit, can loan it to his child if he wishes to read it.[5] The intrusion of the Board here upon any first amendment constitutional right of any category of plaintiffs is not only not "sharp" or "direct", it is miniscule.

Appellants' reliance upon Ginsberg v. New York, 390 U.S. 629, 88 S.Ct. 1274, 20 L.Ed.2d 195 (1968) is puzzling. In that case the Court upheld the constitutionality of a New York statute (N.Y. Penal Law § 484-h (McKinney's Consol.Laws, c. 40, 1967)) which made it a crime to sell defined obscene material to minors under 17 years of age, whether or not the material would be obscene for adults. In upholding the concept of "variable obscenity" the court found the statute to be a rational legislative determination that the exposure of minors to such materials might be harmful and that the statute did not involve any invasion of constitutionally protected freedoms. Appellants' reading of the case as authority for the proposition that minors have an unqualified first ammendment right of access to books, unless they are obscene under the statute, is totally unjustified. It equates the public school library, which has a function as an adjunct to the educational venture, with the entrepreneur seller of books who has no comparable responsibility. The public school library obviously does not have to become the repository, at public expense, for books which are deemed by the proper authorities to be without merit either as works of art or science, simply because they are not obscene within the statute. If someone authored a book advocating that the earth was flat, it could hardly be argued that the work could not be removed from the public school library unless it was also obscene. Appellants concede, or at least do not reject, the proposition that the Board has ultimate authority for the initial selection of the public school library collection. They suggest, however, that we have a different case where, as here, the book was once shelved and is now removed. They analogize the shelving and unshelving of a book to the constitutional right of a person to obtain public employment and his rights to retain such employment when it is sought to be terminated. This concept of a book acquiring tenure by shelving is indeed novel and unsupportable under any theory of constitutional law we can discover. It would seem clear to us that books which become obsolete or irrelevant or where improperly selected initially, for whatever reason, can be removed by the same authority which was empowered to make the selection in the first place.

Tinker v. Des Moines Independent Community School District, 393 U.S. 503, 89 S.Ct. 733, 21 L.Ed.2d 731 (1969) is equally far afield. There the court did intrude into the field of public education by invalidating a regulation of school principals which suspended students who wore black armbands to classes symbolizing their objection to hostilities in Vietnam. This was deemed a violation of their right to free speech under the first amendment in the absence of a showing that the conduct of the students materially disrupted classwork or involved substantial disorder or invasion of the rights of others. The appellant conveniently ignores the factual setting of *Tinker* but would have us apply its test. Since the shelving of *Down These Mean Streets* did not create any disruption or disorder, it is argued, it should remain on the shelf. There is here no problem of freedom of speech or the expression of opinions on the part of parents, teachers, students or librarians. As we have pointed out, the discussion of the book or the problems which it encompasses or the ideas it espouses have not been prohibited by the Board's action in removing the book.

The administration of any library, whether it be a university or particularly a public junior high school, involves a constant process of selection and winnowing based not only on educational needs but financial and architectural realities. To suggest that the shelving or unshelving of books presents a constitutional issue, particularly where there is no showing of a curtailment of freedom of speech or thought, is a proposition we cannot accept.[6]

Appellant finally urges upon us two cases Keefe v. Geanakos, 418 F.2d 359 (1st Cir.1969) and Parducci v. Rutland, 316 F.Supp. 352 (M.D.Ala.1970). Both of these cases involved high school teachers of junior and senior students who assigned material for outside reading which school officials found offensive and inappropriate. Upon a refusal to comply with the orders of school authorities to desist, the teachers were discharged. To the extent that these cases hold that first amendment rights have been violated whenever a district court disagrees with the judgment of school officials as to the propriety of material assigned by a teacher to students, we are not in accord.[7] In any event, both cases involved the discharge of teachers with concomitant issues of procedural due process which are not present here and therefore the cases are not controlling.[8]

In view of the facts in the record before us and the controlling precedents, we find no constitutional infirmity in the resolutions of the Board.

Affirmed.

NOTES

1. N.Y.Educ.Law, McKinney's Consol.Laws, c. 16, § 2590-e(3) (McKinney 1970) provides:

    § 2590-e. Powers and duties of community boards

    Each community board shall have all the powers and duties, vested by law in, or duly delegated to, the local school board districts and the board of education of the city district on the effective date of this article, not inconsistent with the provisions of this article and the policies established by the city board, with respect to the control and operation of all pre-kindergarten, nursery, kindergarten, elementary, intermediate and junior high schools and programs in connection therewith in the community district. The foregoing shall not be limited by the enumeration of the following, each community board shall have the power and duty to:

    .   .   .   .

    3. determine matters relating to the instruction of students, including the selection of textbooks and other instructional materials; provided, however, that such textbooks and other instructional materials shall first have been approved by the chancellor.

2. N.Y.Educ.Law § 310(5)-(6) (McKinney 1970) provides for an appeal to the state commissioner of education by any person "conceiving himself aggrieved" by the action by the trustees of any school library in relation to the books therein or by any action by any district meeting in relation to the library. See *e.g.*, In the Matter of Kornblum, 70 St.Dept.Rep. (Educ.) 19 (1949) where the commissioner held that a citizen and taxpayer had no constitutional right to compel the Board of Education of the City of New York to retain the magazine, "The Nation", in its school libraries.

    Further, N.Y.Educ.Law §2590-l (McKinney 1970) empowers the chancellor of the city school district of the City of New York to override any decision of a community board inconsistent with the educational policies of the city board.

3. See *e.g.*, Rosenberg v. Board of Educ., 196 Misc. 542, 92 N.Y.S.2d 344 (Sup.Ct. 1949).

4. The regulations of the Commissioner of Education of New York State provide:

    "The book collection in the secondary schools shall consist of books approved as satisfactory for: (1) Supplementing the curriculum, (2) reference and general information, (3) appreciation and (4) pleasure reading. The course of study and the interest of boys and girls of given ages and grades are factors which should play a large part in the selection of books for a school library. Books of established quality and authority in sufficient quantity to meet all school needs are recognized as necessary tools and materials of instruction." 8 N.Y.Code, Rules & Regs. (Educ.) §91.1(b) (1966).

5. In Ginsberg v. New York, 390 U.S. 629 at

639, 88 S.Ct. 1274, 20 L.Ed.2d 195 (1968) Mr. Justice Brennan, recognizing the prime responsibility of parents for the well-being of their children, pointed out that the statute barring the sale of salacious material to children did not preclude the parent from purchasing it for their children. Here the school at state expense is making the book available to parents who may wish their children to read it.

6. Other Supreme Court cases relied upon by appellants are inapposite. In Shelton v. Tucker, 364 U.S. 479, 81 S.Ct. 247, 5 L.Ed.2d 231 (1960) the court found unconstitutional an Arkansas statute requiring public school teachers to file annual affidavits listing all organizational affiliations without limitation for a five year retroactive period; in Keyishian v. Board of Regents, 385 U.S. 589, 87 S.Ct. 675, 17 L.Ed.2d 629 (1967) the court invalidated New York teacher oath and loyalty laws as vague and ambiguous. In contrast, there is no inhibition of extramural teacher or librarian association whatsoever in the case before us. If the Board ordered a list of all books read or owned by the staff, these cases might be in point.

7. While the First Circuit has indicated that it does not "regret" its decision in Keefe v. Geanakos, *supra*, its enthusiasm for intrusion into academic issues seems to be lessening, see Mailloux v. Kiley, 436 F.2d 565, 566 (1st Cir. 1971) and Mailloux v. Kiley, 448 F.2d 1242 (1st Cir. 1971).

8. That the discharge of the teacher in Keefe v. Geanakos, *supra*, was a vital fact is apparent from its decision (418 F.2d at 362), when it emphasized this element to distinguish the facts from Parker v. Board of Educ., 237 F.Supp. 222 (D.Md.1965). In that case the teacher was not discharged, but since he had no tenure, there was no obligation to renew his contract. On this point the lower court was affirmed in 348 F.2d 464 (4th Cir. 1965) cert. denied, 382 U.S. 1030, 86 S.Ct. 653, 15 L.Ed.2d 543 (1966).

The students in Presidents Council, District 25, ask the United States Supreme Court to hear their case: "Petitioners respectfully pray that a writ of *certiorari* issue to review the judgment of the United States Court of Appeals for the Second Circuit entered in the above entitled case on March 21, 1972."

Petitioners' Brief for a Writ of Certiorari in *Presidents Council, Dist. 25* v. *Community School Bd. No. 25*

PETITION FOR A WRIT OF CERTIORARI TO THE UNITED STATES COURT OF APPEALS FOR THE SECOND CIRCUIT

Petitioners respectfully pray that a writ of certiorari issue to review the judgment of the United States Court of Appeals for the Second Circuit entered in the above entitled case on March 21, 1972.

Opinions Below

The opinion of the district court is not officially reported. It is set out in the Appendix, *infra*, pp. 12a to 25a. The opinion of the Court of Appeals is reported at 457 F.2d 289 and is set out in the Appendix, *infra*, pp. 2a to 11a.

Jurisdiction

The judgment of the Court of Appeals was entered on March 21, 1972. On June 8, 1972, Mr. Justice Marshall issued an order extending the time within which to file this petition for writ of certiorari up to and including July 19, 1972. The jurisdiction of this Court is invoked under 28 U.S.C. 1254(1).

Question Presented

Whether a school board violates the First Amendment rights of the librarian and students when it orders the removal from a school library of a critically acclaimed and serious book, concededly lawful for distribution to minors, because it contains four-letter words and describes sexual activities.

Statement of the Case

This civil rights action concerns a book entitled *Down These Mean Streets*, by Piri Thomas, a highly acclaimed work portraying the process of growing up in the Puerto Rican ghetto of East Harlem in New York City. Copies of the book were purchased by the librarians for three junior high schools in New York City's Community School District No. 25. The copies remained in the libraries, available for student use, until a parent complained that *Down These Mean Streets* contained four-letter words and described sexual activities. In response to the parent's complaint, Community School Board No. 25 adopted the following resolution by a vote of 5-3, on April 19, 1971:

"The Superintendent is hereby directed to remove *Down These Mean Streets* from all student libraries in the district."

This lawsuit, brought on behalf of a librarian, a principal, teachers, students and parents of students at schools at District 25, followed. Subsequently, on June 2, 1971, the Board passed a so-called "parent option plan" which permitted those schools which originally had the book to permit its direct loan to parents. Other schools in the district remained under the ban imposed by the Board's original resolution.

The librarian and teachers who used the book in class submitted affidavits expressing the belief that it was a particularly effective portrayal of life in the ghetto and an important adjunct to the junior high school curriculum. Those supporting the ban, however, thought that the book's language was too harsh and that its occasional depictions of sex would adversely affect the emotional and psychological development of the early teenage youngsters reading it.

In reply affidavits, junior high school students made light of the suggestion that they were unfamiliar with or would be led astray by the language or sex scenes in the book, adding that the book made them more sensitive to the conditions endured by those who live in the slums. Several eminent psychologists and psychiatrists dismissed as simplistic and unsupportable the contention that the scenes depicted in *Down These Mean Streets* could have an adverse impact on the psychological development of children.

Reasons For Granting The Writ

Despite the frequency with which local pressure groups succeed in persuading school boards to purge controversial books,[1] the constitutional issues presented by this practice have never been decided by this Court. It is the issue touched upon but left undecided in *Epperson* v *Arkansas*, 393 U.S. 97 (1968), namely, to what extent are school professionals at the mercy of politically responsive, often elected, lay boards of education in determining what their students may read and learn in the schools. More than loyalty oaths, more than security investigations, more than armbands, it is an issue which lies at the heart of academic freedom. The issue was framed in *Epperson* as follows:

"By and large, public education in our Nation is committed to the control of state and local authorities....On the other hand, '[t]he vigilant protection of constitutional freedoms is nowhere more vital than in the community of American schools,' *Shelton* v. *Tucker*, 364 U.S. 479, 487...." *Id.* at 104.

Given the recurrence of attacks on school books, it is hardly an exaggeration to suggest that the resolution of those conflicting principles may well determine whether any book which challenges the current orthodoxy will be permitted in the schools. Regrettably, the courts below, showing almost unquestioning deference to the judgment of the school board, have indicated that libraries are not an area in which constitutional freedoms need receive "vigilant protection." While the limits of that viewpoint are not spelled out, the courts below would apparently not interfere with school boards which systematically purged the libraries of all books advocating peace or integration, or their curricula of all courses treating the United Nations. And, although the opinion suggests some solicitude for teachers who are actually dismissed, the courts' reasoning leaves little doubt that teachers who persisted in mentioning those subjects over the objections of the school board would do so wholly without constitutional protection. When this Court has so consistently defended the academic profession against the vagaries of political influence, *e.g.*, *Sweezy* v. *New Hampshire*, 354 U.S. 234 (1957); *Shelton* v. *Tucker*, 364 U.S. 479 (1960); *West Virginia State Bd. of Educ.* v. *Barnette*, 319 U.S. 624 (1943), it would be ironic indeed if the federal judiciary were now to indulge such direct political intrusion into the materials that teachers will be permitted to assign.

Some recent newspaper stories illustrate the issues which are at stake here. In Connecticut, a school board ordered the book *Boss*, a political biography of Chicago Mayor Richard Daley, removed from a high school reading list because, as one Board member explained, it "slandered" local law enforcement officials and "doesn't tell the truth." *New York Times*, April 12, 1972. A New Jersey school board forbade its high school library from purchasing four books, including John Kenneth Galbraith's *The Affluent Society*, as reference materials for a federally funded American studies course. As the president of the Board of Education explained, "In my opinion, the books were too liberal and I disagree with their points of view." *New York Times*, June 17, 1972.

For the court below, this is only "intramural strife" which does not justify "intrusion of the judiciary into the internal affairs of the school." But if the judiciary does not intervene, to whom may parents, students and professionals look when their libraries and their curricula are stripped of books which happen to be in political disfavor with a shifting majority of the school board? Who, if not the federal courts, will prevent our nation's schools from becoming instruments of majoritarian propaganda? If, as appears to be the case, school boards are especially responsive to demands that schools not carry books which honestly deal with race relations in America,[2] will minorities ever be able to secure the promise of *Brown* v. *Board of Education*, 347 U.S. 483 (1954)? To abstain from controversies such as this will indeed create a "pall of orthodoxy," *Keyishian* v. *Board of Regents*, 385 U.S. 589, 603 (1967), over our public schools.

The point was well made by a *New York Times* editorial entitled "Censors at Work," prompted by the Connecticut incident.

"[C]ontrary to all denials, the exercise of the veto power over reading lists or library collections by school boards amounts to establishment of censorship--the removal of books for other than educational reasons. Teachers, librarians and school administrators naturally make choices concerning books --including textbooks--which are appropriate to the schools' purpose. But the introduction of either literary or political criteria by school board members--or of the even more elusive judgment of what constitutes 'truth' in a political volume--is a threat both to education and to freedom." April 14, 1972.

That philosophy has been given judicial expression in *Stanley* v. *Georgia*, 394 U.S. 557, 565 (1969):

"Our whole constitutional heritage rebels at the thought of giving government the power to control men's minds."

I.

Constitutional principles of academic freedom limit the power of school boards even over allegedly educational matters.

To plaintiffs' contention that the ban of *Down These Mean Streets* from the shelves of the school district's libraries is unconstitutional,[3] the court below answers matter-of-factly that someone, after all, "has to make a determination as to what the library collection will be." Since the school board is given, by statute, ultimate responsibility for instruction within its schools, the court suggests that *any* determination which the board makes regarding its library collection is beyond judicial review. That position is not consistent with long-standing precedents of this court. To say that the school board has the conceded power to make educational decisions affords those decisions no greater immunity from constitutional principles than previous attempts to disguise unconstitutional actions with an educational veneer. *Meyer* v. *Nebraska*, 262 U.S. 390 (1923); *Bartels* v. *Iowa*, 262 U.S. 404 (1923); *West Virginia State Board of Education* v. *Barnette*, 319 U.S. 624 (1943); *Epperson* v. *Arkansas*, 393 U.S. 97 (1968); *Tinker* v. *Des Moines Indep. Community School Dist.*, 393 U.S. 503 (1969). In the words of one circuit court, "[d]iscretionary power does

not carry with it the right to its arbitrary exercise." *Shachtman* v. *Dulles*, 225 F.2d 938, 941 (D.C. Cir. 1955).

Two recent cases involving the dismissals of teachers using teaching materials of which the school boards disapproved are illustrative. In *Keefe* v. *Geanakos*, 418 F.2d 359 (1st Cir. 1969) and *Parducci* v. *Rutland*, 316 F. Supp. 352 (M.D. Ala. 1970), the school boards, as here, objected to the use of books which contained profanities and "vulgar" terms. Both courts found that interests of academic freedom outweighed the boards' conceded interest in regulating educational matters in their schools and reinstated the teachers. To the extent that the courts below dismiss those cases as inapplicable because the teachers there had been fired, while the librarian here had not, they impose a burden on challengers of unconstitutional action which is as unfair as it is unprecedented. See, e.g., *Epperson* v. *Arkansas*, 393 U.S. 97 (1968); *Keyishian* v. *Board of Regents*, 385 U.S. 589 (1967). It was the school board's order removing the book, and not the librarian's response, which implicated First Amendment values. It should not be and is not the law that she had to defy the ban and risk dismissal, with its attendant disruption of school functions, before having the right to challenge it.

This is an easier case than either *Keefe* or *Parducci*. In those cases, the books were *assigned* as a part of the classroom curriculum, thereby precluding alternative instructional materials which the school board could argue were more educationally valuable. In this case, the judgment of the librarians conflicted with no interest of the school board. The books' retention in the library would exclude no other books considered more valuable nor take up any class time that could be put to better use. Thus, the broad implications of this Court's opinion in *Meyer* v. *Nebraska*, 262 U.S. 390 (1923), need not be considered. See generally, Hutchins, "The Constitution of Public Education," *The Center Forum*, Vol. II, No. 4 (July 1969).

II.

The removal of the book deprived students of their First Amendment right to know.

The court below, interpreting the students' argument as claiming an "unqualified first amendment right of access to books, unless they are obscene," found no constitutional deficiency in the removal of the book. But the students claim no such unqualified right. Rather, they assert three propositions: (1) that they no longer have access to a book previously available to them; (2) that their right to know has, to that extent, been impaired; and (3) that no "compelling" or "substantial" state interest justified that impairment. *NAACP* v. *Button*, 371 U.S. 415, 438, 444 (1963). The court's search for an unqualified right in this case is misplaced. The focus instead must be on what state interest is served by the board's action. "[T]he view that a 'right must be in-fringed before a remedy can be fashioned, has been steadily eroded; the focus of inquiry has shifted from identification of individual rights to an examination of the reasonableness of government action." Note, "Dismissal of Federal Employees--The Emerging Judicial Role," 66 *Col. L. Rev.* 719, 734 (1966). See, e.g., *Garrity v. New Jersey*, 385 U.S. 493 (1967); *Shelton v. Tucker*, 364 U.S. 479 (1960).

If such compelling state interests were apparent, such as the "financial and architectural realities" suggested by the Second Circuit, the board's decision would raise no constitutional issues. But those realities were never even hinted at in this case. The school board was not engaged in the process of selecting books for its libraries. If it were, its decision to spend its limited dollars on books other than *Down These Mean Streets* would be defensible on educational grounds and beyond judicial review. Nor was there ever the suggestion that "architectural" considerations, such as limited shelf space, motivated the book's removal.

Two decisions of this Court treating the rights of minors, *Tinker v. Des Moines Independent Community School District*, 393 U.S. 503 (1969) and *Ginsberg v. New York*, 390 U.S. 629 (1968), provide the framework for determining whether a sufficient state interest can be shown to justify removal of the book. The court below conceded that the book had created no "substantial disorder" and expressed no opinion as to whether the book was obscene for minors.

The Court of Appeals sums up its rejection of plaintiffs' constitutional claims by pointing out that "discussion of the book or the problems which it encompasses or the ideas it espouses have not been prohibited by the Board's action . . . ." Conveniently ignored is the fact that the book itself cannot be read. To permit school boards arbitrarily to deprive students of the opportunity to read books previously available in the school library violates the principle that "government should leave the mind and spirit of man absolutely free . . . . [P]ublic officials cannot be constitutionally vested with powers to select the ideas people can think about. . . ." *Adler v. Board of Education*, 342 U.S. 485, 497 (1952) (Black, J., dissenting).

CONCLUSION

For the reasons stated above certiorari should be granted.

Respectfully submitted,

Alan H. Levine
c/o New York Civil
Liberties Union
84 Fifth Avenue
New York, New York
Attorney for Petitioners

Burt Neuborne
Melvin L. Wulf
Of Counsel

July 19, 1972

NOTES

1. Campaigns against school books have been waged by, among others, the American Legion and Veterans of Foreign Wars (texts were "un-American"), the Ku Klux Klan (books favored "papists and anti-Christian Jews of the Bolshevik Socialist stripe"), DAR (insufficient emphasis on military history), National Council for Prevention of War (insufficient emphasis on the peace-loving qualities of American heroes), organized labor, WCTU, and the National Association of Manufacturers (books "laced with anti-business sentiment and economic determinist and socialistic theories"). Nelson and Roberts, *The Censors and the Schools*, 28-37 (1963).

Nor is the problem one which has been confined to the distant past. A perusal of issues of the American Library Association *Newsletter on Intellectual Freedom* for the past two years reveals attacks on libraries for shelving books such as Cleaver, *Soul On Ice*; Roth, *Goodbye Columbus*; Brown, *Manchild in the Promised Land*; Griffin, *Black Like Me*; Carmichael, *Black Power*; Salinger, *Catcher in the Rye*; an anthology of modern literature because it contained such reputedly Communist authors as Langston Hughes, Richard Wright, Woody Guthrie, Martin Luther King, Malcolm X and Dick Gregory. It is noteworthy that books by non-white authors appear to come under particular attack.

2. See note 1, *supra*.

3. Although the court makes reference to the availability of "administrative procedures" and state judicial remedies for review of the "wisdom or the efficacy" of the school board's action, it is clear that the court did pass on the question of its constitutionality. It is, of course, settled law that persons seeking redress of constitutional rights by means of a 1983 action need not exhaust state judicial, *Monroe v. Pape*, 365 U.S. 167 (1961) or administrative remedies. *Damico v. California*, 389 U.S. 416 (1967); *McNeese v. Board of Education*, 373 U.S. 668 (1963).

The New York Community School Board, No. 25, presents its brief in opposition to a petition for a writ of certiorari to the United States Supreme Court.

Respondents' Brief in Opposition to Petition for Certiorari in *Presidents Council, Dist. 25* v. *Community School Bd. No. 25*

BRIEF IN OPPOSITION TO PETITION FOR CERTIORARI

Preliminary Statement

The petitioners' civil rights complaint was dismissed, for failure to present a federal question, by the District Court for the Eastern District of New York. The Court of Appeals for the Second Circuit affirmed.

Question Presented

A book entitled *Down These Mean Streets*, by Piri Thomas, about life in East Harlem, had been purchased for the libraries in three junior high schools in Community School District 25. Following a parent's complaint as to the book's language and descriptions of heterosexual and homosexual acts, the duly elected Community School Board considered the matter and, at a public meeting, adopted a resolution directing that the book be removed from all student libraries in the district.

This lawsuit followed. Later, the Community School Board adopted another resolution, modifying the original resolution, to provide that copies of the book shall be kept at the schools which previously had the book in their libraries and that the book should be loaned directly to parents of children attending those schools, if the parents request it. Each of the petitioners is associated with one of the three schools which originally had, and still has, a copy of the book in its library.

Each side to the controversy claims professional support for its views.

Do 11 to 15 years old children attending a public junior high school, their parents, some teachers, a principal and a librarian have a constitutional right to compel retention of any particular book in the school libraries in the district?

Opinion Below

The opinion of both the Court of Appeals and the District Court are reprinted in full in the appendix attached to the instant petition (District Court at pp. 12a to 25a; Court of Appeals at pp. 1a to 11a). Both courts found no merit to the claim that Community School Board's resolutions violated the Constitution.

The Court of Appeals began by noting that there was no dispute as to the following: the challenged resolutions were duly adopted by the duly and legally elected Community School Board at public meetings; the selection of textbooks and other instructional material has been delegated by the Legislature of the State of New York to the Community School Board; the children in the schools affected range from 11 to 15 years of age; there are state administrative and judicial procedures available to review the actions of the Community School Board (3a-4a). [Numbers in parentheses refer to pages of the appendix attached to the petition for a writ of certiorari.]

The Court described the book and noted that (4a), "Acts of criminal violence, sex, normal and perverse, as well as episodes of drug shooting are graphically described." The Court then noted the differing opinions as to whether the book would have an adverse effect on 11 to 15 year old children (5a).

The Court found that since the responsibility for the selection of books in school libraries rests with the Community School Board, and since state administrative and judicial review procedures are available, it was not appropriate for the Court to review the wisdom of the Community School Board's determination, but only whether the Board violated any First Amendment rights (5a-6a). According to the Court (6a):

> "Since we are dealing not with the collection of a public book store but with the library of a public junior high school, evidently some authorized person or body has to make a determination as to what the library collection will be. It is predictable that no matter what choice of books may be made * * * some other person or group may well dissent. The ensuing shouts of book burning, witch hunting and violation of academic freedom hardly elevate this intramural strife to first amendment constitutional proportions."

Epperson v. Arkansas, 393 U.S. 97 (1968), where the Supreme Court struck down a statute making it unlawful for a teacher in a public school to teach or use a textbook which teaches evolution, was distinguished by the Court on two grounds: 1) The *Epperson* statute was found to be an unconstitutional aid to religion, and here there is no religious freedom question; 2) Here, unlike *Epperson*, there is no ban on the teaching of any theory or doctrine (7a). The Court noted (7a):

> "The problem of the youth in the ghetto,

crime, drugs and violence have not been placed off limits by the Board. A book has been removed but the librarian has not been penalized, and the teacher is still free to discuss the Barrio and its problems in the classroom. The action of the Board does not even preclude the teacher from discussing *Down These Mean Streets* in class or from assigning it for outside reading".

Tinker v. Des Moines School Dist., 393 U.S. 503 (1969), a case involving students' freedom of expression was similarly distinguished (9a). The Court also noted that in those schools which have the book, a parent may borrow it and give it to his child to read (7a).

The Court rejected the contention that, if a book is not legally obscene for purposes of sale to children by a public bookstore, it cannot be excluded from a public school library (8a). It said that such an argument, "equates the public school library, which has a function as an adjunct to the educational venture, with the entrepreneur seller of books who has no comparable responsibility" (8a).

The Court also answered the claim that a book achieves some sort of "tenure" once it has been selected. It said that the same authority which has the power to make the initial selection clearly also has the power to remove books which become obsolete or irrelevant or were "improperly selected initially, for whatever reason" (8a-9a).

The Court noted that those cases [*Keefe v. Geanakos*, 418 F. 2d 359 (1st Cir., 1969) and *Parducci v. Rutland*, 316 F. Supp. 352 (M.D. Ala., 1970)] where the discharge of teachers for assigning certain outside reading was held to be improper, unlike the case at bar, involved the discharge of teachers and procedural due process problems and were, therefore, not in point (10a). The Court also said (10a): "To the extent that these cases hold that first amendment rights have been violated whenever a district court disagrees with the judgment of school officials as to the propriety of material assigned by a teacher to students, we are not in accord."

ARGUMENT

The petitioners have no constitutional right to compel the purchase or retention of a particular book in a public school library.

The Legislature of the State of New York has given to each locally elected community school board the power to select the books offered to students in the school libraries within its district. N.Y. Education Law § 2590-e, subd. 3. The book collection of a public school library is an important and integral part of the total education offered to public school children, and the selection of books for the collection is directly related to the instructional goals of the schools. See Regulations of the

N.Y. State Commissioner of Education § 91.1. The decision of the Community School Board for District 25, that a particular book ought not to be made available to children aged 11 to 15 years by the school libraries or that it should be made available (in those three libraries in its district which already possessed it) only if requested by a parent, was within its discretion and violated no constitutional right of any of the petitioners.

As this Court stated in *Epperson v. Arkansas*, 393 U.S. 97, 104 (1968):

"Courts do not and cannot intervene in the resolution of conflicts which arise in the daily operation of school systems and which do not directly and sharply implicate basic constitutional values."

See "Developments in the Law--Academic Freedom," 81 HARV. L. REV. 1045, 1051-1054 (1968), cited by the Court at p. 104. The case at bar does not involve any of the elements of constitutional infirmity which have justified the rare occurrences of judicial intervention in curriculum and school book matters.

The Community School Board exercised its considered judgment as to the suitability of *Down These Mean Streets* for 11 to 15 year old children. As noted by both courts below, the wisdom and efficacy of its judgment is subject to state administrative and judicial review procedures. See N.Y. Education Law §§2590-*l* and 310; N.Y. CPLR Article 78. The petitioners, however, suggest that the power of the Community School Board to select books for school libraries is limited to excluding those books which are legally obscene for children.

They cite *Ginsberg v. New York*, 390 U.S. 629 (1968). However, that case merely established that, as to sales of books to children, a different standard of obscenity from the standard for adults may be imposed on public booksellers. As stated by the Court of Appeals below, the petitioner's argument improperly "equates the public school library, which has a function as an adjunct to the educational venture, with the entrepreneur seller of books who has no comparable responsibility" (8a). If the power of selection for educational purposes is to have any meaning, it must include the power to choose between books and to exclude those which are found inadequate, irrelevant, or otherwise inappropriate for the particular children to be served, and not merely the power to exclude those books which have been held to be illegal for sale to minors.

We recognize, of course, that while the Community School Board has broad powers of selection, that power may not be abused so as to make it a means of implementing an unconstitutional state policy. In *Epperson v. Arkansas*, 393 U.S. 97 (1968), state law made it a misdemeanor to teach, or use a textbook which teaches, the theory of evolution. The Supreme Court found that the sole state policy being served by this bar was the favoring of particular religious views, and it held the law to be an unconstitutional establishment of religion. Here, in contrast, no such unconstitutional reason formed the basis of the book's exclusion.

Moreover, in *Epperson*, there was a ban not simply on a particular book's discussion of evolution, but on the entire body of literature on evolution, and there was a ban on teaching the theory as well. Cf. *Meyer v. Nebraska*, 262 U.S. 390 (1923). Here, there has been no restriction whatever on teaching about the Barrio or its problems. As the Court below noted (7a): "The action of the Board does not even preclude the teacher from discussing *Down These Mean Streets* in class or from assigning it for outside reading." The Board has simply decided that the book ought not to be offered to 11 to 15 year old children in their public school libraries, where they are free to take books and read them without the guidance of any teacher. The petitioners' suggestion in their brief (p. 5) that, in rejecting their claims in this case, a court would be sanctioning the actions of "school boards which systematically purged the libraries of all books advocating peace or integration, or their curricula of all courses treating the United Nations" is absurd and ignores the vastly different facts of this case.

In *Keefe v. Geanakos*, 418 F. 2d 359 (1st Cir., 1969) and *Parducci v. Rutland*, 316 F. Supp. 352 (M.D. Ala., 1970), relied upon by the petitioners, teachers were dismissed for assigning and discussing works which their supervisors found offensive. As already noted, here there has been no such restriction on teaching or assignments, and thus no violation of any teacher's academic freedom. In addition, both cases involved issues of procedural due process not present here. See also *Mailloux v. Kiley*, 323 F. Supp. 1387 (D. Mass., 1971), affd. with opin., 448 F. 2d 1242 (1st Cir., 1971), a case with similar facts, where the courts relied solely on due process considerations in upholding the teacher.

Assuming arguendo that a public school librarian has any constitutionally protected right to unfettered choice in the selection of books for a public school library, the petitioner librarian here cannot possibly show the deprivation of such a right. She is employed at one of the schools which previously had *Down These Mean Streets* in its library. That library remains in possession of the book, and the librarian may lend it to parents who request it and who may, at their option, allow their children to read it. Surely such a limitation cannot be said to violate the librarian's professional freedom.

The parents of the children likewise have not been deprived of any constitutional right. Each parent in a school district will have his own views, often in direct opposition to those of other parents, as to what books are best suited for a school library's collection. The role of the elected Community School Board, acting in furtherance of its educational goals, and *in loco parentis*, is to make the choice. That a parent may disagree with that choice does not give him a constitutional right to compel the purchase or retention of any particular book, or to compel that it be available directly to students rather than to their parents.

The students have not been deprived of any "right to know." As with the teachers, there has been no ban on the discussion or teaching of any field of study or on the assignment or reading of any book. The mere fact that students in some schools will not have a particular book available to them in their school library, which is of course a library of limited space and financial resources, and (what the petitioners ignore) a library with special educational purposes, does not deprive the students of their right to read the book, either as part of an assignment by a teacher or on their own. Nor has there been any restriction of the students' freedom to express their political beliefs or any other beliefs or ideas. Cf. *Tinker v. Des Moines School Dist.*, 393 U.S. 503 (1969).

Unless the exclusion is otherwise improper, the mere fact that a book has been on the shelves and then has been excluded does not enhance the petitioners' claim of unconstitutionality. The power to select necessarily implies a continuing authority to choose new books and omit those which are no longer considered suitable. Moreover, the book was previously available in the school libraries of all the student petitioners and as to those schools the Board has directed that it be kept there and be available for loan on a parent-option basis. Such a plan, where the students have no constitutional right to have the book available at all in their school libraries, raises no constitutional issue.

A school board's judgment concerning what books are appropriate for availability in its school libraries may depend on the age of the children attending the schools. For mature children, it may be improper to exclude certain books. Yet for younger children, it may be clearly constitutionally proper to exclude the same books or place restrictions on their availability. Here the age of the children was 11 to 15. Such a group is sufficiently immature to warrant some limitation on the kind of books made freely available to them.

CONCLUSION

The petition for a writ of certiorari should be denied.

August 28, 1972.

Respectfully submitted,

NORMAN REDLICH,
*Corporation Counsel of the
City of New York,
Attorney for Respondents.*

STANLEY BUCHSBAUM,
NINA G. GOLDSTEIN,
Of Counsel.

The Committee for Parent's Rights in Public Education, a committee opposed to the return of Down These Mean Streets *to the open shelves of the junior high school libraries in Community School District No. 25, submits its brief in opposition to a petition for a writ of certiorari to the United States Supreme Court.*

Brief of Committee for Parents' Rights in Public Education in Opposition to a Petition for a Writ of Certiorari in *Presidents Council, Dist. 25* v. *Community School Bd. No. 25*

Brief in Opposition to a Petition for a Writ of Certiorari to the United States Supreme Court.

This brief is submitted on behalf of the defendant Antoinette McCarthy, individually and as representative of the Committee for Parent's Rights in Public Education. Mrs. McCarthy was not an original defendant but moved to intervene subsequent to the filing of the complaint. The motion was granted by the District Court. The Committee for Parent's Rights in Public Education submitted over 700 parents' signatures to a petition opposing the return of the book *Down These Mean Streets* to the open shelves of the Junior High School Libraries in Public School District No. 25.

Facts.

The following facts were either conceded or uncontested in the District Court:

1. The Board is the duly and legally elected Community School Board of Community School District No. 25.

2. The power of the state to determine matters relating to the education of students, including the prescription of a curriculum and the selection of textbooks and other instructional material, has been delegated by the New York State Legislature to the duly elected Community School Boards in New York City (New York Education Law, Section 2590-E).

3. Pursuant to resolution duly adopted by the Board, the book *Down These Mean Streets* by Piri Thomas was removed from the school libraries from Junior High Schools No. 185, 189 and 218 pursuant to the resolution adopted by the Board on April 19, 1971.

4. The students at Junior High Schools No. 185, 189 and 218 range in age from eleven (11) to fifteen (15) years.

5. The State of New York has provided administrative procedures for the review of arbitrary actions on the part of Community School Boards and final administrative action is reviewable under Article 78 of the New York Civil Practice Law and Rules (A-224-225).

6. Those schools which previously had the book in their respective libraries, were directed by the School Board to implement a procedure to loan said book directly to the parents of the children attending those schools who request the book (A-113).

Reasons for Denying the Writ.

Contained in petitioner's brief (pp. 4 through 7) under the heading *"Reasons for Granting The Writ"* is an analysis of the purported constitutional issues that the petitioner claims is involved in the case at bar, and which said issues the petitioner claims are important that this court review.

The petitioner has stated that "* * * local pressure groups succeed in persuading School Boards to purge controversial books, * * *" and that the issue to be decided by the court is "* * * to what extent are school professionals at the mercy of politically responsive, often elected, lay boards of education in determining what their students may read and learn in the schools." Petitioners further urge that the court below "* * * indicated that libraries are not an area in which constitutional freedoms need receive 'vigilant protection'," and that "* * * the courts below would apparently not interfere with School Boards which systematically purge the library of all books advocating peace or integration, or their curricula of all courses treating the United Nations." The petitioner further urges that the Federal Judiciary not "* * * indulge such direct political intrusion into the materials that teachers will be permitted to assign." And that the plaintiffs are turning to the Federal Courts because "* * * their libraries and their curricula are stripped of books which happen to be in political disfavor with a shifting majority of the School Board * * *"

These extraordinary distortions of the issues presented in the case at bar constitute an outrageous imposition upon this court. There is not one shred of evidence in the record that "local pressure groups succeeded in persuading School Boards to purge controversial books" nor is there one shred of evidence in the record that there was any "political intrusion into the materials that teachers will be permitted to assign."

As stated by Circuit Judge Mulligan, writing for the United States Court of Appeals Second Circuit of New York (p. 7A of the Appendix):

"The problems of the youth in the ghetto, crime, drugs and violence have not been placed off limits by the Board. A book has been removed but the librarian has not been penalized, and the teacher is still free to discuss the Barrio and its problems in the classroom. The action of the Board does not even preclude the teacher from discussing "Down These Mean Streets" in class or for assigning it for outside reading. In those libraries which have the book, the parent can borrow it and, if he sees fit, can loan it to his child if he wishes to read it" (p. 9A of Appendix).

"There is here no problem of freedom of speech or the expression of opinions on the part of parents, teachers, students or librarian. As we have pointed out, the discussion of the book or the problems which it encompasses or the ideas it espouses have not been prohibited by the Board's action in removing the book."

The defendant Board has rightfully determined that the book Down These Mean Streets is not a fit and proper educational tool to remain on the open shelves of a Junior High School library available for 11 to 15-year-olds. Judge Mulligan described this book as follows:
Page 4A of Appendix:

"The book, which has created the controversy and provoked the action of the Board, Down These Mean Streets, is an autobiographical account by Pirie Thomas, of a Puerto Rican youth growing up in the East Side Barrio (Spanish Harlem) in New York City. Predicably, the scene is depressing, ugly and violent. The argot of the vicinage is replete with four-letter and 12-letter obscenities unreported by Tom Swift or even Tom Jones. Acts of criminal violence, sex, normal and pervert as well as episodes of drug shooting are graphically described."

The decision of the duly constituted School Board acting under its lawful authority (there is no claim that the law under which the School Board derived its authority is in any way unconstitutional) determined in their wisdom and discretion that the aforesaid book was not a proper vessel and means for educating the students. In no way, shape or form did the action of the School Board in any way prevent, stop or terminate the teaching of any ideas or subjects in these Junior High Schools. In fact, the record showed that, in the social studies courses, problems of the ghetto are taught and discussed and, in addition, the schools have sex education courses. The petitioner argues that the United States Court of Appeals "matter of factly" answered that someone has to make a determination as to what the library collection will be and that the court below further suggests that "*any determination*" which the Board makes is beyond "judicial review" (p.8, petitioner's brief). The petitioner further states that the Court of Appeals "conveniently ignored * * * the fact that the book itself cannot be read."

Here, again, the petitioner levels uncalled for and unfair strictures upon the learned and scholarly judge who wrote the unanimous decision of the United States Court of Appeals. These liberties are very frankly further impositions on this court.

There was nothing "matter of fact" about the scholarly decision of Judge Mulligan nor that of Judge Mishler, the Presiding Judge of the United States Court, Eastern District of New York. The Court of Appeals never suggested that "any determination which the Board makes regarding its library collection is beyond judicial review." Nor did the Court of Appeals "conveniently ignore" anything. Conveniently ignored by the petitioner is the fact that this book is available to the parent of any student in Junior High School who wishes to borrow the book and said parent is then free to allow his child to read the book if the parent so wishes. Conveniently ignored by the petitioner is the fact that the facts of the case at bar present no intrusion upon the subject matters which students in these schools may be exposed to and learn. Conveniently ignored by the petitioner is the fact that the crux of the dispute is a disagreement as to whether this book is a suitable educational tool for use on the open shelves of a Junior High library.

A decision has been made by a majority of the duly elected local School Board based solely upon their belief as to what is best educationally and psychologically for the 11 to 15-year-old under their jurisdiction. If this decision were arbitrary or capricious, the plaintiffs have available adequate administrative remedies under the laws of the State of New York. The claim that this book was removed from the school library because it was "in political disfavor" with a shifting majority of the School Board is an outrageous fiction. On the contrary, the plaintiffs are attempting to use the Federal Court as a means of imposing their educational values and judgements upon the majority of the parents of the students in Junior High School who are represented by the majority of the School Board.

As stated by Judge Mulligan (p. 6A, Appendix):

"Our function is purely one of constitutional adjudication on the facts and the record before us: Has the Board transgressed the first amendment rights of the plaintiff teachers, parents, librarian and children."

The decision by Judge Mishler in the District Court and by Judge Mulligan speaking on behalf of the unanimous Court of Appeals clearly demonstrate that there has been no constitutional abridgment of any first amendment rights of the plaintiffs.

Conclusion.

The application for a writ of certiorari submitted by the petitioner should be denied.

Respectfully submitted,

JOSEPH R. GUARDINO,
Attorney for Defendant-Appellee,
MacCarthy intervened Defendant,
88-14 Sutphin Boulevard,
Jamaica, N. Y. 11435,
212 OL 7-5757.
7-5757.

STEPHEN W. O'LEARY,
THOMAS J. MASON,
W. ROBERT DEVINE,
STEPHEN W. O'LEARY, JR.,
STEVEN E. PEGALIS,
    Of Counsel.

The Authors League of America, a national society of writers and dramatists, requests permission to file a brief as amicus curiae and submits a brief arguing that the petition for certiorari be granted in the case of Presidents Council Dist. 25.

Brief of The Authors League of America for a Writ of Certiorari in *Presidents Council, Dist. 25* v. *Community School Bd. No. 25*

MOTION FOR LEAVE TO FILE BRIEF
AS *AMICUS CURIAE*

The Authors League of America, Inc. respectfully petitions for leave to file the annexed brief *amicus curiae* in this proceeding. The Authors League is a national society of professional writers and dramatists. One of its principal purposes is to express the views of its members in cases involving the rights of free speech and press. Because determination of the issues involved in this case will significantly affect those fundamental rights, the Authors League respectfully applies for leave to file its brief *amicus curiae*.

Counsel for the Applicant is familiar with the questions involved in this case, and the scope of their presentation, and believes that there is necessity for additional argument on the points specified in the brief.

The right to circulate books, which is protected by the First Amendment (*Bantam Books v. Sullivan*, 372 U.S. 58, 65 (1963), is of paramount importance to authors and publishers. Without it, freedom to write and publish can be made meaningless formalities. School libraries and public libraries are the most important means of circulating books to teenage and college students, more so than bookstores. The Circuit Court's opinion places in the hands of local school and library boards unlimited power to infringe that right of circulation by removing or banning from library shelves those books which are repugnant to the personal views of transitory majorities of laymen on these boards.

If District Board No. 25 can remove DOWN THESE MEAN STREETS from its libraries' shelves, then it or any other school or library board---applying only the subjective opinions of its majority--can remove from their library's shelves books of merit which had been chosen by competent professionals. This form of grass

roots restraint on free speech is far more pre-
vasive and damaging that the occasional criminal prosecution of a book's publisher or seller,
which can be defeated in an adversary judicial
procedure. Allowed to go unchecked, it poses a
real, not a theoretical, threat to freedom of
expression--and freedom to read.

For the reasons set forth in the attached
brief, we submit that the Board's order, on its
face, violated the First Amendment; and that
the Order and the Statute and Regulations which
authorized it, were so vague and ambiguous as
to violate the First and Fourteenth Amendments.

Because the Authors League of America believes that vital First Amendment rights of authors and publishers are involved, it respectfully requests permission to file the within
brief *amicus curiae*.

Respectfully submitted,

IRWIN KARP
*Attorney for the Authors League
of America, Inc.*

BRIEF OF THE AUTHORS LEAGUE OF AMERICA

Interest of The Authors League

The Authors League, a national society of
writers and dramatists, is deeply concerned
with preservation of the First Amendment freedoms to write, publish, circulate and read
books. The decisions of the Court of Appeals
and District Court pose a serious threat to the
freedom to circulate books to students through
school libraries and public libraries. The Authors League believes that these decisions, and
the opinions of the Courts, open the door to
widespread grass roots censorship of these libraries.

Summary of Argument

I. The basic issue is whether a transitory
majority of laymen on a school board can remove
or ban a book from the school libraries because
it offends their personal sensibilities. A
school board must comply with the First Amendment. The action of the District No. 25 Board
in removing DOWN THESE MEAN STREETS from the
junior high school libraries, for which it had
been selected by the District's professional
librarian, infringed the right of circulation
protected by the First Amendment. Moreover,
the Statute and Regulations on which the order
depended were so vague and ambiguous as to violate the First and Fourteenth Amendments. The
District and Circuit Courts correctly recognized that they had jurisdiction to decide the
substantive constitutional issues presented, on
the merits.

II. The Board's actions violated the First
Amendment right of the author and publisher to
have the book which had been selected by the

professional librarian circulated in the school
libraries of District No. 25.

III. The Board's action violated the First
Amendment rights of the District's libraries,
teachers and students.

POINT I

The Board's Order Violated First Amendment
Rights.

(i) The Nature and Scope of the Issue

The Court of Appeals turned the issue inside
out when it suggested it was protecting "academic freedom" by sustaining the Board's order. It said that "Academic freedom is scarcely fostered by the intrusion of three or even
nine federal jurists making curriculum or library choices for the community of scholars."

What actually happened was that five laymen,
a majority of the Board, intruded on the academic freedom of the professional librarian and
teachers--the real "community of scholars"--who
had selected DOWN THESE MEAN STREETS for the
libraries of District 25's three junior high
schools. And the real issue is whether that
"intrusion," by laymen on the community of
scholars--on its face, and absent any specific
and clear-cut statutory guidelines--violated
the First Amendment rights of the author and
publisher, the librarian and teacher, the parents and students--and the public of the School
District.

The members of the District 25 Board were
not scholars or experts in curriculum and
library selection. Nor did they evidence any
expertise in (or understanding of) First
Amendment principles, or the application of
these principles to book selection or book
removal. They were far less qualified than
Federal judges to decide whether DOWN THESE
MEAN STREETS should be banned, or placed in
coventry; although it was selected by
professional librarians and teachers, had been
well reviewed and recommended for teenagers,
and did not violate New York laws against
obscene material for minors.

The constitutional issue is, of course, far
more extensive than the one book. The Court of
Appeals denigrated the dispute, seeing it only
as "ensuing shouts" in an "intramural strife"
over the choice of books. What is really
involved is the power of laymen, elected for a
brief term, to remove or ban books from school
libraries (throughout the State, and the
country) because the books offend their
personal sensibilities. Members of the New
York City Community School Boards are elected
for a two-year term (Sec. 2590-c, N.Y. Educ.
Law). Under the Court's opinion, a new
majority could purge the junior high school
library of books selected by this board (no
less resanctify DOWN THESE MEAN STREETS as
suitable for teenagers). And two years later,
another transitory majority could remove or
ostracize any book selected by librarians and
teachers during the prior board's regime--and
prevent or restrict their circulation by the

libraries, and thus the right of teenage students to read them. Moreover, the Court of Appeals opinion gives school board majorities carte blanche to ban books (selected by the professional staff) which offend their personal political or social sensibilities, as well as those which describe life in a ghetto so vividly as to upset them.

When a handful of laymen, temporarily ensconced as a "school board", decide that a book of general interest must be removed from the library shelves of a school system, or barred from those shelves--they are taking an official action which affects rights to publish, circulate and read the book, rights which are protected by the First Amendment. The board's action must not, in itself, violate the First Amendment and the regulations and guidelines under which it is taken must not violate the First Amendment. We respectfully submit that on both counts, the District 25 order was unconstitutional.

(ii) A School Board Must Comply with the First Amendment

In *Tinker v. Des Moines School District*, 393 U.S. 503, 507 (1969) the Court emphasized that the Bill of Rights applies to the State "and all of its creatures--Boards of Education not excepted" and that their duty to

"...educat(e) the young for citizenship is reason for scrupulous protection of Constitutional freedoms of the individual, if we are not to strangle the free mind at its source and teach youth to discount important principles of our government as mere platitudes."

(iii) The Board's Order Violated the Right of Circulation protected by the First Amendment

The Court has held that the First Amendment protects "the circulation of books as well as their publication. *Lovell v. Griffin*, 303 U.S. 444, 452..."*Bantam Books v. Sullivan*, 372 U.S. 58, 65 (1963). Otherwise the State could compel books to be published in a vacuum, by banning their circulation--thus suppressing the author's freedom to communicate with the public.

The "circulation" of books by school and public libraries is essential to the process of communication protected by the the First Amendment. For Americans in schools and colleges, it is the paramount means of circulation, far exceeding book stores in importance and reach. If the Queens District Attorney had prosecuted a District 25 school librarian for distributing DOWN THESE MEAN STREETS, or threatened prosecution, the Federal Courts would have acted to prevent that restraint on the First Amendment right to circulate the book to teenagers [since it was not obscene under the standards of *Ginsberg v. State of New York*, 390 U.S. 629 (1968)]. See cases collected in note 8 at p. 67, *Bantam Books v. Sullivan*, supra.

The Board's order was also a restraint on that right of circulation. DOWN THESE MEAN STREETS was on the District 25 library shelves and was being circulated when the Board acted--to take it off the shelves and prevent it from being circulated and read. This was a deliberate and official restraint on that right of circulation. The book had not become "obsolete", any more than the "Barrio" whose life it depicted. Indeed, the Board did not claim to remove the book because it was obsolete or because the shelf space was needed for other books. The Board's majority terminated the book's right to be circulated through the school's libraries because they were offended by its language and its portrayal of life in a New York ghetto.

It must be emphasized that here the Board was removing a book already selected; not refusing to approve the purchase of a book not yet on the shelves. Certainly where a transitory majority of a school board acts to *remove* or *restrict* a book already selected and circulating, the minimal protection the First Amendment requires (in addition to the safeguards discussed in IV *infra*) is a clear-cut statement by the Board of the specific educational factors on which it bases its action, to guard against the obvious danger that the majority may order book removals or bans because of its personal political or social viewpoints rather than sound educational considerations.

Moreover, the Board's actions in first removing the book (a power which the Court of Appeals clearly held it possessed) and then directing it could only be loaned to parents were both unconstitutional. The latter step prevented students from having access to the book; and placed a taint on it which is likely to discourage the timid parent or student from requesting this now "forbidden fruit." This type of restraint by inhibition was held unconstitutional in *Lamont v. Postmaster General*, 381 U.S. 301, 309 (1965). It effectively restrains the author's and publisher's right to have the book circulated to those who want to read it. cf. *Bantam Books v. Sullivan*, 372 U.S. 58 (1963).

(iv) The Statute and Regulations underlying the order violated the First Amendment

The statutory sanction for the Board's action was so vague and indefinite as to restrain rights guaranteed by the First and Fourteenth Amendments. *Winters v. New York*, 333 U.S. 507, 509 (1948). Here the School Board acted as legislator, judge and jury. The basis for its action was not even a vague regulation. The only standard for judging the book was the subjective opinions of some of the Board members.

According to the Circuit Court, the Board's action was authorized under a Regulation of the New York Commissioner of Education and Sec. 2590-e(3) of the New York Education Law. The Law gives the Board power to "determine matters relating to the instruction of students, including the selection of textbooks and other instructional materials..." provided they are approved by the Chancellor. The Commissioner's regulation says that secondary school book collections "shall consist of books approved as satisfactory for (1) supplementing the curriculum (2) reference and general information (3) appreciation and (4) pleasure reading." (8 N.Y. Code, Rules & Regs.) (Educ. Sec 91.1(b) (1966).

We respectfully submit that these broadly worded provisions afford no standards whatsoever to guide laymen in applying First Amendment principles when deciding whether to remove or bar "reference and general information" books from the libraries of their district schools (even though the books have been approved by the Chancellor and selected by professional librarians and teachers). The unlimited power of selection or banning gives the transitory majority of a board great opportunities to impose their personal social and political views on the teachers and public of the school district, through the selection process—thus restraining the constitutional rights to circulate and read books. The First Amendment requires that the standards guiding these lay officials in this sensitive work be specific, not vague and ambiguous. *Bantam Books v. Sullivan*, 372 U.S. 58, 66 (1963); *Shelton v. Tucker*, 364 U.S. 479, 488-9 (1960); *Speiser v. Randall*, 357 U.S. 513, 525 (1958). Certainly the statute and regulation empowering the Board's book-banning order do not meet these First Amendment requirements. Moreover, the Regulations and Statute do not provide adequate procedural safeguards. *Freedman v. Maryland*, 380 U.S. 51 (1965).

(v) The District Court had Jurisdiction to Decide these First Amendment Issues

The Circuit Court, in deciding the substantive issues involved, recognized that the District Court had jurisdiction of the controversy. That is consistent with the New York courts' interpretation of Sec. 310 of the New York Education Law, which permits administrative appeals to the Commissioner of Education from decisions of District School Boards (including those involving book selection or banning). The New York courts have consistently held that where a constitutional issue, or the legality of an administrative ruling, is involved, those aggrieved may appeal directly to the courts and need not first exhaust this "administrative" remedy. *Board of Education, Otego v. Rickard, et al.*, 32 A D 2d 135, 300 N.Y. Supp. 2d 472 (3d Dept., 1969); *Matter of Figari v. N.Y. Tel. Co.*, 32 A D 2d 434, 303 N.Y. Supp. 2d 245 (2d Dept. 1969).

As Mr. Justice Brennan declared in *Jacobellis v. Ohio*, 378 U.S. 184 (1964), in cases

"...involving rights derived from the First Amendment guarantees of free expression, this Court cannot avoid making an independent constitutional judgment on the facts of the case as to whether the material involved is constitutionally protected." (p.190)

Moreover since the Board's action was unconstitutional, the plaintiffs were not compelled to exhaust whatever "administrative remedies"

might have been available to them. *Staub v. City of Baxley*, 355 U.S. 313 (1958). To require the plaintiffs to undergo the expense and burden of additional "administrative" procedures before they could turn to the courts for protection of First Amendment rights would seriously diminish those vital rights.

POINT II

The Board Violated the First Amendment Right of the Author and Publisher of DOWN THESE MEAN STREETS.

The Court has upheld the right of authors and publishers to oppose restraints directed at others who distribute and circulate their books, since these measures infringe the First Amendment freedoms of the writer and his publisher. *Bantam Books v. Sullivan*, 272 U.S. 58 (1963).

The author and publisher of DOWN THESE MEAN STREETS were not parties to the action. But the plaintiffs had standing to ask for the protection of the First Amendment rights involved, whether these be considered "their" rights, those of the author and publisher—or rights existing "for the benefit of all of us." (*Time, Inc. v. Hill*, 385 U.S. 374, 389). Moreover, the Authors League, as *amicus curiae* in the District Court and Circuit Court, urged that the Board's order be vacated because it violated the author's and publisher's First Amendment rights, as well as those of the students, teachers and parents.

In *Barrows v. Jackson*, 346 U.S. 249, 257 (1953), the Court held that there are unique situations in which the parties to a suit may assert the constitutional rights of others who are not before the Court. The Court observed that there are situations "in which it would be difficult if not impossible for the persons whose rights are asserted" to present their grievances (at p. 257). (See also: *Pierce v. Society of Sisters*, 268 U.S. 510.) Since a book can be subject to innumerable local restraints and actions designed to inhibit its circulation, it is often economically impossible for its author or publisher to directly protect their First Amendment rights by defending every suit or proceeding aimed at the book. The only effective safeguard for an author's and publisher's freedom of expression in a particular community may be the claim of First Amendment protection for their book by teachers, students, librarians or readers, in the community, who choose to defend it against unconstitutional restraints upon its circulation.

POINT III

The Board's Order Violated the First Amendment Rights of the District's Teachers and Students.

The Board has treated as "a mere platitude" the First Amendment rights of librarians and teachers to circulate to students books which they, in their professional judgment, deem suitable. Their rights were infringed by the Board's order, and must be protected. In *Epperson v. Arkansas,* 393 U.S. 97 (1968) the Court said:

"'[t]he vigilant protection of constitutional freedoms is nowhere more vital than in the community of American schools,' *Shelton v. Tucker,* 364 U.S. 479, 487 (1960). As this Court said in *Keyishian v. Board of Regents,* the First Amendment 'does not tolerate laws that cast a pall of orthodoxy over the classroom.' 385 U.S. 589, 603 (1967)." (p. 104)
"It is much too late to argue that the State may impose upon the teachers in its schools any conditions that it chooses, however restrictive they may be of constitutional guarantees. *Keyishian v. Board of Regents,* 385 U.S. 589, 605-606 (1967)." (at p. 107)

The Board's order also infringed the First Amendment rights of the District's junior high school students. In *Lamont v. Postmaster General,* 381 U.S. 301 (1965) the Court held that the First Amendment protects the rights to receive and read literature, as well as the rights to publish and circulate. These rights apply to the students who use the District junior high school libraries, as well as to adults who use public libraries. In *Tinker v. Des Moines School District,* 393 U.S. 503 (1969), the Court said:

"First Amendment rights, applied in light of the special characteristics of the school environment, are available to teachers and students. It can hardly be argued that either students or teachers shed their constitutional rights to freedom of speech or expression at the schoolhouse gate. This has been the unmistakable holding of this Court for almost 50 years." (at p. 506)

As the Court noted, "The principle of these cases is not confined to the supervised and ordained discussion which takes place in the classroom." (at p. 512) It applies to other aspects of education. One of the most important of these, we submit, is the reading a teenage student does in his school library; "...it is also an important part of the educational process." (at p.512) The library makes available to students a wide range of books, with a rich diversity of ideas and viewpoints, rather than "supervised and ordained" reading of text books. It permits:

". . . train (ing) through wide exposure to that robust exchange of ideas which discovers truth 'out of a multitude of tongues, [rather] than through any kind of authoritative selection.'" *Keyishian v. Board of Regents,* 385 U.S. 589, 603 (1967)

The students' freedom to read Down These

Mean Streets in District 25's libraries was unconstitutionally restrained by the Board's order, and by the Statute and Regulation which sanctioned the order.

CONCLUSION

It is respectfully submitted that the Petition for Certiorari should be granted.

Respectfully submitted,

IRWIN KARP
*Attorney for the Authors League
of America, Inc., as Amicus
Curiae*
120 Broadway
New York, New York 10005

In the case of Presidents Council, Dist. 25 *v.* Community School Board No. 25, *the United States Supreme Court denies certiorari. Justice William O. Douglas, however, explains in his dissent why he "would hear argument in this case." After pointing out that "at school the children are allowed to discuss the contents of the book and the social problems it portrays," Justice Douglas declares: "The First Amendment is a preferred right and is of great importance in the schools. In* Tinker, *the Court held that the First Amendment can only be restricted in the schools when a disciplinary problem is raised. No such allegation is asserted here. What else can the School Board now decide it does not like? How else will its sensibilities be offended? Are we sending children to school to be educated by the norms of the School Board or are we educating our youth to shed the prejudices of the past, to explore all forms of thought, and to find solutions to our world's problems?"*

Presidents Council, Dist. 25 v.
Community School Bd. No. 25, 409
U. S. 998 (1972)

No. 72-109. PRESIDENTS COUNCIL, DISTRICT 25, ET AL. *v.* COMMUNITY SCHOOL BOARD NO. 25 ET AL. C.A. 2d Cir. Motion of Authors League of America, Inc., for leave to file a brief as *amicus curiae* granted. Certiorari denied. MR. JUSTICE STEWART would grant the petition for certiorari and set case for oral argument. Reported below: 457 F. 2d 289.

Mr. JUSTICE DOUGLAS, dissenting.

A book entitled Down These Mean Streets by Piri Thomas was purchased by the librarians of three junior high schools in School District 25 in Queens, New York. The novel describes in graphic detail sexual and drug and drug-related activities that are a part of everyday life for those who live in Spanish Harlem. Its purpose was to acquaint the youth of Queens with the problems of their contemporaries in this social setting. The book was objected to by some parents and, after a public meeting, the School Board by a vote of 5-3 banned it from the libraries.˙ A later vote by the Board amended the order so the book is now kept on the shelves for direct loan to any parent who wants his or her children to have access to it. No child can borrow it directly.

This suit was brought on behalf of a principal, a librarian, and various parents and children who request that the court declare the resolution adopted by the Board unconstitutional, and order the defendants to place the book in normal circulation in the libraries and enjoin them from interfering with other school libraries within their jurisdiction which de-

sire to purchase the book.

Actions of school boards are not immune from constitutional scrutiny. *Meyer v. Nebraska,* 262 U.S. 390 (1923); *Bartels v. Iowa,* 262 U.S. 404 (1923); *Epperson v. Arkansas,* 393 U.S. 97 (1968); *Tinker v. Des Moines School Dist.,* 393 U.S. 503 (1969). Academic freedom has been upheld against attack on various fronts. *Sweezy v. New Hampshire,* 354 U.S. 234 (1957); *Wieman v. Updegraff,* 344 U.S. 183 (1952); *Keyishian v. Board of Regents,* 385 U.S. 589 (1967). The First Amendment involves not only the right to speak and publish, but also the right to hear, to learn, to know. *Martin v. Struthers,* 319 U.S. 141, 143 (1943); *Stanley v. Georgia,* 394 U. S. 557, 564 (1969); *Thomas v. Collins,* 323 U.S. 516, 534 (1945); *Red Lion Broadcasting Co. v. FCC,* 395 U.S. 367, 386, 390 (1969). And this Court has recognized that this right to know is "'nowhere more vital' than in our schools and universities," *Kleindienst v. Mandel,* 408 U.S. 753, 763 (1972); *Shelton v. Tucker,* 364 U.S. 479, 487 (1960); *Sweezy v. New Hampshire,* 354 U.S., at 250 (opinion of Warren, C. J.); *Keyishian v. Board of Regents,* 385 U.S., at 603. The book involved is not alleged to be obscene either under the standards of *Roth v. United States,* 354 U.S. 476 (1957), or under the stricter standards for minors set forth in *Ginsberg v. New York,* 390 U.S. 629 (1968).

The Board, however, contends that a book with such vivid accounts of sordid and perverted occurrences is not good for junior high students. At trial both sides produced expert witnesses to prove the value or harm of the novel. At school the children are allowed to discuss the contents of the book and the social problems it portrays. They can do everything but read it. This in my mind lessens somewhat the contention that the subject matter of the book is not proper.

The First Amendment is a·preferred right and is of great importance in the schools. In *Tinker,* the Court held that the First Amendment can only be restricted in the schools when a disciplinary problem is raised. No such allegation is asserted here. What else can the School Board now decide it does not like? How else will its sensibilities be offended? Are we sending children to school to be educated by the norms of the School Board or are we educating our youth to shed the prejudices of the past, to explore all forms of thought, and to find solutions to our world's problems?

Another requirement of the First Amendment is that any statute that imposes restrictions on the freedoms it protects must be narrowly drawn so as to impose any limitation in only the least restrictive way. N.Y. Educ. Law § 2590-e (3) (1970) gives the Board power to "determine matters relating to the instruction of students, including the selection of textbooks and other instructional materials..." provided they are approved by the Chancellor. The regulation of the State Commissioner of Education says that secondary school book collections "shall consist of books approved as satisfactory for (1) supplementing the curriculum (2) reference and general information (3) appreciation and (4) pleasure reading," 8 N.Y. Code, Rules & Regs. Educ., § 91.1 (b) (1966). Even a casual reading of these regulations shows that they contain no discrete limitations of the type spoken of in *Cantwell v. Connecticut*, 310 U.S. 296 (1940), *Speiser v. Randall*, 357 U. S. 513 (1958), or *Shelton v. Tucker, supra*.

Because the issues raised here are crucial to our national life, I would hear argument in this case.

A United States District Court decides that the First Amendment rights of students were not violated when the Strongsville, Ohio School Board refused to purchase for the school library and for classroom use certain novels, including Catch-22 *and* Cat's Cradle, *books which the professional teaching staff recommended for purchase, the District Court judge declaring: "The Legislature of Ohio having by law duly determined that the responsibility for the selection and determination of materials for use in the high school curriculum and public school libraries of the City of Strongsville City School District is to be vested in the Board of Education, the constitutionality of the relevant statutory enactments pertaining thereto being conceded, the Court deems it inappropriate to consider the wisdom of the board's determination."*

Minarcini v. *Strongsville City School Dist.*, 384 F.Supp. 698 (1974)

MEMORANDUM, OPINION AND ORDER

KRUPANSKY, District Judge.

This is an action instituted pursuant to the Civil Rights Act of 1871, 42 U.S.C. § 1983, wherein five minor plaintiffs, by next friends, purporting to represent a class of themselves and all other students enrolled in schools of the Strongsville City School District and thus similarly situated with plaintiffs, seek declaratory judgment and injunctive relief restraining defendants from continuing to violate plaintiffs' First and Fourteenth Amendment constitutional rights to academic freedom, freedom of speech, due process, and equal protection of the laws by the commission of acts which impose prior restraints upon publications and communications.

The thrust of plaintiffs' Complaint is to challenge the authority of the Board of Education of the Strongsville City School District (hereinafter Board) and the individually elected members thereof while acting within their official capacity and under color of law in accordance with Ohio Revised Code Chapter 3329, more specifically Ohio Rev. Code § 3329.-07, to determine by a majority of votes which textbooks should have been purchased and used in the schools under its control during the academic year 1972-73. Ohio Rev.Code § 3329.07 provides in part as follows:

> The board of education of each city, exempted village, and local school district shall cause it to be ascertained and at a

regular meeting determine which, and the number of each of the textbooks the schools under its charge require. . . .

Plaintiffs in this action concede the constitutionality of the foregoing legislative enactment.

The Complaint charges in substance that accepting the constitutional validity of Ohio Rev.Code § 3329.07, the Board's action in implementing said statutes by refusing to accept recommendations of the professional teaching staff was arbitrary and capricious thus resulting in an unconstitutional censorship of classroom material selected by said professional teaching staff in the exercise of its professional academic judgment thereby denying to plaintiffs their right to academic learning freedom, and thereby constituting a prior restraint on the freedoms of speech and press all in violation of plaintiffs' rights, privileges, and immunities sought to be secured and guaranteed by the free speech, due process and equal protection clauses of the First and Fourteenth Amendment to the Constitution of the United States.

The action was tried to the Court on July 9 and 10, 1974.

The record of testimony discloses little if any factual conflict as between the parties to this action. During 1970, the Board adopted the procedure here in issue to implement its legislative mandate to purchase textbooks for the schools within its District. The promulgated procedure provided that initial recommendations for proposed textbooks to be purchased during any given academic year be initiated by the Faculty Textbook Selection Committee (hereinafter Faculty Committee). The Faculty Committee in turn through its faculty department heads solicited individual faculty members within their respective departments for recommendations for curriculum text for use in their course assignments, designating such recommendations in an order of priority in the form of first, second, third or fourth. Thereafter the Faculty Committee submitted its recommendations to the Director of Secondary Education who in turn provided copies of the proposed texts to a Citizens Textbook Committee. The Citizens Textbook Committee had a composite membership of 16 residents from the School District. One representative to the Committee was designated by each of the five Board members; one representative was designated by the respective PTA's of each of the nine schools within the School District; one representative was designated by the PTA Council of the District and one representative was designated by the preschool PTA of the District. Subsequent to its consideration of the Faculty Committee's suggestions the Citizens Textbook Committee submitted its evaluations and suggestions to the Director of Secondary Education who in turn presented the recommendations of both the Faculty Committee and the Citizens Textbook Committee to the Board's Educational Program and Policy Committee composed of two Board members. The Educational Program and Policy Committee thereafter presented the recommendations of the Faculty Committee, the Citizens Textbook Committee and its own evaluation to the entire Board for its final consideration and selection.

Only the English Department's proposed selections are here in issue.

During the spring of 1972, the English Department through its Chairman, Mrs. Carol Petersen, recommended that the following textbooks be purchased by the Board for the academic year 1972-73 [Plaintiffs' Exhibit 4, page 37]:

TITLE	PUBLISHER	AUTHOR	EDIT.	COURSE	PRICE	EST. QUANT.
		ENGLISH 9 LITERATURE				
Outlooks Through Literature	Scott Foresman	Pooley	1969	Eng. 9	4.95	425
I (Me)	Holt, Rinehart & Winston	Brooks	1971	Eng.9 (Low)	80.00 per set	2 sets
		HIGH SCHOOL LITERATURE				
		Modern				
Catch 22	Dell	Miller [sic Heller]	2nd	Eng. 10-12	1.25	170
		Romantics				
The Portable Mark Twain	Viking Press	Bernard De Voto Ed.	1968	Eng. 10-12	3.95	180
		Early Romantics				
Edgar Allen Poe: Selected Poetry and Prose	Random House	Thomas Mabott Ed.	——	Eng. 10-12	1.15	180
		Drama				
Six Modern American Plays	Modern Library	O'Neill	——	Eng. 10-12	1.45	90
Long Days Journey Into Night	Yale Univ. Press	O'Neill	——	Eng.	1.95	90
		20th Century Novelist				
William Faulkner: Selected Short Stories	Random House	William Faulkner	1962	Eng. 10-12	2.95	180

On April 4, 1972, subsequent to a review and discussion of all the textbooks proposed by the Faculty Committee the Citizens Textbook Committee made the following report to the Board's Educational Program and Policy Committee [Plaintiffs' Exhibit 11:

Literature

OUTLOOKS THROUGH LITERATURE
I (ME)
REFLECTIONS IN LITERATURE   --not objectionable
GOD BLESS YOU MR. ROSEWATER   --not objectionable
CATCH 22--The majority of the committee found this book objectionable. It was felt that there would be no objection to having the students read this selection if it was not a required text. Although GOD BLESS YOU MR. ROSEWATER was found not objectionable, the entire committee felt that between the two selections in the Modern section, CATCH 22 surpassed GOD BLESS YOU MR. ROSEWATER and should have precedence if no other choice is to be made. In the discussion of Modern writing it was agreed by the majority that there must be better books from which to make a selection.

HUCKLEBERRY FINN
THE PORTABLE MARK TWAIN
THE PORTABLE POE   --not objectionable
EDGAR ALLEN POE: SELECTED POETRY & PROSE

SIX MODERN AMERICAN PLAYS--The majority finds no objection to the entire book. A minority objects to the offensive language in the play "Mr. Roberts."

LONG DAYS JOURNEY INTO NIGHT--The committee did not receive any copies of this book to review. A few members read a library copy and found no objection. A minority objected to the crude language.

THE PRICE
WILLIAM FAULKNER: SELECTED SHORT
    STORIES   --not objectionable

Board member Mrs. Ellen J. Wong, Chairman of the Educational Program and Policy Committee, presented that Committee's report together with recommendations of the Faculty Committee, and the Citizens Textbook Committee to the entire Board. Thereafter the Board collectively approved for purchase all initial recommendations of the Faculty Committee with the exception of the novel "Catch 22" by Joseph Heller. "Catch 22" represented faculty member John Lohr's first choice text recommendation for his Modern Literature English Course. Final action thereon was deferred by the Board in order to afford it an opportunity to meet with members of the English Department faculty to further discuss the proposal.

On May 18, 1972, the members of the Board met with Raymond J. Kestner, Director of Secondary Education of the Strongsville City School District, Mrs. Carol Petersen, Chairman of the Strongsville High School English Department, and various other faculty members of the said English Department, including John Lohr and David Edmonds. As previously stated the purpose of the meeting was "so the staff could communicate to the Board their reasons for recommending 'Catch 22' as part of the English text for 1972-73." During the course of the meeting the merits of purchasing "Catch 22" were openly discussed between all parties in a climate of calm objective deliberation free of emotional displays of anger or veiled intimidation. The discussions encompassed the English Department's suggestion of "God Bless You, Mr. Rosewater" by Kurt Vonnegut, Jr. as a substi-

tute selection for "Catch 22". The latter text represented the second choice of John Lohr, the Instructor assigned to teach the Modern Literature Course.

On June 8, 1972, at a duly convened meeting the Board voted not to purchase the novel "Catch 22" for use as a textbook during the 1972-73 academic year.

On June 17, 1972, at a duly convened special meeting of the Board it refused to consider "God Bless You, Mr. Rosewater" by Kurt Vonnegut, Jr., the English Department's second choice for the Modern Literature Course, as a substitute text for "Catch 22."

At a duly convened special meeting of the Board on August 19, 1972, the Board refused to consider the English Department's third choice selection of "Cat's Cradle" by Kurt Vonnegut, Jr., as a substitute text for the Modern Literature Course, although it appears from the testimony that the novel had been previously utilized as a text by the English Department during the year 1969.

On September 14, 1972, at a duly convened meeting of the Board, John Lohr's fourth selection of "Travels With Charlie" by John Steinbeck was approved as a text for the Modern Literature Course during the academic year here in question.

It should be noted that throughout the period of time during which the Board considered the various proposals here in issue, roughly from the middle of April through mid-September, 1972, its members discussed the proposals with its professional administrative staff including the Director of Secondary Education, faculty members assigned to the English Department, members of the Citizens Textbook Committee, and various interested members of the public. Although the evidence is conflicting, it appears further that prior to final action on each novel the individual Board members had read parts of each of the books, reviewed them, or scanned through them and were in a general manner personally familiar with the substance of the novels.

All Board meetings during which curriculum text purchases were discussed, with the exception of the Board's conference with faculty members of the English Department on May 18, 1972, were matters of public knowledge and open to public participation. No individual was denied the right to appear before the Board to express an opinion or discuss pending action; no individual was ruled out of order at any such meeting, nor were any motions proffered or approved to eliminate debate thereon. Additionally, all Board members were readily available to the public for comment about the books which are the subject of this controversy. At all times each Board member acted in good faith and in a manner that each considered to be in the best interest of the School District.

The reasons expressed by Board members in support of their action refusing the purchase of the initially proposed novels are not unreasonable. Those reasons in substance reflect an attitude that the proposed novels were adult-orientated and, therefore, less suitable for use as curriculum text for grades 10 through 12 than other available novels, and that the books were better suited for college level instruction and study.

Literary value of the three novels having been conceded by the parties, consideration by the Court of testimony presented by Kurt Vonnegut, Jr., and Dr. Mary Joanne Monahan together with the deposition of Joseph Heller in support thereof is unnecessary. Similarly, obscenity as defined in the Supreme Court's pronouncements set forth in Miller v. California, 413 U.S. 15, 93 S.Ct. 2607, 37 L.Ed.2d 419 (1973), as subsequently interpreted by Jenkins v. Georgia, 418 U.S. 153, 94 S.Ct. 2750, 41 L.Ed.2d 642 (decided June 24, 1974), is eliminated as an issue herein by agreement of counsel.

Thus, apparent from the foregoing, the novels "Catch 22" by Joseph Heller, "God Bless You, Mr. Rosewater" and "Cat's Cradle" by Kurt Vonnegut, Jr., are not on trial in this proceeding. Rather, the only issue of concern for the Court's determination is the Board's authority to ultimately select, in the manner implemented herein, textbooks to be purchased for use in the Strongsville City School District.

Absent emotionally charged cries of censorship, violation of academic freedom, repression and book burning; there evolves a reality of modern day society where censorship, or "editorial judgment" however characterized in whatever degree, is an inescapable aspect of operating a school system, a library, a televised news program, a monthly or weekly magazine, or a daily newspaper. Some individual or group must ultimately decide that a particular news item is worthy of reporting or printing or disregarding as worthless, that a book is worthy of publication or shelving. The responsibility embraces the authority to declare a book, a news item, or event a matter of great public interest or worthless and unfit to print. In the same fashion news commentators on a daily basis disregard hundreds of stories and items before fashioning the network's evening news programs. Syndicated news columnists annually discard enumerable column ideas as unworthy of discussion. Every editor, publisher, program director, librarian, teacher, school board member, or business executive is confronted with the same decision-making process of inclusion or exclusion on a daily basis. Each believes the adopted decision right and proper to the possible dissent of others.

Ideological conflicts within communities of a free society exacerbate and subside with the ever changing moods and structure of its population. The endless cycle moves from thesis to antithesis through synthesis and back to thesis only to renew itself from ever evolving dissent. Peaceful transition through the cycle, i. e., synthesis of antithesis, is insured in an open society by proportionate legislative representation founded in the elective process. The Court should not and cannot interfere with the orderly procedure except as an impartial arbiter insuring equal protection of the laws and constitutional guarantees free of arbitrary and capricious action or abuse of authority by the antagonists.

Confronted with the removal by the New York City Community School Board of the novel "Down These Mean Streets" by Piri Thomas from all Junior High School libraries in the School District, the Second Circuit Court of Appeals in 1972 deciding Presidents Council, Dist. 25 v. Community Sch. Brd. No. 25, 457 F.2d 289 (2nd Cir. 1972), cert. denied, 409 U.S. 998, 93 S.Ct. 308, 34 L.Ed.2d 260 (1972) stated:

. . . Since we are dealing not with the collection of a public book store but with the library of a public junior high school, evidently some authorized person or body has to make a determination as to what the library collection will be. It is predictable that no matter what choice of books may be made by whatever segment of academe, some other person or group may well dissent. The ensuing shouts of book burning, witch hunting and violation of academic freedom hardly elevate this intramural strife to first amendment constitutional proportions. If it did, there would be a constant intrusion of the judiciary into the internal affairs of the school. Academic freedom is scarcely fostered by the intrusion of three or even nine federal jurists making curriculum or library choices for the community of scholars. When the court has intervened, the circumstances have been rare and extreme and the issues presented totally distinct from those we have here. . . . 457 F.2d at

291-292.

The Second Circuit further noted that:

> The administration of any library, wheth-
> er it be a university or particularly a pub-
> lic junior high school, involves a constant
> process of selection and winnowing based not
> only on educational needs but financial and
> architectural realities.   To suggest that
> the shelving or unshelving of books presents
> a constitutional issue, particularly where
> there is no showing of a curtailment of
> freedom of speech or thought, is a proposi-
> tion we cannot accept [footnote omitted].
> *Id.* at 293.

The events of the two years since the
Board's initial action in 1972 dramatically
demonstrates the dynamics and the pragmatism of
the cycle in operation.   As reflected by the
stipulations herein, on January 1, 1974, two
new members were elected to the Board.   The
events disclose that thereafter the newly constituted Board in a controversial decision approved the purchase of the novel "Manchild in
the Promised Land" by Clarence Brown as curriculum text for use in elective high school English course styled "Street Literature," over
the protest of a segment of the community.   The
Board, as constituted in 1972, moved from its
original decision to exclude the purchase of
certain controversial novels as curriculum text
for the academic year 1972-73 to a decision of
the Board, as presently constituted, to include
a controversial novel of similar substantive
and literary composition as those here in issue
for the academic year 1974-75.

Obvious from the clear and concise language
of § 3329.07 of the Ohio Revised Code, the legislative mandate charged the Board of Education
of each city school district, an elective body,
with the ultimate authority and responsibility
to ascertain and determine which, and the number of textbooks the schools under its charge
require.   Apparent from Ohio Revised Code Chapter 3329 including §§ 3329.01 through 3329.11,
wide discretion was vested in the elective
Boards to implement the mandate.

The Legislature of Ohio having by law duly
determined that the responsibility for the selection and determination of materials for use
in the high school curriculum and public school
libraries of the City of Strongsville City
School District is to be vested in the Board of
Education, the constitutionality of the relevant statutory enactments pertaining thereto
being conceded, the Court deems it inappropriate to consider the wisdom of the Board's determination.   *Presidents Council, Dist. 25,
supra.*

Although the Court may sympathize, in certain respects, with real or imagined ideological and personality conflicts between professional teaching staffs and respective Boards of
Education in the area of curriculum planning
and/or implementation, any change thereof must
develop through the legislative process rather
than judicial decision.   The State having duly
and legally acted thereon, absent constitution-

al infringements, the Court cannot and will not
substitute its individual judgment for that of
the Ohio Legislature.   The Court's function
herein is necessarily limited to one of constitutional inquiry and adjudication on the facts
and the record before it, namely, has the Board
transgressed the First Amendment rights of the
plaintiff students herein.   In Epperson v.
Arkansas, 393 U.S. 97, 89 S.Ct. 266, 21 L.Ed.2d
228 (1968), the United States Supreme Court
stated:

> By and large, public education in our
> Nation is committed to the control of
> state and local authorities.   Courts do
> not and cannot intervene in the resolu-
> tion of conflicts which arise in the
> daily operation of school systems and
> which do not directly and sharply impli-
> cate basic constitutional values. 393
> U.S. at 104, 89 S.Ct. at 270.

The gravamen of plaintiffs' challenge to the
Board's action is its asserted failure to
specify standards and procedures for purchasing
textbooks (pursuant to Ohio Revised Code Chapter 3329), i.e., failure to provide for outside
psychological and professional consultation in
order to confirm or disregard the English Department's proposals, said acts, individually
and collectively, constituting arbitrary and
capricious conduct on the part of the Board in
violation of the plaintiffs' First and Fourteenth Amendment rights.   Plaintiffs' assertion
is contrary to the weight of evidence as reflected in the review procedure voluntarily
adopted by the Board as hereinbefore set forth.

The procedure viewed in its entirety was
fair, equitable and logical.   It provided input
from faculty members assigned to instruct given
courses through appropriate department heads,
through the Faculty Committee representing the
professional staff on the one hand and evaluation by a 16 member Citizens Textbook Committee
representing a broad cross section of the entire School District on the other hand; through
the Board's Educational and Program Policy Committee to the entire Board for final consideration and selection after consultation with its
in-house professional and administrative staff.

Nor does the record disclose arbitrary or
capricious acts by the Board taken either collectively or individually in administering the
procedure.   Affirmatively, the record reflects
a series of open Board hearings, consultation
with members of the English department, discussions with various members of the professional
administrative staff, with members of the Citizens Textbook Committee and any and all other
interested parties before its ultimate action.
All meetings of the Board and professional
staff were conducted in a calm restrained atmosphere free of emotionalism, vindictiveness
or intimidation.   Individual Board members ar-
rived at decisions in good faith after conscientious consideration of the over-all problem.

Considering further the resources available
to and utilized by the Board members individu-

ally and collectively for evaluating and deciding the issues confronting them together with the educational and experience level of each member thereof, the necessity for outside professional assistance suggested by the plaintiffs herein is without merit under the circumstances.

At this juncture the Court is constrained to comment upon the implications of First and Fourteenth Amendment infringements inferred by plaintiffs' legal precedent and application of said precedent as it bears upon the facts and issues developed herein.

In Epperson v. Arkansas, *supra*, cited by plaintiffs herein, the United States Supreme Court invalidated a state statute making it unlawful for a teacher in any state supported school to use a textbook which teaches theories of evolution. The Supreme Court vitiated the statute on the specific ground that "the State may not adopt programs or practices in its public schools or colleges which 'aid or oppose' any religion". 393 U.S. at 106, 89 S.Ct. at 271. "The State's undoubted right to prescribe curriculum for its public schools does not carry with it the right to prohibit, on pain of criminal penalty, a teaching of a scientific theory or doctrine where the prohibition is based upon reasons that violate the First Amendment." *Id*. at 107, 89 S.Ct. at 272. The action herein obviously does not present a religious establishment or free exercise issue, nor, as reflected by the weight of the evidence, did the Board's action ban the teaching of any theory or doctrine. The literary style or content of either author was not placed off limits by the Board. The Board resolved not to purchase the English Department's first, second and third choice novels for use as a textbook. The Board's action per se did not preclude any teacher or librarian within the school system from discussing the novels in the classroom with any students or from assigning any or all of such novels as outside or supplemental reading. The evidence is firm and uncontradicted that the Board passed no resolution, issued no directive either written or oral precluding any instructor from discussing any or all of the novels in class or assigning any such novel as outside reading or the subject of research or book review. The record further discloses some testimony that John Lohr and David Edmonds both discussed to some degree one or more of the novels as part of their respective courses. The plaintiff Susan Lee Minarcini testified that she had read all three novels at some time or other, with parental consent. It is equally apparent from the record that no teacher was intimidated nor reprisals threatened for any classroom discussions or assignments related to the novels. Although the plaintiffs infer that the teaching contract of John Lohr was not renewed as a direct or indirect result of his first, second and third choice recommendations for his Modern Literature Course, the Court is satisfied that his proposals here in issue were in no way related to the Board's refusal to renew his teaching contract at the close of the 1973 academic year.

Plaintiffs further cite three teacher discharge cases, namely, Keefe v. Geanakos, 418 F.2d 359 (1st Cir. 1969); Mailloux v. Kiley, 448 F. 2d 1242 (1st Cir. 1971), and Parducci v. Rutland, 316 F. Supp. 352 (M.D.Ala.1970). Factually the cited cases are distinguishable from the case at bar for the reason that, as previously stated, no teacher was discharged or threatened with discharge nor were any members of the Strongsville teaching staff instructed not to discuss the novels or utilize them as outside or supplemental reading. Additionally, the Court is in complete accord with the underlying principles of plaintiffs' authority, namely, the professional teacher's obligation to utilize individual teaching methodology, which was not violated by the Board's action herein.

In citing Tinker v. Des Moines Independent Community School District, 393 U.S. 503, 89 S.Ct. 733, 21 L.Ed.2d 731 (1969) plaintiffs advance the argument that absent resulting disruption or disorder arising from use of the controversial novels here in issue the Board is constitutionally bound to purchase said novels as curriculum textbooks for utilization in classroom instruction. There is no issue before this Court conflicting with the principles established in the Supreme Court's pronouncements in *Tinker*, namely:

First Amendment rights, applied in light of the special characteristics of the school environment, are available to teachers and students. It can hardly be argued that either students or teachers shed their constitutional rights to freedom of speech or expression at the schoolhouse gate. This has been the unmistakable holding of this Court for almost 50 years. *Id*. at 506, 89 S.Ct. at 736.

Apparent therefrom, the Supreme Court did intrude into the field of public education by invalidating a school principal's regulation suspending students displaying black armbands symbolizing objection to Vietnam hostilities. The regulation was deemed in violation of the student's rights to free speech absent evidence to support a finding that the students' conduct materially disrupted class work or the invasion of rights of others. *Tinker, supra,* is thus distinguishable upon its facts and application to this proceeding. Collateral cases of Antonelli v. Hammond, 308 F.Supp. 1329 (D.Mass.1970) and James v. Brd. of Educ., 461 F.2d 566 (2nd Cir. 1972), cert. denied, 409 U.S. 1042, 93 S.Ct. 529, 34 L.Ed.2d 491 (1972) [high school teacher discharged for wearing black armband] for the same reason are equally not applicable.

One final matter remains for the Court's consideration. Defendant-Intervenors move the Court to dismiss that part of plaintiffs' Complaint designating a class action. Plaintiffs request that they be permitted to maintain this action as a class action pursuant to Rule 23, Fed.R.Civ.P., which class composes all students enrolled in the schools operated and maintained by the Strongsville City School District.

Intervenors contend that plaintiffs' class designation is improper pursuant to Rule 23 for the reason that a majority of Strongsville students and parents thereof are not in sympathy with plaintiffs' views, and are, therefore, not "similarly situated". Intervenor's argument is without merit. All members of the purported class are affected by actions taken by the Board of Education of the Strongsville City School District. The Court need not speculate how many students therein may need or desire to invoke First Amendment protection against such action; the ultimate fact that each student is subject thereto is sufficient. *See,* Arkansas Educ. Ass'n v. Board of Ed., Portland, Ark. Sch. Dist., 446 F.2d 763 (8th Cir. 1971); Norwalk Core v. Norfolk Redevelopment Agency, 395 F.2d 920, 937 (2d Cir. 1968); Sullivan v. Houston Independent School District, 307 F. Supp. 1328 (S.D. Texas 1969); Wright, Class Actions, 47 F.R.D. 169 (1969). Accordingly, the Court finds that this action is maintainable as a class action pursuant to Rule 23(a), (b) (2), Fed.R.Civ.P., and is, therefore, certified as such. The class shall comprise all students enrolled in the schools operated and maintained by the Strongsville City School District.

Conclusions

Upon the pleadings, the evidence in its entirety including the exhibits, the briefs and arguments of counsel, the Court concludes:

1. This action is properly maintained as a class action pursuant to Rule 23, Fed.R.Civ.P., and the class is designated as all students enrolled in the schools operated and maintained by the Strongsville City School District;

2. Chapter 3329 of the Ohio Revised Code more particularly § 3329.07 mandates the Board of Education of each City School District to ascertain and determine at regularly scheduled meetings which, and the number of each of the textbooks the schools under its charge require;

3. The Board promulgated a broad and equitable representative procedure for initial recommendations to originate with various faculty members and department heads within the District with evaluation by a Citizens Textbook Committee composed of representatives from each of the various schools within the District and consultation with its professional administrative staff members as an information resource available as an aid in textbook selection;

4. The procedure thus adopted was openly implemented and faculty members were not foreclosed or limited either formally or informally, directly or indirectly, to utilize individual teaching methodology or from discussing any subject including the books here in issue or assigning said books as outside or supplemental reading or the subject of a review in the course of classroom instruction. No faculty member was intimidated, reprimanded, discharged or threatened with such action as a result of circumstances here involved;

5. Each of the novels here in issue have literary value and are not obscene within the purview of contemporary legal precedent;

6. Final action of the Board in determining which books were to be purchased by the Strongsville City School District for use during the academic year 1972-73 was taken in good faith and predicated upon available information, from reviewing the books, consulting with the administrative professional staff including faculty members of the English department, members of the Citizens Textbook Committee and other interested representatives of the community,

7. The action of the Board as reflected by the evidence in its entirety was not arbitrary and capricious;

8. Considering the educational and experience level of each elected Board member together with its resources of information available to it through its professional administrative staff, faculty members, and Citizens Textbook Committee, outside professional consultants, psychologists and/or educational counselors were neither required nor necessary under the circumstances herein;

9. The three novels here in issue were available to students and/or members of the community through commercial outlets and public libraries and no student was directly or indirectly imposed upon not to read or discuss any of the novels;

10. The plaintiffs herein were not deprived of academic freedom nor did the Board's action constitute a limitation of First and Fourteenth Amendment rights nor any infringement thereof.

The foregoing shall constitute the Court's findings of fact and conclusions of law consistent with Rule 52(a), Fed. R.Civ.P.

It is so ordered.

The United States Court Of Appeals, Sixth Circuit, reverses that part of the lower court order which had held constitutional the Strongsville, Ohio, School Board's removal of certain books from the school library, the Court of Appeals declaring: "A public school library is also a valuable adjunct to classroom discussion. If one of the English teachers considered Joseph Heller's Catch 22 *to be one of the more important modern American novels (as, indeed, at least one did), we assume that no one would dispute that the First Amendment's protection of academic freedom would protect both his right to say so in class and his students' right to hear him and to find and read the book. Obviously, the students' success in this last endeavor would be greatly hindered by the fact that the book sought had been removed from the school library. The removal of books from a school library is a much more serious burden upon freedom of classroom discussion than the action found unconstitutional in* Tinker...."

Minarcini v. *Strongsville City School Dist.*, 541 F.2d 577 (1977)

EDWARDS, Circuit Judge.

This record presents a vivid story of heated community debate over what sort of books should be 1) selected as high school text books, 2) purchased for a high school library, 3) removed from a high school library, or 4) forbidden to be taught or assigned in a high school classroom. The setting of this controversy is the high school in Strongsville, Ohio, a suburb of Cleveland.

This case originated as a class action brought under 42 U.S.C. § 1983 (1970) and 28 U.S.C. § 1343(3) (1970) against the Strongsville City School District, the members of the Board of Education and the Superintendent of the school district by five public high school students through their parents, as next friends. The suit claimed violation of First and Fourteenth Amendment rights in that the school board, disregarding the recommendation of the faculty, refused to approve Joseph Heller's *Catch 22* and Kurt Vonnegut's *God Bless You, Mr. Rosewater* as texts or library books, ordered Vonnegut's *Cat's Cradle* and Heller's *Catch 22* to be removed from the library, and issued resolutions which served to prohibit teacher and student discussion of these books in class or their use as supplemental reading.

The original complaint produced a counterclaim for "malicious prosecution" by one of the defendant school board members, Arthur L. Cain, and a motion to intervene as defendants filed on behalf of still other students in the high school by their parents, indicating that plaintiffs' requested relief was entirely an-

tagonistic to the wishes and interests of the intervenors. The District Judge denied motions for summary judgment by defendants and intervenors, dismissed the counterclaims of defendant Cain, tried the case on the original complaint, and dismissed it after entering findings of fact and conclusions of law holding that the defendants had not violated any First or Fourteenth Amendment rights of the plaintiffs.

On review of the briefs and records filed in this court, and the oral arguments heard before us, we affirm the dismissal of the counterclaims of defendant Arthur L. Cain for the reasons set forth in the District Judge's order of March 22, 1974. Likewise for the reasons set forth on this point in the District Judge's Memorandum Opinion and Order filed August 9, 1974, we affirm his determination of the class represented by plaintiffs pursuant to Rule 23 of the Federal Rules of Civil Procedure thereby rejecting the appellate arguments of the intervenors.

Turning now to the principal issues in this case, we shall discuss them separately.

I. THE BOARD'S DECISION NOT TO APPROVE OR PURCHASE CERTAIN TEXTS

It appears clear to this court that the State of Ohio has specifically committed the duty of selecting and purchasing textbooks to local boards of education. O.R.C. § 3329.07 (1975) provides as follows:

§ 3329.07 Determination of textbooks required; order; payment; transportation charges. (GC § 4854-6)

The board of education of each city, exempted village, and local school district shall cause it to be ascertained and at a regular meeting determine which, and the number of each of the textbooks the schools under its charge require. The clerk at once shall order the books agreed upon from the publisher, who on receipt of such order must ship them to the clerk without delay. He forthwith shall examine the books, and, if found right and in accordance with the order, remit the amount to the publisher. The board must pay for the books so purchased and in addition all charges for the transportation of the books out of the general fund of said district or out of such other funds as it may have available for such purchase of textbooks. If such board at any time can secure from the publishers books at less than such maximum price, they shall do so, and without unnecessary delay may make effort to secure such lower price before adopting any particular textbooks.

Clearly, discretion as to the selection of textbooks must be lodged somewhere and we can find no federal constitutional prohibition which prevents its being lodged in school board officials who are elected representatives of the people. To the extent that this suit concerns a question as to whether the school faculty may make its professional choices of textbooks prevail over the considered decision of the Board of Education empowered by state law to make such decisions, we affirm the decision of the District Judge in dismissing that portion of plaintiffs' complaint. In short, we find no federal constitutional violation in this Board's exercise of curriculum and textbook control as empowered by the Ohio statute.

[3] Nor do we think that the Board's decisions in selecting texts were arbitrary and capricious or offended procedural due process. There was a Board committee appointed to make recommendations on textbooks. It met with the faculty committee and with a citizens' committee to discuss the books recommended by the faculty before the Board received its committee's recommendations and acted thereon. As to the appellants' complaints of arbitrary and capricious action, we again affirm the District Court.

In this determination and in those which follow, we keep in mind the admonitions of the United States Supreme Court in the leading case of *Epperson v. Arkansas*, 393 U.S. 97, 104-05, 89 S.Ct. 266, 270, 21 L.Ed.2d 228 (1968):

Judicial interposition in the operation of the public school system of the Nation raises problems requiring care and restraint. Our courts, however, have not failed to apply the First Amendment's mandate in our educational system where essential to safeguard the fundamental values of freedom of speech and inquiry and of belief. By and large, public education in our Nation is committed to the control of state and local authorities. Courts do not and cannot intervene in the resolution of conflicts which arise in the daily operation of school systems and which do not directly and sharply implicate basic constitutional values. On the other hand, "[t]he vigilant protection of constitutional freedoms is nowhere more vital than in the community of American schools," *Shelton v. Tucker*, 364 U.S. 479, 487 [81 S.Ct. 247, 251, 5 L.Ed.2d 231] (1960). As this Court said in *Keyishian v. Board of Regents*, the First Amendment "does not tolerate laws that cast a pall of orthodoxy over the classroom." 385 U.S. 589, 603 [87 S.Ct. 675, 683, 17 L.Ed.2d 629] (1967). (Footnote omitted.)

II THE REMOVAL OF CERTAIN BOOKS FROM THE SCHOOL LIBRARY

The record discloses that at a special meeting of the Strongsville Board of Education on August 19, 1972, according to the official minutes, the following motion was made and adopted:

Dr. Cain moved, seconded by Mr. Henzey, that the textbook entitled *Cat's Cradle* not be used any longer as a text or in the library in the Strongsville Schools.
Discussion.
Dr. Cain moved the question.
Mr. Henzey requested the Clerk to call for

the vote.
Roll call: Ayes: Dr. Cain, Mr. Henzey, Mrs. Wong
Nays: Mr. Woollett
Motion carried.

Similarly at a meeting of the Strongsville School Board on August 31, 1972, the following action was recorded in the minutes:

Mrs. Wong moved, seconded by Dr. Cain, that the textbook *Catch 22* be removed from the Library in the Strongsville Schools.
Roll call: Ayes: Mr. Ramsey, Mrs. Wong, Dr. Cain
Nays: Mr. Woollett
Motion carried.

In his opinion the District Judge held that "the novels *Catch 22* by Joseph Heller, *God Bless You, Mr. Rosewater* and *Cat's Cradle* by Kurt Vonnegut, Jr., are not on trial in this proceeding." Further he stated, "Literary value of the three novels [has] been conceded by the parties . . ." and that "obscenity as defined in the Supreme Court's pronouncements is eliminated as an issue herein by agreement of counsel." These holdings do not appear to be disputed on this appeal, and we accept them.

The District Judge, in dismissing the complaint concerning removal from the library of Heller's *Catch 22* and Vonnegut's *Cat's Cradle*, relied strongly upon a Second Circuit opinion in *Presidents Council, District 25* v. *Community School Board No. 25*, 457 F.2d 289 (2nd Cir.), *cert. denied*, 409 U.S. 998, 93 S.Ct. 308, 34 L.Ed.2d 260 (1972). In that case, after noting, as we have above, that some authorized body has to make a determination as to the choice of books for texts or for the library, the Second Circuit continued by discussing a parallel right on the part of a board to "winnow" the library:

The administration of any library, whether it be a university or particularly a public junior high school, involves a constant process of selection and winnowing based not only on educational needs but financial and architectural realities. To suggest that the shelving or unshelving of books presents a constitutional issue, *particularly where there is no showing of a curtailment of freedom of speech or thought*, is a proposition we cannot accept. *Id.* at 293. (Emphasis added.) (Footnote omitted.)

The District Judge in our instant case appears to have read this paragraph as upholding an absolute right on the part of this school board to remove from the library and presumably to destroy any books it regarded unfavorably without concern for the First Amendment. We do not read the Second Circuit opinion so broadly (see qualifying clause italicized above). If it were unqualified, we would not follow it.

A library is a storehouse of knowledge. When created for a public school it is an important privilege created by the state for the benefit of the students in the school. That privilege is not subject to being withdrawn by succeeding school boards whose members might desire to "winnow" the library for books the content of which occasioned their displeasure or disapproval. Of course, a copy of a book may wear out. Some books may become obsolete. Shelf space alone may at some point require some selection of books to be retained and books to be disposed of. No such rationale is involved in this case, however.

The sole explanation offered by this record is provided by the School Board's minutes of July 17, 1972, which read as follows:

Mrs. Wong reviewed the Citizens Committee report regarding adoption of "God Bless You Mr. Rosewater".

Dr. Cain presented the following minority report:

1. It is recommended that *God Bless You Mr. Rosewater* not be purchased, either as a textbook, supplemental reading book or library book. The book is completely sick. One secretary read it for one-half hour and handed it back to the reviewer with the written comment, "GARBAGE".

2. Instead, it is recommended that the autobiography of Captain Eddie Rickenbacker be purchased for use in the English course. It is modern and it fills the need of providing material which will inspire and educate the students as well as teach them high moral values and provide the opportunity to learn from a man of exceptional ability and understanding.

3. For the same reason, it is recommended that the following books be purchased for immediate use as required supplemental reading in the high school social studies program:

> *Herbert Hoover*, a biography by Eugene Lyons;
> *Reminiscences of Douglas MacArthur*

4. It is also recommended in the interest of a balanced program that *One Day in The Life of Ivan Denisovich* by A. I. Solzhenitsyn, be purchased as a supplemental reader for the high school social studies program.

5. It is also recommended that copies of all of the above books be placed in the library of each secondary school.

6. It is also recommended that *Cat's Cradle*, which was written by the same character (Vennegutter) who wrote, using the term loosely, *God Bless You Mr. Rosewater*, and which has been used as a textbook, although never legally adopted by the Board, be withdrawn immediately and all copies disposed of in accordance with statutory procedure.

7. Finally, it is recommended that the McGuffy Readers be bought as supplemental readers for enrichment program purposes for the elementary schools, since they seem to offer so many advantages in vocabulary, con-

tent and sentence structure over the drivel being pushed today.

While we recognize that the minute quoted above is designated as a "minority report," we find it significant in view of intervenor Cain's active role in the removal process and the fact that it offers the only official clue to the reasons for the School Board majority's two book removal motions. The Board's silence is extraordinary in view of the intense community controversy and the expressed professional views of the faculty favorable to the books concerned.

In the absence of any explanation of the Board's action which is neutral in First Amendment terms, we must conclude that the School Board removed the books because it found them objectionable in content and because it felt that it had the power, unfettered by the First Amendment, to censor the school library for subject matter which the Board members found distasteful.

Neither the State of Ohio nor the Strongsville School Board was under any federal constitutional compulsion to provide a library for the Strongsville High School or to choose any particular books. Once having created such a privilege for the benefit of its students, however, neither body could place conditions on the use of the library which were related solely to the social or political tastes of school board members.[1]

The Supreme Court long ago said: "It is too late in the day to doubt that the liberties of religion and expression may be infringed by the denial of or placing conditions upon a benefit or privilege." *Pickering v. Board of Education*, 391 U.S. 563, 568, 88 S.Ct. 1731, 20 L.Ed.2d 811 (1968); *Keyishian v. Board of Regents*, 385 U.S. 589, 606, 87 S.Ct. 675, 685 17 L.Ed.2d 629 (1967). See also *Douglas v. California*, 372 U.S. 353, 83 S.Ct. 814, 9 L.Ed.2d 811 (1963); *Griffin v. Illinois*, 351 U.S. 12, 76 S.Ct. 585, 100 L.Ed. 891 (1956).

A public school library is also a valuable adjunct to classroom discussion. If one of the English teachers considered Joseph Heller's *Catch 22* to be one of the more important modern American novels (as, indeed, at least one did), we assume that no one would dispute that the First Amendment's protection of academic freedom would protect both his right to say so in class and his students' right to hear him and to find and read the book. Obviously, the students' success in this last endeavor would be greatly hindered by the fact that the book sought had been removed from the school library. The removal of books from a school library is a much more serious burden upon freedom of classroom discussion than the action found unconstitutional in *Tinker v. Des Moines Independent Community School District*, 393 U.S. 503, 89 S.Ct. 733, 21 L.Ed.2d 731 (1969).

Further, we do not think this burden is minimized by the availability of the disputed book in sources outside the school. Restraint on expression may not generally be justified by the fact that there may be other times, places, or circumstances available for such expression. *Southeastern Promotions, Ltd. v. Conrad,* 420 U.S. 546, 556, 95 S.Ct. 1239, 43 L.Ed.2d 448 (1975); *Spence v. Washington,* 418 U.S. 405, 411 n.4, 94 S.Ct. 2727, 41 L.Ed.2d 842 (1974); *Schneider v. State,* 308 U.S. 147, 163, 60 S.Ct. 146, 84 L.Ed. 155 (1939). *Cf. Cox v. New Hampshire,* 312 U.S. 569, 61 S.Ct. 762, 85 L.Ed. 1049 (1941).

A library is a mighty resource in the free marketplace of ideas. *See Abrams v. United States,* 250 U.S. 616, 40 S.Ct. 17, 63 L.Ed. 1173 (1919) (Holmes, J., dissenting). It is specially dedicated to broad dissemination of ideas. It is a forum for silent speech. See *Tinker v. Des Moines Independent Community School District, supra;* Brown v. Louisiana, 383 U.S. 131, 86 S.Ct. 719, 15 L.Ed.2d 637 (1966).

We recognize of course, that we deal here with a somewhat more difficult concept than a direct restraint on speech. Here we are concerned with the right of students to receive information which they and their teachers desire them to have. First Amendment protection of the right to know has frequently been recognized in the past. *See Procunier v. Martinez,* 416 U.S. 396, 94 S.Ct. 1800, 40 L.Ed.2d 224 (1974); *Kleindienst v. Mandel,* 408 U.S. 753, 763, 92 S.Ct. 2576, 33 L.Ed.2d 683 (1972); *Red Lion Broadcasting Co. v. FCC,* 395 U.S. 367, 386, 390, 89 S.Ct. 1794, 23 L.Ed.2d 371 (1969); *Stanley v. Georgia,* 394 U.S. 557, 564, 89 S.Ct. 1243, 22 L.Ed.2d 542 (1969); *Lamont v. Postmaster General,* 381 U.S. 301, 85 S.Ct. 1493, 14 L.Ed.2d 398 (1965); *Thomas v. Collins,* 323 U.S. 516, 534, 65 S.Ct. 315, 89 L.Ed. 430 (1945); *Martin v. Struthers,* 319 U.S. 141, 143, 63 S.Ct. 862, 87 L.Ed. 1313 (1943). Nonetheless, we might have felt that its application here was more doubtful absent a very recent Supreme Court case. In *Virginia State Board of Pharmacy v. Virginia Citizens Consumers Council, Inc.,* 425 U.S. 748, 96 S.Ct. 1817, 1823, 48 L.Ed.2d 346 (1976), Mr. Justice Blackmun wrote for the Court:

Freedom of speech presupposes a willing speaker. But where a speaker exists, as is the case here, the protection afforded is to the communication, to its source and to its recipients both. This is clear from the decided cases. In *Lamont v. Postmaster General,* 381 U.S. 301 [85 S.Ct. 1493, 14 L.Ed.2d 398] (1965), the Court upheld the First Amendment rights of citizens to receive political publications sent from abroad. More recently, in *Kleindienst v. Mandel,* 408 U.S. 753, 762-763 [92 S.Ct. 2576, 2581, 33 L.Ed.2d 683, 691] (1972), we acknowledged that this Court has referred to a First Amendment right to "receive information and ideas," and that freedom of speech "'necessarily protects the right to receive.'" And in *Procunier v. Martinez,* 416 U.S. 396, 408-409 [94 S.Ct. 1800, 1808-1809, 40 L.Ed.2d 224, 237-238] (1974), where censorship of prison inmates' mail was under examination, we thought it unnecessary

to assess the First Amendment rights of the inmates themselves, for it was reasoned that such censorship equally infringed the rights of noninmates to whom correspondence was addressed. There are numerous other expressions to the same effect in the Court's decisions. See, e. g., *Red Lion Broadcasting Co. v. FCC,* 395 U.S. 367, 390 [89 S.Ct. 1794, 1806-1807, 23 L.Ed.2d 371, 389] (1969); *Stanley v. Georgia,* 394 U.S. 557, 564 [89 S.Ct. 1243, 1247-1248, 22 L.Ed.2d 542, 549] (1969); *Griswold v. Connecticut,* 381 U.S. 479, 482 [85 S.Ct. 1678, 1680-1681, 14 L.Ed.2d 510, 513-514] (1965); *Marsh v. Alabama,* 326 U.S. 501, 505 [66 S.Ct. 276, 278, 90 L.Ed. 265, 267-268] (1946); *Thomas v. Collins,* 323 U.S. 516, 534 [65 S.Ct. 315, 324-325, 89 L.Ed. 430, 442-443] (1945); *Martin v. Struthers,* 319 U.S. 141, 143 [63 S.Ct. 862, 863, 87 L.Ed. 1313, 1316-1317] (1943). If there is a right to advertise, there is a reciprocal right to receive the advertising, and it may be asserted by these appellees.

We believe that the language just quoted, plus the recent cases of *Kleindienst v. Mandel, supra,* and *Procunier v. Martinez, supra,* serve to establish firmly both the First Amendment right to know which is involved in our instant case and the standing of the student plaintiffs to raise the issue.

As to this issue, we must reverse.

III ACADEMIC FREEDOM CLAIMS

Plaintiffs-appellants contend that the Board also violated the First Amendment by prohibiting teachers from referring to any of the three books under consideration in classroom discussion.[2] As to this issue the District Judge entered the following finding of fact:

The procedure thus adopted was openly implemented and faculty members were not foreclosed or limited either formally or informally, directly or indirectly, to utilize individual teaching methodology or from discussing any subject including the books here in issue or assigning said books as outside or supplemental reading or the subject of a review in the course of classroom instruction. No faculty member was intimidated, reprimanded, discharged or threatened with such action as a result of circumstances here involved . . . .

As to this issue we have examined the record carefully. We have no doubt that the two School Board resolutions we have already dealt with would have had a somewhat chilling effect upon classroom discussion. If so, the invalidation of these resolutions should be an adequate remedy. What the testimonial record does not support is a holding by this court that the just quoted finding of fact from the District Judge is clearly erroneous. The testimony does not clearly establish that the Board ever directed the faculty (or directed the principal to direct the faculty) not to refer to any particular books in classroom teaching. For these reasons we affirm the District Judge upon this issue.

The judgment of the District Court is affirmed as to issues numbered one (I) and three (III) of this opinion. It is vacated and reversed as to issue numbered two (II). The District Court is ordered to amend the judgment so as to declare the School Board resolutions of August 19, 1972 and August 31, 1972, null and void as violative of the First Amendment to the United States Constitution and to direct the members of the Strongsville School Board to replace in the library the books with which these resolutions dealt by purchase, if necessary, out of the first sums available for library purposes.

NOTES

1. On the other hand, it would be consistent with the First Amendment (although not required by it) for every library in America to contain enough books so that every citizen in the community could find at least some which he or she regarded as objectionable in either subject matter, expression or idea.
2. Plaintiffs also made the same contention as to the high school principal. There were proofs which tended to support this contention. However, the then principal has left the school system, and there is no complaint as to his replacement.

The *Chelsea, Massachusetts School Committee* decides to bar from the high school library *Male and Female Under 18*, an anthology of writings by adolescents, because of the inclusion of an "offensive" and "damaging" poem, "The city to a young girl," written by a 15-year-old girl. Students, parents, and others seek a court order requiring that the anthology be returned to the library. A United States District Court in deciding that the book cannot be banned from the library declares: "The library is 'a mighty resource in the marketplace of ideas,' Minarcini v. Strongsville City School District. . . . There a student can literally explore the unknown, and discover areas of interest and thought not covered by the prescribed curriculum. The student who discovers the magic of the library is on the way to a life-long experience of self-education and enrichment. That student learns that a library is a place to test or expand upon ideas presented to him, in or out of the classroom. The most effective antidote to the poison of mindless orthodoxy is ready access to a broad sweep of ideas and philosophies. There is no danger from such exposure. The danger is in mind control. The committee's ban of the anthology *Male & Female* is enjoined."

Right to Read Defense Committee v. School Committee, Etc., 454 F.Supp. 703 (1978)

TAURO, District Judge.

At issue is the decision by a majority of the Chelsea School Committee (Committee) to bar from the High School Library an anthology of writings by adolescents entitled "Male and Female Under 18" (*Male & Female*). The Committee's action was prompted by a Chelsea parent's objection to the language in one selection, "The City to a Young Girl" (*City*), a poem written by a fifteen year old New York City high school student.[1]

Plaintiffs[2] commenced this action against the Committee and the School Superintendent[3] on August 3, 1977 under 42 U.S.C. § 1983,[4] seeking an order requiring the anthology returned to the library intact. The essence of plaintiffs' position is that the Committee's action violated First Amendment rights of the High School's students, faculty and library staff. The Committee defends its decision principally on the ground that its action in ordering the anthology removed was well within its statutory authority to oversee the curriculum and support services of the Chelsea High School.[5]

Following a contested hearing on plaintiffs' request for temporary restraining order, this court ordered the anthology returned intact to the library, and made available to students having written permission of a parent or guardian.[6]

Following several weeks of discovery, a six day bench trial and post trial submission of memoranda, the merits of the case were taken under advisement on March 21, 1978.

I.

Chelsea High School has approximately 1200 students in grades nine through twelve. The English Department offers a wide variety of courses including Adolescent Literature, Hispano-American Literature, Poetry, Creative Writing, and Women in Literature. The English curriculum includes literature that, in street language, deals with such provocative themes as homosexuality, drug abuse, sexual experiences, and ghetto life. The High School Library facilities include approximately 7,400 volumes.

The librarian, Coleman, became interested in a reading program sponsored by the Prentice Hall Publishing Company that made available 1000 paperback books at an attractive cost. This collection of books was assembled by professional librarians and teachers for the purpose of stimulating student interest in reading. Coleman decided to purchase the Prentice Hall program, with the understanding that any titles unsuitable for the High School could be exchanged. She followed standard Chelsea procurement procedures in ordering the Prentice Hall collection. After they were delivered to the High School she reviewed all of them, although she was unable to read every page of all 1000 books.

The collection included the challenged *Male & Female,* which is an anthology of prose and poetry written by students aged 8 to 18. Coleman read the book's introduction and scanned its contents, but did not read *City,* the poem which is the subject of this litigation.

Coleman felt that *Male & Female* would be useful for students taking adolescent literature and creative writing courses, particularly because it would give them an opportunity to see the variety of ways in which other students expressed themselves. She recognized the anthology's two editors as highly regarded professionals, and the publisher, Avon Books, as having a good reputation in the area of young adult literature. These considerations, plus her own review, caused Coleman to place the anthology in the High School Library during March of 1976.[7]

On May 19, 1977, Committee Chairman Quigley received a telephone call from a parent of a high school student complaining about offensive language in *City* that was included in the volume *Male & Female* his daughter had borrowed from the High School Library. Quigley went that evening to the parent's home, obtained the volume and assured the parent that the incident would be carefully reviewed by the Committee. He later read the poem and concluded that *Male & Female* should be removed from the High School Library because of the "filthy" and "offensive" language in *City.* He made this determination without reading any

other part of the anthology. The only person he consulted was the complaining parent.

The same evening Quigley scheduled an emergency meeting of the Committee for Monday, May 23, 1977, to consider the subject of "objectionable, salacious and obscene material being made available in books in the High School Library." He also wrote an article that evening that appeared the next day in his newspaper, *The Chelsea Record,* in which he commented:

I think it can be said without contradiction that I am certainly no prude in certain matters—but the complaint of a father made to me yesterday about passages in a book his daughter obtained at the high school library has almost made me sick to my stomach to think that such a book could be obtained in any school—let alone one here in Chelsea.

I want to bring this matter to the attention of our Administrators and I want to make certain that no such filth will be distributed in our schools.

Quite frankly, more than that, I want a complete review of how it was possible for such garbage to even get on bookshelves where 14 year old high school—ninth graders—could obtain them.[8]

Superintendent McGee first became aware of a controversy concerning *Male & Female* when he read Quigley's article in the May 20 *Chelsea Record.* Because Quigley was out of town over the weekend, McGee did not obtain the book from him until 2:00 P.M. on Monday, May 23rd.

On May 23rd, Quigley distributed copies of *City* prior to the Committee meeting to each of its other three male members. He did not give a copy to any of the three women members, because of the poem's "crude" and "offensive" language. Quigley assumed that at least two of the women members, Moore and Montesano, would accept his characterization of the poem and, therefore, would agree to conduct an inquiry as to how the book got into the library.

At the May 23rd meeting, Quigley characterized the poem as "objectionable" and "outright obscene." He commented that it was "a serious mistake" to allow "this filth on the library shelves," and that he wanted to "make certain it doesn't happen again." Defendant Tiro concurred saying, "the book is lewd and leaves nothing to the imagination. It's outright obnoxious." Quigley then moved that the Superintendent be requested to report to the Committee as to how books, *Male & Female* in particular, were selected for the High School Library. Defendant Morochnick unsuccessfully sought to amend Quigley's motion by suggesting that, after the receipt of the Superintendent's report, the Committee meet in executive session with the librarian, the headmaster and complaining parent. McGee stated that it was inappropriate to handle this complaint in an open school meeting, and that Quigley was "setting in motion a chain of events that might lead to censorship."

In the May 25, 1978 *Chelsea Record,*

Quigley chastized McGee in an editorial entitled "Mr. McGee's Censorship." That editorial characterized *City* as "obviously obscene," "filthy" and "vile and offensive garbage."

Quigley called another special meeting of the Committee for May 26, 1977, to confer with the complaining parent. At this meeting, McGee submitted a report based on his reading of the entire book. He identified *City* as its "objectionable portion." He stated that, other than the poem *City* and an objectionable word which appeared in another poem, there was no "obscene terminology" in the book. McGee's conclusion was that,

> the text reflects the goals the editors were attempting to accomplish. I believe the book is sound and has educational value with the exception of the passage objected to and one other word in one other poem.

McGee reported that the book would be removed from the library until a decision was made as to whether to keep the entire book off the shelf or only to remove the offending pages. The book was then turned over to the principal, Franco, who had also submitted a report on High School Library procedures. Franco's report included an explanation by Coleman of the library selection process, as well as her description of a procedure recommended by the American Library Association for considering challenges to the suitability of library material. Quigley requested McGee to determine if Coleman had knowingly put "trash" in the library. The Committee would then determine whether she was "the type of person we want to continue in that position."

On June 14, 1977, Coleman published a statement in *The Chelsea Record* in which she opined that *City* was not obscene, that both students and faculty should have access to it, and that the book should not have been removed from the library without the type of hearing recommended by the American Library Association. In response, Quigley was quoted in his newspaper as being

> shocked and extremely disappointed to have our high school librarian claim there is nothing lewd, lascivious, filthy, suggestive, licentious, pornographic or obscene about this particular poem in this book of many poems.

A special committee meeting with Coleman was called for July 20, 1977, for the purpose of determining how a book such as *Male & Female* could have been placed in the High School Library. At this meeting, Coleman defended the work and its use by students and faculty. Quigley's assessment, however, was that *City* was "low down dirty rotten filth, garbage, fit only for the sewer." Although not a lawyer, Quigley mentioned the case of *Miller v. California,* 413 U.S. 15, 93 S.Ct. 2607, 37 L.Ed.2d 419 (1973), and observed that, under local community standards in Chelsea, *City* was obscene. Defendant Moore classified the work as a "dirty, filthy, rotten poem," written

by "a sick child." Defendant Tiro agreed with Quigley that, under *Miller,* the Committee could apply local community standards and that he would vote to ban the book. Defendant Kornechuk was interested in determining whether Coleman knew that the poem was in the book.

The next special meeting of the Committee was called by Quigley for July 28, 1977. The stated purpose was for "considering and voting upon motions pertaining to the book entitled *Male & Female Under 18* at the high school." Quigley moved that the action of the Superintendent in removing and not returning *Male & Female* be affirmed by the Committee. Morochnick offered an amendment that the book remain in the library but be circulated to students under 18 only if they had written permission from their parents. The amendment was defeated 6-1, with only Morochnick voting in favor of it. Quigley's motion was adopted 6-0, with Morochnick abstaining.[9]

The regular July 28, 1977 School Committee meeting was convened immediately following the special meeting at which the aforementioned vote was taken on *Male & Female*. Quigley moved that consideration be given to transferring Coleman from the library to a classroom because of her "mistake" in having selected *Male & Female* for the library. Tiro moved that Coleman be transferred immediately because she was "out of the mainstream of contact with the youngsters in a classroom situation." Moore moved to table the motions so that Coleman could "think things over." She also moved that a committee be formed for the "careful selection of books from 'good standard lists' for use in the libraries of the Chelsea School System." Quigley moved that the matter be referred to McGee for a feasibility study. Morochnick moved that McGee also study the feasibility of "reviewing and acting upon complaints from parents or others on any books." The Morochnick amendment was defeated and the motion as amended by Quigley was passed. The Morochnick amendment was defeated and the motion as amended by Quigley was passed.

McGee later informed Franco that the page containing *City* was to be removed from *Male & Female*. Franco removed the page, but kept the book in his office. It does not appear that the Committee members had read any of *Male & Female*, other than *City*, prior to voting to ban the entire anthology.

On August 3, 1977, this lawsuit was filed. When Quigley learned of the suit he was quoted as follows in his newspaper, *The Chelsea Record*:

> Who needs employees like that? Who needs employees that will fight to keep the kind of tasteless, filthy trash that is contained in the poem we voted to remove? I may even call a special meeting to discuss what we'll do with these insubordinate teachers.

In a *Chelsea Record* editorial on August 4, 1977, Quigley observed that the Committee "may seek to reassign the School Librarian; or . . . seek the resignations of those teachers who have taken the legal action to restore the poem to the High School Library," and that "it may be necessary to institute a petition to let the people know just what the 'community standards' do NOT include accepting the 'filth' of that poem."

Quigley circulated such petitions for the purpose of demonstrating to this court that *City* was not acceptable under Chelsea's local community standards. A Quigley editorial entitled "'Obscene' Poem Petition" appeared in the August 5th *Chelsea Record*.

> These next few days could be very important to the people of Chelsea who feel this poem is in fact "filthy" or "obscene" or to give it the benefit of every doubt it is certainly in 'bad taste.'
> And we submit it is not the type of poem that the overwhelming majority of parents—AND STUDENTS—want on any library shelf.
> We therefore will be printing petitions which we hope hundreds and hundreds of Chelsea people will sign so that the Judge hearing this case can get some idea of just what 'community standards' are in the City of Chelsea.

At a special meeting of the School Committee on August 10, 1977, its attorney, Robert Tatel, recommended a newspaper survey be conducted to determine community standards, and that a citizens' conference be conveyed for the same purpose. Implementing counsel's suggestion, the Committee sent letters, enclosing copies of the poem, to thirty Chelsea clergy soliciting their evaluation of *City*. Two clergy responded. Both supported the Committee's position.

Another special meeting was held on August 17, 1977 at which Tatel presented the Committee with two resolutions for adoption. The first reaffirmed its decision to remove *Male & Female* from the library on the grounds that 1) the book dealt with "sex education," not a school subject; 2) that *City* had a potentially unhealthy and counter-productive effect on some children; and 3) the Committee preferred that even sex education books in the library not contain words and phrases considered "filthy, shocking and obscene by a large section of the community." The second resolution insulated Coleman, the faculty and student body from any sanctions arising out of the *Male & Female* incident.

This was the first occasion on which counsel had ever presented the Committee with fully prepared resolutions for its adoption. They were prepared for submission to this court at a hearing scheduled the next day, August 18, 1977.[10]

After that hearing, this court issued its temporary restraining order. See n. 6, *supra*.

On August 29, 1977, an article entitled "Parent of Chelsea Student Complaints to Superintendent McGee About Sections In Book" appeared in *The Chelsea Record*. Prior to its publication, Quigley had received a complaint from a parent of a high school student about a book entitled *Growing Up Puerto Rican* that had been used in the Adolescent Literature

course taught by plaintiff Bartlett.

In an editorial appearing the same day entitled "More 'Filthy' Books . . .", Quigley said that Bartlett's use of that book in her class was "an absolute outrage" and that this federal court case "must not and cannot be allowed to intimidate the Committee from doing what has to be done to root out all the 'filthy' literature that is being circulated in the High School under the guise of 'education.'" The editorial concluded that "[s]uch instances of this type of 'filth' MUST NOT—CANNOT—AND WILL NOT be permitted in Chelsea Schools."

II.

The School Committee defends against this suit by claiming an unconstrained authority to remove books from the shelves of the school library. This authority is said to derive from various state statutes giving it "general charge" of the public schools within its jurisdiction, and directing it to purchase textbooks and other supplies for the schools.[11] The Committee argues further that it was not required to purchase *Male & Female* for the library and, therefore, could remove it at will. This court disagrees, and determines that, under the circumstances of this case, the defendants' removal of *Male & Female* from the library was an infringement of the First Amendment rights of the students and faculty of Chelsea High School.

III.

The Supreme Court has commented that "[t]he vigilant protection of constitutional freedoms is nowhere more vital than in the community of American schools." *Shelton v. Tucker*, 364 U.S. 479, 487, 81 S.Ct. 247, 251, 5 L.Ed.2d 231 (1960). The fundamental notion underlying the First Amendment is that citizens, free to speak and hear, will be able to form judgments concerning matters affecting their lives, independent of any governmental suasion or propaganda. Consistent with that noble purpose, a school should be a readily accessible warehouse of ideas.

> The Nation's future depends upon leaders trained through wide exposure to that robust exchange of ideas which discovers truth 'out of a multitude of tongues, [rather] than through any kind of authoritative selection.'

Keyishian v. Board of Regents, 385 U.S. 589, 603, 87 S.Ct. 675, 683, 17 L.Ed.2d 629 (1967), *quoting United States v. Associated Press*, 52 F.Supp. 362, 372 (S.D.N.Y.1943).

Recognizing the important interplay between First Amendment goals and the function of our schools, courts have occasionally found it necessary to intervene in the administration of school affairs. It has been declared unconstitutional for a state to forbid instruction, other than in the English language, to students below the eighth grade, *Meyer v. Nebraska*,

262 U.S. 390, 43 S.Ct. 625, 67 L.Ed. 1042 (1923), and to prohibit the teaching of evolution in public schools, *Epperson v. Arkansas*, 393 U.S. 97, 89 S.Ct. 266, 21 L.Ed.2d 228 (1968). Students have the right to express themselves in non-disruptive political protest, *Tinker v. Des Moines School District*, 393 U.S. 503, 890 S.Ct. 733, 21 L.Ed.2d 731 (1969), and the right not to be forced to express ideas with which they disagree, *West Virginia Board of Education v. Barnette*, 319 U.S. 624, 63 S.Ct. 1178, 87 L.Ed. 1628 (1943). In short, the First Amendment is not merely a mantle which students and faculty must doff when they take their places in the classroom.[12]

It is clear despite such intervention, however, that local authorities are, and must continue to be, the principal policy makers in the public schools. School committees require a flexible and comprehensive set of powers to discharge the challenging tasks that confront them. As the Court stated in *Epperson v. Arkansas*, 393 U.S. 97, 104, 89 S.Ct. 266, 270, 21 L.Ed.2d 228 (1968):

> By and large, public education in our Nation is committed to the control of state and local authorities. Courts do not and cannot intervene in the resolution of conflicts which arise in the daily operation of school systems and which do not directly and sharply implicate basic constitutional values.

It is the tension between these necessary administrative powers and the First Amendment rights of those within the school system that underlies the conflict in this case. Clearly, a school committee can determine what books will go into a library and, indeed, if there will be a library at all. But the question presented here is whether a school committee has the same degree of discretion to order a book removed from a library.

Two federal courts of appeal addressed this issue in cases involving factual patterns similar to that involved here. In *Presidents Council District 25 v. Community School Board No. 25*, 457 F.2d 289 (2d Cir.), *cert. denied*, 409 U.S. 998, 93 S.Ct. 308, 34 L.Ed.2d 260 (1972), the Second Circuit upheld a school board's removal of the book *Down These Mean Streets* from a high school library. In contrast, the school board's removal of a Kurt Vonnegut novel from a school library was set aside by the Sixth Circuit in the case of *Minarcini v. Strongsville City School District*, 541 F.2d 577 (1976). Defendants' heavy reliance on *Presidents Council* presumes incorrectly that the holding there would afford a school committee the absolute right to remove a disfavored book from a library, without any concern for the First Amendment rights of students and faculty. Such reliance overlooks the Second Circuit's implicit acknowledgment that, however absolute may be a school board's discretion in selecting books, there are boundaries to its authority to remove a book from a library.

It would seem clear to us that books which become obsolete or irrelevant or where improperly selected initially, for whatever reason, can be removed by the same authority which was empowered to make the selection in the first place.
457 F.2d at 293.[13]

Here, there is no evidence that the challenged anthology is obsolete. Indeed, there was ample evidence to support the plaintiffs' assertion that the work is relevant to a number of courses taught at Chelsea High School. No contention has been made that the book was improperly selected, insofar as Chelsea procurement regulations were concerned. Despite their continuing objection to the language employed, defendants do not now contend the work is obscene. Limitations of resources such as money and shelf space are not factors here. The book has already been purchased and paid for. It is a small paperback approximately one inch thick. There has been no suggestion that its presence in the library has contributed to any shelf space problem.

The record leaves this court with no doubt that the reason the Committee banned *Male & Female* was because it considered the theme and language of *City* to be offensive. At the time the book was removed, and during their testimony at trial, the members consistently expressed their opinion that *City* was "filthy," "obscene," "disgusting." A number also objected to its theme, as they interpreted it.

Defendants contend that the Committee's reasons for banning *Male & Female* were formulated on the date of removal and were memorialized by a formal resolution of the Committee dated August 17, 1977 (Section I, *supra*). This resolution recited reasons in addition to the poem's language and theme for its removal. This court finds, however, that the August 17 resolution of the Committee was a self-serving document that rewrote history in an effort to meet the issues of this litigation. In simple terms, it was a pretext.[14]

Of course, not every removal of a book from a school library implicates First Amendment values. But when, as here, a book is removed because its theme and language are offensive to a school committee, those aggrieved are entitled to seek court intervention. The Supreme Court has recently acknowledged that the reasons underlying the actions of school officials may determine their constitutionality. In *Mount Healthy City Board of Education v. Doyle*, 429 U.S. 274, 97 S.Ct. 568, 50 L.Ed.2d 471 (1977), an untenured teacher claimed that his contract was not renewed in violation of his First Amendment rights. The Court remanded for further review, commenting:

> Doyle's claims under the First and Fourteenth Amendments are not defeated by the fact that he did not have tenure. Even though he could have been discharged for no reason whatever, and had no constitutional right to a hearing prior to the decision not to rehire him . . . he may nonetheless es-

tablish a claim to reinstatement if the decision not to rehire him was made by reason of his exercise of constitutionally protected First Amendment freedoms.
429 U.S. at 283-4, 97 S.Ct. at 574.

The Committee was under no obligation to purchase *Male & Female* for the High School Library, but it did. It is a familiar constitutional principle that a state, though having acted when not compelled, may consequentially create a constitutionally protected interest.[15]

In *Minarcini*, the court commented,

> Neither the State of Ohio nor the Strongsville School Board was under any federal constitutional compulsion to provide a library for the Strongsville High School to choose any particular books. Once having created such a privilege for the benefit of its students, however, neither body could place conditions on the use of the library which were related solely to the social or political tastes of school board members.
> 541 F.2d at 582 (footnote omitted).[16]

In *Tinker v. Des Moines School District*, 393 U.S. 503, 89 S.Ct. 733, 21 L.Ed.2d 731 (1969), three junior high school students were suspended for wearing black arm bands to school to protest the Vietnam War. The Court found the action unconstitutional, and commented:

> In order for the State in the person of school officials to justify prohibition of a particular expression of opinion, it must be able to show that its action was caused by something more than a mere desire to avoid the discomfort and unpleasantness that always accompany an unpopular viewpoint. Certainly where there is no finding and no showing that engaging in the forbidden conduct would 'materially and substantially interfere with the requirements of appropriate discipline in the operation of the school,' the prohibition cannot be sustained.
> *Burnside v. Byars, supra*, at 749.
> 393 U.S. at 509, 89 S.Ct. at 738.

Tinker points the way to the applicable standard to be applied here. When First Amendment values are implicated, the local officials removing the book must demonstrate some substantial and legitimate government interest. *Tinker* does not require the Committee to demonstrate that the book's presence in the library was a threat to school discipline, but it does stand for the proposition that an interest comparable to school discipline must be at stake. *See also Lamont v. Postmaster General*, 381 U.S. 301, 85 S.Ct. 1493, 14 L.Ed.2d 398 (1965).
No substantial governmental interest was served by cutting off students' access to *Male & Female* in the library. The defendants acted because they felt *City's* language and theme might have a damaging impact on the High School students. But the great weight of expert tes-

timony presented at trial left a clear picture that *City* is a work of at least some value that would have no harmful effect on the students. Defendants' case was premised on the assumption that language offensive to the Committee and some parents had no place in the Chelsea educational system. In *Keefe v. Geanakos*, 418 F.2d 359, 361-62, Judge Aldrich met a comparable contention handily.

> With the greatest of respect to such parents, their sensibilities are not the full measure of what is proper education.

In *Keefe*, the First Circuit granted a temporary injunction to a teacher threatened with discipline for assigning an article containing vulgarities to an English class of high school seniors, and discussing one of the vulgar words with them. Finding that the teacher had a probability of success on the merits, the court commented:

> Hence the question in this case is whether a teacher may, for demonstrated educational purposes, quote a 'dirty' word currently used in order to give special offense, or whether the shock is too great for high school seniors to stand. If the answer were that the students must be protected from such exposure, we would fear for their future.
> 418 F.2d at 361.[17]

City is not a polite poem. Its language is tough, but not obscene. Whether or not scholarly, the poem is challenging and thought-provoking. It employs vivid street language, legitimately offensive to some, but certainly not to everyone. The author is writing about her perception of city life in rough but relevant language that gives credibility to the development of a sensitive theme. *City's* words may shock, but they communicate. As the Supreme Court has noted,

> [W]ords are often chosen as much for their emotive as their cognitive force. We cannot sanction the view that the Constitution, while solicitous of the cognitive content of individual speech, has little or no regard for that emotive function which, practically speaking, may often be the more important element of the overall message sought to be communicated.
> *Cohen v. California*, 403 U.S. 15, 26, 91 S.Ct. 1780, 1788, 29 L.Ed.2d 284 (1971).

The Committee claims an absolute right to remove *City* from the shelves of the school library. It has no such right, and compelling policy considerations argue against any public authority having such an unreviewable power of censorship. There is more at issue here than the poem City. If this work may be removed by a committee hostile to its language and theme, then the precedent is set for removal of any other work. The prospect of successive school committees "sanitizing" the school li-

brary of views divergent from their own is a-
larming, whether they do it book by book or one
page at a time.[18]

What is at stake here is the right to read
and be exposed to controversial thoughts and
language--a valuable right subject to First
Amendment protection.   As the Court commented
in *Red Lion Broadcasting Co. v. FCC*, 395 U.S.
367, 386-390, 89 S.Ct. 1794, 1806, 23 L.Ed.2d
371 (1969):

> It is the purpose of the First Amendment to
> preserve an uninhibited marketplace of ideas
> in which truth will ultimately prevail . . . .
> It is the right of the public to receive
> suitable access to social, political, es-
> thetic, moral and other ideas and experi-
> ences which is crucial here.

The Court has underscored the importance of
that principle to our nation's schools:

> In our system, students may not be regarded
> as closed-circuit recipients of only that
> which the State chooses to communicate.
> They may not be confined to the expression
> of those sentiments that are officially
> approved.
> *Tinker v. Des Moines School District*,
> *supra*,
> 393 U.S. at 511, 89 S.Ct. at 739.[19]

Conclusion

The library is "a mighty resource in the
marketplace of ideas." *Minarcini v. Strongsville City School District*, *supra* at 582.
There a student can literally explore the unknown, and discover areas of interest and
thought not covered by the prescribed curriculum. The student who discovers the magic of
the library is on the way to a life-long experience of self-education and enrichment.
That student learns that a library is a place
to test or expand upon ideas presented to him,
in or out of the classroom.

The most effective antidote to the poison of
mindless orthodoxy is ready access to a broad
sweep of ideas and philosophies. There is no
danger in such exposure. The danger is in mind
control. The Committee's ban of the anthology
Male & Female is enjoined.[20]

An order will issue.

NOTES

1. The text of the poem is as follows:
    THE CITY TO A YOUNG GIRL
    The City is
    One million horney lip-smacking men
    Screaming for my body.
    The streets are long conveyor belts
    Loaded with these suckling pigs.
    All begging for
    a lay

a little pussy
a bit of tit
a leg to rub against
a handful of ass
the connoisseurs of cunt
Every day, every night
Pressing in on me closer and closer.
I swat them off like flies
but they keep coming back.
I'm a good piece of meat.
    --Jody Caravaglia, 15, F.
    Brooklyn, New York

Although the poem is replete with street
language, the defendants do not now contend
that it is obscene within the meaning of
Miller v. California, 413 U.S. 15, 93
S.Ct. 2607, 37 L.Ed.2d 419 (1973).

2. Plaintiffs include Dorothea Filipowich,
    Lisa Jarvis and Sharon Ultsch, students at
    the High School; Walter and Barbara Ultsch,
    parents of a student plaintiff; Sonja
    Coleman, Librarian at the Chelsea High
    School; Danna Crowley, Chairwoman of the
    High School's English Department; Johanna
    Bartlett, an English teacher at the High
    School; the Right to Read Defense Committee
    of Chelsea, formed at the time of the
    School Committee action; and the
    Massachusetts Library Association.

    The Massachusetts Library Association,
    and Walter and Barbara Ultsch, are dis-
    missed from this action for lack of stand-
    ing. All other plaintiffs have alleged a
    sufficient stake in the outcome of the lit-
    igation to warrant standing in this action.

3. The Committee is a seven member body that
    has statutory authority for administering
    the Chelsea public school system, Mass.Gen.
    Laws ch. 71, § 37 and Mass.Gen.Laws ch. 71,
    § 48. At all times relevant to this liti-
    gation, defendant Andrew P. Quigley was the
    Committee's chairman, as well as owner and
    publisher of *The Chelsea Record*, that
    community's daily newspaper. Defendants
    Lucy Brown, Paul Kornechuk, Frances
    Montesano, Nancy Moore, Abraham Morochnick,
    and Anthony Tiro were members of the Com-
    mittee. Defendant Vincent McGee was the
    Chelsea Superintendent of Schools.

4. 42 U.S.C. § 1983 states, in relevant part:
    Every person who, under color of any
    statute . . . of any State . . . subjects .
    . . any citizen of the United States . . .
    to the deprivation of any rights, privi-
    leges, or immunities secured by the Consti-
    tution and laws, shall be liable to the
    party injured in an action at law, suit in
    equity, or other proper proceeding for re-
    dress.

5. Mass.Gen.Laws   ch.   71,   §   37   and
    Mass.Gen.Laws ch. 71 § 48.

6. The text of this court's August 19, 1977
    temporary order is as follows:
    "After hearing on the plaintiffs' mo-
    tion for a temporary restraining order, the
    court ORDERS that the defendants, their
    officers, agents, servants, employees, at-
    torneys, and all those in active concert
    with them shall be enjoined consistent with

their stipulation recited at hearing.

1. from transferring or removing plaintiff Coleman from her position as librarian or from taking any other action against her in reprisal for having purchased *Male & Female Under 18* or for having joined in this action as a plaintiff; and

2. from transferring or removing plaintiff Crowley from her position as chairperson of the English Department and plaintiff Bartlett from her position as English teacher, or from taking any other action against them or against any of the student plaintiffs in reprisal for having protested defendants' actions in censoring *Male & Female Under 18* or for having joined in this action as plaintiffs.

The court understands that this reflects the position of the defendant School Committee.

The court further ORDERS that the defendants shall immediately return the book *Male & Female Under 18* without any deletions to the custody of the librarian; and that, pending final determination of this suit, the librarian shall not permit access to the book *Male & Female Under 18* to any student unless the student presents the librarian with written permission from his or her parent or guardian.

The court further ORDERS that a pre-trial conference will be held in this case on September 14, 1977 at 2:15 p.m."

7. *Male & Female* is classified as an anthology of literature under the Library of Congress Classification System, and under the Dewey Decimal system.

8. Quigley acknowledged authorship of *The Chelsea Record* editorials discussed in this opinion, as well as the accuracy of statements attributed to him in that paper.

9. In a *Chelsea Record* editorial the next day, July 29th, Quigley characterized Morochnick's abstention as a "vote without conscience."

10. This court finds the adoption of these resolutions to have been a tactical subterfuge by the Committee and counsel. See further discussion on this point in Section III *infra*.

11. Mass.Gen.Laws ch. 71 § 37 and Mass.Gen.Laws ch. 71, § 48.

12. The First Circuit has recognized the responsibility of courts to intervene in school policy in order to vindicate constitutional liberties. In connection with the school desegregation process, it reminded the Boston School Committee that "its duties 'must be exercised consistently with federal constitutional requirements.'" *Morgan v. McDonough*, 548 F.2d 28, 32 (1st Cir. 1977). In a case involving the discipline of a teacher for use of a vulgarity in class, the First Circuit noted that it would have to superimpose its judgment on school authorities if, in a constitutional area, their decision was "plainly wrong."

Mailloux v. Kiley, 436 F.2d 565, 566 (1st Cir. 1971).

13. The Sixth Circuit in *Minarcini* reached a similar conclusion in its analysis of *Presidents Council*, rejecting any contention that the Second Circuit had upheld an absolute right on the part of a school board to remove books from a library. 541 F.2d at 581.

14. In disregarding that resolution as pretextual, this court is following the analytical principles of *Tardif v. Quinn*, 545 F.2d 761 (1st Cir. 1976).

There, plaintiff alleged she had been fired from her teaching position for wearing short skirts. Defendants responded that she was discharged for failing to meet outside course requirements, but the Court of Appeals commented:

> [I]n the light of [the contract rationale's] late appearance, coupled with defendants' total failure to support other reasons given, causes us to believe, following familiar principles in Labor Board cases, that it should be disregarded as 'pretextual'.

545 F.2d at 762 (footnote omitted). *Accord, Mabey v. Reagan*, 537 F.2d 1036 (9th Cir. 1976).

15. *See, e. g., Southeastern Promotions, Ltd. v. Conrad*, 420 U.S. 546, 95 S.Ct. 1239, 43 L.Ed.2d 448 (1975); *Griffin v. Illinois*, 351 U.S. 12, 76 S.Ct 585, 100 L.Ed. 891 (1956); *Escalera v. New York City Housing Authority*, 425 F.2d 853 (2d Cir.), *cert. denied*, 400 U.S. 853, 91 S.Ct 54, 27 L.Ed.2d 91 (1970); *Brooks v. Auburn University*, 412 F.2d 1171 (5th Cir. 1969).

The First Circuit's decision in *Advocates for the Arts v. Thomson*, 532 F.2d 792 (1st Cir.), *cert. denied*, 429 U.S. 894, 97 S.Ct. 254, 50 L.Ed.2d 177 (1976), is not to the contrary. There, the court rejected plaintiffs' claim that the state's decision to stop funding their literary magazine because of offensive language contained in one of the published poems violated plaintiffs' First Amendment rights. The court noted that the state committee's selection of grantees worthy of support did not constitute suppression of speech:

> [P]ublic funding of the arts seeks 'not to abridge, restrict, or censor speech, but rather to use public money to facilitate and enlarge' artistic expression. . . . A disappointed grant applicant cannot complain that his work has been suppressed, but only that another's has been promoted in its stead.

532 F.2d at 795 (*citing Buckley v. Valeo*, 424 U.S. 1, 96 S.Ct. 612, 46 L.Ed.2d 659 (1976).

Nor does *Close v. Lederle*, 424 F.2d 988 (1st Cir.), *cert. denied*, 400 U.S. 903, 91 S.Ct. 141, 27 L.Ed.2d 140 (1970), further defendants' contentions. There, the First Circuit upheld the removal of a professor's sexually explicit art works from the corridor of a state university building prior to the expiration of the time allotted the exhibit. Significant to the court's holding, however, was the finding that the students were a "captive audience." 424 F.2d 988 at 990.

16. A thoughtful comment on *Minarcini* observes:

> Selection of books to be shelved . . . requires choosing from an infinite variety of books since no public high school facility has the cataloguing staff, the space, or the budget to carry more than a fraction of published works that might be mentioned in class. Employing content as one of many criteria in textbook selection is different from adopting content as the sole basis for excising a particular book. The countervailing government interests--scarce funds, limited personnel, and restricted space--that outweigh the constitutional interests of students in a book selection situation disappear when school officials remove a particular book merely because its content is offensive to their personal tastes.

Note, *Student's Right to Receive Information Precludes Board's Removal of Allegedly Offensive Books from High School Library*, 30 Vand. L. Rev. 85, 98 (1977).

17. In *Papish v. Missouri Curators*, 410 U.S. 667, 93 S.Ct. 1197, 35 L.Ed.2d 618 (1973), a college student was expelled for distributing a newspaper with vulgar words on a university campus. The Court held that it is "clear that the mere dissemination of ideas--no matter how offensive to good taste--on a state university campus may not be shut off in the name alone of 'conventions of decency.'" 410 U.S. at 670, 93 S.Ct. at 1199. Some of the Chelsea students are younger than those students affected in *Keefe* and *Papish*, but defendants produced no credible evidence that the age difference was consequential.

A commentator has noted:
> It is true that *Lamont* and the cases on controversial campus speakers involved adults or college students who are generally more mature than high school students. Moreover, a high school classroom would seem to be a more controlled and restricted marketplace of ideas than the mail or college campuses, if only because of compulsory attendance and, frequently, a uniformly required curriculum. Nevertheless, . . . it is clear that students cannot be insulated from controversial subjects in school. If this applies to student expression through worn symbols [and] underground newspapers . . . then it would seem both inconsistent and educationally unworkable to prohibit student access to controversial subjects through supervised classroom presentations

Nahmod, *Controversy in the Classroom: The High School Teacher and Freedom of Expression*, 39 Geo.Wash.L.Rev. 1032, 1055 (1971).

18. Defendants' suggestion that *Male & Female* may be returned to the library shelf upon excision of *City* serves to underscore rather than solve the problem here. An anthology is a collection of selected literary works. It would be no less offensive to First Amendment principles for a School Committee to bowdlerize an anthology by removing one poem, than it would be for it to excise objectionable passages in a novel.

19. Plaintiffs contend that defendants' ban deprived them of their access to *Male & Female* in the High School Library. Defendants counter that:

> The plaintiffs did not prove that a single living person has ever exhibited an interest in reading this material and has been prevented from doing so by the actions of the Chelsea School Committee.
>
> If one wanted to own a personal copy of the book, it is available for $1.50 from the publisher. There was no evidence that students at the Chelsea High School could or would be inhibited by this price from purchasing any book they had any serious desire to read.

Defendants' Post-Trial Memorandum at 2.

Defendants' contention is without merit. At least since 1939 it has been settled that "[o]ne is not to have the exercise of his liberty of expression in appropriate places abridged on the plea that it may be exercised in some other place." *Schneider v. State*, 308 U.S. 147, 163, 60 S.Ct. 146, 151, 84 L.Ed. 155 (1939). *See also Southeastern Promotions, Ltd. v. Conrad*, 420 U.S. 546, 556, 95 S.Ct. 1239, 43 L.Ed.2d 448 (1975); *Spence v. Washington*, 418 U.S. 405, 411, n. 4, 94 S.Ct. 2727, 41 L.Ed.2d 842 (1974); *Minarcini v. Strongsville City School Dist.*, 541 F.2d 577 (6th Cir. 1976).

20. In a recent opinion, *F.C.C. v. Pacifica Foundation*, No. 77-528 (July 3, 1978), the Supreme Court approved a decision by the F.C.C. proscribing the broadcast of several words, some of which coincidentally are contained in *City*. That decision, however, is inapposite to the issues here. In *Pacifica*, the Court sustained the F.C.C. action primarily on the ground that broadcasts have the unique potential for invading the privacy of the home. Here we are dealing with a library setting where there is no comparable danger of invasion. The fundamental issue here is whether there should be the opportunity for selection.

MS magazine is removed from a New Hampshire high school library by order of the Nashua School Board. A United States District Court decides for the student, teacher, and adult residents who had brought action against the school board, the court concluding: "The court finds and rules that the defendants herein have failed to demonstrate a substantial and legitimate government interest sufficient to warrant the removal of MS magazine from the Nashua High School library. Their action contravenes the plaintiffs' First Amendment rights, and as such it is plainly wrong."

Salvail v. *Nashua Board of Education,*
469 F.Supp. 1269 (1979)

ORDER AND OPINION

DEVINE, District Judge.

The issue before the Court concerns the extent of the authority of the Nashua School Board to remove certain periodicals from the senior high school library. This issue is apparently one of current national interest.[1]

Plaintiff Rhonda Salvail is a sixteen-year old eleventh grade student at Nashua High School; plaintiff William Hodge teaches English at said high school; plaintiffs Suzanne Coletta and Albert Burrelle are adult residents and taxpayers in Nashua; and plaintiff David E. Cote is a 1978 graduate of Nashua High School who was present when the incidents which give rise to this litigation occurred. Defendants are the Nashua Board of Education ("Board"); Board members Dr. Paul Ouellette, Alan Thomaier, Frank Ulcickas, Thomas Stylianos, Carolyn Mason, T. Harrison Whalen, Judith Berman, Anthony Mirandos, Marlo Sheer, together with Berard Masse, School Superintendent.

The plaintiffs claim deprivation of due process and rights under the First Amendment, and bring this action under 42 U.S.C. § 1983, invoking jurisdiction pursuant to 28 U.S.C. §§ 1343 and 2201. The matter came before the Court, which held a hearing on the merits pursuant to the provisions of Rule 65(a)(2), Federal Rules of Civil Procedure. The Court has reviewed the testimony at such hearing, together with the exhibits, pleadings, legal memos, and other documents on file.

THE FACTS

In March of 1977, the New Hampshire State Department of Education forwarded to each of the 186 school districts certain guidelines for the selection of instructional materials and for review of any challenges to same (Defendants' Exhibit B). Reginald Comeau, consultant of the Libraries and Learning Resources Program of the State Department of Education, testified that although these guidelines were advisory in nature, they were designed to be applicable to challenges to the material made by the members of any school board.

The Nashua Board of Education is composed of nine members elected at large by the voters of that city. *Sullivan v. Flynn*, 116 N.H. 547, 551, 365 A.2d 1052, 1055 (1976). The duties of school boards in New Hampshire include the purchase of textbooks and other supplies required for use in the public schools. RSA 189:16.[2]

Upon receipt of the suggested guidelines from the State Department of Education, the Nashua Board established a committee which in turn drafted certain interim "Guidelines For Selecting Instructional Materials" (Plaintiffs' Exhibit 4), which interim guidelines were in effect at the time of the incidents which gave rise to this litigation. These guidelines provided a method for selection of materials whereby the Board conceded its legal responsibility for all matters relating to the operation of the Nashua schools, but delegated the selection of instructional materials to the "professionally trained personnel employed by the school district." (Plaintiffs' Exhibit 4, p. 2.) It was required by the guidelines that the materials be consistent with the general educational goals of the school district, meet high standards of quality in factual content and presentation, be appropriate for the subject area and for the age, maturation, ability level, and social development of the students; have aesthetic, literary, or social value, be designed to help the students gain an awareness and understanding of the contributions made by both sexes, and by religious, ethnic and cultural groups to American heritage; and that a selection of materials on controversial issues be directed toward maintaining a balanced collection representing various views. (Plaintiffs' Exhibit 4, pp. 1, 2.)

In the event a member of the public raised a question or complaint, the guidelines provided for the appointment of an Instructional Materials Reconsideration Committee composed of professional library-media personnel, the principal or his representative, the appropriate assistant superintendent, the person or persons involved in the original selection of the material, and the person or persons using the materials in the individual school. (Plaintiffs' Exhibit 4, p. 4.) This committee was required to reexamine the material and furnish a report to the superintendent who in turn was to forward copies of same to the complainant. (Plaintiffs' Exhibit 4, p. 4.) The complaining party was granted a right to appeal the decision of the Reconsideration Committee to the superintendent and, if not satisfied with his decision, to refer the decision to the Board. (Plaintiffs' Exhibit 4, p. 4.)

Board member Thomaier held strong religious and patriotic views as to the types of reading material that should be available to pupils in a senior high school. In late 1977 and early 1978, he expressed concern about MS magazine, which was carried in the school library and was available upon request to students in the senior high school. At a meeting of the Board on

March 13, 1978, he presented a formal resolution to withdraw the magazine from the school library (Plaintiffs' Exhibit 2, Resolution of Alan C. Thomaier) appending thereto photocopies of classified advertisement sections from one of the issues of the magazine (Plaintiffs' Exhibit 5). At the meeting of the Board on March 27, 1978, Thomaier moved, seconded by member Stylianos, to have this resolution voted upon. Board members Sheer, Berman, and Chairman Ouellette suggested that the interim guidelines should be followed, and the procedure for review was explained by Superintendent Masse. Stylianos took the position that the Board members were not bound by these interim guidelines and that "in some cases they should act instantaneously" (Plaintiffs' Exhibit 2). By a five to three vote, the motion carried, and subsequently the subscription to MS magazine was canceled and all issues were removed from the school library (Plaintiffs' Exhibit 10).

Thomaier's objection to the periodical focused largely on the fact that it contained advertisements for "vibrators", contraceptives, materials dealing with lesbianism and witchcraft, and gay material. He also objected to advertisements for what he described as a pro-communist newspaper ("The Guardian") and advertisements suggesting trips to Cuba. In addition he felt that the magazines encouraged students and teachers to send away for records made by known communist folk singers. Board member Stylianos, a former school teacher and principal, took the position that the proper test for material to be available for reading by high school students was whether it could be read aloud to his daughter in a classroom.

Plaintiff Salvail testified that she found MS of value in her assigned high school courses, as it discussed important social issues from a feminist viewpoint. She further testified that sexual matters were openly discussed at the Nashua senior high school and that she worked afternoons in a store where vibrators were sold. Ann Hostage, an English teacher, testified that she had assigned research in the magazine to several of her pupils, and plaintiff Hodge, another English teacher, said that he often assigned writings to his students on topics to be chosen by them and that his students had found the magazine valuable as a research tool.

Joseph Dionne, holder of a Master's degree in Library Science, himself a former assistant librarian at Nashua Public Library, testified that he had reviewed the issues of MS for the months of October 1977 through April 1978. He testified flatly that the magazine was neither obscene, patently offensive, nor in contravention of community standards, and that he felt that it was of value as a research tool. He also produced evidence that the magazine is indexed in the traditional type of reference volumes available to librarians for selection of books and periodicals. (Plaintiffs' Exhibits 7, 8.)

Joan McNamara, coordinator of instructional materials for the Concord senior high school, also possessed of a Master's degree in Library Science, testified that her high school has used MS magazine since 1975, that it is not obscene, that it is not patently offensive, that it does not contravene community standards, and that it has a substantial degree of use by students at Concord High School. Board members Ouellette, Sheer, and Berman who had cast dissenting votes at the March 27, 1978, meeting, testified that they had done so because they felt that the Board should have followed the interim guidelines.

At a meeting of the Board on April 10, 1978, which was largely attended by the public, a number of letters (including one from member Carolyn Mason who had been unable to attend the meeting on March 27) from teachers and others were introduced relative to the failure to follow the review procedure with respect to MS magazine. In addition, a number of people spoke both pro and con relative to the action of the Board.

Subsequent to the commencement of the litigation herein, the Board met on March 27, 1979, having reviewed and scrutinized the issues of MS which had been removed from the library. At the meeting they voted to return the December 1977 and January 1978 issues of the magazine with classified ads excised. The Board also approved at such meeting final revised guidelines for the selection of instructional material which, as worded, were clearly applicable to (any Nashua resident) and would therefore include any member of the Board (Defendants' Exhibit C).

THE LAW

It is, of course, clear that the Board is required neither to provide a library for the Nashua senior high school nor to choose any particular books therefor, but, once having created such a privilege for the benefits of its students, it could not place conditions on the use of the library related solely to the social or political tastes of Board members. *Minarcini v. Strongsville City School District*, 541 F.2d 577, 582 (6th Cir. 1976). The duties of school boards must be exercised "consistently with federal constitutional requirements". *Morgan v. McDonough*, 548 F.2d 28, 32 (1st Cir. 1977). It is a familiar constitutional principle that a state, having so acted when not compelled, may consequentially create a constitutionally protected interest. *Right to Read Defense Committee v. School Committee*, 454 F.Supp. 703, 712 (D.Mass.1978).

The Court has reviewed the October 1977, November 1977, December 1977, January 1978, February 1978, March 1978, April 1978, and September 1978 issues of MS magazine (Defendants' Exhibit A; Plaintiffs' Exhibits 9A, 9B, 9C, 9D, 9E, 9F, 9G), and finds that although there are certain articles and works of fiction therein which would be offensive to some, that the periodicals do contain material which would be of interest to someone researching the current feminist viewpoint on matters of social interest, and that the materials themselves are not obscene within any recognized legal definition.

The evidence presented to the Court makes it clear that these magazines "taken as a whole" *do not lack* "serious literary, artistic, political, or scientific value". *Miller v. California*, 413 U.S. 15, 24, 93 S.Ct. 2607, 2614, 37 L.Ed.2d 419 (1973). The First Amendment generally prohibits governments from "cleans[ing] public debate to the point where it is grammatically palatable to the most squeamish among us." *Cohen v. California*, 403 U.S. 15, 25, 91 S.Ct. 1780, 1788, 29 L.Ed.2d 284 (1971). "[I]t is . . . often true that one man's vulgarity is another's lyric." *Id.*[3] Defendants argue that the Board correctly decided that the "interim guidelines" were not applicable to it, stressing that New Hampshire law makes clear that interpretation by an administrative body of its own rules will be honored by a reviewing court unless the interpretation is patently unreasonable. The cases cited in support of this contention (*Bellows Falls, etc., Co. v. State*, 94 N.H. 187, 49 A.2d 511 [1946]; *New Hampshire Retail Grocers Association v. State Tax Commission*, 113 N.H. 511, 309 A.2d 890 [1973]; *Farrelly v. Timberlane Regional School District*, 114 N.H. 560, 324 A.2d 723 [1974]) so hold, but they are inapplicable in the context of the instant case. In cases of constitutional interpretation, the customary deference to an agency's interpretation of its own regulations is inappropriate. *Pacifica Foundation v. FCC*, 181 U.S.App.D.C. 132, 145, n. 12, 556 F 2d 9, 22, n. 12 (1977--concurring opinion of Bazelon, C.J.); *National Broadcasting Co., Inc. v. FCC*, 170 U.S.App. D.C. 173, 516 F.2d 1101 (1974). In the instant case it is clear that Board members Ouellette, Sheer, and Berman, together with Superintendent Masse and Reginald Comeau, were all of the opinion that the "interim guidelines" were applicable to the Nashua School Board. The Court finds and rules that, having adopted such "interim guidelines", the Board was required to follow them in its attempts at removal of MS magazine from the shelves of the high school library. *McDonald v. NCAA*, 370 F.Supp. 625 (C.D.Cal.1974); *Behagen v. Intercollegiate Conference of Faculty Representatives*, 346 F.Supp. 602 (D.Minn.1972).

Defendants' reliance on *Presidents Council, District 25 v. Community School Board No. 25*, 457 F.2d 289 (2d Cir.), *cert. denied*, 409 U.S. 998, 93 S.Ct. 308, 34 L.Ed.2d 260 (1972), is misplaced. In the course of its opinion, that court said:

> [t]o suggest that the shelving or unshelving of books presents a constitutional issue, *particularly where there is no showing of a curtailment of freedom of speech or thought,* is a proposition we cannot accept.

Id., at 293 (emphasis supplied) (footnote omitted). A fair reading of the language above emphasized makes clear that *Presidents Council* does not stand for an absolute right on the part of a school board to remove from the

library any books it regarded unfavorably without concern for the First Amendment. *Minarcini, supra*, at 581.

Furthermore, *Presidents Council* was decided prior to *Virginia State Board of Pharmacy v. Virginia Citizens Consumer Council, Inc.*, 425 U.S. 748, 96 S.Ct. 1817, 48 L.Ed.2d 346 (1976), where in striking down a statute which declared unprofessional conduct for a licensed pharmacist to advertise the price of prescription drugs, the court stated in pertinent part:

> Freedom of speech presupposes a willing speaker. But where a speaker exists, as is the case here, the protection afforded is to the communication, to its source and to its recipients both. This is clear from the decided cases.

Id., at 756, 96 S.Ct. at 1823.

And in a recent note discussing the implications of the effect of *Virginia Pharmacy* on *Presidents Council*, it has been stated:

> Clearly the library of a public high school is a 'forum for silent speech' with communication evidenced by the presence of a source (books) and a recipient (student-reader). Since such communications are protected by the first amendment, any justification offered for denying student access to particular books must meet constitutional standards. Thus, in justifying restrictions on students' right to receive information, school authorities must bear the burden of showing a substantial government interest to be served by the restriction. Admittedly, the burden is less stringent than when such restrictions arise in a truly public form, since students' first amendment rights must be limited to some extent due to the special administrative needs of the school environment. Nevertheless, the decision to remove a book from library use should be based upon 'educational' considerations, obsolescence, or architectural necessity. Such objective criteria would minimize the danger that book removal will be based on constitutionally impermissible grounds, such as the political and social tastes of board members.

Note, *First Amendment Limitations on the Power of School Boards to Select and Remove High School Text and Library Books*, 52 St. John's L.R., 457, at 471 (1978).

Ironically, the dislike of certain of the Board members for articles and advertisements contained in MS magazine apparently does not extend to similar materials in other publications which are contained in the Nashua High School library.[4] The Court finds that despite protestations contained in the testimony of these parties, it is the "political" content of MS magazine more than its sexual overtones that led to its arbitrary displacement. Such a basis for removal of the publication is constitutionally impermissible.

The reliance of defendants on the recent decision of *FCC v. Pacifica Foundation*, 438 U.S. 726, 98 S.Ct. 3026, 57 L.Ed.2d 1073 (1978) is likewise misplaced. That case is inapposite to the issues here presented.

In *Pacifica*, the Court sustained the F.C.C. action primarily on the ground that broadcasts have the unique potential for invading the privacy of the home. Here we are dealing with a library setting, where there is no comparable danger of invasion. The fundamental issue here is whether there should be the opportunity for selection.

Right to Read Defense Committee v. School Committee, supra, at 715, n. 20.
The court also finds that the actions of the Board taken at their meeting of March 27, 1979, wherein all issues of MS were reviewed and two were returned to the library shelves is pretextual and self-serving. *Right to Read Defense Committee v. School Committee, supra*, at 712 and n. 14. Here as in *Right to Read, supra*, the publication was banned by the Board without reading it, the female Board members were "sheltered" from the alleged improper material, and no claim is advanced or supported that the publication is obsolete or worn out or that adequate shelf space is unavailable. Those cases which deal with "captive audiences" (*Close v. Lederle*, 424 F.2d 988 [1st Cir.], *cert. denied*, 400 U.S. 903, 91 S.Ct. 141, 27 L.Ed.2d 140 [1970]) or with whether a magazine containing an allegedly "filthy" poem should be promoted rather than suppressed (*Advocates for Arts v. Thomson*, 532 F.2d 792 [1st Cir.], *cert. denied*, 429 U.S. 894, 97 S.Ct. 254, 50 L.Ed.2d 177 [1976]) are inapposite.
The vigilant protection of constitutional freedoms is nowhere more vital than in the community of American schools. *Shelton v. Tucker*, 364 U.S. 479, 487, 81 S.Ct. 247, 5 L.Ed.2d 231 (1960). When First Amendment values are implicated, the local officials removing a publication must demonstrate some substantial and legitimate government interests. *Right to Read Defense Committee, supra*, at 713. We deal here with publications of obvious research value to *senior high school students*, *i.e.*, sophomores, juniors, and seniors ranging in age from 15 to 19. In *Keefe v. Geanakos*, 418 F.2d 359 (1st Cir. 1969), injunctive relief was granted a teacher threatened with discharge to assigning an article containing vulgarities to an English class of high school seniors, and discussing one of the vulgar words with them. In the course of its opinion, the court there said:

Hence the question in this case is whether a teacher may, for demonstrated educational purposes, quote a 'dirty' word currently used in order to give special offense, or whether the shock is too great for high school seniors to stand. If the answer were that the students must be protected from such exposure, we would fear for their future. We do not question the good faith of the defendants in believing that some pa-

rents have been offended. With the greatest of respect to such parents, their sensibilities are not the full measure of what is proper education.

Id. at 361, 362.

The defendants' contention as to the limited impact of the removal of MS magazine to the high school population, members of which are free to purchase or to read the publication in a public library, is without merit.[5] "Restraint on expression may not generally be justified by the fact that there may be other times, places, or circumstances available for such expression." *Minarcini, supra*, at 582 (and cases cited therein).
A library is "a mighty resource in the free marketplace of ideas . . . specially dedicated to broad dissemination of ideas . . . a forum for silent speech." *Minarcini, supra*, at 582, 583.

There a student can literally explore the unknown and discover areas of interest and thought not covered by the prescribed curriculum. The student who discovers the magic of the library is on the way to a lifelong experience of self-education and enrichment. That student learns that a library is a place to test or expand upon ideas presented to him, in or out of the classroom.
The most effective antidote to the poison of mindless orthodoxy is ready access to a broad sweep of ideas and philosophies. There is no danger in such exposure. The danger is in mind control.

Right to Read, supra, at 715.

The Court finds and rules that the defendants herein have failed to demonstrate a substantial and legitimate government interest sufficient to warrant the removal of MS magazine from the Nashua High School library. Their action contravenes the plaintiffs' First Amendment rights, and as such it is *plainly wrong*. *Mailloux v. Kiley*, 436 F.2d 565, 566 (1st Cir. 1971). The plaintiffs are entitled to relief at the hands of this Court.

CONCLUSION

Upon the pleadings, the evidence in its entirety including the exhibits, and the briefs of counsel, the Court concludes:
1. This action is properly maintained as a class action pursuant to Rule 23, Federal Rules of Civil Procedure. There are three subclasses, the first of which includes all students at Nashua High School (of which subclass plaintiff Salvail is a representative party); the second of which includes all faculty members at the Nashua High School (of which plaintiff Hodge is a representative party); and the third of which includes all students at Nashua High School who were in such posi-

tion at the time of the events which give rise to this litigation (of which subclass plaintiff Cote is a representative party).[6]

2. The resolutions of the Nashua Board of Education of March 27, 1978, and March 27, 1979, are hereby declared null and void as in violation of the First Amendment to the United States Constitution.

3. The Nashua Board of Education and the members thereof are hereby enjoined from the continued withdrawal of MS magazine from the shelves of the Nashua High School library and are ordered to replace the issues they have caused to be removed and to resubscribe to MS magazine, such replacement and resubscription to be made, if necessary, by purchase out of the first sums available for library purposes.

4. The Nashua Board of Education and the members thereof are herewith enjoined and ordered to follow the current guidelines relative to any complaints about any publications in the Nashua High School library, whether said complaints are generated by a member of the Board or by any other Nashua resident.

The foregoing shall constitute the Court's findings of fact and conclusions of law, consistent with Rule 52(a), Federal Rules of Civil Procedure.

SO ORDERED.

NOTES

1. *See*: "Censorship of Textbooks Is Found On Rise in Schools Around Nation", p. B15, New York Times, March 27, 1979.

2. RSA 189:16 provides that school boards "shall purchase, at the expense of the city or town in which the district is situated, textbooks and other supplies required for use in the public schools; and shall loan same to the pupils of such schools free of charge, subject to such regulations for their care and custody as the board may prescribe; and shall sell such books at cost to pupils of the school wishing to purchase them for their own use."

3. Constitutional protection has accordingly been afforded to such items as displays of nudity on drive-in movie screens (*Erznoznik v. City of Jacksonville*, 422 U.S. 205, 95 S.Ct. 2268, 45 L.Ed.2d 125 [1975]); utterance of a vulgar epithet (*Lewis v. City of New Orleans*, 415 U.S. 130, 94 S.Ct. 970, 39 L.Ed.2d 214 [1974]); utterance of a vulgar remark (*Hess v. Indiana*, 414 U.S. 105, 94 S.Ct. 326, 38 L.Ed.2d 303 [1973]); indecent remarks in a campus newspaper (*Papish v. University of Missouri Curators*, 410 U.S. 667, 93 S.Ct. 1197, 35 L.Ed.2d 618 [1973]); utterance of racial slurs (*Brandenburg v. Ohio*, 395 U.S. 444, 89 S.Ct. 1827, 23 L.Ed.2d 430 [1969]); and an alluring portrayal of adultery as proper behavior (*Kingsley Pictures Corp. v.*

Regents, 360 U.S. 684, 79 S.Ct. 1362, 3 L.Ed.2d 1512 [1959]).

4. Examples of this are found in Plaintiffs' Exhibit 12A (Redbook, Jan. 1979), which contains an article entitled, *Your Sexuality--Questions About The Diaphragm; Pills And Weight Gain* (p. 43), and advertisements for "early pregnancy tests" (p. 53), contraceptives (p. 143), and bust developers (p. 145). Plaintiffs' Exhibit 12B (Mademoiselle, Jan. 1979) contains an article entitled, *Sex: Is It Finally Time to Shut Up About It?* (p. 88), and advertisements for bust developers (pp. 131, 141) and an "illustrated encyclopedia" of sexual anatomy and function (p. 142). Plaintiffs' Exhibit 12C (Family Health, Jan. 1979) contains advertisements for early pregnancy tests (p. 5), for contraceptives and vibrators (p. 56), and for a book entitled, *Conception: A Matter of Timing* (p. 55).

5. Plaintiff Salvail and students similarly situated who work after school are perforce limited to research in the school library during school hours. In such cases, reduction of the materials available for research effectively forecloses their right to conduct same.

6. The Court finds and rules that plaintiffs Coletta and Burrelle, described as "concerned residents and taxpayers" of Nashua lack standing in this action, and the action is therefore dismissed as to them.

*The Board of Education of the Island Trees Un-
ion Free School District removes from its
school libraries such "objectionable" books as*
Slaughterhouse Five, Go Ask Alice, Black
Boy, The Naked Ape, Down These Mean
Streets, Soul On Ice, *and other books that
contain "obscenities, blasphemies, brutality,
and perversion beyond description." Several
students bring suit challenging the board's removal of the books from the school libraries
and curriculum of the Island Trees Union Free
School District. A United States District
Court finds for the school board and against
the students, stating: "The school's action
here involved no religious question, either
free exercise or establishment; nor was there a
ban on the teaching of any theory or doctrine;
nor has there been a restriction imposed on
classroom discussion, or a penalty inflicted on
any teacher or librarian. Moreover, these restrictions have denied no student the right to
silent or open speech....the board has restricted access only to certain books which the
board believed to be, in essence, vulgar.
While removal of such books from a school library may, indeed in this court's view does,
reflect a misguided educational philosophy, it
does not constitute a sharp and direct infringement of any first amendment right."*

Pico v. *Board of Ed., Island Trees
Union Free School*, 474 F.Supp. 387
(1979)

MEMORANDUM AND ORDER

GEORGE C. PRATT, District Judge:

On January 4, 1977, plaintiffs filed this
action for injunctive and declaratory relief in
New York State Supreme Court alleging violation
of their rights under the federal and state
constitutions and 42 U.S.C. § 1983. Basically,
the suit challenges defendant board of education's removal of certain books from the school
libraries and curriculum of the Island Trees
Union Free School District.

On January 29, 1977, defendants filed their
petition for removal to this court. Plaintiffs' motion to remand was denied by memorandum and order filed August 16, 1977, because
this case, unlike *Presidents Council, District
25* v. *Community School Board #25*, 457 F.2d 289
(CA2) *cert.* denied, 409 U.S. 998, 93 S.Ct.
308, 34 L.Ed.2d 260 (1972), presented substantial questions of federal constitutional law.
Thereafter, plaintiffs moved for certification
of this case as a class action and both sides
moved for summary judgment. These are the
motions now before the court.

FACTS

Both parties agree to the following

facts.[1] In September, 1975, the president,
vice-president and another member of the board
of education (board) of the Island Trees Union
Free School District attended a conference
sponsored by a conservatively oriented parents
group called Parents of New York United
(PONY-U). There, they obtained a collection of
excerpts from books which PONY-U had classified
as "objectionable."

On November 7, 1975, the president and
vice-president of the board searched the card
catalogue of the Island Trees High School and
found cards for nine of the "objectionable"
books.[2] The president of the board then
asked the principal of the junior high school
to check his school's catalogue, which was
found to contain cards for one additional "objectionable" book.[3] Subsequently, a school
official discovered another "objectionable"
book[4] in the curriculum of a 12th grade literature course; the board had approved its inclusion in 1972. On February 24, 1976, at a
"private session" of the board, attended as
well by the superintendent of schools and the
principals of the junior and senior high
schools, the board gave an "unofficial direction" that the objectionable books be removed.

On March 3, 1976, the president of the board
issued a memorandum to the superintendent, re-
iterating "the board's desire that all copies
of the library books in question be removed
from the libraries to the board's office * *
*". These eleven books were immediately re-
moved by the superintendent,[5] pending further
board action, and delivered to the board's office, where board members could personally review the books.

On March 19, 1976, the board issued a press
release, attached to the complaint as Exhibit
A. It read:

PRESS RELEASE - March 19/76
The Board of Education finds it necessary
to call this press conference because of
distortions, misinformation, and the obvious
attempt by the New York Daily News in a car-
toon published this morning, to characterize
two members of the Board as a pair of shady
hoods who surreptitiously sneak into school
buildings under cover of darkness to snatch
library books.

It comes as no surprise to this Board of
Education that it is once again the subject
of attack by Teacher Union leaders, headed
by Walter Compare. With the election of
school board candidates just two months
away, the Teachers' Union is once again attempting to discredit the Board and win the
seats for two union-backed lackeys.

While at the conference, we learned of
books found in schools throughout the country which were anti-American, anti-Christian, anti-Semetic (sic), and just plain
filthy. Upon their return, Ahrens & Martin
in early November went to the Senior High
School to check the card catalog to see if
any of these objectionable books were in our
library. We discovered nine such books. We
neither removed books, nor cards from the

card file.

At the next meeting of the Board, the entire Board discussed how to handle this situation, realizing that to make the titles of the books public might cause a sudden run on the library by the students.

The Board decided that the Principals of the Senior and Junior High Schools would be called in and be directed to gather up the books in question and bring them to the entire Board, for review. This order was carried out earlier this month. The Board is presently reviewing the content of the books.

To date, what we have found is that the books do, in fact, contain material which is offensive to Christians, Jews, Blacks, and Americans in general. In addition, these books contain obscenities, blasphemies, brutality, and perversion beyond description.

This Board of Education wants to make it clear that we in no way are BOOK BANNERS or BOOK BURNERS. While most of us agree that these books have a place on the shelves of the public library, we all agree that these books simply DO NOT belong in school libraries, where they are so easily accessible to children whose minds are still in the formulative stage, and where their presence actually entices children to read and savor them. As U.S. Commissioner of Education, T.H. Bell, has said, "Parents have a right to expect that the schools, in their teaching approaches and their selection of instructional materials, will support the values and standards that their children are taught at home. And if the schools cannot support those values, they must at least avoid deliberate destruction of them."

We who are elected by the community, are the eyes and ears of the parents. It is our duty, our moral obligation, to protect the children in our schools from this moral danger as surely as from physical and medical dangers.

We have some books which have been reviewed, marked, and underlined. However, if they are read in front of a television camera, the FCC would never permit it to be aired. This stuff is too strong for adult viewers, but some of our educators feel it is appropriate for child consumption.

We are sure that when most of our teachers are given the opportunity to review the material, they will side with the Board, and against the Executive Committee of their own union. When most of the parents review these books, we are confident they will back us to the hilt, grateful that we have done our job and remained as they elected us . . . their faithful Watchdogs.

Finally, we have the books here for your inspection. We will gladly make copies of individual pages to (sic) the UNbelievers.
BOARD OF EDUCATION
Island Trees Union Free
School District
March 19, 1976.

On March 30, 1976, the board met and rati-

fied the already accomplished transfer of the "objectionable" books to the office of the board. At the same meeting, the board appointed four Island Trees parents along with four staff members (not including a librarian) to act as a "Book Review Committee" to make recommendations to the board on the educational suitability of the books.

In its first report to the board on April 30, 1976, the committee recommended return of one book[6] to the libraries and curriculum subject to parental approval. On July 1, 1976, the committee submitted its final report, recommending that four books[7] be "retained" by the school libraries, and that two books[8] be "removed". As to the remaining four books, the members of the committee could not agree about two of them,[9] recommended that parental approval be required for access to another,[10] and took no position on the last[11] because not all the members had been able to read it.

On July 28, 1976, the board acted on the committee report, resolving that one book be returned without restriction,[12] that one book be returned with students' access conditioned on parental approval,[13] and that the remaining nine books, "be removed from elementary and secondary libraries and for use in the curriculum." Explaining the meaning of this last phrase, the president of the board stated in his deposition that these nine books should not be assigned as required, optional, or even suggested reading although the books might still be discussed in class.[14]

Besides agreeing about the occurrence of the above events, the parties substantially agree about the motivation behind the board's actions. In his affidavit, the president of the board explains:

I am basically a conservative in my general philosophy and feel that the community I represent as a school board member shares that philosophy. It is to this that I attribute my re-election on a number of occasions. I feel that it is my duty to apply my conservative principles to the decision making process in which I am involved as a board member and I have done so with regard to fiscal matters, student discipline, teacher performance, union negotiations, curriculum formation and content and other educational matters.

*   *   *   *   *   *

My objection is to the obscenity and bad taste contained in [the books] as well as their irrelevance, in my opinion, to the basic curriculum of the district and to the values which I, as a board member and president, feel the community wishes inculcated in its youth. The whole thing has been blown out of proportion. The best way to indicate the basic reasons of the board as a whole for the actions taken is to annex various statements made by the board to the public as these events were taking place. * * * A review of these materials * * * will indicate that the excerpts about which we were concerned (and later the books themselves) contain every form of obscenity and sexual allusion imagineable (sic). Granted one * * * also makes ridiculous disparaging remarks about Christ and one * * * about Jews. This does not mean that my objection is based on religious grounds or a desire to favor or exclude one religion over another. I just plain think it is in terrible taste and irrelevant to the educational process in my district--not to mention being obscene. * * *

We are the elected members of a board charged with the custody of thousands of youngsters during the school day. We stand in the shoes of their parents during that time. These students do not have the same rights to be exposed to obscenities as an adult. I will certainly not be an instrument of it. If they wish to read the "banned" books they are welcome to while not in school as long as their parents do not object. Most of these volumes are in the public library so there are alternative sources. As long as I have the legal right to exercise my discretion in the way I have, I shall continue to do so. This is the essence of the concept of community standards and local control of school boards.

Despite the board president's opinion quoted above, defendants in their Rule 9(g) statement concede that the books are not obscene; instead they argue that the "objectionable" books are in bad taste and irrelevant to the curriculum. Defendants' reply memorandum to the brief of amicus curiae American Jewish Committee puts the point as follows:

Amicus' memorandum states that * * the Court should intercede "when a school board, acting on the basis of its political or religious views violates these [first amendment] rights." *We agree fully.* Amicus also states that * * * defendants (sic) acts were "Guided by their political views. . . ." and * * * that the decision was made "on the basis of its [the board's] political orientation." That this is not so is obvious from a reading of defendants' affidavits and the exhibits annexed thereto as well as Messrs. Ahrens' and Martin's depositions. These documents (most of which are public school records) are replete with proof that religious and political considerations were far from defendants' minds, but that *their conservative philosophy of morals and traditional values was the dominant factor.* * * *

Additional reference to the depositions of Frank Martin * * * and Richard Ahrens * * * as well as a reading of the whole of the depositions sustain the conclusion that *defendants' basic concern was morality and vulgarity and its relevance to the educational process as well as the obvious bad taste exhibited* in the volumes in question --not politics and religion. (emphasis supplied)

The pleadings and affidavits submitted by

all parties and *amici* demonstrate that the board acted not on religious principles but on its conservative educational philosophy, and on its belief that the nine books removed from the school library and curriculum were irrelevant, vulgar, immoral, and in bad taste, making them educationally unsuitable for the district's junior and senior high school students. Absent any dispute over a material fact, there is nothing to prevent decision of the cross-motions for summary judgment.

ISSUES

The motions present four issues. (A) subject matter jurisdiction; (B) class certification; (C) the constitutionality of the board's action in removing or restricting access to the library books; and (D) the constitutionality of the board's action in removing the books from "use in the curriculum."

A. *Jurisdiction.*

Plaintiffs allege jurisdiction over both the school board and its members in their official capacities under 42 U.S.C. § 1983 and 28 U.S.C. § 1343. Defendants respond that neither the board nor its members in their official capacities are "persons" subject to suit under 42 U.S.C. § 1983, because the board is a municipal corporation and its members are municipal officers, all of whom are immune from suit under § 1983 under *Monroe v. Pape*, 365 U.S. 167, 81 S.Ct. 473, 5 L.Ed.2d 492 (1961) and *Monell v. Department of Social Services of the City of New York*, 532 F.2d 259 (CA2 1976). Since the filing of defendants' brief, *Monell* has been reversed by the Supreme Court, 436 U.S. 658, 98 S.Ct. 2018, 56 L.Ed.2d 611 (1978). In language directly applicable here, Justice Brennan, for the majority, wrote that:

Local governing bodies, therefore, can be sued directly under section 1983 for monetary, declaratory, or injunctive relief where, as here, the action that is alleged to be unconstitutional implements or executes a policy statement, ordinance, regulation, or decision affirmatively adopted and promulgated by that body's officers. *Id.* 98 S.Ct. at 2036.

Since these books were removed from the Island Trees school library pursuant to a decision affirmatively adopted and promulgated by the board, the court does have subject matter jurisdiction under § 1983 over the board and its individual members in their official capacities. *Id.* at footnote 55.

B. *Class Certification.*

Plaintiffs have moved for class action certification under FRCP 23(b)(2). To qualify, plaintiffs must satisfy the following requirements of FRCP 23(a) & (b)(2):

(a) One or more members of a class may sue

or be sued as representative parties on behalf of all only if (1) the class is so numerous that joinder of all members is impracticable, (2) there are questions of law or fact common to the class, (3) the claims or defenses of the representative parties are typical of the claims or defenses of the class, and (4) the representative parties will fairly and adequately protect the interests of the class.
(b) An action may be maintained as a class action if the prerequisites of subdivision (a) are satisfied, and in addition:
*   *   *   *   *   *
(2) the party opposing the class has acted or refused to act on grounds generally applicable to the class, thereby making appropriate final injunctive relief or corresponding declaratory relief with respect to the class as a whole * * *."

Plaintiffs fail to qualify in two respects. First, the claims of the named plaintiffs are not typical of the claims which might be asserted by all members of the proposed class, namely, all students in the Island Trees junior and senior high schools. The named plaintiffs and their parents who represent them as "next friends" oppose the restrictions on access to school library books, but there is reason to believe that at least some students, and perhaps even a majority of parents, in the district feel otherwise.

Second, there is no advantage to class action certification in this case. In terms of FRCP 23(b)(2), there have not been events, "making appropriate final injunctive relief or corresponding declaratory relief with respect to the class as a whole." A disposition either way would be as effective without the procedural complexities that attend class certification. The motion for class certification is therefore denied.

C. *The Constitutionality of the Board's Action in Removing or Restricting Access to Library Books*

It is necessary to begin by focusing the issue. The complaint alleges five separate causes of action based on the board's removal and restriction of access to library books: (1) violation of New York State Constitution Art. 1 §8, guaranteeing liberty of speech; (2) violation of the same provision insofar as it guarantees academic freedom to librarians; (3) violation of the first amendment to the United States Constitution, guaranteeing freedom of expression; (4) violation of the same amendment insofar as it guarantees academic freedom to librarians; and (5) violation of 42 U.S.C. § 1983.

These five causes of action reduce to a single claim for purposes of this decision. The claims to freedom of speech and academic freedom under the New York State Constitution are governed by the same principles that apply under the first amendment to the federal constitution. *East Meadow Community Concerts As-*

sociation v. Board of Ed. of Union Free School District No. 3, 18 N.Y.2d 129, 272 N.Y.S.2d 341, 219 N.E.2d 172, *on remand* 27 A.D.2d 819, 273 N.Y.S.2d 736, *affirmed* 19 N.Y.2d 605, 278 N.Y.S.2d 393, 224 N.E.2d 888 (1967). Moreover, an independent, direct cause of action under the first amendment is superfluous, since the same allegations support a cause of action for violation of first amendment rights under 42 U.S.C. § 1983. *Turpin v. Mailet*, 579 F.2d 152 (CA2 1978).

Finally, plaintiffs have no standing to assert the rights of librarians to academic freedom under either the New York State or federal constitutions.

[O]ne to whom application of a statute is constitutional will not be heard to attack the statute on the ground that impliedly it might also be taken as applying to other persons or other situations in which its application might be unconstitutional. *United States v. Raines*, 362 U.S. 17, 22, 80 S.Ct. 519, 522, 4 L.Ed.2d 524 (1960).

And there is no reason to relax this bar against third-party claims here, where there is no showing that the librarians of Island Trees could not have joined this action as plaintiffs or intervenors, had they wanted to do so, and where none of the classic exceptions to the bar against third-party claims applies. Tribe, *American Constitutional Law*, § 3-26.

Thus, for purposes of this decision, the five causes of action in the pleadings reduce to a single cause of action under 42 U.S.C. § 1983, alleging that the school board's removal of the library books violates the first amendment rights of the student plaintiffs.

To support this first amendment claim, plaintiffs lean heavily on the three most recent federal court decisions involving school board bans on library books: *Minarcini v. Strongsville City School Dist.*, 541 F.2d 577 (CA6 1976), *Right to Read Defense Committee of Chelsea v. School Committee of the City of Chelsea*, 454 F.Supp. 703 (D.Mass.1978) and *Salvail v. Nashua Board of Education*, (D.C.N.H. 1979). Each of these cases struck down school board restrictions on or removal of library books as unconstitutional, and distinguished *Presidents Council, supra*, 457 F.2d 289 (CA2) *cert. denied*, 409 U.S. 998, 93 S.Ct. 308 (1972), the only federal case to uphold similar school board restrictions on library books and the only case on point in this circuit. For reasons set forth below, this court concludes that *Presidents Council*, and not the three more recent federal cases, governs the case at bar and mandates summary judgment in favor of defendants on the issue of restrictions on library books.

In *Presidents Council*, the Second Circuit had to pass on the constitutionality of a New York City local school board's restriction on access to a single book in a junior high school. Upholding the school board, the court, through Judge Mulligan, began by noting the extensive review procedures, both administrative and judicial, available under New York law to challenge the determination of a local school board, procedures which would make it not "appropriate for this court to review either the wisdom or the efficacy of the determinations of the Board." *Id.* at 291. The court then looked for the test to be applied by a federal court in reviewing the constitutionality of school board restrictions. That test was found in *Epperson v. Arkansas*, 393 U.S. 97, 89 S.Ct. 266, 21 L.Ed.2d 228 (1968):

By and large, public education in our Nation is committed to the control of state and local authorities. Courts do not and cannot, intervene in the resolution of conflicts which arise in the daily operations of school systems and which do not directly and sharply implicate basic constitutional values. *Id.* at 104, 89 S.Ct. at 270.

Applying this standard the court found "no impingement upon any basic constitutional values." *Id.* at 291. Placing the controversy in context, Judge Mulligan noted:

Since we are dealing not with the collection of a public book store but with the library of a public junior high school, evidently some authorized person or body has to make a determination as to what the library collection will be. It is predictable that no matter what choice of books may be made by whatever segment of academe, some other person or group may well dissent. The ensuing shouts of book burning, witch hunting and violation of academic freedom hardly elevate this intramural strife to first amendment constitutional proportions. If it did, there would be a constant intrusion of the judiciary into the internal affairs of the school. Academic freedom is scarcely fostered by the intrusion of three or even nine federal jurists making curriculum or library choices for the community of scholars. When the court has intervened, the circumstances have been rare and extreme and the issues presented totally distinct from those we have here. *Id.* at 291-92.

Turning specifically to the facts at hand, the Second Circuit panel concluded:

Here, patently we have no religious establishment or free exercise question, and neither do we have the banning of the teaching of any theory or doctrine. The problems of the youth in the ghetto, crime, drugs and violence have not been placed off limits by the Board. A book has been removed but the librarian has not been penalized, the teacher is still free to discuss the Barrio and its problems in the classroom. The action of the Board does not even preclude the teacher from discussing [the restricted book] in class or from assigning it for outside reading. In those libraries which have the book, the parent can borrow it and, if he sees fit, can loan it to his child if he

wishes to read it. [footnote omitted] The intrusion of the Board here upon any first amendment constitutional right of any category of plaintiffs is not only not "sharp" or "direct", it is miniscule. *Id.* at 292.

The panel found "unsupportable under any theory of constitutional law we can discover" the concept of "a book acquiring tenure". Appellants had argued that although the board had ultimate authority in the initial selection of books for the school library, a different case was presented where the book, once shelved, is now removed. Rejecting the analogy to tenure in public employment, the court found it clear that "books which become obsolete or irrelevant or were improperly selected initially, *for whatever reason*, can be removed by the same authority which was empowered to make the selection in the first place." *Id.* at 293 (emphasis supplied).

Despite this apparently clear rejection of the concept of book tenure by the Second Circuit, plaintiffs here reassert the concept, relying on one subsequent Sixth Circuit case, *Minarcini v. Strongsville City School District, supra*, and two federal district court decisions, *Right to Read Committee of Chelsea v. School Committee of the City of Chelsea, supra*, and *Salvail v. Nashua Board of Education, supra*. Although each of these cases purports to "distinguish" *Presidents Council*, upon analysis it is clear that in both language and result they simply adopt the book tenure concept that was rejected by the Second Circuit, and hold that once a school library book has been selected and acquired, the first amendment prevents the school board from later removing it because of its content.

In *Minarcini*, the Sixth Circuit concluded that

the School Board removed the books because it found them objectionable in content and because it felt that it had the power, unfettered by the First Amendment, to censor the school library for subject matter which the Board members found distasteful. 541 F.2d at 582.

It then noted that

Neither the State of Ohio nor the Strongsville School Board was under any federal constitutional compulsion to provide a library for the Strongsville High School or to choose any particular books. Once having created such a privilege for the benefit of its students, however, neither body could place conditions on the use of the library which were related solely to the social or political tastes of school board members. *Id.* at 582.

In reaching its conclusions that a content-based removal of a school library book infringed the students' first amendment rights, the court argued that a public school library is a valuable adjunct to classroom discussion, that removal of library books is a serious burden on such discussion and that the burden is not minimized because a book is available in sources outside the school. Referring to libraries generally, the court reminded us that "a library is a mighty resource in the free marketplace of ideas", "specially dedicated to broad dissemination of ideas", and asserted that it is "a forum for silent speech". *Id.* at 582–83. Recognizing that it is the book's speech, not the student's, that was limited by removing a book from the library, the court drew on the "right to receive" doctrine expounded in *Virginia State Board of Pharmacy v. Virginia Citizens Consumers Council, Inc.*, 425 U.S. 748, 96 S.Ct. 1817, 48 L.Ed.2d 346, and other Supreme Court cases, and concluded that the students right to receive information, their "right to know", was unconstitutionally infringed when the board removed books because of their content.

With similar reasoning the district courts in *Right to Read, supra* and *Salvail, supra* also found to be unconstitutional content-based removal of reading material from school libraries. With all due deference to those courts and the Sixth Circuit, they do not accurately interpret the Second Circuit's holding in *Presidents Council.* It is true that a variety of considerations may affect the decision of what books to maintain in a school library at a given time. Availability of funds, shelf space and personnel are all significant, but the principal reason for selecting and keeping books is their content. Indeed, in deciding what books to place in a school library a school board not only may, but must choose on the basis of content; to do less would be to neglect their statutory duty. Yet, *Minarcini, Right to Read* and *Salvail* each would require a school board to be content-blind and act only for reasons such as space, physical obsolescence or other considerations that are "neutral" under the first amendment.

At the heart of the controversy is the constitutional role of the school board in public education. In New York, control of the public schools is committed to locally elected bodies, a commitment that "requires significant public control over what is said and done in school." *East Hartford Education Assn. v. Board of Education*, 562 F.2d 838, 856, (CA2, *en banc*, 1977). One of the principal functions of public education is indoctrinative, to transmit the basic values of the community. *James v. Board of Education*, 461 F.2d 566, 573 (CA2 1972), *cert. den.* 409 U.S. 1042, 93 S.Ct. 529, 34 L.Ed.2d 491. A constitutionally required "book tenure" principle would infringe upon an elected school board's discretion in determining what community values were to be transmitted.

Here, the Island Trees School Board removed certain books because it viewed them as vulgar and in bad taste, a removal that clearly was content-based. Whether they were correct in their evaluation of the books is not the issue. Nor is the issue whether, assuming the books to be vulgar and in bad taste, it is a

wise or even desirable educational decision to sanitize the library by removing them, thereby sheltering the students from their influence. Such issues should be decided and remedied either by the school district's voters, or by the State Commissioner of Education on an appropriate administrative appeal.

Here, the issue is whether the first amendment requires a federal court to forbid a school board from removing library books which its members find to be inconsistent with the basic values of the community that elected them. *Presidents Council* resolved that issue by holding that a book that was improperly selected "for whatever reason" could be removed "by the same authority which was empowered to make the selection in the first place". *Presidents Council* is controlling here.

Even if this court were not bound by the Second Circuit's holding, it would reach the same result. Although *Minarcini, Right to Read* and *Salvail* seek to distinguish book removal from book acquisition, the attempted distinction is not grounded in any sound constitutional principle, and inevitably would break down in actual practice. Maintenance of a school library is an ongoing process. Periodically, books are added and removed, as school officials balance considerations of cost, space, educational need, student demand and faculty interest. As already noted, within the constraints of money and space, content is the primary criterion for selection.

If, as in *Minarcini, Right to Read* and *Salvail*, a federal court must guard a book against *removal* because of its content, then how could that same court avoid passing upon a school board's content-based refusal of a student's request to *acquire* a particular book when the funds were available? Disregarding the volume of potential litigation, a court simply is not competent to decide what books are to be in a school's library. The proper agency is the school board, and it would be illogical and unrealistic to deprive a board of its most relevant criterion, content, for making that decision.

Significantly, the school board's action here involved no religious question, either free exercise or establishment; nor was there a ban on the teaching of any theory or doctrine; nor has there been a restriction imposed on classroom discussion, or a penalty inflicted on any teacher or librarian. Moreover, these restrictions have denied no student the right to silent or open speech as did the restrictions in *Tinker v. Des Moines Independent Community School District*, 393 U.S. 503, 89 S.Ct. 733, 21 L.Ed.2d 731 (1969); they have not directly inhibited discussion in the classroom or elsewhere in the schools; and they have focused upon no particular student or group.

The board has restricted access only to certain books which the board believed to be, in essence, vulgar. While removal of such books from a school library may, indeed in this court's view does, reflect a misguided educational philosophy, it does not constitute a sharp and direct infringement of any first amendment right.

D. *The Constitutionality of the Board's Action in Removing the Books from "Use in the Curriculum".*

Plaintiffs in this action are students. No teacher has joined in, nor do plaintiffs establish that any teacher currently desires to use any of the restricted books in the curriculum.[15] While a student may, under the "right to receive" doctrine, *Virginia State Board of Planning v. Virginia Citizens Consumers Council, Inc., supra,* have standing to present a first amendment academic freedom claim, before such a claim may be sustained there must at least be a real, not an imagined controversy. Here, plaintiffs' contention that the board's action interferes with what teachers in the district want to teach, is diffuse, speculative and factually unsupported.

In the absence of a sharp, focused issue of academic freedom, the court concludes that respect for the traditional values of the community and deference to the school board's substantial control over educational content, see *East Hartford Education Assn. v. Board of Education, supra,* 562 F.2d at 859, preclude any finding of a first amendment violation arising out of removal of any of the books from use in the curriculum. As the Second Circuit, *en banc,* noted in *East Hartford,* at 859:

The very notion of public education implies substantial public control. Educational decisions must be made by someone; there is no reason to create a constitutional preference for the views of individual teachers over those of their employers.

Even less should such a constitutional preference be created for the views of students.

CONCLUSION

The challenged action by the school board did not sharply and directly implicate basic first amendment values. It fell, therefore, within the broad range of discretion constitutionally afforded to educational officials who are elected by the community.

Accordingly, defendants' motion for summary judgment is granted and plaintiffs' cross-motion for summary judgment is denied. The motion for class certification is also denied. The clerk shall enter judgment dismissing the complaint, without costs.

SO ORDERED.

NOTES

1. Both parties submitted Rule 9(g) statements in support of their motions for summary judgment. The court accepts as undisputed all facts alleged in each 9(g) statement except where the 9(g) statements conflict.

2. (1) *Slaughter House Five* by Kurt Vonnegut, Jr.;

(2) *The Naked Ape,* by Desmond Morris;

(3) *Down These Mean Streets,* by Piri Thomas;

(4) *Best Short Stories by Negro Writers,* edited by Langston Hughes;

(5) *Go Ask Alice,* Anonymous;

(6) *Laughing Boy,* by Oliver LaFarge;

(7) *Black Boy,* by Richard Wright;

(8) *A Hero Aint Nothing But A Sandwich,* by Alice Childress;

(9) *Soul On Ice,* by Eldridge Cleaver;

3. (10) *A Reader for Writers,* edited by Jerome Archer;

4. (11) *The Fixer,* by Bernard Malamud

5. There is some uncertainty about the exact date of removal. The books may have been removed as early as February 25, 1976. It is clear, however, that they were not delivered to the board's office until after March 3, 1976.

6. *The Fixer.* This book, though previously in the curriculum, was not found in the libraries.

7. *Laughing Boy, Black Boy, Go Ask Alice,* and *Best Short Stories by Negro Writers.*

8. *The Naked Ape, Down These Mean Streets.*

9. *Soul On Ice* and *A Hero Aint Nothing But A Sandwich.*

10. *Slaughter House Five.*

11. *A Reader for Writers.*

12. *Laughing Boy.*

13. *Black Boy.*

14. Whether the curriculum restrictions applied to *Black Boy,* which was put on restricted access, is unclear from the record.

15. One book, *The Fixer,* was a part of the curriculum in one class, until the book was removed by the board in the spring of 1976. There is no assertion by any party that any teacher now wishes to assign this book for use inside or outside the classroom.

*In deciding to reverse the lower court's judg-
ment against the students who had objected to
the removal from the school library of* Down
These Mean Streets, The Naked Ape, *and* Soul
On Ice *and the placing of* Slaughterhouse
Five *on a restricted shelf in the library, the
United States Court of Appeals stated: "Among
the procedural and other irregularities which
warrant an inference that the welfare and education of the children of the Island Trees
School District were not the true motivating
concerns which led to the removal of the books
from school libraries in that District are, in
addition to those already mentioned: defendants' substantive confusion, not to say incoherence, as to the reasons the books were being
removed from the libraries; the informal and
dilatory manner in which the matter was pursued, including the lapse of three months from
the time the presence of the offending books
was discovered in the libraries until the principals of the schools were asked to take some
action to prevent children from reading
them...; the ex post facto appointment of a
committee to review the removal of the books,
the determinations of which were then, without
explanation, not followed by the Board...; and,
finally, the 'substantive' irregularities...of
removing works by such generally recognized
authors as Swift, the late Richard Wright, and
Bernard Malamud, whose book,* The Fixer, *was,
indeed, an assigned high school reading text."*

Pico v. *Board of Ed., Island Trees
Union Free School,* 638 F.2d 404
(1980)

SIFTON, District Judge.

This appeal arises from a judgment entered
in the United States District Court for the
Eastern District of New York granting defendants' application for summary judgment and dismissing plaintiffs' class action complaint
which sought injunctive and declaratory relief
with respect to alleged violations of the first
amendment to the United States Constitution and
Article 1, Section 8 of the New York State Constitution.[1]   These violations were alleged in
the complaint to have arisen as a result of defendant School Board's removal of three works
of fiction, four autobiographies, two anthologies, and one work of non-fiction, from the
school libraries and curriculum of the Island
Trees Union Free School District on Long Island.[2]   Since the majority of the panel concludes that defendants were not entitled to

judgment as a matter of law, we reverse the
judgment below.   Because the majority is not in
agreement as to whether the present record is
sufficient to entitle plaintiffs to judgment in
their favor, we remand for a trial to develop a
plenary record on which that issue may be determined.

FACTUAL BACKGROUND

On September 19, 20, and 21, 1975, three
members of the Board of Education of the Island
Trees Union Free School District[3] in Nassau
County, including defendants Frank Martin,
Patrick Hughes and the Board's President, defendant Richard Ahrens, attended a conference
in Watkins Glen, New York, sponsored by an organization called People of New York United, an
organization described by defendant Ahrens below as a "conservative organization ... composed of parents concerned about education legislation in this State."   Attending the conference, besides the three defendants, were among
others, according to Ahrens,

"... an attorney from Washington, D.C. who
represented the Heritage Foundation, a conservatively oriented organization, George
Archibald, a legislative assistant to Rep.
John Conlon of Arizona, and other speakers
with reputations in education circles who
spoke about current topics about which the
conservative community was concerned including litigation involving the control of text
books and library books in the schools.   The
speaker on this topic was a Mr. Fike from
Kanawa County, West Virginia which had un-
dergone such litigation."

At the conference, according to Ahrens, defendants obtained "lists of books considered objectionable by some persons together with excerpts from them containing the more objectionable material."   These "lists" consisted, at
least in part, of two sets of crudely typed and
reproduced sheets, one relating to a Randolph
High School in Randolph, New York, the other,
to an inspection in March of 1975 by an organization called Concerned Citizens and Taxpayers
for Decent School Books of Baton Rouge, Louisiana of the card catalogue and shelves of the
Tara High School library in an unidentified
town in that State.   The lists included titles,
authors and quotations, with page references.
Interspersed with the quotations, themselves
presented with editorial underlining, were comments of which the following are a sample:

"Title: *Soul on Ice* by Eldridge Cleaver
(Leader of Black panther [sic] and not al-
lowed to live in America.)"
"THIS BOOK WAS RETAINED FOR SENIORS ONLY IN
RANDOLPH.   THE BOOK IS FULL OF ANTI-AMERICAN
MATERIAL AND HATE FOR WHITE WOMEN.   WHY
WOULD TEACHERS WANT HIGH SCHOOL STUDENTS TO
READ THIS????   OUR GROUP IS GOING TO FILE A
COMPLAINT AGAINST THIS BOOK ON SEDITIOUS AND
DISLOYAL MATTER."

*   *   *   *   *   *

"TITLE: *Go Ask Alice* by Anonymous. (*Suppose* to be diary of 15 year old girl)"
"NOTE: This book, after being reviewed by three teachers was retained. Parents, do not be fooled by the movie version of this book. It reads a lot different. If teachers cannot find a better book than this to illustrate drugs are bad then what are we paying them for. They justify their viewpoint because the girl dies in the end. A lot of teachers think this is a great book????????"
"[Handwritten] LEGISLATORS: KEEP MORATORIUM ON SEX ED! PROVIDE CRIMINAL PENALTIES SO D.A.'S CAN PROSECUTE VIOLATORS! PROTECT THE CHILDREN."

       *   *   *   *   *   *

"1. *Our Sexual Evolution* by Helen Colton— This library book displayed in the Tara High School Library appears to be in violation of Act 500 of the Louisiana legislature. It belittles parents, presents no moral judgments, is anti-Christian and contrary to laws of God. It has chapters on Group Marriage, Communes, Abortion, Contraceptives etc. It also promotes women's lib. It costs $5.95 of our tax dollars."

"2. *A Reader for Writers—A Critical Anthology of Prose Readings* by Jerome W. Archer. This book was used in advanced composition class at Tara High School. It equates Malcolm X, considered by many to be a traitor to this country, with the founding fathers of our country."

The excerpts themselves, in contrast to the more politically oriented comments quoted above, are devoted principally to quotations of vulgar and indecent language referring to sexual and other bodily functions and crude descriptions of sexual behavior, although the manner of excerpting, including the use of underlinings, elisions, apparent errors, and interspersed editorial comment leaves no great sense of confidence in the literal accuracy of the quotations. Several books appear on the list without any excerpts at all, but simply with a critical appraisal, e. g., *A Reader for Writers*. Another is listed without comment next to what purports to be quotations from three of the book's pages.[4]
Although acquired in September, nothing was done by defendants with these lists[5] until November 7, 1975, when defendants Martin and Ahrens attended "Winter School Night" at the District's senior high school. According to Ahrens and Martin, they asked a school custodian to let them into the school library and, by comparing Martin's lists of objectionable books with the library card index files, determined that nine "objectionable" texts were in the school library. The school's principal apparently interrupted their work. According to Ahrens, the two men "told him briefly what we were doing."
Nothing more was done about the matter thereafter until late February 1976[6] when, at a regular meeting of the Board, according to Ahrens,

"... we asked the two high school principals to stay after the meeting which they did. We had a lengthy discussion with them ... during which there was much concern and wringing of hands over the potential of the situation. One principal, after reading the excerpts said 'If this stuff is in the books they don't belong in the school.' We had not at that time checked the junior high school library so we asked that principal to check it (he did so and found two more books that were on Mr. Martin's list)."

As a result of this informal meeting, the Board directed the principals of the schools to remove the books from the library shelves forthwith.
Three days later the Superintendent of the School District,[7] Richard Morrow, sent a memorandum to the Board which had as its subject, "List of Books to be Banned." The memorandum stated, *inter alia*:

"My objection to direct action banning all the books on the list purchased [sic] at Watkins Glen is that we don't know who developed the list, nor the criteria they used. I don't believe we should accept and act on someone else's list, unless we first study the books ourselves.
"... [W]e already have a policy ... designed expressly to handle such problems. It calls for the Superintendent, upon receiving an objection to a book or books, to appoint a committee to study them and make recommendations. I feel it is a good policy—and it is Board policy—and that it should be followed in this instance. Furthermore, I think it can be followed quietly and in such a way as to reduce, perhaps avoid, the public furor which has always attended such issues in the past.
"... I have no doubt (but of course no proof) that such a local committee would end up agreeing about most of the books on the list. The Board's feelings on them are not so different from the staff's and parents'— after all, that is shown by the fact that the large majority of the books listed are not and apparently never have been recommended and used by the staff.
"... [U]nilateral banning by the Board without inputs from the staff, would surely create a furious uproar—not only in the staff, but across the community, Long Island and the state. I don't believe you want such an uproar, and I certainly don't."

The Superintendent further reported that one of the books directed to be removed from the library, Malamud's *The Fixer*, was being used as part of a senior course in literature, having been "approved as part of that course in January, 1972, by the Board of Education."
Morrow's memorandum of February 27, 1976

was answered by a memorandum of March 3 from defendant Ahrens directing again that "*all copies* of the books in question" (emphasis in the original) be removed immediately from the libraries.

Shortly thereafter, as Superintendent Morrow had predicted in his memorandum, the Board's action became known, and newspaper articles concerning the events began to appear in the New York press. Defendants responded to these articles by means of a press conference at which a release was distributed which read in part as follows:

"It comes as no surprise to this Board of Education that it is once again the subject of attack by Teacher Union leaders, headed by Walter Compare. With the election of School Board candidates just two months away, the Teachers' Union is once again attempting to discredit the Board and win the seats for two union-backed lackeys."

Referring to the Watkins Glen conference, the press release continued:

"While at the conference, we learned of books found in schools throughout the country which were anti-American, anti-Christian, anti-Semetic [sic], and just plain filthy. Upon their return, Ahrens & Martin in early November went to the Senior High School Library to check the card catalog to see if any of these objectionable books were in our library. We discovered nine such books. We neither removed books, nor cards from the card file.

"At the next meeting of the Board, the entire Board discussed how to handle this situation, realizing that to make the titles of the books public might cause a sudden run on the library by the students.
   *   *   *   *   *   *
"To date, what we have found is that the books do, in fact, contain material which is offensive to Christians, Jews, Blacks, and Americans in general. In addition, these books contain obscenities, blasphemies, brutality, and perversion beyond description.
   *   *   *   *   *   *
"We are sure that when most of our teachers are given the opportunity to review the material, they will side with the Board, and against the Executive Committee of their own union. When most of the parents review these books, we are confident they will back us to the hilt, grateful that we have done our job and remained as they elected us ... their faithful Watchdogs."

Also during the month of March, the Board released an issue of its regular *Newsletter* to the residents of the School District stating, "[t]he entire contents of this special newsletter will be devoted to the library book issue" and asking the people of the District to attend the Board meeting of March 30, 1976, where "[y]ou will have the opportunity to ex-

amine the books yourselves." The *Newsletter*, after again attributing the newspaper stories concerning the issue to "lies and misinformation which has been spread by the teachers' union," stated:

"Mr. Compare is fighting to keep books in our schools which are offensive to Christians, Jews, Blacks, and all Americans in general. One such book [apparently referring to Vonnegut's *Slaughterhouse Five*] refers to Jesus Christ as a 'man with no connections.' One must ask oneself what motivates this man? ... Why ... does Mr. Compare insist that these books remain in the hands of our children."

In this atmosphere the Board held a public meeting on the subject on March 30, 1976. At this meeting Superintendent Morrow again stated his position in a prepared statement that it was "wrong for the Board--or any other single group--to act to remove books without prolonged prior consideration of the views of both the parents whose children read these books, and the teachers who use these books to instruct;" that it was "wrong to judge any book on the basis of brief excerpts from it [since m]any books--among them widely acclaimed classics--contain brief passages which, if taken out of context, would seem to condemn them;" that it was "wrong to take action based on a list prepared by someone outside the Island Trees community;" and that "it was wrong to bypass the established procedure for reviewing the challenged books." Further, Morrow recommended that, pending review by a committee, "the challenged books be returned to the shelves, with the understanding that every parent has the right and the responsibility to supervise the materials his child reads." Instead, the Board ratified its earlier action removing the books, but directed that a committee of eight, composed of four school staff members and four parents, "read ... and make recommendations to the board" concerning "the educational suitability of these books and whether they are in good taste, appropriate and relevant." This latter language was taken from a provision of the union's contract with the Board which provided:

"Accordingly, it is agreed that teachers shall have the right to introduce and explore controversial material, provided only that the material and manner in which it is presented are in good taste, appropriate to grade level, and relevant to course content. Every effort will be made to present all sides of controversial issues."[8]

Coincidentally, the Board fixed May 26, 1976, as the date for the election of new Board members and directed that nominating petitions be filed by April 26, 1976.

On April 2, 1976, the Superintendent in a memorandum to the Board again urged that, pending review by the committee to be appointed, the books be returned to the library since the reason for their removal had been satisfied. The books were, however, not returned. On April 6, 1976, a book review committee was selected by the Board and the Superintendent. On April 30, 1976 the committee met, having apparently read some of the books.

"After a very comprehensive discussion regarding the book *THE FIXER* by Bernard Malamud, the vote to return the book to our modern literature curriculum was: 6 YES and 2 NO. It was further recommended that the book would be returned subject to parental approval."[9]

A second meeting of the committee on May 12, 1976, led to a memorandum from the committee to defendent Ahrens inquiring with respect to the two anthologies, *Best Short Stories by Negro Writers* and *A Reader for Writers,* "whether you object to specific stories or the entire book." There is nothing in the record to indicate whether this inquiry was ever answered and some indication that it was not. At this meeting the committee also voted unanimously that Oliver LaFarge's *Laughing Boy* be returned to the library and by a vote of 5 to 3 that *Slaughterhouse Five* be returned to a restricted shelf in the library. At meetings of May 26, June 16, and June 30, 1976, the committee voted to return *Black Boy*, *Go Ask Alice*, and *Best Short Stories by Negro Writers* to the shelves. It voted not to restore *The Naked Ape, Down These Mean Streets,* and *Soul on Ice.* The committee reported itself unable to make a recommendation with regard to *A Reader for Writers* since "[t]his book seems to be unavailable in this area."

Following the committee's report to the Board on July 1, 1976, the Board met again publicly on July 28, 1976, and took up what the minutes describe as the "Book Issue," voting separately on each of the books covered by the committee's recommendations. As a result of these separate votes, only *Laughing Boy* and *Black Boy* were returned to the library shelves generally. The other books at issue were directed to be "removed [sic] from elementary and secondary libraries, and for use in the curriculum."

At the same time as the book committee was considering each book, two of the incumbent members of the Board of Education ran again for office. According to defendant Ahrens, the "book banning issue was the major one in the campaign. Nevertheless (or more probably because of this) the incumbent members were re-elected."

A further press release defending the Board's position was issued by defendant Ahrens in August 1976. In January 1977 this lawsuit was filed. The Board responded to the lawsuit with a press release stressing the repellent and vulgar language present in the books. Counsel for defendants, in a procedure of questionable propriety,[10] mailed a questionnaire to 4,979 mailing addresses in the District asking whether the recipient was a parent of public school children and whether the re-

cipient "supported" the Board's action in removing "the books in question." The results of this mailing, "done at our attorney's request due to the alleged class action nature of the suit," but reported in defendants' response to plaintiffs' motion for summary judgment, were 508 (or 59% of those responding) supporting the Board, 358 (or 41% of those responding) opposed.

Following denial of plaintiffs' motion to remand the case to state court, defendants moved for summary judgment dismissing plaintiffs' complaint. In support of their motion defendants set forth the history and documents referred to above. In addition, they alleged:

"Defendants Ahrens and Martin objected to the books for numerous reasons including the presence of profanities and obscenities, explicit sexual allusions, depictions of deviant sex, the glorification of sex and drugs, ungrammatical usage, and excerpts offensive to racial, religious or ethnic groups."

The two defendants identified the offending essay in *A Reader for Writers*, not as the essay which equated Malcolm X with the Founding Fathers, but rather, as Swift's "A Modest Proposal." Defendant Ahrens found the subject of that 18th Century satire on England's treatment of Ireland "irrelevant to the curriculum." Defendant Martin averred that he "felt it to be inappropriate"--apparently referring to the standard of appropriateness of grade level contained in the union contract. Plaintiffs sought depositions of defendants and then themselves cross-moved for summary judgment. On August 2, 1979, Judge Pratt, relying principally on the decision of this Court in *President's Council, District 25 v. Community School Board # 25*, 457 F.2d 289 (2d Cir.), *cert. denied,* 409 U.S. 998, 93 S.Ct. 308, 34 L.Ed.2d 260 (1972), granted the motion of defendants for summary judgment in their favor.

DISCUSSION

I

We start with an awareness that the application of the prohibitions of the First Amendment to secondary school education present complexities not encountered in other areas of government activity. We are dealing with the care of children by a government concerned with the "well-being of its youth." *F.C.C. v. Pacifica Foundation*, 438 U.S. 726, 749, 98 S.Ct. 3026, 3040, 57 L.Ed.2d 1073 (1978), *quoting Ginsberg v. New York*, 390 U.S. 629, 640, 88 S.Ct. 1274, 1281, 20 L.Ed.2d 195 (1968). Moreover, "a principal function of all elementary and secondary education is indoctrinative--whether it be to teach the ABC's or multiplication tables or to transmit the basic values of the community." *James v. Board of Education*, 461 F.2d 566, 573 (2d Cir.), *cert. denied,* 409 U.S. 1042, 93 S.Ct 529, 34 L.Ed.2d 491 (1972). Further, "[b]y and large, public education in our Nation is committed to the control of State and local authorities." *Epperson v.*

Arkansas, 393 U.S. 97, 104, 89 S.Ct. 266, 270, 21 L.Ed.2d 228 (1968). Finally, we must accommodate "our concern for the First Amendment rights of students with a cautious deference to the expertise of educational officials within the academic environment." *Thomas v. Board of Education*, 607 F.2d 1043, 1050 (2d Cir. 1979), *cert. denied*, 444 U.S. 1081, 100 S.Ct. 1034, 62 L.Ed.2d 765 (1980).

At the same time, "First Amendment rights, applied in the light of the special characteristics of the school environment, are available to teachers and students." *Tinker v. Des Moines School District*, 393 U.S. 503, 506, 89 S.Ct. 733, 736, 21 L.Ed.2d 731 (1969). Moreover, "[t]he Fourteenth Amendment, as now applied to the States, protects the citizen against the State itself and all of its creatures--Boards of Education not excepted." *West Virginia State Board of Education v. Barnette*, 319 U.S. 624, 637, 63 S.Ct. 1178, 1185, 87 L.Ed. 1628 (1943). As Justice Jackson also wrote in the same decision, "[p]robably no deeper division of our people could proceed from any provocation than from finding it necessary to choose what doctrine and whose program public educational school officials may compel youth to unite in embracing.... [T]he First Amendment to our Constitution was designed to avoid these ends by avoiding these beginnings." *Id*. at 641, 63 S.Ct. at 1186. With respect to the relative expertise of courts and educational officials, the same opinion reminds us, "we act in these matters not by the authority of our competence but by force of our commissions. We cannot, because of modest estimates of our competence in such specialties as public education, withhold the judgment that history authenticates as the function of this Court when liberty is infringed." *Id*. at 640, 63 S.Ct. at 1186.

It is, however, not only the unusual number of potentially conflicting values which compete for attention in matters relating to secondary education that makes these cases difficult. There is, in addition, the generally acknowledged proposition that "freedom of expression demands breathing room." *James v. Board of Education,* supra, 461 F.2d at 572. That conclusion, based on an awareness of the "chilling effect upon the exercise of vital First Amendment rights," *Keyishian v. Board of Regents*, 385 U.S. 589, 604, 87 S.Ct. 675, 684, 17 L.Ed.2d 629 (1967), of determinations, whether by school officials or by courts, which attempt with either excessive breadth or excessive precision to delimit the areas of protected and prohibited speech reminds us to proceed with caution to consider not just the general outlines, but the specific facts of the case before us.[11]

As Judge Kaufman noted in *James v. Board of Education, supra*, 461 F.2d at 575:

> "It is characteristic of resolutions of first amendment cases, where the price of freedom of expression is so high and the horizons of conflict between countervailing interests seemingly infinite, that they do not yield simplistic formulas or handy scales for weighing competing values. 'The best one can hope for is to discern lines of analysis and advance formulations sufficient to bridge past decisions with new facts....' *Eisner v. Stamford Board of Education*, 440 F.2d 803, 804 n.1 (2d Cir. 1971)."

Such considerations are relevant not only to our approach to the facts of the case before us, but also to an appreciation of the significance of past precedents. In circumstances in which so many interests and public policies converge, relatively minor changes in the pattern of facts presented "often deprive precedents of reliability and cast us more than we would choose upon our own judgment." *West Virginia State Board of Education v. Barnette, supra*, 319 U.S. at 640, 63 S.Ct. at 1186. "It is a frustrating process which does not admit of safe analytical harbors." *Eisner v. Stamford Board of Education*, 440 F.2d 803, 804-05 n.1 (2d Cir. 1971).[12]

II

The presence of these conflicting considerations affects, initially, the definition of what constitutes a *prima facie* case. Powers to prescribe what may or may not be said and what may or may not be read--powers which are "denied to most public officials," *Thomas v. Board of Education, supra*, 607 F.2d at 1049 n.10--are accorded to school officials because they are the necessary prerequisites to the information of a school curriculum and the necessary prerequisites to the stocking of a school library. "Courts do not and cannot intervene in the resolution of conflicts which arise in the daily operation of school systems and which do not directly and sharply implicate basic constitutional values." *Epperson v. Arkansas, supra*, 393 U.S. at 104, 89 S.Ct. at 270. As this Court has pointed out in *Presidents Council v. Community School Board, supra*, one cannot bring to court every decision by a school official involving the shelving or unshelving of a book in a school library without truly exposing the country to the danger which was the concern of the Supreme Court in *Minersville School District v. Gobitis*, 310 U.S. 586, 598, 60 S.Ct. 1010, 1014, 84 L.Ed. 1375 (1940), *overruled, West Virginia State Board of Education, supra*, that the federal courts will become "the school board for the country."

It is not simply the onerousness of the task of policing every decision involving the contents of course curriculum or a school library for First Amendment violations which led to dismissal of the complaint in cases such as *President's Council*. The need for policing in such circumstances is, generally speaking, not there. The authority and responsibilities of our public school officials in the area are, by and large, so well understood and well performed that, absent extraordinary circumstances, there is no uncertain or "chilling" effect attendant on a decision to teach one subject rather than another or to select one from among many book titles competing for limited space on the library shelf. Just as it is well understood that "education would be impossible if teachers were forbidden to sanction incorrect responses or substandard essays with failing grades," *Thomas v. Board of Education, supra*, 607 F.2d at 1049, so it is well understood that the school library offers a more restricted choice than the public library and that what is not taught in high school will be available in college. The everyday administration of a school's curriculum or a school library does not, either directly or indirectly, impinge on the free expression of ideas.

In these circumstances, bare allegations that books have been removed from the shelves of secondary school libraries by responsible officials do not make out a *prima facie* First Amendment violation, even if the books have a controversial reputation so that one available inference is that they were removed to prohibit the expression of the ideas they contain. Such activities, being part of "the daily operation of school systems" do not "directly and sharply implicate basic constitutional values." *Epperson v. Arkansas, supra*, 393 U.S. at 104, 89 S.Ct at 270. On the contrary, the activity is on its face entirely consistent with the performance of the ' educational function conferred on school officials. Were it the case here, as in *President's Council*, that nothing more was at issue than the conflicting inferences to be drawn from the act of removal of a controversial text from the shelf of a high school library, we would affirm the decision of the district court because no prima facie case was established.

In this case, however, we are presented with more than the inferences to be drawn from the act of removing controversial texts from library shelves, and more than the clearly understood, routine and regular task of selecting titles for a school library. What we have instead is an unusual and irregular intervention in the school libraries' operations by persons not routinely concerned with such matters. Moreover, this intervention has occurred under circumstances, including the explanations for their actions given by the participants, which so far from clarifying the scope and intentions behind the official action, create instead grave questions concerning both subjects. In circumstances of such irregularity and ambiguity, a *prima facie* case is made out and intervention of a federal court is warranted because of the very infrequency with which it may be assumed such intervention will be necessary and because of the real threat that the school officials' irregular and ambiguous handling of the issue will, even despite the best intentions, create misunderstanding as to the scope of their activities which will serve to suppress freedom of expression.

III

The cases, however, which have recognized a *prima facie* First Amendment violation in some irregular and apparently arbitrary intervention in the daily operation of secondary school affairs have at the same time recognized that, because of the complexity of social policies at work in the secondary school context, defenses --short of clear and present danger--must be recognized to permit the school official to establish that the education of the young cannot be handled entirely by routine procedures and even that "an added increment of chilling effect", *Thomas v. Board of Education supra*, 607 F.2d at 1051, may have to be tolerated to perform adequately the task of educating the young. Thus, speech which "materially disrupts classwork or involves substantial disorder or invasion of the rights of others is, of course, not immunized by the constitutional guarantee of freedom of speech." *Tinker v. Des Moines*, 393 U.S. at 513, 89 S.Ct. at 740. Justice Fortas' concern for "the rights of others" has found particularized recognition in this Circuit in the regulation of language to protect the psychological well being of the young, *Trachtman v. Anker*, 563 F.2d 512 at 517 (2d Cir. 1977), *cert. denied*, 435 U.S. 925, 98 S.Ct. 1491, 55 L.Ed.2d 519 (1978), and "to promote standards of civility and decency among school children," *Thomas v. Board of Education, supra*, 607 F.2d at 1057 (Newman, J., concurring).

To be sure, the burden of demonstrating such defenses rests with the school officials and the burden is one of persuasion, not of pleading.

> "As for the burden oт proof, *Tinker*, as well as other federal cases establish that, if students choose to litigate, school authorities must demonstrate a reasonable basis for interference with student speech, and that courts will not rest content with officials' bare allegation that such a basis existed." *Eisner v. Stamford Board of Education, supra*, 440 F.2d at 810 (citations omitted).

Nor is the burden a light one.

> "Any limitation on the exercise of constitutional rights can be justified only by a conclusion, based on reasonable inferences flowing from concrete facts and not abstractions, that the interests of discipline or sound education are materially and substantially jeopardized...." *James v. Board of Education, supra*, 461 F.2d at 571.

Moreover, and of principal importance to the resolution of the issues presented by this case, the burden is not simply to demonstrate that there is a basis for the school officials' actions. As stated in this Circuit in *Eisner v. Stamford Board of Education, supra*, 440 F.2d at 806, while we are concerned, first, with whether the Board's policy [is] justified as included within one or more of the categories of exceptional cases" in which regulation of speech is permitted in the schools,

"[s]econd, is the policy as narrowly drawn as may reasonably be expected so as to advance the social interests that justify it or, to the contrary, does it unduly restrict protected speech, to an extent 'greater than is essential to the furtherance of' those interests? *See United States v. O'Brien*, 391 U.S. 367, 377, 88 S.Ct. 1673, 1679, 20 L.Ed.2d 672 (1968). In light of *Freedman [v. Maryland* 380 U.S. 51, 85 S.Ct. 734, 13 L.Ed.2d 649 (1965)], the latter question might usefully be addressed, alternatively, to the substantive and to the procedural aspects of the policy--that is, first to the criteria by which school officials are permitted to bar literature from the school and second to the means by which the bar is to be effected." *Id.*

The rationale for this concern with the manner in which the regulation is carried out is that summarized in *Keyishian v. Board of Regents, supra,* 385 U.S. at 603-04, 87 S.Ct. at 683-684:

"We emphasize once again that '[p]recision of regulation must be the touchstone in an area so closely touching our most precious freedoms,' *N.A.A.C.P. v. Button,* 371 U.S. 415, 438, 83 S.Ct. 328, 340, 9 L.Ed.2d 405 ... 'Because First Amendment freedoms need breathing space to survive, government may regulate in the area only with narrow specificity.' *Id.* at 432, 433, 83 S.Ct., at 337-338.... When one must guess what conduct or utterance may lose him his position, one necessarily will 'steer far wider of the unlawful zone....' *Speiser v. Randall,* 357 U.S. 513, 526, 78 S.Ct. 1332, 1342, 2 L.Ed.2d 1460. For '[t]he threat of sanctions may deter ... almost as potently as the actual application of sanctions.' *N.A.A.C.P. v. Button, supra,* 371 U.S. at 433, 83 S.Ct. at 338. The danger of that chilling effect upon the exercise of vital First Amendment rights must be guarded against by sensitive tools which clearly inform ... what is being proscribed."

Whatever may be said in favor of the good intentions of the school officials in this case--and more will be said on that subject, *infra*--little may be said in support of their sensitivity or precision in dealing with the First Amendment issues in this case. On the substantive side, the criteria for removal suggested by the evidence suffer from excessive generality and overbreadth. Whatever definiteness there may be in a complaint that a book is "filthy," *Hamling v. United States,* 418 U.S. 87, 94 S.Ct. 2887, 41 L.Ed.2d 590 1974), there is certainly no precision, sufficient to provide the kind of reasonably clear guidance necessary for free and open debate, in the complaints that books are "anti-Christian" or "anti-American." *See Keyishian v. Board of Regents, supra,* 385 U.S. at 598-99, 87 S.Ct. at 681-682. The very nature of this broad brush approach must inevitably be to suggest that the school officials' concern is less to cleanse the libraries of all books containing material insulting to members of one or another religious group or which evidences an inaccurate view of the nation's history, than it is to express an official policy with regard to God and country of uncertain and indefinite content which is to be ignored by pupils, librarians and teachers at their peril.

However, quite apart from the articulated criteria for selection of the books for removal, precision of regulation and sensivity to First Amendment concerns are hardly established by the erratic, arbitrary and free-wheeling manner in which the defendant school officials proceeded in this case. The books were removed from school library shelves before any concerned school official had read them, solely on the basis of mimeographed quotations collected by anonymous readers whose editorial comments revealed political concerns reaching far beyond the education and well-being of the children of the Island Trees Union Free School District. Moreover, so far from seeking to insure that the "prejudices of the community" not infringe individual free speech and so far from recognizing "that the will of the transient majority can prove devastating to freedom of expression," *James v. Board of Education, supra,* 461 F.2d at 575, defendants conducted themselves, despite warnings by their school Superintendent, in a manner calculated to create public uproar. By drawing the "book issue" into the School Board election, a labor dispute, public meetings (at which "we are confident" that "most of the parents ... will back us to the hilt") and then into a district-wide plebiscite, they insured that the impression would be created that freedom of expression in the District would be determined in some substantial measure by the majority's will. Having proceeded in this fashion, defendants are hardly in a position to carry their burden of establishing that they have not, in pursuit of their functions, "unduly restricted protected speech to an extent greater than is essential" to the furtherance of the interests sought to be protected. *Eisner v. Stamford Board of Education, supra,* 440 F.2d at 806. On the contrary, the Board's erratic and free-wheeling procedures inevitably leave it a matter of guesswork for teachers, librarians and students in the District whether other efforts at self-expression on their part will be curtailed with equally little notice and equally little opportunity for defense, in the name of policies having equally little to do with the local concerns of the educational community, subject to the equally uncertain outcome of public debate. As this Court has said, the erratic, unfair and arbitrary administration of policy with regard to speech in schools is as much to be feared as the contents of the policy itself as a source of first amendment violations. *Eisner v. Stamford Board of Education, supra*, 440 F.2d at 809. We require greater "sensitivity to some of the teaching reflected in relevant constitutional doctrine and to the dangers lurking in improper and unconstitutional administration" than is demonstrated by the Board of Education in this case. *Id.* at 809-10. Not only must there be "narrow specificity" in the criteria applied, but there must be the use of "sensitive tools" in their application. *Keyishian v. Board of Regents, supra*, 385 U.S. at 603-04, 87 S.Ct. at 683-684.

Finally, even were defendants in a position to carry their burden of establishing that there was a substantial and material basis for their actions and that their actions were possessed of sufficient procedural regularity to give a better basis than guesswork as to how the Board of Education would act in the future with regard to similar issues, plaintiffs below should have, in all events, been offered an opportunity to persuade a finder of fact that the ostensible justifications for defendants' actions--be it indecency or ungrammatical usage, as one defendant suggested, or some other ground--were simply pretexts for the suppression of free speech. As was recognized in *Cohen v. California*, 403 U.S. 15, 26, 91 S.Ct. 1780, 1788, 29 L.Ed.2d 284 (1970), government may not "seize upon the censorship of particular words as a convenient guise for banning the expression of unpopular views." *See FCC v. Pacifica Foundation, supra*, 438 U.S. at 746, 98 S.Ct. at 3038.

Clearly, mere reference by a defendant to personal standards of taste or political philosophy as one factor in a decision involving first amendment values cannot, in and of itself, provide a basis for rationally inferring an intent to suppress the different views of others. Courts cannot prohibit and, indeed, should encourage, within limits, the thoughtful application of personal standards of taste and morality and of political belief in the performance of governmental functions. Where, however, as in this case, evidence that the decisions made were based on defendants' moral or political beliefs appears together with evidence of procedural and substantive irregularities sufficient to suggest an unwillingness on the part of school officials to subject their political and personal judgments to the same sort of scrutiny as that accorded other decisions relating to the education of their charges, an inference emerges that political views and personal taste are being asserted not in the interests of the children's well-being, but rather for the purpose of establishing those views as the correct and orthodox ones for all purposes in the particular community. What was said in *Village of Arlington Heights v. Metropolitan Housing Development Corporation*, 429 U.S. 252, 267, 97 S.Ct. 555, 564, 50 L.Ed.2d 450 (1977), applies here:

"The historical background of the decision is one evidentiary source.... The specific sequence of events leading up to the challenged decision also may shed some light on the decisionmakers' purposes.... Departures from the normal procedural sequence also might afford evidence that improper purposes are playing a role. Substantive departures too may be relevant, particularly if the factors usually considered important by the decisionmaker strongly favor a decision contrary to the one reached."

Among the procedural and other irregularities which warrant an inference that the welfare and education of the children of the Island Trees School District were not the true motivating concerns which led to the removal of the books from school libraries in that District are, in addition to those already mentioned: defendants' substantive confusion, not to say incoherence, as to the reasons the books were being removed from the libraries; the informal and dilatory manner in which the matter was pursued, including the lapse of three months from the time the presence of the offending books was discovered in the libraries until the principals of the schools were asked to take some action to prevent children from reading them, *cf. Thomas v. Board of Education, supra*, 607 F.2d at 1052 n.17 (delay of six days by school officials in acting on complaint); the *ex post facto* appointment of a committee to review the removal of the books, the determinations of which were then, without explanation, not followed by the Board; the strong opposition of professional personnel, including the District Superintendent, to the procedures used by the Board, *cf. Thomas v. Board of Education, supra*, 607 F.2d at 1051 (noting the origin of the complaint with the President of the Board of Education, rather than with school administrative officials); and, finally, the "substantive" irregularities, as *Arlington Heights* puts it, of removing works by such generally recognized authors as Swift, the late Richard Wright, and Bernard Malamud, whose book, *The Fixer*, was, indeed, an assigned high school reading text.

In summary, the writer concludes that plaintiffs made out a *prima facie* case of a first amendment violation and that defendants failed to carry their burden of establishing that the manner, if not the motive for their actions, did not violate the First Amendment.[13] In addition, the writer is of the view that, even had defendants' case in support of their actions been more compelling, plaintiffs were improperly deprived of an opportunity to persuade the finder of fact that the proffered justifications were mere pretext for an intentional violation of plaintiffs' rights. While neither the right of free expression nor the freewheeling style of the Board of Education in the Island Trees Union Free School District may seem, from all perspectives, of great significance, as Justice Jackson said with characteristic conciseness in the seminal case in this area, *West Virginia v. Barnette, supra*, 319 U.S. at 638, 63 S.Ct. at 1185 (1943):

"There are village tyrants as well as village Hampdens, but none who acts under color of law is beyond the reach of the Constitution."

Since the majority is of the view that defendants were not entitled to judgment below and that plaintiffs are entitled to proceed with the prosecution of their claims, we reverse and remand to the district court for trial.

MANSFIELD, Circuit Judge (dissenting):

I dissent. The majority unjustifiably overrules our sound decision in the indistinguishable case of *President's Council District 25 v. Community School Board No. 25*, 457 F.2d 289 (2d Cir.), *cert. denied*, 409 U.S. 998, 93 S.Ct. 308, 34 L.Ed.2d 260 (1972), wherein we held that removal by school authorities from a school library of a book containing vulgarities and indecent matter on the ground that the book was educationally inappropriate for school children did not infringe any First Amendment rights.

In my view the majority's action represents an unwarranted interference with the rational exercise by the Board of Education of the Island Trees Union Free School District (the Board) of its statutory duty to prescribe appropriate materials for the education of the children in the district. Despite undisputed evidence that all but one of the eight books discontinued by the Board in this case contained indecent matter, vulgarities, profanities, explicit sexual descriptions or allusions, sexual perversion, or disparaging remarks about Blacks, Jews or Christ, and despite the freedom of the school's faculty and students to discuss in or out of school the ideas contained in the discontinued books, the majority would find a violation of the First Amendment based on possible violation of some vague, undefined rights of expression or on possible suppression of ideas on the part of secondary school children attending the school. Absent some evidence that speech or ideas by anyone are likely to be suppressed I believe this court should keep its hands off. The effect of the majority's decision is improperly to substitute a court's view of what student curriculum is appropriate for that of the Board.

The majority takes some liberties with the record, substituting suspicions for undisputed evidence. In the first place the best evidence of whether the eight discontinued books are unsuitable for the education of secondary school children is the text of the books themselves rather than the conclusory editorial comments of third parties which Judge Sifton cites while studiously avoiding quotation of the actual text objected to by the Board as indecent and improper. Accordingly, adopting the Supreme Court's practice in similar cases, see e. g. *Federal Communications Commission v. Pacifica Foundation*, 438 U.S. 726, 98 S.Ct. 3026, 57 L.Ed.2d 1073 (1978), I have set forth in the margin those portions of the text of the books which led the Board to investigate their suit-

ability as educational tools and to discontinue eight of the books.[1] Despite Judge Sifton's conclusion that the excerpts leave "no great sense of confidence in the literary accuracy of the quotations," I find, upon reading the books, that except for minor errors the quotations are indeed accurate. I also note that some of the books contain additional indecent statements not found in the original excerpts.

The suggestion by Judge Sifton that the Board was engaged in "an unusual and irregular intervention" into the operation of the school's library by persons not "concerned with their contents" flies in the face of the uncontroverted facts and the Board's duties under New York law. Under N.Y. Education Law § 1709 a local school board such as the Board here has both the power and duty to prescribe the books to be used in its schools.[2] There is also no support for statements by Judge Sifton that the Board acted arbitrarily, impulsively, confusingly, incoherently, erratically, dilatorily or in a "free-swinging" manner. This was no bookburning or banning on the part of zealous intermeddlers. Nor was its action in disregard of the rights and views of others. On the contrary, the Board acted carefully, conscientiously and responsibly after according due process to all parties concerned.

The Board's first step was not to remove the books permanently, as the majority suggests, but to transfer them to the School's Residence Reference Room for review by the Board. The decision to do this was not made until February 26, 1976, after all members had seen the objectionable excerpts and some had read at least a few of the books. The actual transfer within the confines of the school occurred on March 3, 1976 after the President of the Board (Ahrens), implementing the Board's decision, requested the school's superintendent Richard G. Morrow to have the books taken "to the Board's office at the rear of the Residents Reference Room in Stokes *for review by the Board*," (emphasis supplied). In view of the excerpts (quoted in Footnote 1, supra), the impressions gained by members who had read some of the books in order to form their judgments (every one of the limited number of copies would obviously be needed for the purpose), the transfer of the books was eminently sensible. The Board's appointment of an eight-person advisory committee to read the books and make recommendations and the Board's later vote continuing two of the ten books as part of the curriculum demonstrate that the March 3rd action was far from final.

That the Board did not prejudge the educational suitability of the books is attested to by its decision not to take any action until it had the views of others, including a cross-section of the school staff and the community. On March 30, 1976, it held a public meeting at which its seven members voted unanimously to appoint an eight-person committee comprised of four members of the school staff and four parents to review and make recommendations regarding the educational suitability of the books and whether they were in good taste, appropriate for the age and grade level, and relevant.[3]   In early April it appointed the Committee. The four community members consisted of a recently graduated student attending college, a former PTA president, a former Board president and a mailman; the four staff members were an English teacher, a social studies teacher, a high school principal and an elementary school principal. The appointment of the Committee had been recommended and was approved by the School Superintendent, Richard G. Morrow.

During the weeks that followed the eight Committee members read all but one of the 10 books under consideration,[4] held a series of meetings, and on July 1, 1976, submitted its report to the Board. Its recommendations were as follows: (1) that *The Fixer* be "returned to the Modern Literature curriculum, subject to parental approval"; (2) that four others, *Laughing Boy*, *Black Boy*, *Go Ask Alice* and *Best Short Stories by Negro Writers*, be "retained" (i. e. kept in the library); (3) that two books, *The Naked Ape* and *Down These Mean Streets*, be "removed from the library" and (4) *Slaughterhouse Five* be "put on a restricted shelf." Except for three books on which the 8-person Committee's vote was unanimous, its votes were divided, ranging from 7-1 to 5-3. With respect to two books, *Soul on Ice* and *A Hero Ain't Nothing but a Sandwich*, the Committee could not agree, four voting in each case for retention and four for removal. The Committee was unable to make a recommendation with respect to the tenth book, *A Reader for Writers* because not all members had read it.

On July 28, 1976, the seven-person Board, having had a chance to review the books again in light of the Committee's recommendations, made its decision with respect to each of the 10 books under consideration. The Board decided: (1) unanimously to retain *Laughing Boy*, (2) by a 6-1 vote to retain *Black Boy* on a restricted basis, (3) by a unanimous vote to discontinue *Slaughterhouse Five*, *The Naked Ape*, *Down These Mean Streets*, *Soul on Ice*, *Best Short Stories by Negro Writers* and *A Reader for Writers*, from use in the School's curriculum, (4) by a 6-1 vote to remove *Go Ask Alice* from use in the curriculum, one member voting to retain it on a restricted basis, (5) by a 5-2 vote to remove *A Hero Ain't Nothing But a Sandwich* from use in the curriculum, 2 members (including Martin) voting to retain it on a restricted basis, (6) by a 5-3 vote to remove *The Fixer* from use in the curriculum, 2 members (including Martin) voting to retain it on a restricted basis and 1 member to retain it with no restrictions.

The retention of two of the ten books by the Board and its divided vote with respect to three is in my view wholly inconsistent with a claim that the Board acted erratically, arbitrarily, or in a "free-swinging style." Since the Board could not delegate its statutory duty and the Committee's recommendations were advisory only, the Board was entitled to differ from the Committee's recommendations, provided a rational basis existed for its doing so. Five members of the Board later attested to

such a basis when they swore,

"2. That we have read each of the books reviewed by the committee referred to in the affidavits of Mr. Martin and Mr. Ahrens.
3. That we each thoroughly considered the recommendations of such committee, the opinions of the superintendent of schools and of members of the community before casting our respective votes with respect to these books (Exhibit 'A-15').
4. That our reasons for casting votes to remove or restrict certain volumes were that they contained obscenities, were irrelevant to our curriculum, were inappropriate and were in bad taste. They contained foul language, gross sexual allusions and language that just wasn't necessary to the story line. Our votes were, however, split on certain works as a result of varying degrees of concern about the relevancy, educational applicability and degree of bad taste exhibited.
5. That we feel we represented the basic values of the community in our actions and that we have exercised our duties in an intelligent, thoughtful and reasonable manner."

Similar, more detailed affidavits and depositions were furnished by Richard Ahrens, President of the Board and Frank Martin, Vice-President (who, after reading the books, voted in favor of retention of some which other members voted to remove from the curriculum). Specific reasons have been given by each for his action with respect to each book. Martin voted to place on the restricted list books in which vulgarity appeared reasonably necessary to the story line but to remove those that indulged in vulgarity, deviant behavior and explicit sex scenes solely for their own sake. Mr. Ahrens objected to the degrading treatment of blacks and the vulgarity in *Soul on Ice*, the poor grammar in *A Hero Ain't Nothing But a Sandwich*, glorification of sex and drugs in *Go Ask Alice*, the explicitness of sex in *The Naked Ape*, which violated the Board's policy against teaching sex education, the vulgarities and anti-Semitism in *The Fixer* and the sadism of *Slaughterhouse Five*.

DISCUSSION

The general principles governing judicial intervention into secondary school education for the purpose of protecting First Amendment rights of students and teachers are fairly well settled. Students do not surrender all of their individual rights by submitting to the public educational process. Their speech and free exchange of ideas will be protected as long as they do not interfere with, obstruct or disrupt the functioning of the teaching system, including the choice of curriculum and methods prescribed by those vested with the duty of providing them with a formal education. For instance, a student may not be punished for refusing to salute the American flag, *West Virginia State Board of Education v. Barnette*,

319 U.S. 624, 63 S.Ct. 1178, 87 L.Ed. 1628 (1943), or wearing an armband in symbolic opposition to Viet Nam hostilities, *Tinker v. Des Moines Independent Community School District*, 393 U.S. 503, 89 S.Ct. 733, 21 L.Ed.2d 731 (1969). Nor may he be barred from off-campus printing and distribution of an indecent publication, *Thomas v. Board of Education*, 607 F.2d 1043 (2nd Cir. 1979). Similarly, an instructor may not be disciplined or barred from teaching because he symbolically expresses his personal political views by wearing a black armband in class, *James v. Board of Education*, 461 F.2d 566 (2nd Cir.), *cert. denied* 409 U.S. 1042, 93 S.Ct. 529, 34 L.Ed.2d 491 (1972), because he is labelled a "subversive," *Keyishian v. Board of Regents*, 385 U.S. 589, 87 S.Ct. 675, 17 L.Ed.2d 629 (1967), or because he or she refuses to salute the flag, *Russo v. Central School District No. 1*, 469 F.2d 623 (2nd Cir. 1972).

On the other hand, the process of public education, if it is to succeed, mandates that "school officials must have some latitude within the school in punishing and prohibiting ordinarily protected speech both out of regard for fellow students who constitute a captive audience, and in recognition of the fact that the school has a substantial educational interest in avoiding the impression that it has authorized a specific expression," *Thomas, supra*, 607 F.2d at 1049. "School authorities can regulate indecent language because its circulation on school grounds undermines their responsibility to try to promote standards of decency and civility among school children," *Id.* 1057 (Newman, J., concurring).

Public secondary school education can function effectively only if school boards are accorded rather broad discretionary authority to determine the subjects to be taught, the curriculum deemed most suitable, the methods of teaching to be employed, and the disciplines to be followed by teachers and students within the school, including the educational tools to be used, whether those tools be test tubes in the laboratory or books in the library. If each student were free to insist that the curriculum, including library books, be changed or augmented to suit his ideas or those of his parents, chaos would ensue. The result would be no different than if a student were permitted to speak out in class whenever he wished or to refrain from studying prescribed subjects that were unappealing to him. Such conduct does not fall within protected First Amendment rights. *Tinker, supra*, 607 F.2d at 1049.

For these reasons the Supreme Court emphasized in *Epperson v. Arkansas*, 393 U.S. 97, 104, 89 S.Ct. 266, 270, 21 L.Ed.2d 228 (1968) that

"Judicial interposition in the operation of the public school system of the Nation raises problems requiring care and restraint..... By and large, public education in our Nation is committed to the control of state and local authorities. Courts do not

and cannot intervene in the resolution of conflicts which arise in the daily operation of school systems and which do not directly and sharply implicate basic constitutional values."

As the Court had warned in in *Abington School Dist. v. Schempp*, 374 U.S. 203, 300-301, 83 S.Ct. 1560, 1612-1613, 10 L.Ed.2d 844 (1963) (Brennan, J., concurring):

"We should heed Mr. Justice Jackson's caveat that any attempt by this Court to announce curricular standards would be 'to decree a uniform, rigid and, if we are consistent, an unchanging standard for countless school boards representing and serving highly localized groups which not only differ from each other but which themselves from time to time change attitudes.'" *Illinois ex rel. McCollum v. Board of Education, supra*, [333 U.S. 203] at 237, 68 S.Ct. 461 at 477, 92 L.Ed. 649.

Recognizing the deference that must be paid to school authorities in such matters, the Court in *Epperson, supra*, established as a standard that we may not intervene in decisions of school systems unless they "*directly and sharply* implicate basic constitutional values," 393 U.S. at 104, 89 S.Ct. at 270 (emphasis supplied). This test clearly requires, as a condition precedent to judicial intervention, a showing that the school's action (1) violates the students' right of expression and (2) is not reasonably related or necessary to the performance by the school of its educational function. A school board's decision as to curriculum, moreover, may properly reflect local community views and values as to educational content and analysis, *James v. Board of Education*, 461 F.2d 566, 573 (2nd Cir.), *cert. denied*, 409 U.S. 1042, 93 S.Ct. 529, 34 L.Ed.2d 491 (1972):

"The interest of the state in promoting the efficient operation of its schools extends beyond merely securing an orderly classroom. Although the pros and cons of progressive education are debated heatedly, a principal function of all elementary and secondary education is indoctrinative—whether it be to teach the ABC's or multiplication tables or *to transmit the basic values of the community*. '[S]ome measure of public regulation is inherent in the very provision of public education.' Note, Developments in the Law—Academic Freedom, 81 Harv.L.Rev. 1045, 1053 (1968). Accordingly, courts consistently have affirmed that curriculum controls belong to the political process and local school authorities." (Emphasis supplied)

This inherent function of school administration was relied on by the Seventh Circuit in its recent opinion in *Zykan v. Warsaw Community School Corp.*, 631 F.2d 1300 (1980), which held that actions similar to those involved in this case (including the removal of *Go Ask Alice* from the library) simply did not rise to the level of constitutional violations. The court said, it is "permissible and appropriate for local boards to make educational decisions based upon their personal social, political and moral views." At 1305.

Recognizing these principles, this circuit upheld a school board's prohibition or regulation of the use on school property of expressions and subject matter that would be fully protected outside the school premises. In *President's Council, District 25 v. Community School Board*, No. 25, 457 F.2d 289 (2nd Cir.), *cert. denied*, 409 U.S. 998, 93 S.Ct. 308, 34 L.Ed.2d 260 (1972), for instance, we upheld the right of a community school board to remove from all junior high school libraries one of the books that was discontinued by the Board here, *Down These Mean Streets* by Piri Thomas.[5] In holding that the board's removal of the book did not impinge on any basic constitutional rights, we stated:

"Since we are dealing not with the collection of a public book store but with the library of a public junior high school, evidently some authorized person or body has to make a determination as to what the library collection will be. It is predictable that no matter what choice of books may be made by whatever segment of academe, some other person or group may well dissent. The ensuing shouts of book burning, witch hunting and violation of academic freedom hardly elevate this intramural strife to first amendment constitutional proportions. If it did, there would be a constant intrusion of the judiciary into the internal affairs of the school. Academic freedom is scarcely fostered by the intrusion of three or even nine federal jurists making curriculum or library choices for the community of scholars. When the court has intervened, the circumstances have been rare and extreme and the issues presented totally distinct from those we have here. See Developments in the Law--Academic Freedom, 81 Harv.L.Rev. 1045, 1051-54 (1968).... Here, patently we have no religious establishment or free exercise question, and neither do we have the banning of the teaching of any theory or doctrine. The problems of the youth in the ghetto, crime, drugs and violence have not been placed off limits by the Board. A book has been removed but the librarian has not been penalized, and the teacher is still free to discuss the Barrio and its problems in the classroom. ... The intrusion of the Board here upon any first amendment constitutional right of any category of plaintiffs is not only not 'sharp' or 'direct', it is minuscule." 457 F.2d at 292.

In *East Hartford Education Association et al. v. Board of Education*, 562 F.2d 838, 857 (2nd Cir. 1977) (en banc), we upheld a school board's right to enforce a dress code requirement for teachers, stating:

"Federal courts must refrain, in most instances, from interfering with the decision of school authorities. Even though decisions may appear foolish or unwise, a federal court may not overturn them unless the standard set forth in *Epperson* is met. The Supreme Court recently emphasized this point in *Wood v. Strickland*, 420 U.S. 308, 95 S.Ct. 992, 43 L.Ed.2d 214 (1975), in which a high school's summary disciplinary proceedings were challenged on due process grounds:

It is not the role of the federal courts to set aside decisions of schools administrators which the court may view as lacking a basis in wisdom or compassion. . . . The system of public education that has evolved in this Nation relies necessarily upon the discretion and judgment of school administrators and school board members, and § 1983 was not intended to be a vehicle for federal-court corrections of errors in the exercise of that discretion which do not rise to the level of violations of specific constitutional guarantees."

Id. 420 U.S. at 326, 95 S.Ct. at 1003 (citations omitted).

Similarly in *Eisner v. Stamford Board of Education*, 440 F.2d 803 (2nd Cir. 1971) we recognized that school authorities may adopt a policy prohibiting distribution of literature on school property without prior permission from the school administration and in *Trachtman v. Anker*, 563 F.2d 512 (2nd Cir. 1977), *cert. denied*, 435 U.S. 925, 98 S.Ct. 1491, 55 L.Ed.2d 519 (1978) we upheld school officials' refusal to allow distribution within the school of a sexually explicit questionnaire prepared by a student group.

Prohibiting exposure of children to indecent language has been upheld by the Supreme Court not only on school premises but in other locations as well, even where the unique demands of the educational process did not play a part. In *Ginsberg v. New York*, 390 U.S. 629, 88 S.Ct. 1274, 20 L.Ed.2d 195 (1968), for instance, the Court held that the State of New York could constitutionally prohibit the sale to minors under 17 years of sex magazines that would not be obscene for adults, based on the state's interest in protecting the children's welfare and safeguarding them from abuses. And in *Federal Communications Commission v. Pacifica Foundation*, 438 U.S. 726, 98 S.Ct. 3026, 57 L.Ed.2d 1073 (1978), the Court upheld the FCC's authority to impose administrative sanctions on broadcasting of indecent language. In his plurality opinion Justice Stevens based the decision not only on the ground that the ideas expressed in indecent language could have been conveyed by less offensive language but also on the ground that the government had a proper interest in protecting minors from exposure to indecencies. 438 U.S. at 749-50, 98 S.Ct. at 3040, 3041. As we said in *Thomas*, *supra*, 607 F.2d at 1057 (Newman, J., concurring),

"When, as in this case, the audience at which a publication is specifically directed consists solely of high school students, and distribution is demanded at a school building attended by students down to the age of 11, First Amendment protection is not available for language that is indisputably indecent. If the F.C.C. can act to keep indecent language off the afternoon airwaves, a school can act to keep indecent language from circulating on high school grounds."

Application of the foregoing principles mandates an affirmance of the Board's action in the present case. Whatever may be a judge's personal view as to the wisdom of its decision, the Board acted on rational and specific grounds relevant to the education and welfare of the school children within its jurisdiction, and it did so fairly and conscientiously. It discontinued the handful of books because all but one contain either vulgar and indecent language, profanities, explicit sex, sexual perversion, poor grammar, glorification of sex and drugs, or anti-Jewish, anti-Black, or anti-Christian remarks.[6] In the Board's view the books lacked sufficient redeeming value to outweigh the threatened harm from the objectionable portions.

The Board's action does not hinder or destroy anybody's rights of free expression. The Board did not seek to inculcate students with any particular social or political views (e.g., legalized abortion or anti-abortion, adherence to the views of any political party or religion, promotion of the Equal Rights Amendment or the like). No free exchange of ideas was suppressed. No one was imposing views, whether labelled "orthodox" or otherwise, on anybody else. No one has been or will be disciplined as a result of the removal of the books. Nor will anyone be denied an education in line with basic community values.[7] Both parties agree that teachers and students are free to discuss and comment on the themes and ideas of the books in class or on school premises.[8] Students may also be able to purchase the books outside of school or borrow them from a public library. In short there are no First Amendment or other constitutional interests at stake, because, as the Seventh Circuit said in *Zykan*:

"the rule [is] that complaints filed by secondary school students to contest the educational decisions of local authorities are sometimes cognizable but generally must cross a relatively high threshold before entering upon the field of a constitutional claim suitable for federal court litigation. Such a balance of legal interests means that panels such as the Warsaw School Board will be permitted to make even ill advised and imprudent decisions without the risk of judicial interference. Nothing in these principles suggests that the courts should condone short-sighted board decision-making. But nothing in the Constitution permits the courts to interfere with local educational discretion until local author-

ities begin to substitute rigid and exclusive indoctrination for mere exercise of their prerogative to make pedagogic choices regarding matters of legitimate dispute." At 1306.

Here we do not find any effort by school authorities to suppress speech or ideas on the part of teachers or pupils or to force them to "speak" against their will, such as existed in *Tinker*, *Epperson*, *West Virginia State Board of Education*, *Keyishian*, *James*, *Thomas* and *Eisner*, *supra*, or any ban on teaching or expressing certain views essential to a basic education, such as occurred in *Epperson*, *supra* (theory of evolution) and *Meyer v. Nebraska*, 262 U.S. 390, 43 S.Ct. 625, 67 L.Ed. 1042 (1922) (statute prohibiting teaching of any foreign language to grades lower than the eighth). The handful of books discontinued by the Board leaves on the school's shelves hundreds of volumes for the students' edification and learning. The action therefore does not create any "pall of orthodoxy" or impermissible indoctrination such as might exist if exchange of ideas between teachers and pupils were prohibited. The ideas expressed in the removed books may also be freely discussed, in or out of the classroom, without using the profanities, vulgarities, and indecencies objected to by the Board. As Justice Stevens stated in *FCC v. Pacifica Foundation supra*, 438 U.S. at 743, n.18, 98 S.Ct. at 3037: "A requirement that indecent language be avoided will have its primary effect on the form, rather than the content, of serious communication. There are few, if any, thoughts that cannot be expressed by the use of less offensive language."

For these reasons, I find no constitutional infringement of individual rights of anyone in the removal of a handful of books containing indecent expressions. As Judge Mulligan pointed out in *President's Council*, *supra*, 457 F.2d 293:

"There is here no problem of freedom of speech or the expression of opinions on the part of parents, teachers, students or librarians. As we have pointed out, the discussion of the book or the problems which it encompasses or the ideas it espouses have not been prohibited by the Board's action in removing the book."

The same may be said of the present case. There is no legally significant distinction between this case and *President's Council*, *supra*, where we held that the removal from the school library by school authorities of a book containing vulgar language and explicit sexual allusions did not sharply and directly infringe upon freedom of speech and thought within the meaning of *Epperson*. That holding represents the law of this Circuit, by which we are bound. The suggestion that *President's Council* may be distinguished on the ground that in the present case eight of the school's hundreds of books were withdrawn (2 of the original 10 were continued) instead of the one in that case is unpersuasive, absent some evidence of inhibition of free expression within the school, of which there is none. Even assuming a First Amendment interest in gaining general access to the information in instructional material, the loss here is *de minimis*.

Nor has *President's Council* been weakened in any way by the Supreme Court's later decision in *Virginia State Board of Pharmacy v. Virginia Citizens Consumer Council, Inc.*, 425 U.S. 748, 96 S.Ct. 1817, 48 L.Ed.2d 346 (1976), which upheld the right to receive information as the "reciprocal right of the speaker." Here no speaker exists claiming a constitutional right to address the students with respect to the text of the removed books unless it is the teachers, who are not prevented from speaking on the subject matter. The publishers and authors of the books do not claim any constitutional right mandating use of their books in the school. The only persons having the right to choose the books are the members of the Board, who have made their decision on rational grounds. Since under *Virginia State Board* the right of students to receive information is no greater than that of the speaker to furnish it, the decision has no application to facts of this case.

The reasons advanced by Judges Sifton and Newman for not following *President's Council* are curious, vague and unsupported by the record. At one point Judge Sifton states (p. 414) that the Board's discontinuance of the eight books was impermissible as "an unusual and irregular intervention in the school libraries' operations by persons not routinely concerned with their contents." The simple answer is that § 1709 of the New York Education Law expressly imposes a duty on the Board to be concerned with the books to be used by school children within its jurisdiction,--indeed, to prescribe those books. At another point (p. 414) he suggests that the Board's action was ambiguous, overbroad, or indefinite, and that a board may not act without an adequate definition of the "scope" of its action. But here the action was specific, being limited to 8 books, and the scope of and reasons for the action have been clearly explained. The Board acted because of the patently indecent matter in almost all of the books, quoted above in Footnote 1. It is difficult to conceive of a more specific description of the scope and basis of the action at issue. At still another point (p. 415) it is suggested that the book removal was improperly motivated, expressing "an official policy with regard to God and country of uncertain and indefinite content," whatever this means. But the undisputed evidence of the motivation for the Board's action was the perfectly permissible ground that the books were indecent, in bad taste, and unsuitable for educational purposes. If by "official policy" Judge Sifton means an expression of

community values, we have recognized this as a valid ground for action by school authorities. *James v. Board of Education, supra*, 461 F.2d at 573; see also, *Zykan, supra*, 631 F.2d at 1305.

In an apparent shift of tactics Judge Sifton next concedes (p. 416) that "[c]ourts cannot prohibit and, indeed, should encourage, within limits, the thoughtful application [by school authorities] of personal standards of taste and morality and of political belief in the performance of governmental functions" but that the action here must nevertheless be condemned because of procedural irregularity, stating that the Board acted in an "erratic, arbitrary and free-wheeling manner" which lacked "precision of regulation" (p. 415). The record here is wholly to the contrary. From the outset the Board made clear that its investigation into the educational suitability of the books was prompted by the excerpts of indecent matter quoted in Footnote 1. The initial transfer of the books from the school library to the Board Room was solely for the purpose of review to determine whether the books should be discontinued.

Nor do I find support in the record for Judge Sifton's statements that there was "confusion" and "incoherence" on the part of the Board as to the reasons the books were being removed, that the matter was pursued by the Board in an "informal or dilatory manner," that there was an "*ex post facto* appointment of a review committee", that there was "strong opposition of professional personnel, including the District Superintendent", and that some of the books were appropriate for educational purposes because they were written by recognized authors". The reasons for discontinuance of the books have been clearly stated by the Board members and are supported by the text of the books themselves. There was nothing dilatory, informal or unfair about the procedure adopted for determining whether the books should be discontinued. The initial removal on March 3, 1976, was solely for the purpose of enabling the Board to read and review the books, and did not represent a discontinuance of them as part of the curriculum. The period required to enable the 7-person Board and the 8-person Committee to read the few available copies and for the Board to reach a final decision with respect to the educational suitability of the books was reasonable. There is no evidence that during this period any faculty or students needed the books for educational purposes. Indeed, for at least a month and a half of the period New York public schools were not in session.

Nor was the appointment of the Committee "*ex post facto*." Although some Board members, after reading some of the books, had expressed the view that the books were inappropriate, the Board did not make a final decision until July 28, 1976, at which time it demonstrated its open-mindedness by deciding that two volumes, *Laughing Boy* and *Black Boy*, should be retained as part of the curriculum and at least three Board members, including

Vice-President Martin, changed their initially
expressed views as to others. There was nothing irrational about the Board's refusal to accept some of the Committee's recommendations.
The procedure by which the Board reached its
decisions was eminently fair, final action
being taken only after much debate, public
meetings, and receipt of a report from the
specially-appointed Committee. Lastly, although we may differ as to the merits of the
Board's action, its rationality is manifest,
being based on the text and contents of the
books themselves, which the majority studiously
avoids discussing. There was thus no impropri-
ety in the procedures used by the Board to
reach its decision.

For several reasons I cannot agree with
Judge Newman's view that the case should be remanded for a trial to determine whether the
Board's action was a "politically motivated effort to suppress ideas". In the first place,
the term "politically motivated" is amorphous.
If this phrase means a desire to implement the
Board's conservative philosophy with respect to
educational policies in the choice of books for
the school's library, there is nothing constitutionally impermissible about the Board's
adopting such a view, which apparently accords
with the views of the community of the Island
Trees Union Free School District. *Zykan*,
supra, 631 F.2d at 1305. Those who disagree
may avail themselves of democratic election
processes, which they apparently have done
without success. The evidence, moreover, is
clear that the injection of the "book issue"
into the election of Board members and teacher
labor disputes was not initiated by the Board
but by the media and persons who disagreed with
the Board's policy. For a federal court to in-
ject itself into this type of local imbroglio
is in my view unwise.

The important fact is not whether the
Board's decision was "politically" motivated,
whatever that means, but whether the discontinuance of the eight books threatens to suppress
any discussion of ideas by students or teachers. On this issue the evidence is overwhelming, if not conclusive, that no ideas are being
suppressed. Removal of a few books and denial
of self-expression by a student body are separate concepts. Both sides agree that students
and teachers remain free to discuss the ideas
in the books.

Even if the Board's motivation were a factor, and I doubt whether it plays any material
role in this case, the quoted texts from the
books, the Board's contemporaneous expressions,
and the later affidavits of its members, none
of which were refuted as required by Rule
56(e), F.R.Civ.P.,[9] demonstrate beyond cavil
that the Board acted on rational grounds and
not with the purpose of suppressing any ideas.

Appellants' reliance on *Minarcini v.
Strongsville City School District*, 541 F.2d
577 (6th Cir. 1976), which refused to follow
President's Council, is misplaced. To the
extent that *Minarcini* relied on the inter-
vening Supreme Court decision in *Virginia
State Board of Pharmacy*, *supra*, I have noted

that since the publishers and authors of the
removed books have and can claim no constitutional right to maintenance of their books in
the School library, no reciprocal *Virginia
State Board* right on the part of students to
receive the books exists and that decision does
not apply here. Moreover, the *Minarcini*
court's reasoning that, although a school board
may lawfully refuse to *acquire* a book for a
school library it may not *remove* a book once
acquired, is logically flawed. If a school
board has the right to select a book to be
placed on the school library shelves, and
neither of my brothers question that right, it
has an equal right to remove them. As Judge
Mulligan aptly stated in *President's Council*,
"the concept of a book acquiring tenure by
shelving is indeed novel and unsupportable under any theory of constitutional law we can
discover," 457 F.2d at 293. Accord, *Zykan*,
supra, 631 F.2d at 1308. A school board may
remove a book upon rationally concluding that
it made a mistake in acquiring the book in the
first place.

In short, the First Amendment entitles students to reasonable freedom of expression but
not to freedom from what some may consider to
be excessively moralistic or conservative selection by school authorities of library books
to be used as educational tools. A secondary
school authority's regulatory function includes
the power to refuse to continue in the school's
library collection books that are rationally
found unsuitable for educational purpose. This
action does not violate any First Amendment
rights of the student body. I would therefore
affirm Judge Pratt's decision.

NEWMAN, Circuit Judge, concurring in the result:

The use of governmental power to condemn a
book touches the central nervous system of the
First Amendment. The core value of the First
Amendment is the free expression of ideas.
Books communicate ideas, more permanently and
often more persuasively than any other form of
expression. Perhaps no single event has more
evocative power to signal the suppression of
free speech than the burning of a book. If
this case involved governmental prohibition of
a book because of its political content, there
is no doubt the panel would be unanimous in
finding a First Amendment violation. But the
case is not so simple. It involves books, and
governmental power is alleged to have been motivated at least in part by the political content of the books. But the governmental action
is not prohibition, it is removal from one lo-
cation--a school library. And the action is
sought to be justified by the acknowledged power of school authorities to make decisions concerning the education of children. Not surprisingly, a case of this sort elicits differing judicial responses. Judge Sifton would decide the case in favor of the plaintiffs.
Judge Mansfield would decide the case in favor
of the defendants. In my view the case pre-

sents a sufficient claim of constitutional violation, but requires a trial to determine whether the claim is supported by the facts.

Applying First Amendment principles in the context of public schools is a subtle and complex endeavor. Neither "students [n]or teachers shed their constitutional rights to freedom of speech or expression at the schoolhouse gate," *Tinker v. Des Moines Independent School District*, 393 U.S. 503, 506, 89 S.Ct. 733, 736, 21 L.Ed.2d 731 (1969), but it is equally clear that the school context profoundly affects the nature of their rights. It must be recognized that schools are specialized environments devoted to the inculcation of both knowledge and social values in children, that our society has made a political decision to grant its public school authorities considerable discretion in determining how that educational process is to occur, and that such a process, by its very nature, involves informal, day-to-day relationships that are normally inappropriate for legal supervision. It is not a First Amendment violation every time a teacher tells a student not to speak, nor does a school administrator violate the First Amendment every time he includes one subject in the educational curriculum and excludes another. The school library is also subject to broad control by school authorities; as a general matter, they may decide how the library should be administered, which books should be acquired, and which books should be removed.

The plenary power of school officials transgresses First Amendment limits, however, when their actions tend to suppress ideas. It is one thing to teach, to urge the correctness of a point of view.[1] But it is quite another to take any action that condemns an idea, that places it beyond the pale of free discussion and scrutiny. Teaching implies that the strengths and weaknesses of ideas will be closely examined. Some will be favored, others criticized. This is the academic freedom that has its own strong claim to First Amendment protection. See *Epperson v. Arkansas*, 393 U.S. 97, 116, 89 S.Ct. 266, 276, 21 L.Ed.2d 228 (1968) (Stewart, J., concurring); *Wilson v. Chancellor*, 418 F.Supp. 1358 (D. Or. 1976); *Parducci v. Rutland*, 316 F.Supp. 352 (M.D. Ala. 1970); cf. *Sweezy v. New Hampshire*, 354 U.S. 234, 77 S.Ct. 1203, 1 L.Ed.2d 1311 (1975) (university level). But the First Amendment does not permit the freedom of the teacher to become an instrument for suppression of the thoughts of the students. Nor may any school official take action that tends to suppress ideas within the school community. Teachers and students alike have a right to freedom from "a pall of orthodoxy." *Keyishian v. Board of Regents*, 385 U.S. 589, 603, 87 S.Ct 675, 683, 17 L.Ed.2d 629 (1967); see *Cary v. Board of Education*, 427 F.Supp. 945, 956 (D. Colo. 1977).

The suppression of ideas against which the First Amendment protects need not be manifested by action taken directly against a student, see *Tinker v. Des Moines Independent School District*, supra, or a teacher, *Keyishian v.*

Board of Regents supra; *Sweezy v. New Hampshire*, supra. Prohibiting expression of views is obviously the most obnoxious violation of the First Amendment, and regulation that only restricts free expression merits the most careful scrutiny. In an open society like our own, acts of disapproval by public authorities, unaccompanied by any imposed or threatened sanctions, will generally not create sufficient risk of suppressing ideas to warrant judicial intervention. Consequently, claims of this sort have rarely been raised.[2] In the school setting, however, where a group of relatively "impressionable children," *James v. Board of Education*, supra, are compelled to attend and pay attention, official action carries an undue risk of suppressing ideas. Those in a school community have a right to be free not only from prohibition and unwarranted regulation of expression. They have a right to be free from official conduct that tends to suppress ideas--conduct conveying the message that some idea or viewpoint is not merely unsound, but is not acceptable to be aired within the school community.[3] First Amendment values are not only precious; they are fragile. In the context of this case they are easily threatened by inhibiting action that stops short of prohibition or restrictive regulation.[4]

Of course actions of school officials tending to suppress ideas must be sufficiently specific and serious to trigger First Amendment inquiry. Cf. *Aebisher v. Ryan*, 622 F.2d 651 (2d Cir. 1980). To regard every disapproving comment as a potential First Amendment violation would unduly intrude upon the prerogatives of the school authorities. A different situation is presented, however, when school authorities take clearly defined and carefully planned action to condemn an idea, especially when such action is taken with respect to an entire school or school district. The implication of such action is unmistakable, and its inhibiting effect is likely to be significant.

The removal of a book from a school library will often be the sort of clearly-defined, school-wide action that carries with it the potential for impermissible suppression of ideas. It is possible, of course, for removal to be a casual, insignificant decision, as when the school librarian replaces an obsolete book, or discards a rarely-used one to make shelf space available for other volumes. But the deliberate decision, taken by leading school officials, that a book is to be removed from the school library because of its ideas can hardly be placed in the same category. Actions such as these can too easily lead to suppression. They signal to the students and the teachers an official message that the ideas presented in those books are unacceptable, are wrong, and should not be discussed or considered. The chilling effect of this message on those who would express the idea is all too apparent.

The symbolic effect of a school's action in removing a book solely because of its ideas will often be more significant than the resulting limitation upon access to it. The fact that the book barred from the school library may be available elsewhere is not decisive. What is significant is that the school has used its public power to perform an act clearly indicating that the views represented by the forbidden book are unacceptable. The impact of burning a book does not depend on whether every copy is on the fire. Removing a book from a school library is a less offensive act, but it can also pose a substantial threat of suppression.[5]

The risk that removing a book from a library will communicate suppression of an idea is markedly increased when the decision to remove is politically motivated. While the mere act of singling out a certain type of speech for disapproval will often be sufficient to render the state's action impermissible, this is not necessarily true in the context of schools. The latitude properly accorded to teaching must tolerate some expressions of disapproval, not only of inappropriate conduct but even of disfavored ideas. But when the disapproval is political in nature--when exclusion of particular views is motivated by authorities' opinion about the proper way to organize and run society in general--then it verges into impermissible suppression.

There may be motivations other than political that increase the risk that removing books will be perceived as condemning unacceptable views and thereby risk suppression of those views. But political thought is a particularly important and sensitive area. Our society depends for its choice of leaders and its basic policy decisions on the independent thinking of its citizens, and on the vitality of the marketplace of ideas, see *Abrams v. United States*, 250 U.S. 616, 630, 40 S.Ct. 17, 22, 63 L.Ed. 1173 (Holmes, J., dissenting). As the Supreme Court has stated, "speech concerning public affairs is more than self-expression; it is the essence of self-government." *Garrison v. Louisiana*, 379 U.S. 64, 74-75, 85 S.Ct. 209, 215-216, 13 L.Ed.2d 125 (1964). Education plays a significant role in preparing students for these responsibilities of citizenship. See *Wisconsin v. Yoder*, 406 U.S. 205, 221, 92 S.Ct. 1526, 1536, 32 L.Ed.2d 15 (1972); *Wieman v. Updegraff*, 344 U.S. 183, 194, 73 S.Ct. 215, 220, 97 L.Ed. 216 (1952) (Frankfurter, J., concurring). When schools are used to suppress independent thinking, rather than to encourage it, they threaten the very process they are designed to foster. Moreover, politics is an area where feelings naturally run high, and the temptation for state officials to impose their views on those within their power is too often present. Special vigilance is needed to ensure that schools are not used in this manner.

Prior to this case and *Bicknell v. Vergennes Union High School Board of Directors*, 638 F.2d 438 (2d Cir. 1980), also decided this day, at least five federal courts have considered First Amendment challenges to the removal of books from school libraries. Three of these courts have concluded that the challenged removal was unconstitutional. *Minarcini v. Strongsville City School District*, 541 F.2d 577 (6th Cir. 1976); *Salvail v. Nashua Board of Education*, 469 F.Supp. 1269 (D.N.H.1979); *Right to Read Defense Committee v. School Committee*, 454 F.Supp. 703 (D.Mass. 1978). A fourth case, decided by this Court, held that the challenged book removal did not violate the First Amendment. *Presidents Council, District 25 v. Community School Board No. 25*, 457 F.2d 289 (2d Cir.), cert. denied, 409 U.S. 998, 93 S.Ct. 308, 34 L.Ed.2d 260 (1972). *Presidents Council* characterized the infringement of First Amendment rights as "minuscule" on the basis of the facts of that case. *Id.* at 292. A single book had been removed because of its "obscenities and explicit sexual interludes," *id.* at 291, and no political motivation for that removal was alleged or proven. *Presidents Council* did not hold that the removal of books would not constitute a First Amendment violation if that action had the effect of discouraging or suppressing particular political ideas. In fact, the Court explicitly noted that the case involved "no showing of a curtailment of freedom of speech or thought." *Id.* at 293. The fifth case, recently decided by the Seventh Circuit, also found no constitutional violation on the facts as pleaded, but remanded the case to afford the plaintiffs an opportunity to amend their complaint to allege that the book removal was part of an effort to remove volumes conflicting with the school board's "orthodoxy." *Zykan v. Warsaw Community School Corp.*, 631 F.2d 1300, 1308 (7th Cir. 1980). Judge Swygert concurred in the result, concluding that the complaint was already sufficient to require trial on the claim that the book removal burdened free expression because several of the books dealt with the topic of feminism. *Id.* at 1309.

Presidents Council establishes that the act of removing a book from a school library does not, by itself, violate constitutional rights. As the Court said, the "concept of a book acquiring tenure by shelving is indeed novel and unsupportable under any theory of constitutional law we can discover." *Ibid.* The right at issue is not that of the book; it is the right of the students and other members of the school community. Their rights are impaired when books are the focal point of official action designed to suppress the ideas that the books contain. In some circumstances even the action of not acquiring a book could inhibit free expression within the school, but normally removal of a book will more likely risk an impermissibly inhibiting effect. To refuse to acquire a book merely makes that book one of innumerable others that have not been acquired, unless, because of extraordinary attention already drawn to that book, it has been specifically barred from acquisition. On the other hand, removal singles out that book for disapproval. In addition, removal, more than failure to acquire, is likely to suggest that an impermissible political motivation may be present. There are many reasons why a book is not acquired, the most obvious being limited resources, but there are few legitimate reasons why a book, once acquired, should be removed from a library not filled to capacity. Thus book removal has an evidentiary significance for determining whether the action of school authorities has created a sufficient risk of suppressing ideas to establish a First Amendment violation.

On this view of First Amendment principles, I conclude that the judgment of the District Court granting summary judgment for the defendants must be reversed, and the matter remanded for fact-finding. The allegations of the plaintiffs, fully presented in Judge Sifton's opinion, are clearly adequate, if proved, to sustain the conclusion that the school has violated the First Amendment. It is conceded that nine books were removed from the Island Trees High School and Junior High School libraries. There is no claim that shelf space was scarce or that these books contained obsolete or disproven statements of fact. These books were singled out for disapproval. There is also no question that the removal was a positive, clearly-defined act by school authorities. By the time the books were removed, the action had become a major policy decision, and there could be little doubt in the minds of the Island Trees students about the message that the school authorities intended to communicate.

Plaintiffs rely on numerous uncontested facts to contend that the removal was designed to suppress ideas. They point to the fact that three members of the School Board, Ahrens, Martin, and Hughes, became concerned about the book issue when attending a conference sponsored by an issue-oriented education group known as PONY-U.[6] The book list distributed at this conference identifies the objectionable nature of many of the books by a number of comments on the ideas or viewpoints of the books. *A Reader for Writers*, for example, is marked for condemnation because it "equates Malcolm X, considered by many to be a traitor to this country, with the founding fathers of our country." *Soul on Ice* is described as "full of anti-American material and hate for white women." Moreover, several of the comments in the newsletter distributed by the Board and in the affidavits and depositions of Board members also indicate concern with what are portrayed as objectionable ideas.[7]

The defendants dispute any politically motivated effort to suppress ideas, contending that the books were removed because of vulgar language and explicit sexual descriptions, matters on which school authorities have considerable latitude. See *Thomas v. Board of Education*, 607 F.2d 1043, 1053 (2d Cir. 1979) (Newman, J., concurring); *Frison v. Franklin County Board of Education*, 596 F.2d 1192 (4th Cir. 1979); *Brubaker v. Board of Education*, 502 F.2d 973 (7th Cir. 1974), *cert denied*, 421 U.S. 965, 95 S.Ct. 1953, 44 L.Ed.2d 451 (1975). If at trial the defendants offer to justify the removal on this ground, the trial court must be satisfied that the school's policing of language has not exceeded even the generous First Amendment limits appropriate in the context of young students. Moreover, the bona fides of a

school's claim of concern with vulgarity or sexual explicitness may be refuted by evidence that other books with similar passages were not removed. A school's effort to regulate vulgarity is not unconstitutional because it is not completely thorough, but if only isolated examples are condemned, the inference will be strengthened that vulgarity was the excuse, not the reason, for book removal whose principal, or at least partial motivation was political.

Judge Mansfield, in dissent, is confident that the Board removed the books solely in the exercise of its acknowledged power to regulate vulgar and sexually explicit materials. In the absence of a trial, I am unable from this vantage point to perform similar fact-finding as to the true motives of the Board members. However, I am satisfied that the Board members' self-professed motives, as set forth in their affidavits, should not be accepted without a trial, especially in light of the evidence the plaintiffs have offered to submit to show that the Board members' motivation was significantly political. Indeed one basis for doubting that their motivation was solely concerned with the vulgarity and sexual explicitness is set forth in the dissenting opinion. The books were removed, the dissent observes, because they contain "*either* vulgar and indecent language, profanities, explicit sex, sexual perversion, poor grammar, glorification of sex and drugs, *or* anti-Jewish, anti-Black, or anti-Christian remarks." *Infra*, p. 6063 (emphasis added). And, as Judge Mansfield acknowledges, the removal of *A Reader for Writers* cannot even be claimed to be attributed to any of these rather varied motives. That book, according to the dissent, was removed because of the book's bad taste in including Jonathan Swift's "A Modest Proposal," the classic satire suggesting that overpopulation and hunger among the Irish should be solved by eating 100,000 Irish children. Surely a fact issue concerning motive is created when the plaintiffs offer to prove (and defendants do not deny) that this book was originally marked for removal because the PONY-U organization objected to the book's inclusion of a different selection, the one containing laudatory comments about Malcolm X.[8]

The possibility of mixed motivation—permissible concern with vulgarity or sexual explicitness and impermissible concern with political content—could call into question the relevance of the Supreme Court's decision in *Mt. Healthy City School District Board of Education v. Doyle*, 429 U.S. 274, 97 S.Ct. 568, 50 L.Ed.2d 471 (1977). *Mt. Healthy* held that an untenured teacher may be dismissed for a legitimate reason related to teaching performance, even if an impermissible reason, expression of protected speech, also entered into the decision to dismiss. This might suggest that a school's permissible reason for removal of books would suffice, even though an impermissible reason also motivated the decision. However, in many contexts the existence of an impermissible motivation renders the challenged action unlawful, even if that motivation is not exclusive. See, *e.g.*, *Robinson v. 12 Lofts*

Realty, Inc., 610 F.2d 1032, 1042 (2d Cir. 1979) (racial discrimination); *Williams v. Matthews Co.*, 499 F.2d 819, 826 (8th Cir. 1974) (same); *NLRB v. J. P. Stevens & Co.*, 563 F.2d 8, 20 (2d Cir. 1977), *cert. denied*, 434 U.S. 1064, 98 S.Ct. 1240, 55 L.Ed.2d 765 (1978) (union harassment); *NLRB v. Jamestown Sterling Corp.*, 211 F.2d 725 (2d Cir. 1954) (same).

The *Mt. Healthy* exception to the more traditional response to mixed motivation should not apply to a school's decision to remove library books. The *Mt. Healthy* rule was designed to avoid placing the teacher "in a better position as a result of the exercise of constitutionally protected conduct than he would have occupied had he done nothing." 429 U.S. at 285, 97 S.Ct. at 575. That reasoning has no application to the removal of a book, which neither exercises a protected right nor can be viewed as gaining by "doing nothing." Moreover, assessing even the alleged permissible motivation for removing a book always involves some consideration of First Amendment protection, for it is that Amendment that determines how far school authorities may go in maintaining standards of decency in expression. See *Thomas v. Board of Education*, *supra*, 607 F.2d at 1057-58. By contrast, the sufficiency of permissible grounds for dismissing an untenured teacher may, in many instances, be assessed without any consideration of First Amendment protection. Finally, the content of a book and its manner of expression are too intimately related to be subjected to entirely separate analysis. The untenured teacher's misconduct in the classroom can be analyzed entirely separately from his out-of-school protected expression. But ideas and the language used to express them always are related. See *Cohen v. California*, 403 U.S. 15, 26, 91 S.Ct. 1780, 1788, 29 L.Ed.2d 284 (1971). Because of that relationship First Amendment values would be imperiled if a motivation concerned with the language of a book were permitted to justify an act of suppression also motivated by the book's political content.

In this case plaintiffs have alleged that the removal of books from the Island Trees School library was motivated in part by the School Board's objection to the political views expressed in those books. The complaint further alleges that this politically motivated action was taken under circumstances that pose a threat to the free expression and exchange of ideas within the school community that is protected by the First Amendment. In opposing the defendants' motion for summary judgment, the plaintiffs have submitted substantial evidence to support their claim. A trial is required to determine precisely what happened, why it happened, and whether, in the circumstances of this case, the School Board's actions, looking forward from the time they were taken,[9] created a sufficient risk of suppressing ideas to constitute a violation of the First Amendment.

JUDGE NEWMAN'S OPINION NOTES

1. This Court has even acknowledged that "a principal function of all elementary and secondary education is indoctrinative." *James v. Board of Education*, 461 F.2d 566 (2d Cir. 1972). It is clear from the context of this statement that it was simply intended to describe the school's role in transmitting values. As the Court said, "The interest of the state in promoting the efficient operation of its schools extends beyond merely securing an orderly classroom...Accordingly, courts consistently have affirmed that curriculum controls belong to the political process and local school authorities." *Ibid*. *James* pointedly condemns "indoctrination" in the sense of endeavoring to insist that one set of values must be accepted by the students. *Ibid*. There is no suggestion in *James*, or in any other federal case, that the power of school officials extends beyond curriculum control to the suppression of ideas.

2. Another reason why such indirect claims have not been frequently raised is that most actions infringing on free speech are taken against the speaker himself, who generally makes a direct claim that his First Amendment rights are violated. In situations like the present case, however, where an isolated book removal limits the free expression of the author so slightly that he makes no claim on his own behalf, the impact of the government's action on those indirectly affected by it comes to the forefront.

3. The crucial role of open inquiry in public schools has been increasingly recognized in recent years. *See Keefe v. Geanakos*, 418 F.2d 359 (1st Cir. 1969) (teacher may not be dismissed for assigning serious magazine article containing single vulgar word); *Cary v. Board of Education*, *supra* (school may not exercise unlimited control over teachers); *Parducci v. Rutland*, *supra* (teacher may not be dismissed for assigning non-vulgar short story); *Citizens for Parental Rights v. San Mateo County Board*, 51 Cal.App.3d 1, 124 Cal.Rptr. 68 (1975) (First Amendment considerations opposed to effort by parents to exclude particular material from school curriculum). *See*, generally, Project, *Education and the Law: State Interests and Individual Rights*, 74 Mich.L. Rev. 1373, 1433-42 (1976); *Developments in the Law--Academic Freedom*, 81 Harv.L.Rev. 1045, 1112-13 (1968).

4. A related principle is illustrated by those cases, discussed in Judge Sifton's opinion, that have invalidated laws granting public authorities broad discretion to punish speech. *See Shuttlesworth v. City of Birmingham*, 394 U.S. 147, 89 S.Ct. 935, 22 L.Ed.2d 162 (1969); *Eisner v. Stamford Board of Education*, 440 F.2d 803 (2d Cir. 1971). Judge Sifton finds this broad dis-

cretion, and the lack of precisely drawn rules for determining which books are to be permitted in the school library, sufficient to invalidate the School Board's action. In my view, this case cannot be decided on this basis. Cases such as *Shuttlesworth* and *Eisner* involved punishment imposed for certain types of speech. The vice of granting board discretion in this context is that it will have a chilling effect on all speakers; those whose speech is protected will be uncertain whether they can be punished, and will consequently hesitate to speak. In this case, however, no punishment was imposed, and there is nothing to indicate that the removal of the books carried any threat of future punishment. The connection between the action of the school and the exercise of First Amendment rights is not so direct, and the case thus requires a more detailed inquiry into the sufficiency of the threatened impact of the Board's action on the students.

5. Lest it be thought that book burning is an extreme event, unlikely to follow the mere removal of a book, it is worth noting the facts presented by the plaintiffs in *Zykan v. Warsaw Community School Corp.*, 631 F.2d 1300 (7th Cir. 1980). The books removed from a school library in that case were conveyed to a local senior citizen's group for a public burning. Id. at 1302.

6. The acronym signifies Parents of New York United, according to the briefs of the parties. Board member Ahrens calls the organization People of New York United.

7. In addition to the examples catalogued in Judge Sifton's opinion, mention should be made of two Board members' comments concerning the removal of *A Hero Ain't Nothing But A Sandwich*. In the book Nigeria Greene, a Black teacher in a predominantly Black school, calls her students' attention to the fact that George Washington was a slave owner. To the reader she expresses her thoughts about the irony of Washington's stature in the materials taught in the school. In their depositions, two Board members concluded that Ms. Greene's thoughts were anti-American and were one reason for removing the book.

8. Though plaintiffs have acknowledged that defendants have not precluded discussion about the removed books or the themes of the books, I do not share Judge Mansfield's confidence that no free exchange of ideas was suppressed by the Board's action. I wonder how willing members of the school community are to discuss the virtues of Malcolm X after the School Board has condemned a book listed for disapproval because it equated Malcolm X with the founding fathers of our country. Judge Mansfield finds the evidence overwhelming that no ideas are being suppressed. I prefer to assess the sufficiency of the evidence after, not before, the trial. Furthermore, the issue at trial should not be simply whether ideas have been suppressed,

but whether the action taken, in light of its motivation, posed a sufficient *threat* to the suppression of ideas.

9. The assessment of risk to protected freedom must be made prospectively, whether or not the risk actually resulted in suppression. This is the same approach that governs when a school asserts the authority to regulate student activity; school authorities must demonstrate facts that might reasonably have led them "to forecast substantial disruption of or material interference with school activities." *Tinker v. Des Moines Independent School District*, supra, 393 U.S. at 514, 89 S.Ct. at 740. The need for a prospective assessment is especially important in evaluating the risk to First Amendment freedoms. If the removal of books, under the circumstances in which it occurred, dissuaded some members of the school community from expressing views because of the message they derived from the Board's action, they may be reluctant publicly to acknowledge that they hold such views and thereby risk the Board's displeasure.

JUDGE MANSFIELD'S OPINION NOTES

1. The excerpts which led the Board to look into the educational suitability of the books in question are set out (with minor corrections after comparison with the text of the books themselves) below. The pagination and the underlinings are retained from the original report used by the board. In newer editions of some of the books, the quotes appear at different pages.
   1) *SOUL ON ICE* by Eldridge Cleaver
   PAGE QUOTE
   157-158   "...There are white men who will pay you to fuck their wives. They approach you and say, 'How would you like to fuck a

white woman?' 'What is this?' you ask. 'On the up-and-up,' he assures you. 'It's all right. She's my wife. She needs black rod, is all. She has to have it. It's like a medicine or drug to her. She has to have it. I'll pay you. It's all on the level, no trick involved. Interested?' You go with him and he drives you to their home. The three of you go into the bedroom. There is a certain type who will leave you and his wife alone and tell you to pile her real good. After it is all over, he will pay you and drive you to wherever you want to go. Then there are some who like to peep at you through a keyhole and watch you have his woman, or peep at you through a window, or lie under the bed and listen to the creaking of the bed as you work out. There is another type who likes to masturbate while he stands beside the bed and watches you pile her. There is the type who likes to eat his woman up after you get through piling her. And there is the type who only wants you to pile her for a little while, just long enough to thaw her out and kick her motor over and arouse her to heat, then he wants you to jump off real quick and he will jump onto her and together they can make it from there by themselves."

2) *A HERO AIN'T NOTHING BUT A SANDWICH* by Alice Childress
    PAGE QUOTE
    10 "Hell, no! *Fuck the society.*
    64-65 "The hell with the junkie, the wino, the capitalist, the welfare checks, the world...yeah, and *fuck* you too!"
    75-76 "They can have back the spread and curtains, I'm too old for them *fuckin* bunnies anyway."

3) *THE FIXER* by Bernard Malamud
    PAGE QUOTE
    52 "What do you think goes on in the wagon at night: Are the drivers on their knees *fucking their mothers*?"
    90 "*Fuck yourself*, said the blinker, etc."
    92 "Who else would do anything like that but a *motherfucking* Zhid?"
    146 "No more noise out of you or I'll shoot your *Jew cock off*."
    189 "Also there's a lot of *fucking in the Old Testament*, so how is that religious?"
    192 "You better go *fuck yourself*, Bok, said Kogin, I'm onto your Jew tricks."
    215 "Ding-dong, giddyap. A *Jew's cock's* in the devil's hock."
    216 "You *cocksucker* Zhid, I ought to make you lick it up off the floor."

4) *GO ASK ALICE* by *Anonymous*
    PAGE QUOTE
    31 "I wonder if sex without acid could be so exciting, so wonderful, so indescribable. I always thought it just took a minute, or that it would be like dogs mating."
    47 "Chris and I walked into Richie and Ted's apartment to find the bastards

stoned and making love to each other... low class queer."
81 "shitty, goddamned, pissing, ass, goddamned beJesus, screwing life's, ass, shit. Doris was ten and had *humped* with who knows how many men in between...her current stepfather started having sex with her but good...*sonofabitch balling her*"
83 "but now when I face a girl its like facing a boy. I get all excited and turned on. *I want to screw with the girl*..."
84 "I'd rather screw with a guy...sometimes I want one of the girls to kiss me. I want her to touch me, to have her sleep under me."
84 "Another day, another *blow job*...If I don't give *Big Ass a blow* he'll cut off my supply...and Little Jacon is yelling, 'Mama, *Daddy can't come now. He's humping Carla.*'"
85 "Shit, goddamn, goddamn prick, son-of-a-bitch, ass, pissed, bastard, goddamn, bullshit
94 "I hope you have a *nice orgasm with your dog tonight*."
110 "You *fucking* Miss Polly pure
117 "Then he said that all I needed was a good *fuck*."
146 "It might be great because I'm practically a virgin in the sense that I've never had sex except when I've been stoned..."

5) *SLAUGHTERHOUSE FIVE* by Kurt Vonnegut, Jr.
    PAGE QUOTE
    29 "'Get out of the road, you dumb *motherfucker*.' The last word was still a novelty in the speech of white people in 1944. It was fresh and astonishing to Billy, who had never *fucked* anybody..."
    32 "You stake a guy out on an anthill in the desert--see? He's facing upward, and you put *honey* all over his *balls and pecker*, and you cut off his eyelids so he has to stare at the sun till he dies."
    34 "He had a prophylactic kit containing two tough condoms 'For the prevention of disease only!'... He had a dirty picture of a *woman* attempting *sexual intercourse* with a *shetland pony*."
    94 & 95 "But the Gospels actually taught this: Before you kill somebody, make absolutely sure he isn't well connected ...The flaw in the Christ stories, said the visitor from outer space, was that Christ who didn't look like much, was actually the son of the Most Powerful Being in the Universe. Readers understood that, so, when they came to the crucifixion, they naturally thought.. Oh boy-- they sure picked the wrong guy to lynch this time! And that thought had a brother: There are right people to lynch. People not well connected .... The visitor from outer space made a gift to Earth of a new Gospel. In it, Jesus really WAS a nobody, and a pain in the neck to a lot

of people with better connections than he had .... So the people amused themselves one day by nailing him to a cross and planting the cross in the ground. There couldn't possibly be any repercussions, the lynchers thought .. since the new Gospel hammered home again and again what a nobody Jesus was. And then just before the nobody died .... The voice of God came crashing down. He told the people that he was adopting the bum as his son ... God said this: *From this moment on, He will punish horribly anybody who torments a bum who has no connections.*"

99 "They told him that there could be no Earthling babies without male homosexuals. There could be babies without female homosexuals."

120 "Why don't you go *fuck* yourself? Don't think I haven't tried .. he was going to have revenge, and that revenge was sweet ... It's the sweetest thing there is, said Lazzaro. People *fuck* with me, he said, and *Jesus Christ* are they ever fucking sorry."

122 "And he'll pull out a gun and *shoot his pecker off.* The stranger'll let him think a couple of seconds about who Paul Lazzaro is and what life's going be like without a *pecker.* Then he'll shoot him once in the guts and walk away. ... He died on account of this silly *cocksucker* here. So I promised him I'd have this silly *cocksucker* shot after the war."

134 "In my prison cell I sit ... With my *britches full of shit*, And my *balls are bouncing* gently on the floor. And I see the bloody snag when she bit me in the bag ... Oh, I'll never *fuck a Polack* any more."

173 "And the *peckers* of the young men would still be *semierect*, and their *muscles* would be *bulging like cannonballs.*"

175 "They didn't have *hard-ons* ... Everybody else did."

177 "The magazine, which was published for *lonesome men to jerk off to.*"

178 "and one critic said.... "To describe *blow-jobs* artistically.'"

6) *THE BEST SHORT STORIES BY NEGRO WRITERS*
Ed. by Langston Hughes
PAGE QUOTE
176 "like bat's shit and camel piss,"

228 "that no-count bitch of a daughter of yours is up there up North making a whore of herself."

237 "they made her get out and stand in front of the headlights of the car and pull down her pants and raise her dress-- they said that was the only way they could be sure. And you can imagine what they said and what they did--."

303 "You need some pussy. Come on, let's go up to the whore house on the hill." "Oh, these bastards, these bastards, this God damned Army and the bastards in it. The sons of bitches!"

436 "he produced a brown rag doll, looked at her again, then grabbed the doll by its legs and tore it part way up the middle. Then he jammed his finger into the rip between the doll's legs. The other men laughed...."

444 "The pimps, hustlers, lesbians, and others trying to misuse me."

462 "But she had straight firm legs and her breasts were small and upright. No doubt if she'd had children her breasts would be hanging like little empty purses."

464 "She first became aware of the warm tense nipples on her breasts." Her hands went up gently to clam them." "In profile, his penis hung like a stout tassle. She could even tell that he was circumcised."

406 "Cadillac Bill was busy following Luheaster around, rubbing her stomach and saying, 'Magic Stomach, Magic Stomach, bring me a little baby cadillac.'" "One of the girls went upstairs with Red Top and stayed for about forty five minutes."

7) *BLACK BOY* by Richard Wright
PAGE QUOTE
70-71 "We black children--seven or eight or nine years of age--used to run to the Jew's store and shout:

...Bloody Christ Killers
Never trust a Jew
Bloody Christ Killers
What won't a Jew do ...
Red, white and blue
Your pa was a Jew
Your ma a dirty dago
What the hell is you?"

265 "Crush that nigger's nuts, nigger!" "Hit that nigger!" "Aw, fight, you goddam niggers!" "Sock 'im, in his f-k-g piece!" "Make 'im bleed!"

8) *LAUGHING BOY* by Oliver LaFarge
PAGE QUOTE
38 "I'll tell you, she is all bad; for two bits she will do the worst thing."

258-9 "I was frightened when he wanted me to lie with him, but he made me feel all right. He knew all about how to make women forget themselves, that man."

9) *THE NAKED APE* by Desmond Morris
PAGE QUOTE
73-74 "Also, the frontal approach provides the maximum possibility for stimulation of the female's clitoris during the pelvic thrusting of the male. It is true that it will be passively, stimulated by the pulling effect of the male's thrusts, regardless of his body position in relation to the female, but in a face-to-face mating there will in addition be the direct rhythmic pressure of the male's pubic region on the clitoral area, and this will considerably heighten the stimulation ..." "So it seems plausible to consider that face-to-face copulation is basic to our species. There are, of course, a number of variations that do not eliminate the frontal element: male

above, female above, side by side, squat-
ting, standing, and so on, but the most
efficient and commonly used one is with
both partners horizontal, the male above
the female...."
80 "... This broadening of the penis results in the female's external genitals
being subjected to much more pulling and
pushing during the performance of pelvic
thrusts. With each inward thrust of the
penis, the clitoral region is pulled
downwards and then, with each withdrawal,
it moves up again. Add to this the
rhythmic pressure being exerted on the
clitoris region by the pubic region of
the frontally copulating male, and you
have a repeated massaging of the clitoris
that--were she a male--would virtually be
masturbatory."
94-99 "... If either males or females
cannot for some reason obtain sexual access to their opposite numbers, they will
find sexual outlets in other ways. They
may use other members of their own sex,
or they may even use members of other
species, or they may masturbate...."
10) READER FOR WRITERS. See note 6 infra.

2. N.Y. Education Law § 1709 (McKinney's) reads
in pertinent part as follows:
"§ 1709. Powers and Duties of Boards of
Education
The said board of education of every union
free school district shall have the power
and it shall be its duty:
         *   *   *   *   *
3. To prescribe the course of study by
which the pupils of the school shall be
graded and classified....
4. To prescribe the text-books to be used
in the schools....
         *   *   *   *   *
9. To take charge and possession of ....
the books, apparatus, and all school property within its district; and the title of
the same shall be vested respectively in
said board of education....
         *   *   *   *   *
13. To have in all respects the superinten-
dence, management and control of said union
free schools....
33. To have in all respects the superinten-
dence, management and control of the educational affairs of the district, and, therefore, shall have all the powers reasonably
granted expressly or by implication by this
chapter or other statutes."
§ 701 of the Education Law, subdivision 1
states in pertinent part:
"In the several cities and school districts
of the state, boards of education ... shall
designate textbooks to be used in the
schools under their charge."
§ 91.1 of the Regulations of the Commissioner of Education states:
"A school library shall be established and
maintained in each school. The library in
each elementary school shall meet the needs
of the pupils, and shall provide an adequate

complement to the various areas of the curriculum."
It also requires a minimum of 1,000 titles
each for a junior and senior high school library.
3. Judge Sifton's opinion quotes at length (at
pp. 409-410) portions of a memorandum by
Superintendent Richard G. Morrow to the
Board dated February 27, 1976, disapproving
a procedure whereby the Board might act un-
ilaterally or precipitously on the basis of
excerpts or lists prepared by others without
first reading the books. The opinion also
quotes portions of a Board press release
issued on March 19, 1976, in response to
articles in the press regarding the book issue. The impression given by these partial
quotations is that the Board had prejudged
the issue of whether the 10 books should be
discontinued as part of the School's curriculum, had permanently removed them, to
which Superintendent Morrow was objecting.
    However, the balance of Mr. Morrow's me-
morandum, as well as his later similar memorandum to the public dated March 30, 1976
(entitled "Statement Concerning the Book
Issue"), when the Board held a public hearing on the issue, reveals that he was recommending that a joint parent-school authority
Committee be appointed to study the books
and make recommendations to the Board. This
was substantially the procedure adopted by
the Board at its March 30, 1980, public
meeting with Superintendent Morrow's approval, and instituted in early April.
4. Because of the unavailability of sufficient
copies of A Reader for Writers most members of the Committee were unable to read
the book within a reasonable length of time
and could not therefore make a recommendation.
5. Judge Mulligan summarized the contents of
Down These Mean Streets as follows:

    "The book, which has created the con-
    troversy and provoked the action of the
    Board, Down These Mean Streets, is an
    autobiographical account by Piri Thomas,
    of a Puerto Rican youth growing up in the
    East Side Barrio (Spanish Harlem) in New
    York City. Predictably the scene is de-
    pressing, ugly and violent. The argot of
    the vicinage is replete with four letter
    and twelve letter obscenities unreported
    by Tom Swift or even Tom Jones. Acts of
    criminal violence, sex, normal and per-
    verse, as well as episodes of drug shoot-
    ing are graphically described." 457 F.2d
    291.

6. A Reader for Writers, an anthology edited
by Jerome W. Archer and Joseph Schwartz,
while not apparently containing vulgar or
indecent language, does contain a story
which members of the Board considered to be
in sufficiently bad taste to justify its removal from the library. An article in the
book by Jonathan Swift, entitled A Modest
Proposal for Preventing the Children of Poor

People in Ireland From Being a Burden to their Parents or Country, suggests at length that the overpopulation problem could be solved by having 100,000 one-year old children slaughtered and served as food, with the skins to be artificially dressed and made into gloves and boots, and describes the proposed process in detail. I cannot label the Board's decision to discontinue the book as irrational or designed to suppress freedom of expression by students, particularly in the absence of evidence that the book was in demand for any of its other writings.

7. Community values may not be underestimated as a factor to be taken into account by a Board in selecting those books suitable for the part to be played by a school library in performance of the school's educational function. According to the Eighth Annual Gallup Poll of the Public Attitude toward the Public Schools, as reported in *Phi Delta Kappa* Magazine for October 1976 (which was during the period of the events in question in this case), most persons answered that "high moral standards" represented the quality most neglected by public schools in the overall development of children. Seven out of ten parents replied that schools should share with them the responsibility for the moral behavior of their children.

8. The parties' statements of facts, about which no dispute exists, filed pursuant to Rule 9(g) of the General Rules of the Southern District of New York, contain the following pertinent provisions:

Plaintiffs: "Although the books themselves were excluded from use in schools in any way, defendants have not precluded discussion about the themes of the books or the books themselves."
Defendants: "No teacher has been instructed not to discuss the books which were removed or to refrain from discussion or comment upon the ideas and positions they represent."

9. As we recently reiterated in *SEC v. Research Automation Corp.*, 585 F.2d 31, 33 (2d Cir. 1978):

"Rule 56(e) provides that when a motion for summary judgment is supported by the documents listed in Rule 56(c)-depositions, affidavits, answers to interrogatories, and admissions-an adverse party may not rest upon mere conclusory allegations or denials. The party opposing the motion must set forth 'concrete particulars' [citation omitted] ... It is not sufficient merely to assert a conclusion without supplying supporting arguments or facts in opposition to the motion."

See also, *Donnelly v. Guion*, 467 F.2d 290, 291 (2d Cir. 1972); *Applegate v. Top Associates, Inc.*, 425 F.2d 92, 96 (2d Cir. 1970).

JUDGE SIFTON'S OPINION NOTES

1. The complaint was originally filed in state court and was thereafter removed to federal district court pursuant to 28 U.S.C. § 1441. Plaintiffs' motion to remand to the state court was denied, a ruling not complained of here and which was, in all events, correct, since the complaint raised substantial issues which the federal court had jurisdiction to decide under 28 U.S.C. § 1343. *See* 28 U.S.C. § 1441(b).

2. The books at issue are: *The Fixer*, by Bernard Malamud; *Slaughterhouse Five*, by Kurt Vonnegut; *The Naked Ape*, by Desmond Morris; *Down These Mean Streets*, by Piri Thomas; *Best Short Stories by Negro Writers*, edited by Langston Hughes; *Go Ask Alice*, by an anonymous author; *A Hero Ain't Nothing But a Sandwich*, by Alice Childress; *Black Boy*, by Richard Wright; *Laughing Boy*, by Oliver LaFarge; *Soul on Ice*, by Eldridge Cleaver; and an anthology entitled, *A Reader for Writers*, edited by Jerome Archer.

3. Union Free School Districts are the product of New York State's first attempt in 1853 to encourage rural school districts to consolidate resources in an effort to enrich elementary education and make possible secondary school facilities not otherwise available to the separate communities. L.1853, c. 433. Graves, "Development of the Education Law in New York," McKinney's Education Law, Sections 1 to 600, pp. xxi-xxii (1969 Ed.).

4. The entry for Oliver LaFarge's *Laughing Boy* reads in its entirety as follows:

"*Laughing Boy* by Oliver Lafarge
"Page 38-'I tell you, she is all bad; for two bits she will do the worst thing.'
"Pages 258-9-'I was frightened when he wanted me to lie with him, but he made me feel all right. He knew all about how to make women forget themselves, that man.'"

5. An affidavit of defendant Martin states he made a second list entitled "Objectionable Books" from the materials acquired at the conference. Since this list includes titles and authors beyond those covered by the lists identified as acquired at the Watkins Glen conference, e.g., *Why I am not a Christian*, by Bertrand Russell; *Law and the Consumer*; and *Down These Mean Streets*, by Richard Yates [sic], it seems clear either that lists were obtained at the Watkins Glen conference which are not part of the record, or that other sources were consulted by Martin.

6. According to Ahrens, "I think we mentioned our concerns to the other board members and to the [District] Superintendent in a rather informal manner" at an executive session of the Board in November. The Board also met in Janaury.

7. Superintendents of Union Free School Districts possess the following powers, among

others, under New York Education Law
1711(5):

> "a.   To be the chief executive officer of
> the school district and the educational
> system, and to have the right to speak on
> all matters before the board, but not to
> vote.
>
> * * * * * *
>
> "c.   To prepare the content of each
> course of study authorized by the board
> of education....
> "d.   To recommend suitable lists of text-
> books to be used in the schools.
>
> * * * * * *
>
> "f.   To have supervision and direction
> over ... all other matters pertaining to
> ... libraries, lectures, and all other
> education activities under the manage-
> ment, direction and control of the board
> of education."

8. Apparently, in March the union had filed a
grievance against the Board stating that
the Board had violated this clause of the
union contract.

9. Neither this recommendation nor any of the
other recommendations made by formal vote
of the committee at later meetings in May
and June were acted upon prior to the July
Board of Education meeting when all of the
committee's recommendations were considered
together.

10. *Manual for Complex Litigation*, Sec. 1.41
(1973).   *Compare AAMCO Automatic Transmis-
sions, Inc. v. Tayloe*, 67 F.R.D., 440,
447 (E.D.Pa. 1975) and *Weight Watchers of
Philadelphia v. Weight Watchers International*, 53 F.R.D. 647 (E.D.N.Y. 1971) with
Matarazzo v. Friendly Ice Cream Corp.,
62 F.R.D. 65 (E.D.N.Y. 1974). *Cf. Coles
v. Marsh*, 560 F.2d 186 (3d Cir.), *cert.
denied*, 434 U.S. 985, 98 S.Ct. 611, 54
L.Ed.2d 479 (1977). And *see Erhardt* v.
Prudential Group, Inc., 429 F.2d 843 (2d
Cir., 1980).

11. It is significant that the precise language
of Justice Fortas' decision in *Tinker* v.
Des Moines School District, *supra*, 393
U.S. at 514, 89 S.Ct. at 740, defining the
boundaries of permissible regulation of
student speech became incorporated in a
school board rule regulating the distribution of literature on school premises which
this Court was obliged to strike down in
Eisner v. *Stamford Board of Education*,
440 F.2d 803, 807 (2d Cir. 1971). As noted
by this Court in *Thomas* v. *Board of
Education*, *supra*, 607 F.2d at 1049, First
Amendment problems in the school area "are
not easy of solution and much depends upon
the specific facts before us."

12. Thus, although both *James* and *Taylor*
involved school regulations barring the
wearing of black arm bands in secondary
schools to protest the Vietnam war, this
Court noted in *James*, *supra*, "there is
merit to appellees' argument that *Tinker*
does not control this case." 461 F.2d at

573.   *Tinker* itself cited with approval
both *Burnside v. Byars*, 363 F.2d 744 (5th
Cir. 1966) and *Blackwell v. Issaquena
County Board of Education*, 363 F.2d 749
(5th Cir. 1966) decided on the same day by
the same panel, one upholding and the other
striking down school board regulations prohibiting the wearing of freedom buttons on
school property, because of a difference in
the manner in which the children wearing
the buttons had comported themselves at the
two schools involved. *Tinker v. Des
Moines School District*, *supra* 393 U.S. at
509, 513, 89 S.Ct. at 737, 740.

13. Judge Newman concludes that a trial is required to determine the effect of defendants' conduct on plaintiffs' exercise of
their first amendment rights, since plaintiffs have not been threatened with punishment for expressing ideas contained in the
offending books.   As Judge Newman points
out in his opinion, however, what is at
issue is the degree of risk that ideas will
be suppressed as a result of defendants'
conduct.   Once all copies of the books containing the offending ideas have been
ordered removed from the school library under the circumstances here presented, it
hardly requires a trial, in my view, to
determine that the risk is overwhelming
that students will conclude that they are
not at liberty to express the same thoughts
themselves and that they will be appropriately punished if they do so.   To hold, as
Judge Newman would, that potential plaintiffs must, when faced with similar conduct
by school boards in the future, contemplate
the prospect of plenary trial in our congested district courts in order to vindicate their First Amendment rights is, in my
view, to impose too great a burden on free
speech.

   Judge Mansfield is mistaken in reading
the majority opinion as condemning the
application by school boards of personal
taste, political beliefs or local community standards to decisions concerning
the contents of school libraries in this
Circuit.   *Cf. Zykan v. Warsaw Community
School Corp.*, 631 F.2d 1300 (7th Cir.,
1980).   The opinion says the contrary.
There is, however, a difference between
applying one's personal taste or political views to the formulation of school
policy and simply requiring conformity by
students and teachers with subjective and
intangible standards of personal morality
or political philosophy.   What is required in order to avoid the effect of
governing school affairs simply by a vague and indefinite pall of orthodoxy is the
development of a set of sufficiently
objective criteria for the identification
of speech which will be objected to and a
sufficiently regular procedure for applying those criteria in concrete cases to
permit students to determine with a reasonable degree of certainty what speech
will be prohibited and when.   This is not

accomplished by the Board's March Newsletter to all families in the District expressing the Board's loosely stated findings ("... the books ... contain material that is offensive to Christians, Jews, Blacks, and Americans in general. In addition, these books contain obscenities, blasphemies, brutality, and perversion beyond description"), its peremptory conclusion ("... we all agree that these books simply DO NOT belong in the school libraries ..."), and its vague warning ("It is our duty, our moral obligation, to protect the children of our schools from this moral danger as surely as from physical and medical dangers"). This message, of course, preceded the April appointment of the book review committee as well as the later efforts by the Board members, in response to the plaintiffs' motion for summary judgment in this case, to explain their actions principally, although still not entirely, in terms of the books' vulgarity and indecency. Nothing in this later history, in my view, serves to dispel the effect upon first amendment rights of the Board's initial manner of dealing with the issue, and, as noted in the body of this opinion, much occurred thereafter which only served to make the situation worse.

The United States Supreme Court decides (5-4) that the students who had objected to the banning of Soul on Ice, Go Ask Alice, Slaughterhouse Five *and other books from the Island Trees School libraries were entitled to a trial to determine what the motives of the School Board were in banning the books, Justice Brennan declaring in the plurality opinion: "Our Constitution does not permit the official suppression of* ideas. *Thus whether petitioners' [School Board] removal of books from their school libraries denied respondents their First Amendment rights depends upon the motivation behind petitioners' actions .... Respondents' allegations and some of the evidentiary materials presented below do not rule out the possibility that petitioners' removal procedures were highly irregular and ad hoc -- the antithesis of those procedures that might tend to allay suspicions regarding petitioners' motivations."*

Bd. of Education, Island Trees Union Free School Dist. v. Pico, 42 CCH S. Ct. Bull. B3921, 50 LW 4831 (1982)

JUSTICE BRENNAN announced the judgment of the Court, and delivered an opinion in which JUSTICE MARSHALL and JUSTICE STEVENS joined, and in which JUSTICE BLACKMUN joined except for Part II-A-(1).

The principal question presented is whether the First Amendment[1] imposes limitations upon the exercise by a local school board of its discretion to remove library books from high school and junior high school libraries.

I

Petitioners are the Board of Education of the Island Trees Union Free School District No. 26, in New York, and Richard Ahrens, Frank Martin, Christina Fasulo, Patrick Hughes, Richard Melchers, Richard Michaels, and Louis Nessim. When this suit was brought, Ahrens was the President of the Board, Martin was the Vice-President, and the remaining petitioners were Board members. The Board is a state agency charged with responsibility for the operation and administration of the public schools within the Island Trees School District, including the Island Trees High School and Island Trees Memorial Junior High School. Respondents are Steven Pico, Jacqueline Gold, Glenn Yarris, Russell Rieger, and Paul Sochinski. When this suit was brought, Pico, Gold, Yarris, and

Rieger were students at the High School, and Sochinski was a student at the Junior High School.

In September 1975, petitioners Ahrens, Martin, and Hughes attended a conference sponsored by Parents of New York United (PONYU), a politically conservative organization of parents concerned about education legislation in the State of New York. At the conference these petitioners obtained lists of books described by Ahrens as "objectionable," App. 22, and by Martin as "improper fare for school students," id., at 101.[2] It was later determined that the High School library contained nine of the listed books, and that another listed book was in the Junior High School library.[3] In February 1976, at a meeting with the superintendent of schools and the principals of the High School and Junior High School, the Board gave an "unofficial direction" that the listed books be removed from the library shelves and delivered to the Board's offices, so that Board members could read them.[4] When this directive was carried out, it became publicized, and the Board issued a press release justifying its action. It characterized the removed books as "anti-American, anti-Christian, anti-Semitic, and just plain filthy," and concluded that "It is our duty, our moral obligation, to protect the children in our schools from this moral danger as surely as from physical and medical dangers." 474 F. Supp. 387, 390.

A short time later, the Board appointed a "Book Review Committee," consisting of four Island Trees parents and four members of the Island Trees schools staff, to read the listed books and to recommend to the Board whether the books should be retained, taking into account the books' "educational suitability," "good taste," "relevance," and "appropriateness to age and grade level." In July, the Committee made it's final report to the Board, recommending that five of the listed books be retained[5] and that two others be removed from the school libraries.[6] As for the remaining four books, the Committee could not agree on two,[7] took no position on one,[8] and recommended that the last book be made available to students only with parental approval.[9] The Board substantially rejected the Committee's report later that month, deciding that only one book should be returned to the High School library without restriction,[10] that another should be made available subject to parental approval,[11] but that the remaining nine books should "be removed from elementary and secondary libraries and [from] use in the curriculum." 474 F.Supp., at 391.[12] The Board gave no reasons for rejecting the recommendations of the Committee that it had appointed.

Respondents reacted to the Board's decision by bringing the present action under 42 U.S.C. § 1983 in the United States District Court for the Eastern District of New York. They alleged that petitioners had

"ordered the removal of the books from school libraries and proscribed their use in the curriculum because particular passages in the books offended their social, political, cal and moral tastes and not because the books, taken as a whole, were lacking in educational value." App.4.

Respondents claimed that the Board's actions denied them their rights under the First Amendment. They asked the court for a declaration that the Board's actions were unconstitutional, and for preliminary and permanent injunctive relief ordering the Board to return the nine books to the school libraries and to refrain from interfering with the use of those books in the schools' curricula. App.5-6.

The District Court granted summary judgment in favor of petitioners. 474 F.Supp. 387 (1979). In the court's view, "the parties substantially agree[d] about the motivation behind the board's actions," id., at 391—namely, that

"the board acted not on religious principles but on its conservative educational philosophy, and on its belief that the nine books removed from the school library and curriculum were irrelevant, vulgar, immoral, and in bad taste, making them educationally unsuitable for the district's junior and senior high school students." Id., at 392.

With this factual premise as its background the court rejected respondents' contention that their First Amendment rights had been infringed by the Board's actions. Noting that statute, history, and precedent had vested local school boards with a broad discretion to formulate educational policy.[13] the court concluded that it should not intervene in "'the daily operations of school systems'" unless "'basic constitutional values'" were "'sharply implicate[d],'"[14] and determined that the conditions for such intervention did not exist in the present case. Acknowledging that the "removal [of the books]...clearly was content-based," the court nevertheless found no constitutional violation of the requisite magnitude:

"The board has restricted access only to certain books which the board believed to be, in essence, vulgar. While removal of such books from a school library may... reflect a misguided educational philosophy, it does not constitute a sharp and direct infringement of any first amendment right." Id., at 397.

A three judge panel of the United States Court of Appeals for the Second Circuit reversed the judgment of the District Court, and remanded the action for a trial on respondents' allegations. 638 F. 2d 404 (1980). Each judge on the panel filed a separate opinion. Delivering the judgment of the court, Judge Sifton treated the case as involving "an unusual and irregular intervention in the school libraries' operations by persons not routinely concerned with such matters," and concluded that petitioners were obliged to demonstrate a reasonable basis for interfering with respondents' First Amendment rights. *Id.*, at 414-415. He then determined that, at least at the summary judgment stage, petitioners had not offered sufficient justification for their action,[15] and concluded that respondents "should have...been offered an opportunity to persuade a finder of fact that the ostensible justifications for [petitioners'] actions ... were simply pretexts for the suppression of free speech." *Id.*, at 417.[16] Judge Newman concurred in the result. *Id.*, at 432-438. He viewed the case as turning on the contested factual issue of whether petitioners' removal decision was motivated by a justifiable desire to remove books containing vulgarities and sexual explicitness, or rather by an impermissible desire to supress ideas. *Id.*, at 436-437.[17] We granted certiorari, ---- U.S.---- (1981).

II

We emphasize at the outset the limited nature of the substantive question presented by the case before us. Our precedents have long recognized certain constitutional limits upon the power of the State to control even the curriculum and classroom. For example, *Meyer* v. *Nebraska*, 262 U.S. 390 (1923), struck down a state law that forbade the teaching of modern foreign languages in pulbic and private schools, and *Epperson* v. *Arkansas*, 393 U.S. 97 (1968), declared unconstitutional a state law that prohibited the teaching of the Darwinian theory of evolution in any state-supported school. But the current action does not require us to re-enter this difficult terrain, which *Meyer* and *Epperson* traversed without apparent misgiving. For as this case is presented to us, it does not involve textbooks, or indeed any books that Island Trees students would be required to read.[18] Respondents do not seek in this Court to impose limitations upon their school board's discretion to prescribe the curricula of the Island Trees schools. On the contrary, the only books at issue in this case are *library* books, books that by their nature are optional rather than required reading. Our adjudication of the present case thus does not intrude into the classroom, or into the compulsory courses taught there. Furthermore, even as to library books, the action before us does not involve the *acquisiton* of books. Respondents have not sought to compel their school board to add to the school library shelves any books that students desire to read. Rather, the only action challenged in this case is the *removal* from school libraries of books originally placed there by the school authorities, or without objection from them.

The substantive question before us is still further constrained by the procedural posture of this case. Petitioners were granted summary judgment by the District Court. The Court of Appeals reversed that judgment, and remanded the action for a trial on the merits of respondents' claims. We can reverse the judgment of the Court of Appeals, and grant petitioners' request for reinstatment of the summary judg-

ment in their favor, only if we determine that "there is no genuine issue as to any material fact," and that petitioners are "entitled to a judgment as a matter of law." Fed. Rule Civ. Proc.56(c). In making our determination, any doubt as to the existence of a genuine issue of material fact must be resolved against petitioners as the moving party. *Adickes* v. *Kress & Co.*, 398 U.S. 144, 157-159 (1970). Furthermore, "On summary judgment the inferences to be drawn from the underlying facts contained...in the affidavits, attached exhibits, and depositions submitted below...must be viewed in the light most favorable to the party opposing the motion." *United States* v. *Diebold, Inc.*, 369 U.S. 654, 655 (962).

In sum, the issue before us in this case is a narrow one, both substantively and procedurally. It may best be restated as two distinct questions. First, Does the First Amendment impose *any* limitations upon the discretion of petitioners to remove library books from the Island Trees High School and Junior High School? Second, If so, do the affidavits and other evidentiary materials before the District Court, construed most favorably to respondents, raise a genuine issue of fact whether petitioners might have exceeded those limitations? If we answer either of these questions in the negative, then we must reverse the judgment of the Court of Appeals and reinstate the District Court's summary judgment for petitioners. If we answer both questions in the affirmative, then we must affirm the judgment below. We examine these questions in turn.

A
(1)

The Court has long recognized that local school boards have broad discretion in the management of school affairs. See, *e.g.*, *Meyer* v. *Nebraska*, 262 U.S. 390, 402 (1923); *Pierce* v. *Society of Sisters*, 268 U.S. 510, 543 (1925). *Epperson* v. *Arkansas, supra*, at 104, reaffirmed that, by and large, "public education in our Nation is committed to the control of state and local authorities," and that federal courts should not ordinarily "intervene in the resolution of conflicts which arise in the daily operation of school systems." *Tinker* v. *Des Moines School Dist.*, 393 U.S. 503, 507 (1969), noted that we have "repeatedly emphasized...the comprehensive authority of the States and of school officials...to prescribe and control conduct in the schools." We have also acknowledged that public schools are vitally important "in the preparation of individuals for participation as citizens," and as vehicles for "inculcating fundamental values necessary to the maintenance of a democratic political system." *Ambach* v. *Norwick*, 441 U.S. 68, 76-77 (1979). We are therefore in full agreement with petitioners that local school boards must be permitted "to establish and apply their curriculum in such a way as to transmit community values, "and that there is a legitimate and substantial community interest in promoting respect for authority and traditional values be they social, moral, or political." Brief for Petitioners 10.[19]

At the same time, however, we have necessarily recognized that the discretion of the States and local school boards in matters of education must be exercised in a manner that comports with the transcendent imperatives of the First Amendment. In *West Virginia* v. *Barnette*, 319 U.S. 624 (1943), we held that under the First Amendment a student in a public school could not be compelled to salute the flag. We reasoned that

"Boards of Education...have, of course, important, delicate, and highly discretionary functions, but none that they may not perform within the limits of the Bill of Rights. That they are educating the young for citizenship is reason for scrupulous protection of Constitutional freedoms of the individual, if we are not to strangle the free mind at its source and teach youth to discount important principles of our government as mere platitudes." *Id.*, at 637.

Later cases have consistently followed this rationale. Thus *Epperson* v. *Arkansas, supra,* invalidated a State's anti-evolution statute as violative of the Establishment Clause, and reaffirmed the duty of federal courts "to apply the First Amendment's mandate in our educational system where essential to safeguard the fundamental values of freedom of speech and inquiry." 393 U.S., at 104. And *Tinker* v. *Des Moines School Dist., supra,* held that a local school board had infringed the free speech rights of high school and junior high school students by suspending them from school for wearing black armbands in class as a protest against the Government's policy in Vietnam; we stated there that the "comprehensive authority...of school officials" must be exercised "consistent with fundamental constitutional safeguards." 393 U.S., at 507. In sum, students do not "shed their rights to freedom of speech or expression at the schoolhouse gate," *id.*, at 506, and therefore local school boards must discharge their "important, delicate, and highly discretionary functions" within the limits and constraints of the First Amendment.

The nature of students' First Amendment rights in the context of this case requires further examination. *West Virginia* v. *Barnette, supra,* is instructive. There the Court held that students' liberty of conscience could not be infringed in the name of "national unity" or "patriotism." 319 U.S., at 640-641. We explained that

"the action of the local authorities in compelling the flag salute and pledge transcends constitutional limitations on their power and invades the sphere of intellect and spirit which it is the purpose of the First Amendment to our Constitution to reserve from all official control." *Id.*, at 642.

Similarly, *Tinker* v. *Des Moines School*

Dist., supra, held that students' rights to freedom of expression of their political views could not be abridged by reliance upon on "undifferentiated fear or apprehension of disturbance" arising from such expression:

"Any departure from absolute regimentation may cause trouble. Any variation from the majority's opinion may inspire fear. Any word spoken, in class, in the lunchroom, or on the campus, that deviates from the views of another person may start an argument or cause a disturbance. But our Constitution says we must take this risk, *Terminiello* v. *Chicago*, 337 U.S. 1 (1949); and our history says that it is this sort of hazardous freedom--this kind of openness--that is the basis of our national strength and of the independence and vigor of Americans who grow up and live in this...often disputatious society." 393 U.S., at 508-509.

In short, "First Amendment rights, applied in light of the special characteristics of the school environment, are available to...students." *Id.*, at 506.

Of course, courts should not "intervene in the resolution of conflicts which arise in the daily operations of school systems" unless "basic constitutional values" are "directly and sharply implicate[d]" in those conflicts. *Epperson* v. *Arkansas*, 393 U.S., at 104. But we think that the First Amendment rights of students may be directly and sharply implicated by the removal of books from the shelves of a school library. Our precedents have focused "not only on the role of the First Amendment in fostering individual self-expression but also on its role in affording the public access to discussion, debate, and the dissemination of information and ideas." *First National Bank of Boston* v. *Bellotti*, 435 U.S. 765, 783 (1978). And we have recognized that "the State may not, consistently with the spirit of the First Amendment, contract the spectrum of available knowledge." *Griswold* v. *Connecticut*, 381 U.S. 479,482 (1965). In keeping with this principle, we have held that in a variety of contexts "the Constitution protects the right to receive information and ideas." *Stanley* v. *Georgia*, 394 U.S. 557,564 (1969); see *Kleindienst* v. *Mandel*, 408 U.S. 753, 762-763 (1972) (citing cases). This right is an inherent corollary of the rights of free speech and press that are explicitly guaranteed by the Constitution, in two senses. First, the right to receive ideas follows ineluctably from the *sender's* First Amendment right to send them: "The right of freedom of speech and press...embraces the right to distribute literature,...and necessarily protects the right to receive it." *Martin* v. *Struthers*, 318 U.S. 141, 143 (1943) (citation omitted). "The dissemination of ideas can accomplish nothing if otherwise willing addressees are not free to receive and consider them. It would be a barren marketplace of ideas that had only sellers and no buyers." *Lamont* v. *Postmaster General*, 381

U.S. 301, 308 (1965) (BRENNAN, J., concurring).

More importantly, the right to receive ideas is a necessary predicate to the *recipient's* meaningful exercise of his own rights of speech, press, and political freedom. Madison admonished us that

"A popular Government, without popular information, or the means of acquiring it, is but a Prologue to a Farce or a Tragedy; or, perhaps both. Knowledge will forever govern ignorance: And a people who mean to be their own Governors, must arm themselves with with [sic] the power which knowledge gives." 9 Writings of James Madison 103 (G. Hunt ed. 1910).[20]

As we recognized in *Tinker*, students too are beneficiaries of this principle:

"In our system, students may not be regarded as closed-circuit recipients of only that which the State chooses to communicate... [S]chool officials cannot suppress 'expressions of feeling with which they do not wish to contend.'" 393 U.S., at 511 (quoting *Burnside* v. *Byars*, 363 F. 2d 744, 749 (CA5 1966)).

In sum, just as access to ideas makes it possible for citizens generally to exercise their rights of free speech and press in a meaningful manner, such access prepares students for active and effective participation in the pluralistic, often contentious society in which they will soon be adult members. Of course all First Amendment rights accorded to students must be construed "in light of the special characteristics of the school environment." *Tinker* v. *Des Moines School Dist.*, *supra*, at 506. But the special characteristics of the school *library* make that environment especially appropriate for the recognition of the First Amendment rights of students.

A school library, no less than any other public library, is "a place dedicated to quiet, to knowledge, and to beauty." *Brown* v. *Louisiana*, 383 U.S. 131, 142 (1966) (Opinion of Fortas, J.). *Keyishian* v. *Board of Regents*, 385 U.S. 589 (1967), observed that "students must always remain free to inquire, to study and to evaluate, to gain new maturity and understanding."[21] The school library is the principal locus of such freedom. As one District Court has well put it, in the school library

"a student can literally explore the unknown, and discover areas of interest and thought not covered by the prescribed curriculum....Th[e] student learns that a library is a place to test or expand upon ideas presented to him, in or out of the classroom." *Right to Read Defense Comm.* v. *School Comm.*, 454 F. Supp. 703, 715 (D. Mass, 1978)

Petitioners emphasize the inculcative function of secondary education, and argue that they

must be allowed *unfettered* discretion to "transmit community values" through the Island Trees schools. But that sweeping claim overlooks the unique role of the school library. It appears from the record that use of the Island Trees school libraries is completely voluntary on the part of students. Their selection of books from these libraries is entirely a matter of free choice; the libraries afford them an opportunity at self-education and individual enrichment that is wholly optional. Petitioners might well defend their claim of absolute discretion in matters of *curriculum* by reliance upon their duty to inculcate community values. But we think that petitioners' reliance upon that duty is misplaced where, as here, they attempt to extend their claim of absolute discretion beyond the compulsory environment of the classroom, into the school library and the regime of voluntary inquiry that there holds sway.

(2)

In rejecting petitioners' claim of absolute discretion to remove books from their school libraries, we do not deny that local school boards have a substantial legitimate role to play in the determination of school library content. We thus must turn to the question of the extent to which the First Amendment places limitations upon the discretion of petitioners to remove books from their libraries. In this inquiry we enjoy the guidance of several precedents. *West Virginia* v. *Barnette*, *supra*, stated that

"If there be any fixed star in our constitutional constellation, it is that no official, high or petty, can prescribe what shall be orthodox in politics, nationalism, religion, or other matters of opinion.... If there are any circumstances which permit an exception, they do not now occur to us." 319 U.S., at 642.

This doctrine has been reaffirmed in later cases involving education. For example, *Keyishian* v. *Board of Regents*, *supra*, at 603, noted that "the First Amendment...does not tolerate laws which cast a pall of orthodoxy over the classroom;" see also *Epperson* v. *Arkansas*, *supra*, at 104-105. And *Mt. Healthy City Board of Ed.* v. *Doyle*, 429 U.S. 274 (1977), recognized First Amendment limitations upon the discretion of a local school board to refuse to rehire a non-tenured teacher. The school board in *Mt. Healthy* had declined to renew respondent Doyle's employment contract, in part because he had exercised his First Amendment rights. Although Doyle did not have tenure, and thus "could have been discharged for no reason whatever," *Mt. Healthy* held that he could "nonetheless establish a claim to reinstatement if the decision not to rehire him was made by reason of his exercise of constitutionally protected First Amendment freedoms." 429 U.S., at 283-284. We held further that once Doyle had shown "that his conduct was constitutionally protected, and that his conduct was a 'substantial factor'...in the Board's decision not to rehire him," the school board was obliged to show "by a preponderance of the evidence that it would have reached the same decision as to respondent's re-employment even in the absence of the protected conduct." *Id.*, at 287.

With respect to the present case, the message of these precedents is clear. Petitioners rightly possess significant discretion to determine the content of their school libraries. But that discretion may not be exercised in a narrowly partisan or political manner. If a Democratic school board, motivated by party affiliation, ordered the removal of all books written by or in favor of Republicans, few would doubt that the order violated the constitutional rights of the students denied access to those books. The same conclusion would surely apply if an all-white school board, motivated by racial animus, decided to remove all books authored by blacks or advocating racial equality and integration. Our Constitution does not permit the official suppression of *ideas*. Thus whether petitioners' removal of books from their school libraries denied respondents their First Amendment rights depends upon the motivation behind petitioners' actions. If petitioners *intended* by their removal decision to deny respondents access to ideas with which petitioners disagreed, and if this intent was the decisive factor in petitioners' decision,[22] then petitioners have exercised their discretion in violation of the Constitution. To permit such intentions to control official actions would be to encourage the precise sort of officially prescribed orthodoxy unequivocally condemned in *Barnette*. On the other hand, respondents implicitly concede that an unconstitutional motivation would *not* be demonstrated if it were shown that petitioners had decided to remove the books at issue because those books were pervasively vulgar. Tr. of Oral Arg. 36. And again, respondents concede that if it were demonstrated that the removal decision was based solely upon the "educational suitability" of the books in question, then their removal would be "perfectly permissible." *Id.*, at 53. In other words, in respondents' view such motivations, if decisive of petitioners' actions, would not carry the danger of an official suppression of ideas, and thus would not violate respondents' First Amendment rights.

As noted earlier, nothing in our decision today affects in any way the discretion of a local school board to choose books to *add* to the libraries of their schools. Because we are concerned in this case with the suppression of ideas, our holding today affects only the discretion to *remove* books. In brief, we hold that local school boards may not remove books from school library shelves simply because they dislike the ideas contained in those books and seek by their removal to "prescribe what shall be orthodox in politics, nationalism, religion, or other matters of opinion." *West Virginia v. Barnette*, 319 U.S., at 642. Such purposes stand inescapably condemned by our precedents.

B

We now turn to the remaining question presented by this case: Do the evidentiary materials that were before the District Court, when construed most favorably to respondents, raise a genuine issue of material fact whether petitioners exceeded constitutional limitations in exercising their discretion to remove the books from the school libraries? We conclude that the materials do raise such a question, which forecloses summary judgment in favor of petitioners.

Before the District Court, respondents claimed that petitioners' decision to remove the books "was based upon [their] personal values, morals and tastes." App. 139. Respondents also claimed that petitioners objected to the books in part because excerpts from them were "anti-American." *Id.*, at 140. The accuracy of these claims was partially conceded by petitioners,[23] and petitioners' own affidavits lent further support to respondents' claims.[24] In addition, the record developed in the District Court shows that when petitioners offered their first public explanation for the removal of the books, they relied in part on the assertion that the removed books were "anti-American," and "offensive to ... Americans in general." 474 F. Supp., at 390.[25] Furthermore, while the Book Review Committee appointed by petitioners was instructed to make its recommendations based upon criteria that appear on their face to be permissible--the books' "educational suitability," "good taste," "relevance," and "appropriateness to age and grade level," App. 67--the Committee's recommendations that five of the books be retained and that only two be removed were essentially rejected by petitioners, without any statement of reasons for doing so. Finally, while petitioners originally defended their removal decision with the explanation that "these books contain obscenities, blasphemies, and perversion beyond description," 474 F. Supp., at 390, one of the books, *A Reader for Writers*, was removed even though it contained no such language. 638 F. 2d, at 428, n. 6 (Mansfield, J., dissenting).

Standing alone, this evidence respecting the substantive motivations behind petitioners' removal decision would not be decisive. This would be a very different case if the record demonstrated that petitioners had employed established, regular, and facially unbiased procedures for the review of controversial materials. But the actual record in the case before us suggests the exact opposite. Petitioners' removal procedures were vigorously challenged below by respondents, and the evidence on this issue sheds further light on the issue of petitioners' motivations.[26] Respondents alleged that in making their removal decision petitioners ignored "the advice of literary experts," the views of "librarians and teachers within the Island Trees School system," the advice of the superintendent of schools, and the guidance of "publications that rate books for junior and senior high school students." App. 128-129. Respondents also claimed that petitioners' decision was based solely on the fact that the books were named on the PONYU list received by petitioners Ahrens, Martin, and Hughes, and that petitioners "did not undertake an independent review of other books in the [school] libraries." *Id.*, at 129-130. Evidence before the District Court lends support to these claims. The record shows that immediately after petitioners first ordered the books removed from the library shelves, the superintendent of schools reminded them that "we already have a policy...designed expressly to handle such problems," and recommended that the removal decision be approached through this established channel. See n. 4, *supra*. But the Board disregarded the superintendent's advice, and instead resorted to the extraordinary procedure of appointing a Book Review Committee--the advice of which was later rejected without explanation. In sum, respondents' allegations and some of the evidentiary materials presented below do not rule out the possibility that petitioners' removal procedures were highly irregular and ad hoc--the antithesis of those procedures that might tend to allay suspicions regarding petitioners' motivations.

Construing these claims, affidavit statements, and other evidentiary materials in a manner favorable to respondents, we cannot conclude that petitioners were "entitled to a judgment as a matter of law." The evidence plainly does not foreclose the possibility that petitioners' decision to remove the books rested decisively upon disagreement with constitutionally protected ideas in those books, or upon a desire on petitioners' part to impose upon the students of the Island Trees High School and Junior High School a political orthodoxy to which petitioners and their constituents adhered. Of course, some of the evidence before the District Court might lead a finder of fact to accept petitioners' claim that their removal decision was based upon constitutionally valid concerns. But that evidence at most creates a genuine issue of material fact on the critical question of the credibility of petitioners' justifications for their decision: On that issue, it simply cannot be said that there is no genuine issue as to any material fact.

The mandate shall issue forthwith.

Affirmed.

JUSTICE BLACKMUN, concurring in part and concurring in the judgment.

While I agree with much in today's plurality opinion, and while I accept the standard laid down by the plurality to guide proceedings on remand, I write separately because I have a somewhat different perspective on the nature of the First Amendment right involved.

I

To my mind, this case presents a particularly complex problem because it involves two competing principles of constitutional stature. On the one hand, as the dissenting opinions demonstrate, and as we all can agree, the Court has acknowledged the importance of the public schools "in the preparation of individuals for participation as citizens, and in the preservation of values on which our society rests." *Ambach* v. *Norwick*, 441 U.S. 68, 76 (1979). See, also, *ante*, at 9-10 (plurality opinion). Because of the essential socializing function of schools, local education officials may attempt "to promote civic virtues," *Ambach* v. *Norwick*, 441 U.S., at 80, and to "awake[n] the child to cultural values." *Brown* v. *Board of Education*, 347 U.S. 483, 493 (1954). Indeed, the Constitution presupposes the existence of an informed citizenry prepared to participate in governmental affairs, and these democratic principles obviously are constitutionally incorporated into the structure of our government. It therefore seems entirely appropriate that the State use "public schools [to]...inculcat[e] fundamental values necessary to the maintenance of a democratic political system." *Ambach* v. *Norwick*, 441 U.S., at 77.

On the other hand, as the plurality demonstrates, it is beyond dispute that schools and school boards must operate within the confines of the First Amendment. In a variety of academic settings the Court therefore has acknowledged the force of the principle that schools, like other enterprises operated by the State, may not be run in such a manner as to "prescribe what shall be orthodox in politics, nationalism, religion, or other matters of opinion." *West Virginia State Board of Education* v. *Barnette*, 319 U.S. 624, 642 (1943). While none of these cases define the limits of a school board's authority to choose a curriculum and academic materials, they are based on the general proposition that "state-operated schools may not be enclaves of totalitarianism.... In our system, students may not be regarded as closed-circuit recipients of only that which the State chooses to communicate." *Tinker* v. *Des Moines School Dist.*, 393 U.S. 503, 511 (1969).

The Court in *Tinker* thus rejected the view that "a State might so conduct its schools as to 'foster a homogeneous people.'" *Id.*, at 511, quoting *Meyer* v. *Nebraska*, 262 U.S. 390, 402 (1923). Similarly, *Keyishian* v. *Board of Regents*, 385 U.S. 589 (1967)--a case that involved the State's attempt to remove "subversives" from academic positions at its universities, but that addressed itself more broadly to public education in general--held that "[t]he classroom is peculiarly the 'marketplace of ideas'"; the First Amendment therefore "does not tolerate laws that cast a pall of orthodoxy over the classroom." *Id.*, at 603. And *Barnette* is most clearly applicable here: its holding was based squarely on the view that "[f]ree public education, if faithful to the ideal of secular instruction and political neutrality, will not be partisan or enemy of any class, creed, party, or faction." The Court therefore made it clear that imposition of "ideological discipline" was not a proper undertaking for school authorities. 319 U.S., at 637.

In combination with more generally applicable First Amendment rules, most particularly the central proscription of content-based regulations of speech, see *Police Department of Chicago* v. *Mosley*, 408 U.S. 92 (1972), the cases outlined above yield a general principle: the State may not suppress exposure to ideas -- for the sole *purpose* of suppressing exposure to those ideas--absent sufficiently compelling reasons. Because the school board must perform all its functions "within the limits of the Bill or Rights," *Barnette*, 319 U.S., at 637, this principle necessarily applies in at least a limited way to public education. Surely this is true in an extreme case: as the plurality notes, it is difficult to see how a school board, consistent with the First Amendment, could refuse for political reasons to buy books written by Democrats or by Negroes, or books that are "anti-American" in the broadest sense of that term. Indeed, JUSTICE REHNQUIST appears "cheerfully [to] concede" this point. *Post*, at 5 (dissenting opinion).

In my view, then, the principle involved here is both narrower and more basic than the "right to receive information" identified by the plurality. I do not suggest that the State has any affirmative obligation to provide students with information or ideas, something that may well be associated with a "right to receive." See *post*, at 4(THE CHIEF JUSTICE, dissenting); *post*, at 13-15 (REHNQUIST, J., dissenting). And I do not believe, as the plurality suggests, that the right at issue here is somehow associated with the peculiar nature of the school library, see *ante*, at 14-15; if schools may be used to inculcate ideas, surely libraries may play a role in that process.[1] Instead, I suggest that certain forms of state discrimination *between* ideas are improper. In particular, our precedents command the conclusion that the State may not act to deny access to an idea simply because state officials disapprove of that idea for partisan or political reasons.[2]

Certainly, the unique environment of the school places substantial limits on the extent to which official decisions may be restrained by First Amendment values. But that environment also makes it particularly important that *some* limits be imposed. The school is designed to, and inevitably will, inculcate ways of thought and outlooks; if educators intentionally may eliminate all diversity of thought, the school will "strangle the free mind at its source and teach youth to discount important principles of our government as mere platitudes." *Barnette*, 319 U.S., at 637. As I see it, then, the question in this case is how to make the delicate accommodation between the limited constitutional restriction that I think is imposed by the First Amendment, and

the necessarily broad state authority to regulate education. In starker terms, we must reconcile the schools' "inculcative" function with the First Amendment's bar on "prescriptions of orthodoxy."

II

In my view, we strike a proper balance here by holding that school officials may not remove books for the *purpose* of restricting access to the political ideas or social perspectives discussed in them, when that action is motivated simply by the officials' disapproval of the ideas involved. It does not seem radical to suggest that state action calculated to suppress novel ideas or concepts is fundamentally antithetical to the values of the First Amendment. At a minimum, allowing a school board to engage in such conduct hardly teaches children to respect the diversity of ideas that is fundamental to the American system. In this context, then, the school board must "be able to show that its action was caused by something more than a mere desire to avoid the discomfort and unpleasantness that always accompany an unpopular viewpoint," *Tinker* v. *Des Moines School Dist.*, 393 U.S., at 509, and that the board had something in mind in addition to the suppression of partisan or political views it did not share.

As I view it, this is a narrow principle. School officials must be able to choose one book over another, without outside interference, when the first book is deemed more relevant to the curriculum, or better written, or when one of a host of other politically neutral reasons is present. These decisions obviously will not implicate First Amendment values. And even absent space or financial limtiations, First Amendment principles would allow a school board to refuse to make a book available to students because it contains offensive language, cf. *FCC* v. *Pacifica Foundation*, 438 U.S. 726,757 (1978)(POWELL,J., concurring), or because it is psychologically or intellectually inappropriate for the age group, or even, perhaps, because the ideas it advances are "manifestly inimical to the public welfare." *Pierce* v. *Society of Sisters*, 268 U.S. 510, 534(1925). And, of course, school officials may choose one book over another because they believe that one subject is more important, or is more deserving of emphasis.

As is evident from this discussion, I do not share JUSTICE REHNQUIST's view that the notion of "suppression of ideas" is not a useful analytical concept. See *post*, at 15-17 (dissenting opinion). Indeed, JUSTICE REHNQUIST's discussion itself demonstrates that "access to ideas" has been given meaningful application in a variety of contexts. See *id.*, at 8-19, 11 ("[e]ducation consists of the selective presentation and explanation of ideas"). And I believe that tying the First Amendment right to the *purposeful* suppression of ideas makes the concept more manageable than JUSTICE REHNQUIST acknowledges. Most people would recognize that refusing to allow discussion of current events in Latin class is a policy designed to "incul-cate" Latin, not to suppress ideas. Similarly, removing a learned treatise criticizing American foreign policy from an elementary school library because the students would not understand it is an action unrelated to the *purpose* of suppressing ideas. In my view, however, removing the same treatise because it is "anti-American" raises a far more difficult issue.

It is not a sufficient answer to this prob-lem that a State operates a school in its role as "educator," rather than its role as "sove-reign," see *post*, at 5-7 (REHNQUIST, J., dis-senting), for the First Amendment has applica-tion to all the State's activities. While the State may act as "property owner" when it pre-vents certain types of expressive activity from taking place on public lands, for example, see *post*, at 6, few would suggest that the State may base such restrictions on the content of the speaker's message, or may take its action for the purpose of suppressing access to the ideas involved. See *Police Department of Chicago* v. *Mosley*, 408 U.S., at 96. And while it is not clear to me from JUSTICE REHNQUIST's dis-cussion whether a State operates its public li-braries in its "role as sovereign," surely dif-ficult constitutional problems would arise if a State chose to exclude "anti-American" books from its public libraries--even if those books remained available at local bookstores.

Concededly, a tension exists between the properly inculcative purposes of public educa-tion and any limitation on the school board's absolute discretion to choose academic materi-als. But that tension demonstrates only that the problem here is a difficult one, not that the problem should be resolved by choosing one principle over another. As the Court has rec-ognized, school officials must have the author-ity to make educationally appropriate choices in designing a curriculum: "the State may 're-quire teaching by instruction and study of all in our history and in the structure and organi-zation of our government, including the guaran-ties of civil liberty, which tend to inspire patriotism and love of country.'" *Barnette*, 319 U.S., at 631, quoting *Minersville School District* v. *Gobitis*, 310 U.S. 586, 604 (1940) (Stone, J., dissenting). Thus school officials may seek to instill certain values "by persuasion and example," 319 U.S., at 640, or by choice of emphasis. That sort of positive educational action, however, is the converse of an intentional attempt to shield students from certain ideas that officials find politically distasteful. Arguing that the ma-jority in the community rejects the ideas in-volved, see *post*, at 5, 7-8 (THE CHIEF JUSTICE, dissenting), does not refute this principle: "The very purpose of a Bill of Rights was to withdraw certain subjects from the vicissitudes of political controversy, to place them beyond the reach of majorities and officials...." *Barnette*, 319 U.S.. at 638.

As THE CHIEF JUSTICE notes, the principle involved here may be difficult to apply in an individual case. See *post*, at 6 (dissenting opinion). But on a record as sparse as the one

before us, the plurality can hardly be faulted for failing to explore every possible ramifaca-tion of its decision. And while the absence of a record "underscore[s] the views of those of us who originally felt that the [case] should not be taken," *Ferguson* v. *Moore-McCormack Lines*, 352 U.S. 521, 559 (1957) (Harlan, J., concurring and dissenting), the case is here, and must be decided.

Because I believe that the plurality has de-rived a standard similar to the one compelled by my analysis, I join all but Part IIA(1) of the plurality opinion.

JUSTICE WHITE, concurring in the judgment.

The District Court found that the books were removed from the school library because the school board believed them "to be, in essence, vulgar". 474 F. Supp. 387, 397 (EDNY 1979). Both Court of Appeals judges in the majority concluded, however, that there was a material issue of fact that precluded summary judgment sought by petitioners. The unresolved factual issue, as I understand it, is the reason or reasons underlying the school board's removal of the books. I am not inclined to disagree with the Court of Appeals on such a fact-bound issue and hence concur in the judgment of af-firmance. Presumably this will result in a trial and the making of a full record and find-ings on the critical issues.

The Court seems compelled to go further and issue a dissertation on the extent to which the First Amendment limits the discretion of the school board to remove books from the school library. I see no neccessity for doing so at this point. When findings of fact and conclu-sions of law are made by the District Court, that may end the case. If, for example, the District Court concludes after a trial that the books were removed for their vulgarity, there may be no appeal. In any event, if there is an appeal, if there is dissatisfaction with the subsequent Court of Appeals' judgment, and if certiorari is sought and granted, there will be time enough to address the First Amendment is-sues that may then be presented.

I thus prefer the course taken by the Court in *Kennedy* v. *Silas Mason Co.*, 334 U.S. 249 (1948), a suit involving overtime compensation under the Fair Labor Standards Act. Summary judgment had been granted by the District Court and affirmed by the Court of Appeals. This Court reversed, holding that summary judgment was improvidently granted, and remanded for trial so that a proper record could be made. The Court expressly abjured issuing its advice on the legal issues involved. Writing for the Court, Justice Jackson stated:

"We consider it the part of good judicial administration to withhold decision of the ultimate questions involved in this case un-til this or another record shall present a more solid basis of findings based on liti-gation or on a comprehensive statement of agreed facts. While we might be able, on the present record, to reach a conclusion that would decide the case, it might well be found later to be lacking in the thoroughness that should precede judgment of this importance and which it is the purpose of the judicial process to provide.

"Without intimating any conclusion on the merits, we vacate the judgments below and remand the case to the District Court for reconsideration and amplification of the record in the light of this opinion and of present contentions." 334 U.S., at 257.

We took a similar course in a unanimous *per curiam* opinion in *Dombrowski* v. *Eastland*, 387 U.S. 82 (1967). There we overturned a summary judgment since it was necessary to resolve a factual dispute about collaboration between one of the respondents and a state legislative committee. We remanded, saying: "In the absence of the factual refinement which can occur only as a result of trial, we need not and, indeed, could not express judgment as to the legal consequences of such collaboration, if it occurred." 387 U.S., at 84.

The *Silas Mason* case turned on issues of statutory construction. It is even more important that we take a similar course in cases like *Dombrowski*, which involved Speech or Debate Clause immunity and in this one, which poses difficult First Amendment issues in a largely uncharted field. We should not decide constitutional questions until it is necessary to do so, or at least until there is better reason to address them than are evident here. I therefore concur in the judgment of affirmance.

CHIEF JUSTICE BURGER, with whom JUSTICE POWELL, JUSTICE REHNQUIST, and JUSTICE O'CONNOR join, dissenting.

The First Amendment, as with other parts of the Constitution, must deal with new problems in a changing world. In an attempt to deal with a problem in an area traditionally left to the states, a plurality of the Court, in a lavish expansion going beyond any prior holding under the First Amendment, expresses its view that a school board's decision concerning what books are to be in the school library is subject to federal court review.[1] Were this to become the law, this Court would come perilously close to becoming a "super censor" of school board library decisions. Stripped to its essentials, the issue comes down to two important propositions: *first*, whether local schools are to be administered by elected school boards, or by federal judges and teenage pupils; and *second*, whether the values of morality, good taste, and relevance to education are valid reasons for school board decisions concerning the contents of a school library. In an attempt to place this case within the protection of the First Amendment, the plurality suggests a new "right" that, when shorn of the plurality's rhetoric, allows this Court to impose its own views about what books must be made available to students.[2]

I
A

I agree with the fundamental proposition that "students do not 'shed their rights to freedom of speech or expression at the schoolhouse gate.'" *Ante*, at 11. For example, the Court has held that a school board cannot compel a student to participate in a flag salute ceremony, *West Virginia Bd. of Education* v. *Barnette*, 319 U.S. 624 (1943), or *prohibit* a student from expressing certain views, so long as that expression does not disrupt the educational process. *Tinker* v. *Des Moines School Dist.*, 393 U.S. 503 (1969). Here, however, no restraints of any kind are placed on the students. They are free to read the books in question, which are available at public libraries and bookstores; they are free to discuss them in the classroom or elsewhere. Despite this absence of any direct external control on the students' ability to express themselves, the plurality suggest that there is a new First Amendment "entitlement" to have access to particular books in a school library.

The plurality cites *Meyer* v. *Nebraska*, 262 U.S. 390 (1923), which struck down a state law that restricted the teaching of modern foreign languages in public and private schools, and *Epperson* v. *Arkansas*, 393 U.S. 97 (1968), which declared unconstitutional under the Establishment Clause a law banning the teaching of Darwinian evolution, to establish the validity of federal court interference with the functioning of schools. The plurality finds it unnecessary "to re-enter this difficult terrain," *ante*, at 7, yet in the next breath relies on these very cases and others to establish the previously unheard of "right" of access to particular books in the public school library.[3] The apparent underlying basis of the plurality's view seems to be that students have an enforceable "right" to receive the information and ideas that are contained in junior and senior high school library books. *Ante*, at 12. This "right" purportedly follows "ineluctably" from the sender's First Amendment right to freedom of speech and as a "necessary predicate" to the recipient's meaningful exercise of his own rights of speech, press, and political freedom. *Ante*, at 12-13. No such right, however, has previously been recognized.

It is true that where there is a willing distributor of materials, the government may not impose unreasonable obstacles to dissemination by the third party. *Virginia State Board of Pharmacy* v. *Virginia Citizens Consumer Council, Inc,*, 425 U.S. 748 (1976). And where the speaker desires to express certain ideas, the government may not impose unreasonable restraints. *Tinker* v. *Des Moines School Dist., supra*. It does not follow, however, that a school board must affirmatively aid the speaker in its communication with the recipient. In short the plurality suggests today that if a writer has something to say, the government through its schools must be the courier. None of the cases cited by the plurality establish this broad-based proposition.

First, the plurality argues that the right to receive ideas is derived in part from the sender's first amendment rights to send them. Yet we have previously held that a sender's rights are not absolute. *Rowan* v. *Post Office Dept.*, 397 U.S. 728 (1970).[4] Never before today has the Court indicated that the government has an *obligation* to aid a speaker or author in reaching an audience.

Second, the plurality concludes that "the right to receive ideas is a necessary predicate to the *recipient's* meaningful exercise of his own rights of speech, press, and political freedom." *Ante*, at 13 (emphasis in original). However, the "right to receive information and ideas," *Stanley* v. *Georgia*, 394 U.S. 557, 564 (1969), cited *ante*, at 12, does not carry with it the concomitant right to have those ideas affirmatively provided at a particular place by the government. The plurality cites James Madison to emphasize the importance of having an informed citizenry. *Ante*, at 13. We all agree with Madison, of course, that knowledge is necessary for effective government. Madison's view, however, does not establish a *right* to have particular books retained on the school library shelves if the school board decides that they are inappropriate or irrelevant to the school's mission. Indeed, if the need to have an informed citizenry creates a "right," why is the government not also required to provide ready access to a variety of information? This same need would support a constitutional "right" of the people to have public libraries as part of a new constitutional "right" to continuing adult education.

The plurality also cites *Tinker, supra*, to establish that the recipient's right to free speech encompasses a right to have particular books retained in the school library shelf. *Ante*, at 14. But the cited passage of *Tinker* notes only that school officials may not *prohibit* a student from expressing his or her view on a subject unless that expression interferes with the legitimate operations of the school. The government does not "contract the spectrum of available knowledge." *Griswold* v. *Connecticut*, 381 U.S. 479, 482 (1965), cited *ante*, at 12, by choosing not to retain certain books on the school library shelf; it simply chooses not to be the conduit for that particular information. In short, even assuming the desirability of the policy expressed by the plurality, there is not a hint in the First Amendment, or in any holding of this Court, of a "right" to have the government provide continuing access to certain books.

B

Whatever role the government might play as a conduit of information, schools in particular ought not be made a slavish courier of the material of third parties. The plurality pays homage to the ancient verity that in the administration of the public schools "'there is a legitimate and substantial community interest in promoting respect for authority and traditional values be they social, moral, or political.'" *Ante*, at 10. If, as we have held, schools may legitimately be used as vehicles for "inculcating fundamental values necessary to the maintenance of a democratic political system," *Ambach* v. *Norwick*, 441 U.S. 68, 77 (1979), school authorities must have broad discretion to fulfill that obligation. Presumably all activity within a primary or secondary school involves the conveyance of information and at least an implied approval of the worth of that information. How are "fundamental values" to be inculcated except by having school boards make content-based decisions about the appropriateness of retaining materials in the school library and curriculum. In order to fulfill its function, an elected school board *must* express its views on the subjects which are taught to its students. In doing so those elected officials express the views of their community; they may err, of course, and the voters may remove them. It is a startling erosion of the very idea of democratic government to have this Court arrogate to itself the power the plurality asserts today.

The plurality concludes that under the Consititution school boards cannot choose to retain or dispense with books if their discretion is exercised in a "narrowly partisan or political manner." *Ante*, at 16. The plurality concedes that permissible factors are whether the books are "pervasively vulgar," *ante*, at 17, or educationally unsuitable. *Ibid.* "Educational suitability, however, is a standardless phrase. This conclusion will undoubtedly be drawn in many -- if not most -- instances because of the decisionmaker's content-based judgment that the ideas contained in the book or the idea expressed from the author's method of communication are inappropriate for teenage pupils.

The plurality also tells us that a book may be removed from a school library if it is "pervasively vulgar." But why must the vulgarity be "pervasive" to be offensive? Vulgarity might be concentrated in a single poem or a single chapter or a single page, yet still be inappropriate. Or a school board might reasonably conclude that even "random" vulgarity is inappropriate for teenage school students. A school board might also reasonably conclude that the school board's retention of such books gives those volumes an implicit endorsement. Cf. *FCC* v. *Pacifica Foundation*, 438 U.S. 726 (1978).

Further, there is no guidance whatsoever as to what constitutes "political" factors. This Court has previously recognized that public education involves an area of broad public policy and "go[es] to the heart of representative government.'" *Ambach* v. *Norwick*, 441 U.S. 68, 74 (1979). As such, virtually all educational decisions necessarily involve "political" determinations.

What the plurality views as valid reasons for removing a book at their core involve partisan judgments. Ultimately the federal courts

will be the judge of whether the motivation for
book removal was "valid" or "reasonable." Undoubtedly the validity of many book removals
will ultimately turn on a judge's evaluation of
the books. Discretion must be used, and the
appropriate body to exercise that discretion is
the local elected school board, not judges.[5]

We can all agree that as a matter of *educational policy* students should have wide access
to information and ideas. But the people elect
school boards, who in turn select administrators, who select the teachers, and these are
the individuals best able to determine the substance of that policy. The plurality fails to
recognize the fact that local control of education involves democracy in a microcosm. In
most public schools in the United States the
parents have a large voice in running the
school.[6] Through participation in the election of school board members, the parents influence, if not control, the direction of their
children's education. A school board is not a
giant bureaucracy far removed from accountabil-
ity for its actions; it is truly "of the people
and by the people." A school board reflects
its constituency in a very real sense and thus
could not long exercise unchecked discretion in
its choice to acquire or remove books. If the
parents disagree with the educational decisions
of the school board, they can take steps to remove the board members from office. Finally,
even if parents and students cannot convince
the school board that book removal is inappropriate, they have alternative sources to the
same end. Books may be acquired from book
stores, public libraries, or other alternative
sources unconnected with the unique environment
of the local public schools.[7]

II

No amount of "limiting" language could rein
in the sweeping "right" the plurality would
create. The plurality distinguishes library
books from textbooks because library books "by
their nature are optional rather than required
reading." *Ante*, at 8. It is not clear, however, why this distinction requires *greater*
scrutiny before "optional" reading materials
may be removed. It would appear that required
reading and textbooks have a greater likelihood
of imposing a "'pall of orthodoxy'" over the
educational process than do optional reading.
Ante, at 16. In essence, the plurality's
view transforms the availability of this "optional" reading into a "right" to have this
"optional" reading maintained at the demand of
teenagers.

The plurality also limits the new right by
finding it applicable only to the *removal* of
books once acquired. Yet if the First Amendment commands that certain books cannot be *removed,* does it not equally require that the
same books be *acquired?* Why does the coinci-
dence of timing become the basis of a constitutional holding? According to the plurality,
the evil to be avoided is the "official suppression of ideas." *Ante*, at 17. It does
not follow that the decision to *remove* a book

is less "official suppression" than the decision not to acquire a book desired by someone.[8] Similarly, a decision to eliminate
certain material from the curriculum, history
for example, would carry an equal -- probably
greater -- prospect of "official suppression."
Would the decision be subject to our review?

III

Through use of bits and pieces of prior
opinions unrelated to the issue of this case,
the plurality demeans our function of constitu-
tinal adjudication. Today the plurality suggests that the *Constitution* distinguishes between school libraries and school classrooms,
between *removing* unwanted books and *acquiring* books. Even more extreme, the plurality concludes that the Constitution *requires*
school boards to justify to its teenage pupils
the decision to remove a particular book from
the school library. I categorically reject
this notion that the Constitution dictates that
judges, rather than parents, teachers, and local school boards, must determine how the
standards of morality and vulgarity are to be
treated in the classroom.

JUSTICE POWELL, dissenting.

The plurality opinion today rejects a basic
concept of public school education in our country: that the States and locally elected school
boards should have the responsibility for determining the educational policy of the public
schools. After today's decision any junior
high school student, by instituting a suit
against a school board or teacher, may invite a
judge to overrule an educational decision by
the official body designated by the people to
operate the schools.

I

School boards are uniquely local and democratic institutions. Unlike the governing bodies of cities and counties, school boards have
only one responsibility: the education of the
youth of our country during their most formative and impressionable years. Apart from
health, no subject is closer to the hearts of
parents than their children's education during
those years. For these reasons, the governance
of elementary and secondary education traditionally has been placed in the hands of a local board, responsible locally to the parents
and citizens of school districts. Through parent-teacher associations (PTA's), and even less
formal arrangements that vary with schools,
parents are informed and often may influence
decisions of the board. Frequently, parents
know the teachers and visit classes. It is
fair to say that no single agency of government
at any level is closer to the people whom it
serves than the typical school board.

I therefore view today's decision with genuine dismay. Whatever the final outcome of this
suit and suits like it, the resolution of educational policy decisions through litigation,
and the exposure of school board members to liability for such decisions, can be expected to

corrode the school board's authority and effectiveness. As is evident from the generality of the plurality's "standard" for judicial review, the decision as to the educational worth of a book is a highly subjective one. Judges rarely are as competent as school authorities to make this decision; nor are judges responsive to the parents and people of the school district.[1]

The new constitutional right, announced by the plurality, is described as a "right to receive ideas" in a school. *Ante*, at 12. As the dissenting opinions of THE CHIEF JUSTICE and JUSTICE REHNQUIST so powerfully demonstrate, however, this new found right finds no support in the First Amendment precedents of this Court. And even apart from the inappropriateness of judicial oversight of educational policy, the new constitutional right is framed in terms that approach a meaningless generalization. It affords little guidance to courts, if they—as the plurality now authorizes them—are to oversee the inculcation of ideas. The plurality does announce the following standard: A school board's "discretion may not be exercised in a narrowly partisan or political manner." *Ante*, at _____. But this is a standardless standard that affords no more than subjective guidance to school boards, their counsel, and to courts that now will be required to decide whether a particular decision was made in a "narrowly partisan or political manner." Even the "chancellor's foot" standard in ancient equity jurisdiction was never this fuzzy.

As JUSTICE REHNQUIST tellingly observes, how does one limit—on a principled basis —today's new constitutional right? If a 14 year old child may challenge a school board's decision to remove a book from the library, upon what theory is a court to prevent a like challenge to a school board's decision not to purchase that identical book? And at the even more "sensitive" level of "receiving ideas," does today's decision entitle student oversight of which courses may be added or removed from the curriculum, or even of what a particular teacher elects to teach or not teach in the classroom? Is not the "right to receive ideas" as much—or indeed even more—implicated in these educational questions?[2]

                    II

The plurality's reasoning is marked by contradiction. It purports to acknowledge the traditional role of school boards and parents in deciding what should be taught in the schools. It states the truism that the schools are "vitally important 'in the preparation of individuals for participation as citizens,' and as vehicles for 'inculcating fundamental values necessary to the maintenance of a democratic political system.'" *Ante*, at _____. Yet when a school board, as in this case, takes its responsibilities seriously and seeks to decide what the fundamental values are that should be imparted, the plurality finds a constitutional violation.

Just this term the Court held, in an opinion I joined, that the children of illegal aliens must be permitted to attend the public schools. See *Plyler* v. *Doe*, _____ U.S. _____ (1982). Quoting from earlier opinions, the Court noted that "the public school [is] a most vital civic institution for the preservation of a democratic system of government" and that the public schools are "the primary vehicle for transmitting 'the values on which our society rests.'" *Id.*, at _____. By denying to illegal aliens the opportunity "to absorb the values and skills upon which our social order rests" the law under review placed a lifelong disability upon these illegal alien children. *Ibid.*

Today the plurality drains much of the content from these apt phrases. A school board's attempt to instill in its students the ideas and values on which a democratic system depends is viewed as an impermissible suppression of other ideas and values on which other systems of government and other societies thrive. Books may not be removed because they are indecent; extoll violence, intolerance and racism; or degrade the dignity of the individual. Human history, not the least of the twentieth century, records the power and political life of these very ideas. But they are not our ideas or values. Although I would leave this educatonal decision to the duly constituted board, I certainly would not *require* a school board to promote ideas and values repugnant to a democratic society or to teach such values to *children*.

In different contexts and in different times, the destruction of written materials has been the symbol of despotism and intolerance. But the removal of nine vulgar or racist books from a high school library by a concerned local school board does not raise this specter. For me, today's decision symbolizes a debilitating encroachment upon the institutions of a free people.

Attached as an Appendix hereto is Judge Mansfield's summary of excerpts from the books at issue in this case.

APPENDIX

"The excerpts which led the Board to look into the educational suitability of the books in question are set out (with minor corrections after comparison with the text of the books themselves) below. The pagination and the underlinings are retained from the original report used by the board. In newer editions of some books, the quotes appear at different pages.

"1) *SOUL ON ICE* by Eldrige Cleaver
PAGE QUOTE
157-158'. . . There are white men who will pay you to fuck their wives. They approach you and say, 'How would you like to fuck a white woman?' 'What is this?' you ask. 'On the up-and-up,' he assures you. 'It's all right. She's my wife. She needs black rod, is all. She has to have it. It's like a medicine or drug to her. She has to have it. I'll pay you. It's all on the level, no trick involved. Interested?' You go with him and he drives you to their home. The three of you go into the bedroom. There is a certain type who will leave you and his wife alone and tell you to pile her real good. After it is all over, he will pay you and drive you to wherever you want to go. Then there are some who like to peep at you through a keyhole and watch you have his woman, or peep at you through a window, or lie under the bed and listen to the creaking of the bed as you work out. There is another type who likes to masturbate while he stands beside the bed and watches you pile her. There is the type who likes to eat his woman up after you get through piling her. And there is the type who only wants you to pile her for a little while, just long enough to thaw her out and kick her motor over and arouse her to heat, then he wants you to jump off real quick and he will jump onto her and together they can make it from there by themselves.'

"2) *A HERO AIN'T NOTHING BUT A SANDWICH*
  by Alice Childress
PAGE QUOTE
10 'Hell, no! *Fuck the society.*'
64-65 'The hell with the junkie, the wino, the capitalist, the welfare checks, the world . . . yeah, and *fuck* you too!'
75-76 'They can have the spread and curtains, I'm too old for them *fuckin* bunnies anyway.'
"3) *THE FIXER* by Bernard Malamud
PAGE QUOTE
52 'What do you think goes on in the wagon at night: Are the drivers on their knees *fucking their mothers?*'
90 '*Fuck yourself*, said the blinker, etc.'
92 'Who else would do anything like that but a *motherfucking* Zhid?'
146 'No more noise out of you or I'll shoot your *Jew cock off.*'
189 'Also there's a lot of *fucking in the Old Testament*, so how is that religious?'
192 'You better go *fuck yourself*, Bok, said Kogin, I'm onto your Jew tricks.'
215 'Ding-dong giddyap. A *Jew's cock's* in the devil's hock.'
216 'You *cocksucker* Zhid, I ought make you

lick it up off the floor.'
"4) *GO ASK ALICE* by Anonymous
PAGE QUOTE
31 'I wonder if sex without acid could be so exciting, so wonderful, so indescribable. I always thought it just took a minute, or that it would be like dogs mating.'
47 'Chris and I walked into Richie and Ted's apartment to find the bastards stoned and making love to each other . . . low class queer.'
81 'shitty, goddamned, pissing, ass, goddamned beJesus, screwing life's, ass, shit. Doris was ten and had *humped* with who knows how many men in between . . . her current stepfather started having sex with her but good . . . *sonofabitch balling her*'
83 'but now when I face a girl its like facing a boy. I get all excited and turned on. *I want to screw with the girl . . .* '
84 'I'd rather screw with a guy . . . sometimes I want one of the girls to kiss me. I want her to touch me, to have her sleep under me.'
84 'Another day, another *blow job . . .* If I don't give *Big Ass a blow* he'll cut off my supply . . . and LittleJacon is yelling, 'Mama, *Daddy can't come now. He's humping Carla.*'
85 'Shit, goddamn, goddamn prick, son-of-a-bitch, ass, pissed, bastard, goddamn, bullshit
94 'I hope you have a *nice orgasim with your dog tonight.*'
110 'You *fucking* Miss Polly pure
117 'Then he said that all I needed was a good *fuck.*'
146 'It might be great because I'm practically a virgin in the sense that I've never had sex except when I've been stoned. . . . '
"5) *SLAUGHTERHOUSE FIVE* by Kurt Vonnegut, Jr.
PAGE QUOTE
29 "Get out of the road, you dumb *motherfucker.*' The last word was still a novelty in the speech of white people in 1944. It was fresh and astonishing to Billy, who had never *fucked* anybody . . . '
32 'You stake a guy out on an anthill in the desert-see? He's facing upward, and you put *honey* all over his *balls and pecker*, and you cut off his eyelids so he has to stare at the sun till he dies.'
34 'He had a prophylactic kit containing two tough condoms 'For prevention of disease only!' . . . He had a dirty picture of a *woman* attempting *sexual intercourse with a shetland pony.*'
94 & 95 'But the Gospels actually taught this: Before you kill somebody, make absolutely sure he isn't well connected . . .
The flaw in the Christ stories, said the visitor from outer space, was that Christ who didn't look like much, was actually the son of the Most Powerful Being in the Universe. Readers understood that, so, when they came to the crucifixion, they naturally thought . . . Oh boy-they sure picked the wrong guy to lynch this time! And that thought had a brother: There are right people to lynch. People not well connected . . . . The visitor from outer space made a gift to Earth of a new Gospel. In it, Jesus really WAS a nobody, and a pain in the neck to a lot of people with better connec-

tions than he had . . . . So the people amused themselves one day by nailing him to a cross and planting the cross in the ground. There couldn't possibly be any repercussions, the lynchers thought . . . since the new Gospel hammered home again and again what a nobody Jesus was. And then just before the nobody dies . . . . The voice of God came crashing down. He told the people that he was adopting the bum as his son . . . God said this: *From this moment on, He will punish horribly anybody who torments a bum who has no connections.*'

99 'They told him that there could be no Earthling babies without male homosexuals. There could be babies without female homosexuals.'

120 'Why don't you go *fuck* yourself? Don't think I haven't tried . . . he was going to have revenge, and that revenge was sweet . . . It's the sweetest thing there is, said Lazaro. People *fuck* with me, he said, and *Jesus Christ* are they ever fucking sorry.'

122 'And he'll pull out a gun and *shoot his pecker off*. The stranger'll let him think a couple of seconds about who Paul Lazzaro is and what life's gonna be like without a *pecker*. Then he'll shoot him once in the guts and walk away. . . . He died on account of this silly *cocksucker* here. So I promised him I'd have the silly *cocksucker* shot after the war.'

134 'In my prison cell I sit . . . With my *britches full of shit*, And my *balls are bouncing* gently on the floor. And I see the bloody snag when she bit me in the bag . . . Oh, I'll never *fuck a Polack* any more.'

173 'And the *peckers* of the young men would still be *semierect*, and their *muscles* would be *bulging like cannonballs*.' .

175 'They didn't have *hard-ons* . . . Everybody else did.'

177 'The magazine, which was published for *lonesome men to jerk off to*.'

178 'and one critic said. . . . 'To describe *blow-jobs* artistically."

"6) *THE BEST SHORT STORIES BY NEGRO WRITERS*
Ed. by Langston Hughes
PAGE QUOTE
176 'like bat's shit and camel piss.'
228 'that no-count bitch of a daughter of yours is up there up north making a whore of herself.'
237 'they made her get out and stand in front of the headlights of the car and pull down her pants and raise her dress--they said that was the only way they could be sure. And you can imagine what they said and what they did--.'
303 'You need some pussy. Come on, let's go up to the whore house on the hill.' 'Oh these bastards, these bastards, this God damned Army and the bastards in it. The sons of bitches!'
436 'he produced a brown rag doll, looked at her again, then grabbed the doll by its legs and tore it part way up the middle. Then he jammed his finger way into the rip between the doll's legs. The other men laughed. . . . '
444 'The pimps, hustlers, lesbians, and others trying to misuse me.'
462 'but she had straight firm legs and her breasts were small and upright. No doubt if she'd had children her breasts would be hanging like little empty purses.'

464 'She first became aware of the warm tense nipples on her breasts. Her hands went up gently to clam them.' 'In profile, his penis hung like a stout tassle. She could even tell that he was circumcised.'
406 'Cadillac Bill was busy following Luheaster around, rubbing her stomach and saying, 'Magic Stomach, Magic Stomach, bring me a little baby cadillac." 'One of the girls went upstairs with Red Top and stayed for about forty five minutes.'

"7) *BLACK BOY* by Richard Wright
PAGE QUOTE
70-71 'We black children-seven or eight or nine years of age-used to run to the Jew's store and shout:

    . . . Bloddy Christ Killers
    Never trust a Jew
    Bloody Christ Killers
    What won't a Jew do . . .
    Red, white and blue
    Your pa was a Jew
    Your ma a dirty dago
    What the hell is you?'

265 'Crush that nigger's nuts, nigger!' 'Hit that nigger!' 'Aw, fight, you goddam niggers!' 'Sock 'im, in his f-k-g-piece' 'Make 'im bleed!'

"8) *LAUGHING BOY* by Oliver LaFarge
PAGE QUOTE
38 "I'll tell you, she is all bad; for two bits she will do the worst thing.'
258-9 'I was frightened when he wanted me to lie with him, but he made me feel right. He knew all about how to make women forget themselves, that man.'

"9) *THE NAKED APE* by Desmond Morris
PAGE QUOTE
73-74 "Also, the frontal approach provides the maximum possibility for stimulation of the female's clitoris during the pelvic thrusting of the male. It is true that it will be passively, stimulated by the pulling effect of the male's thrusts, regardless of his body position in relation to the female, but in a face-to-face mating there will in addition be the direct rhythmic pressure of the male's pubic region on to the clitoral area, and this will considerably heighten the stimulation . . . '
'So it seems plausible to consider that face-to-face copulation is basic to our species. There are, of course, a number of variations that do not eliminate the frontal element: male above, female above, side by side, squating, standing, and so on, but the most efficient and commonly used one is with both partners horizontal, the male above the female. . . . '
80 '. . . This broadening of the penis results in the female's external genitals being subjected to much more pulling and pushing during the performance of pelvic thrusts. With each inward thrust of the penis, the clitoral region is pulled downwards and then with each withdrawal, it moves up again. Add to this the rhythmic pressure being exerted on the clitoris region by the pubic region of the frontal copulating male, and you have a repeated massaging

of the clitoris that--were she a male--would virtually be masturbatory.'
94-99 ' . . . If either males or females cannot for some reason obtain sexual access to their opposite numbers, they will find sexual outlets in other ways. They may use other members of their own sex, or they may even use members of other species, or they may masturbate. . . . '
10) *READER FOR WRITERS* . . . "
638 F. 2d 404, 419-422 n. 1 (Mansfield, J., dissenting).

JUSTICE REHNQUIST, with whom THE CHIEF JUSTICE and JUSTICE POWELL join, dissenting.

Addressing only those aspects of the constitutional question which must be decided to determine whether or not the District Court was correct in granting summary judgement, I conclude that it was. I fully agree with the views expressed by THE CHIEF JUSTICE, and concur in his opinion. I disagree with JUSTICE BRENNAN's opinion because it is largely hypothetical in character, failing to take account of the facts as admitted by the parties pursuant to local rules of the District Court for the Eastern District of New York, and because it is analytically unsound and internally inconsistent.[1]

I
A

JUSTICE BRENNAN's opinion deals far more sparsely with the procedural posture of this case than it does with the constitutional issues which it conceives to arise under the First Amendment. It first launches into a confusing, discursive exegesis on the constitutional issues as applied to junior high school and high school libraries, *ante*, at 9-18, and only thereafter does it discuss the state of the record before the Court. *Ante*, at 18-21. Because the record facts should always establish the limits of the Court's Constitutional analysis, and are particularly relevant in cases where the trial court has granted summary judgement, I think that JUSTICE BRENNAN's approach violates our "long . . . considered practice not to decide abstract, hypothetical or contingent questions, or to decide any Constitutional question in advance of the necessity for its descision." *Alabama State Federation of Labor* v. *McAdory*, 325 U.S. 450, 461 (1944).

When JUSTICE BRENNAN finally does address the state of the record, he refers to snippets and excerpts of the relevant facts to explain why a grant of summary judgment was improper. But he totally ignores the effect of Rule 9(g) of the local rules of the District Court, under which the parties set forth their version of the disputed facts in this case.[2] Since summary judgment was entered against respondents, they are entitled to have their version of the facts, as embodied in their Rule 9(g) statement, accepted for purposes of our review. Since the parties themselves are presumably the best judges of the extent of the factual dispute between them, however, respondents certainly are not entitled to any more favorable

version of the facts than that contained in their own Rule 9(g) statement. JUSTICE BRENNAN's combing through the record of affidavits, school bulletins, and the like for bits and snatches of dispute is therefore entirely beside the point at this stage of the case.

Considering only the respondents' description of the factual aspects of petitioners' motivation, JUSTICE BRENNAN's apparent concern that the Board's action may have been a sinister political plot "to suppress ideas" may be laid to rest. The members of the Board, in deciding to remove these books were undoubtedly influenced by their own "personal values, morals, and tastes,"[3] just as any member of a school board is apt to be so influenced in making decisions as to whether a book is educationally suitable. Respondents essentially conceded that some excerpts of the removed books "contained profanities, some were sexually explicit, some were ungrammatical, some were anti-American, and some were offensive to racial, religious, or ethnic groups."[4]

Respondents also agreed that "[a]lthough the books themselves were excluded from use in the schools in any way, [petitioners] have not precluded discussion about the themes of the books themselves." App. 140. JUSTICE BRENNAN's concern with the "suppresion of ideas" thus seems entirely unwarranted on this state of the record, and his creation of Constitutional rules to cover such eventualities is entirely gratuitous. Though for reasons stated in part II of this opinion I entirely disagree with JUSTICE BRENNAN's treatment of the Constitutional issue, I also disagree with his opinion for the entirely separate reason that it is not remotely tailored to the facts presented by this case.

In the course of his discussion, JUSTICE BRENNAN states:

"Petitioners rightly possess significant discretion to determine the content of their school libraries. But that discretion may not be exercised in a narrowly partisan or political manner. If a Democratic school board , motivated by party affiliation, ordered the removal of all books written by or in favor of Republicans, few would doubt that the order violated the Constitutional rights of the students. . . . The same conclusion would surely apply if an all-white school board, motivated by racial animus, decided to remove all books authored by blacks or advocating racial equality and integration. Our Constitution does not permit the official suppression of *ideas*. Ante, 16-17 (emphasis in original).

I can cheerfully concede all of this, but as in so many other cases the extreme examples are seldom the ones that arise in the real world of Constitutional litigation. In *this case* the facts taken most favorably to respondents suggest that nothing of this sort happened. The nine books removed undoubtedly did contain "ideas," but in the light of the excerpts from them found in the dissenting opinion of Judge Mansfield in the Court of Appeals, it is apparent that eight of them contained demonstrable amounts of vulgarity and profanity, see 638 F. 2d, at 419-422 n. 1, and the ninth contained nothing that could be considered partisan or political, see *id.*, at 428 n. 6. As already demonstrated, respondents admitted as much. Petitioners did not, for the reasons stated hereafter, run afoul of the First and Four-teenth Amendments by removing these particular books from the library in the manner in which they did. I would save for another day--feeling quite confident that that day will not arrive--the extreme examples posed in JUSTICE BRENNAN's opinion.

B

Considerable light is shed on the correct resolution of the Constitutional question in this case by examining the role played by peti-tioners. Had petitioners been the members of a town council, I suppose all would agree that, absent a good deal more than is present in this record, they could not have prohibited the sale of these books by private booksellers within the municipality. But we have also recognized that the government may act in other capacities than as sovereign, and when it does the First Amendment may speak with a different voice:

> "[I]t cannot be gainsaid that the State has interests as an employer in regulating the speech of its employees that differ signifi-cantly from those it possesses in connection with regulation of the speech of the citi-zenry in general. The problem in any case is to arrive at a balance between the in-terests of the teacher, as a citizen, in commenting upon matters of concern and the interests of the State, as an employer, in promoting the efficiency of the public ser-vices it performs through its employees." *Pickering* v. *Board of Education*, 391 U.S. 563, 568 (1968).

By the same token, expressive conduct which may not be prohibited by the State as sovereign may be proscribed by the State as property owner: "The State, no less than a private owner of property, has the power to preserve the proper-ty under its control for the use to which it is lawfully dedicated." *Adderley* v. *Florida*, 385 U.S. 39, 47 (1967) (upholding state prohibition of expressive conduct on certain state property).

With these differentiated roles of govern-ment in mind, it is helpful to assess the role of government as educator, as compared with the role of government as sovereign. When it acts as an educator, at least at the elementary and secondary school level, the government is en-gaged in inculcating social values and know-ledge in relatively impressionable young peo-ple. Obviously there are innumerable decisions to be made as to what courses should be taught, what books should be purchased, or what teach-ers should be employed. In every one of these areas the members of the school board will act on the basis of their own personal or moral

values, will attempt to mirror those of the community, or will abdicate the making of such decisions to so-called "experts."[5] In this connection I find myself entirely in agreement with the observation of the Court of Appeals for the Seventh Circuit in *Zykan* v. *Warsaw Community School Corp.* 631 F. 2d 1300, 1305 (1980), that it is permissible and appropriate for local boards to make educational decisions based upon their personal social, political and moral views." In the very course of adminis-tering the many faceted operations of a school district, the mere decision to purchase some books will necessarily preclude the possibility of purchasing others. The decision to teach a particular subject may preclude the possiblity of teaching another subject. A decision to re-place a teacher because of ineffectiveness may by implication be seen as a disparagement of the subject matter taught. In each of these instances, however, the book or the exposure to the subject matter may be acquired elsewhere. The managers of the school district are not proscribing it as to the citizenry in general, but are simply determining that it will not be included in the curriculum or school library. In short, actions by the government as educator do not raise the same First Amendment concerns as actions by the government as sovereign.

II

JUSTICE BRENNAN would hold that the First Amendment gives high school and junior high school students a "right to receive ideas" in the school. *Ante*, at 12. This right is a curious entitlement. It exists only in the li-brary of the school, and only if the idea pre-viously has been acquired by the school in book form. It provides no protection against a school board's decision not to acquire a par-ticular book, even though that decision denies access to ideas as fully as removal of the book from the library, and it prohibits removal of perviously acquired books only if the remover "dislike[s] the ideas contained in those books," even though removal for any other rea-son also denies the students access to the books. *Ante*, at 17-18.

But it is not the limitations which JUSTICE BRENNAN places on the right with which I dis-agree; they simply demonstrate his discomfort with the new doctrine which he fashions out of whole cloth. It is the very existence of a right to receive information, in the junior high school and high school setting, which I find wholly unsupported by our past decisions and inconsistent with the necessarily selective process of elementary and secondary education.

A

The right described by JUSTICE BRENNAN has never been recognized in the decisions of this Court and is not supported by their rationale. JUSTICE BRENNAN correctly observes that stu-dents do not "shed their rights to freedom of speech or expression at the schoolhouse gate." *Tinker* v. *Des Moines School Dist.*, 393 U.S.

503, 506 (1969). But, as this language from *Tinker* suggests, our past decisions in this area have concerned freedom of speech and expression, not the right of access to particular ideas. We have held that students may not be prevented from symbolically expressing their political views by the wearing of black arm bands, *Tinker* v. *Des Moines School District, supra,* and that they may not be forced to participate in the symbolic expression of saluting the flag, *West Virginia* v. *Barnette,* 319 U.S. 624 (1943). But these decisions scarcely control the case before us. Neither the District Court nor the Court of Appeals found that petitioners' removal of books from the school libraries infringed respondents' right to speak or otherwise express themselves.

Despite JUSTICE BRENNAN's suggestion to the contrary, this Court has never held that the First Amendment grants junior high school and high school students a right of access to certain information in school. It is true that the Court has recognized a limited version of that right in other settings, and JUSTICE BRENNAN quotes language from five such decisions and one of his own concurring opinions in order to demonstrate the viability of the right-to-receive doctrine. *Ante,* at 12-13. But not one of these cases concerned or even purported to discuss elementary or secondary educational institutions.6 JUSTICE BRENNAN brushes over this significant omission in First Amendment law by citing *Tinker* v. *Des Moines School District* for the proposition that "students too are the beneficiaries of this [right-to-receive] principle." *Ante,* at 14. But *Tinker* held no such thing. One may read *Tinker* in vain to find any recognition of a First Amendment right to receive information. *Tinker,* as already mentioned, was based entirely on the students' right to *express* their political views.

Nor does the right-to-receive doctrine recognized in our past decisions apply to schools by analogy. JUSTICE BRENNAN correctly characterizes the right of access to ideas as "an inherent corollary of the rights of free speech and press" which "follows ineluctably from the *sender's* First Amendment right to send them." *Ante,* at 12-13 (emphasis in original). But he then fails to recognize the predicate right to speak from which the students' right to receive must follow. It would be ludicrous, of course, to contend that all authors have a constitutional right to have their books placed in junior high school and high school libraries. And yet without such a right our prior precedents would not recognize the reciprocal right to receive information. JUSTICE BRENNAN disregards this inconsistency with our prior cases and fails to explain the constitutional or logical underpinnings of a right to hear ideas in a place where no speaker has the right to express them.

JUSTICE BRENNAN also correctly notes that the reciprocal nature of the right to receive information derives from the fact that it "is a necessary predicate to the *recipient's* meaningful exercise of his own rights of speech,

press, and political freedom." *Ante,* at 13 (emphasis in original). But the denial of access to ideas inhibits one's own acquisition of knowledge only when that denial is relatively complete. If the denied ideas are readily available from the same source in other accessible locations, the benefits to be gained from the exposure to those ideas have not been foreclosed by the State. This fact is inherent in the right-to-receive cases relied on by JUSTICE BRENNAN, every one of which concerned the complete denial of access to the ideas sought.7 Our past decisions are thus unlike this case where the removed books are readily available to students and non-students alike at the corner bookstore or the public library.

B

There are even some greater reasons for rejecting JUSTICE BRENNAN's analysis, however, than the significant fact that we have never adopted it in the past. "The importance of public schools in the preparation of individuals for participation as citizens, and in the preservation of the values on which our society rests, has long been recognized by our decisions." *Ambach* v. *Norwick,* 441 U.S. 68, 76 (1979). Public schools fulfill the vital role of teaching students the basic skills necessary to function in our society, and of "inculcating fundamental values necessary to the maintenance of a democratic political system." *Id.,* at 77. The idea that such students have a right of access, *in the school,* to information other than that thought by their educators to be necessary is contrary to the very nature of an inculcative education.

Education consists of the selective presentation and explanation of ideas. The effective acquisition of knowledge depends upon an orderly exposure to relevant information. Nowhere is this more true than in elementary and secondary schools, where, unlike the broad-ranging inquiry available to university students, the courses taught are those thought most relevant to the students' individual development. Of necessity, elementary and secondary educators must separate the relevant from the irrelevant, the appropriate from the inappropriate. Determining what information *not* to present to the students is often as important as identifying relevant material. This winnowing process necessarily leaves much information to be discovered by students at another time or in another place, and is fundamentally inconsistent with any constitutionally required eclecticism in public education.

JUSTICE BRENNAN rejects the idea, claiming that it "overlooks the unique role of the school library." *Ante,* at 15. But the unique role referred to appears to be one of JUSTICE BRENNAN's own creation. No previous decision of this Court attaches unique First Amendment significance to the libraries of elementary and secondary schools. And in his paean of praise to such libraries as the "environment especially appropriate for the recognition of the First Amendment rights of students," *Ante,* at

14-15, JUSTICE BRENNAN turns to language about *public* libraries from the three-justice plurality in *Brown* v. *Louisiana*, 383 U.S. 131 (1966), and to language about universities and colleges from *Keyishian* v. *Board of Regents*, 385 U.S. 589 (1967). *Ante*, at 14. Not only is his authority thus transparently thin, but also, and more importantly, his reasoning misapprehends the function of libraries in our public school system.

As already mentioned, elementary and secondary schools are inculcative in nature. The libraries of such schools serve as supplements to this inculcative role. Unlike university or public libraries, elementary and secondary school libraries are not designed for free-wheeling inquiry; they are tailored, as the public school curriculum is tailored, to the teaching of basic skills and ideas. Thus, JUSTICE BRENNAN cannot rely upon the nature of school libraries to escape the fact that the First Amendment right to receive information simply has no application to the one public institution which, by its very nature, is a place for the selective conveyance of ideas.

After all else is said, however, the most obvious reason that petitioners' removal of the books did not violate respondents' right to receive information is the ready availability of the books elsewhere. Students are not denied books by their removal from a school library. The books may be borrowed from a public library, read at a university library, purchased at a bookstore, or loaned by a friend. The government as educator does not seek to reach beyond the confines of the school. Indeed, following the removal from the school library of the books at issue in this case, the local public library put all nine books on display for public inspection. Their contents were fully accessible to any inquisitive student.

C

JUSTICE BRENNAN's own discomfort with the idea that students have a right to receive information from their elementary or secondary schools is demonstrated by the artificial limitations which he places upon the right--limitations which are supported neither by logic nor authority and which are inconsistent with the right itself. The attempt to confine the right to the library is one such limitation, the fallacies of which have already been demonstrated.

As a second limitation, JUSTICE BRENNAN distinguishes the act of removing a previously acquired book from the act of refusing to acquire the book in the first place: "[N]othing in our decision today affects in any way the discretion of a local school board to choose books to *add* to the libraries of their schools. . . . [O]ur holding today affects only the discretion to *remove* books." *Ante*, at 17 (emphasis in original). If JUSTICE BRENNAN truly has found a "right to receive ideas," *Ante*, at 12, 13, however, this distinction between acquisition and removal makes little sense. The failure of a library to acquire a book denies access to its contents just as effectively as does the

removal of the book from the library's shelf. As a result of either action the book cannot be found in the "principal locus" of freedom discovered by JUSTICE BRENNAN. *Ante*, at 14.

The justification for this limiting distinction is said by JUSTICE BRENNAN to be his concern in this case with "the suppression of ideas." *Ante*, at 17. Whatever may be the analytical usefulness of this appealing sounding phrase, see subpart D, *infra*, the suppression of ideas surely is not the identical twin of the denial of access to information. Not every official act which denies access to an idea can be characterized as suppression of the idea. Thus unless the "right to receive information" and the prohibition against "the suppression of ideas" are each a kind of mother-hubbard catch phrase for whatever First Amendment doctrines one wishes to cover, they would not appear to be interchangeable.

JUSTICE BRENNAN's reliance on the "the suppression of ideas" to justify his distinction between acquisition and removal of books has additional logical pitfalls. Presumably the distinction is based upon the greater visibility and the greater sense of conscious decision thought to be involved in the removal of a book, as opposed to that involved in the refusal to acquire a book. But if "suppression of ideas" is to be the talisman, one would think that a school board's public announcement of its refusal to acquire certain books would have every bit as much impact on public attention as would an equally publicized decision to remove the books. And yet only the latter action would violate the First Amendment under JUSTICE BRENNAN's analysis.

The final limitation placed by JUSTICE BRENNAN upon his newly discovered right is a motive requirement: the First Amendment is violated only "[i]f petitioners *intended* by their removal decision to deny respondents access to ideas with which petitioners disagreed." *Ante*, at 17 (emphasis in original). But bad motives and good motives alike deny access to the books removed. If JUSTICE BRENNAN truly recognizes a constitutional right to receive information, it is difficult to see why the reason for the denial makes any difference. Of course JUSTICE BRENNAN's view is that intent matters because the First Amendment does not tolerate an officially prescribed orthodoxy. *Ante*, at 17-18. But this reasoning mixes First Amendment apples and oranges. The right to receive information differs from the right to be free from an officially prescribed orthodoxy. Not every educational denial of access to information casts a pall of orthodoxy over the classroom.

It is difficult to tell from JUSTICE BRENNAN's opinion just what motives he would consider constitutionally impermissible. I had thought that the First Amendment proscribes content-based restrictions on the marketplace of ideas. See *Widmar* v. *Vincent*, ____ U.S. ____, ____ (1981). JUSTICE BRENNAN concludes that a removal decision based solely upon the "educational suitability" of a book or upon its perceived vulgarity is "'perfectly permissible.'" *Ante*, at 17 (quoting Tr. of Oral Arg. 53.) But such determinations are based as much on the content of the book as determinations that the book espouses pernicious political views.

Moreover, JUSTICE BRENNAN's motive test is difficult to square with his distinction between acquisition and removal. If a school board's removal of books might be motivated by a desire to promote favored political or religious views, there is no reason that its acquisition policy might not also be so motivated. And yet the "pall of orthodoxy" cast by a carefully executed book-acquisition program apparently would not violate the First Amendment under JUSTICE BRENNAN's view.

D

Intertwined as a basis for JUSTICE BRENNAN's opinion, along with the "right to receive information," is the statement that "our Constitution does not permit the official suppression of *ideas*." *Ante*, at 17 (emphasis in original). There would be few champions, I suppose, of the idea that our Constitution *does* permit the official suppression of ideas; my difficulty is not with the admittedly appealing catchiness of the phrase, but with my doubt that it is really a useful analytical tool in solving difficult First Amendment problems. Since the phrase appears in the opinion "out of the blue," without any reference to previous First Amendment decisions of this Court, it would appear that the Court for years has managed to decide First Amendment cases without it.

I would think that prior cases decided under established First Amendment doctrine afford adequate guides in this area without resorting to a phrase which seeks to express "a complicated process of constitutional adjudication by a deceptive formula." *Kovacs* v. *Cooper*, 336 U.S. 77, 96 (1949) (Frankfurter, J., concurring). A school board which publicly adopts a policy forbidding the criticism of United States foreign policy by any student, any teacher, or any book on the library shelves is indulging in one kind of "suppression of ideas." A school board which adopts a policy that there shall be no discussion of current events in a class for high school sophomores devoted to second-year Latin "suppresses ideas" in quite a different context. A teacher who had a lesson plan consisting of 14 weeks of study of United States history from 1607 to the present time, but who because of a week's illness is forced to forego the most recent 20 years of American history, may "suppress ideas" in still another way.

I think a far more satisfactory basis for addressing these kinds of questions is found in the Court's language in *Tinker* v. *Des Moines School District* where we noted that

"a particular idea—black arm bands worn to exhibit opposition to this Nation's involvement in Vietnam—was singled out for prohibition. Clearly, the prohibition of expression of one particular opinion, at least

without evidence that it is necessary to avoid material and substantial interference with school work or discipline, is not constitutionally permissible." 393 U.S., at 510-511.

In the case before us the petitioners may in one sense be said to have "suppressed" the "ideas" of vulgarity and profanity, but that is hardly an apt description of what was done. They ordered the removal of books containing vulgarity and profanity, but they did not attempt to preclude discussion about the themes of the books or the books themselves. App. 140. Such a decision, on respondents' version of the facts in this case, is sufficiently related to "educational suitability" to pass muster under the First Amendment.

E

The inconsistencies and illogic of the limitations placed by JUSTICE BRENNAN upon his notion of the right to receive ideas in school are not here emphasized in order to suggest that they should be eliminated. They are emphasized because they illustrate that the right itself is misplaced in the elementary and secondary school setting. Likewise, the criticism of JUSTICE BRENNAN's newly found prohibition against the "suppression of ideas" is by no means intended to suggest that the Constitution permits the suppression of ideas; it is rather to suggest that such a vague and imprecise phrase, while perhaps wholly consistent with the First Amendment, is simply too diaphanous to assist careful decision of cases such as these.

I think the Court will far better serve the cause of First Amendment jurisprudence by candidly recognizing that the role of government as sovereign is subject to more stringent limitations than is the role of government as employer, property owner, or educator. It must also be recognized that the government as educator is subject to fewer strictures when operating an elementary and secondary school system than when operating an institution of higher learning. *Cf. Tilton* v. *Richardson*, 403 U.S. 672, 685-686 (1971) (Opinion of BURGER, C.J.). With respect to the education of children in elementary and secondary schools, the school board may properly determine in many cases that a particular book, a particular course, or even a particular area of knowledge is not educationally suitable for inclusion within the body of knowledge which the school seeks to impart. Without more, this is not a condemnation of the book or the course; it is only a determination akin to that referred to by the Court in *Village of Euclid* v. *Ambler Realty Co.*, 272 U.S. 365, 388 (1926): "A nuisance may be merely a right thing in the wrong place—like a pig in the parlor instead of the barnyard."

III

Accepting as true respondents' assertion that petitioners acted on the basis of their own "personal values, morals, and tastes," App. 139, I find the actions taken in this case hard to distinguish from the myriad choices made by school boards in the routine supervision of elementary and secondary schools. "Courts do not and cannot intervene in the resolution of conflicts which arise in the daily operation of school systems and which do not directly and sharply implicate basic constitutional values." *Epperson* v. *Arkansas*, 393 U.S., at 104. In this case respondents' rights of free speech and expression were not infringed, and by respondents' own admission no ideas were "suppressed." I would leave to another day the harder cases.

JUSTICE O'CONNOR, dissenting.

If the school board can set the curriculum, select teachers, and determine initially what books to purchase for the school library, it surely can decide which books to discontinue or remove from the school library so long as it does not also interfere with the right of students to read the material and to discuss it. As JUSTICE REHNQUIST persuasively argues, the plurality's analysis overlooks the fact that in this case the government is acting in its special role as educator.

I do not personally agree with the board's action with respect to some of the books in question here, but it is not the function of the courts to make the decisions that have been properly relegated to the elected members of school boards. It is the school board that must determine educational suitability, and it has done so in this case. I therefore join THE CHIEF JUSTICE's dissent.

JUSTICE BRENNAN'S OPINION NOTES

1. The Amendment provides in pertinent part that "Congress shall make no law...abridging the freedom of speech, or of the press." It applies to the states by virtue of the Fourteenth Amendment. *Gitlow* v. *New York*, 268 U.S. 652, 666 (1925); *Grosjean* v. *American Press Co.*, 297 U.S. 233, 244 (1936).

2. The District Court noted, however, that petitioners "concede that the books are not obscene." 474 F. Supp. 387,. 392 (1979).

3. The nine books in the High School library were: *Slaughter House Five*, by Kurt Vonnegut, Jr.; *The Naked Ape*, by Desmond Morris; *Down These Mean Streets*, BY Piri Thomas; *Best Short Stories of Negro Writers*, edited by Langston Hughes; *Go Ask Alice*, of anonymous authorship; *Laughing Boy*, by Oliver LaFarge; *Black Boy*, by Richard Wright; *A Hero Ain't Nothin' But A Sandwich*, by Alice Childress; and *Soul On Ice*, by Eldridge Cleaver. The book in the Junior High School library was *A Reader for Writers*, edited by Jerome Archer. Still another listed book, *The Fixer*, by Bernard Malamud, was found to be included in the curriculum of a twelfth grade literature course. 474 F. Supp. 387, 389 and nn. 2-4.

4. The superintendent of schools objected to the Board's informal directive, noting that:"we already have a policy...designed expressly to handle such problems. It calls for the Superintendent, upon receiving an objection to a book or books, to appoint a committee to study them and make recommendations. I feel it is good policy--and it is Board policy--and that it should be followed in this instance. Further, I think it can be followed quietly and in such a way as to reduce, perhaps avoid, the public furor which has always attended such issues in the past." App. 44.

The Board responded to the superintendent's objection by repeating its directive 'that *all copies* of the library books in question be removed from the libraries to the Board's office." App. 47 (emphasis in original).

5. *The Fixer, Laughing Boy, Black Boy, Go Ask Alice*, and *Best Short Stories by Negro Writers*. 474 F. Supp., at 391, nn. 6-7.

6. *The Naked Ape* and *Down These Mean Streets*. 474 F. Supp., at 391,n.8.

7. *Soul On Ice* and *A Hero Ain't Nothin' But A Sandwich*. 474 F. Supp., at 391, n.9.

8. *A Reader for Writers*. 474 F. Supp., at 391, n. 11. The reason given for this disposition was that all members of the Committee had not been able to read the book. *Id.*, at 391.

9. *Slaughter House Five*. 474 F. Supp., at 391, n. 10.

10. *Laughing Boy*. 474 F. Supp., at 391, n. 12.

11. *Black Boy*. 474 F. Supp., at 391, n. 13.

12. As a result, the nine removed books could not be assigned or suggested to students in connection with school work. *Ibid.* However, teachers were not instructed to refrain from discussing the removed books or the ideas and positions expressed in them. App. 131.

13. *Id.,* at 396-397, citing *Presidents Council, District 25* v. *Community School Board #25*, 457 F. 2d 289 (CA2 1972); *James* v. *Board of Education*, 461 F. 2d 566,573 (CA2 1972);*East Hartford Educational Assn.* v. *Board of Education*, 562 F. 2d 838, 856 (CA2 1977) (en banc).

14. 474 F. Supp., at 395-397, quoting *Presidents Council, District 25* v. *Community School Board #25, supra,* at 291 (in turn quoting *Epperson* v. *Arkansas*, 393 U.S. 97, 104 (1968)).

15. After criticizing "the criteria for removal" employed by petitioners as "suffer[ing] from generality and overbreadth," and the procedures used by petitioners as "erratic, arbitrary and free-wheeling," Judge Sifton observed that "precision of regulation and sensitivity to First Amendment concerns" were "hardly established" by such procedures. 638 F. 2d, at 416.

16. Judge Sifton stated that it could be inferred from the record that petitoners' "political views and personal taste [were] being asserted not in the interests of the children's well-being, but rather for the purpose of establishing those views as the correct and orthodox ones for all purposes in the particular community." *Id.,* at 417.

17. Judge Mansfield dissented, 638 F. 2d, at 419-432, based upon a distinctly different reading of the record developed in the District Court. According to Judge Mansfield, "the undisputed evidence of the motivation for the Board's action was the perfectly permissible ground that the books were indecent, in bad taste, and unsuitable for educational purposes." *Id.,* at 430. He also asserted that in reaching its decision "the Board [had] acted carefully, conscientiously and responsibly after according due process to all parties concerned." *Id.,* at 422. Judge Mansfield concluded that "the First Amendment entitles students to reasonable freedom of expression but not to freedom from what some may consider to be excessively moralistic or conservative selection by school authorities of library books to be used as educational tools." *Id.,* at 432.

18. Four of respondents' five causes of action complained of petitioners' "resolutions ordering the removal of certain books from the school libraries of the Distict and prohibiting the use of those books in the curriculum." App.5. The District Court concluded "that respect for the school board's substantial control over educational content...precludes any finding of a first amendment violation arising out of removal of any of the books from use in the curriculum." 474 F. Supp., at 397. This holding is not at issue here. Respondents' fifth cause of action complained that petitioners' "resolutions prohibiting the use of certain books in the curriculum of schools in the District" had "imposed upon teachers in the District arbitrary and unreasonable restrictions upon their ability to function as teachers in violation of principles of academic freedom." App.6. The District Court held that respondents had not proved this cause of action: "before such a claim may be sustained there must at least be a real, not an imagined controversy." 474 F. Supp., at 397. Respondents have not sought review of that holding in this Court.

19. Respondents also agree with these propositions. Tr. of Oral Arg. 28, 41.

20. For a modern version of this observation, see A. Meiklejohn, Free Speech and Its Relation to Self-Government 26 (1948): "Just so far as... the citizens who are to decide an issue are denied acquaintance with information or opinion or doubt or disbelief or criticism which is relevant to that issue, just so far the result must be ill-considered, ill-balanced planning, for the general good." See also *Butler* v. *Michigan*, 352 U.S. 380, 383-384 (1957); *Procunier* v. *Martinez*, 416 U.S. 396, 408-409 (1974); *Houchins* v. *KQED, Inc.,* 438 U.S. 1, 30 (1978)(STEVENS,J., dissenting)("[The] First Amendment protects not only the dissemination but also the receipt of information and ideas."); *Saxbe* v. *Washington Post Co.,*417 U.S. 843, 862-863 (1974) (POWELL, J., dissenting) ("[P]ublic debate must not only be unfettered; it must be informed. For that reason this Court has repeatedly stated that First Amendment concerns encompass the receipt of information and ideas as well as the right of free expression.").

21. 385 U.S., at 603, quoting *Sweezy* v. *New Hampshire*, 354 U.S. 234, 250 (1957) (Opinion of Warren, C.J.).

22. By "decisive factor" we mean a "substantial factor" in the absence of which the opposite decision would have been reached. See *Mt. Healthy City Board of Ed.* v. *Doyle*, 429 U.S., at 287.

23. Petitioners acknowledged that their "evaluation of the suitability of the books was based on [their] personal values, morals, tastes and concepts of educational suitability " App. 142. But they did not accept, and thus apparently denied, respondents' assertion that some excerpts were objected to as "anti-American." *Ibid.*

24. For example, petitioner Ahrens stated that:

"I am basically a conservative in my general philosophy and feel that the community I represent as a school board member shares that philosophy.... I feel that it is my duty to apply my conservative principles to the decision making process in which I am involved as a board member and I have done so with regard to...curriculum formation and content and other educational matters.

. . . . . .

"We are representing the community which first elected us and re-elected us and our actions have reflected its intrinsic values and desires." App. 21,27.

Petitioners Fasulo, Hughes, Melchers, Michaels and Nessim made a similar statement, that they had "represented the basic values of the community in [their] actions." *Id.*, at 120.

25. When asked to give an example of "anti-Americanism" in the removed books, petitioners Ahrens and Martin both adverted to *A Hero Ain't Nothin' But a Sandwich*, which notes at one point that George Washington was a slaveholder. See *A Hero Ain't Nothin' But A Sandwich* 43; Deposition of Petitioner Ahrens 89; Deposition of Petitioner Martin 20-22. Petitioner Martin stated that "I believe it is anti-American to present one of the nation's heroes, the first President,...in such a negative and obviously one-sided life. That is one example of what I would consider anti-American." Deposition of Petitioner Martin 22.

26. We have recognized in numerous precedents that when seeking to distinguish activities unprotected by the First Amendment from other, protected activities, the State must employ "sensitive tools" in order to achieve a precision of regulation that avoids the chilling of protected activities. See, *e.g.*, *Speiser* v. *Randall*, 357 U.S. 513, 525-526 (1957); *N.A.A.C.P.* v. *Button*, 371 U.S. 415, 433 (1963); *Keyishian* v. *Board of Regents*, 385 U.S. 589, 603-604 (1966); *Blount* v. *Rizzi*, 400 U.S. 410, 417 (1971). In the case before us, the presence of such sensitive tools in petitioners' decisionmaking process would naturally indicate a concern on their part for the First Amendment rights of respondents; the absence of such tools might suggest a lack of such concern. See 638 F. 2d, at 416-417 (Opinion of Sifton,J.).

JUSTICE BLACKMUN'S OPINION NOTES

1. As a practical matter, however, it is difficult to see the First Amendment right that I believe is at work here playing a role in a school's choice of curriculum. The school's finite resources--as well as the limited number of hours in the day--require that education officials make sensitive choices between subjects to be offered and competing areas of academic emphasis; subjects generally are excluded simply because school officials have chosen to devote their resources to one rather than to another subject. As is explained below, a choice of this nature does not run afoul of the First Amendment. In any event, the

Court has recognized that students' First Amendment rights in most cases must give way if they interfere "with the schools' work or ... [with] the rights of other students to be secure and to be let alone," *Tinker* v. *Des Moines School Dist.*, 393 U.S. 503, 508 (1969),and such interference will rise to intolerable levels if public participation in the management of the curriculum becomes commonplace. In contrast, library books on a shelf intrude not at all on the daily operation of a school.

I also have some doubt that there is a theoretical distinction between removal of a book and failure to acquire a book. But as Judge Newman observed, there is a profound practical and evidentiary distinction between the two actions: "removal, more than failure to acquire, is likely to suggest that an impermissible political motivation may be present. There are many reasons why a book is not acquired, the most obvious being limited resources, but there are few legitimate reasons why a book, once acquired, should be removed from a library not filled to capacity." 638 F. 2d 404, 436 (CA2 1980) (Newman, J., concurring in the result).

2. In effect, my view presents the obverse of the plurality's analysis: while the plurality focuses on the failure to provide information, I find crucial the State's decision to single out an idea for disapproval and then deny access to it.

JUSTICE BURGER'S OPINION NOTES

1. At the outset, the plurality notes that certain school board members found the books in question "objectionable" and "improper" for junior and senior high school students. What the plurality apparently finds objectionable is that the inquiry as to the challenged books was initially stimulated by what is characterized as "a politically conservative organization of parents concerned about education," which had concluded that the books in question were "improper fare for school students." *Ante*, at 2. As noted by the District Court, however, and in the plurality opinion, *ante*, at 5, both parties substantially agreed about the motivation of the school board in removing the books:

"[T]he board acted not on religious principles but on its conservative educational philosophy, and on its belief that the nine books removed from the school library and curriculum were irrelevant, vulgar, immoral, and in bad taste, making them educationally unsuitable for the district's junior and senior high school students." 474 F. Supp. 387,392 (1979).

2. In oral argument counsel advised the Court that of the original plaintiffs, only "[o]ne of them is still in school ... until this June, and will assumedly graduate in June. *There is a potential question of*

mootness." Transcript of Oral Argument 4-5 (Emphasis added.) The sole surviving plaintiff has therefore either recently been graduated from high school or is within days or even hours of graduation. Yet the plurality expresses views on a very important constitutional issue. Fortunately, there is no binding holding of the Court on the critical constitutional issue presented.

We do well to remember the admonition of Justice Frankfurter that "the most fundamental principle of constitutional adjudication is not to face constitutional questions but to avoid them, if at all possible." *United States* v. *Lovett*, 328 U.S. 303,320 (1946) (Frankfurter, J., concurring.) In the same vein, Justice Stone warned that "the only check upon our own exercise of power is our own sense of self-restraint." *United States* v. *Butler*, 297 U.S. 1, 79 (1936) (Stone,J., dissenting.)

3. Of course, it is perfectly clear that, unwise as it would be, the board could wholly dispense with the school library, so far as the First Amendment is concerned.

4. In *Rowan* a unanimous Court upheld the right of a homeowner to direct the local post office to stop delivery of unwanted materials that the householder viewed as "erotically arousing or sexually provocative."

5. Indeed, this case is illustrative of how essentially all decisions concerning the retention of school library books will become the responsibility of federal courts. As noted above, *supra*, n.1, the parties agreed that the school board in this case acted not on religious principles but "on its belief that the nine books removed from the school library and curriculum were irrelevant, vulgar, immoral, and in bad taste, making them educationally unsuitable for the district's junior and senior high school students."
Despite this agreement as to motivation, the case is to be remanded for a determination of whether removal was in violation of the standard adopted by the plurality. The school board's error appears to be that they made their own determination rather than relying on experts. *Ante*, at 20.

6. *Epperson* v. *Arkansas*, *supra*, at 104. There are approximately 15,000 school districts in the country. U.S. Bureau of the Census, Statistical Abstract of the United States (102 ed. 1981)(Table 495: Number of Local Governments, by Taxing Power and Type, and Public School Systems--States: 1971 and 1977). See aslo Diamond, The First Amendment and Public Schools: The Case Against Judicial Intervention, 59 TX L. Rev. 477, 506-507, n. 130 (1981).

7. Other provisions of the Constitution, such as the Establishment Clause, *Epperson* v. *Arkansas*, *supra*, and the Equal Protection Clause, also limit the discretion of the school board.

8. The formless nature of the "right" found by the plurality in this case is exemplified by this purported distinction. Presumably a school district could, for any reason, choose not to purchase a book for its library. Once it purchases that book, however, it is "locked in" to retaining it on the school shelf until it can justify a reason for its removal. This anomolous result of "book tenure" was pointed out by the District Court in this case. 474 F. Supp. 387, 395-396. See also *Presidents Council* v. *Community School Board*, 457 F. 2d 289,293 (CA2 1972). Under the plurality view, if a school board wants to be assured that it maintains control over the education of its students, every page of every book sought to be acquired must be read before a purchase decision is made.

JUSTICE POWELL'S OPINION NOTES

1. The plurality speaks of the need for "sensitive" decisionmaking, pursuant to "regular" procedures. See *ante*, at ____ . One wonders what indeed does this mean. In this case, for example, the board did not act precipitously. It simply did not agree with the recommendations of a committee it had appointed. Would the plurality require-- as a constitutional matter--that the board delegate unreviewable authority to such a committee?

2. The plurality suggests that the books in a school library derive special protection under the constitution because the school library is a place in which students exercise unlimited choice. See *ante*, at ____ . This suggestion is without support in law or fact. It is contradicted by this very case. The school board in this case does not view the school library as a place in which students pick from an unlimited range of books--some of which may be inappropriate for young people. Rather, the school libary is analogous to an assigned reading list within which students may exercise a degree of choice.

JUSTICE REHNQUIST'S OPINION NOTES

1. I also disagree with JUSTICE WHITE's conclusion that he need not decide the constitutional issue presented by this case. That view seems to me inconsistent with the "rule of four"--"that any case warranting consideration in the opinion of [four Justices] of the Court will be taken and disposed of" on the merits, *Ferguson* v. *Moore-McCormack Lines*, 352 U.S. 521, 561 (1957) (Harlan,J., concurring and dissenting)--which we customarily follow in exercising our certiorari jurisdiction. His concurrence, although not couched in such language, is in effect a single vote to dismiss the writ of certiorari as improvidently granted. Justice Harlan debated this issue with Justice Frankfurter in *Ferguson* v. *Moore-*

McCormack Lines, supra, and his view ultimately attracted the support of six out of
the seven remaining members of the Court.
He stated:
"In my opinion due adherence to [the 'rule
of four'] requires that once certiorari has
been granted a case should be disposed of on
the premise that it is properly here, in the
absence of considerations appearing which
were not manifest or fully apprehended at
the time certiorari was granted. In [this
case] I am unable to say that such considerations exist, even though I do think that
the arguments on the merits underscored the
views of those of us who originally felt
that the [case] should not be taken because
[it] involved only issues of fact, and presented nothing of sufficient general importance to warrant this substantial expendi-
ture of the Court's time." 352 U.S., at 559.

The case upon which JUSTICE WHITE relies,
Kennedy v. *Silas Mason Co.*, 334 U.S. 219
(1948), was disposed of in an opinion which
commanded the votes of seven of the nine
members of the Court. There could therefore
be no question of an infringement of the
"rule of four." Certainly any intimation
from that case that this Court should not
review questions of law in cases where the
District Court has granted summary judgment
is belied by subsequent decisions too numerous to catalogue. See, e.g., *Ernst & Ernst*
v. *Hochfelder*, 425 U.S. 185 (1976); *Cox
Broadcasting Corp.* v. *Cohn*, 420 U.S. 469
(1975); *Mills* v. *Alabama*, 384 U.S. 214
(1966).

2. Rule 9(g) of the local rules of the
United States District Court for the Eastern
District of New York provides:
"Upon any motion for summary judgment
pursuant to Rule 56 of the Rules of Civil
Procedure, there shall be annexed to the notice of motion a separate, short and concise
statement of the material facts as to which
it is contended that there exists a genuine
issue to be tried.

The papers opposing a motion for summary
judgment shall include a separate, short and
concise statement of the material facts as
to which it is contended that there exists a
genuine issue to be tried.

All material facts set forth in the
statement required to be served by the moving party will be deemed to be admitted unless controverted by the statement required
to be served by the opposing party.

3. Paragraph 4 of respondents' Rule 9(g)
statement asserts that petitioners' "evaluation of the suitability of the books was
based on [their] personal values, morals,
and tastes." App. 139.

4. Paragraph 7 of respondents' Rule 9(g)
statement reads:
"Defendants Ahrens and Martin objected to
those excerpts because some contained profanities, some were sexually explicit, some
were ungrammatical, some were anti-American,
and some were offensive to racial, religious
or ethnic groups." App. 140.

5. There are intimations in JUSTICE
BRENNAN's opinion that if petitioners had
only consulted literary experts, librarians,
and teachers their decision might better
withstand First Amendment attack. *Ante*,
at 20. These observations seem to me wholly
fatuous; surely ideas are no more accessible
or no less suppressed if the school board
merely ratifies the opinion of some other
group rather than following its own opinion.

6. The right of corporations to make expenditures or contributions in order to influence ballot issues was the question presented in *First National Bank of Boston* v.
Bellotti, 435 U.S. 765,783 (1978), and the
language which JUSTICE BRENNAN quotes from
that decision, *ante*, at 12, was explicitly
limited to "the Court's decisions involving
corporations in the business of communications or entertainment." 435 U.S., at 783.
In *Kleindienst* v. *Mandel*, 408 U.S. 753
(1972), the Court upheld the power of
Congress and the Executive Branch to prevent
the entry into this country of a Marxist
theoretician who had been invited to lecture
at an American university, despite the First
Amendment rights of citizens who wished to
hear him. *Stanley* v. *Georgia*, 394 U.S.
557 (1969), held that the First Amendment
prohibits States from making the private
possession of obscene material a crime, and
Griswold v. *Connecticut*, 381 U.S. 479
(1965), held that the right of privacy prohibits States from forbidding the use of
contraceptives. Finally, *Martin* v.
Struthers, 319 U.S. 141 (1943), held that
the First Amendment protects the door-to-
door distribution of religious literature.

JUSTICE BRENNAN's concurring opinion appears in a case which considered the constitutionality of certain postal statutes.
Lamont v. *Postmater General*, 381 U.S.
301 (1965).

7. In *First National Bank of Boston* v.
Bellotti, *supra*, public access to
corporate viewpoints on ballot issues not
directly affecting the corporations was
foreclosed by the Massachusetts law
prohibiting corporate expenditures to
express such viewpoints. In *Kleindienst*
v. *Mandel*, *supra*, the Court noted that the
potential recipients of Mandel's ideas were
completely deprived the "particular
qualities inherent in sustained,
face-to-face debate, discussion and questioning." 408 U.S., at 765. The Georgia
law in *Stanley* v. *Georgia*, *supra*, criminalized all private possession of obscene
material, and the statute in *Griswold* v.
Connecticut, *supra*, criminalized all use
of contraceptive devices or actions encouraging the use of such devices. The ordinance at issue in *Martin* v. *Struthers*,
supra, forbade all door-to-door distribution of religious literature, while the
statute challenged in *Lamont* v. *Postmaster General*, *supra*, required persons receiving communist propoganda in the mails
affirmatively to state their desire to receive such mailings.

The Vergennes Union High School Board of Directors orders the removal of Dog Day Afternoon and The Wanderers from the school library because the books contained materials which are "vulgar," "obscene," "immoral," and "perverted." Several students and others challenge the Board's right to ban certain books from the high school library. In finding against the students and for the school board, a United States District Court declares: "Although the court does not entirely agree with the policies and actions of the defendants we do not find that those policies and actions directly or sharply infringe upon the basic constitutional rights of the students of Vergennes Union High School...neither the board's failure to purchase a work nor its decision to remove or restrict access to a work in the school library violate the First Amendment rights of the student plaintiffs before this court....Nor do we believe that school librarians have an independent First Amendment right to control the collection of the school library under the rubric of academic freedom."

Bicknell v. Vergennes Union High School Board, 475 F.Supp. 615 (1979)

OPINION AND ORDER

COFFRIN, District Judge

The parties in this action brought, we assume, pursuant to 42 U.S.C. § 1983 as well as 28 U.S.C. § 1343, have placed before the court a controversy involving one of our most fundamental and most carefully guarded political rights--the right to freedom of speech. The court is asked to determine whether the administrators of a public school district may remove books from the shelves of a high school library, or restrict student access to books, on the basis of their personal opinions that the book is "vulgar," "obscene" or otherwise inappropriate for student readers. Plaintiffs contend that school administrators violate the free speech and due process rights of students, school librarians, and teachers when they make such decisions based solely on their personal opinions. The defendants contend, on the other hand, that the selection and removal of library books is within the range of discretion granted to school authorities and that the exercise of this discretion does not infringe the first amendment or fourteenth amendment rights of students or school employees. The case is presently before the court on the defendants' motion to dismiss.

For the purposes of this motion, the court accepts as admitted the well-pleaded material allegations of the complaint, and we construe those allegations liberally. 2A *Moore's Federal Practice* ¶ 12.08 (2d ed. 1975). Nevertheless, based on the arguments of counsel and their memoranda of law, and for the reasons given below, we find that plaintiffs have failed to state a claim upon which relief can be granted and we grant the defendants' motion.

I. Factual Background

In spite of the complexity and depth of the political controversy that has surrounded this case, the legally relevant facts are straightforward. On August 10, 1977, after almost twelve months of controversy surrounding certain books in circulation at the Vergennes Union High School Library, the elected Board of Directors (the Board) of the High School adopted a formal, written "Library/Media Policy" pertaining to "the philosophy and procedure for operating and maintaining the school library." That promulgation, patterned after the "School Library Bill of Rights" approved by the American Association of School Librarians Board of Directors, contains a number of policy statements covering the objectives of the school library media center, and the "rights" and "responsibilities" of various persons connected with the library, as well as an outline of procedures and criteria for materials selection. The promulgation also contains a statement, entitled "Board Guidelines for Selection of Library Materials," setting forth criteria for materials selection and establishing a procedure for responding to citizen complaints about materials in the library collection. Despite a series of idealistic statements of library goals and policies, the August, 1977, promulgation hardly qualifies as a "library bill of rights" for students, teachers, or librarians. It does, however, repeatedly reaffirm the Board's decision to retain direct control over library acquisition and removal decisions. It states that it is the "right" of the members of the Board of Directors "[t]o adopt policy and procedure, consistent with statute and regulation - that they feel is in the best interests of students, parents, teachers and community." Policy at 2. The rights and responsibilities of professional personnel, on the other hand, are limited "in accordance with Board policy." *Id.*

The procedure for determining whether a book should be removed from the library also places final authority with the Board itself. The August, 1977, procedures provide that a parent or local citizen objecting to a book in the library may initiate a review of the work by completing a form entitled "Citizen's Request for Professional Reconsideration of a Work," and submitting it to the High School Principal. The Principal must provide copies of the request to the librarian and Superintendent of Schools and must inform the Board of the request. The librarian must then review the request and submit a written report of "action taken" to the Board. Finally, the procedures provide that "unresolved issues shall be settled by a majority vote of the Board or its designees." Policy at 5.

In the spring of 1978 defendants employed the procedures outlined above in the review of two books: *The Wanderers*, by Richard Price and *Dog Day Afternoon*, by Patrick Mann. A complaint about *The Wanderers* was submitted by Harold Leach and on April 5, 1978, the Board passed a motion to remove the book from the school library "because it is obscene and vulgar." Mr. and Mrs. Kittridge Haven, Mr. and Mrs. James Parkinson and Mr. and Mrs. Harold Leach also filed a complaint about *Dog Day Afternoon*, asking that the book be removed from the library because of its "vulgar language" and "obscene material," and because it was "immoral, perverted" and portrayed "too much violence." At its April 5 meeting the Board voted not to remove the book from the library permanently, but to place it in the Principal's office pending creation of a special restricted shelf in the library.

Following these decisions, the Board also acted to restrict the professional discretion of the school librarian in the selection and acquisition of additional works for the library. At the April 5 meeting the Board voted to prohibit the librarian from purchasing any additional major fictional works until further vote of the Board. On July 12, 1978, the Board ordered that any book purchases other than those in the category of "Dorothy Canfield Fisher, science fiction and high interest-low vocabulary" be reviewed by the school administration with the assistance of the Board. For the purposes of our decision on this motion, the court assumes that the Board policies freezing major new purchases and screening most new acquisitions are still in effect.

Plaintiffs in this action include several students at Vergennes Union High School, minors who sue by their guardians; four parents of students at the high school; Elizabeth Phillips, the school librarian; Ruth Orr, a library employee; and the Right to Read Defense Committee of Vergennes, an unincorporated association organized to oppose restrictions on the school library collection. The complaint names as defendants the Vergennes Union High School Board of Directors; David Potter, the Superintendent of the school system; and Charles Memoe, the Principal of the high school.

II. *Discussion*

Although the plaintiffs have not delineated precisely the constitutional bases of their challenge to defendants' actions, the court reads the complaint to raise five claims of constitutional infringement:

1. Defendants' removal of *The Wanderers* and *Dog Day Afternoon* from the library infringes the students' first amendment right to receive information.
2. By imposing a freeze on new library acquisitions and permanently screening all major acquisitions, defendants have impermissibly conditioned a government created privilege and have thus violated the student plaintiffs' first amendment rights.
3. Defendants' book removal and library acquisition policies violate the students' rights under the district's own Library/ Media Policy "to freely exercise their right to read and to free access to library materials" and thus infringe their rights to due process of law.
4. Defendants have violated the due process rights of the school librarians by creating and enforcing the August, 1977, reconsideration and removal policy and by freezing and screening new library acquisitions.
5. Defendants' actions have denied teachers at the high school their constitutional rights "by creating a repressive atmosphere where their right to freely discuss literature has been chilled." *See* Complaint (filed September 28, 1978).

A. *Students' Claims*

Plaintiffs' most serious arguments are those concerning the rights of the students. We begin with the observations that "the educational needs of a free people are of utmost importance," *East Hartford Education Association v. Board of Education*, 562 F.2d 838, 842 (2d Cir. 1977), and that "[t]he vigilant protection of constitutional freedoms is nowhere more vital than in the community of American schools." *Shelton v. Tucker*, 364 U.S. 479, 487, 81 S.Ct. 247, 251, 5 L.Ed.2d 231 (1960). We believe, along with the Supreme Court, that "[t]he Nation's future depends upon leaders trained through wide exposure to that robust exchange of ideas which discovers truth 'out of a multitude of tongues, [rather] than through any kind of authoritative election.'" *Tinker v. Des Moines Independent Community School District*, 393 U.S. 503, 512, 89 S.Ct. 733, 739, 21 L.Ed.2d 731 (1969), *quoting Keyishian v. Board of Regents*, 385 U.S. 589, 603, 87 S.Ct. 675, 17 L.Ed.2d 629 (1967). A library is a vital institution in the continuing American struggle to create a society rich in freedom and variety of thought, broad in its understanding of diverse views and cultures and justifiably proud of its democratic institutions. The life and utility of a library are severely impaired whenever works can be removed merely because they are offensive to the personal, political or social tastes of individual citizens, whether or not those citizens represent the majority of opinion in a community.[1] To this extent we agree with the arguments presented by plaintiffs herein.

Nevertheless, we cannot agree with plaintiffs' legal conclusions; what is desirable as a matter of policy is not necessarily commanded as a matter of constitutional law:

By and large, public education in our Nation is committed to the control of state and local authorities. Courts do not and cannot intervene in the resolution of conflicts which arise in the daily operation of school systems and which do not directly and sharply implicate basic constitutional values.

Epperson v. Arkansas, 393 U.S. 97, 104, 89 S.Ct. 266, 270, 21 L.Ed.2d 228 (1968)(footnote omitted). Although the court does not entirely agree with the policies and actions of the defendants we do not find that those policies and actions directly or sharply infringe upon the basic constitutional rights of the students of Vergennes Union High School.

In making this determination we are required as a lower court to accept the law found in a Second Circuit case strikingly similar to the one at bar. In *Presidents Council, District 25 v. Community School Board No. 25*, 457 F.2d 289 (2d Cir.), *cert. denied*, 409 U.S. 998, 93 S.Ct. 308, 34 L.Ed.2d 260 (1972), the court of appeals reviewed a school board's decision to restrict junior high school students' access to the book *Down These Mean Streets* in their school libraries. Observing that New York state law placed responsibility for the selection of materials in public school libraries with local school boards, the court reasoned that:

> some authorized person or body has to make a determination as to what the library collection will be. It is predictable that no matter what choice of books may be made by whatever segment of academe, some other person or group may well dissent. The ensuing shouts of book burning, witch hunting and violation of academic freedom hardly elevate this intramural strife to first amendment constitutional proportions.

Presidents Council, 457 F.2d at 291-92.

Plaintiffs have urged upon this court allegedly critical distinctions between the situation in *Presidents Council* and the case at bar. We do not find any of them constitutionally meaningful. Plaintiffs admit that in Vermont, as in New York, local school boards are by statute afforded considerable authority and discretion with respect to the administration of the schools, including the acquisition and use of materials for school library collections.[2] Moreover, we do not find the difference in the ages of the students involved in the two cases to be critical in determining this issue. Finally, contrary to plaintiffs' assertions, *Presidents Council* does not hold that school authorities must base their decision to purchase or remove a book on articulable educational grounds. To the contrary, the court of appeals stated that it was not appropriate for the federal courts "to review either the wisdom or efficacy of the determinations of the Board," and concluded, "[t]o suggest that the shelving or unshelving of books presents a constitutional issue . . . is a proposition we cannot accept." *Id.* at 291 (footnote omitted).

The court is aware that two other courts

that have reviewed similar public school library controversies have not followed and have sought to distinguish the Second Circuit's decision in *Presidents Council*. *Minarcini v. Strongsville City School District*, 541 F.2d 577 (6th Cir. 1976); *Right to Read Defense Committee v. School Committee*, 454 F.Supp. 703 (D.Mass.1978). Those cases hold that although a school board can determine what books will go into a library, and may even determine whether to create a library at all, it may not exercise the same wide discretion in removing works from the shelves after they are purchased: "[o]nce having created such a privilege for the benefit of its students, however, neither body could place conditions on the use of the library which were related solely to the social or political tastes of school board members." *Minarcini*, 541 F.2d at 582. Whatever merit there may be in such constitutional analysis, it is not the rule we are bound to follow in this circuit. The court of appeals explicitly addressed this argument in *Presidents Council*, holding, "[t]his concept of a book acquiring tenure by shelving is indeed novel and unsupportable under any theory of constitutional law we can discover." *Presidents Council*, 457 F.2d at 293.[3]

Plaintiffs urge the court to find that the underlying premises of *Presidents Council* have been altered by the Supreme Court's recent decisions on the first amendment right to receive information. *Virginia State Board of Pharmacy v. Virginia Citizens Consumer Council*, 425 U.S. 748, 96 S.Ct. 1817, 48 L.Ed.2d 346 (1976); *Kleindienst v. Mandel*, 408 U.S. 753, 92 S.Ct. 2576, 33 L.Ed.2d 683 (1972). We are not persuaded by this line of argument. The right to receive information in the free speech context is merely the reciprocal of the right of the speaker. *See Virginia Board of Pharmacy*, 425 U.S. at 757, 96 S.Ct. at 1823 ("If there is a right to advertise, there is a reciprocal right to receive the advertising...."). Plaintiffs do not contend, nor could they reasonably argue, that the publishers of certain works have a constitutionally protected right to have their works purchased by the Vergennes Union High School Library or retained on the open shelves after purchase. The students' right to review those works through the school library, expressed as the constitutional right to receive information, is no broader. Finally, we note that there has been neither evidence nor argument in this case that the Board's actions have in fact abridged the student plaintiffs' constitutional rights of free expression. Students remain free to purchase the books in question from private bookstores, to read them in other libraries, to carry them to school and to discuss them freely during the school day. Neither the Board's failure to purchase a work nor its decision to remove or restrict access to a work in the school library violate the first amendment rights of the student plaintiffs before this court.[4]

The student plaintiffs' final claim is that

the Board's disputed book acquisition and removal policies violate rights guaranteed them by the district's Library/Media Policy "to freely exercise their right to read and to free access to library materials," and thus violate the due process clause of the fourteenth amendment. The protections of the due process clause extend only to bona fide liberty or property interests created by federal or state law. *Bishop v. Wood*, 426 U.S. 341, 344, 96 S.Ct. 2074, 48 L.Ed.2d 684 (1976); *Paul v. Davis*, 424 U.S. 693, 96 S.Ct. 1155, 47 L.Ed.2d 405 (1976). Since we have found no independent constitutional right to the library policies plaintiffs advocate their due process claim rests on state law alone, and ultimately on the words of the high school's Library/Media Policy. Reading that promulgation in its entirety, the court is unable to find a violation of plaintiffs' rights by the Board. As stated above, the Policy repeatedly reasserts the primacy of the Board itself in the operation of the school library. It also sets forth in detail the process for removing from the collection, a process which plaintiffs do not even claim to have been violated by the Board. If we were to impute such legal content to the high-minded phrases of the "library bill of rights," those general phrases would effectively nullify the specific procedures outlined in the same promulgation. Well-developed rules of statutory construction, as well as common sense, require us to read as a whole the Library/Media Policy and its procedures. Viewing it in its entirety, the court does not find that it creates any "right to read" or "right of access" to library books apart from those rights secured by statute and constitutional law. The student plaintiffs' due process claim must therefore fail.

B. *School Employees' Claims*

We turn now to the claims of the school employees. Since the complaint and supporting papers do not precisely delineate the constitutional claims raised by the high school's library employees, the court assumes that they intend to join in the students' first amendment protest of the Board's book removal policies. *Presidents Council* also forecloses this claim. In that case, upon consideration of the claims of students, parents, parent-teacher associations, teachers and librarians the Second Circuit held that "[t]he intrusion of the Board here upon any first amendment constitutional right of any category of plaintiffs is not only not 'sharp' or 'direct', it is miniscule." *Presidents Council*, 457 F.2d at 292. Nor do we believe that school librarians have an independent first amendment right to control the collection of the school library under the rubric of academic freedom. The selection of works for the library is a curricular rather than a methodological matter, and "public secondary school boards have considerable discretion as to the substantive content" of the curriculum. *East Hartford Education Association v. Board of Education*, 562, F.2d 838, 843

(2d Cir. 1977).[5]

Plaintiffs next argue that the Board's removal of *The Wanderers* from the collection, the imposition of restrictions on *Dog Day Afternoon* and the Board's policy of screening all new major fictional additions to the collection violate the librarians' rights under the Library/Media Policy to "freely select" the media collection for the high school library. This claim is similarly unavailing. As we have pointed out above, the promulgation must be read in its entirety, and the detailed procedures set forth for removing works from the collection obviously condition the general statements of the rights of those persons affected by the Policy. Furthermore, the rights of professional personnel under that Policy "to freely select" materials for the collection are explicitly limited by the phrase "in accordance with Board policy." Policy at 2. Under the heading "Procedures for Materials Selection" the Policy states: "In selecting materials for purchase the media specialist ... 5. Selects materials consistent with Board policy." Policy at 3. In addition, the "Criteria for Materials Selection" explicitly includes that they are to be considered on the basis of "consistency with Board Guidelines," Policy at 3, and the Board Guidelines that follow conclude with the statement that "[u]nresolved issues shall be settled by a majority vote of the Board or its designees." Policy at 5. The court finds nothing in the Board's Library/Media Policy to restrict the Board's prerogatives under state statute to control strictly and closely the collection of the high school library. The Board may exercise that authority by reviewing individual works, by screening all proposed additions to the collection, or by prohibiting new additions to the library altogether. Since the defendants' actions are consistent with the Board's policy and procedural promulgations, there has been no violation of the plaintiffs' due process rights.

For the foregoing reasons, the court grants the defendants' motion to dismiss. As the plaintiffs are not prevailing parties, their motion for attorney's fees under 42 U.S.C. § 1988 is hereby denied. The parties will bear their own costs.

So ORDERED.

NOTES

1. Unfortunately, this is not an isolated problem. *See* King, "Censorship of Textbooks Is Found on Rise in Schools Around Nation," N.Y. Times, Mar. 27, 1979 at B15, Col. 1.
2. Vt.Stat.Ann. tit. 16, § 563 defines the powers of school boards, which include authority to:
   (1) Determine the educational policies of the school district, and prescribe rules and regulations for the conduct and management of the public schools in the district. . .

(2) . . . take any action, which is required for the sound administration of
the school district. . . .

(14) Provide, at the expense of the district, subject to the approval of the
superintendent, all text books, learning
materials, equipment and supplies.

(15) Exercise the general powers given to
a legislative branch of a municipality.

Id. By virtue of Vt.Stat.Ann. tit. 16, §
701(a), the powers afforded the school
boards of other school districts are also
afforded the school boards of union school
districts.

The scope of authority granted Vermont
school boards is comparable to that granted
to school boards in New York and at issue in
Presidents Council. *Presidents Council,*
457 F.2d at 290 n. 1. *See* N.Y.Educ.Law c.
16, § 2590-e(3) (McKinney 1970).

3. Plaintiffs attempt to avoid this holding by
claiming that the school board's discretion
is *equally restricted* with respect to both
acquisition and retention decisions:
"Plaintiffs submit that Defendants' authority and discretion with respect to the selection of books for the library is no
broader than its authority and discretion
with respect to the removal of books contained therein." (Plaintiffs' Memorandum of
Law in Opposition to Defendants' Motion to
Dismiss at 16 n. 8 (filed Nov. 12, 1978).
We find no merit in the argument that a
school board must articulate an educationally related reason for refusing to purchase
any one of the thousands of works that might
be desired by a student, parent or other
person interested in the school library.

4. For these reasons we also reject the conclusory argument in the complaint that the
defendants' actions "have denied teachers at
the High School their Federal and State constitutional rights by creating a repressive
atmosphere where their right to freely discuss literature has been chilled." Complaint at 6 (filed Sept. 28, 1978). The
complaint contains no specific allegation
concerning any restriction on the expression
of opinion by anyone in the school. Although some teachers may be members of the
plaintiff committee, there is no allegation
to that effect, nor is any teacher a named
plaintiff. In these circumstances we believe that the plaintiff has an obligation
to plead specific acts by which the defendants allegedly deprived them of their constitutional rights. "Complaints relying on
the civil rights statutes are plainly insufficient unless they contain some specific
allegations of fact indicating a deprivation
of civil rights, rather than state simple
conclusions." *Koch v. Yunich,* 533 F.2d,
80, 85 (2d Cir. 1976) (citations omitted).
See also Ostrer v. Aronwald, 567 F.2d 551
(2d Cir. 1977).

5. In the absence of any cognizable constitutional claim it is not for this court to say
whether the ultimate responsibility for the
selection, acquisition and removal of books
more appropriately should rest with the
Board or the school librarian. We cannot
assume that librarians are naturally more
vigilant protectors of constitutional liberties than school board members. Nor can we
accept the argument, implicitly made by
plaintiffs here, that a decision to select
or remove a work is constitutionally suspect
when made by a school board but not suspect
when based on the professional discretion or
personal judgment of a library employee.
There is no constitutional basis for making
such a distinction.

United States Court of Appeals Judge Newman decides to uphold the removal by the Vergennes High School's Board of Directors of Dog Day Afternoon *and* The Wanderers *from the school library; Judge Mansfield concurs and Judge Sifton dissents. Both of the latter disagree with Newman's reasoning in deciding the case, Mansfield asserting: "I concur in the result. For the reasons stated in my dissent in* Pico..., *I disagree with Judge Newman's conclusion that there is a legally significant distinction between this case and* Pico. *I would dismiss the complaints in both cases on the grounds of my* Pico *dissent." Judge Sifton declared: "The distinctions perceived by Judge Newman between this case and* Pico..., *decided today, seem to me without basis. The same 'constitutionally protected right of access on school property to material, which...is fairly characterized as vulgar and indecent' exists in this case as exists in* Pico."*

Bicknell v. *Vergennes Union High School Board,* 638 F.2d 438 (1980)

NEWMAN, Circuit Judge:

This case, like *Pico v. Board of Education,* 638 F.2d 404 (2d Cir. 1980), decided this day, involves a school board's decision to remove books from a school library. In *Pico* a divided panel concluded that the allegations of the complaint and the supporting affidavits presented a triable issue as to whether the book removal had created a sufficient risk of suppressing ideas within the school community to constitute a First Amendment violation. In this case the allegations are insufficient to warrant a trial, and we therefore affirm the decision of the District Court for the District of Vermont (Albert W. Coffrin, Judge), dismissing the complaint for failure to state a claim on which relief can be granted.

The complaint alleged the following facts. In response to an ongoing controversy concerning some of the books at the Vergennes Union High School library, the High School's Board of Directors established a written policy governing the selection and removal of books. That document, entitled the "School Library Bill of Rights for School Library Media Center Program," specifies the rights and responsibilities of the Board, the professional staff, the parents, and the students in this area. The "rights" of the Board are: "To adopt policy and procedure, consistent with statute and regulation--that they feel is in the best interests of students, parents, teachers and community." The "rights" of the professional staff are: "To freely select, in accordance with Board policy, organize and administer the media collection to best serve teachers and students." The "rights" of the students are: "To freely exercise the right to read and to free access to library materials." After specifying some procedures and criteria for the selection of materials, the document then lists some general "Board Guidelines for the Selection of Library Materials." These include a procedure allowing parents to submit requests for reconsideration of a particular book. Upon receipt of such a request, the librarian is to meet with the parents to resolve the issue; any matters that remain unresolved are to be settled by a majority vote of the Board.

Some months after this procedure was adopted, two complaints from parents reached the Board. The books involved were *Dog Day Afternoon* by Patrick Mann and *The Wanderers* by Richard Price; in both cases, the objection of the parents was to the vulgarity and indecency of language in the books. The Board voted to remove *The Wanderers* from the library and to place *Dog Day Afternoon* on a restricted shelf.[1] The complaint acknowledges that the Board acted in both instances because of the books' vulgar and indecent language. The Board also voted to prohibit the school librarian from purchasing any additional major works of fiction, and subsequently voted that any book purchases other than those in the category "Dorothy Canfield Fisher, science fiction and high interest-low vocabulary" must be reviewed by the school administration in consultation with the Board. Following these actions, a group of students, their parents, library employees, and an unincorporated association known as the Right to Read Defense Fund brought suit to enjoin removal of the books and alteration of the school's library policy.

Appellants appear to present two theories on which the alleged facts might establish a violation of constitutionally protected rights. First, they claim that their First Amendment rights have been violated, primarily because the Board's action was motivated solely by the "personal taste and values" of the Board members.[2] (Appellants' Br. 7). Second, they claim that the Board's action has denied them due process of law because the Board has violated its own internal policies and procedures.

In *Pico* a majority of the Court recognized a First Amendment right of members of a school community to be free of the inhibiting effects upon free expression that result when the circumstances surrounding the removal of books create a risk of suppressing ideas. In this case there are no allegations of any facts to indicate that such a risk was created by the circumstances under which the two books were removed. The attention of the Board was first directed to the two books by complaint about their vulgar and indecent language. There is no suggestion that the books were complained about or removed because of their ideas, nor that the Board members acted because of political motivation. On the contrary, appellants acknowledge that the books were removed because of vulgarity and obscenity.[3] Nor is there any claim that the passages found objectionable were beyond the allowable scope accorded school authorities to regulate vulgarity and explicit sexual content. See *Thomas v. Board of Education,* 607 F.2d 1043, 1053 (2d Cir. 1979) (Newman, J., concurring); *Frison v. Franklin County Board of Education,* 596 F.2d 1192 (4th Cir. 1979); *Brubaker v. Board of Education,* 502 F.2d 973 (7th Cir. 1974), *cert. denied,* 421 U.S. 965, 95 S.Ct. 1953, 44 L.Ed.2d 451 (1975).

Appellants do not dispute that the Board has the power to remove these two books because of their language. Their point is that the decision to remove is unlawful when the determination of whether the books are vulgar or indecent is made solely on the basis of Board members' personal tastes and values. But so long as the materials removed are permissibly considered to be vulgar or indecent, it is no cause for legal complaint that the Board members applied their own standards of taste about vulgarity.[4]

Appellants' due process theory is also without merit. Whatever deprivation of rights can result from the removal of books from a school library, it is not the sort of deprivation that entitles a student or librarian to a hearing before that removal takes place. The nature of the deprivation that triggers due process protection has been a subject of much debate. See *Paul v. Davis,* 424 U.S. 693, 96 S.Ct. 1155, 47 L.Ed.2d 405 (1976); *Board of Regents v. Roth,* 408 U.S. 564, 92 S.Ct. 2701, 33 L.Ed.2d 548 (1972); L. Tribe, American Constitutional Law 514-32 (1978). It is generally agreed, however, that the deprivation must involve some particularized and personal interest on the part of the person asserting the right. The right recognized in *Pico* is not of that nature; on proper facts, it may be vindicated in a court challenge, but does not assure an opportunity to contest the removal of books before such action is taken.

The school librarian has presented a more particularized claim, but she has not alleged that the board has taken any adverse action of the sort that would require due process protection prior to that action's being taken. The Board did not dismiss her, or reprimand her in any official way; it merely removed certain

functions from her job assignment. In general, an employee of a government agency has no constitutionally protected interest in the particular duties of a job assignment.[5] Finally, to the extent the appellants are alleging that the procedures of the library policy were not followed, it is clear that state procedural requirements do not create interests entitled to due process protection.[6] *Boothe v. Hammock,* 605 F.2d 661, 664 (2d Cir. 1979); *Frison v. Franklin County Board of Education, supra,* 596 F.2d at 1194; *Cofone v. Manson,* 594 F.2d 934, 938-39 (2d Cir. 1979).

The dismissal of the complaint is affirmed.

MANSFIELD, Circuit Judge, concurring in the result:

I concur in the result. For the reasons stated in my dissent in *Pico v. Board of Education,* 638 F.2d 404 (2d Cir. 1980), I disagree with Judge Newman's conclusion that there is a legally significant distinction between this case and *Pico.* I would dismiss the complaints in both cases on the grounds stated in my *Pico* dissent.

SIFTON, District Judge (dissenting):

The distinctions perceived by Judge Newman between this case and *Pico v. Board of Education,* 638 F.2d 404 (2d. Cir.), decided today, seem to me without basis. The same "constitutionally protected right of access on school property to material that, which ... is fairly characterized as vulgar and indecent" exists in this case as exists in *Pico.* That is, access to such material should not be denied to plaintiffs in a fashion or based on criteria of such indefiniteness and ambiguity as to strike not at the vulgarities and indecencies in the books, but rather at the ideas the books express. As Judge Newman aptly states in his concurring opinion in *Pico,* what is significant is whether "the school has used its public power to perform an act clearly indicating that the views represented by the forbidden book are unacceptable." *Pico v. Board of Education, supra,* 638 F.2d at 404 (Newman, C. J., concurring). In my opinion, plaintiffs, in this case, should be given an opportunity through discovery and a trial to prove that this is just what has been done by the Vergennes Union High School Board of Directors. Plaintiffs have, in other words, in my view, alleged in their pleading a *prima facie* case of the type described in *Pico.*

Plaintiffs refer in their complaint to a statement of policy and procedure recently established by defendants for operating and maintaining the Vergennes Union High School library and, specifically, for dealing with decisions concerning the contents of the library of the sort here at issue. Indeed, the statement of policy and procedure is annexed as an exhibit to the complaint. The complaint alleges that this statement of policy and procedure was violated by defendants' action; and, in their brief to this Court, plaintiffs state what they would certainly be entitled to prove under the complaint's allegations--that defendants' actions "were undertaken without even a semblance or pretense of following either the substantive, objective criteria or the expressly articulated procedure set forth in the library policy adopted by them...." Specifically, plaintiffs seek an opportunity to prove that defendants ignored the established objective criteria for selection of library materials, disregarded a five-step procedure for the selection of library materials, and by-passed the personnel whose expertise the same defendants had recently determined should be consulted before school book removal could be accomplished. While Judge Coffrin states in his opinion below that defendants employed the procedures set forth in the statement of policy to remove two books from the library, this factual finding by the district judge is completely in conflict with the allegations of the complaint and, accordingly, not the type of decision appropriately made, as here, on a motion to dismiss pursuant to Rule 12(b)(6) of the Federal Rules of Civil Procedure.

The sort of substantive and procedural irregularity alleged in the complaint does not, in my view, irrevocably condemn defendants' conduct; I agree with Judge Newman that there is no due process argument here. However, it seems to me that detailed allegations of this sort of substantive and procedural irregularity do, for the reasons indicated in my opinion in *Pico*, establish a *prima facie* case deserving of answer, discovery and trial. Plaintiffs should, in other words, be entitled to explore whether the reasons for these irregularities were, as they also allege, that the school board wanted the two books out of the library because of improper ideas they expressed, regardless of what might have been shown concerning the reasons for retaining the books in the library, had the prescribed procedures and criteria been followed. I would reverse and remand for discovery and trial.

NOTES

1. Pending establishment of a restricted shelf, *Dog Day Afternoon* was placed in the principal's office, apparently unavailable to students on any basis.
2. Appellants also urge that removal of the books infringes First Amendment rights because it impairs the students' access to the removed volumes. Whatever the scope of a right of access in other contexts, *Virginia State Board of Pharmacy v. Virginia Citizens Consumer Council*, 425 U.S. 748, 96 S.Ct. 1817, 48 L.Ed.2d 346 (1976); *Procunier v. Martinez*, 416 U.S. 396, 94 S.Ct. 1800, 40 L.Ed.2d 224 (1974), young students have no constitutionally protected right of access on school property to material that, whatever its literary merits, is fairly characterized as vulgar and indecent in the school context.

3. "Obscenity" in the context of this case does not mean the Supreme Court's test of obscenity, *Miller v. California*, 413 U.S. 15, 93 S.Ct. 2607, 37 L.Ed.2d 419 (1973), which must be met before general distribution of material may be constitutionally punished. It refers, instead, only to that degree of sexual explicitness that renders material inappropriate for availability in a school attended by young children.
4. Appellants' objection to the Board's reliance on its own standards of taste is not entirely clear. Their point seems to be that the Board's view of vulgarity and indecency is insufficient to permit book removal in the absence of some demonstration that the removed materials have the capacity to inflict psychological harm. (Appellants' Br. 33). Whatever the standards may be in the context of regulating a student's right of expression, *see Trachtman v. Anker*, 563 F.2d 512 (2d Cir. 1977), *cert. denied*, 435 U.S. 925, 98 S.Ct. 1491, 55 L.Ed.2d 519 (1978), such standards do not apply to a school board's decision concerning the availability of materials within a school facility. If appellants are concerned that standards of taste permit the exercise of unfettered discretion, that concern also warrants relief only in contexts in which the exercise of such discretion is used to penalize expression rather than to limit availability. *See Shuttlesworth v. City of Birmingham*, 394 U.S. 147, 89 S.Ct. 935, 22 L.Ed.2d 162 (1969); *Eisner v. Stamford Board of Education*, 440 F.2d 803 (2d Cir. 1971).
5. It is conceivable that a drastic change in duties could be tantamount to a dismissal, entitling the employee to a prior hearing to contest the lawfulness of such a change. *See Frison v. Franklin County Board of Education*, *supra* (demotion from career teacher to tutor). But the actions taken by the Board in this case do not approach that level of impact.
6. In the view of the majority in *Pico v. Board of Education*, *supra*, a failure to observe local procedures, while not raising due process issues, could have evidentiary significance on the issue of whether removal of books was improperly motivated by political concerns. That issue does not arise in this case because there is no dispute that the two books were removed because of vulgarity and indecency.

After the Warsaw, Indiana, School Board ordered the removal of certain books from the high school classroom and library, student Brooke Zykan brought suit seeking to reverse the board's orders. The district court dismissed Zykan's "amended complaint for lack of subject matter jurisdiction." Zykan appealed and the United States Court of Appeals, Seventh Circuit, declared: "We agree that the complaint must be dismissed, but vacate the district court order and remand with instructions to grant plaintiffs leave to amend." The court indicated that an administrator "would be irresponsible if he or she failed to monitor closely the contents of the library...," but, said the court, this is not to say that an administrator may remove a book from the library as part of a purge of all material offensive to a single exclusive perception of the way of the world, anymore than he or she may originally stock the library on this basis.

Zykan v. *Warsaw Community School Corp.*, 621 F.2d 1300 (1980)

CUMMINGS, Circuit Judge.

Plaintiff Brooke Zykan, a Warsaw, Indiana high school student suing by her parents and next friends, Anthony and Jacqueline Zykan, and plaintiff Blair Zykan, a former Warsaw high school student, field this action under Section 1983 of the Civil Rights Act, alleging violations of their First and Fourteenth Amendment rights by defendants Warsaw Community School Corporation, the Warsaw School Board of Trustees, and six individual members of that Board. In their initial complaint filed on March 21, 1979, plaintiffs sought certification as a class to contest various curriculum-related decisions made by the Board and several of its present and former employees, including Charles Bragg, the Superintendent of Schools, William Goshert, former Assistant Superintendent, and C. J. Smith, former principal of Warsaw High School. Plaintiffs filed an amended complaint on April 6, 1979. On June 18, defendants asked that the district court dismiss the amended complaint for failure to state a claim for relief or for lack of subject matter jurisdiction, or, in the alternative, that it abstain pending resolution of certain state law issues or grant summary judgment on their behalf. On December 3, 1979, the district court dismissed the amended complaint for lack of subject matter jurisdiction, and this appeal followed. We agree that the complaint must be dismissed, but vacate the district court order and remand with instructions to grant plaintiffs leave to amend.

This case arises from a series of decisions made in 1977 and 1978 by the defendant School Board and its various members and employees primarily regarding the English curriculum at Warsaw High School, the use of certain books in that curriculum, and the rehiring of teachers for English courses. The amended complaint essentially concerns six incidents that, when viewed together, are said by plaintiffs to amount to violations of their First and Fourteenth Amendment rights.[1] The first four of these incidents involve the removal of books from certain courses and the school library. They include:

1) that defendants ordered the removal from the school premises and the destruction of the textbook *Values Clarification*[2] and did so "without proper consultation with teachers, parents or students and without taking adequate steps to determine the literary and scholastic value of the text * * *" (par. 17);
2) that former principal Smith told English teacher Teresa Burnau to return to the publisher one book[3] she had planned to use in her course "Women in Literature" and not to use three others[4] (pars. 21,22);
3) that defendants promulgated a policy prohibiting the use of reading materials that "'might be objectionable'" and that as a consequence of this policy, Smith required a teacher to excise certain portions of *Student Critic,* a book long in use in the high school[5] (pars. 23-26);
4) that defendants have permanently removed the book *Go Ask Alice* from the school library (pars. 27-29).[6]

Plaintiffs allege that defendants took these actions because "* * * particular words in the books offended their social, political and moral tastes and not because the books, taken as a whole, were lacking in educational value" (par. 32). They also assert that in each case defendants acted in defiance of the "Croft Policy," which, they say, established the regular procedure for handling censorship decisions. The amended complaint also charges defendants with eliminating seven courses from the high school curriculum "because the teaching methods and/or content of the courses offended their social, political and moral beliefs" (par. 34). Plaintiffs once again allege that defendants took this action without compliance with the Croft Policy. A final set of allegations concerns defendants' decision not to rehire English teacher Teresa Burnau and another teacher, which plaintiffs contend has deprived them "of the opportunity to learn from and associate with these capable teachers" and has created an "atmosphere of tension and fear among present teachers * * * resulting in a diminution or loss of academic freedom on the part of all teachers and students in the District" (pars. 35-37). Plaintiffs' factual allegations conclude with the assertions that plaintiff Blair Zykan's "right to know was directly violated by defendants' actions, which capriciously and unreasonably infringed upon his right to read literary works in their entirety," that plaintiff Brooke Zykan suffers directly from defendants' "capricious and arbitrary actions in censoring courses and books" (par. 38), and finally that defendants' actions have had and continue to have "a chilling effect on the free exchange of knowledge" in the Warsaw schools (par. 39).

In addition to requesting class certification to represent all former, present and future students at Warsaw High School, plaintiffs sought, *inter alia,* declaratory relief adjudging defendants' conduct in violation of the First and Fourteenth Amendments, an injunction ordering the restoration to the curriculum of the discontinued books, and an order directing the reversal of all curriculum changes. They also requested an order restraining defendants from further changing the school curriculum and reading materials "until a reasonable and impartial procedure * * * has been formulated and * * * complied with" and from interfering with "reasonable" selections of course materials by teachers or access to such materials by students. As noted, defendants opposed the complaint with a variety of motions, including one to dismiss the complaint for lack of subject matter jurisdiction.

On December 3, Judge Sharp granted the motion to dismiss on the ground that he lacked jurisdiction over the subject matter. He concluded that the "complaint fail[ed] to allege a violation of either the First Amendment's guarantee of religious freedom or the First Amendment's guarantee of a right to receive a constitutionally protected communication." (R. Item 17 at 3). He found that the precedents of this Circuit have otherwise placed few constitutional constraints on the exercise of discretion by school officials. In particular he stated that:

"the function of school officials is not constitutionally restricted to determining the most efficient method of exposing students to as many facts and opinions as possible; rather, it is legitimate for school officials to develop an opinion about what type of citizens are good citizens, to determine what curriculum and material will best develop good citizens, and to prohibit the use of texts, remove library books, and delete courses from the curriculum as a part of the effort to shape students into good citizens. *See Ambach v. Norwick,* [441 U.S. 68], 99 S.Ct. 1589, 60 L.Ed.2d 49 (1979). And there is no way for school officials to make the determinations involved except on the basis of personal moral beliefs. To allege that school officials have made decisions regarding classroom texts, library books, and curriculum courses solely on the basis of personal 'social, political, and moral' beliefs is insufficient to allege a violation of constitutionally protected 'academic freedom.'" (R. Item 17 at 4.)

This Case Is Not Moot

Defendants argue in their brief that this case should be dismissed as moot. They note that Indiana law requires local school boards to select new textbooks every five years and that pursuant to this directive, the Warsaw Board adopted in 1978 an entirely new English curriculum in which the course offerings are more traditional and the disputed books have no place.[7] They assert that the factual allegations of the complaint did not challenge the decision to adopt this new curriculum and therefore that the administrative action subsequent to the incidents at issue here has rendered the relief sought by plaintiffs inappropriate.

The short answer to defendants' argument is that both the facts alleged and relief sought in the complaint easily survive the Board's change in curriculum. For example, plaintiffs have alleged that a book has been improperly removed from the library and not returned and that teachers have not been rehired for improper motives. These actions and others are said to have had a chilling effect on academic freedom and to have caused harm to one plaintiff and to be causing harm to another. Further, the relief sought by plaintiffs plainly reaches beyond the specific incidents alleged, for plaintiffs have sought an injunction requiring defendants to adopt and comply with impartial procedures for implementing curriculum changes. Plaintiffs clearly argue that they have suffered a legal injury greater than the sum of the specific factual allegations involved, and defendants have cited no authority for their assertion that in such a context plaintiffs' broad claims for relief must be narrowed to correspond to the specific facts alleged. At the same time, plaintiffs' request for relief is sufficiently broad to cover even the legislatively-sanctioned decision to revise the high school English curriculum. Accordingly, plaintiffs' complaint is not moot.

Failure to State a Constitutional Claim

Nevertheless, plaintiffs' complaint does not state a violation of constitutional rights and therefore is not cognizable in federal court under Civil Rights Act Section 1983 and Section 1343 of the Judicial Code. This conclusion stems from a careful consideration of the competing interests presented by a complaint charging infringement of students' academic freedom. It is now settled of course that students do not "shed their constitutional rights to freedom of speech or expression at the schoolhouse gate," *Tinker v. Des Moines Independent Community School District,* 393 U.S. 503, 506, 89 S.Ct. 733, 736, 21 L.Ed.2d 731. It is also clear that in line with such concepts as the "marketplace of ideas" the First Amendment guarantees are sufficiently broad to provide some protection for what has been called "academic freedom," which recognizes the importance to the scholarly and academic communities of being free from ideological coercion. *Healey v. James*, 408 U.S. 169,180-181, 92 S.Ct. 2338, 2345-46, 33 L.Ed.2d 266, *Clark v. Holmes*, 474 F.2d 928 (7th Cir. 1972), certiorari denied, 411 U.S. 972, 93 S.Ct. 2148, 36 L.Ed.2d 695; see also *Developments In The Law--Academic Freedom*, 81 Harv.L.Rev. 1045 (1968). Less clear are the precise contours of this constitutionally protected academic freedom, and particularly its appropriate role when the concern is not the rarified atmosphere of the college or university, but rather the heartier environment of the secondary school.

Secondary school students certainly retain an interest in some freedom of the classroom, if only through the qualified "freedom to hear" that has lately emerged as a constitutional concept. See *Virginia Pharmacy Board v. Virginia Citizens Consumer Concil*, 425 U.S. 748, 96 S.Ct. 1817, 48 L.Ed.2d 346. But two factors tend to limit the relevance of "academic freedom" at the secondary school level. First, the student's right to and need for such freedom is bounded by the level of his or her intellectual development. A high school student's lack of the intellectual skills necessary for taking full advantage of the marketplace of ideas engenders a correspondingly greater need for direction and guidance from those better equipped by experience and reflection to make critical educational choices. Second, the importance of secondary schools in the development of intellectual faculties is only one part of a broad formative role encompassing the encouragement and nurturing of those fundamental social, political, and moral values that will permit a student to take his place in the community. *Ambach v. Norwick*, 441 U.S. 68, 76-77, 99 S.Ct. 1589, 1594-95, 60 L.Ed.2d 49; *James v. Board of Education*, 461 F.2d 566, 573 (2d Cir. 1972), certiorari denied, 409 U.S. 1042, 93 S.Ct. 529, 34 L.Ed.2d 491. As a result, the community has a legitimate, even a vital and compelling interest in "the choice [of] and adherence to a suitable curriculum for the benefit of our young citizens * * * ." *Palmer v. Board of Education*, 603 F.2d 1271, 1274 (7th Cir. 1979), certiorari denied, 444 U.S. 1026, 100 S.Ct. 689, 62 L.Ed.2d 659.

The need for intellectual and moral guidance from a body capable of transmitting the mores of the community has led most state legislatures to lodge primary responsibility for secondary school education in local school boards, which generally have considerable authority to regulate the specifics of the classroom. In accordance with these principles, Indiana, pursuant to statute, has entrusted the governance of secondary school education to such local boards (Ind. Code 20-4-1-8) who have nearly plenary powers concerning curriculum, textbooks and other educational matters (Ind. Code 20-5-2-1; 20-5-2-2; see also Ind.Code 20-10.1-4-4). The breadth of these powers in part reflects the perception that at the secondary school level the need for educational guidance predominates over many of the rights and interests comprised by "academic freedom."

The Supreme Court itself has sanctioned this balance of interests, noting that

"[b]y and large, public education in our Nation is committed to the control of state and local authorities. Courts do not and cannot intervene in the resolution of conflicts which arise in the daily operation of school systems and which do not *directly and sharply* implicate basic constitutional values." *Epperson v. Arkansas*, 393 U.S. 97, 104, 89 S.Ct. 266, 270, 21 L.Ed.2d 228 (emphasis supplied).

Virtually every judicial body that has commented on the matter has acknowledged the need for broad discretionary powers in local school boards. *E. g. Cary v. Board of Education*, 598 F.2d 535 (10th Cir. 1979); *East Hartford Education Assn. v. Board of Education*, 562 F.2d 838 (2d Cir. 1977) (en banc); *Minarcini v. Strongsville City School District*, 541 F.2d 577 (6th Cir. 1976); *Presidents Council, District 25 v. Community School Board*, 457 F.2d 289 (2d Cir. 1972), certiorari denied, 409 U.S. 998, 93 S.Ct. 308, 34 L.Ed.2d 260; *James v. Board of Education*, 461 F.2d 566 (2d Cir. 1972), certiorari denied, 409 U.S. 1042, 93 S.Ct. 529, 34 L.Ed.2d 491; *Pico v. Board of Education*, 474 F.Supp. 387 (E.D. N.Y.1979); *Right to Read Defense Committee of Chelsea v. School Committee of Chelsea*, 454 F.Supp. 703 (D.Mass.1978); *Mercer v. Michigan State Board of Education*, 379 F.Supp. 580 (E.D.Mich.1974), affirmed, 419 U.S. 1081, 95 S.Ct. 673, 42 L.Ed.2d 678; *Parducci v. Rutland*, 316 F.Supp. 352 (M.D.Ala.1970); see also *Ambach v. Norwick*, 441 U.S. 68, 99 S.Ct. 1589, 60 L.Ed.2d 49; *Shelton v. Tucker*, 364 U.S. 479, 81 S.Ct. 247, 5 L.Ed.2d 231.

This grant of broad discretion specifically means that there are only limited constitutional constraints on the form and content of decisions of local school boards acting within the bounds of their statutory powers. Educational decisions necessarily involve choices regarding what students should read and hear, and particularly in light of the formative purpose of secondary school education, local discretion thus means the freedom to form an opinion regarding the instructional content that will best transmit the basic values of the community. As a result, it is in general permissible and appropriate for local boards to make educational decisions based upon their personal social, political and moral views. *Cary v. Board of Education*, 598 F.2d 535, 544 (10th Cir. 1979).

To be sure, the discretion lodged in local school boards is not completely unfettered by constitutional considerations. Control of matters not immediately affecting classroom activities is subject to numerous qualifications. See *Tinker v. Des Moines Independent School District*, 393 U.S. 503, 89 S.Ct. 733, 21 L.Ed.2d 731; *Thomas v. Board of Education*, 607 F.2d 1043 (2d Cir. 1979), certiorari denied *sub nom.*, *Granville Central School District v. Thomas*, 444 U.S. 1081, 100 S.Ct. 1034, 62

L.Ed.2d 765. In the classroom there are recognized limits on local control of educational matters. School boards are for example not free to fire teachers for every random comment in the classroom. See, e. g., *Sterzing v. Fort Bend Independent School District*, 376 F.Supp. 657 (S.D.Tex. 1972). In the case of the students themselves, local school boards must respect certain strictures that for example bar them from insisting upon instruction in a religiously-inspired dogma to the exclusion of all other points of view (*Epperson v. Arkansas, supra*), or from placing a flat prohibition on the mention of certain relevant topics in the classroom (but see *Mercer v. Michigan State Board of Education*, 379 F.Supp. 580 (E.D.Mich.1974), affirmed, 419 U.S 1081, 95 S.Ct. 673, 42 L.Ed.2d 678), or from forbidding students to take an interest in subjects not directly covered by the regular curriculum. At the very least, academic freedom at the secondary school level precludes a local board from imposing "a pall of orthodoxy" on the offerings of the classroom (*Keyishian v. Board of Regents*, 385 U.S. 589, 602, 87 S.Ct. 675, 683, 17 L.Ed.2d 629), which might either implicate the state in the propagation of an identifiable religious creed or otherwise impair permanently the student's ability to investigate matters that arise in the natural course of intellectual inquiry.

From these principles derives the rule that complaints filed by secondary school students to contest the educational decisions of local authorities are sometimes cognizable but generally must cross a relatively high threshold before entering upon the field of a constitutional claim suitable for federal court litigation. Such a balance of legal interests means that panels such as the Warsaw School Board will be permitted to make even ill advised and imprudent decisions without the risk of judicial interference. Nothing in these principles suggests that the courts should condone short-sighted board decision-making. But nothing in the Constitution permits the courts to interfere with local educational discretion until local authorities begin to substitute rigid and exclusive indoctrination for the mere exercise of their prerogative to make pedagogic choices regarding matters of legitimate dispute. A reading of the amended complaint confirms that these plaintiffs have failed to allege sufficient facts regarding such a flagrant abuse of discretion by defendants to justify intervention by this Court at this point.

First, some of the allegations seem too ephemeral when measured against the gravity of these constitutional concerns. Thus plaintiff Blair Zykan's summary assertion that defendants "capriciously and unreasonably infringed upon his right to read literary works in their entirety" posits an interference with a right of uncertain constitutional genealogy. Second, plaintiffs' more cogent allegations with respect to the removal of *Values Clarification* from one course, the deletion of certain materials from the "Women in Literature" course, the excision of "objectional" parts of a text-

book, and even the discontinuance of certain courses simply do not rise to the level of a constitutional claim. *Cf. Arundar v. DeKalb County School District*, 620 F.2d 493 (5th Cir. 1980) (finding no due process right to enroll in classes of a certain content). The amended complaint nowhere suggests that in taking these actions defendants have been guided by an interest in imposing some religious or scientific orthodoxy or a desire to eliminate a particular kind of inquiry generally.

Plaintiffs' assertions that the decisions of the Board and its employees have stemmed from their social, political and moral tastes and not from educational criteria suggest a constitutional analysis based on the very facile categorization that the principles expressed above should foreclose. The Constitution neither disparages the application of social, political and moral tastes to secondary school educational decisions nor specifies that such criteria are irrelevant or alien to the legitimate exercise of educational choice. Noticeably absent from the amended complaint is any hint that the decisions of these administrators flow from some rigid and uniform view of the sort the Constitution makes unacceptable as a basis for educational decision-making or from some systematic effort to exclude a particular type of thought, or even from some identifiable ideological preference. Plaintiffs have also not alleged that the Board's decisions have deprived them of all contact with the material in question by, for example, forbidding students to have or to read the materials or making them wholly unavailable to them from other sources. See *Minarcini v. Strongsville City School District, supra* at 583-584; *Bicknell v. Vergennes Union High School Board of Directors*, 475 F.Supp. 615, 621 (D.Vt.1979).

As for the Croft Policy that defendants are alleged to have defied, the text of its procedures, which plaintiffs have affixed to both their complaints, belies any suggestion that the channel it offers to the public for voicing displeasure with curricular decisions made by the Board constitutes an established constraint on the Board's own exercise of its powers. In addition, it is highly questionable whether, even if construed as applicable to the Board, these informal procedures, which presumably do not have the force of law, could achieve the status of a constitutionally enforced due process restraint on Board action, particularly given the freedom school boards traditionally have in electing how to make their decisions. At the same time, plaintiffs' complaint lacks any allegation that the Board exceeded its statutory powers, failed to act consistently with them,[8] or improperly delegated responsibilities to others. Plaintiffs have also not alleged that the various employees acted beyond the authority properly granted to them by the Board.

Plaintiffs' allegations regarding teacher hiring decisions are creative but no more availing. On the one hand, if these allegations are construed to contest directly the motives and procedures surrounding the Board's

decision not to rehire two teachers, they would
engender serious standing problems. If colorable, such claims are properly litigated not by
the students, whose injury is highly attenu-
ated, but by the teachers who have suffered the
harm. Accordingly, the teachers involved in
this case have apparently filed actions in the
appropriate forum.[9] On the other hand,
plaintiffs cannot successfully circumvent this
difficulty merely by couching their vague interests in such lofty First Amendment phrases
as the right of association, or by appealing to
the asserted right to have the teachers control
the classroom. It has been generally recognized that secondary school teachers occupy a
unique position for influencing secondary
school students (*Ambach v. Norwick*, 441 U.S.
at 78-80, 99 S.Ct. at 1595-96), an observation
that has given rise to a concomitant power on
the part of local authorities to choose the
teachers (*id.*), regulate their pedagogical
methods (*Hetrick v. Martin*, 480 F.2d 705, 709
(6th Cir. 1973), certiorari denied, 414 U.S.
1075, 94 S.Ct. 592, 38 L.Ed.2d 482), and establish basic standards for what they will
teach. *Palmer v. Board of Education*, 603 F.2d
1271, 1274 (7th Cir. 1979), certiorari denied,
444 U.S. 1026, 100 S.Ct. 689, 62 L.Ed.2d 659;
Cary v. Board of Education, 598 F.2d 535, 543
(10th Cir. 1979); *East Hartford Education
Assn. v. Board of Education*, 562 F.2d 838, 859
(2d Cir. 1977) (*en banc*); *James v. Board of
Education*, 461 F.2d 566, 575 (2d Cir. 1972),
certiorari denied, 409 U.S. 1042, 93 S.Ct. 529,
34 L.Ed.2d 491; *Clark v. Holmes*, 474 F.2d
928, 931 (7th Cir. 1972), certiorari denied,
411 U.S. 972, 93 S.Ct. 2148, 36 L.Ed.2d 695;
Ahern v. Board of Education, 456 F.2d 399,
403-404 (8th Cir. 1970); *Mercer v. Michigan
State Board of Education*, 379 F.Supp. 580, 585
(E.D.Mich.1974), affirmed, 419 U.S. 1081, 95
S.Ct. 673, 42 L.Ed.2d 678. *Contra, Keefe v.
Geanakos*, 418 F.2d 359 (1st Cir. 1969); but
see *Mailloux v. Kiley*, 436 F.2d 565, 566 (1st
Cir. 1971) and *Mailloux v. Kiley*, 448 F.2d
1242 (1st Cir. 1971) (seemingly limiting
Geanakos to its facts).

It is difficult to conceive how a student
may assert a right to have the teacher control
the classroom when the teacher herself does not
have such a right. As a result, whatever
rights secondary school students may have outside the classroom to meet and discuss with a
particular teacher, their associational interests do not afford them a right to be taught
in the classroom by that instructor or in accordance with that teacher's own sense of the
best material. *Pico v. Board of Education*,
474 F.Supp. at 397-398. A student's appreciation of a teacher's skills simply does not in-
vest a teacher with a constitutionally-based
tenure when the actions of the school board
have given that teacher none. Of course, it is
possible that failure to rehire a particular
teacher may further evidence an attempt by the
local board to impose an identifiable orthodoxy, thereby fueling plaintiffs' case for
specific curricular relief without raising directly a teacher's own claim to reinstatement.

But again this amended complaint is inadequate
to support such a theory, for it suggests nothing more than the allowable application by the
local board of its preferences in the choice of
formative models for local schooling.

Our basic principles for handling academic
freedom claims by secondary school students
would seem to dispose as well of the claim regarding the removal of one book from the school
library. The amended complaint does not allege
that the book has been made completely unavailable to plaintiffs, that students are prohibited from discussing its contents in school, or
even that the removal was part of an action to
cleanse the library of materials conflicting
with the School Board's orthodoxy. Nevertheless
at least three courts have held that once a
book has been offered as part of the school library collection, school authorities may not
remove it because they object to its content.
*Minarcini v. Strongsville City School Dis-
trict*, 541 F.2d 577 (6th Cir. 1976); *Salvail
v. Nashua Board of Education*, 469 F.Supp. 1269
(D.N.H.1979); *Right to Read Defense Committee
of Chelsea v. School Committee of Chelsea*, 454
F.Supp. 703 (D.Mass.1978). However, there is
substantial authority on the other side
(*Presidents Council, District 25 v. Community
School Board*, 457 F.2d 289 (2d Cir. 1972),
certiorari denied, 409 U.S. 998, 93 S.Ct. 308,
34 L.Ed.2d 260; see also *Bicknell v. Vergennes
Union High School Board of Directors*, 475
F.Supp. 615 (D.Vt.1979); *Pico v. Board of
Education*, 474 F.Supp. 387 (E.D.N.Y.1979)),
and we join with these courts in rejecting the
suggestion that a particular book can gain a
kind of tenure on the shelf merely because the
administrators voice some objections to its
contents.

To be sure, a library is a general resource
the purpose of which is to foster intellectual
curiosity and serve the intellectual needs of
its users. *Minarcini v. Strongsville City
School District*, supra at 582; *Bicknell v.
Vergennes Union High School Board of Directors*,
supra at 619. But such sentiments should not
obscure practical realities. School libraries
are small auxiliary facilities often run on
limited budgets. *Pico v. Board of Education*,
supra at 397. They must, despite their limitations, cater to the needs of an often diverse
student body, primarily by providing materials
that properly supplement the basic readings assigned through the standard curriculum. An administrator would be irresponsible if he or she
failed to monitor closely the contents of the
library and did not remove a book when an appraisal of its content fails to justify its
continued use of valuable shelf space. See
*Presidents Council, District 25 v. Community
School Board*, supra at 291-293; *Pico v. Board
of Education*, supra at 396.

This is not to say that an administrator may
remove a book from the library as part of a
purge of all material offensive to a single,
exclusive perception of the way of the world,
anymore than he or she may originally stock the
library on this basis. Nor can school authorities prohibit students from buying or reading a

particular book or, under most circumstances, from bringing it to school and discussing it there. But no such allegations appear in plaintiffs' pleading, which only recites the aforementioned phrase regarding defendants' reliance on their personal moral, political and social judgment in removing the book. See note 2 *supra*. Accordingly, we agree with Judge Sharp that the amended complaint has failed in all its particulars as well as its overall tenor to allege a constitutional violation from which subject matter jurisdiction may be drawn.

Nevertheless, the articulation of the principles at issue here is sufficiently novel and important that plaintiffs should be given leave to amend their complaint again, if they can, to allege the kind of interference with secondary school academic freedom that has been found to be cognizable as a constitutional claim. This leave is of course without prejudice to the defenses and motions defendants have raised in response to the present amended complaint.[10]

Judgment vacated and remanded with instructions; Rule 18 to apply; costs to defendants.

SWYGERT, Circuit Judge, concurring in the judgment in part.

I concur only in the result that the judgment of dismissal should be vacated and that the case should be remanded for further proceedings under Circuit Rule 18. Other than that, I must with deference, but in all candor, disassociate myself from the approach taken by Judge Cummings.

The Federal Rules of Civil Procedure establishes a "notice" system of pleading in the federal courts. A party is required in the first instance only to plead "a short and plain statement of the claim," Fed.R.Civ.P.8(a)(2), and is not limited to reliance on the legal theory of relief originally pleaded. 2A Moore's Federal Practice (¶)8.14 (2d ed. 1979). A judgment of dismissal under Rule 12(b) should not be granted "unless it appears to a certainty that the plaintiff would be entitled to no relief under any state of facts which could be proved in support of his claim." 2A Moore's Federal Practice (¶)8.13, at 118-19 (2d ed. 1979).

In the case at bar the district court improperly considered plaintiffs' main legal theory--that the Board violated the Constitution by acting on the basis of their personal, moral, political, and social, but not religious beliefs--to the complete exclusion of other legal theories presented by the complaint. The plaintiffs also alleged, for instance, "unreasonable censorship . . that unduly burdens the freedom of protected classroom discussion." Complaint (¶)39. That allegation, when considered with the nature of the specific books allegedly excised, many of which appear to deal with feminism, is sufficient in my view to withstand a motion to dismiss even under the substantive standard adopted by the majority: the censoring of a number of books on the same subject states a claim, for purposes of plead-

ing, that the Board's actions suppressed "a particular kind of inquiry generally." Although I do not think that further amendment of the complaint is necessary, any problem in the pleading will likely be resolved on remand since counsel for plaintiffs indicated at oral argument that he would, if given leave, amend his complaint to allege the suppression of discussion of political and social views more explicitly.

Because the complaint, either as pleaded or as amended, states a claim of infringement of the First Amendment on at least one theory, the majority's lengthy discussion of plaintiffs' main legal theory is inappropriate. Drawing the line between the local school Board's rightful prerogative to decide high school curricula and the methodology of teachers and Board ukases involving infringements of the First Amendment is difficult, to say the least. But however difficult, the line should be drawn, in my judgment, not on pleadings but on concrete facts developed at trial.

NOTES

1. We must of course accept as true the well-pleaded allegations of the complaint. The amended complaint now in the record was filed a fortnight after the initial complaint as a matter of course. See Rule 15(a) of the Federal Rules of Civil Procedure.

2. The amended complaint alleges that defendants eventually granted a request that they convey the books to a local senior citizens group for a public burning. This contemptible ceremony, which has greatly animated the discussion of this case by the *amici curiae*, took place in December 1977. No self-respecting citizen with a knowledge of history can look upon this incident with equanimity, but its relationship to the legal issues in this case is tenuous at best. Its only arguable relevance is as evidence of the purposes of the School Board and its agents in making the educational decisions at issue here. As discussed at length below, we do not regard the allegations with respect to these purposes as sufficient to state a constitutional claim, and the book burning incident requires no change in this conclusion.

3. *Growing Up Female In America.*

4. *Go Ask Alice; The Bell Jar; The Stepford Wives.* There is no suggestion that any of the disputed books is obscene.

5. Defendants' account of this incident is somewhat different, but as noted, we must accept as true the allegations of plaintiffs' complaint.

6. This book, which it should be noted was one of the books eliminated from the "Women in Literature" course, was, according to defendant, checked out of the library to be used in some related litigation spawned by

the incidents at issue here. Defendants
have promised to return the book when that
litigation is completed. For purposes of
our consideration, we will view the book as
simply eliminated from the library collection.

7. According to the defendants, "Women in
   Literature" and the other discontinued
   courses were a part of the experimental
   "Apex" curriculum which replaced the standard curriculum with a series of "mini-
   courses" on selected topics. Periodic review of the English curriculum resulted in
   the discontinuance of the Apex program in
   favor of a more traditional format.

8. There is no need to linger over plaintiffs'
   assertions that the School Board and its
   employees have made decisions "capriciously," "arbitrarily," or "unreasonably."
   Read in context, these allegations plainly
   refer to the use of social, political and
   moral judgments in making curriculum decisions. As noted above, decisions based on
   such judgments are neither capricious nor
   arbitrary nor unreasonable. Furthermore,
   nothing in the School Board's statutory authority requires it to make its decisions
   according to some formal procedure and we
   do not regard the Constitution as imposing
   such a requirement.

9. According to defendants (Br. at 9 n. 16),
   the two teachers brought suit in the district court against the Warsaw School
   Board, contesting their terminations. In
   one instance the court entered judgment for
   the defendants. The second case has now
   apparently proceeded through the trial
   stage, but the parties have not informed
   this Court of the outcome.

10. Accordingly, we express no view on the ar-
    gument defendants have pressed here that
    the amended complaint should be dismissed
    for want of exhaustion of administrative
    remedies.

PART TWO

United States Supreme Court Decisions Relied On by the Lower Courts in Library Censorship Cases

In deciding that it was unconstitutional for the state to compel students of the Jehovah's Witnesses faith to salute the flag at school, the United States Supreme Court declared: "The Fourteenth Amendment, as now applied to the States, protects the citizen against the State itself and all of its creatures--Boards of Education not excepted. These have, of course, important, delicate, and highly discretionary functions, but none that they may not perform within the limits of the Bill of Rights. That they are educating the young for citizenship is reason for scrupulous protection of Constitutional freedoms of the individual, if we are not to strangle the free mind at its source and teach youth to discount important principles of our government as mere platitudes....The very purpose of a Bill of Rights was to withdraw certain subjects from the vicissitudes of political controversy, to place them beyond the reach of majorities and officials and to establish them as legal principles to be applied by the courts. One's right to life, liberty, and property, to free speech, a free press, freedom of worship and assembly, and other fundamental rights may not be submitted to vote; they depend on the outcome of no elections....If there is any fixed star in our Constitutional constellation, it is that no official, high or petty, can prescribe what shall be orthodox in politics, nationalism, religion, or other matters of opinion or force citizens to confess by word or act their faith therein."

West Virginia State Bd. of Education v. Barnette, 319 U. S. 624 (1943)

MR. JUSTICE JACKSON delivered the opinion of the Court.

Following the decision by this Court on June 3, 1940, in *Minersville School District* v. *Gobitis*, 310 U.S. 586, the West Virginia legislature amended its statutes to require all schools therein to conduct courses of instruction in history, civics, and in the Constitutions of the United States and of the State "for the purpose of teaching, fostering and perpetuating the ideals, principles and spirit of Americanism, and increasing the knowledge of the organization and machinery of the government." Appellant Board of Education was directed, with advice of the State Superintendent of Schools, to "prescribe the courses of study covering these subjects" for public schools. The Act made it the duty of private, parochial and denominational schools to prescribe courses of study "similar to those required for the public schools."[1]

The Board of Education on January 9, 1942, adopted a resolution containing recitals taken largely from the Court's *Gobitis* opinion and ordering that the salute to the flag become "a regular part of the program of activities in the public schools," that all teachers and pupils "shall be required to participate in the salute honoring the Nation represented by the Flag; provided, however, that refusal to salute the Flag be regarded as an act of insubordination, and shall be dealt with accordingly."[2]

The resolution originally required the "commonly accepted salute to the Flag" which it defined. Objections to the salute as "being too much like Hitler's" were raised by the Parent and Teachers Association, the Boy and Girl Scouts, the Red Cross, and the Federation of Women's Clubs.[3] Some modification appears to have been made in deference to these objections, but[4] no concession was made to Jehovah's Witnesses. What is now required is the "stiff-arm" salute, the saluter to keep the right hand raised with palm turned up while the following is repeated: "I pledge allegiance to the Flag of the United States of America and to the Republic for which it stands; one Nation, indivisible; with liberty and justice for all."

Failure to conform is "insubordination" dealt with by expulsion. Readmission is denied by statute until compliance. Meanwhile the expelled child is "unlawfully absent"[5] and may be proceeded against as a delinquent.[6] His parents or guardians are liable to prosecution,[7] and if convicted are subject to fine not exceeding $50 and jail term not exceeding thirty days.[8]

Appellees, citizens of the United States and of West Virginia, brought suit in the United States District Court for themselves and others similarly situated asking its injunction to restrain enforcement of these laws and regulations against Jehovah's Witnesses. The Witnesses are an unincorporated body teaching that the obligation imposed by law of God is superior to that of laws enacted by temporal government. Their religious beliefs include a literal version of Exodus, Chapter 20, verses 4 and 5, which says: "Thou shalt not make unto thee any graven image, or any likeness of anything that is in heaven above, or that is in the earth beneath, or that is in the water under the earth; thou shalt not bow down thyself to them nor serve them." They consider that the flag is an "image" within this command. For this reason they refuse to salute it.

Children of this faith have been expelled from school and are threatened with exclusion for no other cause. Officials threaten to send them to reformatories maintained for criminally inclined juveniles. Parents of such children have been prosecuted and are threatened with prosecutions for causing delinquency.

The Board of Education moved to dismiss the complaint setting forth these facts and alleging that the law and regulations are an unconstitutional denial of religious freedom, and of freedom of speech, and are invalid under the "due process" and "equal protection" clauses of the Fourteenth Amendment to the Federal Constitution. The cause was submitted on the pleadings to a District Court of three judges. It restrained enforcement as to the plaintiffs and those of that class. The Board of Education brought the case here by direct appeal.[9]

This case calls upon us to reconsider a precedent decision, as the Court throughout its history often has been required to do.[10] Before turning to the *Gobitis* case, however, it is desirable to notice certain characteristics by which this controversy is distinguished.

The freedom asserted by these appellees does not bring them into collision with rights asserted by any other individual. It is such conflicts which most frequently require intervention of the State to determine where the rights of one end and those of another begin. But the refusal of these persons to participate in the ceremony does not interfere with or deny rights of others to do so. Nor·is there any question in this case that their behavior is peaceable and orderly. The sole conflict is between authority and rights of the individual. The State asserts power to condition access to public education on making a prescribed sign and profession and at the same time to coerce attendance by punishing both parent and child. The latter stand on a right of self-determination in matters that touch individual opinion and personal attitude.

As the present CHIEF JUSTICE said in dissent in the *Gobitis* case, the State may "require teaching by instruction and study of all in our history and in the structure and organization of our government, including the guaranties of civil liberty, which tend to inspire patriotism and love of country." 310 U.S. at 604. Here, however, we are dealing with a compulsion of students to declare a belief. They are not merely made acquainted with the flag salute so that they may be informed as to what it is or even what it means. The issue here is whether this slow and easily neglected route to aroused loyalties constitutionally may be short-cut by substituting a compulsory salute and slogan.[12] This issue is not prejudiced by the Court's previous holding that where a State, without compelling attendance, extends college facilities to pupils who voluntarily enroll, it may prescribe military training as part of the course without offense to the Constitution. It was held that those who take advantage of its opportunities may not on ground of conscience refuse compliance with such conditions. *Hamilton* v. *Regents*, 293 U.S. 245. In the present case attendance is not optional. That case is also to be distinguished from the present one because, independently of college privileges or requirements, the State has power to raise militia and impose the duties of service therein upon its citizens.

There is no doubt that, in connection with the pledges, the flag salute is a form of utterance. Symbolism is a primitive but effective way of communicating ideas. The use of an emblem or flag to symbolize some system, idea, institution, or personality, is a short cut from mind to mind. Causes and nations, political parties, lodges and ecclesiastical groups seek to knit the loyalty of their followings to a flag or banner, a color or design. The State announces rank, function, and authority through crowns and maces, uniforms and black robes; the church speaks through the Cross, the Crucifix, the altar and shrine, and clerical raiment. Symbols of State often convey political ideas just as religious symbols come to convey theological ones. Associated with many of these symbols are appropriate gestures of acceptance or respect: a salute, a bowed or bared head, a bended knee. A person gets from a symbol the meaning he puts into it, and what is one man's comfort and inspiration is another's jest and scorn.

Over a decade ago Chief Justice Hughes led this Court in holding that the display of a red flag as a symbol of opposition by peaceful and legal means to organized government was protected by the free speech guaranties of the Constitution. *Stromberg* v. *California*, 283 U.S. 359. Here it is the State that employs a flag as a symbol of adherence to government as presently organized. It requires the individual to communicate by word and sign his acceptance of the political ideas it thus bespeaks. Objection to this form of communication when coerced is an old one, well known to the framers of the Bill of Rights.[13]

It is also to be noted that the compulsory flag salute and pledge requires affirmation of a belief and an attitude of mind. It is not clear whether the regulation contemplates that pupils forego any contrary convictions of their own and become unwilling converts to the prescribed ceremony or whether it will be acceptable if they simulate assent by words without belief and by a gesture barren of meaning. It is now a commonplace that censorship or suppression of expression of opinion is tolerated by our Constitution only when the expression presents a clear and present danger of action of a kind the State is empowered to prevent and punish. It would seem that involuntary affirmation could be commanded only on even more immediate and urgent grounds than silence. But here the power of compulsion is invoked without any allegation that remaining passive during a flag salute ritual creates a clear and present danger that would justify an effort even to muffle expression. To sustain the compulsory flag salute we are required to say that a Bill of Rights which guards the individual's right to speak his own mind, left it open to public authorities to compel him to utter what is not in his mind.

Whether the First Amendment to the Constitution will permit officials to order observance of ritual of this nature does not depend upon whether as a voluntary exercise we would think it to be good, bad or merely innocuous. Any credo of nationalism is likely to include what some disapprove or to omit what others think essential, and to give off different overtones as it takes on different accents or interpretations.[14] If official power exists to coerce acceptance of any patriotic creed, what it shall contain cannot be decided by courts, but must be largely discretionary with the ordaining authority, whose power to prescribe would no doubt include power to amend. Hence validity of the asserted power to force an American citizen publicly to profess any statement of belief or to engage in any ceremony of assent

10

to one, presents questions of power that must be considered independently of any idea we may have as to the utility of the ceremony in question.

Nor does the issue as we see it turn on one's possession of particular religious views or the sincerity with which they are held. While religion supplies appellees' motive for enduring the discomforts of making the issue in this case, many citizens who do not share these religious views hold such a compulsory rite to infringe constitutional liberty of the individual.[15] It is not necessary to inquire whether non-conformist beliefs will exempt from the duty to salute unless we first find power to make the salute a legal duty.

The *Gobitis* decision, however, *assumed*, as did the argument in that case and in this, that power exists in the State to impose the flag salute discipline upon school children in general. The Court only examined and rejected a claim based on religious beliefs of immunity from an unquestioned general rule.[16] The question which underlies the flag salute controversy is whether such a ceremony so touching matters of opinion and political attitude may be imposed upon the individual by official authority under powers committed to any political organization under our Constitution. We examine rather than assume existence of this power and, against this broader definition of issues in this case, reexamine specific grounds assigned for the *Gobitis* decision.

1. It was said that the flag-salute controversy confronted the Court with "the problem which Lincoln cast in memorable dilemma: 'Must a government of necessity be too *strong* for the liberties of its people, or too *weak* to maintain its own existence?'" and that the answer must be in favor of strength. *Minersville School District* v. *Gobitis*, *supra*, at 596.

We think these issues may be examined free of pressure or restraint growing out of such considerations.

It may be doubted whether Mr. Lincoln would have thought that the strength of government to maintain itself would be impressively vindicated by our confirming power of the State to expel a handful of children from school. Such oversimplification, so handy in political debate, often lacks the precision necessary to postulates of judicial reasoning. If validly applied to this problem, the utterance cited would resolve every issue of power in favor of those in authority and would require us to override every liberty thought to weaken or delay execution of their policies.

Government of limited power need not be anemic government. Assurance that rights are secure tends to diminish fear and jealousy of strong government, and by making us feel safe to live under it makes for its better support. Without promise of a limiting Bill of Rights it is doubtful if our Constitution could have mustered enough strength to enable its ratification. To enforce those rights today is not to choose weak government over strong government. It is only to adhere as a means of

strength to individual freedom of mind in preference to officially disciplined uniformity for which history indicates a disappointing and disastrous end.

The subject now before us exemplifies this principle. Free public education, if faithful to the ideal of secular instruction and political neutrality, will not be partisan or enemy of any class, creed, party, or faction. If it is to impose any ideological discipline, however, each party or denomination must seek to control, or failing that, to weaken the influence of the educational system. Observance of the limitations of the Constitution will not weaken government in the field appropriate for its exercise.

2. It was also considered in the *Gobitis* case that functions of educational officers in States, counties and school districts were such that to interfere with their authority "would in effect make us the school board for the country." *Id.* at 598.

The Fourteenth Amendment, as now applied to the States, protects the citizen against the State itself and all of its creatures—Boards of Education not excepted. These have, of course, important, delicate, and highly discretionary functions, but none that they may not perform within the limits of the Bill of Rights. That they are educating the young for citizenship is reason for scrupulous protection of Constitutional freedoms of the individual, if we are not to strangle the free mind at its source and teach youth to discount important principles of our government as mere platitudes.

Such Boards are numerous and their territorial jurisdiction often small. But small and local authority may feel less sense of responsibility to the Constitution, and agencies of publicity may be less vigilant in calling it to account. The action of Congress in making flag observance voluntary[17] and respecting the conscience of the objector in a matter so vital as raising the Army[18] contrasts sharply with these local regulations in matters relatively trivial to the welfare of the nation. There are village tyrants as well as village Hampdens, but none who acts under color of law is beyond reach of the Constitution.

3. The *Gobitis* opinion reasoned that this is a field "where courts possess no marked and certainly no controlling competence," that it is committed to the legislatures as well as the courts to guard cherished liberties and that it is constitutionally appropriate to "fight out the wise use of legislative authority in the forum of public opinion and before legislative assemblies rather than to transfer such a contest to the judicial arena," since all the "effective means of inducing political changes are left free." *Id.* at 597-598, 600.

The very purpose of a Bill of Rights was to withdraw certain subjects from the vicissitudes of political controversy, to place them beyond the reach of majorities and officials and to establish them as legal principles to be applied by the courts. One's right to life, liberty, and property, to free speech, a free press, freedom of worship and assembly, and other fundamental rights may not be submitted to vote; they depend on the outcome of no elections.

In weighing arguments of the parties it is important to distinguish between the due process clause of the Fourteenth Amendment as an instrument for transmitting the principles of the First Amendment and those cases in which it is applied for its own sake. The test of legislation which collides with the Fourteenth Amendment, because it also collides with the principles of the First, is much more definite than the test when only the Fourteenth is involved. Much of the vagueness of the due process clause disappears when the specific prohibitions of the First become its standard. The right of a State to regulate, for example, a public utility may well include, so far as the due process test is concerned, power to impose all of the restrictions which a legislature may have a "rational basis" for adopting. But freedoms of speech and of press, of assembly, and of worship may not be infringed on such slender grounds. They are susceptible of restriction only to prevent grave and immediate danger to interests which the State may lawfully protect. It is important to note that while it is the Fourteenth Amendment which bears directly upon the State it is the more specific limiting principles of the First Amendment that finally govern this case.

Nor does our duty to apply the Bill of Rights to assertions of official authority depend upon our possession of marked competence in the field where the invasion of rights occurs. True, the task of translating the majestic generalities of the Bill of Rights, conceived as part of the pattern of liberal government in the eighteenth century, into concrete restraints on officials dealing with the problems of the twentieth century, is one to disturb self-confidence. These principles grew in soil which also produced a philosophy that the individual was the center of society, that his liberty was attainable through mere absence of governmental restraints, and that government should be entrusted with few controls and only the mildest supervision over men's affairs. We must transplant these rights to a soil in which the *laissez-faire* concept or principle of non-interference has withered at least as to economic affairs, and social advancements are increasingly sought through closer integration of society and through expanded and strengthened governmental controls. These changed conditions often deprive precedents of reliability and cast us more than we would choose upon our own judgment. But we act in these matters not by authority of our competence but by force of our commissions. We cannot, because of modest estimates of our competence in such specialties as public education, withhold the judgment that history authenticates as the function of this Court when liberty is infringed.

4. Lastly, and this is the very heart of the *Gobitis* opinion, it reasons that "National unity is the basis of national security," that the authorities have "the right to select appropriate means for its attainment," and hence reaches the conclusion that such compulsory measures toward "national unity" are constitutional. *Id*. at 595. Upon the verity of this assumption depends our answer in this case.

National unity as an end which officials may foster by persuasion and example is not in question. The problem is whether under our Constitution compulsion as here employed is a permissible means for its achievement.

Struggles to coerce uniformity of sentiment in support of some end thought essential to their time and country have been waged by many good as well as by evil men. Nationalism is a relatively recent phenomenon but at other times and places the ends have been racial or territorial security, support of a dynasty or regime, and particular plans for saving souls. As first and moderate methods to attain unity have failed, those bent on its accomplishment must resort to an ever-increasing severity. As governmental pressure toward unity becomes greater, so strife becomes more bitter as to whose unity it shall be. Probably no deeper division of our people could proceed from any provocation than from finding it necessary to choose what doctrine and whose program public educational officials shall compel youth to unite in embracing. Ultimate futility of such attempts to compel coherence is the lesson of every such effort from the Roman drive to stamp out Christianity as a disturber of its pagan unity, the Inquisition, as a means to religious and dynastic unity, the Siberian exiles as a means to Russian unity, down to the fast failing efforts of our present totalitarian enemies. Those who begin coercive elimination of dissent soon find themselves exterminating dissenters. Compulsory unification of opinion achieves only the unanimity of the graveyard.

It seems trite but necessary to say that the First Amendment to our Constitution was designed to avoid these ends by avoiding these beginnings. There is no mysticism in the American concept of the State or of the nature or origin of its authority. We set up government by consent of the governed, and the Bill of Rights denies those in power any legal opportunity to coerce that consent. Authority here is to be controlled by public opinion, not public opinion by authority.

The case is made difficult not because the principles of its decision are obscure but because the flag involved is our own. Nevertheless, we apply the limitations of the Constitution with no fear that freedom to be intellectually and spiritually diverse or even contrary will disintegrate the social organization. To believe that patriotism will not flourish if patriotic ceremonies are voluntary and spontaneous instead of a compulsory routine is to make an unflattering estimate of the appeal of our institutions to free minds. We can have intellectual individualism and the rich cultural diversities that we owe to exceptional minds only at the price of occasional eccentricity and abnormal attitudes. When they are so harmless to others or to the State as those we deal with here, the price is not too great. But freedom to differ is not limited to things that do not matter much. That would be a mere shadow of freedom. The test of its substance is the right to differ as to things that touch the heart of the existing order.

If there is any fixed star in our constitutional constellation, it is that no official, high or petty, can prescribe what shall be orthodox in politics, nationalism, religion, or other matters of opinion or force citizens to confess by word or act their faith therein. If there are any circumstances which permit an exception, they do not now occur to us.[19]

We think the action of the local authorities in compelling the flag salute and pledge transcends constitutional limitations on their power and invades the sphere of intellect and spirit which it is the purpose of the First Amendment to our Constitution to reserve from all official control.

The decision of this Court in *Minersville School District* v. *Gobitis* and the holdings of those few *per curiam* decisions which preceded and foreshadowed it are overruled, and judgment enjoining enforcement of the West Virginia Regulation is

Affirmed.

NOTES

1. § 1734, West Virginia Code (1941 Supp.):"In all public, private, parochial and denominational schools located within this state there shall be given regular courses of instruction in history of the United States, in civics, and in the constitutions of the United States and of the State of West Virginia, for the purpose of teaching, fostering and perpetuating the ideals, principles and spirit of Americanism, and increasing the knowledge of the organization and machinery of the government of the United States and of the state of West Virginia. The state board of education shall, with the advice of the state superintendent of schools, prescribe the courses of study covering these subjects for the public elementary and grammar schools, public high schools and state normal schools. It shall be the duty of the officials or boards having authority over the respective private, parochial and denominational schools to prescribe courses of study for the schools under their control and supervision similar to those required for the public schools."

2. The text is as follows:"WHEREAS, The West Virginia State Board of Education holds in highest regard those rights and privileges guaranteed by the Bill of Rights in the Constitution of the United States of America and in the Constitution of West Virginia, specifically, the first amendment to the Constitution of the United States as restated in the fourteenth amendment to the same document and in the guarantee of religious freedom in Article III of the Constitution of this State, and

"WHEREAS, The West Virginia State Board of Education honors the broad principle that one's convictions about the ultimate mystery of the universe and man's relation to it is placed beyond the reach of law; that the propagation of belief is protected whether in church or chapel, mosque or synagogue, tabernacle or meeting house; that the Constitutions of the United States and of the State of West Virginia assure generous immunity to the individual from imposition of penalty for offending, in the course of his own religious activities, the religious views of others, be they a minority or those who are dominant in the government, but

"WHEREAS, The West Virginia State Board of Education recognizes that the manifold character of man's relations may bring his conception of religious duty into conflict with the secular interests of his fellowman; that conscientious scruples have not in the course of the long struggle for religious toleration relieved the individual from obedience to the general law not aimed at the promotion or restriction of the religious beliefs; that the mere possession of convictions which contradict the relevant concerns of political society does not relieve the citizen from the discharge of political responsibility, and

"WHEREAS, The West Virginia State Board of Education holds that national unity is the basis of national security; that the flag of our Nation is the symbol of our National Unity transcending all internal differences, however large within the framework of the Constitution; that the Flag is the symbol of the Nation's power; that emblem of freedom in its truest, best sense; that it signifies government resting on the consent of the governed, liberty regulated by law, protection of the weak against the strong, security against the exercise of arbitrary power, and absolute safety for free institutions against foreign aggression, and

"WHEREAS, The West Virginia State Board of Education maintains that the public schools, established by the legislature of the State of West Virginia under the authority of the Constitution of the State of West Virginia and supported by taxes imposed by legally constituted measures, are dealing with the formative period in the development in citizenship that the Flag is an allowable portion of the program of schools thus publicly supported.

"Therefore, be it RESOLVED, That the West Virginia Board of Education does hereby recognize and order that the commonly accepted salute to the Flag of the United States—the right hand is placed upon the breast and following pledge repeated in unison: 'I pledge allegiance to the Flag of the United States of America and to the Republic for which it stands; one Nation, indivisible, with liberty and justice for all'—now becomes a regular part of the program of activities in the public schools, supported in whole or in part by public funds, and that all teachers as defined by law in West Virginia and pupils in such schools shall be required to participate in the salute, honoring the Nation represented by the Flag; provided, however, that refusal to salute the Flag be regarded as an act of insubordination, and shall be dealt with accordingly."

3. The National Headquarters of the United States Flag Association takes the position that the extension of the right arm in this salute to the flag is not the Nazi-Fascist salute, "although quite similar to it. In the Pledge to the Flag the right arm is extended and raised, palm UPWARD, whereas the Nazis extend the arm practically *straight to the front* (the finger tips being about even with the eyes), *palm* DOWNWARD, and the Fascists do the same except they raise the arm slightly higher." James A. Moss, The Flag of the United States: Its History and Symbolism (1914) 108.

4. They have offered in lieu of participating in the flag salute ceremony "periodically and publicly" to give the following pledge:

"I have pledged my unqualified allegiance

and devotion to Jehovah, the Almighty God, and to His Kingdom, for which Jesus commands all Christians to pray.

"I respect the flag of the United States and acknowledge it as a symbol of freedom justice to all.

"I pledge allegiance and obedience to all the laws of the United States that are consistent with God's law, as set forth in the Bible."

5. § 1851 (1), West Virginia Code (1941 Supp.):"If a child be dismissed, suspended, or expelled from school because of refusal of such child to meet legal and lawful requirements of the school and the established regulations of the county and/or state board of education, further admission of the child to school shall be refused until such requirements and regulations be complied with. Any such child shall be treated as being unlawfully absent from school during the time he refuses to comply with such requirements and regulations, and any person having legal or actual control of such child shall be liable to prosecution under the provisions of this article for the absence of such child from school."

6. § 4904 (4), West Virginia Code (1941 Supp.).

7. See Note 5, *supra*.

8. §§ 1847, 1851, West Virginia Code (1941 Supp.).

9. § 266 of the Judicial Code, 28 U.S.C. § 380.

10. See authorities cited in *Helvering* v. *Griffiths*, 318 U.S. 371, 401, note 52.

11. See the nation-wide survey of the study of American history conducted by the New York Times, the results of which are published in the issue of June 21, 1942, and are there summarized on p. 1, col. 1, as follows:

"82 percent of the institutions of higher learning in the United States do not require the study of United States history for the undergraduate degree. Eighteen per cent of the colleges and universities require such history courses before a degree is awarded. It was found that many students complete their four years in college without taking any history courses dealing with this country.

"Seventy-two per cent of the colleges and universities do not require United States history for admission, while 28 per cent require it. As a result, the survey revealed, many students go through high school, college and then to the professional or graduate institution without having explored courses in the history of their country.

"Less than 10 per cent of the total undergraduate body was enrolled in United States history classes during the Spring semester just ended. Only 8 per cent of the freshman class took courses in United States history, although 30 per cent was enrolled in European or world history courses."

12. The Resolution of the Board of Education

did not adopt the flag salute because it was claimed to have educational value. It seems to have been concerned with promotion of national unity (see footnote 2), which justification is considered later in this opinion. No information as to its educational aspect is called to our attention except Olander, Children's Knowledge of the Flag Salute, 35 Journal of Educational Research 300, 305, which sets forth a study of the ability of a large and representative number of children to remember and state the meaning of the flag salute which they recited each day in school. His conclusion was that it revealed "a rather pathetic picture of our attempts to teach children not only the words but the meaning of our Flag Salute."

13. Early Christians were frequently persecuted for their refusal to participate in ceremonies before the statue of the emperor or other symbol of imperial authority. The story of William Tell's sentence to shoot an apple off his son's head for refusal to salute a bailiff's hat is an ancient one. 21 Encyclopedia Britannica (14th ed.) 911-912. The Quakers, William Penn included, suffered punishment rather than uncover their heads in deference to any civil authority. Braithwaite, The Beginnings of Quakerism (1912) 200, 229-230, 232-233, 447, 451; Fox, Quakers Courageous (1941) 113.

14. For example: Use of "Republic," if rendered to distinguish our government from a "democracy," or the words "one Nation," if intended to distinguish it from a "federation," open up old and bitter controversies in our political history; "liberty and justice for all," if it must be accepted as descriptive of the present order rather than an ideal, might to some seem an overstatement.

15. Cushman, Constitutional Law in 1939-40, 35 American Political Science Review 250, 271, observes: "All of the eloquence by which the majority extol the ceremony of flag saluting as a free expression of patriotism turns sour when used to describe the brutal compulsion which requires a sensitive and conscientious child to stultify himself in public." For further criticism of the opinion in the *Gobitis* case by persons who do not share the faith of the Witnesses see: Powell, Conscience and the Constitution, in Democracy and National Unity (University of Chicago Press, 1941) 1; Wilkinson, Some Aspects of the Constitutional Guarantees of Civil Liberty, 11 Fordham Law Review 50; Fennell, The "Reconstructed Court" and Religious Freedom: The Gobitis Case in Retrospect, 19 New York University Law Quarterly Review 31; Green, Liberty under the Fourteenth Amendment, 27 Washington University Law Quarterly 497; 9 International Juridical Association Bulletin 1; 39 Michigan Law Review 149; 15 St. John's Law Review 95.

16. The opinion says "That the flag-salute is

an allowable portion of a school program *for those who do not invoke conscientious scruples* is *surely not debatable*. But for us to insist that, *though the ceremony may be required, exceptional immunity must be given to dissidents*, is to maintain that there is no basis for a legislative judgment that such an exemption might introduce elements of difficulty into the school discipline, might cast doubts in the minds of the other children which would themselves weaken the effect of the exercise." (Italics ours.) 310 U.S. at 599-600. And elsewhere the question under consideration was stated, "When does the constitutional guarantee *compel exemption* from doing what society thinks necessary for the promotion of some great common end, or from a penalty for conduct which appears dangerous to the general good?" (Italics ours.) *Id*. at 593. And again, "...whether school children, like the Gobitis children, must be *excused from conduct required of all the other children* in the promotion of national cohesion...." (Italics ours.) *Id*. at 595.

17. Section 7 of House Joint Resolution 359, approved December 22, 1942, 56 Stat. 1074, 36 U.S.C. (1942 Supp.) § 172, prescribes no penalties for nonconformity but provides:

"That the pledge of allegiance to the flag, 'I pledge allegiance to the flag of the United States of America and to the Republic for which it stands, one Nation indivisible, with liberty and justice for all,' be rendered by standing with the right hand over the heart. However, civilians will always show full respect to the flag when the pledge is given by merely standing at attention, men removing the headdress..."

18. § 5 (a) of the Selective Training and Service Act of 1940, 50 U.S.C. (App.) § 307 (g).

19. The Nation may raise armies and compel citizens to give military service. *Selective Draft Law Cases*, 245 U.S. 366. It follows, of course, that those subject to military discipline are under many duties and may not claim many freedoms that we hold inviolable as to those in civilian life.

In deciding for a member of the Jehovah's Witnesses faith who had been arrested for distributing religious literature on a sidewalk in the company town of Chickasaw, Alabama, the United States Supreme Court spoke of the importance of citizens being informed and being able to receive uncensored information: "Many people in the United States live in company-owned towns. These people, just as residents of municipalities, are free citizens of their State and country. Just as all other citizens they must make decisions which affect the welfare of community and nation. To act as good citizens they must be informed. In order to enable them to be properly informed their information must be uncensored. There is no more reason for depriving these people of the liberties guaranteed by the First and Fourteenth Amendments than there is for curtailing these freedoms with respect to any other citizen."

Marsh v. *Alabama*, 326 U. S. 501 (1946)

MR. JUSTICE BLACK delivered the opinion of the Court.

In this case we are asked to decide whether a State, consistently with the First and Fourteenth Amendments, can impose criminal punishment on a person who undertakes to distribute religious literature on the premises of a company-owned town contrary to the wishes of the town's management. The town, a suburb of Mobile, Alabama, known as Chickasaw, is owned by the Gulf Shipbuilding Corporation. Except for that it has all the characteristics of any other American town. The property consists of residential buildings, streets, a system of sewers, a sewage disposal plant and a "business block" on which business places are situated. A deputy of the Mobile County Sheriff, paid by the company, serves as the town's policeman. Merchants and service establishments have rented the stores and business places on the business block and the United States uses one of the places as a post office from which six carriers deliver mail to the people of Chickasaw and the adjacent area. The town and the surrounding neighborhood, which can not be distinguished from the Gulf property by anyone not familiar with the property lines, are thickly settled, and according to all indications the residents use the business block as their regular shopping center. To do so, they now, as they have for many years, make use of a company-owned paved street and sidewalk located alongside the store fronts in order to enter and leave the stores and the post office. Intersecting company-owned roads at each end of the business block lead into a four-lane public highway which runs parallel to the business block at a distance of thirty feet. There is nothing to stop highway traffic from coming onto the business block and upon arrival a traveler may make free use of the facilities available there. In short the town and its

shopping district are accessible to and freely used by the public in general and there is nothing to distinguish them from any other town and shopping center except the fact that the title to the property belongs to a private corporation.

Appellant, a Jehovah's Witness, came onto the sidewalk we have just described, stood near the post office and undertook to distribute religious literature. In the stores the corporation had posted a notice which read as follows: "This Is Private Property, and Without Written Permission, No Street, or House Vendor, Agent or Solicitation of Any Kind Will Be Permitted." Appellant was warned that she could not distribute the literature without a permit and told that no permit would be issued to her. She protested that the company rule could not be constitutionally applied so as to prohibit her from distributing religious writings. When she was asked to leave the sidewalk and Chickasaw she declined. The deputy sheriff arrested her and she was charged in the state court with violating Title 14, § 426 of the 1940 Alabama Code which makes it a crime to enter or remain on the premises of another after having been warned not to do so. Appellant contended that to construe the state statute as applicable to her activities would abridge her right to freedom of press and religion contrary to the First and Fourteenth Amendments to the Constitution. This contention was rejected and she was convicted. The Alabama Court of Appeals affirmed the conviction, holding that the statute as applied was constitutional because the title to the sidewalk was in the corporation and because the public use of the sidewalk had not been such as to give rise to a presumption under Alabama law of its irrevocable dedication to the public. 21 So. 2d 558. The State Supreme Court denied certiorari, 246 Ala. 539, 21 So. 2d 564, and the case is here on appeal under § 237 (a) of the Judicial Code, 28 U.S.C. § 344 (a).

Had the title to Chickasaw belonged not to a private but to a municipal corporation and had appellant been arrested for violating a municipal ordinance rather than a ruling by those appointed by the corporation to manage a company town it would have been clear that appellant's conviction must be reversed. Under our decision in *Lovell* v. *Griffin*, 303 U. S. 444 and others which have followed that case,[1] neither a State nor a municipality can completely bar the distribution of literature containing religious or political ideas on its streets, sidewalks and public places or make the right to distribute dependent on a flat license tax or permit to be issued by an official who could deny it at will. We have also held that an ordinance completely prohibiting the dissemination of ideas on the city streets can not be justified on the ground that the municipality holds legal title to them. *Jamison* v. *Texas*, 318 U. S. 413. And we have recognized that the preservation of a free society is so far dependent upon the right of each individual citizen to receive such literature as he himself might desire that a municipality could not, without jeopardizing that vital individual freedom, prohibit door to door distribution of literature. *Martin* v. *Struthers*, 319 U.S. 141, 146, 147. From these decisions it is clear that had the people of Chickasaw owned all the homes, and all the stores, and all the streets, and all the sidewalks, all those owners together could not have set up a municipal government with sufficient power to pass an ordinance completely barring the distribution of religious literature. Our question then narrows down to this: Can those people who live in or come to Chickasaw be denied freedom of press and religion simply because a single company has legal title to all the town? For it is the State's contention that the mere fact that all the property interests in the town are held by a single company is enough to give that company power, enforceable by a state statute, to abridge these freedoms.

We do not agree that the corporation's property interests settle the question.[2] The State urges in effect that the corporation's right to control the inhabitants of Chickasaw is coextensive with the right of a homeowner to regulate the conduct of his guests. We cannot accept that contention. Ownership does not always mean absolute dominion. The more an owner, for his advantage, opens up his property for use by the public in general, the more do his rights become circumscribed by the statutory and constitutional rights of those who use it. Cf. *Republic Aviation Corp.* v. *Labor Board*, 324 U.S. 793, 798, 802, n.8. Thus, the owners of privately held bridges, ferries, turnpikes and railroads may not operate them as freely as a farmer does his farm. Since these facilities are built and operated primarily to benefit the public and since their operation is essentially a public function, it is subject to state regulation.[3] And, though the issue is not directly analogous to the one before us, we do want to point out by way of illustration that such regulation may not result in an operation of these facilities, even by privately owned companies, which unconstitutionally interferes with and discriminates against interstate commerce. *Port Richmond Ferry* v. *Hudson County*, *supra*, 234 U.S. at 326 and cases cited, pp. 328-329; cf. *South Carolina Highway Dept.* v. *Barnwell Bros.*, 303 U.S. 177. Had the corporation here owned the segment of the four-lane highway which runs parallel to the "business block" and operated the same under a state franchise, doubtless no one would have seriously contended that the corporation's property interest in the highway gave it power to obstruct through traffic or to discriminate against interstate commerce. See *County Commissioners* v. *Chandler*, 96 U.S. 205, 208; *Donovan* v. *Pennsylvania Co.*, *supra*, 199 U.S. at 294; *Covington Drawbridge Co.* v. *Shepherd*, 21 How. 112, 125. And even had there been no express franchise but mere acquiescence by the State in the corporation's use of its property as a segment of the four-lane highway, operation of all the highway, including the segment owned by the corporation, would still have been performance of a public

function and discrimination would certainly have been illegal.[4]

We do not think it makes any significant constitutional difference as to the relationship between the rights of the owner and those of the public that here the State, instead of permitting the corporation to operate a highway, permitted it to use its property as a town, operate a "business block" in the town and a street and sidewalk on that business block. Cf. *Barney* v. *Keokuk*, 94 U.S. 324, 340. Whether a corporation or a municipality owns or possesses the town the public in either case has an identical interest in the functioning of the community in such manner that the channels of communication remain free. As we have heretofore stated, the town of Chickasaw does not function differently from any other town. The "business block" serves as the community shopping center and is freely accessible and open to the people in the area and those passing through. The managers appointed by the corporation cannot curtail the liberty of press and religion of these people consistently with the purposes of the Constitutional guarantees, and a state statute, as the one here involved, which enforces such action by criminally punishing those who attempt to distribute religious literature clearly violates the First and Fourteenth Amendments to the Constitution.

Many people in the United States live in company-owned towns.[5] These people, just as residents of municipalities, are free citizens of their State and country. Just as all other citizens they must make decisions which affect the welfare of community and nation. To act as good citizens they must be informed. In order to enable them to be properly informed their information must be uncensored. There is no more reason for depriving these people of the liberties guaranteed by the First and the Fourteenth Amendments than there is for curtailing these freedoms with respect to any other citizen.[6]

When we balance the Constitutional rights of owners of property against those of the people to enjoy freedom of press and religion, as we must here, we remain mindful of the fact that the latter occupy a preferred position.[7] As we have stated before, the right to exercise the liberties safeguarded by the First Amendment "lies at the foundation of free government by free men" and we must in all cases "weigh the circumstances and . . . appraise the . . . reasons . . . in support of the regulation. . . of the rights." *Schneider* v. *State*, 308 U.S. 147, 161. In our view the circumstance that the property rights to the premises where the deprivation of liberty, here involved, took place, were held by others than the public, is not sufficient to justify the State's permitting a corporation to govern a community of citizens so as to restrict their fundamental liberties and the enforcement of such restraint by the application of a state statute. Insofar as the State has attempted to impose criminal punishment on appellant for undertaking to distribute religious literature in a company town, its action cannot stand. The case is reversed and the cause remanded for further proceedings not inconsistent with this opinion.

Reversed and remanded.

NOTES

1. *Hague v. C.I.O.*, 307 U.S. 496; *Schneider v. State*, 308 U.S. 147; *Thornhill v. Alabama*, 310 U.S. 88; *Cantwell v. Connecticut*, 310 U.S. 296; dissent of Chief Justice Stone in *Jones v. Opelika*, 316 U.S. 584, 600, adopted as the opinion of the Court, 319 U.S. 103; *Largent v. Texas*, 318 U.S. 418; *Murdock v. Pennsylvania*, 319 U.S. 105; *Follett v. McCormick*, 321 U.S. 573.

2. We do not question the state court's determination of the issue of "dedication." That determination means that the corporation could, if it so desired, entirely close the sidewalk and the town to the public and is decisive of all questions of state law which depend on the owner's being estopped to reclaim possession of, and the public's holding the title to, or having received an irrevocable easement in, the premises. *Demopolis v. Webb*, 87 Ala. 659, 6 So. 408; *Hamilton v. Town of Warrior*, . 215 Ala. 670, 112 So. 136; *Town of Leeds v. Sharp*, 218 Ala. 403, 405, 118 So. 572; *Forney v. Calhoun County*, 84 Ala. 215, 4 So. 153; *Cloverdale Homes v. Cloverdale*, 182 Ala. 419, 62 So. 712. The "dedication" of a road to the public may also be decisive of whether, under Alabama law, obstructing the road constitutes a crime, *Beverly v. State*, 28 Ala. App. 451, 185 So. 768, and whether certain action on or near the road amounts to a tort. *Thrasher v. Burr*, 202 Ala. 307, 80 So. 372. But determination of the issue of "dedication" does not decide the question under the Federal Constitution here involved.

3. *Clark's Ferry Bridge Co. v. Public Service Commission*, 291 U.S. 227; *American Toll Bridge Co. v. Railroad Commission*, 307 U.S. 486; *Mills v. St. Clair County*, 8 How. 569, 581; *Port Richmond Ferry v. Hudson County*, 234 U.S. 317, 327, 331-332; *Covington & L. Turnpike Road Co. v. Sandford*, 164 U.S. 578; *Norfolk & S.*

Turnpike Co. v. Virginia, 225 U.S. 264; *Donovan v. Pennsylvania Co.*, 199 U.S. 279, and cases cited on pp. 293-295.

4. And certainly the corporation can no more deprive people of freedom of press and religion than it can discriminate against commerce. In his dissenting opinion in *Jones v. Opelika*, 316 U.S. 584, 600, which later was adopted as the opinion of the Court, 319 U.S. 103, 104, Mr. Chief Justice Stone made the following pertinent statement: "Freedom of press and religion, explicitly guaranteed by the Constitution, must at least be entitled to the same freedom from burdensome taxation which it has been thought that the more general phraseology of the commerce clause has extended to interstate commerce. Whatever doubts may be entertained as to this Court's function to relieve, unaided by Congressional legislation, from burdensome taxation under the commerce clause, see *Gwin, White & Prince v. Henneford*, 305 U.S. 434, 441, 446-55; *McCarroll v. Dixie Lines*, 309 U.S. 176, 184-85, it cannot be thought that that function is wanting under the explicit guaranties of freedom of speech, press and religion." 316 U.S. at 610-11.

5. In the bituminous coal industry alone, approximately one-half of the miners in the United States lived in company-owned houses in the period from 1922-23. The percentage varied from 9 per cent in Illinois and Indiana and 64 per cent in Kentucky, to almost 80 per cent in West Virginia. U.S. Coal Commission, Report, 1925, Part III, pp. 1467, 1469 summarized in Morris, The Plight of the Coal Miner, Philadelphia 1934, Ch. VI, p. 86. The most recent statistics we found available are in Magnusson, Housing by Employers in the United States, Bureau of Labor Statistics Bulletin No. 263 (Misc. Ser.) p. 11. See also United States Department of Labor, Wage and Hour Division, Data on Pay Roll Deductions, Union Manufacturing Company, Union Point, Georgia, June 1941; Rhyne, Some Southern Cotton Mill Workers and Their Villages, Chapel Hill, 1930 (Study completed under the direction of the Institute for Research in Social Science at the University of North Carolina); Comment, *Urban Redevelopment*, 54 Yale L.J. 116.

6. As to the suppression of civil liberties in company towns and the need of those who live there for Constitutional protection, see the summary of facts aired before the Senate Committee on Education and Labor, *Violations of Free Speech and Rights of Labor*, Hearings pursuant to S. Res. 266, 74th Cong., 2d Sess., 1937, summarized in Bowden, *Freedom for Wage Earners*, Annals of The American Academy of Political and Social Science, Nov. 1938, p. 185; Z. Chafee, *The Inquiring Mind* (New York, 1928), pp. 173-74; Pamphlet published in 1923 by the Bituminous Operators Special Committee under the title *The Company Town*; U.S. Coal Commission, Report, *supra*, Part III, p. 1331.

7. *Jones v. Opelika, supra,* 316 U.S. at
608; *Murdock v. Pennsylvania, supra,*
319 U.S. at 115; *Follett v. McCormick,*
supra, 321 U.S. at 577.

When the New Hampshire Attorney General asked Sweezy questions related to the content of his lectures and related to Progressive Party members, Sweezy refused to answer on the ground that the questions were not pertinent to the subject matter being investigated by the Attorney General. As a result, Sweezy was cited for contempt and his conviction was upheld by the New Hampshire Supreme Court. Upon appeal, however, the United States Supreme Court reversed and stated in its opinion: "No field of education is so thoroughly comprehended by man that new discoveries cannot yet be made. Particularly is that true in the social sciences, where few, if any, principles are accepted as absolutes. Scholarship cannot flourish in an atmosphere of suspicion and distrust. Teachers and students must always remain free to inquire, to study and to evaluate, to gain new maturity and understanding; otherwise our civilization will stagnate and die."

Sweezy v. *New Hampshire,* 354 U.S. 234 (1957)

MR. CHIEF JUSTICE WARREN announced the judgment of the Court and delivered an opinion, in which MR. JUSTICE BLACK, MR. JUSTICE DOUGLAS, and MR. JUSTICE BRENNAN join.

This case, like *Watkins* v. *United States, ante,* p. 178, brings before us a question concerning the constitutional limits of legislative inquiry. The investigation here was conducted under the aegis of a state legislature, rather than a House of Congress. This places the controversy in a slightly different setting from that in *Watkins.* The ultimate question here is whether the investigation deprived Sweezy of due process of law under the Fourteenth Amendment. For the reasons to be set out in this opinion, we conclude that the record in this case does not sustain the power of the State to compel the disclosures that the witness refused to make.

This case was brought here as an appeal under 28 U. S. C. § 1257 (2). Jurisdiction was alleged to rest upon contentions, rejected by the state courts, that a statute of New Hampshire is repugnant to the Constitution of the United States. We postponed a decision on the question of jurisdiction until consideration of the merits. 352 U. S. 812. The parties neither briefed nor argued the jurisdictional question. The appellant has thus failed to meet his burden of showing that jurisdiction by appeal was properly invoked. The appeal is therefore dismissed. Treating the appeal papers as a petition for writ of certiorari, under 28 U.S.C. § 2103, the petition is granted. Cf. *Union National Bank* v. *Lamb,* 337 U. S. 38, 39-40.

The investigation in which petitioner was summoned to testify had its origins in a statute passed by the New Hampshire legislature in 1951.[1] It was a comprehensive scheme of regulation of subversive activities. There was a section defining criminal conduct in the nature of sedition. "Subversive organizations" were declared unlawful and ordered dissolved. "Subversive persons" were made ineligible for employment by the state government. Included in the disability were those employed as teachers or in other capacities by any public educational institution. A loyalty program was instituted to eliminate "subversive persons" among government personnel. All present employees, as well as candidates for elective office in the future, were required to make sworn statements that they were not "subversive persons."

In 1953, the legislature adopted a "Joint Resolution Relating to the Investigation of Subversive Activities."[2] It was resolved:

"That the attorney general is hereby authorized and directed to make full and complete investigation with respect to violations of the subversive activities act of 1951 and to determine whether subversive persons as defined in said act are presently located within this state. The attorney general is authorized to act upon his own motion and upon such information as in his judgment may be reasonable or reliable...."

.   .   .   .   .

"The attorney general is directed to proceed with criminal prosecutions under the subversive activities act whenever evidence presented to him in the course of the investigation indicates violations thereof, and he shall report to the 1955 session on the first day of its regular session the results of this investigation, together with his recommendations, if any, for necessary legislation."[3]

Under state law, this was construed to constitute the Attorney General as a one-man legislative committee.[4] He was given the authority to delegate any part of the investigation to any member of his staff. The legislature conferred upon the Attorney General the further authority to subpoena witnesses or documents. He did not have power to hold witnesses in contempt, however. In the event that coercive or punitive sanctions were needed, the Attorney General could invoke the aid of a State Superior Court which could find recalcitrant witnesses in contempt of court.[5]

Petitioner was summoned to appear before the Attorney General on two separate occasions. On January 5, 1954, petitioner testified at length upon his past conduct and associations. He denied that he had ever been a member of the Communist Party or that he had ever been part of any program to overthrow the government by force or violence. The interrogation ranged over many matters, from petitioner's World War II military service with the Office of Strategic Services to his sponsorship, in 1949, of the Scientific and Cultural Conference for World Peace, at which he spoke.

During the course of the inquiry, petitioner declined to answer several questions. His reasons for doing so were given in a statement he read to the Committee at the outset of the

hearing.[6] He declared he would not answer those questions which were not pertinent to the subject under inquiry as well as those which transgress the limitations of the First Amendment. In keeping with this stand, he refused to disclose his knowledge of the Progressive Party in New Hampshire or of persons with whom he was acquainted in that organization.[7] No action was taken by the Attorney General to compel answers to these questions.

The Attorney General again summoned petitioner to testify on June 3, 1954. There was more interrogation about the witness' prior contacts with Communists. The Attorney General lays great stress upon an article which petitioner had co-authored. It deplored the use of violence by the United States and other capitalist countries in attempting to preserve a social order which the writers thought must inevitably fall. This resistance, the article continued, will be met by violence from the oncoming socialism, violence which is to be less condemned morally than that of capitalism since its purpose is to create a "truly human society." Petitioner affirmed that he styled himself a "classical Marxist" and a "socialist" and that the article expressed his continuing opinion.

Again, at the second hearing, the Attorney General asked, and petitioner refused to answer, questions concerning the Progressive Party, and its predecessor, the Progressive Citizens of America. Those were:

"Was she, Nancy Sweezy, your wife, active in the formation of the Progressive Citizens of America?"
"Was Nancy Sweezy then working with individuals who were then members of the Communist Party?"
"Was Charles Beebe active in forming the Progressive Citizens of America?"
"Was Charles Beebe active in the Progressive Party in New Hampshire?"
"Did he work with your present wife--Did Charles Beebe work with your present wife in 1947?"
"Did it [a meeting at the home of Abraham Walenko in Weare during 1948] have anything to do with the Progressive Party?"

The Attorney General also turned to a subject which had not yet occurred at the time of the first hearing. On March 22, 1954, petitioner had delivered a lecture to a class of 100 students in the humanities course at the University of New Hampshire. This talk was given at the invitation of the faculty teaching that course. Petitioner had addressed the class upon such invitations in the two preceding years as well. He declined to answer the following questions:

"What was the subject of your lecture?"
"Didn't you tell the class at the University of New Hampshire on Monday, March 22, 1954, that Socialism was inevitable in this country?"
"Did you advocate Marxism at that time?"

"Did you express the opinion, or did you make the statement at that time that Socialism was inevitable in America?"

"Did you in this last lecture on March 22 or in any of the former lectures espouse the theory of dialectical materialism?"

Distinct from the categories of questions about the Progressive Party and the lectures was one question about petitioner's opinions. He was asked: "Do you believe in Communism?" He had already testified that he had never been a member of the Communist Party, but he refused to answer this or any other question concerning opinion or belief.

Petitioner adhered in this second proceeding to the same reasons for not answering he had given in his statement at the first hearing. He maintained that the questions were not pertinent to the matter under inquiry and that they infringed upon an area protected under the First Amendment.

Following the hearings, the Attorney General petitioned the Superior Court of Merrimack County, New Hampshire, setting forth the circumstances of petitioner's appearance before the Committee and his refusal to answer certain questions.[8] The petition prayed that the court propound the questions to the witness. After hearing argument, the court ruled that the questions set out above were pertinent.[9] Petitioner was called as a witness by the court and persisted in his refusal to answer for constitutional reasons. The court adjudged him in contempt and ordered him committed to the county jail until purged of the contempt.

The New Hampshire Supreme Court affirmed. 100 N.H. 103, 121 A. 2d 783. Its opinion discusses only two classes of questions addressed to the witness: those dealing with the lectures and those about the Progressive Party and the Progressive Citizens of America. No mention is made of the single question concerning petitioner's belief in Communism. In view of what we hold to be the controlling issue of the case, however, it is unnecessary to resolve affirmatively that that particular question was or was not included in the decision by the State Supreme Court.

There is no doubt that legislative investigations, whether on a federal or state level, are capable of encroaching upon the constitutional liberties of individuals. It is particularly important that the exercise of the power of compulsory process be carefully circumscribed when the investigative process tends to impinge upon such highly sensitive areas as freedom of speech or press, freedom of political association, and freedom of communication of ideas, particularly in the academic community. Responsibility for the proper conduct of investigations rests, of course, upon the legislature itself. If that assembly chooses to authorize inquiries on its behalf by a legislatively created committee, that basic responsibility carries forward to include the duty of adequate supervision of the actions of the committee. This safeguard can be nullified when a committee is invested with a broad and ill-defined jurisdiction. The authorizing resolution thus becomes especially significant in that it reveals the amount of discretion that has been conferred upon the committee.

In this case, the investigation is governed by provisions in the New Hampshire Subversive Activities Act of 1951.[10] The Attorney General was instructed by the legislature to look into violations of that Act. In addition, he was given the far more sweeping mandate to find out if there were subversive persons, as defined in that Act, present in New Hampshire. That statute, therefore, measures the breadth and scope of the investigation before us.

"Subversive persons" are defined in many gradations of conduct. Our interest is in the minimal requirements of that definition since they will outline its reach. According to the statute, a person is a "subversive person" if he, by any means, aids in the commission of any act intended to assist in the alteration of the constitutional form of government by force or violence.[11] The possible remoteness from armed insurrection of conduct that could satisfy these criteria is obvious from the language. The statute goes well beyond those who are engaged in efforts designed to alter the form of government by force or violence. The statute declares, in effect, that the assistant of an assistant is caught up in the definition. This chain of conduct attains increased significance in light of the lack of a necessary element of guilty knowledge in either stage of assistants. The State Supreme Court has held that the definition encompasses persons engaged in the specified conduct "... whether or not done 'knowingly and willfully ....'" *Nelson* v. *Wyman*, 99 N. H. 33, 39, 105 A. 2d 756, 763. The potential sweep of this definition extends to conduct which is only remotely related to actual subversion and which is done completely free of any conscious intent to be a part of such activity.

The statute's definition of "subversive organizations" is also broad. An association is said to be any group of persons, whether temporarily or permanently associated together, for joint action or advancement of views on any subject.[12] An organization is deemed subversive if it has a purpose to abet, advise or teach activities intended to assist in the alteration of the constitutional form of government by force or violence.

The situation before us is in many respects analogous to that in *Wieman* v. *Updegraff*, 344 U.S. 183. The Court held there that a loyalty oath prescribed by the State of Oklahoma for all its officers and employees violated the requirements of the Due Process Clause because it entailed sanctions for membership in subversive organizations without scienter. A State cannot, in attempting to bar disloyal individuals from its employ, exclude persons solely on the basis of organizational membership, regardless of their knowledge concerning the organizations to which they belonged. The Court said:

"There can be no dispute about the consequences visited upon a person excluded from public employment on disloyalty grounds. In the view of the community, the stain is a deep one; indeed, it has become a badge of infamy. Especially is this so in a time of cold war and hot emotions when 'each man begins to eye his neighbor as a possible enemy.' Yet under the Oklahoma Act, the fact of association alone determines disloyalty and disqualification; it matters not whether association existed innocently or knowingly. To thus inhibit individual freedom of movement is to stifle the flow of democratic expression and controversy at one of its chief sources." 344 U. S., at 190-191.

The sanction emanating from legislative investigations is of a different kind than loss of employment. But the stain of the stamp of disloyalty is just as deep. The inhibiting effect in the flow of democratic expression and controversy upon those directly affected and those touched more subtly is equally grave. Yet here, as in *Wieman*, the program for the rooting out of subversion is drawn without regard to the presence or absence of guilty knowledge in those affected.

The nature of the investigation which the Attorney General was authorized to conduct is revealed by this case. He delved minutely into the past conduct of petitioner, thereby making his private life a matter of public record. The questioning indicates that the investigators had thoroughly prepared for the interview and were not acquiring new information as much as corroborating data already in their possession. On the great majority of questions, the witness was cooperative, even though he made clear his opinion that the interrogation was unjustified and unconstitutional. Two subjects arose upon which petitioner refused to answer: his lectures at the University of New Hampshire, and his knowledge of the Progressive Party and its adherents.

The state courts upheld the attempt to investigate the academic subject on the ground that it might indicate whether petitioner was a "subversive person." What he taught the class at a state university was found relevant to the character of the teacher. The State Supreme Court carefully excluded the possibility that the inquiry was sustainable because of the state interest in the state university. There was no warrant in the authorizing resolution for that. 100 N. H., at 110, 121 A. 2d, at 789-790. The sole basis for the inquiry was to scrutinize the teacher as a person, and the inquiry must stand or fall on that basis.

The interrogation on the subject of the Progressive Party was deemed to come within the Attorney General's mandate because that party might have been shown to be a "subversive organization." The State Supreme Court held that the "...questions called for answers concerning the membership or participation of named persons in the Progressive Party which, if given, would aid the Attorney General in determining

whether that party and its predecessor are or were subversive organizations." 100 N. H., at 112, 121 A. 2d, at 791.

The New Hampshire court concluded that the "...right to lecture and the right to associate with others for a common purpose, be it political or otherwise, are individual liberties guaranteed to every citizen by the State and Federal Constitutions but are not absolute rights.... The inquiries authorized by the Legislature in connection with this investigation concerning the contents of the lecture and the membership, purposes and activities of the Progressive Party undoubtedly interfered with the defendant's free exercise of those liberties." 100 N. H., at 113, 121 A. 2d, at 791-792.

The State Supreme Court thus conceded without extended discussion that petitioner's right to lecture and his right to associate with others were constitutionally protected freedoms which had been abridged through this investigation. These conclusions could not be seriously debated. Merely to summon a witness and compel him, against his will, to disclose the nature of his past expressions and associations is a measure of governmental interference in these matters. These are rights which are safeguarded by the Bill of Rights and the Fourteenth Amendment. We believe that there unquestionably was an invasion of petitioner's liberties in the areas of academic freedom and political expression--areas in which government should be extremely reticent to tread.

The essentiality of freedom in the community of American universities is almost self-evident. No one should underestimate the vital role in a democracy that is played by those who guide and train our youth. To impose any strait jacket upon the intellectual leaders in our colleges and universities would imperil the future of our Nation. No field of education is so thoroughly comprehended by man that new discoveries cannot yet be made. Particularly is that true in the social sciences, where few, if any, principles are accepted as absolutes. Scholarship cannot flourish in an atmosphere of suspicion and distrust. Teachers and students must always remain free to inquire, to study and to evaluate, to gain new maturity and understanding; otherwise our civilization will stagnate and die.

Equally manifest as a fundamental principle of a democratic society is political freedom of the individual. Our form of government is built on the premise that every citizen shall have the right to engage in political expression and association. This right was enshrined in the First Amendment of the Bill of Rights. Exercise of these basic freedoms in America has traditionally been through the media of political associations. Any interference with the freedom of a party is simultaneously an interference with the freedom of its adherents. All political ideas cannot and should not be channeled into the programs of our two major parties. History has amply proved the virtue of political activity by minority, dissident groups, who innumerable times have been in the vanguard of democratic thought and whose pro-

grams were ultimately accepted. Mere unortho-
doxy or dissent from the prevailing mores is
not to be condemned. The absence of such
voices would be a symptom of grave illness in
our society.

Notwithstanding the undeniable importance of
freedom in the areas, the Supreme Court of New
Hampshire did not consider that the abridgment
of petitioner's rights under the Constitution
vitiated the investigation. In the view of
that court, "the answer lies in a determination
of whether the object of the legislative investigation under consideration is such as to
justify the restriction thereby imposed upon
the defendant's liberties." 100 N. H., at
113-114, 121 A. 2d, at 791-792. It found such
justification in the legislature's judgment,
expressed by its authorizing resolution, that
there exists a potential menace from those who
would overthrow the government by force and violence. That court concluded that the need for
the legislature to be informed on so elemental
a subject as the self-preservation of government outweighed the deprivation of constitutional rights that occurred in the process.

We do not now conceive of any circumstance
wherein a state interest would justify infringement of rights in these fields. But we
do not need to reach such fundamental questions
of state power to decide this case. The State
Supreme Court itself recognized that there was
a weakness in its conclusion that the menace of
forcible overthrow of the government justified
sacrificing constitutional rights. There was a
missing link in the chain of reasoning. The
syllogism was not complete. There was nothing
to connect the questioning of petitioner with
this fundamental interest of the State. Petitioner had been interrogated by a one-man legislative committee, not by the legislature itself. The relationship of the committee to the
full assembly is vital, therefore, as revealing
the relationship of the questioning to the
state interest.

In light of this, the state court emphasized
a factor in the authorizing resolution which
confined the inquiries which the Attorney General might undertake to the object of the investigation. That limitation was thought to
stem from the authorizing resolution's condition precedent to the institution of any inquiry. The New Hampshire legislature specified
that the Attorney General should act only when
he had information which "...in his judgment
may be reasonable or reliable." The state
court construed this to mean that the Attorney
General must have something like probable cause
for conducting a particular investigation. It
is not likely that this device would prove an
adequate safeguard against unwarranted inquiries. The legislature has specified that the
determination of the necessity for inquiry
shall be left in the judgment of the investigator. In this case, the record does not reveal
what reasonable or reliable information led the
Attorney General to question petitioner. The
state court relied upon the Attorney General's
description of prior information that had come
into his possession.[13]

The respective roles of the legislature and
the investigator thus revealed are of considerable significance to the issue before us. It
is eminently clear that the basic discretion of
determining the direction of the legislative
inquiry has been turned over to the investigative agency. The Attorney General has been
given such a sweeping and uncertain mandate
that it is his decision which picks out the
subjects that will be pursued, what witnesses
will be summoned and what questions will be
asked. In this circumstance, it cannot be
stated authoritatively that the legislature
asked the Attorney General to gather the kind
of facts comprised in the subjects upon which
petitioner was interrogated.

Instead of making known the nature of the
data it desired, the legislature has insulated
itself from those witnesses whose rights may be
vitally affected by the investigation. Incor-
porating by reference provisions from its subversive activities act, it has told the Attorney General, in effect to screen the citizenry
of New Hampshire to bring to light anyone who
fits into the expansive definitions.

Within the very broad area thus committed to
the discretion of the Attorney General there
may be many facts which the legislature might
find useful. There would also be a great deal
of data which that assembly would not want or
need. In the classes of information that the
legislature might deem it desirable to have,
there will be some which it could not validly
acquire because of the effect upon the constitutional rights of individual citizens. Sepa-
rating the wheat from the chaff, from the
standpoint of the legislature's object, is the
legislature's responsibility because it alone
can make that judgment. In this case, the New
Hampshire legislature has delegated that task
to the Attorney General.

As a result, neither we nor the state courts
have any assurance that the questions petitioner refused to answer fall into a category of
matters upon which the legislature wanted to be
informed when it initiated this inquiry. The
judiciary are thus placed in an untenable position. Lacking even the elementary fact that
the legislature wants certain questions answered and recognizing that petitioner's constitutional rights are in jeopardy, we are
asked to approve or disapprove his incarceration for contempt.

In our view, the answer is clear. No one
would deny that the infringement of constitutional rights of individuals would violate the
guarantee of due process where no state interest underlies the state action. Thus, if the
Attorney General's interrogation of petitioner
were in fact wholly unrelated to the object of
the legislature in authorizing the inquiry, the
Due Process Clause would preclude the endanger-
ing of constitutional liberties. We believe
that an equivalent situation is presented in
this case. The lack of any indications that
the legislature wanted the information the Attorney General attempted to elicit from petitioner must be treated as the absence of authority. It follows that the use of the con-

tempt power, notwithstanding the interference with constitutional rights, was not in accordance with the due process requirements of the Fourteenth Amendment.

The conclusion that we have reached in this case is not grounded upon the doctrine of separation of powers. In the Federal Government, it is clear that the Constitution has conferred the powers of government upon three major branches: the Executive, the Legislative and the Judicial. No contention has been made by petitioner that the New Hampshire legislature, by this investigation, arrogated to itself executive or judicial powers. We accept the finding of the State Supreme Court that the employment of the Attorney General as the investigating committee does not alter the legislative nature of the proceedings. Moreover, this Court has held that the concept of separation of powers embodied in the United States Constitution is not mandatory in state governments. *Dreyer* v. *Illinois*, 187 U. S. 71; but cf. *Tenney* v. *Brandhove*, 341 U. S. 367, 378. Our conclusion does rest upon a separation of the power of a state legislature to conduct investigations from the responsibility to direct the use of that power insofar as that separation causes a deprivation of the constitutional rights of individuals and a denial of due process of law.

The judgment of the Supreme Court of New Hampshire is

Reversed.

NOTES

1. N. H. Laws 1951, c. 193; now N. H. Rev. Stat. Ann., 1955, c. 588, §§ 1-16.
2. N. H. Laws 1953, c. 307.
3. The authority of the Attorney General was continued for another two-year period by N. H. Laws 1955, cc. 197, 340.
4. "Having determined that an investigation should be conducted concerning a proper subject of action by it, the Legislature's choice of the Attorney General as its investigating committee, instead of a committee of its own members or a special board or commission, was not in and of itself determinative of the nature of the investigation. His position as the chief law en-

forcement officer of the State did not transform the inquiry which was otherwise legislative into executive action." *Nelson* v. *Wyman*, 99 N. H. 33, 38, 105 A. 2d 756, 762-763.

The Attorney General of New Hampshire is appointed to office by the Governor and the State Council, a group of five persons who share some of the executive responsibilities in the State Government. The principal duties of the Attorney General are set forth in N. H. Rev. Stat. Ann., 1955, c. 7, §§ 6-11. He represents the State in all cases before the State Supreme Court. He prosecutes all criminal cases in which the accused is charged with an offense punishable by twenty-five years in prison or more. All other criminal cases are under his general supervision. He gives opinions on questions of law to the legislature, or to state boards, departments, commissions, officers, etc., on questions relating to their official duties.

5. "Whenever any official or board is given the power to summon witnesses and take testimony, but has not the power to punish for contempt, and any witness refuses to obey such summons, either as to his appearance or as to the production of things specified in the summons, or refuses to testify or to answer any question, a petition for an order to compel him to testify or his compliance with the summons may be filed in the superior court, or with some justice thereof." N. H. Rev. Stat. Ann., 1955, c. 491, § 19. "Upon such petition the court or justice shall have authority to proceed in the matter as though the original proceeding had been in the court, and may make orders and impose penalties accordingly." *Id.*, § 20. See *State* v. *Uphaus*, 100 N. H. 1, 116 A. 2d 887.
6. "Those called to testify before this and other similar investigations can be classified in three categories.

"First there are Communists and those who have reason to believe that even if they are not Communists they have been accused of being and are in danger of harassment and prosecution.

"Second, there are those who approve of the purposes and methods of these investigations.

"Third, there are those who are not Communists and do not believe they are in danger of being prosecuted, but who yet deeply disapprove of the purposes and methods of these investigations.

"The first group will naturally, and I think wholly justifiably, plead the constitutional privilege of not being witnesses against themselves.

"The second group will equally naturally be cooperative witnesses.

"The third group is faced with an extremely difficult dilemma. I know because I belong to this third group, and I have been struggling with its problems for many weeks now. I would like to explain what the nature of that dilemma is. I think it is important that both those conducting these inquiries and the public should understand.

"It is often said: If a person is not a Communist and has nothing to fear, why should he not answer whatever questons are put to him and be done with it? The answer, of course, is that some of us believe these investigations are evil and dangerous, and we do not want to give our approval to them, either tacitly or otherwise. On the contrary, we want to oppose them to the best of our ability and persuade others to do likewise, with the hope of eventually abolishing them altogether.

"Our reasons for opposing these investigations are not captious or trivial. They have deep roots in principle and conscience. Let me explain with reference to the present New Hampshire investigation. The official purpose of the inquiry is to uncover and lay the basis for the prosecution of persons who in one way or another promote the forcible overthrow of constitutional forms of government. Leaving aside the constitutionality of the investigation, which is now before the courts, I think it must be plain to any reasonable person who is at all well informed about conditions in New Hampshire today that strict adherence to this purpose would leave little room for investigation. It is obvious enough that there are few radicals or dissenters of any kind in New Hampshire; and if there are any who advocate use of force and violence, they must be isolated crackpots who are no danger to anyone, least of all to the constitutional form of government of state and nation. The Attorney General should be able to check these facts quickly and issue a report satisfying the mandate laid upon him by the legislature.

"But this is not what he has done. We do not know the whole story, but enough has come out to show that the Attorney General has issued a considerable number of subpoenas and has held hearings in various parts of the state. And so far as the available information allows us to judge, most of those subpoenaed have fallen into one or both of two groups: first professors at Dartmouth and the University of New Hampshire who have gained a reputation for liberal or otherwise unorthodox views, and, second, people who have been active in the Progressive Party. It should be specially noted that whatever may be thought of the Progressive Party in any other respect, it was certainly not devoted to violent overthrow of constitutional forms of government but on the contrary to effecting reforms through the very democratic procedures which are the essence of constitutional forms of government.

"The pattern I have described is no accident. Whatever their official purpose, these investigations always end up by inquiring into the politics, ideas, and beliefs of people who hold what are, for the time being, unpopular views. The federal House Committee on Un-American Activities, for example, is supposed to investigate various kinds of propaganda and has no other mandate whatever. Over the years, however, it has spent almost no time investigating propaganda and has devoted almost all of its energies to 'exposing' people and their ideas, their affiliations, their associations. Similarly, this New Hampshire investigation is supposed to be concerned with violent overthrow of government, but it is actually turning out to be concerned with what few manifestations of political dissent have made themselves felt in the state in recent years.

"If all this is so, and if the very first principle of the American constitutional form of government is political freedom—which I take to include freedoms of speech, press, assembly, and association—then I do not see how it can be denied that these investigations are a grave danger to all that Americans have always claimed to cherish. No rights are genuine if a person, for exercising them, can be hauled up before some tribunal and forced under penalties of perjury and contempt to account for his ideas and conduct.

"Let us now return to the problem of the witness who would have nothing to fear from being what is nowadays styled a 'friendly' witness, but who feels deeply that to follow such a course would be a betrayal of his principles and repugnant to his conscience. What other courses are open to him?

"He can claim the privilege not to be a witness against himself and thus avoid a hateful inquisition. I respect the decision of those who elect to take this course. My own reason for rejecting it is that, with public opinion in its present state, the exercise of the privilege is almost certain to be widely misinterpreted. One of the noblest and most precious guarantees of freedom, won in the course of bitter struggles and terrible suffering, has been distorted in our own day to mean a confession of guilt, the more sinister because undefined and indeed undefinable. It is unfortunate, but true, that the public at large has accepted this distortion and will scarcely listen to those who have invoked the privilege.

"Alternatively, the witness can seek to uphold his principles and maintain his integrity, not by claiming the protection of the Fifth Amendment (or the Fifteenth Article of the New Hampshire Bill of Rights), but by contesting the legitimacy of offensive questions on other constitutional and legal grounds.

"Just how far the First Amendment limits the right of legislative inquiry has not been settled. The Supreme Court of the United States is at this very moment considering a case (the *Emspak* case) which may do much to settle the question. But even before the Court has handed down its decision in the *Emspak* case, it is quite certain that the First Amendment does place *some* limitations on the power of investigation, and it is always open to a witness to challenge a question on the ground that it transgresses these limitations and, if necessary, to take the issue to the courts for decision.

"Moreover, a witness may not be required to answer questions unless they are 'pertinent to the matter under inquiry' (the words are those of the United States Supreme Court).

"What is the 'matter under inquiry' in the present investigation? According to the Act of the New Hampshire legislature directing the investigation, its purpose is twofold: (1) 'to make full and complete investigation with respect to violations of the subversive activities act of 1951,' and (2) 'to determine whether subversive persons as defined in said act are presently located within this state.'

"I have studied the subversive activities act of 1951 with care, and I am glad to volunteer the information that I have absolutely no knowledge of any violations of any of its provisions; further, that I have no knowledge of subversive persons presently located within the state.

"That these statements may carry full conviction, I am prepared to answer certain questions about myself, though in doing so I do not mean to concede the right to ask them. I am also prepared to discuss my views relating to the use of force and violence to overthrow constitutional forms of government.

"But I shall respectfully decline to answer questions concerning ideas, beliefs, and associations which could not possibly be pertinent to the matter here under inquiry and/or which seem to me to invade the freedoms guaranteed by the First Amendment to the United States Constitution (which, of course, applies equally to the several states)."

7. The Progressive Party offered a slate of candidates for national office in the 1948 presidential election. Henry A. Wallace, former Vice President of the United States, was the party's selection for the presidency. Glen Taylor, former United States Senator, was the vice-presidential nominee of the party. Nationwide, the party received a popular vote of 1,156,103. Of this total, 1,970 votes for Progressive Party candidates were cast in New Hampshire. Statistics of the Presidential and Congressional Election of November 2, 1948, pp. 24, 48-49.

8. See note 5, *supra*.

9. The court made a general ruling that questions concerning the opinions or beliefs of the witness were not pertinent. Nevertheless, it did propound to the witness the one question about his belief in Communism.

10. See note 1, *supra*.

11. "'Subversive person' means any person who commits, attempts to commit, aids in the commission, or advocates, abets, advises or teaches, by any means any person to commit, attempt to commit, or aid in the commission of any act intended to overthrow, destroy or alter, or to assist in the overthrow, destruction or alteration of, the constitutional form of the government of the United States, or of the state of New Hampshire, or any political subdivision of either of them, by force, or violence; or who is a member of a subversive organization or a foreign subversive organization." N. H. Rev. Stat. Ann., 1955, c. 588, § 1.

12. "For the purpose of this chapter 'organization' means an organization, corporation, company, partnership, association, trust, foundation, fund, club, society, committee, political party, or any group of persons, whether or not incorporated, permanently or temporarily associated together for joint action or advancement of views on any subject or subjects.

"'Subversive organization' means any organization which engages in or advocates, abets, advises, or teaches, or a purpose of which is to engage in or advocate, abet, advise, or teach activities intended to overthrow, destroy or alter, or to assist in the overthrow, destruction or alteration of, the constitutional form of the government of the United States, or of the state of New Hampshire, or of any political subdivision of either of them, by force, or violence." *Ibid.*

13. The State Supreme Court illustrated the "reasonable or reliable" information underlying the inquiries on the Progressive Party by quoting from a remark made by the Attorney General at the hearing in answer to petitioner's objection to a line of questions. The Attorney General had declared that he had "...considerable sworn testimony...to the effect that the Progressive Party in New Hampshire has been heavily infiltrated by members of the Communist Party and that the policies and purposes of the Progressive Party have been directly influenced by members of the Communist Party." 100 N. H., at 111, 121 A. 2d, at 790-791. None of this testimony is a part of the record in this case. Its existence and weight were not independently reviewed by the state courts.

The court did not point to anything that supported the questioning on the subject of the lecture. It stated that the Attorney General could inquire about lectures only if he "...possesses reasonable or reliable information indicating that the violent overthrow of existing government may have been advocated or taught, either 'knowingly and wilfully' or not." 100 N. H., at 110, 121 A. 2d, at 789-790. What, if anything, indicated that petitioner knowingly or innocently advocated or taught violent overthrow of existing government does not appear. At one point in the hearing, the Attorney General said to petitioner: "I have in the file here a statement from a person who attended your class, and I will read it in part because I don't want you to think I am just fishing. 'His talk this time was on the inevitability of the Socialist program. It was a glossed-over interpretation of the materialist dialectic.'" R. 107. The court did not cite this statement.

In holding unconstitutional an Arkansas statute requiring teachers to file annually an affidavit listing all the organizations to which they belonged or to which they regularly contributed within the previous five years, the United States Supreme Court said: "The vigilant protection of constitutional freedoms is nowhere more vital than in the community of American schools.....'Scholarship cannot flourish in an atmosphere of suspicion and distrust. Teachers and students must always remain free to inquire, to study, and to evaluate....'"

Shelton v. *Tucker*, 364 U.S. 479 (1960)

MR. JUSTICE STEWART delivered the opinion of the Court.

An Arkansas statute compels every teacher, as a condition of employment in a state-supported school or college, to file annually an affidavit listing without limitation every organization to which he has belonged or regularly contributed within the preceding five years. At issue in these two cases is the validity of that statute under the Fourteenth Amendment to the Constitution. No. 14 is an appeal from the judgment of a three-judge Federal District Court upholding the statute's validity, 174 F. Supp. 351. No. 83 is here on writ of certiorari to the Supreme Court of Arkansas, which also held the statute constitutionally valid. 231 Ark. 641, 331 S. W. 2d 701.

The statute in question is Act 10 of the Second Extraordinary Session of the Arkansas General Assembly of 1958. The provisions of the Act are summarized in the opinion of the District Court as follows:

"Act 10 provides in substance that no person shall be employed or elected to employment as a superintendent, principal or teacher in any public school in Arkansas, or as an instructor, professor or teacher in any public institution of higher learning in that State until such person shall have submitted to the appropriate hiring authority an affidavit listing all organizations to which he at the time belongs and to which he has belonged during the past five years, and also listing all organizations to which he at the time is paying regular dues or is making regular contributions, or to which within the past five years he has paid such dues or made such contributions. The Act further provides, among other things, that any contract entered into with any person who has not filed the prescribed affidavit shall be void; that no public moneys shall be paid to such person as compensation for his services; and that any such funds so paid may be recovered back either from the person receiving such funds or from the board of trustees or other governing body making the payment. The filing of a false affidavit is denounced as perjury, punishable by a fine of not less than five hundred nor more than one thousand dollars, and, in addition, the person filing the false affidavit is to lose his teaching license." 174 F. Supp. 353-354.[1]

These provisions must be considered against the existing system of teacher employment required by Arkansas law. Teachers there are hired on a year-to-year basis. They are not covered by a civil service system, and they have no job security beyond the end of each school year. The closest approach to tenure is a statutory provision for the automatic renewal of a teacher's contract if he is not notified within ten days after the end of a school year that the contract has not been renewed. Ark. 1947 Stat. Ann. § 80-1304 (b) (1960); *Wabbaseka School District No. 7* v. *Johnson*, 225 Ark. 982, 286 S. W. 2d 841.

The plaintiffs in the Federal District Court (appellants here) were B.T. Shelton, a teacher employed in the Little Rock Public School System, suing for himself and others similarly situated, together with the Arkansas Teachers Association and its Executive Secretary, suing for the benefit of members of the Association. Shelton had been employed in the Little Rock Special School District for twenty-five years. In the spring of 1959 he was notified that, before he could be employed for the 1959-1960 school year, he must file the affidavit required by Act 10, listing all his organizational connections over the previous five years. He declined to file the affidavit, and his contract for the ensuing school year was not renewed. At the trial the evidence showed that he was not a member of the Communist Party or of any organization advocating the overthrow of the Government by force, and that he was a member of the National Association for the Advancement of Colored People. The court upheld Act 10, finding the information it required was "relevant," and relying on several decisions of this Court, particularly *Garner* v. *Board of Public Works of Los Angeles*, 341 U. S. 716; *Adler* v. *Board of Education*, 342 U. S. 485; *Beilan* v. *Board of Education*, 357 U. S. 399; and *Lerner* v. *Casey*, 357 U. S. 468.[2]

The plaintiffs in the state court proceedings (petitioners here) were Max Carr, an associate professor at the University of Arkansas, and Ernest T. Gephardt, a teacher at Central High School in Little Rock, each suing for himself and others similarly situated. Each refused to execute and file the affidavit required by Act 10. Carr executed an affirmation[3] in which he listed his membership in professional organizations, denied ever having been a member of any subversive organization, and offered to answer any questions which the University authorities might constitutionally ask touching upon his qualifications as a teacher. Gephardt filed an affidavit stating that he had never belonged to a subversive organization, disclosing his membership in the Arkansas Education Association and the American Legion, and also offering to answer any questions which the school authorities might con-

stitutionally ask touching upon his qualifications as a teacher. Both were advised that their failure to comply with the requirements of Act 10 would make impossible their re-employment as teachers for the following school year. The Supreme Court of Arkansas upheld the constitutionality of Act 10, on its face and as applied to the petitioners. 231 Ark. 641, 331 S. W. 2d 701.

I.

It is urged here, as it was unsuccessfully urged throughout the proceedings in both the federal and state courts, that Act 10 deprives teachers in Arkansas of their rights to personal, associational, and academic liberty, protected by the Due Process Clause of the Fourteenth Amendment from invasion by state action. In considering this contention, we deal with two basic postulates.

First. There can be no doubt of the right of a State to investigate the competence and fitness of those whom it hires to teach in its schools, as this Court before now has had occasion to recognize. "A teacher works in a sensitive area in a schoolroom. There he shapes the attitude of young minds towards the society in which they live. In this, the state has a vital concern." *Adler* v. *Board of Education*, 342 U. S. 485, 493. There is "no requirement in the Federal Constitution that a teacher's classroom conduct be the sole basis for determining his fitness. Fitness for teaching depends on a broad range of factors." *Beilan* v. *Board of Education*, 357 U. S. 399, 406.[4]

This controversy is thus not of a pattern with such cases as *N.A.A.C.P.* v. *Alabama*, 357 U. S. 449, and *Bates* v. *Little Rock*, 361 U. S. 516. In those cases the Court held that there was no substantially relevant correlation between the governmental interest asserted and the State's effort to compel disclosure of the membership lists involved. Here, by contrast, there can be no question of the relevance of a State's inquiry into the fitness and competence of its teachers.[5]

Second. It is not disputed that to compel a teacher to disclose his every associational tie is to impair that teacher's right of free association, a right closely allied to freedom of speech and a right which, like free speech, lies at the foundation of a free society. *DeJonge* v. *Oregon*, 299 U. S. 353, 364; *Bates* v. *Little Rock, supra,* at 522-523. Such interference with personal freedom is conspicuously accented when the teacher serves at the absolute will of those to whom the disclosure must be made--those who any year can terminate the teacher's employment without bringing charges, without notice, without a hearing, without affording an opportunity to explain.

The statute does not provide that the information it requires be kept confidential. Each school board is left free to deal with the information as it wishes.[6] The record contains evidence to indicate that fear of public disclosure is neither theoretical nor groundless.[7] Even if there were no disclosure to the general public, the pressure upon a teacher to avoid any ties which might displease those who control his professional destiny would be constant and heavy. Public exposure, bringing with it the possibility of public pressures upon school boards to discharge teachers who belong to unpopular or minority organizations, would simply operate to widen and aggravate the impairment of constitutional liberty.

The vigilant protection of constitutional freedoms is nowhere more vital than in the community of American schools. "By limiting the power of the States to interfere with freedom of speech and freedom of inquiry and freedom of association, the Fourteenth Amendment protects all persons, no matter what their calling. But, in view of the nature of the teacher's relation to the effective exercise of the rights which are safeguarded by the Bill of Rights and by the Fourteenth Amendment, inhibition of freedom of thought, and of action upon thought, in the case of teachers brings the safeguards of those amendments vividly into operation. Such unwarranted inhibition upon the free spirit of teachers ... has an unmistakable tendency to chill that free play of the spirit which all teachers ought especially to cultivate and practice; it makes for caution and timidity in their associations by potential teachers." *Wieman* v. *Updegraff*, 344 U. S. 183, 195 (concurring opinion). "Scholarship cannot flourish in an atmosphere of suspicion and distrust. Teachers and students must always remain free to inquire, to study and to evaluate ...." *Sweezy* v. *New Hampshire*, 354 U. S. 234, 250.

II.

The question to be decided here is not whether the State of Arkansas can ask certain of its teachers about all their organizational relationships. It is not whether the State can ask all of its teachers about certain of their associational ties. It is not whether teachers can be asked how many organizations they belong to, or how much time they spend in organizational activity. The question is whether the State can ask every one of its teachers to disclose every single organization with which he has been associated over a five-year period. The scope of the inquiry required by Act 10 is completely unlimited. The statute requires a teacher to reveal the church to which he belongs, or to which he has given financial support. It requires him to disclose his political party, and every political organization to which he may have contributed over a five-year period. It requires him to list, without number, every conceivable kind of associational tie -- social, professional, political, avocational, or religious. Many such relationships could have no possible bearing upon the teacher's occupational competence or fitness.

In a series of decisions this Court has held that, even though the governmental purpose be legitimate and substantial, that purpose cannot be pursued by means that broadly stifle fundamental personal liberties when the end can be more narrowly achieved.[8] The breadth of legislative abridgment must be viewed in the light of less drastic means for achieving the same basic purpose.[9]

In *Lovell* v. *Griffin*, 303 U. S. 444, the Court invalidated an ordinance prohibiting all distribution of literature at any time or place in Griffin, Georgia, without a license, pointing out that so broad an interference was unnecessary to accomplish legitimate municipal aims. In *Schneider* v. *State*, 308 U. S. 147, the Court dealt with ordinances of four different municipalities which either banned or imposed prior restraints upon the distribution of handbills. In holding the ordinances invalid, the Court noted that where legislative abridgment of "fundamental personal rights and liberties" is asserted, "the courts should be astute to examine the effect of the challenged legislation. Mere legislative preferences or beliefs respecting matters of public convenience may well support regulation directed at other personal activities, but be insufficient to justify such as diminishes the exercise of rights so vital to the maintenance of democratic institutions." 308 U. S., at 161. In *Cantwell* v. *Connecticut*, 310 U. S. 296, the Court said that "[c]onduct remains subject to regulation for the protection of society," but pointed out that in each case "the power to regulate must be so exercised as not, in attaining a permissible end, unduly to infringe the protected freedom." 310 U. S., at 304. Illustrations of the same constitutional principle are to be found in many other decisions of the Court, among them, *Martin* v. *Struthers*, 319 U. S. 141; *Saia* v. *New York*, 334 U. S. 558; and *Kunz* v. *New York*, 340 U. S. 290.

As recently as last Term we held invalid an ordinance prohibiting the distribution of handbills because the breadth of its application went far beyond what was necessary to achieve a legitimate governmental purpose. *Talley* v. *California*, 362 U. S. 60. In that case the Court noted that it had been "urged that this ordinance is aimed at providing a way to identify those responsible for fraud, false advertising and libel. Yet the ordinance is in no manner so limited .... Therefore we do not pass on the validity of an ordinance limited to prevent these or any other supposed evils. This ordinance simply bars all handbills under all circumstances anywhere that do not have the names and addresses printed on them in the place the ordinance requires." 362 U. S., at 64.

The unlimited and indiscriminate sweep of the statute now before us brings it within the ban of our prior cases. The statute's comprehensive interference with associational freedom goes far beyond what might be justified in the exercise of the State's legitimate inquiry into the fitness and competency of its teachers. The judgments in both cases must be reversed.

It is so ordered.

NOTES

1. The statute is in seven sections. Section 1 provides: "It is hereby declared that the purpose of this act is to provide assistance in the administration and financing of the public schools of Arkansas, and institutions of higher learning supported wholly or in part by public funds, and it is hereby determined that it will be beneficial to the public schools and institutions of higher learning and the State of Arkansas, if certain affidavits of membership are required as hereinafter provided."

   Section 2 provides: "No superintendent, principal, or teacher shall be employed or elected in any elementary or secondary school by the district operating such school, and no instructor, professor, or other teacher shall be employed or elected in any institution of higher learning, or other educational institution supported wholly or in part by public funds, by the trustees or governing authority thereof, until, as a condition precedent to such employment, such superintendent, principal, teacher, instructor or professor shall have filed with such board of trustees or governing authority an affidavit as to the names and addresses of all incorporated and/or unincorporated associations and organizations that such superintendent, principal, teacher, instructor or professor is or within the past five years has been a member of, or to which organization or association such superintendent, principal, teacher, instructor, professor, or other teacher is presently paying, or within the past five years has paid regular dues, or to which the same is making or within the past five years has made regular contributions."

   Section 3 sets out the form of affidavit to be used.

   Section 4 provides: "Any contract entered into by any board of any school district, board of trustees of any institution of higher learning, or other educational institution supported wholly or in part by public funds, or by any governing authority thereof, with any superintendent, principal, teacher, instructor, professor, or other instructional personnel, who shall not have filed the affidavit required in Section 2 hereof prior to the employment or election of such person and prior to the making of such contracts, shall be null and void and no funds shall be paid under said contract to such superintendent, principal, teacher, instructor, professor, or other instructional personnel; any funds so paid under said contract to such superintendent, principal, teacher, instructor, professor, or other instructional personnel, may be recovered from the person receiving the same and/or from the board of trustees or other governing authority by suit filed in the circuit court of the county in which such contract was made, and any judgment entered by such court in such cause of action shall be a personal judgment against the defendant therein and upon the official bonds made by such defendants, if any such bonds be in existence."

   Section 5 provides that a teacher filing a false affidavit shall be guilty of perjury, punishable by a fine, and shall forfeit his license to teach in any school or other institution of learning supported wholly or in part by public funds.

   Section 6 is a separability provision.

   Section 7 is an emergency clause, reading in part as follows:

   "It is hereby determined that the decisions of the United States Supreme Court in the school segregation cases require solution of a great variety of local public school problems of considerable complexity immediately and which involve the health, safety and general welfare of the people of the State of Arkansas, and that the purpose of this act is to assist in the solution of these problems and to provide for the more efficient administration of public education."

2. In the same proceeding the court held constitutionally invalid an Arkansas statute making it unlawful for any member of the National Association for the Advancement of Colored People to be employed by the State of Arkansas or any of its subdivisions. 174 F. Supp. 351.

3. The affirmation recited that Carr was "conscientiously opposed to taking an oath or swearing in any form...."

4. The actual holdings in *Adler* and *Beilan*, involving the validity of teachers' discharges, are not relevant to the present case.

5. The declared purpose of Act 10 is "to provide assistance in the administration and financing of the public schools ...." The declared justification for the emergency clause is "to assist in the solution" of problems raised by "the decisions of the United States Supreme Court in the school segregation cases." See note 1. But neither the breadth and generality of the declared purpose nor the possible irrelevance of the emergency provision detracts from the existence of an actual relevant state interest in the inquiry.

6. The record contains an opinion of the State Attorney General that "it is an administrative determination, to be made by the respective Boards, as to the disclosure of information contained in the affidavits." The Supreme Court of Arkansas has held only that "the affidavits *need* not be opened to public inspection...." 231 Ark. 641, 646, 331 S. W. 2d 701, 704. (Emphasis added.)

7. In the state court proceedings a witness who was a member of the Capital Citizens Council testified that his group intended to gain access to some of the Act 10 affidavits with a view to eliminating from the school system persons who supported organizations unpopular with the group. Among such organiza-

tions he named the American Civil Liberties Union, the Urban League, the American Association of University Professors, and the Women's Emergency Committee to Open Our Schools.

8. In other areas, involving different constitutional issues, more administrative leeway has been thought allowable in the interest of increased efficiency in accomplishing a clearly constitutional central purpose. See *Purity Extract Co.* v. *Lynch*, 226 U. S. 192; *Jacob Ruppert* v. *Caffey*, 251 U. S. 264; *Schlesinger* v. *Wisconsin*, 270 U. S. 230, 241 (dissenting opinion); *Queenside Hills Co.* v. *Saxl*, 328 U. S. 80, 83. But cf. *Dean Milk Co.* v. *Madison*, 340 U. S. 349.

9. See Freund, Competing Freedoms in American Constitutional Law, 13 U. of Chicago Conference Series 26, 32-33; Richardson, Freedom of Expression and the Function of Courts, 65 Harv. L. Rev. 1, 6, 23-24; Comment, Legislative Inquiry into Political Activity: First Amendment Immunity From Committee Interrogation, 65 Yale L. J. 1159, 1173-1175.

In holding unconstitutional a U.S. Postal regulation which required the Postmaster General to detain unsealed foreign mailings of "communist political propaganda" and not to deliver the mailings until receipt of a postcard from the addressee indicating desire to receive the materials, the United States Supreme Court said: "We rest on the narrow ground that the addressee in order to receive his mail must request in writing that it be delivered. This amounts in our judgment to unconstitutional abridgment of the addressee's First Amendment rights. The addressee carries an affirmative obligation which we do not think the government may impose on him....The regime of this act is at war with the 'uninhibited, robust, and wide-open' debate and discussion that are contemplated by the First Amendment."

Lamont v. *Postmaster General*, 381 U. S. 301 (1965)

MR. JUSTICE DOUGLAS delivered the opinion of the Court.

These appeals present the same question: is § 305 (a) of the Postal Service and Federal Employees Salary Act of 1962, 76 Stat. 840, constitutional as construed and applied? The statute provides in part:

"Mail matter, except sealed letters, which originates or which is printed or otherwise prepared in a foreign country and which is determined by the Secretary of the Treasury pursuant to rules and regulations to be promulgated by him to be 'communist political propaganda,' shall be detained by the Postmaster General upon its arrival for delivery in the United States, or upon its subsequent deposit in the United States domestic mails, and the addressee shall be notified that such matter has been received and will be delivered only upon the addressee's request, except that such detention shall not be required in the case of any matter which is furnished pursuant to subscription or which is otherwise ascertained by the Postmaster General to be desired by the addressee." 39 U. S. C. 4008 (a).

The statute defines "communist political propaganda" as political propaganda (as that term is defined in § 1 (j) of the Foreign Agents Registration Act of 1938[1]) which is issued by or on behalf of any country with respect to which there is in effect a suspension or withdrawal of tariff concessions or from which foreign assistance is withheld pursuant to certain specified statutes. 39 U. S. C. § 4008 (b). The statute contains an exemption from its provisions for mail addressed to government agencies and educational institutions, or officials thereof, and for mail sent pursuant to a reciprocal cultural international agreement. 39 U. S. C. § 4008 (c).

To implement the statute the Post Office

maintains 10 or 11 screening points through which is routed all unsealed mail from the designated foreign countries. At these points the nonexempt mail is examined by Customs authorities. When it is determined that a piece of mail is "communist political propaganda," the addressee is mailed a notice identifying the mail being detained and advising that it will be destroyed unless the addressee requests delivery by returning an attached reply card within 20 days.

Prior to March 1, 1965, the reply card contained a space in which the addressee could request delivery of any "similar publication" in the future. A list of the persons thus manifesting a desire to receive "communist political propaganda" was maintained by the Post Office. The Government in its brief informs us that the keeping of this list was terminated, effective March 15, 1965. Thus, under the new practice, a notice is sent and must be returned for each individual piece of mail desired. The only standing instruction which it is now possible to leave with the Post Office is *not* to deliver any "communist political propaganda."[2] And the Solicitor General advises us that the Post Office Department "intends to retain its assumption that those who do not return the card want neither the identified publication nor any similar one arriving subsequently."

No. 491 arose out of the Post Office's detention in 1963 of a copy of the *Peking Review #12* addressed to appellant, Dr. Corliss Lamont, who is engaged in the publishing and distributing of pamphlets. Lamont did not respond to the notice of detention which was sent to him but instead instituted this suit to enjoin enforcement of the statute, alleging that it infringed his rights under the First and Fifth Amendments. The Post Office thereupon notified Lamont that it considered his institution of the suit to be an expression of his desire to receive "communist political propaganda" and therefore none of his mail would be detained. Lamont amended his complaint to challenge on constitutional grounds the placement of his name on the list of those desiring to receive "communist political propaganda." The majority of the three-judge District Court nonetheless dismissed the complaint as moot, 229 F. Supp. 913, because Lamont would now receive his mail unimpeded. Insofar as the list was concerned, the majority thought that any legally significant harm to Lamont as a result of being listed was merely a speculative possibility, and so on this score the controversy was not yet ripe for adjudication. Lamont appealed from the dismissal, and we noted probable jurisdiction. 397 U. S. 926.

Like Lamont, appellee Heilberg in No. 848, when his mail was detained, refused to return the reply card and instead filed a complaint in the District Court for an injunction against enforcement of the statute. The Post Office reacted to this complaint in the same manner as it had to Lamont's complaint, but the District Court declined to hold that Heilberg's action was thereby mooted. Instead the District Court

reached the merits and unanimously held that the statute was unconstitutional under the First Amendment. 236 F. Supp. 405. The Government appealed and we noted probable jurisdiction. 379 U.S. 997.

There is no longer even a colorable question of mootness in these cases, for the new procedure, as described above, requires the postal authorities to send a separate notice for each item as it is received and the addressee to make a separate request for each item. Under the new system, we are told, there can be no list of persons who have manifested a desire to receive "communist political propaganda" and whose mail will therefore go through relatively unimpeded. The Government concedes that the changed procedure entirely precludes any claim of mootness and leaves for our consideration the sole question of the constitutionality of the statute.

We conclude that the Act as construed and applied is unconstitutional because it requires an official act (*viz.*, returning the reply card) as a limitation on the unfettered exercise of the addressee's First Amendment rights. As stated by Mr. Justice Holmes in *Milwaukee Pub. Co.* v. *Burleson*, 255 U.S. 407, 437 (dissenting): "The United States may give up the Post Office when it sees fit, but while it carries it on the use of the mails is almost as much a part of free speech as the right to use our tongues ...."[3]

We struck down in *Murdock* v. *Pennsylvania*, 319 U.S. 105, a flat license tax on the exercise of First Amendment rights. A registration requirement imposed on a labor union organizer before making a speech met the same fate in *Thomas* v. *Collins*, 323 U.S. 516. A municipal licensing system for those distributing literature was held invalid in *Lovell* v. *Griffin*, 303 U.S. 444. We recently reviewed in *Harman* v. *Forssenius*, 380 U.S. 528, an attempt by a State to impose a burden on the exercise of a right under the Twenty-fourth Amendment. There, a registration was required by all federal electors who did not pay the state poll tax. We stated:

"For federal elections, the poll tax is abolished absolutely as a prerequisite to voting, and no equivalent or milder substitute may be imposed. Any material requirement imposed upon the federal voter solely because of his refusal to waive the constitutional immunity subverts the effectiveness of the Twenty-fourth Amendment and must fall under its ban." *Id.*, p. 542.

Here the Congress--expressly restrained by the First Amendment from "abridging" freedom of speech and of press--is the actor. The Act sets administrative officials astride the flow of mail to inspect it, appraise it, write the addressee about it, and await a response before dispatching the mail. Just as the licensing or taxing authorities in the *Lovell*, *Thomas*, and *Murdock* cases sought to control the flow of ideas to the public, so here federal agencies regulate the flow of mail. We do not have here, any more than we had in *Hannegan* v. *Esquire, Inc.*, 327 U.S. 146, any question concerning the extent to which Congress may classify the mail and fix the charges for its carriage. Nor do we reach the question whether the standard here applied could pass constitutional muster. Nor do we deal with the right of Customs to inspect material from abroad for contraband. We rest on the narrow ground that the addressee in order to receive his mail must request in writing that it be delivered. This amounts in our judgment to an unconstitutional abridgment of the addressee's First Amendment rights. The addressee carries an affirmative obligation which we do not think the Government may impose on him. This requirement is almost certain to have a deterrent effect, especially as respects those who have sensitive positions. Their livelihood may be dependent on a security clearance. Public officials, like schoolteachers who have no tenure, might think they would invite disaster if they read what the Federal Government says contains the seeds of treason. Apart from them, any addressee is likely to feel some inhibition in sending for literature which federal officials have condemned as "communist political propaganda." The regime of this Act is at war with the "uninhibited, robust, and wide-open" debate and discussion that are contemplated by the First Amendment. *New York Times Co.* v. *Sullivan*, 376 U.S. 254, 270.

We reverse the judgment in No. 491 and affirm that in No. 848.

It is so ordered.

the foreign policies of the United States or promote in the United States racial, religious, or social dissensions, or (2) which advocates, advises, instigates, or promotes any racial, social, political, or religious disorder, civil riot, or other conflict involving the use of force or violence in any other American republic or the overthrow of any government or political subdivision of any other American republic by any means involving the use of force or violence." 22 U.S.C. § 611 (j).

2. A Post Office regulation permits a patron to refuse delivery of any piece of mail (39 CFR § 44.1 (a)) or to request in writing a withholding from delivery for a period not to exceed two years of specifically described items of certain mail, including "foreign printed matter." *Ibid*. And see Schwartz, The Mail Must Not Go Through, 11 U.C.L.A.L. Rev. 805, 847.

3. "Whatever may have been the voluntary nature of the postal system in the period of its establishment, it is now the main artery through which the business, social, and personal affairs of the people are conducted and upon which depends in a greater degree than upon any other activity of government the promotion of the general welfare." *Pike* v. *Walker*, 73 App. D.C. 289, 291, 121 F. 2d 37, 39. And see Gellhorn, Individual Freedom and Governmental Restraints, p. 88 *et seq*. (1956).

NOTES

1. "The term 'political propaganda' includes any oral, visual, graphic, written, pictorial, or other communication or expression by any person (1) which is reasonably adapted to, or which the person disseminating the same believes will, or which he intends to, prevail upon, indoctrinate, convert, induce, or in any other way influence a recipient or any section of the public within the United States with reference to the political or public interests, policies, or relations of a government of a foreign country or a foreign political party or with reference to

In declaring New York's teacher loyalty oaths unconstitutional, the United States Supreme Court stated: "Our Nation is deeply committed to safeguarding academic freedom, which is of transcendent value to all of us and not merely to the teachers concerned. That freedom is therefore a special concern of the First Amendment, which does not tolerate laws that cast a pall of orthodoxy over the classroom. 'The vigilant protection of constitutional freedoms is nowhere more vital than in the community of American schools.' Shelton v. Tucker....The classroom is peculiarly the 'marketplace of ideas.' The nation's future depends upon leaders trained through wide exposure to that robust exchange of ideas which discovers truth 'out of a multitude of tongues, [rather] than through any kind of authoritative selection.' United States v. Associated Press...."

Keyishian v. Board of Regents of the University of the State of New York, 385 U.S. 589 (1967)

Mr. Justice Brennan delivered the opinion of the Court.

Appellants were members of the faculty of the privately owned and operated University of Buffalo, and became state employees when the University was merged in 1962 into the State University of New York, an institution of higher education owned and operated by the State of New York. As faculty members of the State University their continued employment was conditioned upon their compliance with a New York plan, formulated partly in statutes and partly in administrative regulations,[1] which the State utilizes to prevent the appointment or retention of "subversive" persons in state employment.

Appellants Hochfield and Maud were Assistant Professors of English, appellant Keyishian an instructor in English, and appellant Garver, a lecturer in philosophy. Each of them refused to sign, as regulations then in effect required, a certificate that he was not a Communist, and that if he had ever been a Communist, he had communicated that fact to the President of the State University of New York. Each was notified that his failure to sign the certificate would require his dismissal. Hochfield and Garver, whose contracts still had time to run, continue to teach, but subject to proceedings for their dismissal if the constitutionality of the New York plan is sustained. Maud has voluntarily resigned and therefore no longer has standing in this suit.

Appellant Starbuck was a nonfaculty library employee and part-time lecturer in English. Personnel in that classification were not required to sign a certificate but were required to answer in writing under oath the question, "Have you ever advised or taught or were you ever a member of any society or group of persons which taught or advocated the doctrine that the Government of the United States or of any political subdivisions thereof should be overthrown or overturned by force, violence or any unlawful means?" Starbuck refused to answer the question and as a result was dismissed.

Appellants brought this action for declaratory and injunctive relief, alleging that the state program violated the Federal Constitution in various respects. A three-judge federal court held that the program was constitutional. 255 F.Supp. 981.[2] We noted probable jurisdiction of appellants' appeal, 384 U.S. 998. We reverse.

I.

We considered some aspects of the constitutionality of the New York plan 15 years ago in *Adler* v. *Board of Education*, 342 U.S. 485. That litigation arose after New York passed the Feinberg Law which added § 3022 to the Education Law.[3] The Feinberg Law was enacted to implement and enforce two earlier statutes. The first was a 1917 law, now § 3021 of the Education Law, under which "the utterance of any treasonable or seditious word or words or the doing of any treasonable or seditious act" is a ground for dismissal from the public school system. The second was a 1939 law which was § 12-a of the Civil Service Law when *Adler* was decided and, as amended, is now § 105 of that law. This law disqualifies from the civil service and from employment in the educational system any person who advocates the overthrow of government by force, violence, or any unlawful means, or publishes material advocating such overthrow or organizes or joins any society or group of persons advocating such doctrine.

The Feinberg Law charged the State Board of Regents with the duty of promulgating rules and regulations providing procedures for the disqualification or removal of persons in the public school system who violate the 1917 law or who are ineligible for appointment to or retention in the public school system under the 1939 law. The Board of Regents was further directed to make a list, after notice and hearing, of "subversive" organizations, defined as organizations which advocate the doctrine of overthrow of government by force, violence, or any unlawful means. Finally, the Board was directed to provide in its rules and regulations that membership in any listed organization should constitute prima facie evidence of disqualification for appointment to or retention in any office or position in the public schools of the State.

The Board of Regents thereupon promulgated rules and regulations containing procedures to be followed by appointing authorities to discover persons ineligible for appointment or retention under the 1939 law, or because of violation of the 1917 law. The Board also announced its intention to list "subversive" organizations after requisite notice and hearing, and provided that membership in a listed organization after the date of its listing should be regarded as constituting prima facie evidence of disqualification, and that membership prior to listing should be presumptive evidence that membership has continued, in the absence of a showing that such membership was terminated in good faith. Under the regulations, an appointing official is forbidden to make an appointment until after he has first inquired of an applicant's former employers and other persons to ascertain whether the applicant is disqualified or ineligible for appointment. In addition, an annual inquiry must be made to determine whether an appointed employee has ceased to be qualified for retention, and a report of findings must be filed.

Adler was a declaratory judgment suit in which the Court held, in effect, that there was no constitutional infirmity in former § 12-a or in the Feinberg Law on their faces and that they were capable of constitutional application. But the contention urged in this case that both § 3021 and § 105 are unconstitutionally vague was not heard or decided. Section 3021 of the Education Law was challenged in *Adler* as unconstitutionally vague, but because the challenge had not been made in the pleadings or in the proceedings in the lower courts, this Court refused to consider it. 342 U. S., at 496. Nor was any challenge on grounds of vagueness made in *Adler* as to subdivisions 1 (a) and (b) of § 105 of the Civil Service Law.[4] Subdivision 3 of § 105 was not added until 1958. Appellants in this case timely asserted below the unconstitutionality of all these sections on grounds of vagueness and that question is now properly before us for decision. Moreover, to the extent that *Adler* sustained the provision of the Feinberg Law constituting membership in an organization advocating forceful overthrow of government a ground for disqualification, pertinent constitutional doctrines have since rejected the premises upon which that conclusion rested. *Adler* is therefore not dispositive of the constitutional issues we must decide in this case.

II.

A 1953 amendment extended the application of the Feinberg Law to personnel of any college or other institution of higher education owned and operated by the State or its subdivisions. In the same year, the Board of Regents, after notice and hearing, listed the Communist Party of the United States and of the State of New York as "subversive organizations." In 1956 each applicant for an appointment or renewal of an appointment was required to sign the so-called "Feinberg Certificate" declaring that he had read the Regents Rules and understood that the Rules and the statutes constituted terms of employment, and declaring further that he was not a member of the Communist Party, and that if he had ever been a member he had

communicated that fact to the President of the State University. This was the certificate that appellants Hochfield, Maud, Keyishian, and Garver refused to sign.

In June 1965, shortly before the trial of this case, the Feinberg Certificate was rescinded and it was announced that no person then employed would be deemed ineligible for continued employment "solely" because he refused to sign the certificate, In lieu of the certificate, it was provided that each applicant be informed before assuming his duties that the statutes, §§ 3021 and 3022 of the Education Law and § 105 of the Civil Service Law, constituted part of his contract. He was particularly to be informed of the disqualification which flowed from membership in a listed "subversive" organization. The 1965 announcement further provides: "Should any question arise in the course of such inquiry such candidate may request...a personal interview. Refusal of a candidate to answer any question relevant to such inquiry by such officer shall be sufficient ground to refuse to make or recommend appointment." A brochure is also given new applicants. It outlines and explains briefly the legal effect of the statutes and invites any applicant who may have any question about possible disqualification to request an interview. The covering announcement concludes that "a prospective appointee who does not believe himself disqualified need take no affirmative action. No disclaimer oath is required."

The change in procedure in no wise moots appellants' constitutional questions raised in the context of their refusal to sign the now abandoned Feinberg Certificate. The substance of the statutory and regulatory complex remains and from the outset appellants' basic claim has been that they are aggrieved by its application.

III.

Section 3021 requires removal for "treasonable or seditious" utterances or acts. The 1958 amendment to § 105 of the Civil Service Law, now subdivision 3 of that section, added such utterances or acts as a ground for removal under that law also.[5] The same wording is used in both statutes--that "the utterance of any treasonable or seditious word or words or the doing of any treasonable or seditious act or acts" shall be ground for removal. But there is a vital difference between the two laws. Section 3021 does not define the terms "treasonable or seditious" as used in that section; in contrast, subdivision 3 of § 105 of the Civil Service Law provides that the terms "treasonable word or act" shall mean "treason" as defined in the Penal Law and the terms "seditious word or act" shall mean "criminal anarchy" as defined in the Penal Law.

Our experience under the Sedition Act of 1798, 1 Stat. 596, taught us that dangers fatal to First Amendment freedoms inhere in the word "seditious." See *New York Times Co. v. Sullivan*, 376 U. S. 254, 273-276. And the word "treasonable," if left undefined, is no less dangerously uncertain. Thus it becomes important whether, despite the omission of a similar reference to the Penal Law in § 3021, the words as used in that section are to be read as meaning only what they mean in subdivision 3 of § 105. Or are they to be read more broadly and to constitute utterances or acts "seditious" and "treasonable" which would not be so regarded for the purposes of § 105?

Even assuming that "treasonable" and "seditious" in § 3021 and § 105, subd. 3, have the same meaning, the uncertainty is hardly removed. The definition of "treasonable" in the Penal Law presents no particular problem. The difficulty centers upon the meaning of "seditious." Subdivision 3 equates the term "seditious" with "criminal anarchy" as defined in the Penal Law. Is the reference only to Penal Law § 160, defining criminal anarchy as "the doctrine that organized government should be overthrown by force or violence, or by assassination of the executive head or of any of the executive officials of government, or by any unlawful means"? But that section ends with the sentence "The advocacy of such doctrine either by word of mouth or writing is a felony." Does that sentence draw into § 105, Penal Law § 161, proscribing "advocacy of criminal anarchy"? If so, the possible scope of "seditious" utterances or acts has virtually no limit. For under Penal Law § 161, one commits the felony of advocating criminal anarchy if he "...publicly displays any book...containing or advocating, advising or teaching the doctrine that organized government should be overthrown by force, violence or any unlawful means."6 Does the teacher who carries a copy of the Communist Manifesto on a public street thereby advocate criminal anarchy? It is no answer to say that the statute would not be applied in such a case. We cannot gainsay the potential effect of this obscure wording on "those with a conscientious and scrupulous regard for such undertakings." *Baggett* v. *Bullitt*, 377 U. S. 360, 374. Even were it certain that the definition referred to in § 105 was solely Penal Law § 160, the scope of § 105 still remains indefinite. The teacher cannot know the extent, if any, to which a "seditious" utterance must transcend mere statement about abstract doctrine, the extent to which it must be intended to and tend to indoctrinate or incite to action in furtherance of the defined doctrine. The crucial consideration is that no teacher can know just where the line is drawn between "seditious" and nonseditious utterances and acts.

Other provisions of § 105 also have the same defect of vagueness. Subdivision 1 (a) of § 105 bars employment of any person who "by word of mouth or writing wilfully and deliberately advocates, advises or teaches the doctrine" of forceful overthrow of government. This provision is plainly susceptible of sweeping and improper application. It may well prohibit the employment of one who merely advocates the doctrine in the abstract without any attempt to indoctrinate others, or incite others to action in furtherance of unlawful aims.7 See

Herndon v. *Lowry*, 301 U. S. 242; *Yates* v. *United States*, 354 U. S. 298; *Noto* v. *United States*, 367 U. S. 290; *Scales* v. *United States*, 367 U. S. 203. And in prohibiting "advising" the "doctrine" of unlawful overthrow does the statute prohibit mere "advising" of the existence of the doctrine, or advising another to support the doctrine? Since "advocacy" of the doctrine of forceful overthrow is separately prohibited, need the person "teaching" or "advising" this doctrine himself "advocate" it? Does the teacher who informs his class about the precepts of Marxism or the Declaration of Independence violate this prohibition?

Similar uncertainty arises as to the application of subdivision 1 (b) of § 105. That subsection requires the disqualification of an employee involved with the distribution of written material "containing or advocating, advising or teaching the doctrine" of forceful overthrow, and who himself "advocates, advises, teaches, or embraces the duty, necessity or propriety of adopting the doctrine contained therein." Here again, mere advocacy of abstract doctrine is apparently included.8 And does the prohibition of distribution of matter "containing" the doctrine bar histories of the evolution of Marxist doctrine or tracing the background of the French, American, or Russian revolutions? The additional requirement, that the person participating in distribution of the material be one who "advocates, advises, teaches, or embraces the duty, necessity or propriety of adopting the doctrine" of forceful overthrow, does not alleviate the uncertainty in the scope of the section, but exacerbates it. Like the language of § 105, subd. 1 (a), this language may reasonably be construed to cover mere expression of belief. For example, does the university librarian who recommends the reading of such materials thereby "advocate...the...propriety of adopting the doctrine contained therein"?

We do not have the benefit of a judicial gloss by the New York courts enlightening us as to the scope of this complicated plan.9 In light of the intricate administrative machinery for its enforcement, this is not surprising. The very intricacy of the plan and the uncertainty as to the scope of its proscriptions make it a highly efficient *in terrorem* mechanism. It would be a bold teacher who would not stay as far as possible from utterances or acts which might jeopardize his living by enmeshing him in this intricate machinery. The uncertainty as to the utterances and acts proscribed increases that caution in "those who believe the written law means what it says." *Baggett* v. *Bullitt, supra*, at 374. The result must be to stifle "that free play of the spirit which all teachers ought especially to cultivate and practice...."10 That probability is enhanced by the provisions requiring an annual review of every teacher to determine whether any utterance or act of his, inside the classroom or out, came within the sanctions of the laws. For a memorandum warns employees that under the statutes "subversive" activities may take the form of "(t)he writing of articles, the distribution of pamphlets, the endorsement of speeches made or articles written or acts performed by others," and reminds them "that it is a primary duty of the school authorities in each school district to take positive action to eliminate from the school system any teacher in whose case there is evidence that he is guilty of subversive activity. School authorities are under obligation to proceed immediately and conclusively in every such case."

There can be no doubt of the legitimacy of New York's interest in protecting its education system from subversion. But "even though the governmental purpose be legitimate and substantial, that purpose cannot be pursued by means that broadly stifle fundamental personal liberties when the end can be more narrowly achieved." *Shelton* v. *Tucker*, 364 U. S. 479, 488. The principle is not inapplicable because the legislation is aimed at keeping subversives out of the teaching ranks. In *De Jonge* v. *Oregon*, 299 U. S. 353, 365, the Court said:

"The greater the importance of safeguarding the community from incitements to the overthrow of our institutions by force and violence, the more imperative is the need to preserve inviolate the constitutional rights of free speech, free press and free assembly in order to maintain the opportunity for free political discussion, to the end that government may be responsive to the will of the people and that changes, if desired, may be obtained by peaceful means. Therein lies the security of the Republic, the very foundation of constitutional government."

Our Nation is deeply committed to safeguarding academic freedom, which is of transcendent value to all of us and not merely to the teachers concerned. That freedom is therefore a special concern of the First Amendment, which does not tolerate laws that cast a pall of orthodoxy over the classroom. "The vigilant protection of the constitutional freedoms is nowhere more vital than in the community of American schools." *Shelton* v. *Tucker*, *supra*, at 487. The classroom is peculiarly the "marketplace of ideas." The Nation's future depends upon leaders trained through wide exposure to that robust exchange of ideas which discovers truth "out of a multitude of tongues, [rather] than through any kind of authoritative selection." *United States* v. *Associated Press*, 52 F. Supp. 362, 372. In *Sweezy* v. *New Hampshire*, 354 U. S. 234, 250, we said:

"The essentiality of freedom in the community of American universities is almost self-evident. No one should underestimate the vital role in a democracy that is played by those who guide and train our youth. To impose any strait jacket upon the intellectual leaders in our colleges and universities would imperil the future of our Nation. No field of education is so thorough-

ly comprehended by man that new discoveries cannot yet be made. Particularly is that true in the social sciences, where few, if any, principles are accepted as absolutes. Scholarship cannot flourish in an atmosphere of suspicion and distrust. Teachers and students must always remain free to inquire, to study and to evaluate, to gain new maturity and understanding; otherwise our civilization will stagnate and die."

We emphasize once again that "[p]recision of regulation must be the touchstone in an area so closely touching our most precious freedoms," *N.A.A.C.P.* v. *Button*, 371 U. S. 415, 438; "[f]or standards of permissible statutory vagueness are strict in the area of free expression....Because First Amendment freedoms need breathing space to survive, government may regulate in the area only with narrow specificity." *Id.*, at 432-433. New York's complicated and intricate scheme plainly violates that standard. When one must guess what conduct or utterance may lose him his position, one necessarily will "steer far wider of the unlawful zone...." *Speiser* v. *Randall*, 357 U. S. 513, 526. For "[t]he threat of sanctions may deter...almost as potently as the actual application of sanctions." *N.A.A.C.P.* v. *Button*, *supra*, at 433. The danger of that chilling effect upon the exercise of vital First Amendment rights must be guarded against by sensitive tools which clearly inform teachers what is being proscribed. See *Stromberg* v. *California*, 283 U. S. 359, 369; *Cramp* v. *Board of Public Instruction*, 368 U. S. 278; *Baggett* v. *Bullitt*, *supra*.

The regulatory maze created by New York is wholly lacking in "terms susceptible of objective measurement." *Cramp* v. *Board of Public Instruction*, *supra*, at 286. It has the quality of "extraordinary ambiguity" found to be fatal to the oaths considered in *Cramp* and *Baggett* v. *Bullitt*. "[M]en of common intelligence must necessarily guess at its meaning and differ as to its application...." *Baggett* v. *Bullitt*, *supra*. at 367. Vagueness of wording is aggravated by prolixity and profusion of statutes, regulations, and administrative machinery, and by manifold cross-references to interrelated enactments and rules.

We therefore hold that § 3021 of the Education Law and subdivisions 1 (a), 1 (b) and 3 of § 105 of the Civil Service Law as implemented by the machinery created pursuant to § 3022 of the Education Law are unconstitutional.

IV.

Appellants have also challenged the constitutionality of the discrete provisions of subdivision 1 (c) of § 105 and subdivision 2 of the Feinberg Law, which make Communist Party membership, as such, prima facie evidence of disqualification. The provision was added to subdivision 1 (c) of § 105 in 1958 after the Board of Regents, following notice and hearing, listed the Communist Party of the United States and the Communist Party of the State of New

York as "subversive" organizations. Subdivision 2 of the Feinberg Law was, however, before the Court in *Adler* and its constitutionality was sustained. But constitutional doctrine which has emerged since that decision has rejected its major premise. That premise was that public employment, including academic employment, may be conditioned upon the surrender of constitutional rights which could not be abridged by direct government action. Teachers, the Court said in *Adler*, "may work for the school system upon the reasonable terms laid down by the proper authorities of New York. If they do not choose to work on such terms, they are at liberty to retain their beliefs and associations and go elsewhere." 342 U. S., at 492. The Court also stated that a teacher denied employment because of membership in a listed organization "is not thereby denied the right of free speech and assembly. His freedom of choice between membership in the organization and employment in the school system might be limited, but not his freedom of speech or assembly, except in the remote sense that limitation is inherent in every choice." *Id.*, at 493.

However, the Court of Appeals for the Second Circuit correctly said in an earlier stage of this case, "...the theory that public employment which may be denied altogether may be subjected to any conditions, regardless of how unreasonable, has been uniformly rejected." *Keyishian* v. *Board of Regents*, 345 F. 2d 236, 239. Indeed, that theory was expressly rejected in a series of decisions following *Adler*. See *Wieman* v. *Updegraff*, 344 U. S. 183; *Slochower* v. *Board of Education*, 350 U. S. 551; *Cramp* v. *Board of Public Instruction*, *supra*; *Baggett* v. *Bullitt*, *supra*; *Shelton* v. *Tucker*, *supra*; *Speiser* v. *Randall*, *supra*; see also *Schware* v. *Board of Bar Examiners*, 353 U. S. 232; *Torcaso* v. *Watkins*, 367 U. S. 488. In *Sherbert* v. *Verner*, 374 U. S. 398, 404, we said: "It is too late in the day to doubt that the liberties of religion and expression may be infringed by the denial of or placing of conditions upon a benefit or privilege."

We proceed then to the question of the validity of the provisions of subdivision 1 (c) of § 105 and subdivision 2 of § 3022, barring employment to members of listed organizations. Here again constitutional doctrine has developed since *Adler*. Mere knowing membership without a specific intent to further the unlawful aims of an organization is not a constitutionally adequate basis for exclusion from such positions as those held by appellants.

In *Elfbrandt* v. *Russell*, 384 U. S. 11, we said, "Those who join an organization but do not share its unlawful purposes and who do not participate in its unlawful activities surely pose no threat, either as citizens or as public employees." *Id.*, at 17. We there struck down a statutorily required oath binding the state employee not to become a member of the Communist Party with knowledge of its unlawful purpose, on threat of discharge and perjury prosecution if the oath were violated. We

found that "[a]ny lingering doubt that proscription of mere knowing membership, without any showing of 'specific intent,' would run afoul of the Constitution was set at rest by our decision in *Aptheker* v. *Secretary of State*, 378 U. S. 500." *Elfbrandt* v. *Russell*, *supra*, at 16. In *Aptheker* we held that Party membership, without knowlege of the Party's unlawful purposes *and* specific intent to further its unlawful aims, could not constitutionally warrant deprivation of the right to travel abroad. As we said in *Schneiderman* v. *United States*, 320 U. S. 118, 136, "[U]nder our traditions beliefs are personal and not a matter of mere association, and... men in adhering to a political party or other organization...do not subscribe unqualifiedly to all of its platforms or asserted principles." "A law which applies to membership without the 'specific intent' to further the illegal aims of the organization infringes unnecessarily on protected freedoms. It rests on the doctrine of 'guilt by association' which has no place here." *Elfbrandt*, *supra*, at 19. Thus mere Party membership, even with knowledge of the Party's unlawful goals, cannot suffice to justify criminal punishment, see *Scales* v. *United States*, 367 U. S. 203; *Noto* v. *United States*, 367 U. S. 290; *Yates* v. *United States*, 354 U. S. 298;[11] nor may it warrant a finding of moral unfitness justifying disbarment. *Schware* v. *Board of Bar Examiners*, 353 U. S. 232.

These limitations clearly apply to a provision, like § 105, subd. 1 (c), which blankets all state employees, regardless of the "sensitivity" of their positions. But even the Feinberg Law provision, applicable primarily to activities of teachers, who have captive audiences of young minds, are subject to these limitations in favor of freedom of expression and association; the stifling effect on the academic mind from curtailing freedom of association in such manner is manifest, and has been documented in recent studies.[12] *Elfbrandt* and *Aptheker* state the governing standard: legislation which sanctions membership unaccompanied by specific intent to further the unlawful goals of the organization or which is not active membership violates constitutional limitations.

Measured against this standard, both Civil Service Law § 105, subd. 1 (c), and Education Law § 3022, subd. 2, sweep overbroadly into association which may not be proscribed. The presumption of disqualification arising from proof of mere membership may be rebutted, but only by (a) a denial of membership, (b) a denial that the organization advocates the overthrow of government by force, or (c) a denial that the teacher has knowledge of such advocacy. *Lederman* v. *Board of Education*, 276 App. Div. 527, 96 N. Y. S. 2d 466, aff'd, 301 N. Y. 476, 95 N. E. 2d 806.[13] Thus proof of nonactive membership or a showing of the absence of intent to further unlawful aims will not rebut the presumption and defeat dismissal. This is emphasized in official administrative interpretations. For example, it is said in a letter addressed to prospective appointees by the President of the State University, "You will note that...both the Law and regulations are very specifically directed toward the elimination and nonappointment of 'Communists' from or to our teaching ranks...." The Feinberg Certificate was even more explicit: "Anyone who is a *member* of the Communist Party or of any organization that advocates the violent overthrow of the Government of the United States or of the State of New York or any political subdivision thereof cannot be employed by the State University." (Emphasis supplied.) This official administrative interpretation is supported by the legislative preamble to the Feinberg Law, § 1, in which the legislature concludes as a result of its findings that "it is essential that the laws prohibiting persons who are *members* of subversive groups, such as the communist party and its affiliated organizations, from obtaining or retaining employment in the public schools, be rigorously enforced." (Emphasis supplied.)

Thus § 105, subd. 1 (c), and § 3022, subd. 2, suffer from impermissible "overbreadth." *Elfbrandt* v. *Russell*, *supra*, at 19; *Aptheker* v. *Secretary of State*, *supra*; *N.A.A.C.P.* v. *Button*, *supra*; *Saia* v. *New York*, 334 U. S. 558; *Schneider* v. *State*, 308 U. S. 147; *Lovell* v. *Griffin*, 303 U. S. 444; cf. *Hague* v. *C. I. O.*, 307 U. S. 496, 515-516; see generally *Dombrowski* v. *Pfister*, 380 U. S. 479, 486. They seek to bar employment both for association which legitimately may be proscribed and for association which may not be proscribed consistently with First Amendment rights. Where statutes have an overbroad sweep, just as where they are vague, "the hazard of loss or substantial impairment of those precious rights may be critical," *Dombrowski* v. *Pfister*, *supra*, at 486, since those covered by the statute are bound to limit their behavior to that which is unquestionably safe. As we said in *Shelton* v. *Tucker*, *supra*, at 488, "The breadth of legislative abridgment must be viewed in the light of less drastic means for achieving the same basic purpose."

We therefore hold that Civil Service Law § 105, subd. 1 (c), and Education Law § 3022, subd 2, are invalid insofar as they proscribe mere knowing membership without any showing of specific intent to further the unlawful aims of the Communist Party of the United States or of the State of New York.

The judgment of the District Court is reversed and the case is remanded for further proceedings consistent with this opinion.

Reversed and remanded.

NOTES

1. The text of the pertinent statutes and administrative regulations in effect at the time of trial appears in the Appendix to the opinion.

2. The District Court initially refused to convene a three-judge court, 233 F. Supp. 752, and was reversed by the Court of Appeals for the Second Circuit. 345 F. 2d 236.

3. For the history of New York loyalty-security legislation, including the Feinberg Law, see Chamberlain, Loyalty and Legislative Action, and that author's article in Gellhorn, The States and Subversion 231.

4. The sole "vagueness" contention in *Adler* concerned the word "subversive," appearing in the preamble to and caption of § 3022. 342 U. S., at 496.

5. There is no merit in the suggestion advanced by the Attorney General of New York for the first time in his brief in this Court that § 3021 of the Education Law and § 105, subd. 3, of the Civil Service Law are not "pertinent to our inquiry." Section 3022 of the Education Law incorporates by reference the provisions of both, thereby rendering them applicable to faculty members of all colleges and institutions of higher education. One of the reasons why the Court of Appeals ordered the convening of a three-judge court was that a substantial federal question was presented by the fact that "Adler...refused to pass upon the constitutionality of section 3021...[and that] several statutory amendments, such as Section 105 (3) of the Civil Service Law, are all subsequent to Adler." 345 F.2d 236, 238. The three-judge court also properly found these provisions applicable to appellants in holding them constitutional. It is significant that appellees consistently defended the constitutionality of these sections in the courts below. Moreover, the three-judge court rendered its decision upon the basis of a "Stipulation of Fact," paragraph 20 of which recites:

"Section 3022 incorporates in full by reference and implements Section 105 of the Civil Service Law and Section 3021 of the New York State Education Law as follows: Subdivision (1) of Section 3022, as amended...directs the Board of Regents to adopt and enforce rules and regulations for the elimination of persons barred from employment in the public school system or any college or institution of higher education owned by the State of New York or any political subdivision thereof, by reason of violation of any of the provisions of Section 105 of the Civil Service Law or Section 3021 of the New York State Education Law."

6. Penal Law §§ 160-161 are to be replaced effective September 1, 1967, by a single provision entitled "criminal advocacy."

7. The New York State Legislative Committee on Public Employee Security Procedures, in describing this provision, noted:

"In disqualifying for employment those who advocate or teach the 'doctrine' of the violent overthrow of government, [§ 105] is to be distinguished from the language of the Smith Act (18 U. S. C. §§ 371, 2385), which has been construed by the Supreme Court to make it criminal to incite to 'action' for the forcible overthrow of government, but not to teach the 'abstract doctrine' of such forcible overthrow. *Yates* v. *United States*, 354 U. S. 298 (1957)." 1958 N. Y. State Legis. Annual 70, n. 1.

8. Compare the Smith Act, 18 U. S. C. § 2385, which punishes one who "prints, publishes, edits, issues, circulates, sells, distributes, or publicly displays any written or printed matter advocating, advising, or teaching the duty, necessity, desirability, or propriety of "unlawful overthrow, provided he is shown to have an "intent to cause the overthrow or destruction of any such government."

9. This is not a case where abstention pending state court interpretation would be appropriate. *Baggett* v. *Bullitt*, *supra*, at 375–379; *Dombrowski* v. *Pfister*, 380 U. S. 479, 489–490.

10. *Wieman* v. *Updegraff*, 344 U. S. 183, 195 (Frankfurter, J., concurring).

11. Whether or not loss of public employment constitutes "punishment," cf. *United States* v. *Lovett*, 328 U. S. 303, there can be no doubt that the repressive impact of the threat of discharge will be no less direct or substantial.

12. See Lazarsfeld & Thielens, The Academic Mind 92–112, 192–217; Biddle, The Fear of Freedom 155 *et seq.*; Jahoda & Cook, Security Measures and Freedom of Thought: An Exploratory Study of the Impact of Loyalty and Security Programs, 61 Yale L. J. 295 (1952). See generally, MacIver, Academic Freedom in Our Time; Hullfish, Educational Freedom in an Age of Anxiety; Konvitz, Expanding Liberties 86–108; Morris, Academic Freedom and Loyalty Oaths, 28 Law & Contemp. Prob. 487 (1963).

13. In light of our disposition, we need not consider appellants' contention that the burden placed on the employee of coming forward with substantial rebutting evidence upon proof of membership in a listed organization is constitutionally impermissible. Compare *Speiser* v. *Randall*, 357 U. S. 513.

In holding unconstitutional Arkansas's "anti-evolution" statute, the United States Supreme Court said: "Judicial interposition in the operation of the public school system of the Nation raises problems requiring care and restraint. Our courts, however, have not failed to apply the First Amendment's mandate in our educational system where essential to safeguard the fundamental values of freedom of speech and inquiry and of belief. By and large, public education in our Nation is committed to the control of state and local authorities. Courts do not and cannot intervene in the resolution of conflicts which arise in the daily operation of school systems and which do not directly and sharply implicate basic constitutional values. On the other hand, '[t]he vigilant protection of constitutional freedoms is nowhere more vital than in the community of American schools,' Shelton v. Tucker...."

Epperson v. *Arkansas*, 393 U. S. 97 (1968)

MR. JUSTICE FORTAS delivered the opinion of the Court.

I.

This appeal challenges the constitutionality of the "anti-evolution" statute which the State of Arkansas adopted in 1928 to prohibit the teaching in its public schools and universities of the theory that man evolved from other species of life. The statute was a product of the upsurge of "fundamentalist" religious fervor of the twenties. The Arkansas statute was an adaptation of the famous Tennessee "monkey law" which that State adopted in 1925.[1] The constitutionality of the Tennessee law was upheld by the Tennessee Supreme Court in the celebrated *Scopes* case in 1927.[2]

The Arkansas law makes it unlawful for a teacher in any state-supported school or university "to teach the theory or doctrine that mankind ascended or descended from a lower order of animals," or "to adopt or use in any such institution a textbook that teaches" this theory. Violation is a misdemeanor and subjects the violator to dismissal from his position.[3]

The present case concerns the teaching of biology in a high school in Little Rock. According to the testimony, until the events here in litigation, the official textbook furnished for the high school biology course did not have a section on the Darwinian Theory. Then, for the academic year 1965–1966, the school administration, on recommendation of the teachers of biology in the school system, adopted and prescribed a textbook which contained a chapter setting forth "the theory about the origin. . . of man from a lower form of animal."

Susan Epperson, a young woman who graduated

from Arkansas' school system and then obtained her master's degree in zoology at the University of Illinois, was employed by the Little Rock school system in the fall of 1964 to teach 10th grade biology at Central High School. At the start of the next academic year, 1965, she was confronted by the new textbook (which one surmises from the record was not unwelcome to her). She faced at least a literal dilemma because she was supposed to use the new textbook for classroom instruction and presumably to teach the statutorily condemned chapter; but to do so would be a criminal offense and subject her to dismissal.

She instituted the present action in the Chancery Court of the State, seeking a declaration that the Arkansas statute is void and enjoining the State and the defendant officials of the Little Rock school system from dismissing her for violation of the statute's provisions. H. H. Blanchard, a parent of children attending the public schools, intervened in support of the action.

The Chancery Court, in an opinion by Chancellor Murray O. Reed, held that the statute violated the Fourteenth Amendment to the United States Constitution.[4] The court noted that this Amendment encompasses the prohibitions upon state interference with freedom of speech and thought which are contained in the First Amendment. Accordingly, it held that the challenged statute is unconstitutional because, in violation of the First Amendment, it "tends to hinder the quest for knowledge, restrict the freedom to learn, and restrain the freedom to teach."[5] In this perspective, the Act, it held, was an unconstitutional and void restraint upon the freedom of speech guaranteed by the Constitution.

On appeal, the Supreme Court of Arkansas reversed.[6] Its two-sentence opinion is set forth in the margin.[7] It sustained the statute as an exercise of the State's power to specify the curriculum in public schools. It did not address itself to the competing constitutional considerations.

Appeal was duly prosecuted to this Court under 28 U. S. C. § 1257 (2). Only Arkansas and Mississippi have such "anti-evolution" or "monkey" laws on their books.[8] There is no record of any prosecutions in Arkansas under its statute. It is possible that the statute is presently more of a curiosity than a vital fact of life in these States.[9] Nevertheless, the present case was brought, the appeal as of right is properly here, and it is our duty to decide the issues presented.

II

At the outset, it is urged upon us that the challenged statute is vague and uncertain and therefore within the condemnation of the Due Process Clause of the Fourteenth Amendment. The contention that the Act is vague and uncertain is supported by language in the brief opinion of Arkansas' Supreme Court. That court, perhaps reflecting the discomfort which the statute's quixotic prohibition necessarily

engenders in the modern mind,[10] stated that it "expresses no opinion" as to whether the Act prohibits "explanation" of the theory of evolution or merely forbids "teaching that the theory is true." Regardless of this uncertainty, the court held that the statute is constitutional.

On the other hand, counsel for the State, in oral argument in this Court, candidly stated that, despite the State Supreme Court's equivocation, Arkansas would interpret the statute "to mean that to make a student aware of the theory . . . just to teach that there was such a theory" would be grounds for dismissal and for prosecution under the statute; and he said "that the Supreme Court of Arkansas' opinion should be interpreted in that manner." He said: "If Mrs. Epperson would tell her students that 'Here is Darwin's theory, that man ascended or descended from a lower form of being,' then I think she would be under this statute liable for prosecution."

In any event, we do not rest our decision upon the asserted vagueness of the statute. On either interpretation of its language, Arkansas' statute cannot stand. It is of no moment whether the law is deemed to prohibit mention of Darwin's theory, or to forbid any or all of the infinite varieties of communication embraced within the term "teaching." Under either interpretation, the law must be stricken because of its conflict with the constitutional prohibition of state laws respecting an establishment of religion or prohibiting the free exercise thereof. The overriding fact is that Arkansas' law selects from the body of knowledge a particular segment which it proscribes for the sole reason that it is deemed to conflict with a particular religious doctrine; that is, with a particular interpretation of the Book of Genesis by a particular religious group.[11]

III

The antecedents of today's decision are many and unmistakable. They are rooted in the foundation soil of our Nation. They are fundamental to freedom.

Government in our democracy, state and national, must be neutral in matters of religious theory, doctrine, and practice. It may not be hostile to any religion or to the advocacy of no-religion; and it may not aid, foster, or promote one religion or religious theory against another or even against the militant opposite. The First Amendment mandates governmental neutrality between religion and religion, and between religion and nonreligion.[12]

As early as 1872, this Court said: "The law knows no heresy, and is committed to the support of no dogma, the establishment of no sect." *Watson* v. *Jones*, 13 Wall. 679, 728. This has been the interpretation of the great First Amendment which this Court has applied in the many and subtle problems which the ferment of our national life has presented for decision within the Amendment's broad command.

Judicial interposition in the operation of

the public school system of the Nation raises problems requiring care and restraint. Our courts, however, have not failed to apply the First Amendment's mandate in our educational system where essential to safeguard the fundamental values of freedom of speech and inquiry and of belief. By and large, public education in our Nation is committed to the control of state and local authorities. Courts do not and cannot intervene in the resolution of conflicts which arise in the daily operation of school systems and which do not directly and sharply implicate basic constitutional values.[13] On the other hand, "[t]he vigilant protection of constitutional freedoms is nowhere more vital than in the community of American schools," *Shelton* v. *Tucker*, 364 U. S. 479, 487 (1960). As this Court said in *Keyishian* v. *Board of Regents*, the First Amendment "does not tolerate laws that cast a pall of orthodoxy over the classroom." 385 U. S. 589, 603 (1967).

The earliest cases in this Court on the subject of the impact of constitutional guarantees upon the classroom were decided before the Court expressly applied the specific prohibitions of the First Amendment to the States. But as early as 1923, the Court did not hesitate to condemn under the Due Process Clause "arbitrary" restrictions upon the freedom of teachers to teach and of students to learn. In that year, the Court, in an opinion by Justice McReynolds, held unconstitutional an Act of the State of Nebraska making it a crime to teach any subject in any language other than English to pupils who had not passed the eighth grade.[14] The State's purpose in enacting the law was to promote civic cohesiveness by encouraging the learning of English and to combat the "baneful effect" of permitting foreigners to rear and educate their children in the language of the parents' native land. The Court recognized these purposes, and it acknowledged the State's power to prescribe the school curriculum, but it held that these were not adequate to support the restriction upon the liberty of teacher and pupil. The challenged statute, it held, unconstitutionally interfered with the right of the individual, guaranteed by the Due Process Clause, to engage in any of the common occupations of life and to acquire useful knowledge. *Meyer* v. *Nebraska*, 262 U.S. 390 (1923). See also *Bartels* v. *Iowa*, 262 U. S. 404 (1923).

For purposes of the present case, we need not re-enter the difficult terrain which the Court, in 1923, traversed without apparent misgivings. We need not take advantage of the broad premise which the Court's decision in *Meyer* furnishes, nor need we explore the implications of that decision in terms of the justiciability of the multitude of controversies that beset our campuses today. Today's problem is capable of resolution in the narrower terms of the First Amendment's prohibition of laws respecting an establishment of religion or prohibiting the free exercise thereof.

There is and can be no doubt that the First Amendment does not permit the State to require that teaching and learning must be tailored to the principles or prohibitions of any religious sect or dogma. In *Everson* v. *Board of Education*, this Court, in upholding a state law to provide free bus service to school children, including those attending parochial schools, said: "Neither [a State nor the Federal Government] can pass laws which aid one religion, aid all religions, or prefer one religion over another." 330 U. S. 1, 15 (1947).

At the following Term of Court, in *McCollum* v. *Board of Education*, 333 U. S. 203 (1948), the Court held that Illinois could not release pupils from class to attend classes of instruction in the school buildings in the religion of their choice. This, it said, would involve the State in using tax-supported property for religious purposes, thereby breaching the "wall of separation" which, according to Jefferson, the First Amendment was intended to erect between church and state. *Id*., at 211. See also *Engel* v. *Vitale*, 370 U. S. 421 (1962); *Abington School District* v. *Schempp*, 374 U. S. 203 (1963). While study of religions and of the Bible from a literary and historic viewpoint, presented objectively as part of a secular program of education, need not collide with the First Amendment's prohibition, the State may not adopt programs or practices in its public schools or colleges which "aid or oppose" any religion. *Id*., at 225. This prohibition is absolute. It forbids alike the preference of a religious doctrine or the prohibition of theory which is deemed antagonistic to a particular dogma. As Mr. Justice Clark stated in *Joseph Burstyn, Inc.* v. *Wilson*, "the state has no legitimate interest in protecting any or all religions from views distasteful to them . . . ." 343 U. S. 495, 505 (1952). The test was stated as follows in *Abington School District* v. *Schempp, supra*, at 222: "[W]hat are the purpose and the primary effect of the enactment? If either is the advancement or inhibition of religion then the enactment exceeds the scope of legislative power as circumscribed by the Constitution."

These precedents inevitably determine the result in the present case. The State's undoubted right to prescribe the curriculum for its public schools does not carry with it the right to prohibit, on pain of criminal penalty, the teaching of a scientific theory or doctrine where that prohibition is based upon reasons that violate the First Amendment. It is much too late to argue that the State may impose upon the teachers in its schools any conditions that it chooses, however restrictive they may be of constitutional guarantees. *Keyishian* v. *Board of Regents*, 385 U. S. 589, 605-606 (1967).

In the present case, there can be no doubt that Arkansas has sought to prevent its teachers from discussing the theory of evolution because it is contrary to the belief of some that the Book of Genesis must be the exclusive source of doctrine as to the origin of man. No suggestion has been made that Arkansas' law may be justified by considerations of state policy other than the religious views of some of its citizens.[15] It is clear that fundamentalist sectarian conviction was and is the law's reason for existence.[16] Its antecedent, Tennessee's "monkey law," candidly stated its purpose: to make it unlawful "to teach any theory that denies the story of the Divine Creation of man as taught in the Bible, and to teach instead that man has descended from a lower order of animals."[17] Perhaps the sensational publicity attendant upon the *Scopes* trial induced Arkansas to adopt less explicit language.[18] It eliminated Tennessee's reference to "the story of the Divine Creation of man" as taught in the Bible, but there is no doubt that the motivation for the law was the same: to suppress the teaching of a theory which, it was thought, "denied" the divine creation of man.

Arkansas' law cannot be defended as an act of religious neutrality. Arkansas did not seek to excise from the curricula of its schools and universities all discussion of the origin of man. The law's effort was confined to an attempt to blot out a particular theory because of its supposed conflict with the Biblical account, literally read. Plainly, the law is contrary to the mandate of the First, and in violation of the Fourteenth, Amendment to the Constitution.

The judgment of the Supreme Court of Arkansas is   *Reversed.*

NOTES

1. Chapter 27, Tenn. Acts 1925; Tenn. Code Ann. § 49-1922 (1966 Repl. Vol.).
2. *Scopes* v. *State*, 154 Tenn. 105, 289 S. W. 363 (1927). The Tennessee court, however, reversed Scopes' conviction on the ground that the jury and not the judge should have assessed the fine of $100. Since Scopes was no longer in the State's employ, it saw "nothing to be gained by prolonging the life of this bizarre case." It directed that a *nolle prosequi* be entered, in the interests of "the peace and dignity of the State." 154 Tenn., at 121, 289 S. W., at 367.
3. Initiated Act No. 1, Ark. Acts 1929; Ark. Stat. Ann. §§ 80-1627, 80-1628 (1960 Repl. Vol.). The text of the law is as follows:
   "§80-1627.--Doctrine of ascent or descent of man from lower order of animals prohibited.--It shall be unlawful for any teacher or other instructor in any University, College, Normal, Public School, or other institution of the State, which is supported in whole or in part from public funds derived by State and local taxation to teach the theory or doctrine that mankind ascended or descended from a lower order of animals and also it shall be unlawful for any teacher, textbook commission, or other authority exercising the power to select textbooks for above mentioned educational institutions to adopt or use in any such institution a textbook that teaches the doctrine or theory that mankind descended or ascended from a lower order of animals.
   "§ 80-1628.--Teaching doctrine or adopting textbook mentioning doctrine-- Penalties--Positions to be vacated.--Any teacher or other instructor or textbook commissioner who is found guilty of violation of this act by teaching the theory or doctrine mentioned in section 1 hereof, or by using, or adopting any such textbooks in any such educational institution shall be guilty of a misdemeanor and upon conviction shall be fined not exceeding five hundred dollars; and upon conviction shall vacate the position thus held in any educational institutions of the character above mentioned or any commission of which he may be a member."
4. The opinion of the Chancery Court is not officially reported.
5. The Chancery Court analyzed the holding of its sister State of Tennessee in the *Scopes* case sustaining Tennessee's similar statute. It refused to follow Tennessee's 1927 example. It declined to confine the judicial horizon to a view of the law as merely a direction by the State as employer to its employees. This sort of astigmatism, it held, would ignore overriding constitutional values, and "should not be followed," and it proceeded to confront the substance of the law and its effect.
6. 242 Ark. 922, 416 S. W. 2d 322 (1967).
7. "Per Curiam. Upon the principal issue, that of constitutionality, the court holds that Initiated Measure No. 1 of 1928, Ark. Stat. Ann. § 80-1627 and § 80-1628, (Repl. 1960), is a valid exercise of the state's power to specify the curriculum in its public schools. The court expresses no opinion on the question whether the Act prohibits any explanation of the theory of evolution or merely prohibits teaching that the theory is true; the answer not being necessary to a decision in the case, and the issue not having been raised.
   "The decree is reversed and the cause dismissed.
   "Ward, J., concurs. Brown, J., dissents.
   "Paul Ward, Justice, concurring. I agree with the first sentence in the majority opinion.
   "To my mind, the rest of the opinion beclouds the clear announcement made in the first sentence."
8. Miss. Code Ann. §§ 6798, 6799 (1942). Ark. Stat. Ann §§ 80-1627, 80-1628 (1960 Repl. Vol.) The Tennessee law was repealed in 1967. Oklahoma enacted an anti-evolution law, but it was repealed in 1926. The

Florida and Texas Legislatures, in the period between 1921 and 1929, adopted resolutions against teaching the doctrine of evolution. In all, during that period, bills to this effect were introduced in 20 States. American Civil Liberties Union (ACLU), The Gag on Teaching 8 (2d ed., 1937).

9. Clarence Darrow, who was counsel for the defense in the *Scopes* trial, in his biography published in 1932, somewhat sardonically pointed out that States with anti-evolution laws did not insist upon the fundamentalist theory in all respects. He said: "I understand that the States of Tennessee and Mississippi both continue to teach that the earth is round and that the revolution on its axis brings the day and night, in spite of all opposition." The Story of My Life 247 (1932).

10. R. Hofstadter & W. Metzger, in The Development of Academic Freedom in the United States 324 (1955), refer to some of Darwin's opponents as "exhibiting a kind of phylogenetic snobbery [which led them] to think that Darwin had libeled the [human] race by discovering simian rather than seraphic ancestors."

11. In *Scopes* v. *State*, 154 Tenn. 105, 126, 289 S.W.363, 369 (1927), Judge Chambliss, concurring, referred to the defense contention that Tennessee's anti-evolution law gives a "preference" to "religious establishments which have as one of their tenets or dogmas the instantaneous creation of man."

12. *Everson* v. *Board of Education*, 330 U. S. 1, 18 (1947); *McCollum* v. *Board of Education*, 333 U. S. 203 (1948); *Zorach* v. *Clauson*, 343 U.S.306, 313-314 (1952): *Fowler* v. *Rhode Island*, 345 U. S. 67 (1953): *Torcaso* v. *Watkins*, 367 U. S. 488, 495 (1961).

13. See the discussion in Developments in The Law--Academic Freedom, 81 Harv. L. Rev. 1045, 1051-1055 (1968).

14. The case involved a conviction for teaching "the subject of reading in the German language" to a child of 10 years.

15. Former Dean Leflar of the University of Arkansas School of Law has stated that "the same ideological considerations underlie the anti-evolution enactment" as underlie the typical blasphemy statute. He says that the purpose of these statutes is an "ideological" one which "involves an effort to prevent (by censorship) or punish the presentation of intellectually significant matter which contradicts accepted social, moral or religious ideas." Leflar, Legal Liability for the Exercise of Free Speech, 10 Ark. L. Rev. 155, 158 (1956). See also R. Hofstadter & W. Metzger, The Development of Academic Freedom in the United States 320-366 (1955) (*passim*); H. Beale, A History of Freedom of Teaching in American Schools 202-207 (1941); Emerson & Haber, The *Scopes* Case in Modern Dress, 27 U. Chi. L. Rev. 522 (1960); Waller, The Con-

stitutionality of the Tennessee Anti-Evolution Act, 35 Yale L. J. 191 (1925) (*passim*); ACLU, The Gag on Teaching 7 (2d ed., 1937); J. Scopes & J. Presley, Center of the Storm 45-53 (1967).

16. The following advertisement is typical of the public appeal which was used in the campaign to secure adoption of the statute:

"THE BIBLE OR ATHEISM, WHICH?

"All atheists favor evolution. If you agree with atheism vote against Act No. 1. If you agree with the Bible vote for Act No. 1.... Shall conscientious church members be forced to pay taxes to support teachers to teach evolution which will undermine the faith of their children? The Gazette said Russian Bolshevists laughed at Tennessee. True, and that sort will laugh at Arkansas. Who cares? Vote FOR ACT NO. 1." The Arkansas Gazette, Little Rock, Nov. 4, 1928, p. 12, cols. 4-5.

Letters from the public expressed the fear that teaching of evolution would be "subversive of Christianity," *id.*, Oct. 24, 1928, p. 7, col. 2; see also *id.*, Nov. 4, 1928, p. 19, col. 4; and that it would cause school children "to disrespect the Bible," *id.*, Oct. 27, 1928, p. 15, col. 5. One letter read: "The cosmogony taught by [evolution] runs contrary to that of Moses and Jesus, and as such is nothing, if anything at all, but atheism. . . . Now let the mothers and fathers of our state that are trying to raise their children in the Christian faith arise in their might and vote for this anti-evolution bill that will take it out of our tax supported schools. When they have saved the children, they have saved the state." *Id.*, at cols. 4-5.

17. Arkansas' law was adopted by popular initiative in 1928, three years after Tennessee's law was enacted and one year after the Tennessee Supreme Court's decision in the *Scopes* case, *supra*.

18. In its brief, the State says that the Arkansas statute was passed with the holding of the *Scopes* case in mind. Brief for Appellee 1.

In deciding that the wearing of black armbands by three public school students protesting the government's policy in Vietnam was conduct protected by the First Amendment, the United States Supreme Court stated: "It can hardly be argued that either students or teachers shed their constitutional rights to freedom of speech or expression at the schoolhouse gate. This has been the unmistakable holding of this Court for almost 50 years....In our system, state-operated schools may not be enclaves of totalitarianism. School officials do not possess absolute authority over their students. Students in school as well as out of school are 'persons' under our Constitution. They are possessed of fundamental rights which the State must respect, just as they themselves must respect their obligations to the State. In our system, students may not be regarded as closed-circuit recipients of only that which the State chooses to communicate. They may not be confined to the expression of those sentiments that are officially approved."

Tinker v. Des Moines School District, 393 U. S. 503 (1969)

MR. JUSTICE FORTAS delivered the opinion of the Court.

Petitioner John F. Tinker, 15 years old, and petitioner Christopher Eckhardt, 16 years old, attended high schools in Des Moines, Iowa. Petitioner Mary Beth Tinker, John's sister, was a 13-year-old student in junior high school.

In December 1965, a group of adults and students in Des Moines held a meeting at the Eckhardt home. The group determined to publicize their objections to the hostilities in Vietnam and their support for a truce by wearing black armbands during the holiday season and by fasting on December 16 and New Year's Eve. Petitioners and their parents had previously engaged in similar activities, and they decided to participate in the program.

The principals of the Des Moines schools became aware of the plan to wear armbands. On December 14, 1965, they met and adopted a policy that any student wearing an armband to school would be asked to remove it, and if he refused he would be suspended until he returned without the armband. Petitioners were aware of the regulation that the school authorities adopted.

On December 16, Mary Beth and Christopher wore black armbands to their schools. John Tinker wore his armband the next day. They were all sent home and suspended from school until they would come back without their armbands. They did not return to school until after the planned period for wearing armbands had expired--that is, until after New Year's Day.

This complaint was filed in the United

States District Court by petitioners, through their fathers, under § 1983 of Title 42 of the United States Code. It prayed for an injunction restraining the respondent school officials and the respondent members of the board of directors of the school district from disciplining the petitioners, and it sought nominal damages. After an evidentiary hearing the District Court dismissed the complaint. It upheld the constitutionality of the school authorities' action on the ground that it was reasonable in order to prevent disturbance of school discipline. 258 F. Supp. 971 (1966). The court referred to but expressly declined to follow the Fifth Circuit's holding in a similar case that the wearing of symbols like the armbands cannot be prohibited unless it "materially and substantially interfere[s] with the requirements of appropriate discipline in the operation of the school." *Burnside* v. *Byars*, 363 F. 2d 744, 749 (1966).[1]

On appeal, the Court of Appeals for the Eighth Circuit considered the case *en banc*. The court was equally divided, and the District Court's decision was accordingly affirmed, without opinion. 383 F. 2d 988 (1967). We granted certiorari. 390 U. S. 942 (1968).

I.

The District Court recognized that the wearing of an armband for the purpose of expressing certain views is the type of symbolic act that is within the Free Speech Clause of the First Amendment. See *West Virginia* v. *Barnette*, 319 U. S. 624 (1943); *Stromberg* v. *California*, 283 U. S. 359 (1931). Cf. *Thornhill* v. *Alabama*, 310 U. S. 88 (1940); *Edwards* v. *South Carolina*, 372 U. S. 229 (1963); *Brown* v. *Louisiana*, 383 U. S. 131 (1966). As we shall discuss, the wearing of armbands in the circumstances of this case was entirely divorced from actually or potentially disruptive conduct by those participating in it. It was closely akin to "pure speech" which, we have repeatedly held, is entitled to comprehensive protection under the First Amendment. Cf. *Cox* v. *Louisiana*, 379 U. S. 536, 555 (1965); *Adderley* v. *Florida*, 385 U. S. 39 (1966).

First Amendment rights, applied in light of the special characteristics of the school environment, are available to teachers and students. It can hardly be argued that either students or teachers shed their constitutional rights to freedom of speech or expression at the schoolhouse gate. This has been the unmistakable holding of this Court for almost 50 years. In *Meyer* v. *Nebraska*, 262 U. S. 390 (1923), and *Bartels* v. *Iowa*, 262 U. S. 404 (1923), this Court, in opinions by Mr. Justice McReynolds, held that the Due Process Clause of the Fourteenth Amendment prevents States from forbidding the teaching of a foreign language to young students. Statutes to this effect, the Court held, unconstitutionally interfere with the liberty of teacher, student and parent.[2] See also *Pierce* v. *Society of Sisters*, 268 U. S. 510 (1925); *West Virginia*

v. *Barnette*, 319 U. S. 624 (1943); *McCollum v. Board of Education*, 333 U. S. 203 (1948); *Wieman* v. *Updegraff*, 344 U. S. 183, 195 (1952) (concurring opinion); *Sweezy* v. *New Hampshire*, 354 U. S. 234 (1957); *Shelton* v. *Tucker*, 364 U. S. 479, 487 (1960); *Engel* v. *Vitale*, 370 U. S. 421 (1962); *Keyishian* v. *Board of Regents*, 385 U. S. 589, 603 (1967); *Epperson* v. *Arkansas, ante*, p. 97 (1968).

In *West Virginia* v. *Barnette, supra,* this Court held that under the First Amendment, the student in public school may not be compelled to salute the flag. Speaking through Mr. Justice Jackson, the Court said:

"The Fourteenth Amendment, as now applied to the States, protects the citzen against the State itself and all of its creatures—Boards of Education not excepted. These have, of course, important, delicate, and highly discretionary functions, but none that they may not perform within the limits of the Bill of Rights. That they are educating the young for citizenship is reason for scrupulous protection of Constitutional freedoms of the individual, if we are not to strangle the free mind at its source and teach youth to discount important principles of our government as mere platitudes." 319 U. S., at 637.

On the other hand, the Court has repeatedly emphasized the need for affirming the comprehensive authority of the States and of school officials, consistent with fundamental constitutional safeguards, to prescribe and control conduct in the schools. See *Epperson* v. *Arkansas, supra,* at 104; *Meyer* v. *Nebraska, supra,* at 402. Our problem lies in the area where students in the exercise of First Amendment rights collide with the rules of the school authorities.

II.

The problem posed by the present case does not relate to regulation of the length of skirts or the type of clothing, to hair style, or deportment. Cf. *Ferrell* v. *Dallas Independent School District*, 392 F. 2d 697 (1968); *Pugsley* v. *Sellmeyer*, 158 Ark. 247, 250 S. W. 538 (1923). It does not concern aggressive, disruptive action or even group demonstrations. Our problem involves direct, primary First Amendment rights akin to "pure speech."

The school officials banned and sought to punish petitioners for a silent, passive expression of opinion, unaccompanied by any disorder or disturbance on the part of petitioners. There is here no evidence whatever of petitioners' interference, actual or nascent, with the schools' work or of collision with the rights of other students to be secure and to be let alone. Accordingly, this case does not concern speech or action that intrudes upon the work of the schools or the rights of other students.

Only a few of the 18,000 students in the school system wore the black armbands. Only five students were suspended for wearing them. There is no indication that the work of the schools or any class was disrupted. Outside the classrooms, a few students made hostile remarks to the children wearing armbands, but there were no threats or acts of violence on school premises.

The District Court concluded that the action of the school authorities was reasonable because it was based upon their fear of a disturbance from the wearing of the armbands. But, in our system, undifferentiated fear or apprehension of disturbance is not enough to overcome the right to freedom of expression. Any departure from absolute regimentation may cause trouble. Any variation from the majority's opinion may inspire fear. Any word spoken, in class, in the lunchroom, or on the campus, that deviates from the views of another person may start an argument or cause a disturbance. But our Constitution says we must take this risk, *Terminiello* v. *Chicago*, 337 U. S. 1 (1949); and our history says that it is this sort of hazardous freedom—this kind of openness—that is the basis of our national strength and of the independence and vigor of Americans who grow up and live in this relatively permissive, often disputatious, society.

In order for the State in the person of school officials to justify prohibition of a particular expression of opinion, it must be able to show that its action was caused by something more than a mere desire to avoid the discomfort and unpleasantness that always accompany an unpopular viewpoint. Certainly where there is no finding and no showing that engaging in the forbidden conduct would "materially and substantially interfere with the requirements of appropriate discipline in the operation of the school," the prohibition cannot be sustained. *Burnside* v. *Byars, supra,* at 749.

In the present case, the District Court made no such finding, and our independent examination of the record fails to yield evidence that the school authorities had reason to anticipate that the wearing of the armbands would substantially interfere with the work of the school or impinge upon the rights of other students. Even an official memorandum prepared after the suspension that listed the reasons for the ban on wearing the armbands made no reference to the anticipation of such disruption.[3]

On the contrary, the action of the school authorities appears to have been based upon an urgent wish to avoid the controversy which might result from the expression, even by the silent symbol of armbands, of opposition to this Nation's part in the conflagration in Vietnam.[4] It is revealing, in this respect, that the meeting at which the school principals decided to issue the contested regulation was called in response to a student's statement to the journalism teacher in one of the schools that he wanted to write an article on Vietnam and have it published in the school paper. (The student was dissuaded.[5])

It is also relevant that the school authorities did not purport to prohibit the wearing of all symbols of political or controversial significance. The record shows that students in some of the schools wore buttons relating to national political campaigns, and some even wore the Iron Cross, traditionally a symbol of Nazism. The order prohibiting the wearing of armbands did not extend to these. Instead, a particular symbol--black armbands worn to exhibit opposition to this Nation's involvement in Vietnam--was singled out for prohibition. Clearly, the prohibition of expression of one particular opinion, at least without evidence that it is necessary to avoid material and substantial interference with schoolwork or discipline, is not constitutionally permissible.

In our system, state-operated schools may not be enclaves of totalitarianism. School officials do not possess absolute authority over their students. Students in school as well as out of school are "persons" under our Constitution. They are possessed of fundamental rights which the State must respect, just as they themselves must respect their obligations to the State. In our system, students may not be regarded as closed-circuit recipients of only that which the State chooses to communicate. They may not be confined to the expression of those sentiments that are officially approved. In the absence of a specific showing of constitutionally valid reasons to regulate their speech, students are entitled to freedom of expression of their views. As Judge Gewin, speaking for the Fifth Circuit, said, school officials cannot suppress "expressions of feelings with which they do not wish to contend." *Burnside* v. *Byars, supra*, at 749.

In *Meyer* v. *Nebraska, supra*, at 402, Mr. Justice McReynolds expressed this Nation's repudiation of the principle that a State might so conduct its schools as to "foster a homogeneous people." He said:

"In order to submerge the individual and develop ideal citizens, Sparta assembled the males at seven into barracks and intrusted their subsequent education and training to official guardians. Although such measures have been deliberately approved by men of great genius, their ideas touching the relation between individual and State were wholly different from those upon which our institutions rest; and it hardly will be affirmed that any legislature could impose such restrictions upon the people of a State without doing violence to both letter and spirit of the Constitution."

This principle has been repeated by this Court on numerous occasions during the interveing years. In *Keyishian* v. *Board of Regents*, 385 U. S. 589, 603, MR. JUSTICE BRENNAN, speaking for the Court, said:

"'The vigilant protection of constitutional freedoms is nowhere more vital than in the community of American schools.' *Shelton* v. *Tucker*, [364 U. S. 479,] at 487. The classroom is peculiarly the 'marketplace of ideas.' The Nation's future depends upon leaders trained through wide exposure to that robust exchange of ideas which discovers truth 'out of a multitude of tongues, [rather] than through any kind of authoritative selection.'"

The principle of these cases is not confined to the supervised and ordained discussion which takes place in the classroom. The principal use to which the schools are dedicated is to accommodate students during prescribed hours for the purpose of certain types of activities. Among those activities is personal intercommunication among the students.[6] This is not only an inevitable part of the process of attending school; it is also an important part of the educational process. A student's rights, therefore, do not embrace merely the classroom hours. When he is in the cafeteria, or on the playing field, or on the campus during the authorized hours, he may express his opinions, even on controversial subjects like the conflict in Vietnam, if he does so without "materially and substantially interfer[ing] with the requirements of appropriate discipline in the operation of the school" and without colliding with the rights of others. *Burnside* v. *Byars, supra*, at 749. But conduct by the student, in class or out of it, which for any reason--whether it stems from time, place, or type of behavior--materially disrupts classwork or involves substantial disorder or invasion of the rights of others is, of course, not immunized by the constitutional guarantee of freedom of speech. Cf. *Blackwell* v. *Issaquena County Board of Education*, 363 F. 2d 749 (C. A. 5th Cir. 1966).

Under our Constitution, free speech is not a right that is given only to be so circumscribed that it exists in principle but not in fact. Freedom of expression would not truly exist if the right could be exercised only in an area that a benevolent government has provided as a safe haven for crackpots. The Constitution says that Congress (and the States) may not abridge the right to free speech. This provision means what it says. We properly read it to permit reasonable regulation of speech-connected activities in carefully restricted circumstances. But we do not confine the permissible exercise of First Amendment rights to a telephone booth or the four corners of a pamphlet, or to supervised and ordained discussion in a school classroom.

If a regulation were adopted by school officials forbidding discussion of the Vietnam conflict, or the expression by any student of opposition to it anywhere on school property except as part of a prescribed classroom exercise, it would be obvious that the regulation would violate the constitutional rights of students, at least if it could not be justified by a showing that the students' activities would materially and substantially disrupt the work and discipline of the school. Cf. *Hammond* v. *South Carolina State College*, 272 F. Supp. 947 (D. C. S. C. 1967) (orderly protest meeting on state college campus); *Dickey* v. *Alabama State Board of Education*, 273 F. Supp. 613 (D. C. M. D. Ala. 1967) (expulsion of student editor of college newspaper). In the circumstances of the present case, the prohibition of the silent, passive "witness of the armbands," as one of the children called it, is no less offensive to the Constitution's guarantees.

As we have discussed, the record does not demonstrate any facts which might reasonably have led school authorities to forecast substantial disruption of or material interference with school activities, and no disturbances or disorders on the school premises in fact occurred. These petitioners merely went about their ordained rounds in school. Their deviation consisted only in wearing on their sleeve a band of black cloth, not more than two inches wide. They wore it to exhibit their disapproval of the Vietnam hostilities and their advocacy of a truce, to make their views known, and, by their example, to influence others to adopt them. They neither interrupted school activities nor sought to intrude in the school affairs or the lives of others. They caused discussion outside of the classrooms, but no interference with work and no disorder. In the circumstances, our Constitution does not permit officials of the State to deny their form of expression.

We express no opinion as to the form of relief which should be granted, this being a matter for the lower courts to determine. We reverse and remand for further proceedings consistent with this opinion.

Reversed and remanded.

NOTES

1. In *Burnside*, the Fifth Circuit ordered that high school authorities be enjoined from enforcing a regulation forbidding students to wear "freedom buttons." It is instructive that in *Blackwell v. Issaquena County Board of Education*, 363 F. 2d 749 (1966), the same panel on the same day reached the opposite result on different facts. It declined to enjoin enforcement of such a regulation in another high school where the students wearing freedom buttons harassed students who did not wear them and created much disturbance.

2. *Hamilton* v. *Regents of Univ. of Cal.*, 293 U. S. 245 (1934), is sometimes cited for the broad proposition that the State may attach conditions to attendance at a state university that require individuals to violate their religious convictions. The case involved dismissal of members of a religious denomination from a land grant college for refusal to participate in military training. Narrowly viewed, the case turns upon the Court's conclusion that merely requiring a student to participate in school training in military "science" could not conflict with his constitutionally protected freedom of conscience. The

decision cannot be taken as establishing that the State may impose and enforce any conditions that it chooses upon attendance at public institutions of learning, however violative they may be of fundamental constitutional guarantees. See, *e. g.*, *West Virginia* v. *Barnette*, 319 U. S. 624 (1943); *Dixon* v. *Alabama State Board of Education*, 294 F. 2d 150 (C. A. 5th Cir. 1961); *Knight* v. *State Board of Education*, 200 F. Supp. 174 (D. C. M. D. Tenn. 1961); *Dickey* v. *Alabama State Board of Education*, 273 F. Supp. 613 (D. C. M. D. Ala. 1967). See also Note, Unconstitutional Conditions, 73 Harv. L. Rev. 1595 (1960); Note, Academic Freedom, 81 Harv. L. Rev. 1045 (1968).

3. The only suggestions of fear of disorder in the report are these:
"A former student of one of our high schools was killed in Viet Nam. Some of his friends are still in school and it was felt that if any kind of a demonstration existed, it might evolve into something which would be difficult to control."

"Students at one of the high schools were heard to say they would wear arm bands of other colors if the black bands prevailed."

"Moreover, the testimony of school authorities at trial indicates that it was not fear of disruption that motivated the regulation prohibiting the armbands; the regulation was directed against "the principle of the demonstration" itself. School authorities simply felt that "the schools are no place for demonstrations," and if the students "didn't like the way our elected officials were handling things, it should be handled with the ballot box and not in the halls of our public schools."

4. The District Court found that the school authorities, in prohibiting black armbands, were influenced by the fact that "[t]he Viet Nam war and the involvement of the United States therein has been the subject of a major controversy for some time. When the arm band regulation involved herein was promulgated, debate over the Viet Nam war had become vehement in many localities. A protest march against the war had been recently held in Washington, D. C. A wave of draft card burning incidents protesting the war had swept the country. At that time two highly publicized draft card burning cases were pending in this Court. Both individuals supporting the war and those opposing it were quite vocal in expressing their views." 258 F. Supp., at 972-973.

5. After the principals' meeting, the director of secondary education and the principal of the high school informed the student that the principals were opposed to publication of his article. They reported that "we felt that it was a very friendly conversation, although we did not feel that we had convinced the student that our decision was a just one."

6. In *Hammond* v. *South Carolina State College*, 272 F. Supp. 947 (D. C. S. C.

1967), District Judge Hemphill had before him a case involving a meeting on campus of 300 students to express their views on school practices. He pointed out that a school is not like a hospital or a jail enclosure. Cf. *Cox* v. *Louisiana*, 379 U. S. 536 (1965); *Adderley* v. *Florida*, 385 U. S. 39 (1966). It is a public place, and its dedication to specific uses does not imply that the constitutional rights of persons entitled to be there are to be gauged as if the premises were purely private property. Cf. *Edwards* v. *South Carolina*, 372 U. S. 229 (1963); *Brown* v. *Louisiana*, 383 U. S. 131 (1966).

In holding that the First Amendment (as made applicable to the states through the Fourteenth Amendment) prohibits making the mere possession of obscene materials in the privacy of one's home a crime, the United States Supreme Court declared: "It is now well established that the Constitution protects the right to receive information and ideas. 'This freedom [of speech and press]...necessarily protects the right to receive....' Martin v. City of Struthers .... This right to receive information and ideas, regardless of their social worth ... is fundamental to our free society."

Stanley v. *Georgia*, 394 U. S. 557 (1969)

MR. JUSTICE MARSHALL delivered the opinion of the Court.

An investigation of appellant's alleged bookmaking activities led to the issuance of a search warrant for appellant's home. Under authority of this warrant, federal and state agents secured entrance. They found very little evidence of bookmaking activity, but while looking through a desk drawer in an upstairs bedroom, one of the federal agents, accompanied by a state officer, found three reels of eight-millimeter film. Using a projector and screen found in an upstairs living room, they viewed the films. The state officer concluded that they were obscene and seized them. Since a further examination of the bedroom indicated that appellant occupied it, he was charged with possession of obscene matter and placed under arrest. He was later indicted for "knowingly hav[ing] possession of...obscene matter" in violation of Georgia law.[1] Appellant was tried before a jury and convicted. The Supreme Court of Georgia affirmed. *Stanley* v. *State*, 224 Ga. 259, 161 S. E. 2d 309 (1968). We noted probable jurisdiction of an appeal brought under 28 U. S. C. § 1257 (2). 393 U. S. 819 (1968).

Appellant raises several challenges to the validity of his conviction.[2] We find it necessary to consider only one. Appellant argues here, and argued below, that the Georgia obscenity statute, insofar as it punishes mere private possession of obscene matter, violates the First Amendment, as made applicable to the States by the Fourteenth Amendment. For reasons set forth below, we agree that the mere private possession of obscene matter cannot constitutionally be made a crime.

The court below saw no valid constitutional objection to the Georgia statute, even though it extends further than the typical statute forbidding commercial sales of obscene material. It held that "[i]t is not essential to an indictment charging one with possession of obscene matter that it be alleged that such possession was 'with intent to sell, expose or circulate the same.'" *Stanley* v. *State, supra*, at 261, 161 S. E. 2d, at 311. The State and appellant both agree that the question here before us is whether "a statute im-

posing criminal sanctions upon the mere [know-
ing] possession of obscene matter" is constitutional. In this context, Georgia concedes that
the present case appears to be one of "first
impression...on this exact point,"[3] but contends that since "obscenity is not within the
area of constitutionally protected speech or
press," *Roth* v. *United States*, 354 U. S.
476, 485 (1957), the States are free, subject
to the limits of other provisions of the Constitution, see, *e. g.*, *Ginsberg* v. *New
York*, 390 U. S. 629, 637-645 (1968), to deal
with it any way deemed necessary, just as they
may deal with possession of other things
thought to be detrimental to the welfare of
their citizens. If the State can protect the
body of a citizen, may it not, argues Georgia,
protect his mind?

It is true that *Roth* does declare,
seemingly without qualification, that obscenity
is not protected by the First Amendment. That
statement has been repeated in various forms in
subsequent cases. See, *e. g.*, *Smith* v.
California, 361 U. S. 147, 152 (1959);
Jacobellis v. *Ohio*, 378 U. S. 184, 186-187
(1964) (opinion of BRENNAN, J.); *Ginsberg* v.
New York, *supra*, at 635. However, neither
Roth nor any subsequent decision of this
Court dealt with the precise problem involved
in the present case. *Roth* was convicted of
mailing obscene circulars and advertising, and
an obscene book, in violation of a federal obscenity statute.[4] The defendant in a com-
panion case, *Alberts* v. *California*, 354 U.
S. 476 (1957), was convicted of "lewdly keeping for sale obscene and indecent books, and
[of] writing, composing and publishing an obscene advertisement of them...." *Id.*, at
481. None of the statements cited by the Court
in *Roth* for the proposition that "this Court
has always assumed that obscenity is not protected by the freedoms of speech and press"
were made in the context of a statute punishing
mere private possession of obscene material;
the cases cited deal for the most part with use
of the mails to distribute objectionable material or with some form of public distribution
or dissemination.[5] Moreover, none of this
Court's decisions subsequent to *Roth* involved
private possession of obscene materials. Those
cases dealt with the power of the State and
Federal Governments to prohibit or regulate
certain public actions taken or intended to be
taken with respect to obscene matter.[6] Indeed, with one exception, we have been unable
to discover any case in which the issue in the
present case has been fully considered.[7]

In this context, we do not believe that this
case can be decided simply by citing *Roth*.
Roth and its progeny certainly do mean that
the First and Fourteenth Amendments recognize a
valid governmental interest in dealing with the
problem of obscenity. But the assertion of
that interest cannot, in every context, be insulated from all constitutional protections.
Neither *Roth* nor any other decision of this
Court reaches that far. As the Court said in
Roth itself, "[c]easeless vigilance is the
watchword to prevent ... erosion [of First

Amendment rights] by Congress or by the
States. The door barring federal and state intrusion into this area cannot be left ajar; it
must be kept tightly closed and opened only the
slightest crack necessary to prevent encroachment upon more important interests." 354 U.S.
at 488. *Roth* and the cases following it dis-
cerned such an "important interest" in the regulation of commercial distribution of obscene
material. That holding cannot foreclose an examination of the constitutional implications of
a statute forbidding mere private possession of
such material.

It is now well established that the Constitution protects the right to receive information and ideas. "This freedom [of speech and
press] ... necessarily protects the right to
receive ...." *Martin* v. *City of
Struthers*, 319 U. S. 141, 143 (1943); see
Griswod v. *Connecticut*, 381 U. S. 479, 482
(1965); *Lamont* v. *Postmaster General*, 381
U. S. 301, 307-308 (1965) (BRENNAN, J., concurring); cf. *Pierce* v. *Society of Sisters*,
268 U. S. 510 (1925). This right to receive
information and ideas, regardless of their social worth, see *Winters* v. *New York*, 333 U.
S. 507, 510 (1948), is fundamental to our free
society. Moreover, in the context of this
case--a prosecution for mere possession of
printed or filmed matter in the privacy of a
person's own home -- that right takes on an
added dimension. For also fundamental is the
right to be free, except in very limited circumstances, from unwanted governmental intru-
sions into one's privacy.

> "The makers of our Constitution undertook to
> secure conditions favorable to the pursuit
> of happiness. They recognized the signifi-
> cance of man's spiritual nature, of his
> feelings and of his intellect. They knew
> that only a part of the pain, pleasure and
> satisfactions of life are to be found in ma-
> terial things. They sought to protect Amer-
> icans in their beliefs, their thoughts,
> their emotions and their sensations. They
> conferred, as against the Government, the
> right to be let alone--the most comprehen-
> sive of rights and the right most valued by
> civilized man." *Olmstead* v. *United
> States*, 277 U. S. 438, 478 (1928)
> (Brandeis, J., dissenting).

See *Griswold* v. *Connecticut*, *supra*; cf.
NAACP v. *Alabama*, 357 U. S. 449, 462 (1958).

These are the rights that appellant is asserting in the case before us. He is asserting
the right to read or observe what he pleases--
the right to satisfy his intellectual and emotional needs in the privacy of his own home.
He is asserting the right to be free from state
inquiry into the contents of his library.
Georgia contends that appellant does not have
these rights, that there are certain types of
materials that the individual may not read or
even possess. Georgia justifies this assertion
by arguing that the films in the present case
are obscene. But we think that mere categorization of these films as "obscene" is insuffi-

cient justification for such a drastic invasion of personal liberties guaranteed by the First and Fourteenth Amendments. Whatever may be the justifications for other statutes regulating obscenity, we do not think they reach into the privacy of one's own home. If the First Amendment means anything, it means that a State has no business telling a man, sitting alone in his own house, what books he may read or what films he may watch. Our whole constitutional heritage rebels at the thought of giving government the power to control men's minds.

And yet, in the face of these traditional notions of individual liberty, Georgia asserts the right to protect the individual's mind from the effects of obscenity. We are not certain that this argument amounts to anything more than the assertion that the State has the right to control the moral content of a person's thoughts.[8] To some, this may be a noble purpose, but it is wholly inconsistent with the philosophy of the First Amendment. As the Court said in *Kingsley International Pictures Corp.* v. *Regents*, 360 U. S. 684, 688-689 (1959), "[t]his argument misconceives what it is that the Constitution protects. Its guarantee is not confined to the expression of ideas that are conventional or shared by a majority.... And in the realm of ideas it protects expression which is eloquent no less than that which is unconvincing." Cf. *Joseph Burstyn, Inc.* v. *Wilson*, 343 U. S. 495 (1952). Nor is it relevant that obscene materials in general, or the particular films before the Court, are arguably devoid of any ideological content. The line between the transmission of ideas and mere entertainment is much too elusive for this Court to draw, if indeed such a line can be drawn at all. See *Winters* v. *New York, supra,* at 510. Whatever the power of the state to control public dissemination of ideas inimical to the public morality, it cannot constitutionally premise legislation on the desirability of controlling a person's private thoughts.

Perhaps recognizing this, Georgia asserts that exposure to obscene materials may lead to deviant sexual behavior or crimes of sexual violence. There appears to be little empirical basis for that assertion.[9] But more important, if the State is only concerned about printed or filmed materials inducing antisocial conduct, we believe that in the context of private consumption of ideas and information we should adhere to the view that "[a]mong free men, the deterrents ordinarily to be applied to prevent crime are education and punishment for violations of the law...." *Whitney* v. *California*, 274 U. S. 357, 378 (1927) (Brandeis, J., concurring). See Emerson, Toward a General Theory of the First Amendment, 72 Yale L. J. 877, 938 (1963). Given the present state of knowledge, the State may no more prohibit mere possession of obscene matter on the ground that it may lead to antisocial conduct than it may prohibit possession of chemistry books on the ground that they may lead to the manufacture of homemade spirits.

It is true that in *Roth* this Court rejected the necessity of proving that exposure to obscene material would create a clear and present danger of antisocial conduct or would probably induce its recipients to such conduct. 354 U. S., at 486-487. But that case dealt with public distribution of obscene materials and such distribution is subject to different objections. For example, there is always the danger that obscene material might fall into the hands of children, see *Ginsberg* v. *New York, supra,* or that it might intrude upon the sensibilities or privacy of the general public.[10] see *Redrup* v. *New York*, 386 U. S. 767, 769 (1967). No such dangers are present in this case.

Finally, we are faced with the argument that prohibition of possession of obscene materials is a necessary incident to statutory schemes prohibiting distribution. That argument is based on alleged difficulties of proving an intent to distribute or in producing evidence of actual distribution. We are not convinced that such difficulties exist, but even if they did we do not think that they would justify infringement of the individual's right to read or observe what he pleases. Because that right is so fundamental to our scheme of individual liberty, its restriction may not be justified by the need to ease the administration of otherwise valid criminal laws. See *Smith* v. *California*, 361 U. S. 147 (1959).

We hold that the First and Fourteenth Amendments prohibit making mere private possession of obscene material a crime.[11] *Roth* and the cases following that decision are not impaired by today's holding. As we have said, the States retain broad power to regulate obscenity; that power simply does not extend to mere possession by the individual in the privacy of his own home. Accordingly, the judgment of the court below is reversed and the case is remanded for proceedings not inconsistent with this opinion.

It is so ordered.

NOTES

1. "Any person who shall knowingly bring or cause to be brought into this State for sale or exhibition, or shall knowingly sell or offer to sell, or who shall knowingly lend or give away or offer to lend or give away, or who shall knowingly have possession of, or who shall knowingly exhibit or transmit to another, any obscene matter, or who shall knowingly advertise for sale any form of notice, printed, written, or verbal, any obscene matter, or who shall knowingly manufacture, draw, duplicate or print any obscene matter with intent to sell, expose or circulate the same, shall, if such person has knowledge or reasonably should know of the obscene nature of such matter, be guilty of a felony, and, upon conviction thereof, shall be punished by confinement in the penitentiary for not less than one year nor more than five years: Provided, however, in the event the jury so recommends, such per-

son may be punished as for a misdemeanor. As used herein, a matter is obscene if, considered as a whole, applying contemporary community standards, its predominant appeal is to prurient interest, i. e., a shameful or morbid interest in nudity, sex or excretion." Ga. Code Ann. § 26-6301 (Supp. 1968).

2. Appellant does not argue that the films are not obscene. For the purpose of this opinion, we assume that they are obscene under any of the tests advanced by members of this Court. See *Redrup* v. *New York*, 386 U. S. 767 (1967).

3. The issue was before the Court in *Mapp* v. *Ohio*, 367 U. S. 643 (1961), but that case was decided on other grounds. MR. JUSTICE STEWART, although disagreeing with the majority opinion in *Mapp*, would have reversed the judgment in that case on the ground that the Ohio statute proscribing mere possession of obscene material was "not 'consistent with the rights of free thought and expression assured against state action by the Fourteenth Amendment.'" *Id.*, at 672.

4. 18 U.S.C. § 1461.

5. *Ex parte Jackson*, 96 U. S. 727, 736-737 (1878) (use of the mails); *United States* v. *Chase*, 135 U. S. 255, 261 (1890) (use of the mails); *Robertson* v. *Baldwin*, 165 U. S. 275, 281 (1897) (publication); *Public Clearing House* v. *Coyne*, 194 U. S. 497, 508 (1904) (use of the mails); *Hoke* v. *United States*, 227 U. S. 308, 322 (1913) (use of interstate facilities); *Near* v. *Minnesota*, 283 U. S. 697, 716 (1931) (publication); *Chaplinsky* v. *New Hampshire*, 315 U. S. 568, 571-572 (1942) (utterances); *Hannegan* v. *Esquire, Inc.*, 327 U. S. 146, 158 (1946) (use of the mails); *Winters* v. *New York*, 333 U. S. 507, 510 (1948) (possession with intent to sell); *Beauharnais* v. *Illinois*, 343 U. S. 250, 266 (1952) (libel).

6. Many of the cases involved prosecutions for sale or distribution of obscene materials or possession with intent to sell or distribute. See *Redrup* v. *New York*, 386 U. S. 767 (1967); *Mishkin* v. *New York*, 383 U. S. 502 (1966); *Ginzberg* v. *United States*, 383 U.S. 463 (1966); *Jacobellis* v. *Ohio*, 378 U.S. 184 (1964); *Smith* v. *California*, 361 U. S. 147 (1959). Our most recent decision involved a prosecution for sale of obscene material to children. *Ginsberg* v. *New York*, 390 U. S. 629 (1968); cf. *Interstate Circuit, Inc.* v. *City of Dallas*, 390 U. S. 676 (1968). Other cases involved federal or state statutory procedures for preventing the distribution or mailing of obscene material, or procedures for predistribution approval. See *Freedman* v. *Maryland*, 380 U.' S. 51 (1965); *Bantam Books, Inc.* v. *Sullivan*, 372 U. S. 58 (1963); *Manual Enterprises, Inc.* v. *Day*, 370 U. S. 478 (1962). Still another case dealt with an attempt to seize obscene material "kept for the purpose of being sold, published, exhibited...or otherwise distri-

buted or circulated...." *Marcus* v. *Search Warrant*, 367 U. S. 717, 719 (1961); see also *A Quantity of Books* v. *Kansas*, 378 U. S. 205 (1964). *Memoirs* v. *Massachusetts*, 383 U..S. 413 (1966), was a proceeding in equity against a book. However, possession of a book determined to be obscene in such a proceeding was made criminal only when "for the purpose of sale, loan or distribution." *Id.*, at 422.

7. The Supreme Court of Ohio considered the issue in *State* v. *Mapp*, 170 Ohio St. 427, 166 N. E. 2d 387 (1960). Four of the seven judges of that court felt that criminal prosecution for mere private possession of obscene materials was prohibited by the Constitution. However, Ohio law required the concurrence of "all but one of the judges" to declare a state law unconstitutional. The view of the "dissenting" judges was expressed by Judge Herbert:

"I cannot agree that mere private possession of... [obscene] literature by an adult should constitute a crime. The right of the individual to read, to believe or disbelieve, and to think without governmental supervision is one of our basic liberties, but to dictate to the mature adult what books he may have in his own private library seems to the writer to be a clear infringement of his constitutional rights as an individual." 170 Ohio St., at 437, 166 N. E. 2d, at 393.

Shortly thereafter, the Supreme Court of Ohio interpreted the Ohio statute to require proof of "possession and control for the purpose of circulation or exhibition." *State* v. *Jacobellis*, 173 Ohio St. 22, 27-28, 179 N. E. 2d 777, 781 (1962), rev'd on other grounds, 378 U. S. 184 (1964). The interpretation was designed to avoid the constitutional problem posed by the "dissenters" in *Mapp*. See *State* v. *Ross*, 12 Ohio St. 2d 37, 231 N.E. 2d 299 (1967).

Other cases dealing with nonpublic distribution of obscene material or with legitimate uses of obscene material have expressed similar reluctance to make such activity criminal, albeit largely on statutory grounds. In *United States* v. *Chase*, 135 U. S. 255 (1890), the Court held that federal law did not make criminal the mailing of a private sealed obscene letter on the ground that the law's purpose was to purge the mails of obscene matter "as far as was consistent with the rights reserved to the people, and with a due regard to the security of private correspondence...." 135 U. S., at 261. The law was later amended to include letters and was sustained in that form. *Andrews* v. *United States*, 162 U. S. 420 (1896). In *United States* v. *31 Photographs*, 156 F. Supp. 350 (D. C. S. D. N. Y. 1957), the court denied an attempt by the Government to confiscate certain materials sought to be imported into the United States by the Institute for Sex Research, Inc., at Indiana University. The court found, applying the *Roth* formulation, that the materials would not appeal to the "prurient interest" of those seeking to import and utilize the materials. Thus, the statute permitting seizure of "obscene" materials was not applicable. The court found it unnecessary to reach the constitutional questions presented by the claimant, but did note its belief that "the statement...[in *Roth*] concerning the rejection of obscenity must be interpreted in the light of the widespread distribution of the material in Roth." 156 F. Supp., at 360, n. 40. See also *Redmond* v. *United States*, 384 U. S. 264 (1966), where this Court granted the Solicitor General's motion to vacate and remand with instructions to dismiss an information charging a violation of a federal obscenity statute in a case where a husband and wife mailed undeveloped films of each other posing in the nude to an out-of-state firm for developing. But see *Ackerman* v. *United States*, 293 F. 2d 449 (C. A. 9th Cir. 1961).

8. "Communities believe, and act on the belief, that obscenity is immoral, is wrong for the individual, and has no place in a decent society. They believe, too, that adults as well as children are corruptible in morals and character, and that obscenity is a source of corruption that should be eliminated. Obscenity is not suppressed primarily for the protection of others. Much of it is suppressed for the purity of the community and for the salvation and welfare of the 'consumer.' Obscenity, at bottom, is not crime. Obscenity is sin." Henkin, Morals and the Constitution: The Sin of Obscenity. 63 Col. L. Rev. 391, 395 (1963).

9. See, e. g., Cairns, Paul, & Wishner, Sex Censorship: The Assumptions of Anti-Obscenity Laws and the Empirical Evidence, 46 Minn. L. Rev. 1009 (1962): see also M. Jahoda, The Impact of Literature: A Psychological Discussion of Some Assumptions in the Censorship Debate (1954), summarized in the concurring opinion of Judge Frank in *United States* v. *Roth*, 237 F. 2d 796, 814-816 (C. A. 2d Cir. 1956).

10. The Model Penal Code provisions dealing with obscene materials are limited to cases of commercial dissemination. Model Penal Code § 251.4 (Prop. Official Draft 1962); see also Model Penal Code § 207.10 and comment 4 (Tent. Draft No. 6, 1957); H. Packer, The Limits of the Criminal Sanction 316-328 (1968); Schwartz, Morals Offenses and the Model Penal Code, 63 Col. L. Rev. 669 (1963).

11. What we have said in no way infringes upon the power of the State or Federal Government to make possession of other items, such as narcotics, firearms, or stolen goods, a crime. Our holding in the present case turns upon the Georgia statute's infringement of fundamental liberties protected by the First and Fourteenth Amendments. No First Amendment rights are involved in most statutes making mere possession criminal.

Nor do we mean to express any opinion on statutes making criminal possession of other types of printed, filmed, or recorded materials. See, e. g., 18 U. S. C. § 793 (d), which makes criminal the otherwise lawful possession of materials which "the possessor has reason to believe could be used to the injury of the United States or to the advantage of any foreign nation ...." In such cases, compelling reasons may exist for overriding the right of the individual to possess those materials.

*In deciding that those persons who are person-
ally attacked during a broadcast discussion of
a controversial issue and politicians who are
editorially attacked by a station endorsing
another political candidate must be given the
opportunity by the station to answer the charges, in upholding the constitutionality of the
"fairness doctrine," the United States Supreme
Court stated: "It is the right of the viewers
and listeners, not the right of the broadcasters, which is paramount....It is the purpose of
the First Amendment to preserve an uninhibited
marketplace of ideas in which truth will ultimately prevail, rather than to countenance monopolization of that market, whether it be by
the Government itself or a private licensee.... It is the right of the public to receive suitable access to social, political, esthetic, moral, and other ideas and experiences
which is crucial here. That right may not constitutionally be abridged either by Congress or
by the FCC."*

Red Lion Broadcasting Co. v. *FCC,* 395
U. S. 365 (1969)

MR. JUSTICE WHITE delivered the opinion of
the Court.

The Federal Communications Commission has
for many years imposed on radio and television
broadcasters the requirement that discussion of
public issues be presented on broadcast stations, and that each side of those issues must
be given fair coverage. This is known as the
fairness doctrine, which originated very early
in the history of broadcasting and has maintained its present outlines for some time. It
is an obligation whose content has been defined in a long series of FCC rulings in particular cases, and which is distinct from the
statutory requirement of § 315 of the Communications Act[1] that equal time be allotted all
qualified candidates for public office. Two
aspects of the fairness doctrine, relating to
personal attacks in the context of controversial public issues and to political editorializing, were codified more precisely in the form
of FCC regulations in 1967. The two cases before us now, which were decided separately below, challenge the constitutional and statutory
bases of the doctrine and component rules.
Red Lion involves the application of the
fairness doctrine to a particular broadcast,
and *RTNDA* arises as an action to review the
FCC's 1967 promulgation of the personal attack
and political editorializing regulations, which
were laid down after the *Red Lion* litigation
had begun.

I.

A.

The Red Lion Broadcasting Company is licensed to operate a Pennsylvania radio station,
WGCB. On November 27, 1964, WGCB carried a
15-minute broadcast by the Reverend Billy James
Hargis as part of a "Christian Crusade" series. A book by Fred J. Cook entitled
"Goldwater--Extremist on the Right" was discussed by Hargis, who said that Cook had been
fired by a newspaper for making false charges
against city officials; that Cook had then
worked for a Communist-affiliated publication;
that he had defended Alger Hiss and attacked J.
Edgar Hoover and the Central Intelligence
Agency; and that he had now written a "book to
smear and destroy Barry Goldwater."[2] When
Cook heard of the broadcast he concluded that
he had been personally attacked and demanded
free reply time, which the station refused.
After an exchange of letters among Cook, Red
Lion, and the FCC, the FCC declared that the
Hargis broadcast constituted a personal attack
on Cook; that Red Lion had failed to meet its
obligation under the fairness doctrine as expressed in *Times-Mirror Broadcasting Co.,* 24
P & F Radio Reg. 404 (1962), to send a tape,
transcript, or summary of the broadcast to Cook
and offer him reply time; and that the station
must provide reply time whether or not Cook
would pay for it. On review in the Court of
Appeals for the District of Columbia Circuit,[3] the FCC's position was upheld as constitutional and otherwise proper. 127 U. S.
App. D. C. 129, 381 F. 2d 908 (1967).

B.

Not long after the *Red Lion* litigation was
begun, the FCC issued a Notice of Proposed Rule
Making, 31 Fed. Reg. 5710, with an eye to
making the personal attack aspect of the fairness doctrine more precise and more readily enforceable, and to specifying its rules relating
to political editorials. After considering
written comments supporting and opposing the
rules, the FCC adopted them substantially as
proposed, 32 Fed. Reg. 10303. Twice amended,
32 Fed. Reg. 11531, 33 Fed. Reg. 5362, the
rules were held unconstitutional in the *RTNDA*
litigation by the Court of Appeals for the
Seventh Circuit, on review of the rule-making
proceeding, as abridging the freedoms of speech
and press. 400 F. 2d 1002 (1968).

As they now stand amended, the regulations
read as follows:

"Personal attacks; political editorials.

"(a) When, during the presentation of
views on a controversial issue of public importance, an attack is made upon the hon-
esty, character, integrity or like personal
qualities of an identified person or group,
the licensee shall, within a reasonable time
and in no event later than 2 weeks after the
attack, transmit to the person or group attacked (1) notification of the date, time

and identification of the broadcast; (2) a script or tape (or an accurate summary if a script or tape is not available) of the attack; and (3) an offer of a reasonable opportunity to respond over the licensee's facilities.

"(b) The provisions of paragraph (a) of this section shall not be applicable (1) to attacks on foreign groups or foreign public figures; (2) to personal attacks which are made by legally qualified candidates, their authorized spokesmen, or those associated with them in the campaign, on other such candidates, their authorized spokesmen, or persons associated with the candidates in the campaign; and (3) to bona fide newscasts, bona fide news interviews, and on-the-spot coverage of a bona fide news event (including commentary or analysis contained in the foregoing programs, but the provisions of paragraph (a) of this section shall be applicable to editorials of the licensee).

"NOTE: The fairness doctrine is applicable to situations coming within [(3)], above, and in a specific factual situation, may be applicable in the general area of political broadcasts [(2)], above. See, section 315 (a) of the Act, 47 U. S. C. 315 (a); Public Notice: *Applicability of the Fairness Doctrine in the Handling of Controversial Issues of Public Importance*. 29 F. R. 10415. The categories listed in [(3)] are the same as those specified in section 315 (a) of the Act.

"(c) Where a licensee, in an editorial, (i) endorses or (ii) opposes a legally qualified candidate or candidates, the licensee shall, within 24 hours after the editorial, transmit to respectively (i) the other qualified candidate or candidates for the same office or (ii) the candidate opposed in the editorial (1) notification of the date and the time of the editorial; (2) a script or tape of the editorial; and (3) an offer of a reasonable opportunity for a candidate or a spokesman of the candidate to respond over the licensee's facilities: *Provided, however,* That where such editorials are broadcast within 72 hours prior to the day of the election, the licensee shall comply with the provisions of this paragraph sufficiently far in advance of the broadcast to enable the candidate or candidates to have a reasonable opportunity to prepare a response and to present it in a timely fashion." 47 CFR §§ 73.123, 73.300, 73.598, 73.679 (all identical).

C.

Believing that the specific application of the fairness doctrine in *Red Lion*, and the promulgation of the regulations in *RTNDA*, are both authorized by Congress and enhance rather than abridge the freedoms of speech and press protected by the First Amendment, we hold them valid and constitutional, reversing the judgment below in *RTNDA* and affirming the judgment below in *Red Lion*.

II.

The history of the emergence of the fairness doctrine and of the related legislation shows that the Commission's action in the *Red Lion* case did not exceed its authority, and that in adopting the new regulations the Commission was implementing congressional policy rather than embarking on a frolic of its own.

A.

Before 1927, the allocation of frequencies was left entirely to the private sector, and the result was chaos.[4] It quickly became apparent that broadcast frequencies constituted a scarce resource whose use could be regulated and rationalized only by the Government. Without government control, the medium would be of little use because of the cacaphony of competing voices, none of which could be clearly and predictably heard.[5] Consequently, the Federal Radio Commission was established to allocate frequencies among competing applicants in a manner responsive to the public "convenience, interest, or necessity."[6]

Very shortly thereafter the Commission expressed its view that the "public interest requires ample play for the free and fair competition of opposing views, and the commission believes that the principle applies...to all discussions of issues of importance to the public." *Great Lakes Broadcasting Co.*, 3 F. R. C. Ann. Rep. 32,33 (1929), rev'd on other grounds, 59 App. D. C. 197, 37 F. 2d 993, cert. dismissed, 281 U. S. 706 (1930). This doctrine was applied through denial of license renewals or construction permits, both by the FRC, *Trinity Methodist Church, South* v. *FRC*, 61 App. D. C. 311, 62 F. 2d 850 (1932), cert. denied, 288 U. S. 599 (1933), and its successor FCC, *Young People's Association for the Propagation of the Gospel*, 6 F. C. C. 178 (1938). After an extended period during which the licensee was obliged not only to cover and to cover fairly the views of others, but also to refrain from expressing his own personal views, *Mayflower Broadcasting Corp.*, 8 F. C. C. 333 (1940), the latter limitation on the licensee was abandoned and the doctrine developed into its present form.

There is a twofold duty laid down by the FCC's decisions and described by the 1949 Report on Editorializing by Broadcast Licensees, 13 F. C. C. 1246 (1949). The broadcaster must give adequate coverage to public issues, *United Broadcasting Co.*, 10 F. C. C. 515 (1945), and coverage must be fair in that it accurately reflects the opposing views. *New Broadcasting Co.*, 6 P & F Radio Reg. 258 (1950). This must be done at the broadcaster's own expense if sponsorship is unavailable. *Cullman Broadcasting Co.*, 25 P & F Radio Reg. 895 (1963). Moreover, the duty must be met by programming obtained at the licensee's own initiative if available from no other source. *John J. Dempsey*, 6 P & F Radio Reg. 615 (1950); see *Metropolitan Broadcasting Corp.*,

19 P & F Radio Reg. 602 (1960); *The Evening News Assn.*, 6 P & F Radio Reg. 283 (1950). The Federal Radio Commission had imposed these two basic duties on broadcasters since the outset, *Great Lakes Broadcasting Co.*, 3 F. R. C. Ann. Rep. 32 (1929), rev'd on other grounds, 59 App. D. C. 197, 37 F. 2d 993, cert. dismissed, 281 U. S. 706 (1930); *Chicago Federation of Labor v. FRC*, 3 F. R. C. Ann. Rep. 36 (1929), aff'd, 59 App. D. C. 333, 41 F. 2d 422 (1930); *KFKB Broadcasting Assn. v. FRC*, 60 App. D. C. 79, 47 F. 2d 670 (1931), and in particular respects the personal attack rules and regulations at issue here have spelled them out in greater detail.

When a personal attack has been made on a figure involved in a public issue, both the doctrine of cases such as *Red Lion* and *Times-Mirror Broadcasting Co.*, 24 P & F Radio Reg. 404 (1962), and also the 1967 regulations at issue in *RTNDA* require that the individual attacked himself be offered an opportunity to respond. Likewise, where one candidate is endorsed in a political editorial the other candidates must themselves be offered reply time to use personally or through a spokesman. These obligations differ from the general fairness requirement that issues be presented, and presented with coverage of competing views, in that the broadcaster does not have the option of presenting the attacked party's side himself or choosing a third party to represent that side. But insofar as there is an obligation of the broadcaster to see that both sides are presented, and insofar as that is an affirmative obligation, the personal attack doctrine and regulations do not differ from the preceding fairness doctrine. The simple fact that the attacked men or unendorsed candidates may respond themselves or through agents is not a critical distinction, and indeed, it is not unreasonable for the FCC to conclude that the objective of adequate presentation of all sides may best be served by allowing those most closely affected to make the response, rather than leaving the response in the hands of the station which has attacked their candidacies, endorsed their opponents, or carried a personal attack upon them.

B.

The statutory authority of the FCC to promulgate these regulations derives from the mandate to the "Commission from time to time, as public convenience, interest, or necessity requires" to promulgate "such rules and regulations and prescribe such restrictions and conditions...as may be necessary to carry out the provisions of this chapter...." 47 U. S. C. § 303 and § 303 (r).[7] The Commission is specifically directed to consider the demands of the public interest in the course of granting licenses, 47 U. S. C. §§ 307 (a), 309 (a); renewing them, 47 U. S. C. § 307; and modifying them. *Ibid.* Moreover, the FCC has included among the conditions of the Red Lion license itself the requirement that operation of the station be carried out in the public interest,

47 U. S. C. § 309 (h). This mandate to the FCC to assure that broadcasters operate in the public interest is a broad one, a power "not niggardly but expansive," *National Broadcasting Co. v. United States*, 319 U. S. 190, 219 (1943), whose validity we have long upheld. *FCC v. Pottsville Broadcasting Co.*, 309 U. S. 134, 138 (1940); *FCC v. RCA Communications, Inc.*, 346 U. S. 86, 90 (1953); *FRC v. Nelson Bros. Bond & Mortgage Co.*, 289 U. S 266, 285 (1933). It is broad enough to encompass these regulations.

The fairness doctrine finds specific recognition in statutory form, is in part modeled on explicit statutory provisions relating to political candidates, and is approvingly reflected in legislative history.

In 1959 the Congress amended the statutory requirement of § 315 that equal time be accorded each political candidate to except certain appearances on news programs, but added that this constituted no exception *"from the obligation imposed upon them under this Act to operate in the public interest and to afford reasonable opportunity for the discussion of conflicting views on issues of public importance."* Act of September 14, 1959, § 1, 73 Stat. 557, amending 47 U. S. C. § 315 (a) (emphasis added). This language makes it very plain that Congress, in 1959, announced that the phrase "public interest," which had been in the Act since 1927, imposed a duty on broadcasters to discuss both sides of controversial public issues. In other words, the amendment vindicated the FCC's general view that the fairness doctrine inhered in the public interest standard. Subsequent legislation declaring the intent of an earlier statute is entitled to great weight in statutory construction.[8] And here this principle is given special force by the equally venerable principle that the construction of a statute by those charged with its execution should be followed unless there are compelling indications that it is wrong,[9] especially when Congress has refused to alter the administrative construction.[10] Here, the Congress has not just kept its silence by refusing to overturn the administrative construction,[11] but has ratified it with positive legislation. Thirty years of consistent administrative construction left undisturbed by Congress until 1959, when that construction was expressly accepted, reinforce the natural conclusion that the public interest language of the Act authorized the Commission to require licensees to use their stations for discussion of public issues, and that the FCC is free to implement this requirement by reasonable rules and regulations which fall short of abridgment of the freedom of speech and press, and of the censorship proscribed by § 326 of the Act.[12]

The objectives of § 315 themselves could readily be circumvented but for the complementary fairness doctrine ratified by § 315. The section applies only to campaign appearances by candidates, and not by family, friends, campaign managers, or other supporters. Without the fairness doctrine, then, a licensee could ban all campaign appearances by candidates themselves from the air[13] and proceed to deliver over his station entirely to the supporters of one slate of candidates, to the exclusion of all others. In this way the broadcaster could have a far greater impact on the favored candidacy than he could by simply allowing a spot appearance by the candidate himself. It is the fairness doctrine as an aspect of the obligation to operate in the public interest, rather than § 315, which prohibits the broadcaster from taking such a step.

The legislative history reinforces this view of the effect of the 1959 amendment. Even before the language relevant here was added, the Senate report on amending § 315 noted that "broadcast frequencies are limited and, therefore, they have been necessarily considered a public trust. Every licensee who is fortunate in obtaining a license is mandated to operate in the public interest and has assumed the obligation of presenting important public questions fairly and without bias." S. Rep. No. 562, 86th Cong., 1st Sess., 8-9 (1959). See also, specifically adverting to Federal Communications Commission doctrine, id., at 13.

Rather than leave this approval solely in the legislative history, Senator Proxmire suggested an amendment to make it part of the Act. 105 Cong. Rec. 14457. This amendment, which Senator Pastore, a manager of the bill and a ranking member of the Senate Committee, considered "rather surplusage," 105 Cong. Rec. 14462, constituted a positive statement of doctrine[14] and was altered to the present merely approving language in the conference committee. In explaining the language to the Senate after the committee changes, Senator Pastore said: "We insisted that that provision remain in the bill, to be a continuing reminder and admonition to the Federal Communications Commission and to the broadcasters alike, that we were not abandoning the philosophy that gave birth to section 315, in giving the people the right to have a full and complete disclosure of conflicting views on news of interest to the people of the country." 105 Cong. Rec. 17830. Senator Scott, another Senate manager, added that: "It is intended to encompass all legitimate areas of public importance which are controversial," not just politics. 105 Cong. Rec. 17831.

It is true that the personal attack aspect of the fairness doctrine was not actually adjudicated until after 1959, so that Congress then did not have those rules specifically before it. However, the obligation to offer time to reply to a personal attack was presaged by the FCC's 1949 Report on Editorializing, which the FCC views as the prinicipal summary of its *ratio decidendi* in cases in this area:

"In determining whether to honor specific requests for time, the station will inevitably be confronted with such questions as...whether there may not be other available groups or individuals who might be more appropriate spokesmen for the particular point of view than the person making the request. The latter's person-

al involvement in the controversy may also be a factor which must be considered, for elementary considerations of fairness may dictate that time be allocated to a person or group which has been specifically attacked over the station, where otherwise no such oligation would exist." 13 F. C. C., at 1251-1252.

When the Congress ratified the FCC's implication of a fairness doctrine in 1959 it did not, of course, approve every past decision or pronouncement by the Commission on this subject, or give it a completely free hand for the future. The statutory authority does not go so far. But we cannot say that when a station publishes personal attacks or endorses political candidates, it is a misconstruction of the public interest standard to require the station to offer time for a response rather than to leave the response entirely within the control of the station which has attacked either the candidacies or the men who wish to reply in their own defense. When a broadcaster grants time to a political candidate, Congress itself requires that equal time be offered to his opponents. It would exceed our competence to hold that the Commission is unauthorized by the statute to employ a similar device where personal attacks or political editorials are broadcast by a radio or television station.

In light of the fact that the "public interest" in broadcasting clearly encompasses the presentation of vigorous debate of controversial issues of importance and concern to the public; the fact that the FCC has rested upon that language from its very inception a doctrine that these issues must be discussed, and fairly; and the fact that Congress has acknowledged that the analogous provisions of § 315 are not preclusive in this area, and knowingly preserved the FCC's complementary efforts, we think the fairness doctrine and its component personal attack and political editorializing regulations are a legitimate exercise of congressionally delegated authority. The Communications Act is not notable for the precision of its substantive standards and in this respect the explicit provisions of § 315, and the doctrine and rules at issue here which are closely modeled upon that section, are far more explicit than the generalized "public interest" standard in which the Commission ordinarily finds its sole guidance, and which we have held a broad but adequate standard before. *FCC v. RCA Communications, Inc.*, 346 U. S. 86, 90 (1953); *National Broadcasting Co., v. United States*, 319 U. S. 190, 216-217 (1943); *FCC v. Pottsville Broadcasting Co.*, 309 U. S. 134, 138 (1940); *FRC v. Nelson Bros. Bond & Mortgage Co.*, 289 U. S. 266, 285 (1933). We cannot say that the FCC's declaratory ruling in *Red Lion*, or the regulation at issue in *RTNDA*, are beyond the scope of the congressionally conferred power to assure that stations are operated by those whose possession of a license serves "the public interest."

III.

The broadcasters challenge the fairness doctrine and its specific manifestations in the personal attack and political editorial rules on conventional First Amendment grounds, alleging that the rules abridge their freedom of speech and press. Their contention is that the First Amendment protects their desire to use their allotted frequencies continuously to broadcast whatever they choose, and to exclude whomever they choose from ever using that frequency. No man may be prevented from saying or publishing what he thinks, or from refusing in his speech or other utterances to give equal weight to views of his opponents. This right, they say, applies equally to broadcasters.

A.

Although broadcasting is clearly a medium affected by a First Amendment interest, *United States v. Paramount Pictures, Inc.*, 334 U. S. 131, 166 (1948), differences in the characteristics of new media justify differences in the First Amendment standards applied to them.[15] *Joseph Burstyn, Inc. v. Wilson*, 343 U. S. 495, 503 (1952). For example, the ability of new technology to produce sounds more raucous than those of the human voice justifies restrictions on the sound level, and on the hours and places of use, of sound trucks so long as the restrictions are reasonable and applied without discrimination. *Kovacs v. Cooper*, 336 U. S. 77 (1949).

Just as the Government may limit the use of sound-amplifying equipment potentially so noisy that it drowns out civilized private speech, so may the Government limit the use of broadcast equipment. The right of free speech of a broadcaster, the user of a sound truck, or any other individual does not embrace a right to snuff out the free speech of others. *Associated Press v. United States*, 326 U. S. 1, 20 (1945).

When two people converse face to face, both should not speak at once if either is to be clearly understood. But the range of the human voice is so limited that there could be meaningful communications if half the people in the United States were talking and the other half listening. Just as clearly, half the people might publish and the other half read. But the reach of radio signals is incomparably greater than the range of the human voice and the problem of interference is a massive reality. The lack of know-how and equipment may keep many from the air, but only a tiny fraction of those with resources and intelligence can hope to communicate by radio at the same time if intelligible communication is to be had, even if the entire radio spectrum is utilized in the present state of commercially acceptable technology.

It was this fact, and the chaos which ensued from permitting anyone to use any frequency at whatever power level he wished, which made necessary the enactment of the Radio Act of 1927 and the Communications Act of 1934,[16] as the Court has noted at length before. *National Broadcasting Co. v. United States*, 319 U. S. 190, 210-214 (1943). It was this reality which at the very least necessitated first the division of the radio spectrum into portions reserved respectively for public broadcasting and for other important radio uses such as amateur operation, aircraft, police, defense, and navigation; and then the subdivision of each portion, and assignment of specific frequencies to individual users or groups of users. Beyond this, however, because the frequencies reserved for public broadcasting were limited in number, it was essential for the Government to tell some applicants that they could not broadcast at all because there was room for only a few.

Where there are substantially more individuals who want to broadcast than there are frequencies to allocate, it is idle to posit an unabridgeable First Amendment right to broadcast comparable to the right of every individual to speak, write, or publish. If 100 persons want broadcast licenses, but there are only 10 frequencies to allocate, all of them may have the same "right" to a license; but if there is to be any effective communication by radio, only a few can be licensed and the rest must be barred from the airwaves. It would be strange if the First Amendment, aimed at protecting and furthering communications, prevented the Government from making radio communication possible by requiring licenses to broadcast and by limiting the number of licenses so as not to overcrowd the spectrum.

This has been the consistent view of the Court. Congress unquestionably has the power to grant and deny licenses and to eliminate existing stations. *FRC v. Nelson Bros. Bond & Mortgage Co.*, 289 U. S. 266 (1933). No one has a First Amendment right to a license or to monopolize a radio frequency; to deny a station license because "the public interest" requires it "is not a denial of free speech." *National Broadcasting Co. v. United States*, 319, U. S. 190, 227 (1943).

By the same token, as far as the First Amendment is concerned those who are licensed stand no better than those to whom licenses are refused. A license permits broadcasting, but the licensee has no constitutional right to be the one who holds the license or to monopolize a radio frequency to the exclusion of his fellow citizens. There is nothing in the First Amendment which prevents the Government from requiring a licensee to share his frequency with others and to conduct himself as a proxy or fiduciary with obligations to present those views and which would otherwise, by necessity, be barred from the airwaves.

This is not to say that the First Amendment is irrelevant to public broadcasting. On the contrary, it has a major role to play as the Congress itself recognized in § 326, which forbids FCC interference with "the right of free speech by means of radio communication." Because of the scarcity of radio frequencies, the Government is permitted to put restraints on licenses in favor of others whose views should be expressed on this unique medium. But the people as a whole retain their interest in free speech by radio and their collective right to have the medium function consistently with the ends and purposes of the First Amendment. It is the right of the viewers and listeners, not the right of the broadcasters, which is paramount. See FCC v. *Sanders Bros. Radio Station*, 309 U. S. 470, 475 (1940); FCC v. *Allentown Broadcasting Corp.*, 349 U. S. 358, 361-362 (1955); 2 Z. Chafee, Government and Mass Communications 546 (1947). It is the purpose of the First Amendment to preserve an uninhibited marketplace of ideas in which truth will ultimately prevail, rather than to countenance monopolization of that market, whether it be the Government itself or a private licensee. *Associated Press* v. *United States*, 326 U. S. 1, 20 (1945); *New York Times Co.* v. *Sullivan*, 376 U. S. 254, 270 (1964); *Abrams* v. *United States*, 250 U. S. 616, 630 (1919) (Holmes, J., dissenting). "[S]peech concerning public affairs is more than self-expression; it is the essence of self-government." *Garrison* v. *Louisiana*, 379 U. S. 64, 74-75 (1964). See Brennan, The Supreme Court and the Meiklejohn Interpretation of the First Amendment, 79 Harv. L. Rev. 1 (1965). It is the right of the public to receive suitable access to social, political, esthetic, moral, and other ideas and experiences which is crucial here. That right may not constitutionally be abridged either by Congress or by the FCC.

B.

Rather than confer frequency monopolies on a relatively small number of licensees, in a Nation of 200,000,000, the Government could surely have decreed that each frequency should be shared among all or some of those who wish to use it, each being assigned a portion of the broadcast day or the broadcast week. The ruling and regulations at issue here do not go quite so far. They assert that under specified circumstances, a licensee must offer to make available a reasonable amount of broadcast time to those who have a view different from that which has already been expressed on his station. The expression of a political endorsement, or of a personal attack while dealing with a controversial public issue, simply triggers this time sharing. As we have said, the First Amendment confers no right on licensees to prevent others from broadcasting on "their" frequencies and no right to an unconditional monopoly of a scarce resource which the Government has denied others the right to use.

In terms of constitutional principle, and as enforced sharing of a scarce resource, the personal attack and political editorial rules are indistinguishable from the equal-time provision of § 315, a specific enactment of Congress requiring stations to set aside reply time under specified circumstances and to which the fairness doctrine and these constituent regulations are important complements. That provision, which has been part of the law since 1927, Radio Act of 1927, § 18, 44 Stat. 1170, has been held valid by this Court as an obligation of the licensee relieving him of any power in any way to prevent or censor the broadcast, and thus insulating him from liability for defamation. The constitutionality of the statute under the First Amendment was unquestioned.[17] *Farmers Educ. & Coop. Union* v. *WDAY*, 360 U. S. 525 (1959).

Nor can we say that it is inconsistent with the First Amendment goal of producing an informed public capable of conducting its own affairs to require a broadcaster to permit answers to personal attacks occurring in the course of discussing controversial issues, or to require that the political opponents of those endorsed by the station be given a chance to communicate with the public.[18] Otherwise, station owners and a few networks would have unfettered power to make time available only to the highest bidders, to communicate only their own views on public issues, people and candidates, and to permit on the air only those with whom they agreed. There is no sanctuary in the First Amendment for unlimited private censorship operating in a medium not open to all. "Freedom of the press from governmental interference under the First Amendment does not sanction repression of that freedom by private interests." *Associated Press* v. *United States*, 326 U. S. 1, 20 (1945).

C.

It is strenuously argued, however, that if political editorials or personal attacks will trigger an obligation in broadcasters to afford the opportunity for expression to speakers who need not pay for time and whose views are unpalatable to the licensees, then broadcasters will be irresistibly forced to self-censorship and their coverage of controversial public issues will be eliminated or at least rendered wholly ineffective. Such a result would indeed be a serious matter, for should licensees actually eliminate their coverage of controversial issues, the purposes of the doctrine would be stifled.

At this point, however, as the Federal Communications Commission has indicated, that possibility is at best speculative. The communications industry, and in particular the networks, have taken pains to present controversial issues in the past, and even now they do not assert that they intend to abandon their efforts in this regard.[19] It would be better if the FCC's encouragement were never necessary to induce the broadcasters to meet their responsibility. And if experience with the administration of these doctrines indicates that they have the net effect of reducing rather than enhancing the volume and quality of coverage, there will be time enough to reconsider the constitutional implications. The fairness doctrine in the past has had no such overall effect.

That this will occur now seems unlikely, however, since if present licensees should suddenly prove timorous, the Commission is not powerless to insist that they give adequate and fair attention to public issues. It does not violate the First Amendment to treat licensees given the privilege of using scarce radio frequencies as proxies for the entire community, obligated to give suitable time and attention to matters of great public concern. To condition the granting or renewal of licensees on a willingness to present representative community views on controversial issues is consistent with the ends and purposes of those constitutional provisions forbidding the abridgment of freedom of speech and freedom of the press. Congress need not stand idly by and permit those with licenses to ignore the problems which beset the people or to exclude from the airways anything but their own views of fundamental questions. The statute, long administrative practice, and cases are to this effect.

Licenses to broadcast do not confer ownership of designated frequencies, but only the temporary privilege of using them. 47 U. S. C. § 301. Unless renewed, they expire within three years. 47 U. S. C. § 307 (d). The statute mandates the issuance of licenses if the "public convenience, interest, or necessity will be served thereby." 47 U. S. C. § 307 (a). In applying this standard the Commission for 40 years has been choosing licensees based in part on their program proposals. In *FRC* v. *Nelson Bros. Bond & Mortgage Co.,* 289 U. S. 266, 279 (1933), the Court noted that in "view of the limited number of available broadcasting frequencies, the Congress has authorized allocation and licenses." In determining how best to allocate frequencies, the Federal Radio Commission considered the needs of competing communities and the programs offered by competing stations to meet those needs; moreover, if needs or programs shifted, the Commission could alter its allocations to reflect those shifts. *Id.,* at 285. In the same vein, in *FCC* v. *Pottsville Broadcasting Co.,* 309 U. S. 134, 137-138 (1940), the Court noted that the statutory standard was a supple instrument to effect congressional desires "to maintain...a grip on the dynamic aspects of radio transmission" and to allay fears that "in the absence of governmental control the public interest might be subordinated to monopolistic domination in the broadcasting field." Three years later the Court considered the validity of the Commission's chain broadcasting regulations, which among other things forbade stations from devoting too much time to network programs in order that there be suitable opportunity for local programs serving local needs. The Court upheld the regulations, unequivocally recognizing that the Commission was more than a traffic policeman concerned with the technical aspects of broadcasting and that it neither exceeded its powers under the statute nor transgressed the First Amendment in interesting itself in general program format and the kinds of programs broadcast by licensees. *National Broadcasting Co.* v. *United States,* 319 U. S. 190 (1943).

D.

The litigants embellish their First Amendment arguments with the contention that the regulations are so vague that their duties are impossible to discern. Of this point it is enough to say that, judging the validity of the regulations on their face as they are presented here, we cannot conclude that the FCC has been left a free hand to vindicate its own idiosyncratic conception of the public interest or of the requirements of free speech. Past adjudications by the FCC give added precision to the regulations; there was nothing vague about the FCC's specific ruling in *Red Lion* that Fred Cook should be provided an opportunity to reply. The regulations at issue in *RTNDA* could be employed in precisely the same way as the fairness doctrine was in *Red Lion.* Morever, the FCC itself has recognized that the applicability of its regulations to situations beyond the scope of past cases may be questionable, 32 Fed. Reg. 10303, 10304 and n. 6, and will not impose sanctions in such cases without warning. We need not approve every aspect of the fairness doctrine to decide these cases, and we will not now pass upon the constitutionality of these regulations by envisioning the most extreme applications conceivable, *United States* v. *Sullivan,* 332 U. S. 689, 694 (1948), but will deal with those problems if and when they arise.

We need not and do not now ratify every past and future decision by the FCC with regard to programming. There is no question here of the Commission's refusal to permit the broadcaster to carry a particular program or to publish his own views; of a discriminatory refusal to require the licensee to broadcast certain views which have been denied access to airwaves; of government censorship of a particular program contrary to § 326; or of the official government view dominating public broadcasting. Such questions would raise more serious First Amendment issues. But we do hold that the Congress and the Commission do not violate the First Amendment when they require a radio or television station to give reply time to answer personal attacks and political editorials.

E.

It is argued that even if at one time the lack of available frequencies for all who wished to use them justified the Government's choice of those who would best serve the public interest by acting as proxy for those who would present differing views, or by giving the latter access directly to broadcast facilities, this condition no longer prevails so that continuing control is not justified. To this there are several answers.

Scarcity is not entirely a thing of the past. Advances in technology, such as microwave transmission, have led to more efficient utilization of the frequency spectrum, but uses for that spectrum have also grown apace.[20] Portions of the spectrum must be reserved for vital uses unconnected with human communication, such as radio-navigational aids used by aircraft and vessels. Conflicts have even emerged between such vital functions as defense preparedness and experimentation in methods of averting midair collisions through radio warning devices.[21] "Land mobile services" such as police, ambulance, fire department, public utility, and other communications systems have been occupying an increasingly crowded portion of the frequency spectrum[22] and there are, apart from licensed amateur radio operators' equipment, 5,000,000 transmitters operated on the "citizens' band" which is also increasingly congested.[23] Among the various uses for radio frequency space, including marine, aviation, amateur, military, and common carrier users, there are easily enough claimants to permit use of the whole with an even smaller allocation to broadcast radio and television uses than now exists.

Comparative hearings between competing applicants for broadcast spectrum space are by no means a thing of the past. The radio spectrum has become so congested that at times it has been necessary to suspend new applications.[24] The very high frequency television spectrum is, in the the country's major markets, almost entirely occupied, although space reserved for ultra high frequency television transmission, which is a relatively recent development as a commercially viable alternative, has not yet been completely filled.[25]

The rapidity with which technological advances succeed one another to create more efficient use of spectrum space on the one hand, and to create new uses for that space by ever growing numbers of people on the other, makes it unwise to speculate on the future allocation of that space. It is enough to say that the resource is one of considerable and growing importance whose scarcity impelled its regulation by an agency authorized by Congress. Nothing in this record, or in our own researches, convinces us that the resource is no longer one for which there are more immediate and potential uses than can be accommodated, and for which wise planning is essential.[26] This does not mean, of course, that every possible wavelength must be occupied at every hour by some vital use in order to sustain the congressional judgment. The substantial capital investment required for many uses, in addition to the potentiality for confusion and interference inherent in any scheme for continuous kaleidoscopic reallocation of all available space may make this unfeasible. The allocation need not be made at such a breakneck pace that the objectives of the allocation are themselves imperiled.[27]

Even where there are gaps in spectrum utilization, the fact remains that existing broadcasters have often attained their present position because of their initial government selection in competition with others before new technological advances opened new opportunities for further uses. Long experience in broadcasting, confirmed habits of listeners and viewers, network affiliation, and other advantages in program procurement give existing broadcasters a substantial advantage over new entrants, even where new entry is technologically possible. These advantages are the fruit of a preferred position conferred by government. Some present possibility for new entry by competing stations is not enough, in itself to render unconstitutional the Government's effort to assure that a broadcaster's programming ranges widely enough to serve the public interest.

In view of the scarcity of broadcast frequencies, the Government's role in allocating those frequencies, and the legitimate claims of those unable without governmental assistance to gain access to those frequencies for expression of their views, we hold the regulations and ruling at issue here are both authorized by statute and constitutional.[28] The judgment of the Court of Appeals in *Red Lion* is affirmed and that in *RTNDA* reversed and the causes remanded for proceedings consistent with this opinion.

It is so ordered.

NOTES

1. Communications Act of 1934, Tit. III, 48 Stat. 1081, as amended, 47 U. S. C. § 301 *et seq*. Section 315 now reads:

"315. Candidates for public office; facilities; rules.

"(a) If any licensee shall permit any person who is a legally qualified candidate for any public office to use a broadcasting station, he shall afford equal opportunities to all other such candidates for that office in the use of such broadcasting station: *Provided*, That such licensee shall have no power of censorship over the material broadcast under the provisions of this section. No obligation is imposed upon any licensee to allow the use of its station by any such candidate. Appearance by a legally qualified candidate on any--

"(1) bona fide newscast,

"(2) bona fide news interview,

"(3) bona fide news documentary (if the appearance of the candidate is incidental to the presentation of the subject or subjects covered by the news documentary), or

"(4) on-the-spot coverage of bona fide events (including but not limited to political conventions and activities incidental thereto), shall not be deemed to be use of a broadcasting station within the meaning of this subsection. Nothing in the foregoing sentence shall be construed as relieving broadcasters, in connection with the presentation of newscasts, news interviews, news documentaries, and on-the-spot coverage of news events, from the obligation imposed upon them under this chapter to operate in the public interest and to afford reasonable opportunity for the discussion of conflicting views on issues of public importance.

"(b) The charges made for the use of any broadcasting station for any of the purposes set forth in this section shall not exceed the charges made for comparable use of such station for other purposes.

"(c) The Commission shall prescribe appropriate rules and regulations to carry out the provisions of this section"

2. According to the record, Hargis asserted that his broadcast included the following statement:

"Now, this paperback book by Fred J. Cook is entitled, 'GOLDWATER--EXTREMIST ON THE RIGHT." Who is Cook? Cook was fired from the New York World Telegram after he made a false charge publicly on television against an un-named official of the New York City government. New York publishers and NEWSWEEK Magazine for December 7, 1959, showed that Fred Cook and his pal, Eugene Gleason, had made up the whole story and this confession was made to the New York District Attorney, Frank Hogan. After losing his job, Cook went to work for the left-wing publication, THE NATION, one of the most scurrilous publications of the left which has championed many communist causes over many years. Its editor, Carry McWilliams, has been affiliated with many communist enterprises, scores of which have been cited as subversive by the Attorney General of the U. S. or by other government agencies.... Now, among other things Fred Cook wrote for THE NATION, was an article absolving Alger Hiss of any wrong doing ... there was a 208 page attack on the FBI and J. Edgar Hoover; another attack by Mr. Cook was on the Central Intelligence Agency ... now this is the man who wrote the book to smear and destroy Barry Goldwater called 'Barry Goldwater--Extremist Of The Right!'"

3. The Court of Appeals initially dismissed the petition for want of a reviewable order, later reversing itself en banc upon argument by the Government that the FCC rule used here, which permits it to issue "a declaratory ruling terminating a controversy or removing uncertainty," 47 CFR § 1.2, was in fact justified by the Administrative Procedure Act. That Act permits an adjudicating agency, "in its sound discretion, with like effect as in the case of other orders, to issue a declaratory order to terminate a controversy or remove uncertainty." §5, 60 Stat. 239, 5 U. S. C. § 1004 (d). In this case, the FCC could have determined the question of Red Lion's liability to a cease-and-desist order or license revocation, 47 U. S. C. § 312, for failure to comply with the license's condition that the station be operated "in the public interest," or for failure to obey a requirement of operation in the public interest implicit

in the ability of the FCC to revoke licenses for conditions justifying the denial of an initial license, 47 U. S. C. § 312 (a) (2), and the statutory requirement that the public interest be served in granting and renewing licenses, 47 U. S. C. §§ 307 (a), (d). Since the FCC could have adjudicated these questions it could, under the Administrative Procedure Act, have issued a declaratory order in the course of its adjudication which would have been subject to judicial review. Although the FCC did not comply with all of the formalities for an adjudicative proceeding in this case, the petitioner itself adopted as its own the Government's position that this was a reviewable order, waiving any objection it might have had to the procedure of the adjudication.

4. Because of this chaos, a series of National Radio Conferences was held between 1922 and 1925, at which it was resolved that regulation of the radio spectrum by the Federal Government was essential and that regulatory power should be utilized to ensure that allocation of this limited resource would be made only to those who would serve the public interest. The 1923 Conference expressed the opinion that the Radio Communications Act of 1912, 37 Stat. 302, conferred upon the Secretary of Commerce the power to regulate frequencies and hours of operation, but when Secretary Hoover sought to implement this claimed power by penalizing the Zenith Radio Corporation for operating on an unauthorized frequency, the 1912 Act was held not to permit enforcement. *United States v. Zenith Radio Corporation*, 12 F. 2d 614 (D. C. N. D. Ill. 1926). Cf *Hoover v. Intercity Radio Co.*, 52 App. D. C. 339, 286 F. 1003 (1923) (Secretary had no power to deny licenses, but was empowered to assign frequencies). An opinion issued by the Attorney General at Hoover's request confirmed the impotence of the Secretary under the 1912 Act. 35 Op. Atty. Gen. 126 (1926). Hoover thereafter appealed to the radio industry to regulate itself, but his appeal went largely unheeded. See generally L. Schmeckebier, The Federal Radio Commission 1-14 (1932).

5. Congressman White, a sponsor of the bill enacted as the Radio Act of 1927, commented upon the need for new legislation:

"We have reached the definite conclusion that the right of all our people to enjoy this means of communication can be preserved only by the repudiation of the idea underlying the 1912 law that anyone who will may transmit and by the assertion in its stead of the doctrine that the right of the public to service is superior to the right of any individual.... The recent radio conference met this issue squarely. It recognized that in the present state of scientific development there must be a limitation upon the number of broadcasting stations and it recommended that licenses should be issued only to those stations whose operation would render a benefit to the public, are necessary in the public interest, or would contribute to the development of the art. This principle was approved by every witness before your committee. We have written it into the bill. If enacted into law, the broadcasting privilege will not be a right of selfishness. It will rest upon an assurance of public interest to be served." 67 Cong. Rec. 5479.

6. Radio Act of 1927, § 4, 44 Stat. 1163. See generally Davis, The Radio Act of 1927, 13 Va. L. Rev. 611 (1927).

7. As early as 1930, Senator Dill expressed the view that the Federal Radio Commission had the power to make regulations requiring a licensee to afford an opportunity for presentation of the other side on "public questions." Hearings before the Senate Committee on Interstate Commerce on S. 6, 71st Cong., 2d Sess., 1616 (1930):

"Senator Dill. Then you are suggesting that the provision of the statute that now requires a station to give equal opportunity to candidates for office shall be applied to all public questions?

"Commissioner Robinson. Of course, I think in the legal concept the law requires it now. I do not see that there is any need to legislate about it. It will evolve one of these days. Somebody will go into court and say, 'I am entitled to this opportunity,' and he will get it.

"Senator Dill. Has the Commission considered the question of making regulations requiring the stations to do that?

"Commissioner Robinson. Oh, no.

"Senator Dill. It would be within the power of the commission, I think, to make regulations on that subject."

8. Federal Housing Administration v. Darlington, Inc., 358 U. S. 84, 90 (1958); Glidden Co. v. Zdanok, 370 U. S. 530, 541 (1962) (opinion of Mr. Justice Harlan, joined by Mr. Justice Brennan and Mr. Justice Stewart). This principle is a venerable one. Alexander v. Alexandria, 5 Cranch 1 (1809); United States v. Freeman, 3 How. 556 (1845); Stockdale v. The Insurance Companies, 20 Wall. 323 (1874).

9. Zemel v. Rusk, 381 U. S. 1, 11–12 (1965); Udall v. Tallman, 380 U. S. 1, 16–18 (1965); Commissioner v. Sternberger's Estate, 348 U. S. 187, 199 (1955); Hastings & D. R. Co. v. Whitney, 132 U. S. 357, 366 (1889); United States v. Burlington & Missouri River R. Co., 98 U. S. 334, 341 (1879); United States v. Alexander, 12 Wall. 177, 179–181 (1871); Surgett v. Lapice, 8 How. 48, 68 (1850).

10. Zemel v. Rusk, 381 U. S. 1, 11–12 (1965); United States v. Bergh, 352 U. S. 40, 46–47 (1956); Alstate Construction Co. v. Durkin, 345 U. S. 13, 16–17 (1953); Costanzo v. Tillinghast, 287 U. S. 341, 345 (1932).

11. An attempt to limit sharply the FCC's power to interfere with programming practices failed to emerge from Committee in 1943. S. 814, 78th Cong., 1st Sess. (1943). See Hearings on S. 814 before the Senate Committee on Interstate Commerce, 78th Cong., 1st Sess. (1943). Also, attempts specifically to enact the doctrine failed in the Radio Act of 1927, 67 Cong. Rec. 12505 (1926) (agreeing to amendment proposed by Senator Dill eliminating coverage of "question affecting the public"), and a similar proposal in the Communications Act of 1934 was accepted by the Senate, 78 Cong. Rec. 8854 (1934); see S. Rep. No. 781, 73d Cong., 2d Sess., 8 (1934), but was not included in the bill reported by the House Committee, see H. R. Rep. No. 1850, 73d Cong., 2d Sess. (1934). The attempt which came nearest success was a bill, H. R. 7716, 72d Cong., 1st Sess. (1932), passed by Congress but pocket-vetoed by the President in 1933, which would have extended "equal opportunities" whenever a public question was to be voted on at an election or by a government agency. H. R. Rep. No. 2106, 72d Cong., 2d Sess., 6 (1933). In any event, unsuccessful attempts at legislation are not the best of guides to legislative intent. Fogarty v. United States, 340 U. S. 8, 13–14 (1950); United States v. United Mine Workers, 330 U. S. 258, 281–282 (1947). A review of some of the legislative history over the years, drawing a somewhat different conclusion, is found in Staff Study of the House Committee on Interstate and Foreign Commerce, Legislative History of the Fairness Doctrine, 90th Cong., 2d Sess. (Comm. Print. 1968). This inconclusive history was, of course, superseded by the specific statutory language added in 1959.

12. "§ 326. Censorship.

"Nothing in this chapter shall be understood or construed to give the Commission the power of censorship over the radio communications or signals transmitted by any radio station, and no regulation or condition shall be promulgated or fixed by the Commission which shall interfere with the right of free speech by means of radio communication."

13. John P. Crommelin, 19 P & F Radio Reg. 1392 (1960).

14. The Proxmire amendment read: "[B]ut nothing in this sentence shall be construed as changing the basic intent of Congress with respect to the provisions of this act, which recognizes that television and radio frequencies are in the public domain, that the license to operate in such frequencies requires operation in the public interest, and that in newscasts, news interviews, news documentaries, on-the-spot coverage of news events, and panel discussions, all sides of public controversies shall be given as equal an opportunity to be heard as is practically possible." 105 Cong. Rec. 14457.

15. The general problems raised by a technology

which **supplants** atomized, relatively informal **communication** with mass media as a
prime **source** of national cohesion and news
were **discussed** at considerable length by
Zechariah **Chafee** in Government and Mass
Communications (1947). Debate on the par-
ticular **implications of** this view for the
broadcasting **industry** has continued un-
abated. A **compendium of** views appears in
Freedom and **Responsibility** in Broadcasting
(J. Coons ed.) (1961). See also Kalven,
Broadcasting, Public Policy and the First
Amendment, 10 J. Law & Econ. 15 (1967); M.
Ernst, The First Freedom 125-180 (1946); T.
Robinson, Radio Networks and the Federal
Government, especially at 75-87 (1943).
The considerations which the newest technology brings to bear on the **particular** prob-
lem of this litigation are concisely ex-
plored by Louis Jaffe in The **Fairness** Doc-
trine, Equal Time, Reply to **Personal** At-
tacks, and the Local Service Obligation;
Implications of Technological Change,
Printed for Special Subcommittee on Investigations of the House Committee on Interstate and Foreign Commerce (1968).

16. The range of controls which have in fact
been imposed over the last 40 years, without giving rise to successful constitutional challenge in this Court, is discussed in
W. Emery, Broadcasting and Government: Responsibilities and Regulations (1961);
Note, Regulation of Program Content by the
FCC, 77 Harv. L. Rev. 701 (1964).

17. This has not prevented vigorous argument
from developing on the constitutionality of
the ancillary FCC doctrines. Compare
Barrow, The Equal Opportunities and Fairness Doctrines in Broadcasting: Pillars in
the Forum of Democracy, 37 U. Cin. L. Rev.
447 (1968), with Robinson, The FCC and the
First Amendment: Observations on 40 Years
of Radio and Television Regulation, 52
Minn. L. Rev. 67 (1967), and Sullivan,
Editorials and Controversy: The Broadcaster's Dilemma, 32 Geo. Wash. L. Rev. 719
(1964).

18. The expression of views opposing those
which broadcasters permit to be aired in
the first place need not be confined solely
to the broadcasters themselves as proxies.
"Nor is it enough that he should hear the
arguments of adversaries from his own
teachers, presented as they state them, and
accompanied by what they offer as refuta-
tions. That is not the way to do justice
to the arguments, or bring them into real
contact with his own mind. He must be able
to hear them from persons who actually believe them; who defend them in earnest, and
do their very utmost for them." J. Mill,
On Liberty 32 (R. McCallum ed. 1947).

19. The President of the Columbia Broadcasting
System has recently declared that despite
the Government, "we are determined to continue covering controversial issues as a
public service, and exercising our own independent news judgment and enterprise. I,
for one, refuse to allow that judgment and

enterprise to be affected by official intimidation." F. Stanton, Keynote Address,
Sigma Delta Chi National Convention,
Atlanta, Georgia, November 21, 1968. Problems of news coverage from the broadcaster's viewpoint are surveyed in W. Wood,
Electronic Journalism (1967).

20. Current discussions of the frequency allocation problem appear in Telecommunication
Science Panel, Commerce Technical Advisory
Board, U. S. Dept. of Commerce, Electromag-
netic Spectrum Utilization--The Silent
Crisis (1966); Joint Technical Advisory
Committee, Institute of Electrical and
Electronics Engineers and Electronic Indus-
tries Assn., Report on Radio Spectrum Utilization (1964); Note, The Crisis in Elec-
tromagnetic Frequency Spectrum Allocation,
53 Iowa L. Rev. 437 (1967). A recently released study is the Final Report of the
President's Task Force on Communications
Policy (1968).

21. *Bendix Aviation Corp.* v. *FCC*, 106, U.
S. App. D.C. 304, 272 F. 2d 533 (1959),
cert. denied, 361 U. S. 965 (1960).

22. 1968 FCC Annual Report 65-69.

23. New limitations on these users, who can lay
claim to First Amendment protection, were
sustained against First Amendment attack
with the comment, "Here is truly a situation where if everybody could say anything,
many could say nothing." *Lafayette Radio
Electronics Corp.* v. *United States*, 345
F. 2d 278, 281 (1965). Accord, *California
Citizens Band Assn.* v. *United States*,
375 F. 2d 43 (C.A. 9th Cir.), cert. denied,
389 U. S. 844 (1967).

24. *Kessler* v. *FCC*, 117 U. S. App. D.C.
130, 326 F. 2d 673 (1963).

25. In a table prepared by the FCC on the basis
of statistics current as of August 31,
1968, VHF and UHF channels allocated to and
those available in the top 100 market areas
for television are set forth:

COMMERCIAL

Market Areas	Channels Allocated		On the Air, Authorized, or Applied for		Available Channels	
	VHF	UHF	VHF	UHF	VHF	UHF
Top 10....	40	45	40	44	0	1
Top 50...	157	163	157	136	0	27
Top 100..	264	297	264	213	0	84

NONCOMMERCIAL

Market Areas	Channels Reserved		On the Air Authorized, or Applied for		Available Channels	
	VHF	UHF	VHF	UHF	VHF	UHF
Top 10....	7	17	7	16	0	1
Top 50...	21	79	20	47	1	32
Top 100..	35	138	34	69	1	69

1968 FCC Annual Report 132-135.

26. RTNDA argues that these regulations should
be held invalid for failure of the FCC to
make specific findings in the rule-making

proceeding relating to these factual questions. Presumably the fairness doctrine and the personal attack decisions themselves, such as *Red Lion*, should fall for the same reason. But this argument ignores the fact that these regulations are no more than the detailed specification of certain consequences of long-standing rules, the need for which was recognized by the Congress on the factual predicate of scarcity made plain in 1927, recognized by this Court in the 1943 *National Broadcasting Co.* case, and reaffirmed by the Congress as recently as 1959. ."If the number of radio and television stations were not limited by available frequencies, the committee would have no hesitation in removing completely the present provision regarding equal time and urge the right of each broadcaster to follow his own conscience.... However, broadcast frequencies are limited and, therefore they have been necessarily considered a public trust." S. Rep. No. 562, 86th Cong., 1st Sess., 8-9 (1959). In light of this history; the opportunity which the broadcasters have had to address the FCC and show that somehow the situation had radically changed, undercutting the validity of the congressional judgment; and their failure to adduce any convincing evidence of that in the record here, we cannot consider the absence of more detailed findings below to be determinative.

27. The "airwaves [need not] be filled at the earliest possible moment in all circumstances without due regard for these important factors." *Community Broadcasting Co.* v. *FCC*, 107 U. S. App. D.C. 95, 105, 274 F. 2d 753, 763 (1960). Accord, enforcing the fairness doctrine, *Office of Communication of the United Church of Christ* v. *FCC*, 123 U. S. App. D.C. 328, 343, 359 F. 2d 994, 1009 (1966).

28. We need not deal with the argument that even if there is no longer a technological scarcity of frequencies limiting the number of broadcasters, there nevertheless is an economic scarcity in the sense that the Commission could or does limit entry to the broadcasting market on economic grounds and license no more stations than the market will support. Hence, it is said, the fairness doctrine or its equivalent is essential to satisfy the claims of those excluded and of the public generally. A related argument, which we also put aside, is that quite apart from scarcity of frequencies, technological or economic, Congress does not abridge freedom of speech or press by legislation directly or indirectly multiplying the voices and views presented to the public through time sharing, fairness doctrines, or other devices which limit or dissipate the power of those who sit astride the channels of communication with the general public. Cf. *Citizen Publishing Co.* v. *United States*, 394 U.S. 131 (1969).

In deciding for a young man who had worn a jacket in public on the back of which were the words "Fuck the Draft," the United States Supreme Court concluded: "...absent a more particularized and compelling reason for its actions, the state may not, consistently with the First and Fourteenth Amendments, make the simple public display here involved of this single four-letter expletive a criminal offense." Justice Harlan, delivering the opinion of the Court, stated: "Surely the State has no right to cleanse public debate to the point where it is grammatically palatable to the most squeamish among us. Yet no readily ascertainable general principle exists for stopping short of that result were we to affirm the judgment below. For, while the particular four-letter word being litigated here is perhaps more distasteful than most others of its genre, it is nevertheless often true that one man's vulgarity is another's lyric....Finally, and in the same vein, we cannot indulge the facile assumption that one can forbid particular words without also running a substantial risk of suppressing ideas in the process. Indeed, governments might soon seize upon the censorship of particular words as a convenient guise for banning the expression of unpopular views."

Cohen v. *California*, 403 U. S. 15 (1971)

MR. JUSTICE HARLAN delivered the opinion of the Court.

This case may seem at first blush too inconsequential to find its way into our books, but the issue it presents is of no small constitutional significance.

Appellant Paul Robert Cohen was convicted in the Los Angeles Municipal Court of violating that part of the California Penal Code § 415 which prohibits "maliciously and willfully disturb[ing] the peace or quiet of any neighborhood or person . . . by . . . offensive conduct...."[1] He was given 30 days' imprisonment. The facts upon which his conviction rests are detailed in the opinion of the Court of Appeal of California, Second Appellate District, as follows:

"On April 26, 1968, the defendant was observed in the Los Angeles County Courthouse in the corridor outside of division 20 of the municipal court wearing a jacket bearing the words 'Fuck the Draft' which were plainly visible. There were women and children present in the corridor. The defendant was arrested. The defendant testified that he wore the jacket knowing that the words were on the jacket as a means of informing the public of the depth of his feelings against the Vietnam War and the draft.

"The defendant did not engage in, nor threaten to engage in, nor did anyone as the result of his conduct in fact commit or threaten to commit any act of violence. The defendant did not make any loud or unusual noise, nor was there any evidence that he uttered any sound prior to his arrest." 1 Cal. App. 3d 94, 97-98, 81 Cal Rptr. 503, 505 (1969).

In affirming the conviction the Court of Appeal held that "offensive conduct" means "behavior which has a tendency to provoke *others* to acts of violence or to in turn disturb the peace," and that the State had proved this element because, on the facts of this case, "[i]t was certainly reasonably foreseeable that such conduct might cause others to rise up to commit a violent act against the person of the defendant or attempt to forceably remove his jacket." 1 Cal. App. 3d, at 99-100, 81 Cal. Rptr., at 506. The California Supreme Court declined review by a divided vote.[2] We brought the case here, postponing the consideration of the question of our jurisdiction over this appeal to a hearing of the case on the merits. 399 U. S. 904. We now reverse.

The question of our jurisdiction need not detain us long. Throughout the proceedings below, Cohen consistently claimed that, as construed to apply to the facts of this case, the statute infringed his rights to freedom of expression guaranteed by the First and Fourteenth Amendments of the Federal Constitution. That contention has been rejected by the highest California state court in which review could be had. Accordingly, we are fully satisfied that Cohen has properly invoked our jurisdiction by this appeal. 28 U. S. C. § 1257 (2); *Dahnke-Walker Milling Co.* v. *Bondurant*, 257 U. S. 282 (1921).

I

In order to lay hands on the precise issue which this case involves, it is useful first to canvass various matters which this record does *not* present.

The conviction quite clearly rests upon the asserted offensiveness of the *words* Cohen used to convey his message to the public. The only "conduct" which the State sought to punish is the fact of communication. Thus, we deal here with a conviction resting solely upon "speech," cf. *Stromberg* v. *California*, 283 U. S. 359 (1931), not upon any separately identifiable conduct which allegedly was intended by Cohen to be perceived by others as expressive of particular views but which, on its face, does not necessarily convey any message and hence arguably could be regulated without effectively repressing Cohen's ability to express himself. Cf. *United States* v. *O'Brien*, 391 U. S. 367 (1968). Further, the State certainly lacks power to punish Cohen for the underlying content of the message the inscription conveyed. At least so long as there is no showing of an intent to incite disobedience to or disruption of the draft, Cohen could not, consistently with the First and Fourteenth Amendments, be punished for asserting the evident position on the inutility or immorality

of the draft his jacket reflected. *Yates* v. *United States*, 354 U. S. 298 (1957).

Appellant's conviction, then, rests squarely upon his exercise of the "freedom of speech" protected from arbitrary governmental interference by the Constitution and can be justified, if at all, only as a valid regulation of the manner in which he exercised that freedom, not as a permissible prohibition on the substantive message it conveys. This does not end the inquiry, of course, for the First and Fourteenth Amendments have never been thought to give absolute protection to every individual to speak whenever or wherever he pleases, or to use any form of address in any circumstances that he chooses. In this vein, too, however, we think it important to note that several issues typically associated with such problems are not presented here.

In the first place, Cohen was tried under a statute applicable throughout the entire State. Any attempt to support this conviction on the ground that the statute seeks to preserve an appropriately decorous atmosphere in the courthouse where Cohen was arrested must fail in the absence of any language in the statute that would have put appellant on notice that certain kinds of otherwise permissible speech or conduct would nevertheless, under California law, not be tolerated in certain places. See *Edwards* v. *South Carolina*, 372 U.S. 229, 236-237, and n. 11 (1963). Cf. *Adderley* v. *Florida*, 385 U. S. 39 (1966). No fair reading of the phrase "offensive conduct" can be said sufficiently to inform the ordinary person that distinctions between certain locations are thereby created.[3]

In the second place, as it comes to us, this case cannot be said to fall within those relatively few categories of instances where prior decisions have established the power of government to deal more comprehensively with certain forms of individual expression simply upon a showing that such a form was employed. This is not, for example, an obscenity case. Whatever else may be necessary to give rise to the States' broader power to prohibit obscene expression, such expression must be, in some significant way, erotic. *Roth* v. *United States*, 354 U. S. 476 (1957). It cannot plausibly be maintained that this vulgar allusion to the Selective Service System would conjure up such psychic stimulation in anyone likely to be confronted with Cohen's crudely defaced jacket.

This Court has also held that the States are free to ban the simple use, without a demonstration of additional justifying circumstances, of so-called "fighting words," those personally abusive epithets which, when addressed to the ordinary citizen, are, as a matter of common knowledge, inherently likely to provoke violent reaction. *Chaplinsky* v. *New Hampshire*, 315 U. S. 568 (1942). While the four-letter word displayed by Cohen in relation to the draft is not uncommonly employed in a personally provocative fashion, in this instance it was clearly not "directed to the person of the hearer." *Cantwell* v.

Connecticut, 310 U. S. 296, 309 (1940). No individual actually or likely to be present could reasonably have regarded the words on appellant's jacket as a direct personal insult. Nor do we have here an instance of the exercise of the State's police power to prevent a speaker from intentionally provoking a given group to hostile reaction. Cf. *Feiner* v. *New York*, 340 U. S. 315 (1951); *Terminiello* v. *Chicago*, 337 U.S. 1 (1949). There is, as noted above, no showing that anyone who saw Cohen was in fact violently aroused or that appellant intended such a result.

Finally, in arguments before this Court much has been made of the claim that Cohen's distasteful mode of expression was thrust upon unwilling or unsuspecting viewers, and that the State might therefore legitimately act as it did in order to protect the sensitive from otherwise unavoidable exposure to appellant's crude form of protest. Of course, the mere presumed presence of unwitting listeners or viewers does not serve automatically to justify curtailing all speech capable of giving offense. See, *e. g., Organization for a Better Austin* v. *Keefe*, 402 U. S. 415 (1971). While this Court has recognized that government may properly act in many situations to prohibit intrusion into the privacy of the home of unwelcome views and ideas which cannot be totally banned from the public dialogue, *e. g, Rowan* v. *Post Office Dept.*, 397 U. S. 728 (1970), we have at the same time consistently stressed that "we are often 'captives' outside the sanctuary of the home and subject to objectionable speech." *Id.*, at 738. The ability of government, consonant with the Constitution, to shut off discourse solely to protect others from hearing it is, in other words, dependent upon a showing that substantial privacy interests are being invaded in an essentially intolerable manner. Any broader view of this authority would effectively empower a majority to silence dissidents simply as a matter of personal predilections.

In this regard, persons confronted with Cohen's jacket were in a quite different posture than, say, those subjected to the raucous emissions of sound trucks blaring outside their residences. Those in the Los Angeles courthouse could effectively avoid further bombardment of their sensibilities simply by averting their eyes. And, while it may be that one has a more substantial claim to a recognizable privacy interest when walking through a courthouse corridor than, for example, strolling through Central Park, surely it is nothing like the interest in being free from unwanted expression in the confines of one's own home. Cf. *Keefe, supra.* Given the subtlety and complexity of the factors involved, if Cohen's "speech" was otherwise entitled to constitutional protection, we do not think the fact that some unwilling "listeners" in a public building may have been briefly exposed to it can serve to justify this breach of the peace conviction where, as here, there was no evidence that persons powerless to avoid appellant's conduct did in fact object to it, and where that portion of the statute upon which Cohen's conviction rests evinces no concern, either on its face or as construed by the California courts, with the special plight of the captive auditor, but, instead, indiscriminately sweeps within its prohibitions all "offensive conduct" that disturbs "any neighborhood or person." Cf *Edwards* v. *South Carolina, supra.*[4]

II

Against this background, the issue flushed by this case stands out in bold relief. It is whether California can excise, as "offensive conduct," one particular scurrilous epithet from the public discourse, either upon the theory of the court below that its use is inherently likely to cause violent reaction or upon a more general assertion that the States, acting as guardians of public morality, may properly remove this offensive word from the public vocabulary.

The rationale of the California court is plainly untenable. At most it reflects an "undifferentiated fear or apprehension of disturbance [which] is not enough to overcome the right to freedom of expression." *Tinker* v. *Des Moines Indep. Community School Dist.*, 393 U. S. 503, 508 (1969). We have been shown no evidence that substantial numbers of citizens are standing ready to strike out physically at whoever may assault their sensibilities with execrations like that uttered by Cohen. There may be some persons about with such lawless and violent proclivities, but that is an insufficient base upon which to erect, consistently with constitutional values, a governmental power to force persons who wish to ventilate their dissident views into avoiding particular forms of expression. The argument amounts to little more than the self-defeating proposition that to avoid physical censorship of one who has not sought to provoke such a response by a hypothetical coterie of the violent and lawless, the States may more appropriately effectuate that censorship themselves. Cf. *Ashton* v. *Kentucky*, 384 U. S. 195, 200 (1966); *Cox* v. *Louisiana*, 379 U. S. 536, 550-551 (1965).

Admittedly, it is not so obvious that the First and Fourteenth Amendments must be taken to disable the States from punishing public utterance of this unseemly expletive in order to maintain what they regard as a suitable level of discourse within the body politic.[5] We think, however, that examination and reflection will reveal the shortcomings of a contrary viewpoint.

At the outset, we cannot overemphasize that, in our judgment, most situations where the State has a justifiable interest in regulating speech will fall within one or more of the various established exceptions, discussed above but not applicable here, to the usual rule that governmental bodies may not prescribe the form or content of individual expression. Equally important to our conclusion is the constitutional backdrop against which our decision must be made. The constitutional right of free expression is powerful medicine in a society as diverse and populous as ours. It is designed and intended to remove governmental restraints from the arena of public discussion, putting the decision as to what views shall be voiced largely into the hands of each of us, in the hope that use of such freedom will ultimately produce a more capable citizenry and more perfect polity and in the belief that no other approach would comport with the premise of individual dignity and choice upon which our political system rests. See *Whitney* v. *California*, 274 U.S. 357, 375-377 (1927) (Brandeis, J., concurring).

To many, the immediate consequence of this freedom may often appear to be only verbal tumult, discord, and even offensive utterance. These are, however, within established limits, in truth necessary side effects of the broader enduring values which the process of open debate permits us to achieve. That the air may at times seem filled with verbal cacophony is, in this sense not a sign of weakness but of strength. We cannot lose sight of the fact that, in what otherwise might seem a trifling and annoying instance of individual distasteful abuse of a privilege, these fundamental societal values are truly implicated. That is why "[w]holly neutral futilities...come under the protection of free speech as fully as do Keats' poems or Donne's sermons," *Winters* v. *New York*, 333 U.S. 507, 528 (1948) (Frankfurter, J., dissenting), and why "so long as the means are peaceful, the communication need not meet standards of acceptability," *Organization for a Better Austin* v. *Keefe*, 402 U. S. 415, 419 (1971).

Against this perception of the constitutional policies involved, we discern certain more particularized considerations that peculiarly call for reversal of this conviction. First, the principle contended for by the State seems inherently boundless. How is one to distinguish this from any other offensive word? Surely the State has no right to cleanse public debate to the point where it is grammatically palatable to the most squeamish among us. Yet no readily ascertainable general principle exists for stopping short of that result were we to affirm the judgment below. For, while the particular four-letter word being litigated here is perhaps more distasteful than most others of its genre, it is nevertheless often true that one man's vulgarity is another's lyric. Indeed, we think it is largely because governmental officals cannot make principled distinctions in this area that the Constitution leaves matters of taste and style so largely to the individual.

Additionally, we cannot overlook the fact, because it is well illustrated by the episode involved here, that much linguistic expression serves a dual communicative function: it conveys not only ideas capable of relatively precise, detached explication, but otherwise inexpressible emotions as well. In fact, words are often chosen as much for their emotive as their cognitive force We cannot sanction the view that the Constitution, while solicitous of the cognitive content of individual speech, has little or no regard for that emotive function

which, practically speaking, may often be the more important element of the overall message sought to be communicated. Indeed, as Mr. Justice Frankfurter has said, "[o]ne of the prerogatives of American citizenship is the right to criticize public men and measures--and that means not only informed and responsible criticism but the freedom to speak foolishly and without moderation." *Baumgartner* v. *United States*, 322 U. S. 665, 673-674 (1944).

Finally, and in the same vein, we cannot indulge the facile assumption that one can forbid particular words without also running a substantial risk of suppressing ideas in the process. Indeed, governments might soon seize upon the censorship of particular words as a convenient guise for banning the expression of unpopular views. We have been able, as noted above, to discern little social benefit that might result from running the risk of opening the door to such grave results.

It is, in sum, our judgment that, absent a more particularized and compelling reason for its actions, the State may not, consistently with the First and Fourteenth Amendments, make the simple public display here involved of this single four-letter expletive a criminal offense. Because that is the only arguably sustainable rationale for the conviction here at issue, the judgment below must be

Reversed.

NOTES

1. The statute provides in full:
   "Every person who maliciously and willfully disturbs the peace or quiet of any neighborhood or person, by loud or unusual noise, or by tumultuous or offensive conduct, or threatening, traducing, quarreling, challenging to fight, or fighting, or who, on the public streets of any unincorporated town, or upon the public highways in such unincorporated town, run any horse race, either for a wager or for amusement, or fire any gun or pistol in such unincorporated town, or use any vulgar, profane, or indecent language within the presence or hearing of women or children, in a loud and boisterous manner, is guilty of a misdemeanor, and upon conviction by any Court of competent jurisdiction shall be punished by fine not exceeding two hundred dollars, or by imprisonment in the County Jail for not more than ninety days, or by both fine and imprisonment, or either, at the discretion of the Court."

2. The suggestion has been made that, in light of the supervening opinion of the California Supreme Court in *In re Bushman*, 1 Cal. 3d 767, 463 P. 2d 727 (1970), it is "not at all

certain that the California Court of Appeal's construction of § 415 is now the authoritative California construction." *Post*, at 27 (BLACKMUN, J., dissenting). In the course of the *Bushman* opinion, Chief Justice Traynor stated: "[One] may . . . be guilty of disturbing the peace through 'offensive' conduct [within the meaning of § 415] if by his actions he wilfully and maliciously incites others to violence or engages in conduct likely to incite others to violence. (*People* v. *Cohen* (1969) 1 Cal. App. 3d 94, 101, [81 Cal. Rptr. 503].)" 1 Cal. 3d, at 773, 463 P. 2d, at 730.

We perceive no difference of substance between the *Bushman* construction and that of the Court of Appeal, particularly in light of the *Bushman* court's approving citation of *Cohen*.

3. It is illuminating to note what transpired when Cohen entered a courtroom in the building. He removed his jacket and stood with it folded over his arm. Meanwhile, a policeman sent the presiding judge a note suggesting that Cohen be held in contempt of court. The judge declined to do so and Cohen was arrested by the officer only after he emerged from the courtroom. App. 18-19.

4. In fact, other portions of the same statute do make some such distinctions. For example, the statute also prohibits disturbing "the peace or quiet . . . by loud or unusual noise" and using "vulgar, profane, or indecent language within the presence or hearing of women or children, in a loud and boisterous manner." See n. 1, *supra*. This second-quoted provision in particular serves to put the actor on much fairer notice as to what is prohibited. It also buttresses our view that the "offensive conduct" portion, as construed and applied in this case, cannot legitimately be justified in this Court as designed or intended to make fine distinctions between differently situated recipients.

5. The *amicus* urges, with some force, that this issue is not properly before us since the statute, as construed, punishes only conduct that might cause others to react violently. However, because the opinion below appears to erect a virtually irrebuttable presumption that use of this word will produce such results, the statute as thus construed appears to impose, in effect, a flat ban on the public utterance of this word. With the case in this posture, it does not seem inappropriate to inquire whether any other rationale might properly support this result. While we think it clear, for the reasons expressed above, that no statute which merely proscribes "offensive conduct" and has been construed as broadly as this one was below can subsequently be justified in this Court as discriminating between conduct that occurs in different places or that offends only certain persons, it is not so unreasonable to seek to justify its full broad sweep on an alternate rationale such

as this. Because it is not so patently clear that acceptance of the justification presently under consideration would render the statute overbroad or unconstitutionally vague, and because the answer to appellee's argument seems quite clear, we do not pass on the contention that this claim is not presented on this record.

In holding unconstitutional prisoner mail censorship regulations issued by the Director of the California Department of Corrections, the United States Supreme Court declared that the censorship of prisoners' mail "implicates more than the right of prisoners": "Communication by letter is not accomplished by the act of writing words on paper. Rather, it is effected only when the letter is read by the addressee. Both parties to the correspondence have an interest in securing that result, and censorship of the communication between them necessarily impinges on the interest of each. Whatever the status of a prisoner's claim to uncensored correspondence with an outsider, it is plain that the latter's interest is grounded in the First Amendment's guarantee of freedom of speech. And this does not depend on whether the nonprisoner correspondent is the author or intended recipient of a particular letter, for the addressee as well as the sender of direct personal correspondence derives from the First and Fourteenth Amendments a protection against unjustified governmental interference with the intended communication....The wife of a prison inmate who is not permitted to read all that her husband wanted to say to her has suffered an abridgment of her interest in communicating with him as plain as that which results from censorship of her letter to him. In either event, censorship of prisoner mail works a consequential restriction on the First and Fourteenth Amendment rights of those who are not prisoners."

Procunier v. *Martinez,* 416 U. S. 396 (1974)

MR. JUSTICE POWELL delivered the opinion of the Court.

This case concerns the constitutionality of certain regulations promulgated by appellant Procunier in his capacity as Director of the California Department of Corrections. Appellees brought a class action on behalf of themselves and all other inmates of penal institutions under the Department's jurisdiction to challenge the rules relating to censorship of prisoner mail and the ban against the use of law students and legal paraprofessionals to conduct attorney-client interviews with inmates. Pursuant to 28 U. S. C. § 2281 a three-judge United States District Court was convened to hear appellees' request for declaratory and injunctive relief. That court entered summary judgment enjoining continued enforcement of the rules in question and ordering appellants to submit new regulations for the court's approval. 354 F. Supp. 1092 (ND Cal. 1973). Appellants' first revisions resulted in counterproposals by appellees and a court order issued May 30, 1973, requiring further modification of the proposed rules. The second set

of revised regulations was approved by the District Court on July 20, 1973, over appellees' objections. While the first proposed revisions of the Department's regulations were pending before the District Court, appellants brought this appeal to contest that court's decision holding the original regulations unconstitutional.

We noted probable jurisdiction. 412 U. S. 948 (1973). We affirm.

I

First we consider the constitutionality of the Director's rules restricting the personal correspondence of prison inmates. Under these regulations, correspondence between inmates of California penal institutions and persons other than licensed attorneys and holders of public office was censored for nonconformity to certain standards. Rule 2401 stated the Department's general premise that personal correspondence by prisoners is "a privilege, not a right...."[1] More detailed regulations implemented the Department's policy. Rule 1201 directed inmates not to write letters in which they "unduly complain" or "magnify grievances."[2] Rule 1205 (d) defined as contraband writings "expressing inflammatory political, racial, religious or other views or beliefs...."[3] Finally, Rule 2402 (8) provided that inmates "may not send or receive letters that pertain to criminal activity; are lewd, obscene, or defamatory; contain foreign matter, or are otherwise inappropriate."[4]

Prison employees screened both incoming and outgoing personal mail for violations of these regulations. No further criteria were provided to help members of the mailroom staff decide whether a particular letter contravened any prison rule or policy. When a prison employee found a letter objectionable, he could take one or more of the following actions: (1) refuse to mail or deliver the letter and return it to the author; (2) submit a disciplinary report, which could lead to suspension of mail privileges or other sanctions; or (3) place a copy of the letter or a summary of its contents in the prisoner's file, where it might be a factor in determining the inmate's work and housing assignments and in setting a date for parole eligibility.

The District Court held that the regulations relating to prisoner mail authorized censorship of protected expression without adequate justification in violation of the First Amendment and that they were void for vagueness. The court also noted that the regulations failed to provide minimum procedural safeguards against error and arbitrariness in the censorship of inmate correspondence. Consequently, it enjoined their continued enforcement.

Appellants contended that the District Court should have abstained from deciding these questions. In that court appellants advanced no reason for abstention other than the assertion that the federal court should defer to the California courts on the basis of comity. The District Court properly rejected this suggestion, noting that the mere possibility that a state court might declare the prison regulations unconstitutional is no ground for abstention. *Wisconsin* v. *Constantineau*, 400 U. S. 433, 439 (1971).

Appellants now contend that we should vacate the judgment and remand the case to the District Court with instructions to abstain on the basis of two arguments not presented to it. First, they contend that any vagueness challenge to an uninterpreted state statute or regulation is a proper case for abstention. According to appellants, "[t]he very statement by the district court that the regulations are vague constitutes a compelling reason for abstention." Brief for Appellants 8-9. As this Court made plain in *Baggett* v. *Bullitt*, 377 U. S. 360 (1964), however, not every vagueness challenge to an uninterpreted state statute or regulation constitutes a proper case for abstention.[5] But we need not decide whether appellants' contention is controlled by the analysis in *Baggett*, for the short answer to their argument is that these regulations were neither challenged nor invalidated solely on the ground of vagueness. Appellees also asserted, and the District Court found, that the rules relating to prisoner mail permitted censorship of constitutionally protected expression without adequate justification. In light of the successful First Amendment attack on these regulations, the District Court's conclusion that they were also unconstitutionally vague hardly "constitutes a compelling reason for abstention."

As a second ground for abstention appellants rely on Cal. Penal Code § 2600 (4), which assures prisoners the right to receive books, magazines, and periodicals.[6] Although they did not advance this argument to the District Court, appellants now contend that the interpretation of the statute by the state courts and its application to the regulations governing prisoner mail might avoid or modify the constitutional questions decided below. Thus appellants seek to establish the essential prerequisite for abstention—"an uncertain issue of state law," the resolution of which may eliminate or materially alter the federal constitutional question.[7] *Harman* v. *Forssenius*, 380 U. S. 528, 534 (1965). We are not persuaded.

A state court interpretation of § 2600 (4) would not avoid or substantially modify the constitutional question presented here. That statute does not contain any provision purporting to regulate censorship of personal correspondence. It only preserves the right of inmates to receive "newspapers, periodicals, and books" and authorizes prison officials to exclude "obscene publications or writings and mail containing information concerning where, how, or from whom *such matter* may be obtained..." (emphasis added). And the plain meaning of the lauguage is reinforced by recent legislative history. In 1972, a bill was introduced in the California Legislature to restrict censorship of personal correspondence by adding an entirely new subsection to

§ 2600. The legislature passed the bill, but it was vetoed by Governor Reagan. In light of this history, we think it plain that no reasonable interpretation of § 2600 (4) would avoid or modify the federal constitutional question decided below. Moreover, we are mindful of the high cost of abstention when the federal constitutional challenge concerns facial repugnance to the First Amendment. *Zwickler* v. *Koota*, 389 U. S. 241, 252 (1967); *Baggett* v. *Bullitt*, 377 U. S., at 379. We therefore proceed to the merits.

A

Traditionally, federal courts have adopted a broad hands-off attitude toward problems of prison administration. In part this policy is the product of various limitations on the scope of federal review of conditions in state penal institutions.[8] More fundamentally, this attitude springs from complementary perceptions about the nature of the problems and the efficacy of judicial intervention. Prison administrators are responsible for maintaining internal order and discipline, for securing their institutions against unauthorized access or escape, and for rehabilitating, to the extent that human nature and inadequate resources allow, the inmates placed in their custody. The Herculean obstacles to effective discharge of these duties are too apparent to warrant explication. Suffice it to say that the problems of prisons in America are complex and intractable, and, more to the point, they are not readily susceptible of resolution by decree. Most require expertise, comprehensive planning, and the commitment of resources, all of which are peculiarly within the province of the legislative and executive branches of government. For all of those reasons, courts are ill equipped to deal with the increasingly urgent problems of prison administration and reform.[9] Judicial recognition of that fact reflects no more than a healthy sense of realism. Moreover, where state penal institutions are involved, federal courts have a further reason for deference to the appropriate prison authorities.

But a policy of judicial restraint cannot encompass any failure to take cognizance of valid constitutional claims whether arising in a federal or state institution. When a prison regulation or practice offends a fundamental constitutional guarantee, federal courts will discharge their duty to protect constitutional rights. *Johnson* v. *Avery*, 393 U. S. 483, 486 (1969). This is such a case. Although the District Court found the regulations relating to prisoner mail deficient in several respects, the first and principal basis for its decision was the constitutional command of the First Amendment, as applied to the States by the Fourteenth Amendment.[10] The issue before us is the appropriate standard of review for prison regulations restricting freedom of speech. This Court has not previously addressed this question, and the tension between the traditional policy of judicial restraint regarding prisoner complaints and the need to protect constitutional rights has led the federal courts to adopt a variety of widely inconsistent approaches to the problem. Some have maintained a hands-off posture in the face of constitutional challenges to censorship of prisoner mail. *E. g.*, *McCloskey* v. *Maryland*, 337 F. 2d 72 (CA4 1964); *Lee* v. *Tahash*, 352 F. 2d 970 (CA8 1965) (except insofar as mail censorship rules are applied to discriminate against a particular racial or religious group); *Krupnick* v. *Crouse*, 366 F. 2d 851 (CA10 1966); *Pope* v. *Daggett*, 350 F. 2d 296 (CA10 1965). Another has required only that censorship of personal correspondence not lack support "in any rational and constitutionally acceptable concept of a prison system." *Sostre* v. *McGinnis*, 442 F. 2d 178, 199 (CA2 1971), cert. denied *sub nom.* *Oswald* v. *Sostre*, 405 U. S. 978 (1972). At the other extreme some courts have been willing to require demonstration of a "compelling state interest" to justify censorship of prisoner mail. *E. g.*, *Jackson* v. *Godwin*, 400 F. 2d 529 (CA5 1968) (decided on both equal protection and First Amendment grounds); *Morales* v. *Schmidt*, 340 F. Supp. 544 (WD Wis. 1972); *Fortune Society* v. *McGinnis*, 319 F. Supp. 901 (SDNY 1970). Other courts phrase the standard in similarly demanding terms of "clear and present danger." *E. g.*, *Wilkinson* v. *Skinner*, 462 F. 2d 670, 672-673 (CA2 1972). And there are various intermediate positions, most notably the view that a "regulation or practice which restricts the right of free expression that a prisoner would have enjoyed if he had not been imprisoned must be related both reasonably and necessarily to the advancement of some justifiable purpose." *E. g.*, *Carothers* v. *Follette*, 314 F. Supp. 1014, 1024 (SDNY 1970) (citations omitted). See also *Gates* v. *Collier*, 349 F. Supp. 881, 896 (ND Miss. 1972); *LeMon* v. *Zelker*, 358 F. Supp. 554 (SDNY 1972).

This array of disparate approaches and the absence of any generally accepted standard for testing the constitutionality of prisoner mail censorship regulations disserve both the competing interests at stake. On the one hand, the First Amendment interests implicated by censorship of inmate correspondence are given only haphazard and inconsistent protection. On the other, the uncertainty of the constitutional standard makes it impossible for correctional officials to anticipate what is required of them and invites repetitive, piecemeal litigation on behalf of inmates. The result has been unnecessarily to perpetuate the involvement of the federal courts in affairs of prison administration. Our task is to formulate a standard of review for prisoner mail censorship that will be responsive to these concerns.

B

We begin our analysis of the proper standard of review for constitutional challenges to censorship of prisoner mail with a somewhat different premise from that taken by the other federal courts that have considered the question. For the most part, these courts have dealt with challenges to censorship of prisoner mail as involving broad questions of "prisoners' rights." This case is no exception. The District Court stated the issue in general terms as "the applicability of First Amendment rights to prison inmates...," 354 F. Supp., at 1096, and the arguments of the parties reflect the assumption that the resolution of this case requires an assessment of the extent to which prisoners may claim First Amendment freedoms. In our view this inquiry is unnecessary. In determining the proper standard of review for prison restrictions on inmate correspondence, we have no occasion to consider the extent to which an individual's right to free speech survives incarceration, for a narrower basis of decision is at hand. In the case of direct personal correspondence between inmates and those who have a particularized interest in communicating with them,[11] mail censorship implicates more than the right of prisoners.

Communication by letter is not accomplished by the act of writing words on paper. Rather, it is effected only when the letter is read by the addressee. Both parties to the correspondence have an interest in securing that result, and censorship of the communication between them necessarily impinges on the interest of each. Whatever the status of a prisoner's claim to uncensored correspondence with an outsider, it is plain that the latter's interest is grounded in the First Amendment's guarantee of freedom of speech. And this does not depend on whether the nonprisoner corespondent is the author or intended recipient of a particular letter, for the addressee as well as the sender of direct personal correspondence derives from the First and Fourteenth Amendments a protection against unjustified governmental interference with the intended communication. *Lamont* v. *Postmaster General*, U. S. 301 (1965); accord. *Kleindienst* v. *Mandel*, 408 U. S. 753, 762-765 (1972); *Martin* v. *City of Struthers*, 319 U. S. 141, 143 (1943). We do not deal here with difficult questions of the so-called "right to hear" and third-party standing but with a particular means of communication in which the interests of both parties are inextricably meshed. The wife of a prison inmate who is not permitted to read all that her husband wanted to say to her has suffered an abridgment of her interest in communicating with him as plain as that which results from censorship of her letter to him. In either event, censorship of prisoner mail works a consequential restriction on the First and Fourteenth Amendments rights of those who are not prisoners.

Accordingly, we reject any attempt to justify censorship of inmate correspondence merely by reference to certain assumptions about legal status of prisoners. Into this category of argument falls appellants' contention that "an inmate's rights with reference to social correspondence are something fundamentally different than those enjoyed by his free brother."

Brief for Appellants 19. This line of argument and the undemanding standard of review it is intended to support fail to recognize that the First Amendment liberties of free citizens are implicated in censorship of prisoner mail. We therefore turn for guidance, not to cases involving questions of "prisoners' rights," but to decisions of this Court dealing with the general problem of incidental restrictions on First Amendment liberties imposed in furtherance of legitimate governmental activities.

As the Court noted in *Tinker* v. *Des Moines School District*, 393 U. S. 503, 506 (1969), First Amendment guarantees must be "applied in light of the special characteristics of the...environment." *Tinker* concerned the interplay between the right to freedom of speech of public high school students and "the need for affirming the comprehensive authority of the States and of school officials, consistent with fundamental constitutional safeguards, to prescribe and control conduct in the schools." *Id.*, at 507. In overruling a school regulation prohibiting the wearing of antiwar armbands, the Court undertook a careful analysis of the legitimate requirements of orderly school administration in order to ensure that the students were afforded maximum freedom of speech consistent with those requirements. The same approach was followed in *Healy* v. *James*, 408 U. S. 169 (1972), where the Court considered the refusal of a state college to grant official recognition to a group of students who wished to organize a local chapter of the Students for a Democratic Society (SDS), a national student organization noted for political activism and campus disruption. The Court found that neither the identification of the local student group with the national SDS, nor the purportedly dangerous political philosophy of the local group, nor the college administration's fear of future, unspecified disruptive activities by the students could justify the incursion on the right of free association. The Court also found, however, that this right could be limited if necessary to prevent campus disruption, *id.*, at 189-190, n. 20, and remanded the case for determination of whether the students had in fact refused to accept reasonable regulations governing student conduct.

In *United States* v. *O'Brien*, 391 U. S. 367 (1968), the Court dealt with incidental restrictions on free speech occasioned by the exercise of the governmental power to conscript men for military service. O'Brien had burned his Selective Service registration certificate on the steps of a courthouse in order to dramatize his opposition to the draft and to our country's involvement in Vietnam. He was convicted of violating a provision of the Selective Service law that had recently been amended to prohibit knowing destruction or mutilation of registration certificates. O'Brien argued that the purpose and effect of the amendment were to abridge free expression and that the statutory provision was therefore unconstitutional, both as enacted and as applied to him. Although O'Brien's activity involved "conduct" rather than pure "speech," the Court did not define away the First Amendment concern, and neither did it rule that the presence of a communicative intent necessarily rendered O'Brien's actions immune to governmental regulation. Instead, it enunciated the following four-part test:

"[A] government regulation is sufficiently justified if it is within the constitutional power of the Government; if it furthers an important or substantial governmental interest; if the governmental interest is unrelated to the suppression of free expression; and if the incidental restriction on alleged First Amendment freedoms is no greater than is essential to the furtherance of that interest." *Id.*, at 377.

Of course, none of these precedents directly controls the instant case. In *O'Brien* the Court considered a federal statute which on its face prohibited certain conduct having no necessary connection with freedom of speech. This led the Court to differentiate between "speech" and "nonspeech" elements of a single course of conduct, a distinction that has little relevance here. Both *Tinker* and *Healy* concerned First and Fourteenth Amendment liberties in the context of state educational institutions, a circumstance involving rather different governmental interests than are at stake here. In broader terms, however, these precedents involved incidental restrictions on First Amendment liberties by governmental action in furtherance of legitimate and substantial state interest other than suppression of expression. In this sense these cases are generally analogous to our present inquiry.

The case at hand arises in the context of prisons. One of the primary functions of government is the preservation of societal order through enforcement of the criminal law, and the maintenance of penal institutions is an essential part of that task. The identifiable governmental interests at stake in this task are the preservation of internal order and discipline,[12] the maintenance of institutional security against escape or unauthorized entry, and the rehabilitation of the prisoners. While the weight of professional opinion seems to be that inmate freedom to correspond with outsiders advances rather than retards the goal of rehabilitation,[13] the legitimate governmental interest in the order and security of penal institutions justifies the imposition of certain restraints on inmate correspondence. Perhaps the most obvious example of justifiable censorship of prisoner mail would be refusal to send or deliver letters concerning escape plans or containing other information concerning proposed criminal activity, whether within or without the prison. Similarly, prison officials may properly refuse to transmit encoded messages. Other less obvious possibilities come to mind, but it is not our purpose to survey the range of circumstances in which particular restrictions on prisoner mail might be warranted by the legitimate demands of prison administration as they exist from time to time in the various kinds of penal institutions found in this country. Our task is to determine the proper standard for deciding whether a particular regulation or practice relating to inmate correspondence constitutes an impermissible restraint of First Amendment liberties.

Applying the teachings of our prior decisions to the instant context, we hold that censorship of prisoner mail is justified if the following criteria are met. First, the regulation or practice in question must further an important or substantial governmental interest unrelated to the suppression of expression. Prison officials may not censor inmate correspondence simply to eliminate unflattering or unwelcome opinions or factually inaccurate statements. Rather, they must show that a regulation authorizing mail censorship furthers one or more of the substantial governmental interests of security, order, and rehabilitation. Second, the limitation of First Amendment freedoms must be no greater than is necessary or essential to the protection of the particular governmental interest involved. Thus a restriction on inmate correspondence that furthers an important or substantial interest of penal administration will nevertheless be invalid if its sweep is unnecessarily broad. This does not mean, of course, that prison administrators may be required to show with certainty that adverse consequences would flow from the failure to censor a particular letter. Some latitude in anticipating the probable consequences of allowing certain speech in a prison environment is essential to the proper discharge of an administrator's duty. But any regulation or practice that restricts inmate correspondence must be generally necessary to protect one or more of the legitimate governmental interests identified above.[14]

C

On the basis of this standard, we affirm the judgment of the District Court. The regulations invalidated by that court authorized, inter alia, censorship of statements that "unduly complain" or "magnify grievances," expression of "inflammatory political, racial, religious or other views," and matter deemed "defamatory" or "otherwise inappropriate." These regulations fairly invited prison officials and employees to apply their own personal prejudices and opinions as standards for prisoner mail censorship. Not surprisingly, some prison officials used the extraordinary latitude for discretion authorized by the regulations to suppress unwelcome criticism. For example, at one institution under the Department's jurisdiction, the checklist used by the mailroom staff authorized rejection of letters "criticizing policy, rules or officials," and the mailroom sergeant stated in a deposition that he would reject as "defamatory" letters "belittling staff or our judicial system or anything connected with Department of Cor-

rections." Correspondence was also censored for "disrespectful comments," "derogatory remarks," and the like.

Appellants have failed to show that these broad restrictions on prisoner mail were in any way necessary to the furtherance of a governmental interest unrelated to the suppression of expression. Indeed, the heart of appellants' position is not that the regulations are justified by a legitimate governmental interest but that they do not need to be. This misconception is not only stated affirmatively; it also underlies appellants' discussion of the particular regulations under attack. For example, appellants' sole defense of the prohibition against matter that is "defamatory" or "otherwise inappropriate" is that it is "within the discretion of the prison administrators." Brief for Appellants 21. Appellants contend that statements that "magnify grievances" or "unduly complain" are censored "as a precaution against flash riots and in the furtherance of inmate rehabilitation." Id., at 22. But they do not suggest how the magnification of grievances or undue complaining, which presumably occurs in outgoing letters, could possibly lead to flash riots, nor do they specify what contribution the suppression of complaints makes to the rehabilitation of criminals. And appellants defend the ban against "inflammatory political, racial, religious or other views" on the ground that "[s]uch matter clearly presents a danger to prison security...." Id., at 21. The regulation, however, is not narrowly drawn to reach only material that might be thought to encourage violence nor is its application limited to incoming letters. In short, the Department's regulations authorized censorship of prisoner mail far broader than any legitimate interest of penal administration demands and were properly found invalid by the District Court.[15]

D

We also agree with the District Court that the decision to censor or withhold delivery of a particular letter must be accompanied by minimum procedural safeguards. The interest of prisoners and their correspondents in uncensored communication by letter, grounded as it is in the First Amendment, is plainly a "liberty" interest within the meaning of the Fourteenth Amendment even though qualified of necessity by the circumstance of imprisonment. As such, it is protected from arbitrary governmental invasion. See *Board of Regents* v. *Roth*, 408 U. S. 564 (1972); *Perry* v. *Sindermann*, 408 U. S. 593 (1972). The District Court required that an inmate be notified of the rejection of a letter written by or addressed to him, that the author of that letter be given a reasonable opportunity to protest that decision, and that complaints be referred to a prison official other than the person who originally disapproved the correspondence. These requirements do not appear to be unduly burdensome, nor do appellants so contend. Accordingly, we affirm the judgment of the District Court with respect to the Department's regulations relating to prisoner mail.

II

The District Court also enjoined continued enforcement of Administrative Rule MV-IV-02, which provides in pertinent part:

"Investigators for an attorney-of-record will be confined to not more than two. Such investigators must be licensed by the State or must be members of the State Bar. Designation must be made in writing by the Attorney."

By restricting access to prisoners to members of the bar and licensed private investigators, this regulation imposed an absolute ban on the use by attorneys of law students and legal paraprofessionals to interview inmate clients. In fact, attorneys could not even delegate to such persons the task of obtaining prisoners' signatures on legal documents. The District Court reasoned that this rule constituted an unjustifiable restriction on the right of access to the courts. We agree.

The constitutional guarantee of due process of law has as a corollary the requirement that prisoners be afforded access to the courts in order to challenge unlawful convictions and to seek redress for violations of their constitutional rights. This means that inmates must have a reasonable opportunity to seek and receive the assistance of attorneys. Regulations and practices that unjustifiably obstruct the availability of professional representation or other aspects of the right of access to the courts are invalid. *Ex parte Hull*, 312 U. S. 546 (1941).

The District Court found that the rule restricting attorney-client interviews to members of the bar and licensed private investigators inhibited adequate professional representation of indigent inmates. The remoteness of many California penal institutions makes a personal visit to an inmate client a time-consuming undertaking. The court reasoned that the ban against the use of law students or other paraprofessionals for attorney-client interviews would deter some lawyers from representing prisoners who could not afford to pay for their traveling time or that of licensed private investigators. And those lawyers who agreed to do so would waste time that might be employed more efficaciously in working on the inmates' legal problems. Allowing law students and paraprofessionals to interview inmates might well reduce the cost of legal representation for prisoners. The District Court therefore concluded that the regulation imposed a substantial burden on the right of access to the courts.

As the District Court recognized, this conclusion does not end the inquiry, for prison administrators are not required to adopt every proposal that may be thought to facilitate prisoner access to the courts. The extent to which that right is burdened by a particular regulation or practice must be weighed against the legitimate interests of penal administration and the proper regard that judges should give to the expertise and discretionary authority of correctional officials. In this case the ban against the use of law students and other paraprofessional personnel was absolute. Its prohibition was not limited to prospective interviewers who posed some colorable threat to security or to those inmates thought to be especially dangerous. Nor was it shown that a less restrictive regulation would unduly burden the administrative task of screening and monitoring visitors.

Appellants' enforcement of the regulation in question also created an arbitrary distinction between law students employed by practicing attorneys and those associated with law school programs providing legal assistance to prisoners.[16] While the Department flatly prohibited interviews of any sort by law students working for attorneys, it freely allowed participants of a number of law school programs to enter the prisons and meet with inmates. These largely unsupervised students were admitted without any security check other than verification of their enrollment in a school program. Of course, the fact that appellants have allowed some persons to conduct attorney-client interviews with prisoners does not mean that they are required to admit others, but the arbitrariness of the distinction between the two categories of law students does reveal the absence of any real justification for the sweeping prohibition of Administrative Rule MV-IV-02. We cannot say that the District Court erred in invalidating this regulation.

This result is mandated by our decision in *Johnson* v. *Avery*, 393 U. S. 483 (1969). There the Court struck down a prison regulation prohibiting any inmate from advising or assisting another in the preparation of legal documents. Given the inadequacy of alternative sources of legal assistance, the rule had the effect of denying to illiterate or poorly educated inmates any opportunity to vindicate possibly valid constitutional claims. The Court found that the regulation impermissibly burdened the right of access to the courts despite the not insignificant state interest in preventing the establishment of personal power structures by unscrupulous jailhouse lawyers and the attendant problems of prison discipline that follow. The countervailing state interest in *Johnson* is, if anything, more persuasive than any interest advanced by appellants in the instant case.

The judgment is

Affirmed.

NOTES

1. Director's Rule 2401 provided:"The sending and receiving of mail is a privilege, not a right, and any violation of the rules governing mail privileges either by you or by your correspondents may cause suspension of the mail privileges."

2. Director's Rule 1201 provided:"INMATE BEHAVIOR: Always conduct yourself in an orderly manner. Do not fight or take part in horseplay or physical encounters except as part of the regular athletic program. Do not agitate, unduly complain, magnify grievances, or behave in any way which might lead to violence."
    It is undisputed that the phrases "unduly complain" and "magnify grievances" were applied to personal correspondence.

3. Director's Rule 1205 provided: "The following is contraband:

    .   .   .   .   .

    "d. Any writings or voice recordings expressing inflammatory political, racial, religious or other views or beliefs when not in the immediate possession of the originator, or when the originator's possession is used to subvert prison discipline by display or circulation."
    Rule 1205 also provides that writings "not defined as contraband under this rule, but which, if circulated among other inmates, would in the judgment of the warden or superintendent tend to subvert prison order or discipline, may be placed in the inmate's property, to which he shall have access under supervision."

4. At the time of appellees' amended complaint, Rule 2402 (8) included prohibitions against "prison gossip or discussion of other inmates." Before the first opinion of the District Court, these provisions were deleted, and the phrase "contain foreign matter" was substituted in their stead.

5. In *Baggett* the Court considered the constitutionality of loyalty oaths required of certain state employees as a condition of employment. For the purpose of applying the doctrine of abstention the Court distinguished between two kinds of vagueness attacks. Where the case turns on the applicability of a state statute or regulation to a particular person or a defined course of conduct, resolution of the unsettled question of state law may eliminate any need for constitutional adjudication. 377 U. S., at 376-377. Abstention is therefore appropriate. Where, however, as in this case, the statute or regulation is challenged as vague because individuals to whom it plainly applies simply cannot understand what is required of them and do not wish to forswear all activity arguably within the scope of the vague terms, abstention is not required. *Id.*, at 378. In such a case no single adjudication by a state court could eliminate the constitutional difficulty. Rather it would re-

quire "extensive adjudications, under the impact of a variety of factual situations," to bring the challenged statute or regulation "within the bounds of permissible constitutional certainty." *Ibid.*

6. Cal. Penal Code § 2600 provides that "[a] sentence of imprisonment in a state prison for any term suspends all the civil rights of the person so sentenced...," and it allows for partial restoration of those rights by the California Adult Authority. The statute then declares, in pertinent part:
    "This section shall be construed so as not to deprive such person of the following civil rights, in accordance with the laws of this state:

    .   .   .   .   .

    "(4) To purchase, receive, and read any and all newspapers, periodicals, and books accepted for distribution by the United States Post Office. Pursuant to the provisions of this section, prison authorities shall have the authority to exclude obscene publications or writings, and mail containing information concerning where, how, or from whom such matter may be obtained; and any matter of a character tending to incite murder, arson, riot, violent racism, or any other form of violence; and any matter concerning gambling or a lottery...."

7. Appellants argue that the correctness of their abstention argument is demonstrated by the District Court's disposition of Count II of appellees' amended complaint. In Count II appellees challenged the mail regulations on the ground that their application to correspondence between inmates and attorneys contravened the Sixth and Fourteenth Amendments. Appellees later discovered that a case was then pending before the Supreme Court of California in which the application of the prison rules to attorney-client mail was being attacked under subsection (2) of § 2600, which provides:
    "This section shall be construed so as not to deprive [an inmate] of the following civil rights, in accordance with the laws of this state:

    .   .   .   .   .

    "(2) To correspond, confidentially, with any member of the State Bar, or holder of public office, provided that the prison authorities may open and inspect such mail to search for contraband."
    The District Court did stay its hand, and the subsequent decision in *In re Jordan*, 7 Cal. 3d 930, 500 P. 2d 873 (1972) (holding that § 2600 (2) barred censorship of attorney-client correspondence), rendered Count II moot. This disposition of the claim relating to attorney-client mail is, however, quite irrelevant to appellants' contention that the District Court should have abstained from deciding whether the mail regulations are constitutional as

they apply to personal mail. Subsection (2) of § 2600 speaks directly to the issue of censorship of attorney-client mail but says nothing at all about personal correspondence, and appellants have not informed us of any challenge to the censorship of personal mail presently pending in the state courts.

8. See Note, *Decency and Fairness: An Emerging Judicial Role in Prison Reform*, 57 Va. L. Rev. 841, 842-844 (1971).

9. They are also ill suited to act as the front-line agencies for the consideration and resolution of the infinite variety of prisoner complaints. Moreover, the capacity of our criminal justice system to deal fairly and fully with legitimate claims will be impaired by a burgeoning increase of frivolous prisoner complaints. As one means of alleviating this problem, The Chief Justice has suggested that federal and state authorities explore the possibility of instituting internal administrative procedures for disposition of inmate grievances. 59 A. B. A. J. 1125, 1128 (1973). At the Third Circuit Judicial Conference meeting of October 15, 1973, at which the problem was addressed, suggestions also included (i) abstention where appropriate to avoid needless consideration of federal constitutional issues; and (ii) the use of federal magistrates who could be sent into penal institutions to conduct hearings and make findings of fact. We emphasize that we express no view as to the merit or validity of any particular proposal, but we do think it appropriate to indicate the necessity of prompt and thoughtful consideration by responsible federal and state authorities of this worsening situation.

10. Specifically, the District Court held that the regulations authorized restraint of lawful expression in violation of the First and Fourteenth Amendments, that they were fatally vague, and that they failed to provide minimum procedural safeguards against arbitrary or erroneous censorship of protected speech.

11. Different considerations may come into play in the case of mass mailings. No such issue is raised on these facts, and we intimate no view as to its proper resolution.

12. We need not and do not address in this case the validity of a temporary prohibition of an inmate's personal correspondence as a disciplinary sanction (usually as part of the regimen of solitary confinement) for violation of prison rules.

13. Policy Statement 7300.1A of the Federal Bureau of Prisons sets forth the Bureau's position regarding general correspondence by the prisoners entrusted to its custody. It authorizes all federal institutions to adopt open correspondence regulations and recognizes that any need for restrictions arises primarily from considerations of order and security rather than

rehabilitation:

"Constructive, wholesome contact with the community is a valuable therapeutic tool in the overall correctional process. At the same time, basic controls need to be exercised in order to protect the security of the institution, individuals and/or the community-at-large."

The recommended policy guideline adopted by the Association of State Correctional Administrators on August 23, 1972, echoes the view that personal correspondence by prison inmates is a generally wholesome activity:

"Correspondence with members of an inmate's family, close friends, associates and organizations is beneficial to the morale of all confined persons and may form the basis for good adjustment in the institution and the community."

14. While not necessarily controlling, the policies followed at other well-run institutions would be relevant to a determination of the need for a particular type of restriction. For example, Policy Statement 7300.1A of the Federal Bureau of Prisons specifies that personal correspondence of inmates in federal prisons, whether incoming or outgoing, may be rejected for inclusion of the following kinds of material:

"(1) Any material which might violate postal regulations, *i.e.*, threats, blackmail, contraband or which indicate plots of escape.

"(2) Discussions of criminal activities.

"(3) No inmate may be permitted to direct his business while he is in confinement. This does not go to the point of prohibiting correspondence necessary to enable the inmate to protect the property and funds that were legitimately his at the time he was committed to the institution. Thus, an inmate could correspond about refinancing a mortgage on his home or sign insurance papers, but he could not operate a mortgage or insurance business while in the institution.

"(4) Letters containing codes or other obvious attempts to circumvent these regulations will be subject to rejection.

"(5) Insofar as possible, all letters should be written in English, but every effort should be made to accommodate those inmates who are unable to write in English or whose correspondents would be unable to understand a letter written in English. The criminal sophistication of the inmate, the relationship of the inmate and the correspondent are factors to be considered in deciding whether correspondence in a foreign language should be permitted."

15. After the District Court held the original regulations unconstitutional, revised regulations were developed by appellants and approved by the court. Supp. to App. 194-200, 211. Although these regulations are not before us for review, they are indicative of one solution to the pro-

blem. The following provisions govern censorship of prisoner correspondence:
"*CORRESPONDENCE*
"A.   *Criteria for Disapproval of Inmate Mail*
    "1.   *Outgoing Letters*
    "Outgoing letters from inmates of institutions not requiring approval of inmate correspondents may be disapproved for mailing only if the content falls as a whole or in significant part into any of the following categories:
    "a.   The letter contains threats of physical harm against any person or threats of criminal activity.
    "b.   The letter threatens blackmail...or extortion.
    "c.   The letter concerns sending contraband in or out of the institutions.
    "d.   The letter concerns plans to escape.
    "e.   The letter concerns plans for activities in violation of institutional rules.
    "f.   The letter concerns plans for criminal activity.
    "g.   The letter is in code and its contents are not understood by reader.
    "h.   The letter solicits gifts or money from other than family.
    "i.   The letter is obscene.
    "j.   The letter contains information which if communicated would create a clear and present danger of violence and physical harm to a human being. Outgoing letters from inmates of institutions requiring approval of correspondents may be disapproved only for the foregoing reasons, or if the addressee is not an approved correspondent of the inmate and special permission for the letter has not been obtained.
    "2.   *Incoming Letters*
    "Incoming letters to inmates may be disapproved for receipt only for the foregoing reasons, or if the letter contains material which would cause severe psychiatric or emotional disturbance to the inmate, or in an institution requiring approval of inmate correspondents, is from a person who is not an approved correspondent and special permission for the letter has not been obtained.
    "3.   *Limitations*
    "Disapproval of a letter on the basis that it would cause severe psychiatric or emotional disturbance to the inmate may be done only by a member of the institution's psychiatric staff after consultation with the inmate's caseworker. The staff member may disapprove the letter only upon a finding that receipt of the letter would be likely to affect prison discipline or security or the inmate's rehabilitation, and that there is no reasonable alternative means of ameliorating the disturbance of the inmate. Outgoing or incoming letters may not be rejected solely upon the ground that they contain criticism of the

institution or its personnel.
    "4.   *Notice of Disapproval of Inmate Mail*
    "a.   When an inmate is *prohibited from sending* a letter, the letter and a written and signed notice stating one of the authorized reasons for disapproval and indicating the portion or portions of the letter causing disapproval will be given the inmate.
    "b.   When an inmate is *prohibited from receiving* a letter, the letter and a written and signed notice stating one of the authorized reasons for disapproval and indicating the portion or portions of the letter causing disapproval will be given the sender. The inmate will be given notice in writing that a letter has been rejected, indicating one of the authorized reasons and the sender's name.
    "c.   Material from correspondence which violates the provisions of paragraph one may be placed in an inmate's file. Other material from correspondence may not be placed in an inmate's file unless it has been lawfully observed by an employee of the department and is relevant to assessment of the inmate's rehabilitation. However, such material which is not in violation of the provisions of paragraph one may not be the subject of disciplinary proceedings against an inmate. An inmate shall be notified in writing of the placing of any material from correspondence in his file.
    "d.   Administrative review of inmate grievances regarding the application of this rule may be had in accordance with paragraph DP-1003 of these rules."
16.   Apparently, the Department's policy regarding law school programs providing legal assistance to inmates, though well established, is not embodied in any regulation.

In deciding that licensed pharmacists are not guilty of unprofessional conduct if they advertise or promote drugs which may be dispensed only by prescription, the United States Supreme Court spoke of the citizen's right to receive information: "Freedom of speech presupposes a willing speaker. But where a speaker exists, as is the case here, the protection afforded is to the communication, to its source and to its recipients both. This is clear from the decided cases. In Lamont *v.* Postmaster General..., *the Court upheld the First Amendment rights of citizens to receive political publications sent from abroad. More recently, in* Kleindienst *v.* Mandel...., *we acknowledged that this Court has referred to a First Amendment right 'to receive information and ideas,' and that freedom of speech 'necessarily protects the right to receive.'"*

Virginia State Board of Pharmacy v. *Virginia Citizens Consumer Council,*
425 U. S. 748 (1976)

MR. JUSTICE BLACKMUN delivered the opinion of the Court.

The plaintiff-appellees in this case attack, as violative of the First and Fourteenth Amendments,[1] that portion of § 54-524.35 of Va. Code Ann. (1974), which provides that a pharmacist licensed in Virginia is guilty of unprofessional conduct if he "(3) publishes, advertises or promotes, directly or indirectly, in any manner whatsoever, any amount, price, fee, premium, discount, rebate or credit terms...for any drugs which may be dispensed only by prescription."[2] The three-judge District Court declared the quoted portion of the statute "void and of no effect," Jurisdictional Statement, App. 1, and enjoined the defendant-appellants, the Virginia State Board of Pharmacy and the individual members of that Board, from enforcing it. 373 F. Supp. 683 (ED Va. 1974). We noted probable jurisdiction of the appeal. 420 U.S. 971 (1975).

I

Since the challenged restraint is one that peculiarly concerns the licensed pharmacist in Virginia, we begin with a description of that profession as it exists under Virginia law.

The "practice of pharmacy" is statutorily declared to be "a professional practice affecting the public health, safety and welfare," and to be "subject to regulation and control in the public interest." Va. Code Ann. § 54-524.2(a) (1974).[3] Indeed, the practice is subject to extensive regulation aimed at preserving high professional standards. The regulatory body is the appellant Virginia State Board of Pharmacy. The Board is broadly charged by statute with various responsibilities, including the "[m]aintenance of the quality, quantity, integrity, safety and efficacy of drugs or devices distributed, dispensed or administered." § 54-524.16 (a). It also is to concern itself with "[m]aintaining the integrity of, and public confidence in, the profession and improving the delivery of quality pharmaceutical services to the citizens of Virginia." § 54-524.16 (d). The Board is empowered to "make such bylaws, rules and regulations...as may be necessary for the lawful exercise of its powers." § 54-524.17.

The Board is also the licensing authority. It may issue a license, necessary for the practice of pharmacy in the State, only upon evidence that the applicant is "of good moral character," is a graduate in pharmacy of a school approved by the Board, and has had "a suitable period of experience [the period required not to exceed 12 months] acceptable to the Board." § 54-524.21. The applicant must pass the examination prescribed by the Board. *Ibid.* One approved school is the School of Pharmacy of the Medical College of Virginia, where the curriculum is for three years following two years of college. Prescribed prepharmacy courses, such as biology and chemistry, are to be taken in college, and study requirements at the school itself include courses in organic chemistry, biochemistry, comparative anatomy, physiology, and pharmacology. Students are also trained in the ethics of the profession, and there is some clinical experience in the school's hospital pharmacies and in the medical center operated by the Medical College. This is "a rigid, demanding curriculum in terms of what the pharmacy student is expected to know about drugs."[4]

Once licensed, a pharmacist is subject to a civil monetary penalty, or to revocation or suspension of his license, if the Board finds that he "is not of good moral character," or has violated any of a number of stated professional standards (among them that he not be "negligent in the practice of pharmacy" or have engaged in "fraud or deceit upon the consumer...in connection with the practice of pharmacy"), or is guilty of "unprofessional conduct." § 54-524.22:1. "Unprofessional conduct" is specifically defined in § 54-524.35, n. 2, *supra,* the third numbered phrase of which relates to advertising of the price for any prescription drug, and is the subject of this litigation.

Inasmuch as only a licensed pharmacist may dispense prescription drugs in Virginia, § 54-524.48,[5] advertising or other affirmative dissemination of prescription drug price information is effectively forbidden in the State. Some pharmacies refuse even to quote prescription drug prices over the telephone. The Board's position, however, is that this would not constitute an unprofessional publication.[6] It is clear, nonetheless, that all advertising of such prices, in the normal sense, is forbidden. The prohibition does not extend to nonprescription drugs, but neither is it confined to prescriptions that the pharmacist compounds himself. Indeed, about 95% of all prescriptions now are filled with dosage forms prepared by the pharmaceutical manufacturer.[7]

II

This is not the first challenge to the constitutionality of § 54-524.35 and what is now its third-numbered phrase. Shortly after the phrase was added to the statute in 1968,[8] a suit seeking to enjoin its operation was instituted by a drug retailing company and one of its pharmacists. Although the First Amendment was invoked, the challenge appears to have been based primarily on the Due Process and Equal Protection Clauses of the Fourteenth Amendment. In any event, the prohibition on drug price advertising was upheld. *Patterson Drug Co.* v. *Kingery*, 305 F. Supp. 821 (WD Va. 1969). The three-judge court did find that the dispensation of prescription drugs "affects the public health, safety and welfare." *Id.*, at 824-825. No appeal was taken.

The present, and second, attack on the statute is one made not by one directly subject to its prohibition, that is, a pharmacist, but by prescription drug consumers who claim that they would greatly benefit if the prohibition were lifted and advertising freely allowed. The plaintiffs are an individual Virginia resident who suffers from diseases that require her to take prescription drugs on a daily basis,[9] and two nonprofit organizations.[10] Their claim is that the First Amendment entitles the user of prescription drugs to receive information that pharmacists wish to communicate to them through advertising and other promotional means, concerning the prices of such drugs.

Certainly that information may be of value. Drug prices in Virginia, for both prescription and nonprescription items, strikingly vary from outlet to outlet even within the same locality. It is stipulated, for example, that in Richmond "the cost of 40 Achromycin tablets ranges from $2.59 to $6.00, a difference of 140% [*sic*]," and that in the Newport News-Hampton area the cost of tetracycline ranges from $1.20 to $9.00, a difference of 650%.[11]

The District Court seized on the identity of the plaintiff-appellees as consumers as a feature distinguishing the present case from *Patterson Drug Co.* v. *Kingery, supra*. Because the unsuccessful plaintiffs in that earlier case were pharmacists, the court said, "theirs was a prima facie commercial approach," 373 F. Supp., at 686. The present plaintiffs, on the other hand, were asserting an interest in their own health that was "fundamentally deeper than a trade consideration." *Ibid.* In the District Court's view, the expression in *Valentine* v. *Chrestensen*, 316 U. S. 52, 54-55 (1942), to the effect that "purely commercial advertising" is not protected had been tempered, by later decisions of this Court, to the point that First Amendment interests in the free flow of price information could be found to outweigh the countervailing interests of the State. The strength of the interest in the free flow of drug price information was borne

out, the court felt, by the fact that three States by court decision had struck down their prohibitions on drug price advertising. *Florida Board of Pharmacy* v. *Webb's City, Inc.*, 219 So. 2d 681 (Fla. 1969); *Maryland Board of Pharmacy* v. *Sav-A-Lot, Inc.*, 270 Md. 103, 311 A. 2d 242 (1973); *Pennsylvania State Board of Pharmacy* v. *Pastor*, 441 Pa. 186, 272 A. 2d 487 (1971).[12] The District Court recognized that this Court had upheld-- against federal constitutional challenges other than on First Amendment grounds--state restrictions on the advertisement of prices for optometrists' services, *Head* v. *New Mexico Board*, 374 U.S. 424 (1963), for eyeglass frames, *Williamson* v. *Lee Optical Co.*, 348 U.S. 483 (1955), and for dentists' services, *Semler* v. *Dental Examiners*, 294 U.S. 608 (1935).[13] The same dangers of abuse and deception were not thought to be present, however, when the advertised commodity was prescribed by a physician for his individual patient and was dispensed by a licensed pharmacist. The Board failed to justify the statute adequately, and it had to fall. 373 F. Supp., at 686-687.

III

The question first arises whether, even assuming that First Amendment protection attaches to the flow of drug price information, it is a protection enjoyed by the appellees as recipients of the information, and not solely, if at all, by the advertisers themselves who seek to disseminate that information.

Freedom of speech presupposes a willing speaker. But where a speaker exists, as is the case here,[14] the protection afforded is to the communication, to its source and to its recipients both. This is clear from the decided cases. In *Lamont* v. *Postmaster General*, 381 U.S. 301 (1965), the Court upheld the First Amendment rights of citizens to receive political publications sent from abroad. More recently, in *Kleindienst* v. *Mandel*, 408 U.S. 753, 762-763 (1972), we acknowledged that this Court has referred to a First Amendment right to "receive information and ideas," and that freedom of speech "'necessarily protects the right to receive.'" And in *Procunier* v. *Martinez*, 416 U.S. 396, 408-409 (1974), where censorship of prison inmates' mail was under examination, we thought it unnecessary to assess the First Amendment right of the inmates themselves, for it was reasoned that such censorship equally infringed the rights of non-inmates to whom the correspondence was addressed. There are numerous other expressions to the same effect in the Court's decisions. See, *e.g.*, *Red Lion Broadcasting Co.* v. *FCC*, 395 U.S. 367, 390 (1969); *Stanley* v. *Georgia*, 394 U.S. 557, 564 (1969); *Griswold* v. *Connecticut*, 381 U.S. 479, 482 (1965); *Marsh* v. *Alabama*, 326 U.S. 501, 505 (1946); *Thomas* v. *Collins*, 323 U.S. 516, 534 (1945); *Martin* v. *Struthers*, 319 U.S. 141, 143 (1943). If there is a right to advertise, there is a reciprocal right to receive the advertising, and it may be asserted by these appellees.[15]

IV

The appellants contend that the advertisement of prescription drug prices is outside the protection of the First Amendment because it is "commercial speech." There can be no question that in past decisions the Court has given some indication that commercial speech is unprotected. In *Valentine* v. *Chrestensen, supra*, the Court upheld a New York statute that prohibited the distribution of any "handbill, circular...or other advertising matter whatsoever in or upon any street." The Court concluded that, although the First Amendment would forbid the banning of all communication by handbill in the public thoroughfares, it imposed "no such restraint on government as respects purely commercial advertising." 316 U.S., at 54. Further support for a "commercial speech" exception to the First Amendment may perhaps be found in *Breard* v. *Alexandria*, 341 U.S. 622 (1951), where the Court upheld a conviction for violation of an ordinance prohibiting door-to-door solicitation of magazine subscriptions. The Court reasoned: "The selling...brings into the transaction a commercial feature," and it distinguished *Martin* v. *Struthers, supra*, where it had reversed a conviction for door-to-door distribution of leaflets publicizing a religious meeting, as a case involving "no element of the commercial." 341 U.S., at 642-643. Moreover, the Court several times has stressed that communications to which First Amendment protection was given were *not* "purely commercial." *New York Times Co.* v. *Sullivan*, 376 U.S. 254, 266 (1964); *Thomas* v. *Collins*, 323 U.S., at 533; *Murdock* v. *Pennsylvania*, 319 U.S. 105, 111 (1943); *Jamison* v. *Texas*, 318 U.S. 413, 417 (1943).

Since the decision in *Breard*, however, the Court has never *denied* protection on the ground that the speech in issue was "commercial speech." That simplistic approach, which by then had come under criticism or was regarded as of doubtful validity by Members of the Court,[16] was avoided in *Pittsburgh Press Co.* v. *Human Relations Comm'n*, 413 U.S. 376 (1973). There the Court upheld an ordinance prohibiting newspapers from listing employment advertisements in columns according to whether male or female employees were sought to be hired. The Court, to be sure, characterized the advertisements as "classic examples of commercial speech," *id.*, at 385, and a newspaper's printing of the advertisements as of the same character. The Court, however, upheld the ordinance on the ground that the restriction it imposed was permissible because the discriminatory hirings proposed by the advertisements, and by their newspaper layout, were themselves illegal.

Last Term, in *Bigelow* v. *Virginia*, 421 U.S. 809 (1975), the notion of unprotected "commercial speech" all but passed from the scene. We reversed a conviction for violation of a Virginia statute that made the circulation of any publication to encourage or promote the processing of an abortion in Virginia, a misdemeanor. The defendant had published in his newspaper the availability of abortions in New York. The advertisement in question, in addition to announcing that abortions were legal in New York, offered the services of a referral agency in that State. We rejected the contention that the publication was unprotected because it was commercial. *Chrestensen*'s continued validity was questioned, and its holding was described as "distinctly a limited one" that merely upheld "a reasonable regulation of the manner in which commercial advertising could be distributed." 421 U.S., at 819. We concluded that "the Virginia courts erred in their assumptions that advertising, as such, was entitled to no First Amendment protection," and we observed that the "relationship of speech to the marketplace of products or of services does not make it valueless in the marketplace of ideas." *Id.*, at 825-826.

Some fragment of hope for the continuing validity of a "commercial speech" exception arguably might have persisted because of the subject matter of the advertisement in *Bigelow*. We noted that in announcing the availability of legal abortions in New York, the advertisement "did more than simply propose a commercial transaction. It contained factual material of clear 'public interest.'" *Id.*, at 822. And, of course, the advertisement related to activity with which, at least in some respects, the State could not interfere. See *Roe* v. *Wade*, 410 U.S. 113 (1973); *Doe* v. *Bolton*, 410 U.S. 179 (1973). Indeed, we observed: "We need not decide in this case the precise extent to which the First Amendment permits regulation of advertising that is related to activities the State may legitimately regulate or even prohibit." 421 U.S., at 825.

Here, in contrast, the question whether there is a First Amendment exception for "commercial speech" is squarely before us. Our pharmacist does not wish to editorialize on any subject, cultural, philosophical, or political. He does not wish to report any particularly newsworthy fact, or to make generalized observations even about commercial matters. The "idea" he wishes to communicate is simply this: "I will sell you the X prescription drug at the Y price." Our question, then, is whether this communication is wholly outside the protection of the First Amendment.

V

We begin with several propositions that already are settled or beyond serious dispute. It is clear, for example, that speech does not lose its First Amendment protection because money is spent to project it, as in a paid advertisement of one form or another. *Buckley* v. *Valeo*, 424 U.S. 1, 35-59 (1976); *Pittsburgh Press Co.* v. *Human Relations Comm'n*, 413 U.S., at 384; *New York Times Co.* v. *Sullivan*, 376 U.S., at 266. Speech likewise is protected even though it is carried in a form that is "sold" for profit, *Smith* v.

California, 361 U.S. 147, 150 (1959) (books); *Joseph Burstyn, Inc.* v. *Wilson*, 343 U.S. 495, 501 (1952) (motion pictures); *Murdock* v. *Pennsylvania*, 319 U.S., at 111 (religious literature), and even though it may involve a solicitation to purchase or otherwise pay or contribute money. *New York Times Co.*, v. *Sullivan*, *supra*; *NAACP* v. *Button*, 371 U.S. 415, 429 (1963); *Jamison* v. *Texas*, 318 U.S., at 417; *Cantwell* v. *Connecticut*, 310 U.S. 296, 306-307 (1940).

If there is a kind of commercial speech that lacks all First Amendment protection, therefore, it must be distinguished by its content. Yet the speech whose content deprives it of protection cannot simply be speech on a commercial subject. No one would contend that our pharmacist may be prevented from being heard on the subject of whether, in general, pharmaceutical prices should be regulated, or their advertisement forbidden. Nor can it be dispositive that a commercial advertisement is noneditorial, and merely reports a fact. Purely factual matter of public interest may claim protection. *Bigelow* v. *Virginia*, 421 U.S., at 822; *Thornhill* v. *Alabama*, 310 U.S. 88, 102 (1940).

Our question is whether speech which does "no more than propose a commercial transaction," *Pittsburgh Press Co.* v. *Human Relations Comm'n*, 413 U.S., at 385, is so removed from any "exposition of ideas," *Chaplinsky* v. *New Hampshire*, 315 U.S. 568, 572 (1942), and from "'truth, science, morality, and arts in general, in its diffusion of liberal sentiments on the administration of Government,'" *Roth* v. *United States*, 354 U.S. 476, 484 (1957), that it lacks all protection. Our answer is that it is not.

Focusing first on the individual parties to the transaction that is proposed in the commercial advertisement, we may assume that the advertiser's interest is a purely economic one. That hardly disqualifies him from protection under the First Amendment. The interests of the contestants in a labor dispute are primarily economic, but it has long been settled that both the employee and the employer are protected by the First Amendment when they express themselves on the merits of the dispute in order to influence its outcome. See, *e.g.*, *NLRB* v. *Gissel Packing Co.*, 395 U.S. 575, 617-618 (1969); *NLRB* v. *Virginia Electric & Power Co.*, 314 U.S. 469, 477 (1941); *AFL* v. *Swing*, 312 U.S. 321, 325-326 (1941); *Thornhill* v. *Alabama*, 310 U.S., at 102. We know of no requirement that, in order to avail themselves of First Amendment protection, the parties to a labor dispute need address themselves to the merits of unionism in general or to any subject beyond their immediate dispute.[17] It was observed in *Thornhill* that "the practices in a single factory may have economic repercussions upon a whole region and affect widespread systems of marketing." *Id.*, at 103. Since the fate of such a "single factory" could as well turn on its ability to advertise its product as on the resolution of its labor difficulties, we see no satisfactory distinction between the two kinds of speech.

As to the particular consumer's interest in the free flow of commercial information, that interest may be as keen, if not keener by far, than his interest in the day's most urgent political debate. Appellees' case in this respect is a convincing one. Those whom the suppression of prescription drug price information hits the hardest are the poor, the sick, and particularly the aged. A disproportionate amount of their income tends to be spent on prescription drugs; yet they are the least able to learn, by shopping from pharmacist to pharmacist, where their scarce dollars are best spent.[18] When drug prices vary as strikingly as they do, information as to who is charging what becomes more than a convenience. It could mean the alleviation of physical pain or the enjoyment of basic necessities.

Generalizing, society also may have a strong interest in the free flow of commercial information. Even an individual advertisement, though entirely "commercial," may be of general public interest. The facts of decided cases furnish illustrations: advertisements stating that referral services for legal abortions are available, *Bigelow* v. *Virginia*, *supra*; that a manufacturer of artificial furs promotes his product as an alternative to the extinction by his competitors of fur-bearing mammals, see *Fur Information & Fashion Council, Inc.* v. *E.F. Timme & Son*, 364 F. Supp. 16 (SDNY 1973); and that a domestic producer advertises his product as an alternative to imports that tend to deprive American residents of their jobs, cf. *Chicago Joint Board* v. *Chicago Tribune Co.*, 435 F. 2d 470 (CA7 1970), cert. denied, 402 U.S. 973 (1971). Obviously, not all commercial messages contain the same or even a very great public interest element. There are few to which such an element, however, could not be added. Our pharmacist, for example, could cast himself as a commentator on store-to-store disparities in drug prices, giving his own and those of a competitor as proof. We see little point in requiring him to do so, and little difference if he does not.

Moreover there is another consideration that suggests that no line between publicly "interesting" or "important" commercial advertising and the opposite kind could ever be drawn. Advertising, however tasteless and excessive it sometimes may seem, is nonetheless dissemination of information as to who is producing and selling what product, for what reason, and at what price. So long as we preserve a predominantly free enterprise economy, the allocation of our resources in large measure will be made through numerous private economic decisions. It is a matter of public interest that those decisions, in the aggregate, be intelligent and well informed. To this end, the free flow of commercial information is indispensable. See *Dun & Bradstreet, Inc.* v. *Grove*, 404 U.S. 898, 904-906 (1971) (Douglas, J., dissenting from denial of certiorari). See also *FTC* v. *Procter & Gamble Co.*, 386 U.S. 568, 603-604 (1967) (Harlan, J., concurring). And if it is indispensable to the proper allocation of resources in a free enterprise system, it is also indispensable to the formation of intelligent opinions as to how that system ought to be regulated or altered. Therefore, even if the First Amendment were thought to be primarily an instrument to enlighten public decision making in a democracy,[19] we could not say that the free flow of information does not serve that goal.[20]

Arrayed against these substantial individual and societal interests are a number of justifications for the advertising ban. These have to do principally with maintaining a high degree of professionalism on the part of licensed pharmacists.[21] Indisputably, the State has a strong interest in maintaining that professionalism. It is exercised in a number of ways for the consumer's benefit. There is the clinical skill involved in the compounding of drugs, although, as has been noted, these now make up only a small percentage of the prescriptions filled. Yet, even with respect to manufacturer-prepared compounds, there is room for the pharmacist to serve his customer well or badly. Drugs kept too long on the shelf may lose their efficacy or become adulterated. They can be packaged for the user in such a way that the same results occur. The expertise of the pharmacist may supplement that of the prescribing physician, if the latter has not specified the amount to be dispensed or the directions that are to appear on the label. The pharmacist, a specialist in the potencies and dangers of drugs, may even be consulted by the physician as to what to prescribe. He may know of a particular antagonism between the prescribed drug and another that the customer is or might be taking, or with an allergy the customer may suffer. The pharmacist himself may have supplied the other drug or treated the allergy. Some pharmacists, concededly not a large number, "monitor" the health problems and drug consumptions of customers who come to them repeatedly.[22] A pharmacist who has a continuous relationship with his customer is in the best position, of course, to exert professional skill for the customer's protection.

Price advertising, it is argued, will place in jeopardy the pharmacist's expertise and, with it, the customer's health. It is claimed that the aggressive price competition that will result from unlimited advertising will make it impossible for the pharmacist to supply professional services in the compounding, handling, and dispensing of prescription drugs. Such services are time consuming and expensive; if competitors who economize by eliminating them are permitted to advertise their resulting lower prices, the more painstaking and conscientious pharmacist will be forced either to follow suit or to go out of business. It is also claimed that prices might not necessarily fall as a result of advertising. If one pharmacist advertises, others must, and the resulting expense will inflate the cost of drugs. It is further claimed that advertising will lead people to shop for their prescription drugs among the various pharmacists who offer the lowest prices, and the loss of stable pharma-

cist-customer relationships will make individual attention--and certainly the practice of monitoring--impossible. Finally, it is argued that damage will be done to the professional image of the pharmacist. This image, that of a skilled and specialized craftsman, attracts talent to the profession and reinforces the better habits of those who are in it. Price advertising, it is said, will reduce the pharmacist's status to that of a mere retailer.[23]

The strength of these proffered justifications is greatly undermined by the fact that high professional standards, to a substantial extent, are guaranteed by the close regulation to which pharmacists in Virginia are subject. And this case concerns the retail sale by the pharmacist more than it does his professional standards. Surely, any pharmacist guilty of professional dereliction that actually endangers his customer will promptly lose his license. At the same time, we cannot discount the Board's justifications entirely. The Court regarded justifications of this type sufficient to sustain the advertising bans challenged on due process and equal protection grounds in *Head* v. *New Mexico Board, supra*; *Williamson* v. *Lee Optical Co., supra*; and *Semler* v. *Dental Examiners, supra.*

The challenge now made, however, is based on the First Amendment. This casts the Board's justifications in a different light, for on close inspection it is seen that the State's protectiveness of its citizens rests in large measure on the advantages of their being kept in ignorance. The advertising ban does not directly affect professional standards one way or the other. It affects them only through the reactions it is assumed people will have to the free flow of drug price information. There is no claim that the advertising ban in any way prevents the cutting of corners by the pharmacist who is so inclined. That pharmacist is likely to cut corners in any event. The only effect the advertising ban has on him is to insulate him from price competition and to open the way for him to make a substantial, and perhaps even excessive, profit in addition to providing an inferior service. The more painstaking pharmacist is also protected but, again, it is a protection based in large part on public ignorance.

It appears to be feared that if the pharmacist who wishes to provide low cost, and assertedly low quality, services is permitted to advertise, he will be taken up on his offer by too many unwitting customers. They will choose the low-cost, low-quality service and drive the "professional" pharmacist out of business. They will respond only to costly and excessive advertising, and end up paying the price. They will go from one pharmacist to another, following the discount, and destroy the pharmacist-customer relationship. They will lose respect for the profession because it advertises. All this is not in their best interests, and all this can be avoided if they are not permitted to know who is charging what.

There is, of course, an alternative to this highly paternalistic approach. That alternative is to assume that this information is not in itself harmful, that people will perceive their own best interests if only they are well enough informed, and that the best means to that end is to open the channels of communication rather than to close them. If they are truly open, nothing prevents the "professional" pharmacist from marketing his own assertedly superior product, and contrasting it with that of the low-cost, high-volume prescription drug retailer. But the choice among these alternative approaches is not ours to make or the Virginia General Assembly's. It is precisely this kind of choice, between the dangers of suppressing information, and the dangers of its misuse if it is freely available, that the First Amendment makes for us. Virginia is free to require whatever professional standards it wishes of its pharmacists; it may subsidize them or protect them from competition in other ways. Cf. *Parker* v. *Brown*, 317 U.S. 341 (1943). But it may not do so by keeping the public in ignorance of the entirely lawful terms that competing pharmacists are offering. In this sense, the justifications Virginia has offered for suppressing the flow of prescription drug price information, far from persuading us that the flow is not protected by the First Amendment, have reinforced our view that it is. We so hold.

VI

In concluding that commercial speech, like other varieties, is protected, we of course do not hold that it can never be regulated in any way. Some forms of commercial speech regulation are surely permissible. We mention a few only to make clear that they are not before us and therefore are not foreclosed by this case.

There is no claim, for example, that the prohibition on prescription drug price advertising is a mere time, place, and manner restriction. We have often approved restrictions of that kind provided that they are justified without reference to the content of the regulated speech, that they serve a significant governmental interest, and that in so doing they leave open ample alternative channels for communication of the information. Compare *Grayned* v. *City of Rockford*, 408 U.S. 104, 116 (1972); *United States* v. *O'Brien*, 391 U.S. 367, 377 (1968); and *Kovacs* v. *Cooper*, 336 U.S. 77, 85-87 (1949), with *Buckley* v. *Valeo*, 424 U.S. 1; *Erznoznik* v. *City of Jacksonville*, 422 U.S. 205, 209 (1975); *Cantwell* v. *Connecticut*, 310 U.S., at 304-308; and *Saia* v. *New York*, 334 U.S. 558, 562 (1948). Whatever may be the proper bounds of time, place, and manner restrictions on commercial speech, they are plainly exceeded by this Virginia statute, which singles out speech of a particular content and seeks to prevent its dissemination completely.

Nor is there any claim that prescription drug price advertisements are forbidden because they are false or misleading in any way. Untruthful speech, commercial or otherwise, has never been protected for its own sake. *Gertz*

v. *Robert Welch, Inc.*, 418 U.S. 323, 340 (1974); *Konigsberg* v. *State Bar*, 366 U.S. 36, 49, and n. 10 (1961). Obviously, much commercial speech is not provably false, or even wholly false, but only deceptive or misleading. We foresee no obstacle to a State's dealing effectively with this problem.[24] The First Amendment, as we construe it today, does not prohibit the State from insuring that the stream of commercial information flow cleanly as well as freely. See, for example, Va. Code Ann. § 18.2-216 (1975).

Also, there is no claim that the transactions proposed in the forbidden advertisements are themselves illegal in any way. Cf. *Pittsburgh Press Co.* v. *Human Relations Comm'n*, 413 U.S. 376 (1973); *United States* v. *Hunter*, 459 F. 2d 205 (CA4), cert. denied, 409 U.S. 934 (1972). Finally, the special problems of the electronic broadcast media are likewise not in this case. Cf. *Capitol Broadcasting Co.* v. *Mitchell*, 333 F. Supp. 582 (DC 1971), aff'd *sub nom. Capitol Broadcasting Co.* v. *Acting Attorney General*, 405 U.S. 1000 (1972).

What is at issue is whether a State may completely suppress the dissemination of concededly truthful information about entirely lawful activity, fearful of that information's effect upon its disseminators and its recipients. Reserving other questions,[25] we conclude that the answer to this one is in the negative.

The judgment of the District Court is affirmed.

It is so ordered.

NOTES

1. The First Amendment is applicable to the States through the Due Process Clause of the Fourteenth Amendment. See, *e.g.*, *Bigelow* v. *Virginia*, 421 U.S. 809, 811 (1975); *Schneider* v. *State*, 308 U.S. 147, 160 (1939).

2. Section 54-524.35 provides in full:

   "Any pharmacist shall be considered guilty of unprofessional conduct who (1) is found guilty of any crime involving grave moral turpitude, or is guilty of fraud or deceit in obtaining a certificate of registration; or (2) issues, publishes, broadcasts by radio, or otherwise, or distributes or uses in any way whatsoever advertising matter in which statements are made about his professional service which have a tendency to deceive or defraud the public, contrary to the public health and welfare; or (3) publishes, advertises or promotes, directly or indirectly, in any manner whatsoever, any amount, price, fee, premium, discount, rebate or credit terms for professional services or for drugs containing

3. The parties, also, have stipulated that pharmacy "is a profession." Stipulation of Facts ¶ 11, App. 11.

4. *Id.*, ¶ 8, App. 11. See generally *id.*, ¶¶ 6-16, App. 10-12.

5. Exception is made for "legally qualified" practitioners of medicine, dentistry, osteopathy, chiropody, and veterinary medicine. § 54-524.53.

6. Stipulation of Facts ¶ 25, App. 15.

7. *Id.*, ¶ 18, App. 13.

8. Theretofore an administrative regulation to the same effect had been outstanding. The Board, however, in 1967 was advised by the State Attorney General's office that the regulation was unauthorized. The challenged phrase was added to the statute the following year. See *Patterson Drug Co.* v.*Kingery*, 305 F. Supp. 821, 823 n.1 (WD Va. 1969).

9. Stipulation of Facts ¶ 3, App. 9.

10. The organizations are the Virginia Citizens Consumer Council, Inc., and the Virginia State AFL-CIO. Each has a substantial membership (approximately 150,000 and 69,000 respectively) many of whom are users of prescription drugs. *Id.*, ¶¶ 1 and 2, App. 9. The American Association of Retired Persons and the National Retired Teachers Association, also claiming many members who "depend substantially on prescription drugs for their well-being," Brief 2, are among those who have filed briefs *amici curiae* in support of the appellees.

11. Stipulation of Facts ¶¶ 22 (b) and (c), App. 14. The phenomenon of widely varying drug prices is apparently national in scope. The American Medical Association conducted a survey in Chicago that showed price differentials in that city of up to 1200% for the same amounts of a specific drug. A study undertaken by the Consumers Union in New York found that prices for the same amount of one drug ranged from 79¢ to $7.45, and for another from $1.25 to $11.50. *Id.*, ¶¶ 22 (d) and (e), App. 14. *Amici* American Association of Retired Persons and National Retired Teachers Association state that in 1974 they participated in a survey of three prescription drug prices at 28 pharmacies in Washington, D.C., and found pharmacy-to-pharmacy variances in the price of identical drugs as great as 245%. Brief as *Amici Curiae* 10. The prevalence of such discrepancies "throughout the United States" is documented in a recent report. Staff Report to the Federal Trade Commission, Prescription Drug Price Disclosures 119 (1975). The same report indicates that 34 States impose significant restrictions on dissemination of drug price information and, thus, make the problem a national one. *Id.*, at 34.

12. The Florida and Pennsylvania decisions appear to rest on state constitutional grounds. The Maryland decision was based on the Due Process Clause of the Fourteenth Amendment as well as on provisions of the State Constitution.

Accord: *Terry* v. *California State Board of Pharmacy*, 395 F. Supp. 94 (ND Cal. 1975), appeal docketed, No. 75-336. Contra: *Urowsky* v. *Board of Regents*, 38 N.Y. 2d 364, 342 N.E. 2d 583 (1975); *Supermarkets General Corp.* v. *Sills*, 93 N.J. Super. 326, 225 A. 2d 728 (1966).

See Note: Commercial Speech--An End in Sight to *Chrestensen*? 23 De Paul L. Rev. 1258 (1974); Comment, 37 Brooklyn L. Rev. 617 (1971); Comment, 24 Wash. and Lee L. Rev. 299 (1967).

13. In *Head* v. *New Mexico Board*, the First Amendment issue was raised. This Court refused to consider it, however, because it had not been presented to the state courts, nor reserved in the notice of appeal here. 374 U.S., at 432 n. 12. The Court's action to this effect was noted in *Pittsburgh Press Co.* v. *Human Relations Comm'n*, 413 U.S. 376, 387 n. 10 (1973). The appellants at the oral argument recognized that *Head* was a due process case. Tr. of Oral Arg. 10.

14. "In the absence of Section 54-524.35 (3), some pharmacies in Virginia would advertise, publish and promote price information regarding prescription drugs." Stipulation of Facts ¶ 26, App. 15.

15. The dissent contends that there is no such right to receive the information that another seeks to disseminate, at least not when the person objecting could obtain the information in another way, and could himself disseminate it. Our prior decisions, cited above, are said to have been limited to situations in which the information sought to be received "would not be otherwise reasonably available," see *post*, at 782; emphasis is also placed on the appellees' great need for the information, which need, assertedly, should cause them to take advantage of the alternative of digging it up themselves. We are aware of no general principle that freedom of speech may be abridged when the speaker's listeners could come by his message by some other means, such as seeking him out and asking him what it is. Nor have we recognized any such limitation on the independent right of the listener to receive the information sought to be communicated. Certainly, the recipients of the political publications in *Lamont* could have gone abroad and thereafter disseminated them themselves. Those in *Kleindienst* who organized the lecture tour by a foreign Marxist could have done the same. And the addressees of the inmate correspondence in *Procunier* could have visited the prison themselves. As for the recipients' great need for the information sought to be disseminated, if it distinguishes our prior cases at all, it makes the appellees' First Amendment claim a stronger rather than a weaker one.

16. See *Bigelow* v. *Virginia*, 421 U.S., at

820 n. 6, citing Mr. Justice Douglas' observation in *Cammarano* v. *United States*, 358 U.S. 498, 514 (1959) (concurring opinion), that the *Chrestensen* ruling "was casual, almost offhand. And it has not survived reflection"; the similar observation of four Justices in dissent in *Lehman* v. *City of Shaker Heights*, 418 U.S. 298, 314 n. 6 (1974); and expressions of three Justices in separate dissents in *Pittsburgh Press Co.* v. *Human Relations Comm'n*, 413 U.S., at 393, 398, and 401. See also Mr. Justice Douglas' comment, dissenting from the denial of certiorari in *Dun & Bradstreet, Inc.* v. *Grove*, 404 U.S. 898, 904-906 (1971).

17. The speech of labor disputants, of course, is subject to a number of restrictions. The Court stated in *NLRB* v. *Gissel Packing Co.*, 395 U.S., at 618, for example, that an employer's threats of retaliation for the labor actions of his employees are "without the protection of the First Amendment." The constitutionality of restrictions upon speech in the special context of labor disputes is not before us here. We express no views on that complex subject, and advert to cases in the labor field only to note that in some circumstances speech of an entirely private and economic character enjoys the protection of the First Amendment.

18. The point hardly needs citation, but a few figures are illustrative. It has been estimated, for example, that in 1973 and 1974 per capita drug expenditures of persons age 65 and over were $97.27 and $103.17, respectively, more than twice the figures of $41.18 and $45.14 for all age groups. Cooper & Piro, Age Differences in Medical Care Spending, Fiscal Year 1973, 37 Social Security Bull., No. 5, p. 6 (1974); Mueller & Gibson, Age Differences in Health Care Spending, Fiscal Year 1974, 38 Social Security Bull., No. 6, p. 5 (1975). These figures, of course, reflect the higher rate of illness among the aged. In 1971, 16.9% of all Americans 65 years and over were unable to carry on major activities because of some chronic condition, the figure for all ages being only 2.9%. Statistical Policy Division, Office of Management and Budget, Social Indicators 1973, p. 36. These figures eloquently suggest the diminished capacity of the aged for the kind of active comparison shopping that a ban on advertising makes necessary or desirable. Diminished resources are also the general rule for those 65 and over; their income averages about half that for all age groups. *Id.*, at 176.

The parties have stipulated that a "significant portion of income of elderly persons is spent on medicine." Stipulation of Facts ¶ 27, App. 15.

19. For the views of a leading exponent of this position, see A. Meiklejohn, Free Speech And Its Relation to Self-Government

(1948). This Court likewise has emphasized the role of the First Amendment in guaranteeing our capacity for democratic self-government. See *New York Times Co.* v. *Sullivan*, 376 U.S. 254, 269-270 (1964), and cases cited therein.

20. Pharmaceuticals themselves provide a not insignificant illustration. The parties have stipulated that expenditures for prescription drugs in the United States in 1970 were estimated at $9.14 billion. Stipulation of Facts ¶ 17, App. 12. It has been said that the figure for drugs and drug sundries in 1974 was $9.695 billion, with that amount estimated to be increasing about $700 million per year. Worthington, National Health Expenditures 1929-1974, 38 Social Security Bull., No. 2, p. 9 (1975). The task of predicting the effect that a free flow of drug price information would have on the production and consumption of drugs obviously is a hazardous and speculative one. It was recently undertaken, however, by the staff of the Federal Trade Commission in the course of its report, see n. 11, *supra*, on the merits of a possible Commission rule that would outlaw drug price advertising restrictions. The staff concluded that consumer savings would be "of a very substantial magnitude, amounting to many millions of dollars per year." Staff Report, *supra*, n. 11, at 181.

21. An argument not advanced by the Board, either in its brief or in the testimony proffered prior to the summary judgment, but which on occasion has been made to other courts, see, e. g., *Pennsylvania State Board of Pharmacy* v. *Pastor*, 441 Pa. 186, 272 A. 2d 487 (1971), is that the advertisement of low drug prices will result in overconsumption and in abuse of the advertised drugs. The argument prudently has been omitted. By definition, the drugs at issue here may be sold only on a physician's prescription. We do not assume, as apparently the dissent does, that simply because low prices will be freely advertised, physicians will overprescribe, or that pharmacists will ignore the prescription requirement.

22. Monitoring, even if pursued, is not fully effective. It is complicated by the mobility of the patient; by his patronizing more than one pharmacist; by his being treated by more than one prescriber; by the availability of over-the-counter drugs; and by the antagonism of certain foods and drinks. Stipulation of Facts ¶¶ 30-47, App. 16-19. Neither the Code of Ethics of the American Pharmaceutical Association nor that of the Virginia Pharmaceutical Association requires a pharmacist to maintain family prescription records. *Id.*, ¶ 42, App. 18. The appellant Board has never promulgated a regulation requiring such records. *Id.*, ¶ 43, App. 18.

23. Descriptions of the pharmacist's expertise, its importance to the consumer, and its alleged jeopardization by price advertising

are set forth at length in the numerous summaries of testimony of proposed witnesses for the Board, and objections to testimony of proposed witnesses for the plaintiffs, that the Board filed with the District Court prior to summary judgment, the substance of which appellees did not contest. App. 4, 27-48, 52-53; Brief for Appellants 4-5, and n. 2.

24. In concluding that commercial speech enjoys First Amendment protection, we have not held that it is wholly undifferentiable from other forms. There are commonsense differences between speech that does "no more than propose a commercial transaction," *Pittsburgh Press Co.* v. *Human Relations Comm'n*, 413 U. S., at 385, and other varieties. Even if the differences do not justify the conclusion that commercial speech is valueless, and thus subject to complete suppression by the State, they nonetheless suggest that a different degree of protection is necessary to insure that the flow of truthful and legitimate commercial information is unimpaired. The truth of commercial speech, for example, may be more easily verifiable by its disseminator than, let us say, news reporting or political commentary, in that ordinarily the advertiser seeks to disseminate information about a specific product or service that he himself provides and presumably knows more about than anyone else. Also, commercial speech may be more durable than other kinds. Since advertising is the *sine qua non* of commercial profits, there is little likelihood of its being chilled by proper regulation and forgone entirely.

Attributes such as these, the greater objectivity and hardiness of commercial speech, may make it less necessary to tolerate inaccurate statements for fear of silencing the speaker. Compare *New York Times Co.* v. *Sullivan*, 376 U. S. 254 (1964), with *Dun & Bradstreet, Inc.* v. *Grove*, 404 U. S. 898 (1971). They may also make it appropriate to require that a commercial message appear in such a form, or include such additional information, warnings, and disclaimers, as are necessary to prevent its being deceptive. Compare *Miami Herald Publishing Co.* v. *Tornillo*, 418 U. S. 241 (1974), with *Banzhaf* v. *FCC*, 132 U. S. App. D. C. 14, 405 F. 2d 1082 (1968), cert. denied sub nom. *Tobacco Institute, Inc.* v. *FCC*, 396 U. S. 842 (1969). Cf. *United States* v. *95 Barrels of Vinegar*, 265 U. S. 438, 443 (1924) ("It is not difficult to choose statements, designs and devices which will not deceive"). They may also make inapplicable the prohibition against prior restraints. Compare *New York Times Co.* v. *United States*, 403 U. S. 713 (1971), with *Donaldson* v. *Read Magazine*, 333 U. S. 178, 189-191 (1948); *FTC* v. *Standard Education Society*, 302 U. S. 112 (1937); *E. F. Drew & Co.* v. *FTC*, 235 F. 2d 735, 739-740 (CA2 1956), cert.

denied, 352 U. S. 969 (1957).

25. We stress that we have considered in this case the regulation of commercial advertising by pharmacists. Although we express no opinion as to other professions, the distinctions, historical and functional, between professions, may require consideration of quite different factors. Physicians and lawyers, for example, do not dispense standardized products; they render professional *services* of almost infinite variety and nature, with the consequent enhanced possibility for confusion and deception if they were to undertake certain kinds of advertising.

INDEX

215

Veterans of Foreign Wars, 24
Vietnam War, v, xix, 171-74
Vonnegut, Jurt, 6-13, 37-39,
    43-44, 51, 67, 70, 88, 91,
    106, 113

Wanderers, The, xii, xvi, 118-
    19, 121, 123
Washington, George, 113

Washington, George, 113
Why I Am Not a Christian, 91
*William Faulkner: Selected
    Short Stories,* 37-38
Women in literature, 126, 129,
    131-32
Wright, Richard, 24, 67, 75,
    89, 91, 106, 113

Young Adult Services Intellec-
    tual Freedom Committee, ix

Zola, Emile, 11